Holland, Belgium
and Luxembourg

THE ROUGH GUIDE

Rough Guide Credits

Text editor:	Martin Dunford
Series editor:	Mark Ellingham
Editorial:	John Fisher, Jonathan Buckley, Greg Ward, Jules Brown, Graham Parker, Jo Mead, Samantha Cook
Production:	Susanne Hillen, Andy Hilliard, Gail Jammy, Vivien Antwi, Alan Spicer
Cartography:	Melissa Flack
Publicity:	Richard Trillo
Finance:	Celia Crowley, Simon Carloss
Administration:	Tania Hummel

Special thanks to Michael Baert and Pierre Claus at the Belgian Tourist Office, whose help was invaluable in the preparation of this guide. Thanks also to Julia Britchford at British Midland Airways; to Marijke Katsis-Hulst at Netherlands Railways and Marielle Albers of the Netherlands Board of Tourism; to Geerdt Magiels; Andrew Tibber for proofreading and Ros Belford for editorial help; Matt Welton for map revisions; and to Alan Spicer for page makeup.

Thanks are also due to all those who wrote in with comments on suggestions on previous editions: Alison Woodhead, Mattilda Gomez, Georges van den Eshof, Ian Watt, Dave Gorman and Eva Lartey, Mark Silverstein, Richard G. Hovey, Doug Hall, Dave Jarratt, Jim Hynes, Colin Smith, H. Reddy, Paul Aspden, Jonathan Burton, Georgia Wood and Glenn McDonald, Laura Miller, Andrew Thomas, Corinne D. Hayward, Harriet Gutuertz, Emma Louch, Sally Abbott, P. McManus, Raymond Travers, Erika Guttmann, Ursula Liu, Naomi Walton, Daniel Mack and Lorraine Ellis, Kathy Smith, Ian Carr-de Avelon, Paul Zandbergen, Colin Costello, G. Light, Pierre Flener, Michael Hindlay, John Humphries, Jay Davidson, Elaine Hughes, Steve Wood, Wendy Alexander, Edison Montgomery, Giles Curtis-Raleigh. Apologies if we've spelt anyone's name wrong or have missed anyone out – and please keep writing.

The publishers and authors have done their best to ensure the accuracy and currency of all the information in *The Rough Guide to Holland, Belgium and Luxembourg*: however, they can accept no responsibility for any loss, injury, or inconvenience sustained by any traveller as a result of information or advice contained in the guide.

This edition published 1994 by Rough Guides Ltd, 1 Mercer Street, London WC2H 9QJ.
Distributed by The Penguin Group:

Penguin Books Ltd, 27 Wrights Lane, London W8 5TZ
Penguin Books USA Inc., 375 Hudson Street, New York 10014, USA
Penguin Books Australia Ltd, 487 Maroondah Highway, PO Box 257, Ringwood, Victoria 3134, Australia
Penguin Books Canada Ltd, 10 Alcorn Avenue, Toronto, Ontario, Canada M4V 1E4
Penguin Books (NZ) Ltd, 182–190 Wairau Road, Auckland 10, New Zealand

Previous edition published in the UK by Harrap Columbus.
Previous edition published in the United States and Canada as *The Real Guide: Holland, Belgium & Luxembourg.*

Typeset in Linotron Univers and Century Old Style
Printed in the UK by Cox & Wyman Ltd, Reading, Berks.

Illustrations in Part One and Part Three by Ed Briant; Basics illustration by David Loftus; Contexts illustration by Sally Davies.

Front cover photograph © Christian Sarramon, taken from *Living in Amsterdam*, published by Flammarion, Paris.

576pp
includes index

A catalogue record for this book is available from the British Library.

ISBN 1-85828-087-7

Holland, Belgium
and Luxembourg

THE ROUGH GUIDE

written and researched by
**Martin Dunford,
Jack Holland and Phil Lee**

with additional research by
Anna van Kemenade and Emile Bruls

THE ROUGH GUIDES

CONTENTS

Introduction vi

INTRODUCTION

Holland, **Belgium** and **Luxembourg** together make up one of the most densely populated regions of Europe. Historically, all three nations have been closely entwined, sharing the same history of colonial oppression and subsequent independence until 1830, when Belgium and Luxembourg became separate states. As a result, there are cultural similarities which run very deep: in language – Dutch is spoken in both Holland and northern Belgium, French in southern Belgium and Luxembourg; in cuisine – southern Belgium's long and honourable tradition of good food influence the rich dishes of Luxembourg to the east; and in architecture – compare the gabled facades of northern Belgium to those of provincial Holland. The landscape also ignores frontiers, the plains of northern Belgium merging into the flat southern provinces of Holland. Sometimes, travelling around, you would hardly know you had crossed a border: formalities are few, and there's often little obvious change apart from car registration plates and currency – and between Belgium and Luxembourg even that remains the same.

Within this homogeneity, however, differences remain, especially in Belgium, which clearly divides between the north – Flanders – a flat Flemish-speaking region that's home to most of its historic towns, and the hillier French-speaking southern region of Wallonia. Holland is a less obviously divided state, its unifying factor being water, the presence of which is reflected almost everywhere – in the food (plenty of fish), the look of the towns (charmingly cut by canals), and the landscape, the reclaimed polder areas enjoying slender protection from the open sea by means of dykes. In spite of this there are discernible regions. Though only three hours away by train, Friesland – and especially its offshore islands – can seem a world away from Amsterdam and the other Randstad cities, a feeling reinforced by the attitudes of the locals, who look on the capital as a kind of faraway "sin city" that impinges little on their everyday lives.

Despite these distinctions, few travellers stray far beyond the major centres of Bruges, Brussels and Amsterdam, most treating the Low Countries as a sort of weekend-away destination for the work-weary. Certainly few really know – or care to know – the region, which is a shame as there is plenty to discover. The Belgian (and Luxembourg) Ardennes offer some of the wildest, most untamed **scenery** in this part of Europe, fast-flowing rivers and steep gorges sitting beneath green hills and towering crags high enough for some of Europe's most northerly ski resorts. Belgium and Holland also hold some of Europe's most historic **cities** – places like Bruges, Ghent, Antwerp, Leiden, Haarlem and Maastricht, to name only the most memorable – all of which have superbly preserved city centres, while maintaining a lively and relevant cultural life. Of the **capitals**, Belgium has in **Brussels** one of Europe's most cosmopolitan and happening cities, despite its relatively dour reputation; **Amsterdam**, with its delicate balance of seediness and culture, and perhaps the world's most beautifully preserved city centre, needs no introduction; while **Luxembourg** more than compensates for a lack of sights with a marvellously spectacular location.

Among things to do and see, you can enjoy the well-displayed fruits of the region's long and distinguished **artistic tradition** in some wonderful galleries. Outside the urban centres, **cycling** is, not surprisingly, a big activity, both in the low landscapes of north Belgium and Holland and – to a greater degree if anything – in the hills of the Ardennes. **Hiking**, too, is second to none, in the Belgian Ardennes and in Luxembourg, while in northern Holland at low tide people go wadlopen or **mud-walking** across the dank mud flats to the Frisian islands.

Climate and when to go

All three countries enjoy a temperate **climate**, with warm, if fairly mild, summers and cold winters. Generally speaking, temperatures rise the further south you go, with Belgium a couple of degrees warmer than Holland for much of the year. To the east, also, temperatures begin to dip, as the more severe climate of continental Europe begins to assert itself. In all three countries, rain is a possibility all year round.

Holland's climate is influenced by the ubiquitous proximity of water, and in winter city centre canals can make the streets alongside brutally cold – though the western, maritime side of the country is in general warmer than the eastern provinces. **Belgium** enjoys a fairly standard temperate climate, slightly warmer than Holland on the whole, though growing colder the further east you go – something emphasized by the increase in altitude with the Ardennes. In **Luxembourg** temperatures are that little bit more extreme, with sometimes fairly harsh winters that almost always bring snow. In both countries you can expect more rain in the Ardennes and upland regions.

As regards **clothing**, you should take heavy coats, hats and gloves in winter, lighter clothes and warm sweaters for the evening in summer, with some kind of rain protection all year round.

AVERAGE DAILY TEMPERATURES (°C)			
	Holland	Belgium	Luxembourg
January	2	1	0
February	2	4	1
March	5	7	7
April	8	11	11
May	12	13	13
June	15	18	17
July	17	19	19
August	17	18	16
September	15	17	15
October	11	12	9
November	6	7	4
December	3	3	2

PART ONE

THE

BASICS

GETTING THERE FROM BRITAIN AND IRELAND

The wide range of options available to reach Holland, Belgium or Luxembourg means basically deciding between a swift but relatively expensive flight, a low-cost but time-consuming ferry crossing, or, once it has opened, a faster journey by train or car using the Channel Tunnel – although this is of most use if you're travelling to Belgium. Whichever alternative you opt for, you'll find a variety of competitive fares on these busy routes.

BY PLANE

Flying to any of the major airports in the Low Countries – Schiphol (for Amsterdam), Brussels, Antwerp or Maastricht – represents a considerable saving in time compared to the ferry connections: Schiphol, for example, is just 45 minutes' flying time from London.

Fares tend to be slightly more expensive to destinations other than Schiphol or Brussels: the large number of flights passing through both these cities has led to a mass of cheap tickets, however, and it's reasonably easy to find a return fare from London for around £80; a standard, unrestricted ticket will cost upwards of £120. To find the current bargains, study the ads in the Sunday travel sections of the quality newspapers (*The Observer* especially), or, if you live in London, the back pages of the listings magazine *Time Out* and the *Evening Standard*.

Alternatively, go to a **discount flight agent** such as *STA Travel* or *Campus Travel* (addresses over the page), who specialize in youth flights, and, if you're under 26 or a student, can offer savings on the price of a flight; they also offer ordinary discounted tickets.

It's also worth trying the **national scheduled airlines** direct – *British Airways, KLM, Sabena* and *Luxair* – since their fares can be competitive with the cheaper operators. The best deal you'll get with a scheduled airline is with an APEX or Super PEX ticket: these cost around £130 return (£150 upward for Luxembourg) and have to be booked fourteen days in advance; you have to spend one Saturday night abroad, and have no option to change your flight. To gain more flexibility, you'll need to buy a standard return, which can prove more than twice as expensive. The **smaller operators**, such as *British Midland* and *Air UK*, sometimes work out cheaper.

If you don't live in London, bear in mind that there's a huge number of flights leaving from various **UK regional airports**, especially to the capital cities, and that these can be good value alternatives, particularly if you use the smaller operators. Their APEX fares average £138 return, but bargains can occasionally be found. The larger, national carriers tend to be much more expensive. It's also worth considering a **package deal** if you want to stay in one city and have your accommodation arrangements organized beforehand; these can be surprisingly good value (see p.7 for more details).

BY TRAIN

Until the opening of full direct services through the Channel Tunnel, taking a **train** to either Holland or Belgium involves travelling at least part of the way by ferry or jetfoil/hovercraft; and even after the Channel Tunnel is properly up and running, it might be that you prefer the relatively leisurely approach by sea – not to mention the duty-free services.

TO HOLLAND

British Rail operates services to Amsterdam (Centraal Station) from Liverpool Street and Victoria stations. Basically, the choice of route depends on how long you want to spend on the water. Two daily departures run from Liverpool Street via Harwich to the Hook of Holland, passing

AIRLINE ADDRESSES AND ROUTES

Aer Lingus 223 Regent St, London W1 (☎081/569 5555). Birmingham to Brussels, Manchester to Schiphol.

Air UK Stansted Airport (☎0345/666777). London (Heathrow), Aberdeen, Edinburgh, Glasgow, Humberside, Leeds/Bradford, Newcastle, Norwich and Teeside to Schiphol; Stansted to Schiphol and Brussels.

Birmingham European Airways Birmingham Airport (☎021/782 0711). Birmingham to Schiphol.

British Airways 75 Regent St, London W1 (☎081/897 4000). London (Heathrow), Aberdeen, Belfast, Birmingham, Edinburgh, Glasgow, Manchester and Newcastle to Schiphol; London (Heathrow) to Brussels, Antwerp and Luxembourg, Manchester to Brussels. London (Gatwick) to Rotterdam.

British Midland (☎071/581 0864). London (Heathrow), Belfast and East Midlands to Schiphol; Birmingham to Brussels.

Europe Express (☎0345/444737). London (Gatwick) to Rotterdam.

Flexair (☎0800/289447). London (City Airport) to Rotterdam.

KLM 8 Hanover St, London W1 (☎081/750 9000). London (Heathrow), Belfast, Birmingham, Cardiff, Manchester, Newcastle and Southampton to Schiphol. London (Heathrow) to Eindhoven and Rotterdam.

Luxair Terminal 2, Heathrow Airport (☎081/745 4254). London (Heathrow) to Luxembourg.

Netherlines 8 Hanover St, London W1 (☎081/750 9000). Birmingham, Bristol, Luton, Manchester, Southampton and Teeside to Schiphol.

NLM 8 Hanover St, London W1. (☎081/750 9000). London (Gatwick and Heathrow) to Eindhoven and Rotterdam, London (Gatwick) to Maastricht.

Sabena 36 Piccadilly, London W1 (☎081/780 1444). London (Heathrow), Birmingham, Bristol, Edinburgh, Glasgow, Leeds/Bradford, Manchester, Newcastle and Southend to Brussels, London (Heathrow) to Antwerp.

Suckling Airways Ipswich Airport (☎0473/729091). Manchester to Schiphol via Cambridge.

Transavia (☎0293/38181). London (Gatwick) to Schiphol.

DISCOUNT FLIGHT AGENTS

Campus Travel, 52 Grosvenor Gardens, London SW1 (☎071/730 3402); 541 Bristol Rd, Selly Oak, Birmingham (☎021/414 1848); 39 Queen's Rd, Clifton, Bristol (☎0272/292494); 5 Emmanuel St, Cambridge (☎0223/324283); 53 Forest Rd, Edinburgh (☎031/668 3303); 166 Deansgate, Manchester (☎061/273 1721); 13 High St, Oxford (☎0865/242067); also in YHA shops and on university campuses throughout Britain. Student/youth specialists.

Council Travel 28a Poland St, London W1 (☎071/287 3337).

South Coast Student Travel, 61 Ditchling Rd, Brighton (☎0273/570226). A good agent with plenty to offer non-students as well.

Springways Travel, 71 Oxford St, London W1 (☎071/734 0393). Reliable agent for discounted flights.

STA Travel, 74 Old Brompton Rd, London W7 (☎071/937 9962); 25 Queen's Rd, Bristol (☎0272/294 399); 38 Sidney St, Cambridge (☎0223/66966); 75 Deansgate, Manchester (☎061/834 0668); and personal callers at 117 Euston Rd, London NW1; 28 Vicar Lane, Leeds; 36 George St, Oxford; and offices at the universities of Birmingham, London, Kent and Loughborough. Discount fares and special deals for students and young people.

Travel Cuts 295 Regent St, London W1 (☎071/255 1944).

---

through Rotterdam, The Hague, Leiden and Haarlem before reaching Amsterdam; return fares are £63 for a five-day excursion, £83 otherwise. There are also four daily departures from London Victoria via Dover and Ostend in Belgium; on this route, five-day excursions cost £73, longer stays as much as £99, depending on the sailing and the time of year. Total journey times on both routes are ten to twelve hours each way, and tickets are

valid for two months. If you opt to travel at night, cabin supplements start at around £10 per person. Tickets for these services (and to all other destinations in the Low Countries) can be bought from any *British Rail* ticket office, many high street travel agents or *Eurotrain* (see opposite).

To travel to any other city in Holland, there's a flat fare from London of £49 single, £83 return if you travel via the Hook. Travelling via Ostend, individual fares apply unless you opt for a five-day excursion fare for £73.

TO BELGIUM AND LUXEMBOURG

British Rail's services run three times a day from London Victoria via Dover and Ostend, stopping at Bruges and Ghent before reaching **Brussels**. There's an option of ferry or jetfoil services across the Channel: journey times to Brussels are eight to ten hours by boat, six hours by jetfoil. Fares to Brussels are £57 for a five-day excursion ticket, £72 for an ordinary return; jetfoil supplements are £10 each way.

To Luxembourg, take either the jetfoil or ferry options detailed above and change at Brussels' Midi Station; the train arrives in Luxembourg two and a half hours later. Fares are £79 for a five-day excursion, £100 otherwise.

YOUTH FARES

Fares can be cut drastically if you're **under 26**. **BIJ** (youth) tickets are available from *Eurotrain*, 52 Grosvenor Gardens, London SW1 (☎071/730 3402), plus branches nationwide, or most other student/youth travel agents. These cost £62 (return) to Amsterdam, £52 to Brussels, £82 to Luxembourg; tickets are valid for two months and you can stop off en route as many times as you wish. These prices drop considerably in winter months. It is, of course, possible to buy a BIJ ticket to any destination on the rail network in any of the three countries. Eurotrain also offer **"Explorer"** tickets for anyone under 26, which are valid for unlimited rail travel around a prescribed circular route, taking in, say, Paris, Amsterdam and Brussels for around £74.

Another cash-saving possibility for those under 26 (and resident in Europe for six months) is the **InterRail pass**, currently costing £249 from any major UK train station or student/youth travel agents, which is valid for one month's travel on all European (and Moroccan) railways, and gives around a third off rail travel within Britain and fifty percent off certain cross-channel and North Sea ferries. This could cut costs significantly if the Low Countries form part of your European travels (see also the **Benelux Tourrail** card and **EuroDomino** passes, detailed in "Low Countries Connections" on p.10).

An alternative to this, worth considering if you intend only travelling within a limited area of Europe is the **InterRail zonal pass**. Passes for a

single zone, valid for fifteen days, and covering Holland, Belgium, Luxembourg and France, cost £179; monthly passes for two and three zones cost £209 and £229 respectively. Contact the nearest large *British Rail* station or a student travel office for more details.

BY BUS

Travelling by long-distance **bus** is a good option if you're over 26, since fares are roughly the same as for under-26 rail travel. Choices are between bus and hovercraft (via Dover–Calais) and the slower bus and ferry.

Eurolines, operated by *National Express*, offer four daily departures from London's Victoria coach station to **Amsterdam** in summer, via Breda, Rotterdam and The Hague or Breda and Utrecht (one service leaving in the morning, the other overnight). They also run coaches once daily overnight to **Brussels**, via Antwerp. *Eurolines* also act as agents for *Hoverspeed* who offer similar services, but with faster hovercraft crossings. Their twice daily London–Brussels service runs through Bruges and Ghent (daily morning service) or Lille and Mons (daily afternoon service). Tickets for all services are bookable through most travel agents or *British*

BUS COMPANIES AND JOURNEY TIMES

Hoverspeed City Sprint (☎0304/240241)
National Express/Eurolines (☎071/730 8235), plus agents nationwide.

Destination	Eurolines	Hoverspeed
Amsterdam	12hr	10hr
The Hague	11hr 30min	9hr 30min
Rotterdam	11hr	9hr
Brussels	11hr	8hr
Bruges	6hr	—
Antwerp	9hr 30min	7hr 30min
Ghent	6hr 30min	—

Return fares to all destinations are £49

Rail travel centres, and there's an eight percent reduction for under-25s and students.

BY CAR: FERRIES AND LE SHUTTLE

With the opening of the Channel Tunnel – which should be running regular shuttle services for cars by the summer of 1994 – travelling by car, to Belgium at least, will become much easier. However, at the time of writing you could only take your car to the Continent by **ferry** – and this in any case may well continue to be your preferred route to Holland even after the Tunnel is open. Below is a list of the ferry routes that take you into the Low Countries.

High street **travel agents** have fares and brochures on offer; it's worth shopping around for competitive deals. Prices vary with the month, day and even hour that you're travelling, how long you're staying and the size of your car, and the different ferry companies are always offering special fares to outdo their competitors – not to mention the tunnel. In particular, since the price structures tend to be geared around one-way rather than return travel, you don't necessarily have to cross over and back from the same port.

FERRY ROUTES AND FARES

The **most direct ferry crossings into Holland** are via Harwich to the Hook of Holland, and from Sheerness to Vlissingen. It takes about one hour to drive from the Hook to Amsterdam; from Vlissingen it takes roughly two and a half hours.

FERRY DETAILS

Routes and prices

| Destination | Operator | Frequency | Duration | One-way fares | |
				Car, 2 adults, 2 kids	Foot passenger
HOLLAND					
Harwich–Hook of Holland	*Stena Sealink*	2 daily	6hr 45min (day) 8hr 45min (night)	£84–174	£30
Sheerness–Vlissingen	*Olau Lines*	2 daily	7hr (day) 8hr 30min (night)	£91–114	£27.50
Hull–Rotterdam	*North Sea*	1 daily	14hr	£151–179	£47–55
BELGIUM					
Dover–Ostend	*P&O*	6–8 daily	4hr	£70–145	£24
Hull–Zeebrugge	*North Sea*	1 daily	14hr 30min	£151–179	£47–55
Felixtowe–Zeebrugge	*P&O*	2 daily	5hr 45min (day) 8hr (night)	£70–145	£24
FRANCE					
Ramsgate–Dunkerque	*Sally Line*	2hr 30min	5 daily	£59–120	£15

Discount tickets

Olau: 53-hr and 5-day returns for £33; various off-peak and combination tickets.

P&O: 72-hr returns for the price of a single.

Stena Sealink: Foot passenger day returns for £32 on Thurs and Fri; also 5-day returns for same price.

Ferry companies

North Sea Ferries, King George Dock, Hedon Road, Hull HU9 5QA (☎0482/77177).

Olau Lines, 104 Anchor Lane, Sheerness, Kent ME12 1SN (☎0795/666666).

P&O European Ferries, Channel House, Channel View Rd, Dover, Kent , CT17 (☎0304/203388).

Sally Line, 81 Piccadilly, London W1V 9HF (☎071/409 2240).

Stena Sealink, Charter House, Park St, Ashford, Kent TN24 (☎0233/647047).

If you're **heading for Belgium**, or want to spend less time crossing the water, consider instead sailing either from Dover to Ostend, or, if you live in the Midlands or north of England, from Felixstowe to Zeebrugge. Further options from the north of England are the Hull–Rotterdam service, which leaves you just an hour or so's drive from Amsterdam, and the Hull–Zeebrugge service for Belgium and the south.

If you're going for a **weekend break**, check out the short-period excursion fares offered by all the companies; usually 53-hour or five-day returns which can cost the same as a single. If you have kids, *Sealink* have the best deals: on day crossings children under fourteen may travel free, and at night go for fifty percent discount; other companies tend to give a fifty percent discount across the board. All also carry **children** under four free. Note that for those **under 26** or a **student**, *Eurotrain* can knock a few pounds off ferry tickets.

Booking ahead is strongly recommended for motorists; indeed it's essential in high season. Foot passengers can normally just turn up and board, at any time of year.

LE SHUTTLE

The opening of **Le Shuttle** service through the **Channel Tunnel** should go some way to speeding up journey-times for those crossing the Channel by car, although whether it will make the journey any more pleasurable is debatable. Trains run 24 hours a day, carrying cars, motorcycles, coaches and their passengers, and take just 35 minutes between Folkestone and Calais. At peak times, services leave every fifteen minutes, and advance bookings should hopefully be unnecessary; at night services are hourly. Summer fares, basically between May and August, run to a fairly hefty £280–310 return per vehicle (including passengers) – much less than this out of the high season period. Through **trains** will eventually run through the Tunnel, connecting London and Brussels in around three hours.

> **LE SHUTTLE**
> Information and ticket sales ☎0303/271100.

HITCHING

It's relatively easy to get lifts once in Holland or Belgium, so **hitching** can be a good way of cutting costs. Bear in mind, though, that drivers

are nowadays made to account for unauthorized passengers, and it's no longer possible to travel over for free in a truck-driver's cab. To make sure of a lift on arrival, talk to as many people as you can on the ferry and do your best to cajole them into picking you up on the other side of customs.

FROM IRELAND

There are no direct **ferry links** from Ireland to the Dutch or Belgian coasts, but if you are a student under 32, **direct flights to Amsterdam** from Dublin, Cork or Shannon can be had from IR£195 return through *USIT* also have bargain fares for those under 26 that involve a change at Stansted in London and cost upwards of IR£190. Flights **direct to Brussels** for students and/or those under 26 can be had for as little as IR£110. **Flights to Luxembourg** via London (for students/under 26s) cost around IR£230. For non-students and those over 26, fares start at around the same price but escalate quickly: book well in advance for bargains and ask *USIT* for details of regular charters. *USIT* also offer flights from Belfast to Amsterdam (from IR£166 for students/under 26s via London, IR£191 direct), Brussels (from IR£174) and Luxembourg (from IR£197). Their office at *Belfast Student Travel* has details.

> **FLIGHT AGENTS IN IRELAND**
> **Belfast Student Travel**, 13b College Street, Belfast, BT1 6ET (☎0232/324073).
> **USIT**, Aston Quay, O'Connell Bridge, Dublin 2 (☎01/679 8833).

PACKAGE HOLIDAYS

Don't be put off by the idea of going on a **package**: most comprise only travel and accommodation and can work out an easy way of cutting costs and hassle – especially if you live some distance from London, as many operators offer a range of regional flight departures. Depending on the type of hotel you opt for (anything from budget to five-star is available with most companies), city breaks in Amsterdam, Brussels, Luxembourg and other cities start at £70 per person for return coach and hovercraft travel and two nights' accommodation in a one-star hotel with breakfast, or a little over £100 if you fly. A travel agent can advise further on the best deals available, or you can contact one of the **operators** over the page.

PACKAGE HOLIDAY COMPANIES

Amsterdam/Belgian Travel Service Bridge House, Ware SG12 9DF (☎0920/463900). Amsterdam and various Belgian cities. Inexpensive.

Anglo Dutch Sports, 30a Foxgrove Rd, Beckenham, Kent (☎081/650 2347). Specialists in cycling holidays, with a wide and flexible range of destinations.

Cresta Holidays, 32 Victoria St, Altrincham WA14 1ET (☎061/926 8817). City and short breaks in Amsterdam, Brusseis and Bruges.

Hoseasons Holidays, Sunway House, Lowestoft NR32 3LT (☎0502/500555). Boating and self-catering holidays in both Holland and Belgium.

Olau Line Holidays, 104 Anchor Lane, Sheerness, Kent ME12 1SN (☎0795/666666). An interesting variety of short holidays all over the Low Countries.

Thomson Holidays, First Floor, Greater London House, Hampstead Road, London NW1 7SD (☎071/632 6282). Short breaks in Amsterdam and Brussels; often the cheapest.

Time Off, 2a Chester Close, London SW1X 7BQ (☎071/235 8070). Short breaks in Amsterdam, The Hague, Brussels, Bruges and Luxembourg.

Travelscene, 11–15 St Ann's Rd, Harrow, Middlesex (☎081/427 8800). Weekend breaks.

GETTING THERE FROM NORTH AMERICA

Flying direct to Holland and Belgium from the United States should not be a problem, although getting to Luxembourg might take a bit more ingenuity – and money. Most of the major US airlines service either Amsterdam or Brussels, and prices are about the same as travelling to Paris – although more expensive than going to London.

FROM THE USA

KLM, the Dutch national airline, flies from a number of US cities **to Holland**, but, like most national airlines, its fares are not cheap. *KLM* has daily flights to Amsterdam from New York JFK, Baltimore–Washington, Houston, Los Angeles, Chicago, Minneapolis–St Paul and Atlanta, and three flights a week from Orlando, Florida. High season round-trip **fares** from JFK are in the region of $900, while from LA the cost is around $1110. In low season, prices range from $600 on the New York route to $650 if you fly from LA.

To Belgium, the national carrier, *Sabena*, which flies from New York JFK, Boston and Chicago into Brussels, offers almost identical prices to those of *KLM*. *TWA* has a daily flight from JFK to both Brussels and Amsterdam. *American Airlines* flies non-stop to Brussels from JFK and Chicago, with the Chicago fare working

out only $40 more expensive than the regular New York fare of around $900 round trip in high season. The only way to fly direct **to Luxembourg** is by taking *Iceland Air*, which during the summer months flies every day to Findel Airport in Luxembourg, making a 45-minute stopover in Iceland on the way. Fares are $830 round trip in high season, $548 in low season.

FROM CANADA

Sabena flies from Montreal to Brussels three times a week – on Wednesday, Friday and Sunday; while prices fluctuate throughout the year, a high season round trip APEX fare will cost around CDN$930. *Sabena* also has connections from Brussels through to Amsterdam, although *KLM* offers by far the most comprehensive

TOLL-FREE AIRLINE ENQUIRY NUMBERS

Air Canada ☎1-800/776-3000

Air France ☎1-800/237-2747

American Airlines ☎1-800/433-7300

British Airways ☎1-800/247-9297

KLM ☎1-800/777-5553

TWA ☎1-800/221-2000

United Airlines ☎1-800/241-6522

Virgin Atlantic ☎1-800/862-8621

Canadian service to Amsterdam, flying non-stop from Toronto and Montreal daily and direct non-stop three days a week from Calgary, two days a week from Vancouver and Halifax, and just once a week from Ottawa. The cheapest (non-refundable) APEX fare during high season is about CDN$900 travelling from Toronto, CDN$1500 from Vancouver or Calgary. None of the major airlines is cheap – though *Martinair* undercuts *KLM* on the Toronto–Amsterdam route by about CDN$100 – so it's worth it to check with a discount travel agent like *Travel Cuts* (see below for addresses) which can offer useful reductions, although some of their tickets are restricted to students, or travellers under 26.

DISCOUNT FLIGHTS

You can normally cut costs even further if you go through a **specialist flight agent** – either a **consolidator**, who buys up blocks of tickets from the airlines and subsequently sells them at a knock-down price, or a **discount agent**, who wheels and deals in blocks of tickets offloaded by the airlines, and is often able to offer special student and youth fares together with a range of other travel-related services such as travel insurance, rail passes, car rentals, tours and the like. High season round-trip fares to Amsterdam can be picked up for as little as $600, and prices can drop to below $500 during off-peak periods. Bear in mind, though, that the penalties charged for changing your plans can be stiff. Some agents specialize in charter flights, which may be cheaper than anything available on a scheduled flight, but again departure dates are fixed and withdrawal penalties are high (check the company's refund policy). If you travel a lot, **discount travel clubs** are another option – the annual membership fee may be worth it for benefits such as cut-price air tickets and car rental.

DISCOUNT FLIGHT AGENTS

Air Brokers International, 323 Geary St, Suite 411, San Francisco, CA 94102 (☎1-800/883-3273). Consolidator.

Council Charter, 205 E 42nd St, New York, NY 10017 (☎1-800/223-7402). Youth-oriented charter broker.

Council Travel, 205 E 42nd St, New York, NY 10017 (☎212/661-1450); 1093 Broxton Ave, Los Angeles, CA 90024 (☎213/208-3551); 1210 Potomac St, NW Washington, DC 20007 (☎202/337-6464); 1153 North Dearborn St, Chicago IL 60610 (☎312/951-0585); 8141 Maple St, New Orleans, LA 70118 (☎504/866-1767); 729 Boylston St, Suite 201, Boston, MA 02116 (☎617/266-1926); Exec. Tower Office Center, 3300 West Mockingbird, Suite 101, Dallas, TX 75235 (☎214/350-6166); 1314 NE 43rd St, Suite 210, Seattle WA 98105 (☎206/632-2448). North America's largest student travel outfit.

Discount Travel International, Ives Building, 114 Forrest Ave, Suite 205, Narberth, PA 19072 (☎215/668-7184). Discount travel club, membership $45.

Moment's Notice, 425 Madison Ave, New York, NY (☎212/486-0503). Travel club.

Nouvelles Frontières, 19th W 44th St, Suite 1702, New York, NY 10036 (☎212/764-6494); 6363 Wilshire Blvd, Suite 200, Los Angeles, CA 90048 (☎213/658-8955); 209 Post St, Suite 1121,

San Francisco, CA 94108 (☎415/781-4480); 1130 Ouest, bd de Maisonneuve, Montréal, PQ H3A 1M8 (☎514/842-1450); 176 Grand Allée Ouest, Québec, PQ G1R 2G9 (☎418/525-5255).

STA Travel, 273 Newbury St, Boston, MA 02116 (☎617/266-6014); 920 Westwood Blvd, Los Angeles, CA 90024 (☎213/824-1574); 17 East 45th St, New York, NY 10017 (☎212/986-9470); 166 Geary St, Suite 702, San Francisco, CA 94108 (☎415/391-8407).

Stand Buys, 311 W Superior St, Chicago, IL 60610 (☎1-800/548-1116). Travel club.

Travel Cuts, 170812 St NW, Calgary T2M 3M7 (☎403/282-7687); Student Union Building, University of British Columbia, Vancouver V6T 1W5 (☎604/228-6890); University of Manitoba, Winnipeg R3T 2N2 (☎204/269-9530); 6139 South St, Halifax B3H 4J2 (☎902/424-7027); 96 Gerrard St East, Toronto M5B 1G7 (☎416/977-0441). The principal student/youth discount agency in Canada.

UniTravel, 1177 N Warson Rd, St Louis, MO 63132 (☎1-800/325-2222). Consolidator.

Voyages Cuts, 19 rue Ste-Ursule, Québec G1R4E1 (☎418/692-3971); 3480 rue McTavish, Montréal H3A 1X9 (☎514/398-0647); Place Riel Campus Centre, University of Saskatchewan, Saskatoon S7N 0W0 (☎306/343-1601).

GETTING THERE FROM AUSTRALASIA

The rockbottom alternative to the Low Countries from **Australia** is with *Aeroflot*, who fly from Sydney to Amsterdam via Moscow twice a week for Aus$1900 in high season — Aus$1600 off-season. *Garuda* (via Bali, Jakarta and Bangkok) and *Japan Airlines* (via Tokyo) fly similarly regularly from both Australia and New Zealand, although with them you can reckon on paying around Aus$100 more. *KLM* fly four times a week from Sydney to Amsterdam, and although their flights come more expensive — Aus$2400 in high season, Aus$2000 the rest of the time, you receive coupons for four free flights within Europe when you buy your ticket — a potentially good deal if you're making Amsterdam the start of a wider tour. *Lufthansa* do a similar deal, and

they fly from Auckland in **New Zealand** as well as Sydney, both via Frankfurt; they also often have deals on car rental, etc.

AIRLINES
Aeroflot, 388 George St, Sydney (☎02/233 7911).
Garuda, 175 Clarence St, Sydney (☎02/334 9900); 120 Albert St, Auckland (☎09/366 1855).
Japan Airlines, 17 Bligh St, Sydney (☎02/233 5400).
KLM, 5 Elizabeth St, Sydney (☎02/231 6333).
Lufthansa, 143 Macquarie St, Sydney (☎02/367 3800); 109 Queen St, Auckland (☎09/303 1520).

AUSTRALIAN DISCOUNT AGENTS

Anywhere Travel, 345 Anzac Parade, Kingsford, Sydney (☎02/663 0411).

Brisbane Discount Travel, 360 Queen St, Brisbane (☎07/229 9211).

Discount Travel Specialists, Shop 53, Forrest Chase, Perth (☎09/221 1400).

Flight Centres, Circular Quay, Sydney (☎02/241 2422); Bourke St, Melbourne (☎03/650 2899); plus other branches nationwide except the Northern Territory.

Passport Travel, 320b Glenferrie Rd, Malvern, Melbourne (☎03/824 7183).

STA Travel, 732 Harris St, Sydney (☎02/212 1255); 256 Flinders St, Melbourne (☎03/347 4711); other offices in Townsville and state capitals.

Topdeck Travel, 45 Grenfell St, Adelaide (☎08/410 1110).

Tymtro Travel, Suite G12, Wallaceway Shopping Centre, Chatswood, Sydney (☎02/411 1222).

NEW ZEALAND DISCOUNT AGENTS

Budget Travel, PO Box 505, Auckland (☎09/309 4313).

Flight Centres, National Bank Towers, 205–225 Queen St, Auckland (☎09/309 6171); Shop 1M, National Mutual Arcade, 152 Hereford St, Christchurch (☎09/379 7145); 50–52 Willis St,

Wellington (☎04/472 8101); other branches countrywide.

STA Travel, Traveller's Centre, 10 High St, Auckland (☎09/309 9995); 233 Cuba St, Wellington (☎04/385 0561); 223 High St, Christchurch (☎03/379 9098); other offices in Dunedin, Palmerston North and Hamilton.

LOW COUNTRIES CONNECTIONS

Both Holland and Belgium have an extensive rail network, and connections between the two countries are good, with hourly trains linking south Holland (Roosendaal) to Brussels (via Antwerp), and connecting Maastricht in Holland to

Brussels via Liège. Trains to Luxembourg from Brussels pass either though Liège or Namur; from Holland they pass through Brussels or Maastricht and Liège. There are no border formalities imposed when travelling by train.

RAIL PASSES

If you're travelling the whole Low Countries region by train, it's worth considering a **Benelux Tourrail** card. This enables you to travel on all Dutch, Belgian and Luxembourg railways for five out of a specified seventeen days and costs F3760 in Belgium/Luxembourg (F2860 if you're under 26) ƒ217/162 in The Netherlands. It's available from any train station in Holland, Belgium or Luxembourg, or in England from *Belgian Railways*, 439 Premier House, Greycoat Place, London SW1P 1SB (☎071/233 0360), or *Netherlands Railways*, at 25–28 Buckingham Gate, London SW1E 6LD (☎071/630 1735) for £80/60.

Alternatively there's the **EuroDomino ticket**, which gives unlimited rail travel, but only in one country's network. Available from travel agents or any mainline station, either in the country or outside it, they're worth considering if you know that all your travel will be in just one of the Benelux countries. There's a further discount for those under 26 (see the price chart below).

EURODOMINO RAIL PASSES

	3-day	5-day	10-day
Holland	£31/24	£51/38	£92/69
Belgium	£38/31	£41/33	£73/59
Luxembourg	£14/11	£17/14	£30/23

Prices are second class, over 26/under 26

American and Canadian travellers should consider investing in a **Eurail pass**, valid for unlimited first-class travel throughout seventeen countries, including The Netherlands. It's available for periods of 15 days ($498), 21 days ($648), one month ($798), two months ($1098) and three months ($1398). For Americans under 26 years of age, the **Eurail Youthpass** offers one or two months' unlimited second-class rail travel for

TRAIN OFFICES AND AGENCIES IN NORTH AMERICA

British Rail International, 1500 Broadway, New York, NY 10036 (☎1-800/677-8585 or 212/575-2667); 94 Cumberland St, Toronto, ON M5R 1A3 (☎416/929-3333).

CIE Tours International, 108 Ridgedale Ave, Morristown, NJ 07690 (☎1-800/522-5258 or 201/292-3438).

Rail Europe, 226–230 Westchester Ave, White Plains, NY 10604 (☎1-800/848-7245 or 914/682-2999); and branches in Santa Monica, San Francisco, Fort Lauderdale, Chicago, Dallas, Vancouver and Montréal.

$578 and $768 respectively. There's also the option of a **Eurail Flexipass,** which entitles travellers to a range of options: five days of unlimited first-class travel spread out over a fifteen-day period ($255); a one month pass which gives ten days of travel ($402); and a two month pass which gives fifteen days of travel ($540). All passes must be bought before you leave for Europe from an authorized travel agent or from *RailEurope*.

BUS CONNECTIONS

Most **bus stations** in the Low Countries are next to train stations. Bus services often complement train routes, and are more useful for local hops than long-distance journeys. In Luxembourg the bus network is much more extensive than the train, and with a *Benelux Tourrail* card you can travel free on the buses run by Luxembourg Railways.

ROADS AND CAR RENTAL

Road connections are fast, usually with no border formalities to slow you down. If you're taking your own car you may well need a green card from your insurance company, but not an

CAR RENTAL COMPANIES

IN THE UK		IN THE US	
Avis	☎081/848 8733	Avis	☎ 1-800/722 1333
Budget	☎0800/181 181	Budget	☎1-800/527 0700
Eurodollar	☎0895/233300	Dollar	☎1-800/421 6868
Europcar	☎081/950 5050	Hertz	☎1-800/654 3131
Hertz	☎081/679 1799	National	☎1-800/227 7368

international driving licence. **Car rental** costs are comparable with the UK, although considerably higher than in the US: prices for the smallest vehicle (inclusive of collision damage waiver and insurance) start at £200 per week in Holland, £250 in Belgium, and a cheaper £175 in Luxembourg. Of the international companies, *Hertz* tend to be the cheapest: you should make some savings by going to local operators. Bear in mind, too, that it's always cheaper to rent your car before you leave home and pick it up at the airport on arrival: a good agent for this in the UK are *Holiday Autos* (☎071/491 1111). For more on driving, see the *Practicalities* sections for each country.

PLANES

Plane connections might be worth considering as an alternative to a long train trip. The Amsterdam–Brussels route is served by *Sabena* and *NLM*: there are roughly eight flights daily and the cheapest PEX return fare (valid for three months, and you must spend a Saturday night away) works out at £105, plus around £10 in taxes; an ordinary single costs £99. The Amsterdam–Luxembourg route is operated by *Netherlines* and *Luxair*: an APEX return, on which the same restrictions apply, costs £169, and an ordinary, unrestricted single £159.

RED TAPE AND VISAS

Citizens of the UK and Ireland, other EC countries, and Australia and New Zealand, need only a valid passport to stay three months in Holland, Belgium or Luxembourg. A one-year British Visitor's Passport, obtainable from post offices, is also valid for the same period. On arrival, make sure you have enough money to convince officials you can support yourself. Poorer-looking visitors are often checked, and if you can't flash a few travellers' cheques or notes you may not be allowed in.

For longer stays, you officially need an **extension visa**. These are obtainable in advance from the relevant embassy in your own country. In reality, if you hold a European Community passport restrictions are fairly loose –

they're not always date-stamped when entering the country – though if you are definitely planning to stay and work it's probably best to get a stamp anyway.

Non-EC nationals, however, should always have their documents in order. **Residence permits** are preferably obtained from outside the particular country and are issued for a maximum term of one year – upon proof of income from sources other than employment in that country, and sometimes not even then. **Work permits** for non-EC nationals are even harder to get; your prospective employer must apply locally while you simultaneously apply at home; both parties must await its issuance (by no means automatic) before proceeding.

United States and Canadian citizens travelling to Holland, Belgium or Luxembourg do not need an entry visa for trips of ninety days or less: all that is required is a valid passport and a round-trip ticket. Visitors who wish to stay for more than ninety days must apply for a residency permit, which has to be done at the relevant embassy in your home country. One exception to this rule is that US citizens who wish to prolong their stay in The Netherlands can report to the police for a permit within eight days of their arrival in the country.

CUSTOMS

Since the inauguration of the EC Single Market, EC citizens travelling from one EC country to another do not have to make a declaration to

NETHERLANDS EMBASSIES AND CONSULATES

UK Write for an information pack to PO Box 523, London SW1E 6NT.
Information line ☎0891/200277 (24hr: calls charged above normal rate).

Ireland 160 Merrion Road, Dublin 4 (☎01/693 444).

Belgium Wotensehschapsstraat 35/ rue de la Science 35, 1040 Brussels (☎02/2230 3020).

Luxembourg 5 rue C M Spoor, L-2546 Luxembourg (☎275 70).

Australia 130 Empire Circus, Yarralumla, Canberra A.C.T. 2600 (☎62/733 111).

Canada Third Floor, 275 Slater Street, Ottowa, Ontario ONT K1P 5H9 (☎613/237 5030).

Denmark Toldbodgade 95, 1253 Copenhagen K (☎01/156 293).

Norway Oscargate 29, 0352 Oslo 3 (☎02/60 21 93).

Sweden Gotgatan 16A, 11646 Stockholm (☎08/247180).

New Zealand Investment House, Tenth Floor, Balance and Featherstone Street, Wellington (☎04/738 652).

USA
4200 Linnean Ave. NW Washington DC 20008 (☎202/244-5300).

303 E. Whacker Dr. #410, Chicago IL 60601 (☎312/856-0110).

2200 Post Oak Blvd. #610,Houston TX 77056–4783 (☎713/622-8000).

Central Plaza 3460 Wilshire Blvd, Los Angeles CA 90010 (☎213/380-3440).

BELGIAN EMBASSIES AND CONSULATES

UK 103 Eaton Square, London SW1 (☎071/235 5422).

Ireland Shrewsbury House, 2 Shrewsbury Rd, Ballsbridge, Dublin 4 (☎01/69 20 82).

Netherlands Drentestr. 11, 1083 HK, Amsterdam (☎020/42 97 63): Lange Vijverberg 12, 2513 AC, The Hague (☎070/64 49 10).

Luxembourg 4 rue de Girondins 4, Residence Champagne, L. 1626, Luxembourg (☎44 27 46).

Canada The Sandringham, 85 Range Rd, Suite 601–604, Ottawa, Ontario, K1N 8J6 (☎613/236 7267).

Australia 19 Arkana St, Yarralumla, A.C.T. 2600 Canberra (☎062/73 25 01).

New Zealand 1 Willeston St, Wellington (☎04/72 95 58).

Denmark Øster Allé 7, 2100 Copenhagen Ø (☎01/26 03 88).

Norway Drammensveien 103c, 0273 Oslo 2 (☎02/55 22 15).

Sweden 13a Villegatan, Fack 10268, Stockholm (☎08/11 88 58).

USA
3330 Garfield St. NW, Washington DC 20008.

#2306 Peach Tree Center, Cain Towers, 229 Peach Tree St, Atlanta GA 30343 (☎404/659-2150).

333 North Michigan Ave, Chicago IL 60601 (☎312/263-6624).

6100 Wilshire Blvd #1200, Los Angeles CA 90047 (☎213/385-8116).

50 Rockefeller Plaza, New York NY 10020 (☎212/586-5100).

LUXEMBOURG EMBASSIES AND CONSULATES

UK and Ireland 122 Regent St, W1R 5FE (☎071/235 6963).

Netherlands Nassaulaan 8, NL 2514 JS, The Hague (☎070/60 75 16).

Belgium av de Cortenbergh 75, B 1040 Brussels (☎02/733 9977).

USA
2200 Massachusetts Ave. NW, Washington DC 20008 (☎202/265-4171).

801 Second Ave, 13th floor, New York NY 100017 (☎212/370-9870).

1 Sansome St, San Francisco CA 94104 (☎415/788-0816).

customs at their place of entry. In other words, you are effectively permitted to bring as much duty-paid beer or anything else across the water as you can carry (the legal limits being 90 litres of wine or 110 of beer). However, there are still restrictions on the volume of tax- or duty-free goods you can bring into the country. In general, residents of EC countries travelling to other EC states are allowed a duty-free allowance of two hundred cigarettes, one litre of spirits and five litres of wine; for non-EC residents the allowances are usually two hundred cigarettes, one litre of spirits and two litres of wine. Residents of the USA and Canada can take up to two hundred cigarettes and one litre of alcohol back into the country, as can Australian citizens, while New Zealanders must confine themselves to two hundred cigarettes, 4.5 litres of beer or wine, and just over one litre of spirits. Again, if in doubt consult the relevant – or your own – embassy or consulate. When returning home, remember that the importing of food, plants or animals back into Britain, Ireland, the USA, Canada, Australia or New Zealand is prohibited.

British **customs officials** tend to assume that anyone youthful-looking coming directly from Holland, in particular, is a potential dope fiend or pornographer – strip searches and unpleasantness are frequent, particularly at airports. Those with drugs, pornography or flick knives can expect a hard time and most likely arrest. If you are carrying prescribed drugs of any kind, it can be a good idea to have a copy of the prescription to flash at a suspicious customs officer.

HEALTH AND INSURANCE

As fellow members of the European Community, both the UK and Ireland have reciprocal health agreements with Holland, Belgium and Luxembourg.

These provide for free medical advice and treatment on presentation of **certificate E111** – though in practice many doctors and pharmacists charge, and it's up to you to be reimbursed by the Department of Health once you're home: get receipts for all prescriptions and/or treatment. To get an E111, fill in a form at any post office, and you'll be issued with a certificate immediately. Without an E111 you won't be turned away from a doctor or hospital, but will almost certainly have to contribute towards treatment.

For non-EC citizens **travel insurance** is essential, and it's a wise additional protection for everyone, since policies cover your cash and possessions as well as the cost of medicines, medical and dental treatment. Among British insurance companies, *Endsleigh* are about the cheapest. Premiums cost about £20 a month, available from youth/student travel offices, or direct from 97–107 Southampton Row, London WC1 (☎071/580 4311). In America, *STA* and *Council Travel*, along with most other travel agents, offer short- and long-term insurance policies, covering possessions and travel and health provisions. The *STA* plan, using the insurance agent *ISIS*, offers a choice of three policies which cost between $50 and $80 for the minimum fifteen days, rising to between $510 and $750 for a full year. All include medical, dental and flight cover, permanent disablement and loss of luggage, but vary in amounts of financial cover.

Remember that the policy may not cover all medical expenses, and that you'll need to keep **receipts** for any medicines you buy or treatment you pay for, to claim from your insurance company once you're home. Similarly, if you have anything **stolen**, report the theft to the police (see "Police and Trouble"), and keep a copy of your statement.

If you're currently a **student**, you may be covered on your college medical plan, and likewise a **homeowners' policy** may well cover vacations – though you should take a thorough look into the small print of both before setting off. Lastly, don't forget that flights paid for with a major credit or charge card offer an automatic degree of cover.

Minor ailments can be remedied at **pharmacies** (*Drogist* in Dutch, *Pharmacie* in French), which supply toiletries, non-prescription drugs, tampons, condoms and the like. In Holland, an *Apotheek* or pharmacy (usually open Mon–Fri 9.30am–5.30 or 6pm) is where you go to get a prescription filled. To get a prescription or **consult a doctor**, ask at the local tourist office: if you're in a large city, US and British embassies and legations keep a list of local English-speaking doctors.

INFORMATION AND MAPS

Before you leave home, there's a wealth of information which you can pick up from each of the relevant countries' tourist offices detailed below. Each offers glossy leaflets on the various regions, maps, useful accommodation lists and other general information.

HOLLAND

The **Netherlands Board of Tourism** (the NBT) has a mass of information on the country, with useful leaflets on the main tourist attractions, annual events and accommodation. It produces booklets detailing the country's campgrounds, hotels where to find private rooms, as well as special interest leaflets on cycling and water-sports, and publishes a reasonable map of the country.

Once in Holland, simply head for the nearest **VVV**. Just about every town (and even most large villages) will have a VVV office, either in the centre of town or by the train station (sometimes both). In addition to handing out basic maps (often for free) and English info on the main sights, the VVV keeps lists of local accommodation options and, for a small fee, will book rooms for you – useful if you want to avoid a long walk only to find a full hotel. Most VVV offices also keep information on neighbouring towns, which can be a great help for forward planning. Hours vary, and are detailed – along with phone numbers – in the text.

NETHERLANDS BOARD OF TOURISM OFFICES

UK and Ireland Write to PO Box 523, London SW1E 6NT for an information pack. For recorded info, call ☎0891/200277 (48p/36p per minute).

Belgium, Razensteinstant 68, 1000 Brussels (☎02/5118646).

Australia Suite 302, 5 Elizabeth Street, Sydney, NSW 2000 (☎2/27 69 21).

Canada 25 Adelaide St E, Suite 710, Toronto, Ontario M5C 1Y2 (☎416/363 1577).

Sweden Styrmansgatan 8, 114 54 Stockholm (☎08/782 9925).

Germany Laurenplatz 1–3, 500-Köln-1 (☎221/23 62 62).

USA

355 Lexington Avenue, 21st Floor, New York, NY 10017 (☎212/370 7367).

225 N. Michigan Ave, Suite 326, Chicago, IL 60601 (☎312/819 0300).

90 Montgomery St., San Francisco CA 94105 (☎415/543-6772).

BELGIAN TOURIST OFFICES

UK Premier House, 2 Gayton Rd, Harrow, Middlesex HA1 2XU (☎081/861 3300).

Holland Herengracht 435, 1017 BR Amsterdam (☎020/25 12 51).

Italy Piazza Velasca 5, 1-20122 Milan (☎02/86 05 66).

Sweden Markvadsgatan 16, S-104 32 Stockholm (☎08/34 15 75).

Denmark Vester Farimagsgade 7–9, 1606 Copenhagen V (☎01/12 30 27).

Germany Berliner Allee 47, D4000 Düsseldorf 1 (☎0211/32 60 08).

USA 745 Fifth Ave, New York NY 10151 (☎212/758 8130).

LUXEMBOURG TOURIST OFFICES

UK 122 Regent St, London W1R 5FE (☎071/434 2800).

USA 801 Second Ave, thirteenth floor, New York NY 10017 (☎212/370-9850).

Holland Nassaulaan 8, Postbus 18660, 2502 ER, The Hague (☎70/649041).

Belgium Bureau du Tourisme Luxembourgeois, 104 avenue Louise, Boite 1, B-1050, Brussels (☎02/646 0370).

MAPS

For touring purposes, the best road **map** of Holland is the one published by *Kümmerly and Frey*. For more detailed **regional maps**, aside from the NBT's own plan, the Dutch motoring organization *ANWB* publishes an excellent 1:100,000 series that covers the whole country. Although our city maps should be adequate for most purposes, the best large-scale alternatives are the *Falk Plans*, most of which have gazetteers.

BELGIUM AND LUXEMBOURG

The **Belgian Tourist Office** offers a similarly comprehensive service, stocking free booklets detailing hotels and campgrounds across the country, as well as a series of regional booklets packed with useful information. It also offers a free map, complete with basic city plans.

In Belgium there are **tourist offices** in all but the smallest villages. They often have free maps and, in the larger towns, offer an accommodation booking service: in smaller towns you won't find a booking service, though offices will often call ahead and make a reservation for you; in both cases, this will be done without charge.

Branches of the **Luxembourg Tourist Office** abroad publish free booklets of hotel and restaurant listings, with reliable prices and gradings, and publish the usual bumph and maps. Ask also for their annually updated "Tourist Information" booklet, detailing everything from hours when all the country's major tourist sights are open to where to go ballooning. In Luxembourg itself even the very smallest town will have a **tourist office** of some description, with maps of the immediate area and details of accommodation, which they can sometimes book for you.

MAPS

The Belgian Tourist Office gives out a decent free map of the country that incorporates basic city plans. Otherwise, the best value **general road map** of Belgium (and Luxembourg) is the 1:350,000 *Michelin* plan; the 1:300,000 *Kümmerly and Frey* map covers the same area in much the same sort of detail. The most useful **regional maps** are those of Flanders, the Ardennes and Wallonia, published by *Geocart.*

MAP OUTLETS IN THE UK

London

National Map Centre, 22–24 Caxton St, SW1
(☎071/222 4945).

Stanfords, 12–14 Long Acre, WC2
(☎071/836 1321).

The Travellers Bookshop, 25 Cecil Court, WC2
(☎071/836 9132).

Edinburgh

Thomas Nelson and Sons Ltd, 51 York Place, EH1
3JD (☎031/557 3011).

Glasgow

John Smith and Sons, 57–61 St Vincent St
(☎041/221 7472).

Maps by **mail or phone order** are available from *Stanfords* (☎071/836 1321).

MAP OUTLETS IN NORTH AMERICA

Chicago

Rand McNally, 444 N Michigan Ave, IL 60611
(☎312/321-1751).

Montréal

Ulysses Travel Bookshop, 4176 St-Denis
(☎514/289-0993).

New York

British Travel Bookshop, 551 Fifth Ave, NY 10176
(☎1-800/448-3039 or ☎212/490-6688).

The Complete Traveler Bookstore, 199 Madison
Ave, NY 10016 (☎212/685-9007).

Rand McNally, 150 E 52nd St, NY 10022 (☎212/
758-7488).

Traveler's Bookstore, 22 W 52nd St, NY 10019
(☎212/664-0995).

San Francisco

The Complete Traveler Bookstore, 3207 Filmore St,
CA 92123 (☎415/923-1511).

Rand McNally, 595 Market St, CA 94105 (☎415/
777-3131).

Seattle

Elliot Bay Book Company, 101 S Main St, WA
98104 (☎206/624-6600).

Toronto

Open Air Books and Maps, 25 Toronto St, M5R
2C1 (☎416/363-0719).

Vancouver

World Wide Books and Maps, 1247 Granville St
(☎604/687-3320).

Washington DC

Rand McNally, 1201 Connecticut Ave NW,
Washington DC 20036 (☎202/223-6751).

Note that *Rand McNally* now have 24 stores across the US; phone ☎1-800/333-0136 (ext 2111) for the
address of your nearest store, or for **direct mail** maps.

MAP OUTLETS IN AUSTRALIA

Adelaide

The Map Shop, 16a Peel St, Adelaide, SA 5000
(☎08/231 2033).

Brisbane

Hema, 239 George St, Brisbane, QLD 4000 (☎07/
221 4330).

Melbourne

Bowyangs, 372 Little Bourke St, Melbourne, VIC
3000 (☎03/670 4383).

Perth

Perth Map Centre, 891 Hay St, Perth, WA 6000
(☎09/322 5733).

Sydney

Travel Bookshop, 20 Bridge St, Sydney, NSW 2000
(☎02/241 3554).

POLICE AND TROUBLE

There's little reason why you should ever come into contact with the police forces of Holland, Belgium or Luxembourg: this is an area of Europe that's relatively free of street crime. Even in Brussels, Amsterdam and the larger cities you shouldn't have problems, though it's obviously advisable to be on your guard against petty theft: secure your things in a locker when staying in hostel accommodation, and never leave any valuables in a tent or car. If you're on a bike, make sure it is well locked up – bike theft and resale is one of the major industries in most cities.

As far as **personal safety** goes, it's normally possible to walk anywhere in the centres of the larger cities at any time of day, though women should obviously be wary of badly lit or empty streets; public transport, even late at night, isn't usually a problem.

If you are unlucky enough to have **something stolen**, report it immediately to the nearest police station. Get them to write a statement detailing what has been lost for your insurance claim when you get home, and remember to make a note of the report number – or, better still, ask for a copy of the statement itself.

If you find yourself in trouble, or simply need **assistance of a legal or social nature**, there are a couple of organizations in Holland that might be able to help. **JAC** gives free confidential help to young people, especially foreign nationals, on work, alien status, drugs and accommodation matters. There's also **MAIC**, which similarly specializes in legal advice, though not just for young people; and it will also help on other matters. Both organizations have offices in the larger cities; some of them are listed in the text. In Belgium there's **Infor-Jeunes/Info Jeugd**, a nationwide information organization similar to JAC. In large cities, **SOS Jeune** has a 24-hour emergency number listed in the phonebook or available from the operator.

Drugs are predictably visible in all three countries, especially in Holland, and specifically Amsterdam. Although it is effectively legal in Holland to possess up to 28g of cannabis for your own consumption, be aware that the liberal attitude toward its being smoked exists only in the capital and the large cities to the south that form the Randstad. In Belgium and Luxembourg the possession and use of any drugs is totally illegal, and in the current conservative climate would be guaranteed to get you into trouble. Better to leave your dope at the Dutch border.

MONEY AND BANKS

The currency of Holland is the guilder, that used in Belgium is the franc; Luxembourg's currency is also the franc, and it carries the same value as the Belgian franc. However, whereas Belgian francs are always accepted in Luxembourg, the reverse doesn't hold true – ie Luxembourg francs are rarely taken as legal tender in Belgium.

The best way of carrying the bulk of your money is in **travellers' cheques** (US$ travelers'

checks), available from most high street banks (whether or not you have an account) for a usual fee of one percent of the amount ordered. For British residents, an alternative is the **Eurocheque** book and card, issued on request by most British banks to account holders, which can be used to get cash in the majority of European banks and bureaux de change. This works out slightly more expensive than travellers' cheques, but can be more convenient. Bear in mind that you always need to have your passport with you as well as the Eurocheque card to obtain cash at Benelux banks.

PLASTIC MONEY

Visa, Access/*Mastercard*, *Diners Club* and *American Express* cards can be used in most banks and bureaux de change — if you're prepared to withdraw a minimum of the equivalent of (roughly) £70/$120. Credit and charge cards are less popular than you might expect when it comes to purchasing goods and services, although most mainstream shops, hotels and restaurants will take at least one brand. Check before you commit yourself to spending.

CHANGING MONEY

Changing money is rarely problematic and seldom expensive. Banks offer the best exchange rates, but commissions vary and it's worth shopping around. The best bet out of banking hours are the exchange offices found at train stations, which open late and at weekends (the *GWB* offices in Holland are particularly good and reliable): otherwise numerous bureaux de change, hostels, hotels, campgrounds, tourist offices, airports, ferry terminals and ferries offer rates that range from decent to diabolical. See the "Costs, Money and Banks" sections on each country for more details on hours and the various ways of changing money.

BUSINESS HOURS AND PUBLIC HOLIDAYS

The Benelux weekend fades painlessly into the week with many shops staying closed on Monday morning, even in major cities.

Hours are usually from 9am to 5.30 or 6pm; certain shops stay open later on Thursday and Friday evenings for *Koopavond* (shopping nights). *Avondwinkels* are nightshops found in major cities, notably Amsterdam, that usually open at 6pm and close at 1 or 2am. Things shut down a little earlier on Saturday, and only die-hard money makers open on a Sunday.

Most towns have a **market day**, usually midweek (and sometimes Saturday morning), and this is often the liveliest day to be in a town, particularly when the stalls fill the central square or *markt*; very occasionally you'll see elderly women wearing bona fide peasant costume. Though the tradition has died out in all but the smallest towns and villages, some shops close for the **half-day** on Wednesday or Thursday afternoon.

Though closed on Christmas Day, New Year's Day, the day after Christmas, and on Mondays, all state-run museums adopt Sunday hours on the **public holidays** listed below, when most shops and banks are closed.

PUBLIC HOLIDAYS

HOLLAND

New Year's Day
Good Friday (many shops open)
Easter Sunday and Monday
April 30 (Queen's Birthday, many shops open)
Ascension Day (mid-May)
Whit (Pentecost) Sunday and Monday
December 5 (early closing for St Nicholas' day).
Christmas Day
December 26

BELGIUM

New Year's Day
Monday after Easter
Labour Day (May 1)
Ascension Day (mid-May)

All Saints' Day (November 1)
Armistice Day (November 11)
King's Birthday (November 15)
Christmas Day

LUXEMBOURG

New Year's Day
Monday after Easter
May Day (May 1)
Ascension Day (mid-May)
Monday after Pentecost
National Day (June 23)
Assumption Day (August 15)
All Saints' Day (November 1)
Christmas Day
December 26

COMMUNICATIONS: MAIL AND PHONES

up mail take your passport, and make sure they check under middle names and initials, as letters often get misfiled.

Phone booths are plentiful and almost invariably work; most have English instructions which are normally displayed inside. To make a direct call to the UK, dial the code in the box below, wait for the tone and then dial the number, omitting the initial 0. To make a direct call to the US, dial the code in the box below, wait for the tone and then dial 1 followed by the area code and number. To make a reverse charge or collect call, phone the operator (they all speak English).

Post office hours and other details are given under each individual country's section on "Communications." Postal charges are not particularly high, but the cost of stamps and postcards can soon take a chunk out of the daily budget.

You can have letters sent **poste restante/ general delivery** to any post office in Holland (main offices only in Belgium and Luxembourg) by addressing them **"Poste Restante"** followed by the name of the town and country. When picking

DIALLING CODES TO BRITAIN

from **Holland**	☎09 44
from **Belgium**	☎00 44
from **Luxembourg**	☎00 44

DIALLING CODES TO THE USA AND CANADA

from **Holland**	☎09 1
from **Belgium**	☎00 1
from **Luxembourg**	☎00 1

GAY LIFE

As you'd expect, it's in Holland's **cities** that gay life is most visible and enjoyable. **Amsterdam** is probably the best city in Europe in which to be gay – attitudes are tolerant, bars are excellent and plentiful, and support groups and facilities are unequalled. Elsewhere in Holland, while the scene isn't anywhere near as extensive, it's always well organized: Rotterdam, The Hague, Nijmegen and Groningen each have an enjoyable nightlife, and all cities of any size have a branch of *COC*, the national organization for gay men and women, which can offer help, information and usually a coffee bar. The national HQ is at

Rozenstraat 8, Amsterdam (☎020/23 11 92). You'll also find addresses for each city in the "Listings" sections.

Gay life in **Belgium and Luxembourg** isn't so upfront. Brussels and Antwerp are the main centres, but both sit very firmly in Amsterdam's shadow – and most gay travellers overlook what is by and large a far less "international" scene in these two countries. The Belgian national organization for gay men and women is *FWH*, Dambruggestraat 204, Antwerp (☎03/233 25 02). The legal **age of consent** for gay men is 16 in Holland and Belgium, 18 in Luxembourg.

WOMEN

Of all the Low Countries' cities, **Amsterdam** has the most impressive feminist infrastructure: support groups, health centres, and businesses are run by and for women, and there's a good range of bars and discos, a few exclusively for women. Once outside the capital you'll frequently be reminded just how parochial Holland is – attitudes and behaviour acceptable in Amsterdam will be frowned on elsewhere, especially in the Catholic south. Many towns in Holland have a *Vrouwenhuis* or women's centre, a meeting place that organizes various activities, discussion groups and events exclusively for women. These are often the best place to meet local women and make feminist connections; sadly, many have closed in recent years: where still applicable, addresses are given in *the Guide*.

Belgium, with the strong influence of the Catholic Church, has a less liberal tradition: women are still scarce in the upper echelons of business and government, abortion is still illegal (though there are an estimated fifteen thousand abortions a year carried out in feminist clinics), and tax laws discriminate against two-career families. Belgian feminist organizations seem to be operated mainly by lesbians, and, perhaps as a result, the women's movements in Holland and France have been comparatively more successful in involving women from a broader spectrum of backgrounds.

By and large, nowhere in Holland, Belgium, and Luxembourg is **unsafe** for women travelling alone – the seedier areas of the big cities may feel threatening, but with common sense and circumspection you shouldn't have anything to worry about.

The native **lesbian scene** is smaller and more subdued than the gay one. Many politically active lesbians move within tight circles, and it takes time for foreign visitors to find out what's happening. Good places to begin are the women-only cafés listed in the text.

PART TWO

HOLLAND

THE NORTH AND
THE FRISIAN ISLANDS

NORTH
HOLLAND

AMSTERDAM

OVERIJSSEL,
FLEVOLAND
AND GELDERLAND

SOUTH HOLLAND
AND UTRECHT

THE SOUTH

WEST
GERMANY

BELGIUM

0   50 km

Introduction

Holland, or (to give the country its proper name) The Netherlands, is a country reclaimed in part from the waters of the North Sea, an artificially created land, around half of which lies at or below sea level. Land reclamation has been the dominant motif of its history, the result a country of resonant and unique images – flat, fertile landscapes punctuated by windmills and church spires; ornately gabled terraces flanking peaceful canals; huge, open skies; and mile upon mile of grassy dune, backing onto wide stretches of pristine, sandy beach.

A leading colonial power, its mercantile fleets once challenged the best in the world for supremacy, and its standard of living (for the majority at least) was second to none. These days Holland is one of the most developed countries in the world, small and urban, with the highest population density in Europe, its fifteen million or so inhabitants concentrated into an area about the size of the US state of Maine. It's an international, well-integrated place: many people speak English, at least in the heavily populated west of the country; communications and infrastructure are genuinely efficient; and its companies – Philips, Unilever, Shell – are at the forefront of the new, free-trading Europe. Politically, also, the Dutch government's policies (despite something of an Eighties backlash) are those of consensus: among Europe's – and the world's – most liberal, with relaxed laws regarding soft drugs, and forward-thinking attitudes on social issues. The crime rate, too, though on the increase, is relatively low.

■ Where to go

If you say you're going to Holland, everyone will immediately assume you're going to **Amsterdam**. Indeed for such a small and accessible country, Holland is, apart from Amsterdam, relatively unknown territory. Some people may confess to a brief visit to Rotterdam or The Hague, but for most people Amsterdam basically *is* Holland – there's nothing remotely worth seeing outside the capital, so if you're not going there, why go at all?

It's an attitude exacerbated by the chauvinism of Amsterdammers themselves, many of whom rarely set foot outside the limits of their own city. It's true that in many ways the rest of Holland can seem terribly dull after the bright lights of the capital, but to write off the rest of the country would be to miss much, especially considering the size of the place and the efficiency of its transport systems, which make everywhere easily accessible.

Although throughout the guide we have used the name Holland to mean the whole country, in fact it refers to only two of The Netherlands' **twelve provinces – North** and **South Holland**, in the west of the country. These for the most part are unrelentingly flat territory, much of it reclaimed land that has since become home to a grouping of towns known collectively as the **Randstad** (literally "rim town") – a circular urban sprawl that holds the country's largest cities and the majority of its population. Travelling in this part of the country is easy, with trains and buses cheap and efficient and language no problem; at times, you barely feel abroad at all. Amsterdam is rightly the main focus: there's no other city which has its vitality and cosmopolitanism – or, indeed, its features of interest. But the other Randstad towns are worth a visit, too – places like **Haarlem**, **Leiden** and **Delft** with their old canal-girded centres; the gritty port city of **Rotterdam**; the dignified architecture and stately air of **The Hague**, home of the government and the Dutch royal family; not to mention the **bulbfields** which spread all around – in spring, justifiably, the one thing that never fails to draw tourists out of Amsterdam.

Outside of the Randstad life moves more slowly, and although you're never far from civilization, travelling is marginally more time-consuming and the incidence of English-speakers more sporadic. The **islands** of the north, most of them off the coast of the province of **Friesland**, are prime resort territory for the Dutch, though they retain a rather untamed air, sparsely settled after the crowded Randstad cities. The rest of Friesland, too, can feel somewhat cut off, its inhabitants speaking a language, *Frysk*, not spoken – or understood – elsewhere in the country. Which isn't to say it's dull: Friesland's capital, **Leeuwarden**, is a likeable city, and neighbouring **Groningen** is one of the country's busiest cultural centres, given verve by its large resident student population. To the south, the provinces of **Overijssel** and

Gelderland, at least in their eastern portions, herald Holland's first few bumps, the landscape undulating into boggy peat and wasteland around the towns of **Arnhem** and **Apeldoorn**, best experienced in the country's only national park, the **Hoge Veluwe**, and another lively college town, **Nijmegen**. Further south still lie the predominantly Catholic provinces of **Limburg, North Brabant** and **Zeeland**. The latter is well named – literally "Sealand", made up of a series of low-lying islands connected by road and protected from the encroaching waters of the North Sea by one of Holland's most ambitious projects, the Delta Plan. Heading east, **North Brabant** is gently rolling scrub and farmland, centring on the historic cities of **Breda** and **Den Bosch**, and, not least, the modern manufacturing hub of **Eindhoven**, home to the electronics giant Philips. Lastly, **Limburg** occupies the slim scythe of land that reaches down between the Belgian and German borders, perhaps the least Dutch of all Holland's provinces – its landscape, in the south at least, genuinely hilly, and with as cosmopolitan a capital in **Maastricht** as they come.

Getting around

Getting around is never a problem in Holland: it's a small country, distances are short, and the longest journey you'll ever make – say from Amsterdam to Maastricht – takes under three hours by train or car. Public transport in and around towns and cities, too, is efficient and cheap, buses (and sometimes trams) running on an easy-to-understand ticketing system that covers the whole country. The two networks link up together neatly – bus terminuses almost everywhere situated next door to the train station.

■ Trains

The best way of travelling around Holland is to take the **train**. The system, run by *Nederlandse Spoorwegen* or *NS* (*Netherlands Railways*), is one of the best in Europe: trains are fast, modern, frequent and, normally, very punctual; fares are relatively low, and the network of lines comprehensive. **Ordinary fares** are calculated by the kilometre, diminishing proportionally the further you travel. *NS* publishes a booklet detailing costs and distances, so it's easy enough to work out broadly how much a ticket will cost. As a rough guide, reckon on spending about ƒ13 to travel 50km or so; for a round-trip ticket simply double the price of one way; first-class fares cost about fifty percent on top. With any ticket, you're also free to stop off anywhere en route and continue your journey later that day. For a one-way ticket ask for an "enkele reis"; a round-trip is a "retour".

Of a number of ways of saving money on these rates, the **dagretour**, or day return, is the most commonly used, valid for 24 hours and costing around ten percent less than two ordinary one-way tickets. If you're visiting some specific attraction on a day out from somewhere by train, consider also buying a **dagtochtkaart** – a special ticket which includes the price of admission to selected sights (say Enkhuizen's Zuider Zee Museum or the Hoge Veluwe Park) with the price of a return ticket, usually saving a good deal. There are 72 possible excursions in all, though most are only possible between May and September: ask for the booklet *Er Op Uit!*, which has full details, or the *Dagje Uit* leaflet, which is free but only in Dutch.

If you're travelling extensively by train, you should consider buying a **rail pass**. There are a number of different kinds of pass available: **rover tickets,** which entitle the holder to unlimited travel anywhere in Holland at a cost of ƒ63 (second class) for one day, ƒ152 for seven days; and the **Eurodomino Pass**, which gives three days' travel within a month for ƒ83 (ƒ63 if you're 26 or under); ƒ140 for five days' travel (ƒ106 if you're 26 or under); and ten days' travel for ƒ252 (ƒ189 if you're 26 or under). Optional **extras** issued in conjunction with the rover tickets are public transport link cards (ƒ6.50 for one day, ƒ25 for seven days), which allow the additional free use of town and country buses and trams all over the country. Consider also the **Benelux Tourrail Card**, valid for any five days within a specified seventeen on all three national rail networks as well as country buses in Luxembourg. Costs are ƒ162 if you're under 26, ƒ217 if not. In addition to these are various deals and passes available in summer, as well as arrangements for **families and groups** of people travelling together.

Everywhere in Holland buses stop outside train stations, but if you don't wish to take a bus, *NS* has devised a **treintaxi** scheme, whereby for ƒ5 a head in thirty towns across the country, excluding Amsterdam, The Hague, Rotterdam and Utrecht, a taxi will take you anywhere within the city limits,

even if you're travelling alone – though drivers are supposed to wait ten minutes for other passengers. Vouchers for *treintaxis* must be purchased when you buy your train ticket.

Stations aren't the slums you often find in America or Britain, but bright, well-equipped places, with information and facilities that – even in some of the smaller towns – include a coffee shop and restaurant, florist and newspaper/ bookshop and often a GWK bureau de change. The food in the restaurants, incidentally, is usually good, filling and reasonably priced.

Netherlands Railways publishes mounds of **information** annually on the various services, passes, fares and suchlike – most of it in English. It also produces a free condensed timetable detailing inter-city services and a full timetable (*spoorboekje*), available in advance either from the Netherlands Board of Tourism (see p.15 for addresses) or from any Dutch train station (*f*8.75).

■ Buses

Supplementing the extensive train network are **buses** – run by local companies but again ruthlessly efficient, spreading out to span the local surroundings from ranks of bus stops almost always located bang next to the train station. Ticketing is simple, organized on a system that covers the whole country. You need to buy just one kind of ticket wherever you are, a *strippenkaart*. The country is divided into zones: the driver will cancel one strip on your *strippenkaart* for your journey plus one for each of the zones you travel through (on city trams and metro systems it's up to you to cancel it yourself: see the *Amsterdam* chapter). In the larger towns and cities you'll find you only need to use two zones for the centre. You can buy 2-, 3- or 8-strip *strippenkaarts* from bus drivers, or pick up the better value 15-strip (*f*10.75) or 45-strip (*f*31) *strippenkaarts* in advance from train stations, tobacconists and local public transport offices. If you're in Holland during the summer months and are intending to travel around a lot by bus, it's well worth investing in a *Zomerzwerfkaart*, which gives free access to all bus routes. It currently costs *f*14.75 for adults and *f*9.75 for under-12s and over-65s.

■ Driving and hitching

Driving around Holland is pretty much what you would expect – painless and quick. The country has a uniformly good and comprehensive road network, most of the major towns are linked by some kind of motorway or dual carriageway, and things only get congested on the outskirts of the major cities. **Rules of the road** are similar to other mainland European countries: you drive on the right; speed limits are 50kph in built-up areas, 80kph outside, 120kph on motorways – though some motorways have a speed limit of 100kph, indicated by small yellow signs on the side of the road. Drivers and front-seat passengers are required by law to wear seatbelts, and crackdowns on drunken driving are severe. There are no toll roads, and although petrol isn't particu-

larly cheap, at around *f*2 per litre, the short distances mean this isn't much of a factor.

To drive in Holland, British citizens need only an ordinary full British **driver's licence**. If you're driving your own car, check with your insurance company as to whether or not your policy covers you abroad: if not, you'll need a green insurance card, though you can obtain last-minute insurance cover at border exchange offices. Americans need an International Driver's Licence, obtainable from your local branch of the *AAA*, for a small charge. If you **break down**, the Dutch motoring organization, the *ANWB*, offers reciprocal repair and breakdown services to members of most international motoring organizations. Known as the *Wegenwacht*, their nationwide number is ☎06/0888, and there are special telephones by the side of the highway. If you're not a member of your home motoring organization, you can either pay for this service or, for a *f*75 fee, become a temporary (one-month) member.

Car rental is fairly expensive: reckon on paying a minimum of *f*700 for a small car for a week, with unlimited milage, or around *f*50 a day plus 60c per kilometre – though obviously there are much cheaper weekend deals available.

Hitching is feasible throughout the country: the Dutch are usually well disposed towards giving lifts, and the dense population and road network means it's unusual to get stuck anywhere. Bear in mind, though, that highways are hard to avoid, and that it's only legal to hitch on approach roads or at the special places seen on the outskirts of some larger cities, known as *liftplaatsen*.

■ Cycling

If you're not especially short of time, **cycling** is *the* way to see the country. Holland's largely flat landscape makes travelling by bike an almost effortless pursuit, and the short distances involved make it possible to see most of the country this way, using the nationwide system of well-marked cycle paths – which often divert away from the main roads into the countryside. The 1:100,000 *ANWB* maps show all the cycle paths and are perfectly adequate for touring. Ask also for the NBT booklet, *Cycling in Holland*, which details a number of suggested routes and has other advice for cyclists.

The NBT, in association with regional VVV offices, also organize **cycling package holidays** all over the country, which include bicycles, accommodation, maps and other information and are generally excellent value.

Most people, however, either **bring their own bike** or **rent one**. Bikes can be rented from all main train stations for *f*7.50 a day or *f*30 per week plus a *f*50 deposit (*f*200 in larger centres); if you have a valid train ticket, it costs just *f*5 a day with a *treinfiets* voucher. You'll also need some form of ID. The snag is that cycles must be returned to the station from which they were rented, making onward hops by rented bike impossible. Most bike shops rent bicycles out for around the same amount as train stations, though they may be more flexible on deposits – some accept a passport in lieu of cash; otherwise, again expect to leave *f*50–200. Wherever you rent your bike from, in summer it is a good idea to reserve one in advance.

It is possible to take your **bike on trains**, but it isn't encouraged, and a ticket costs *f*9–25 depending on the day and time of year. Be warned that space is limited and you're not allowed to load your bike on at all during the rush hour – between 6.30am and 9am and 4.30pm and 6pm. Bear in mind that you should never, ever, leave your bike **unlocked**, even for a few minutes. In the larger cities especially, used bikes are big business, the prey of thieves armed with bolt-cutters. Almost all train stations have somewhere you can store your bike for around *f*2 a day.

Accommodation

Accommodation is not particularly cheap in Holland, though a wide network of official and unofficial youth hostels and generally well-equipped campsites can help to cut costs. Wherever you stay, you should book during the summer and over holiday periods like Easter, when places can run short.

■ Hotels and private rooms

All **hotels** in Holland are graded on a star system up to five stars. One-star and no-star hotels are rare, and prices for two-star establishments start at around *f*75 for a double room without private bath or shower; count on paying at least *f*85 if you want your own facilities. Three-star hotels cost upwards of about *f*140; for four- and five-star places you'll pay *f*220-plus, which won't always include breakfast. In cheaper places prices usually include a reasonable breakfast, though not always; be sure to check first as some hotels use this as a sneaky way of adding *f*10 or so to your bill.

During the summer, in all parts of the country but especially in Amsterdam and the major tourist centres, it's a good idea to reserve **a room** in advance. You can do this most easily by calling the hotel direct – we've listed phone numbers throughout the guide, and English is almost always spoken so there should be no language problem. You can also make bookings through the *Netherlands Reservations Centre* (NRC), PO Box 404, 2260 AK Leidschendam (Mon–Fri 8am–8pm, Sat 8am–2pm; ☎070/320 50 00), which can book hotel rooms, apartments, and cabins all over the country. Bookings are confirmed in writing and the service is free. In Holland itself, you can make advance bookings in person through VVV offices, for a fee of *f*3.50 per person.

One way of cutting costs is, wherever possible, to use **private accommodation** – rooms in private homes that are let out to visitors on a bed and breakfast basis; they're sometimes known as pensions. Prices are usually quoted per person and are normally around *f*30; breakfast is usually included, but if not will cost about *f*5 on top. You have to go through the VVV to find private rooms: they will either give you a list to follow up independently or will insist they book the accommodation themselves and levy the appropriate booking fee. Bear in mind, also, that not all VVVs are able to offer private accommodation; generally you'll find it only in the larger towns and tourist centres.

■ Hostels, sleep-ins, student rooms

There are about 45 official **youth hostels** in Holland, all affiliated to the IYHF and open to members for around *f*20 per person per night, including breakfast. Accommodation is usually in dormitories, though some hostels have single- and double-bedded rooms. Meals are often available – about ƒ14 for a filling dinner – and in some hostels there are kitchens where you can cook your own food. It is possible for non-members to stay in official hostels, though they'll pay more; given the price of membership, it's worth joining even if you're only going to be doing a little hosteling. You should book in advance if possible during the summer, as some places get crammed. For a full list of Dutch hostels, contact the *Nederlandse Jeugdherberg Central* (*NJHC*), Prof. Tulplein 4, 1018 GX Amsterdam (☎020/551 3155).

In addition to official hostels, the larger cities – particularly Amsterdam – often have a number of **unofficial hostels** offering dormitory accommodation (and invariably double- and triple-bedded rooms, too) at broadly similar prices, though inevitably standards are frequently not as

---

HOTEL PRICE CODES

All the establishments we have listed in Holland have been **graded** according to the following categories. These will sometimes, but not always, correspond to the ratings laid down by the tourist board, who themselves grade all hotels rigorously. Indeed, they are above all a guide to price, and give no indication of the facilities you might expect to find other than the broad outlines given below.

Please note that the **prices** we give in this guide are for the cheapest double room – ie without private bath, etc – during high season. You will find many bottom-end hotels have a mixture of rooms, some with private facilities, some without; thus you may find that a good standard ③ category hotel has quite a number of ④ rooms as well.

① **Up to ƒ30 per person.** Hostel accommodation, either a private hostel or an official youth hostel, (part of the IYHF), where charges are in fact often slightly cheaper – up to ƒ20 a night. At most hostels this price will get you dormitory accommodation, shared facilities, and (sometimes) a frugal breakfast. Both official and private hostels will often have some level of private accommodation too – single-, double-, even triple-bedded rooms, which normally fall into the price range of the following category.

② **ƒ30–65.** Either private rooms arranged through the local tourist office, or the most basic, one-star form of hotel accommodation, not normally with any kind of private facilities beyond a washbasin in the room if you're lucky, and not normally recognised or rated by the tourist office. At this grade, given the choice between a hotel and a private room in someone's home, the latter will invariably be more appealing, if more restricting as regards your comings and goings.

③ **ƒ65–100.** Basic one- and two-star hotel accommodation, where most of the rooms won't have private facilities. This, together with the following, is probably the most commonly recommended category in this guide, although in the larger cities you might find even hotels in this grade a little hard to come by.

④ **ƒ100–140.** Two-star hotel accommodation, where there will often be a choice of shared and private facilities. Probably the most common category we recommend, and definitely the best choice if you're not on too tight a budget and want

to spend more than a night or two somewhere. At this price you may occasionally enjoy the use of a telephone and TV too, but don't count on it.

⑤ **ƒ140–180.** Two-star moving on occasion into three-star hotel accommodation, where facilities will always be private and you will invariably have the benefit of a TV, telephone, etc, though probably not room service.

⑥ **ƒ180–220.** Solid three-star hotels, probably bigger and better-equipped places than the previous category, and always with private facilities, telephone, and TV and room service in larger establishments, even if the rooms aren't likely to be hugely different in quality.

⑦ **ƒ220–260.** The bottom end of four-star hotels. Normally all rooms will have private facilities, telephone, TV and room service. There will usually be other facilities – laundry, etc – and there may even be other bonuses like a gym or swimming pool. Once up to this sort of category, breakfast, oddly enough, is not always included in the price.

⑧ **ƒ260 and over.** We've included this category in order to take in really decent four- and five-star hotels with excellent facilities, and to include really special places, which charge for their location, environment, or simply their service. They're definitely not places at which to spend every night of your trip, even if you could afford it, as there are almost always plenty of very desirable cheaper options. However, if you feel like pampering yourself, or it's a special occasion, they come highly recommended.

high or as reliable as the official *IYHF* places (and some are extremely poor). We've detailed possibilities in the guide. In some cities you may also come across something known as a **Sleep-in** – dormitory accommodation established and run by the local council that's often cheaper than regular hostels and normally only open during the summer. Locations vary from year to year; again, we've tried to give some indication of locations in the guide, but for the most current information contact the VVV. The same goes for **student accommodation**, which is sporadically open to travellers during the summer holidays in some university towns. We've detailed definite possibilities in the guide, but the VVV usually has up-to-date information.

■ **Campsites and cabins**

Camping is a serious option in Holland: there are plenty of sites, most are very well equipped, and they represent a good saving on other forms of accommodation. Prices vary greatly, mainly depending on the number of facilities available, but you can generally expect to pay around *f*5 per person, plus another *f*5–10 for a tent, and another *f*5 or so if you have a car or motorcycle. Everywhere the VVV will have details of the

nearest site, though we've given indications throughout the text. There's also a free NBT list of selected sites, and the *ANWB* publishes an annual list of Dutch campsites (*f*16.50), available from bookstores in Holland itself or in advance from the ANWB direct, at Wassenaarseweg 220, The Hague (☎070/314 7147).

Some sites can also offer **cabins**, known as *trekkershutten* – spartanly furnished affairs that can house a maximum of four people for around *f*45 a night. Again, both the NBT and ANWB can provide a list of these, the latter for *f*2.50, though you should normally book in advance – either by phoning the site direct or through the *Netherlands Reservations Centre* (address and phone number above).

Costs, money and banks

Though Holland is by a slim margin the least expensive country in the Benelux region, costs are never cheap, and while prices won't be too alarming for British visitors, Americans will find price levels for most things a little higher than at home.

If you come for a short time and stay in one place, sleep in youth hostels or camp, and eat out rarely, you can just about get by on around £20–25 ($30–40) a day; staying in modest hotels, travelling around the country, eating out most evenings, and doing some socializing, expect to spend at least £45 ($70) a day.

■ **Money and banks**

Dutch **currency** is the guilder, written as "*f*", "fl" or "Dfl", and made up of 100 cents ("c"). It comes in **coins** worth 5c, (irritatingly tiny) 10c, 25c, *f*1, *f*2.50, and *f*5; denominations of **bills** are *f*10, *f*25, *f*50, *f*100, and – rarely – *f*250 and *f*1000. At the time of writing the exchange rate was just under *f*2 to one dollar, just under *f*3 to one pound.

Many shops and restaurants accept the major **credit cards** – *Visa, Mastercard* (*Eurocard*), *American Express*, and *Diners Club* – and, subject to a roughly *f*300 minimum, *GWK* offices and many banks give (pricy) cash advances on all cards.

As ever, **banks** are the best place to change travellers' cheques and cash. Their hours are Monday to Friday 9am to 4pm. In the larger cities, Amsterdam for example, some banks are also open Thursday 7 to 9pm and occasionally on Saturday mornings, though changing money at odd times is never a problem, as the nationwide network of *De Grenswisselkantoren* (*GWK*) exchange offices, usually at train stations, are open very late every day – sometimes (as in Amsterdam) even 24 hours. At these you can change money or travellers' cheques, obtain cash advances on all the major credit cards, even arrange travel insurance. You can also change money at most VVV offices, though the rate will be less favourable, as it will at numerous bureaux de change dotted about the larger cities – *Change Express* is just one national change office. Hotels, hostels, and campsites will also often change money: only use them when desperate though – they often give rip-off rates. Basically, when stuck, you're better off using *GWK*.

Communications

In a country as small as Holland, essential communications – mail and phones – are easy and efficient, whether sending a postcard or calling the other end of the country.

■ Mail

Dutch **post offices** are plentiful and easy to use, usually open Monday to Friday 8.30am to 5pm and in cities also often on Saturday 8.30am to noon. Be sure to join the right queue, though, if you only want stamps (*postzegelen*), as post offices handle numerous other services. The charges are 70c for postcards within Europe, 90c elsewhere; 90c for letters up to 90g within Europe, ƒ1.60 outside.

Post boxes are everywhere, but make sure you use the correct slot, marked "Overige". If you're receiving mail rather than sending it, poste restante is available at main post offices countrywide; to collect items, you need your passport.

■ Phones

The Dutch **phone system** is similarly straightforward. The green-trim telephone boxes are like the others throughout Europe: you deposit the money before making a call and a digital display tells you the amount of credit remaining. The slots take 25c, ƒ1, and ƒ2.50 coins; only wholly unused coins are returned. Phone booths taking only phonecards are becoming more common, and a card is a good way to avoid waiting in line and convenient for calling abroad. They're available from post offices and train stations – ƒ5 for the equivalent of twenty local calls.

If you are calling home, in the larger cities it might be better to use a post office (except in Amsterdam where there's a separate place known as the "Telehouse"), where you can make your call from a booth and settle up afterward. They're open at least the same hours as post offices, sometimes later. Phone booths accept 25c, ƒ1 and ƒ2.50 coins; there are also blue cardphones. Phonecards for ƒ5, ƒ10 and ƒ25 are sold at post offices and VVVs, and at certain shops.

The discount rate for calls within Europe operates from 8pm to 8am; to the USA and Canada, it's cheaper to call between 7pm and 10am (for the USA) at weekends; and to Australia and New Zealand, between midnight and 7am. You

---

USEFUL NUMBERS

Operator calls ☎06 01 04.
Information ☎008 (daily 8am–10pm). Outside these times dial ☎06 899 11 33, though this is expensive.
International information ☎06 04 18.
Emergencies ☎06 11.

Reverse charge calls ☎06 04 10. Or for calls to the USA and Canada ☎06 022 9111; to the UK ☎06 022 9944; to Australia ☎06 022 0061. These numbers connect directly to national operators and usually provide a quicker service.

INTERNATIONAL DIALLING CODES

USA and Canada ☎09 1
UK ☎09 44
Ireland ☎09 353
Australia ☎09 61
New Zealand ☎09 64

---

can, obviously, also call from hotels, though expect this to be much more expensive than from anywhere else.

■ Media

There's no problem finding **British newspapers**. They're widely available, on the same day of publication in the Randstad towns, the day after elsewhere, for around *f3*. The only **American newspapers** available in Holland are the *International Herald Tribune*, which is published in Paris, and *USA Today*. Current issues of UK and US magazines can be found pretty much all over, and in Amsterdam you'll find *Time Out Amsterdam*, a monthly English-language listings guide to the capital. If you're having problems finding UK or US magazines, train station bookstalls are always a good bet, though most newsagents in the larger cities will stock at least a few overseas newspapers and magazines.

Of the **Dutch press**, the right-leaning down-market *De Telegraaf* is one of the most widely read papers, as is the centre-right but less scandal-ridden *Algemeeen Dagsblad*. *De Volkskrant* is a centre-left daily and *NRC Handelsblad* is a relatively uncommitted paper supposedly favoured by the country's intellectuals.

British TV and radio stations can also be picked up in Holland. BBC Radio 4 is found on 1500m long wave, and the World Service on 463m medium wave and short wave frequencies between 75m and 49m at intervals throughout the day and night. If you're staying somewhere with cable TV, it's possible to tune into BBC1 and BBC2 at most times during the day, and a flick through the stations might also turn up any number of cable and satellite options: Superchannel – an at times dreadfully amateurish mix of videos, soaps, and movies; MTV – 24-hour pop videos; CNN, which gives 24-hour news coverage; or Eurosport – up-to-the-minute footage of contests like the women's world curling championships or European Handball league. There are also the Dutch TV channels, which

regularly run American and British programmes and films with Dutch subtitles. In most parts of the country, you've also got the programmes of the Belgian, French, and German networks to choose from, not to mention BBC1 and BBC2.

Food and drink

Holland is – quite rightly – not renowned for its cuisine, but although much is unimaginative, it's rarely unpleasant. The country has a good supply of ethnic restaurants, especially Indonesian and Chinese; Dutch food holds one or two surprises; and if you're selective prices are rarely high enough to break the bank. Drinking, too, is easily affordable, Dutch beer – and bars – being one of the real pleasures of the country.

■ Food

Dutch food tends to be higher in protein content than in variety: steak, chicken and fish, along with filling soups and stews, are staple fare, usually served up in enormous quantities. It can, however, at its best, be excellent, some restaurants offering increasingly adventurous crossovers with French cuisine at good-value prices, especially *eetcafés* and bars.

Breakfast

In all but the very cheapest hostels or most expensive hotels **breakfast** (*ontbijt*) will be included in the price of the room. Though usually nothing fancy, it's always substantial: rolls, cheese, ham, hard-boiled eggs, jam and honey, or peanut butter are the principal ingredients. If you don't have a hotel breakfast, many bars and cafés serve rolls and sandwiches and some offer a set breakfast.

The **coffee** is normally good and strong, around ƒ2 a cup, served with a little tub of *koffie-melk* (evaporated milk); ordinary milk is rarely used. If you want coffee with warm milk, ask for a *koffie verkeerd*. Most bars also serve cappuccino and espresso coffees, though remember that many stop serving coffee altogether around 11pm. **Tea** generally comes with lemon if anything – if you want milk you have to ask for it. **Chocolate** (*chocomel*) is also popular, hot or cold: for a real treat drink it hot with a layer of fresh whipped cream (*slagroom*) on top. Some coffee shops also sell aniseed-flavoured warm milk or *anijsmelk*.

Snacks, cakes, cheeses

For the rest of the day, eating cheaply and well, particularly on your feet, is no real problem, although those on the tightest of budgets may find themselves dependent on the dubious delights of **Dutch fast food**. This has its own peculiarities. Chips – *frites or patat* – are the most common standby (*vlaamse* or "Flemish" *frites* are the best), sprinkled with salt and smothered with huge gobs of mayonnaise (*fritesaus*) or, alternatively, curry, sate, goulash, or tomato sauce. If you just want salt, ask for "patat zonder"; fries with salt and mayonnaise are "patat met". Chips are complemented with *kroketten* – spiced minced meat covered with breadcrumbs and deep fried – or *fricandel*, a frankfurter-like sausage. All these are available over the counter at evil-smelling fast-food places (*Febo* is the most common chain), or, for a guilder or so, from heated glass compartments outside.

Tastier, and good both as a snack and a full lunch, are the **fish specialities** sold by street vendors: salted raw herring, smoked eel (*gerookte paling*), mackerel in a roll (*broodje makreel*), mussels, and various kinds of deep-fried fish. Look out, too, for "green" or *maatje* herring, eaten raw with onions in early summer. Tip your head back and dangle the fish into your mouth, Dutch-style. A nationwide chain of fish restaurants, *Noordzee*, serves up well-priced fish-based rolls and sandwiches as well as good-value fish lunches.

Another fast snack you'll see everywhere is **shoarma** – kebabs, basically, sold in numerous Middle Eastern restaurants and takeaways. A shoarma in pitta will set you back about ƒ5 on average. Other street foods include **pancakes**, sweet or spicy, also widely available at sit-down restaurants; **waffles**, doused with syrup; and **poffertjes**, shell-shaped dumplings served with masses of melted butter and powdered sugar – an extremely filling snack. Try also **oliebollen**, greasy doughnuts sometimes filled with fruit (often apple) or custard (a *berliner*) and traditionally served at New Year. Dutch **cakes and cookies** are always good, and filling, best eaten in a *banketbakkerij* with a small serving area; or buy a bag and eat them on the hoof. Apart from the ubiquitous *appelgebak* – wedges of apple and cinnamon tart – things to try include *spekulaas*, a cinnamon cookie with gingerbread texture; *stroop-wafels*, butter wafers sandwiched together with runny syrup; *amandelkoek*, cakes with a crisp cookie outside and melt-in-the-mouth almond paste inside. In Limburg you should also sample *Limburgse Vlaai* – a pie with various fruit fillings.

As for the kind of food you can expect to encounter in bars, there are **sandwiches and rolls** (*boterham* and *broodjes*) – often open, and varying from a slice of tired cheese on old bread to something so embellished it's almost a complete meal – as well as different kinds of more substantial fare. A sandwich made with French bread is known as a *stokbrood*. In the winter, *erwtensoep* (or *snert*) – thick pea soup with smoked sausage, served with a portion of smoked bacon on *pumpernickel* – is available in most bars, and at about ƒ6 a bowl makes a great buy for lunch. Or there's an *uitsmijter* (literally, "bouncer"): one, two, or three fried eggs on buttered bread, topped with a choice of ham, cheese, or roast beef – at about ƒ8, another good budget lunch.

Holland's **cheeses** have an unjustified reputation abroad for being bland. This is because they tend to export the lower quality products and keep the best for themselves. In fact, Dutch cheese can be delicious, although there isn't the variety you get in, say, France or Italy. Most are based on the same soft creamy *Goudas*, and differences in taste come with the varying stages of maturity – *jong*, *belegen*, or *oud*. *Jong* cheese has a mild flavour, *belegen* is much tastier, while *oud* can be pungent and strong, with a flaky texture not unlike parmesan. Among the other cheeses you'll find, best known is the round red *Edam*, made principally for export and not eaten much by the Dutch; *Leidse*, simply Gouda with cumin seeds; *Leerdammer* and *Maasdammer*, strong, creamy, and full of holes; and Dutch-made

Emmentals and *Gruyères*. The best way to eat cheese here is the way the Dutch do it, in thin slices (cut with a cheese slice or *kaasschaaf*) rather than in large hunks.

Sit-down eating

Sit-down eating is possible at many different sorts of establishment. The majority of **bars** serve food, everything from sandwiches to a full menu, in which case they may be known as an **eetcafé**. These type of places tend to be open all day, serving both lunch and dinner. Full-blown **restaurants**, on the other hand, tend to open in the evening only, usually from around 5.30pm or 6pm until around 11pm. Bear in mind that everywhere, especially in the smaller provincial towns, the Dutch tend to eat early, usually around 7.30pm or 8pm, and that after about 10pm you'll find many restaurant kitchens closed.

If you're on a budget, stick to **dagschotels** (dish of the day) wherever possible, for which you pay around ƒ15, bottom-line, for a meat or fish dish, heavily garnished with potatoes and other vegetables and salad; bear in mind, though, that it's often only served at lunchtime or between 6pm and 8pm. Otherwise, you can pay up to ƒ25 for a meat course in an average restaurant; fish is generally high quality but rarely cheap at ƒ25–30, on average. The three-course **tourist menu**, which you'll see displayed at some mainstream restaurants, is – at ƒ22 or so – reasonable value, but the food is often dull. Surprisingly enough, **train station restaurants** are a good standby: every station has one serving full meals, in huge portions, for ƒ10–15. Consider also Holland's cheapest option for eating out, the university **mensa restaurants** in larger towns, where, with international student ID you can get a filling, if not especially exciting, meal for under ƒ10.

Eating vegetarian isn't a problem in Holland. Many *eetcafés* and restaurants have at least one meat-free menu item, and you'll find a few vegetarian restaurants in most towns, offering full-course set meals for ƒ10–15. Bear in mind that vegetarian restaurants often close early.

Of foreign cuisines, **Italian** food is ubiquitous and a good cheap standby: pizzas and pasta dishes start at a fairly uniform ƒ12 or so in all but the ritziest places. **Spanish** and **Tex-Mex** eateries serve well-priced, filling food for ƒ15–20. **Surinam** restaurants are a good bet for eating on a budget: try *roti*, flat pancake-like bread served with a spicy curry, hardboiled egg, and

vegetables. **Chinese** and **Indonesian** restaurants, too, are widespread (sometimes they're combined), and are normally well worth checking out. You can eat à la carte – *Nasi Goreng* and *Bami Goreng* (rice or noodles with meat) are good basic dishes, though there are normally more exciting things on the menu, some very spicy and chicken or beef in peanut sauce (*sate*) is always available. Or try a *rijstaffel*: boiled rice and/or noodles served with a huge number of spicy side dishes and hot *sambal* sauce on the side. Eaten with the spoon in the right hand, fork in the left, and with dry white or rosé wine, or beer, this doesn't come cheap, but it's delicious and is normally more than enough for two; indeed that's the usual way to order it – reckon on paying ƒ60–70 for two people.

■ Drinking

Most **drinking** is done either in the cosy surroundings of a **brown café** (*bruin kroeg*) – so named because of the colour of the walls, often stained by years of tobacco smoke – or in more modern-looking **designer bars**, minimally furnished and usually catering for a younger crowd. Most bars open until around 1am during the week, 2am at weekends, though some don't bother to open until lunchtime, a few not until around 4pm. There is another drinking establishment that you may come across, though they're no longer all that common – *proeflokaalen* or **tasting houses**, originally the sampling houses of small distillers, now small, old-fashioned bars that only serve spirits and close up around 8pm. Note that many cafés are a good source of budget **food**, when they're sometimes designated *eetcafés*. Most bars offer sandwiches and soup, or at least hardboiled eggs from the bar.

Beer

Other than in tasting houses, the most commonly consumed beverage is **beer**. This is usually served in small measures (just under a British half-pint); ask for "een pils" – "may I have?" is "mag ik", as in "mag ik een pils?". The Dutch like their beer with a foaming head, and requests to have it poured without a head meet with various responses, but it's worth trying. Prices are fairly standard: you don't pay much over the odds for sitting outside or drinking in a swanky bar or club; reckon on paying about ƒ2.50 a glass pretty much everywhere. Some bars, particularly those

DUTCH FOOD AND DRINK TERMS

Basics

Boter	Butter	Nagerechten	Desserts
Brood	Bread	Peper	Pepper
Broodje	Sandwich/roll	Pindakaas	Peanut butter
Dranken	Drinks	Sla/salade	Salad
Eieren	Eggs	Smeerkaas	Cheese spread
Groenten	Vegetables	Stokbrood	French bread
Gerst	Semolina: the type of grain used in Algerian couscous, popular in vegetarian restaurants	Suiker	Sugar
		Vis	Fish
		Vlees	Meat
		Voorgerechten	Appetizers, hors d'oeuvres
Honing	Honey		
Hoofdgerechten	Entrées	Vruchten	Fruit
Kaas	Cheese	Warm	Hot
Koud	Cold	Zout	Salt

Appetizers and snacks

Erwtensoep/snert	Thick pea soup with bacon or sausage	Uitsmijter	Ham or cheese with eggs on bread
Huzarensalade	Egg salad	Koffietafel	A light midday meal of cold meats, cheese, bread and perhaps soup
Patats/Frites	French fries		
Soep	Soup		

Meat and poultry

Biefstuk (hollandse)	Steak	Kalfsvlees	Veal
Eend	Duck	Karbonade	Chop
Fricandeau	Roast pork	Kip	Chicken
Fricandel	A frankfurter-like sausage	Kroket	Spiced meat in breadcrumbs
Gehakt	Ground meat	Lamsvlees	Lamb
Ham	Ham	Lever	Liver
Hutspot	Beef stew with vegetables	Rookvlees	Smoked beef
		Spek	Bacon
Kalkoen	Turkey	Worst	Sausages

Fish

Forel	Trout	Kabeljauw	Cod	Schol	Flounder
Garnalen	Shrimp	Makreel	Mackerel	Schelvis	Shellfish
Haring	Herring	Mosselen	Mussels	Tong	Sole
Haringsalade	Herring salad	Paling	Eel	Zalm	Salmon

terms

Doorbakken	Well done	Gerookt	Smoked
Gebakken	Fried/baked	Gestoofd	Stewed
Gebraden	Roasted	Half doorbakken	Medium
Gekookt	Boiled	Hollandse saus	Hollandaise (butter and egg sauce)
Gegrild	Grilled		
Geraspt	Grated		

Vegetables

Aardappelen	Potatoes	*Champignons*	Mushrooms	*Rijst*	Rice
Bloemkool	Cauliflower	*Erwten*	Peas	*Sla*	Salad, lettuce
Boerenkool	A kind of	*Knoflook*	Garlic	*Uien*	Onions
	cabbage	*Komkommer*	Cucumber	*Wortelen*	Carrots
Bonen	Beans	*Prei*	Leek	*Zuurkool*	Sauerkraut

Indonesian, Chinese and Surinamese dishes and terms

Ajam	Chicken	*Nasi Goreng*	Fried rice with meat/chicken
Bami	Fried noodles with meat/		and vegetables
	chicken and vegetables	*Nasi Rames*	*Rijsttafel* on a single plate
Daging	Beef	*Pedis*	Hot and spicy
Gado gado	Vegetables in peanut	*Pisang*	Banana
	sauce	*Rijsttafel*	Collection of different spicy
Goreng	Fried		dishes served with plain rice
Ikan	Fish	*Sambal*	Hot, chilli-based sauce
Katjang	Peanut	*Satesaus*	Peanut sauce to accompany
Kroepoek	Shrimp crackers		meat broiled on skewers
Loempia	Egg rolls	*Seroendeng*	Spicy fried, shredded coconut
Nasi	Rice	*Tauge*	Bean shoots

Desserts

Appelgebak	Apple tart or cake	*Oliebollen*	Doughnuts
Drop	Dutch liquorice, available in *zoet*	*Pannekoeken*	Pancakes
	(sweet) or *zout* (salted) varieties	*Poffertjes*	Small pancakes, fritters
	– the latter an acquired taste	*(Slag) room*	(Whipped) cream
Gebak	Pastry	*Speculaas*	Spice- and honey-flavoured
Ijs	Ice cream		biscuit
Koekjes	Cookies	*Stroopwafels*	Waffles
		Vla	Custard

Fruit and nuts

Aardbei	Strawberry	*Druif*	Grape	*Peer*	Pear
Amandel	Almond	*Framboos*	Raspberry	*Perzik*	Peach
Appel	Apple	*Hazelnoot*	Hazelnut	*Pinda*	Peanut
Appelmoes	Apple purée	*Kers*	Cherry	*Pruim*	Plum/prune
Citroen	Lemon	*Kokosnoot*	Coconut		

Drinks

Anijsmelk	Aniseed-	*Koffie*	Coffee	*Pils*	Dutch beer
	flavoured	*Koffie verkeerd*	Coffee with	*Proost !*	Cheers!
	warm milk		warm milk	*Sinaasappelsap*	Orange juice
Appelsap	Apple juice	*Kopstoot*	Beer with a	*Thee*	Tea
Bessenjenever	Blackcurrant gin		jenever	*Tomatensap*	Tomato juice
Chocomel	Chocolate milk		chaser	*Vieux*	Dutch brandy
Citroenjenever	Lemon gin	*Melk*	Milk	*Vruchtensap*	Fruit juice
Droog	Dry	*Met ijs*	With ice	*Wijn*	Wine
Frisdranken	Sodas	*Met slagroom*	With	*(wit/rood/rose)*	(white/red/
Jenever	Dutch gin		whipped		rosé)
Karnemelk	Buttermilk		cream	*Zoet*	Sweet

popular with the local English community, serve beer in larger measures, similar to the British pint, for which you can expect to pay ƒ5–7. Beer is much cheaper from a supermarket, most brands retailing at a little over ƒ1 for a half-litre bottle (a little less than half a pint).

The most common names are *Heineken*, *Amstel*, *Oranjeboom* and *Grolsch*, all of which you can find more or less nationwide. *Grolsch*, with its unique ceramic-topped bottles, is reputedly the strongest. Expect them to be stronger and more distinctive than the watery approximations brewed under licence outside Holland. In the southern provinces of North Brabant and Limburg you'll also find a number of locally brewed beers – *Bavaria* from Brabant, *De Ridder*, *Leeuw*, *Gulpen* and *Brand* (the latter the country's oldest brewer) from Limburg, all of which are worth trying. For something a little less strong, look out for *Donkenbier*, which is about half the strength of an ordinary pilsener beer.

You will also, of course, especially in the south of the country, see plenty of the better-known **Belgian brands**, like *Stella Artois* and the darker *De Koninck*, available on tap, and bottled beers like *Duvel*, *Chimay* and various brands of the cherry-flavoured *Kriek*. There are also a number of beers which are **seasonally available**: *Bokbier* (bock beer) is widespread in autumn; white beers (*witbieren*) like *Hoegaarden*, *Dentergems* and *Raaf* are available in summer, often served with a slice of a lemon – very refreshing. See *Belgium and Luxembourg*, "Eating and drinking".

Wine and spirits

Wine is reasonably priced – expect to pay around ƒ6 or so for an average bottle of French white or red. As for **spirits**, the indigenous drink is **jenever**, or Dutch gin – not unlike British gin, but a bit weaker and oilier, made from molasses and flavoured with juniper berries: it's served in small glasses and is traditionally drunk straight, often knocked back in one gulp with much hearty back-slapping. There are a number of varieties: *Oud* (old) is smooth and mellow, *Jong* (young) packs more of a punch – though neither is extremely alcoholic. *Zeer oude* is very old jenever. The older jenevers are a little more expensive but are stronger and less oily. In a bar, ask for a *borreltje* (straight jenever) or a *bittertje* (with angostura); if you've a sweet tooth, try a *bessenjenever* – blackcurrant-flavoured gin; for a glass of beer with a

jenever chaser, ask for a *kopstoot*. A glass of jenever in a bar will cost you around ƒ2.50; in a supermarket bottles sell for around ƒ14. Imported spirits are considerably more expensive.

Other drinks you'll see include numerous Dutch **liqueurs**, notably *advocaat* or eggnog, the sweet blue *curaçao* and luminous green *pisang ambon*, as well as an assortment of luridly coloured **fruit brandies** best left for experimentation at the end of an evening. There's also the Dutch-produced brandy, *Vieux*, which tastes as if it's made from prunes but is in fact grape-based, and various regional firewaters, such as *elske* from Maastricht – made from the leaves, berries and bark of alder bushes.

Galleries, museums and churches

Holland is strong on museums and galleries: most towns have at least a small collection of Dutch art worth looking at, as well as several other museums.

■ Galleries and museums

There are a number of **different kinds of museum** you'll come across time and again: a *Rijksmuseum* is a state-run museum, housing a national collection on a specific theme; a *Stedelijk* or *Gemeente* museum is run by the local town council and can vary from a small but quality collection of art to dusty arrays of local archeological finds; a *tentoonstelling* is a temporary exhibition, usually of contemporary art. **Hours** are fairly uniform across the country – generally Tuesday to Saturday 10am to 5pm, Sunday 1pm or 2pm to 5pm; entry prices for the more ordinary collections are usually around ƒ2–5, children halfprice. Many museums offer at least some English information, even if it's just a returnable leaflet.

If you're planning to visit a fair number of museums, the *Cultureel Jongeren Paspoort* or **CJP**, if you're under 26 years of age, gets you reductions in museums and on theatre, cinema and concert tickets for ƒ20 – though bear in mind that the discounts vary wildly and in many cases are not that substantial. CJPs are valid across Holland and are available from the Uitburo in Amsterdam. There is also the **Holland Leisure Card**, available before you leave for Holland through the NBT – details on p.15.

■ Churches

Dutch **churches** are normally rather austere – stripped bare after the Reformation, their spartan, white-painted walls emphasizing the effect of their often soaring Gothic lines. Organs are often the only embellishment, with great, ornate cases that put out a terrific – and awesome – noise, and only in the Catholic south of the country does the occasional church still retain anything of the mystery of pre-Calvinist rituals. Hours for visitors vary, though northern churches do usually have set times when visits are possible – assuming, of course, that there's something inside worth seeing. Falling attendances, however, also mean that some churches have been pragmatically turned over to other purposes – exhibition halls, concert halls, even apartments. In the south, unless there's something of special interest, you may find visits confined to services.

Festivals and annual events

Holland has few national annual events, and aside from the carnivals that are celebrated in the southern part of the country and a sprinkling of religious-oriented celebrations, most annual shindigs are arts- or music-based affairs, confined to a particular town or city. In addition there are also markets and folkloric events, rather bogusly sustained for tourists, that take place during summer only, the Alkmaar cheese market being one of the most well-known examples.

Most festivals, as you might expect, take place during the summer. Contact the local VVV for up-to-date details – and remember that wherever you might be staying, huge swathes of the country are no more than a short train ride away.

Of the country's **annual cultural events**, the *Holland Festival*, held in June in Amsterdam, Rotterdam and The Hague, is probably the most diverse, with theatre, opera and classical music, by mainly Dutch performers. The Hague's *North Sea Jazz Festival* in July probably has more prestige and attracts a host of big names. There's more jazz on offer in June with Apeldoorn's *Jazz in the Woods* binge; check out also the Europe-renowned *Pink Pop Festival*, held in Landgraaf, near Maastricht early the same month, which attracts top-level performers.

Outside summer, **other annual events** include, of course, viewing the **bulbfields** – at their best between March and May. There are a number of places you can visit in the bulbfield areas of North and South Holland, notably the dazzling Keukenhof Gardens and – for a taste of the industry in action – the Aalsmeer flower auction. If you're visiting the country in February, a number of towns in Holland's southern provinces host pre-lenten **carnivals**, notably Maastricht; while an event to look out for also in February (though really any time when the weather is cold enough) is the **Elfstedentocht**, Friesland's uniquely exciting and gruelling, canal skating race between the province's eleven towns – though it's only actually been held once in the last twenty years so don't plan your trip around it.

PUBLIC HOLIDAYS

New Year's Day

Good Friday (many shops open)

Easter Sunday and Monday

April 30 (Queen's Birthday, street parties and many shops open)

May 5 Liberation Day

Ascension Day

Whit Sunday and Monday

December 5 (St Nicholas' Day, shops close early)

Christmas Day

December 26

FESTIVALS DIARY

January
Mid-Jan Leiden Jazz Week.
End Jan Rotterdam Film Festival.

February
Mid-Feb West Frisian Flora exhibition, Bovenkarspel.
Third week of Feb Carnivals in Breda, 's Hertogenbosch, Maastricht and in other southern towns.

March
End March–end May Keukenhof Gardens, Lisse: displays in the bulbfields and hothouses.
End March–end May Frans Roozen Nursery, Vogelenzang: displays in gardens and hothouses.
Sunday closest to March 15 Amsterdam: *Stille Ommegang* procession through the city streets to the St Nicolaaskerk.

April
April–Oct Amsterdam: city illuminations on bridges and buildings.
April–Oct Amsterdam: Tramline Museum, trams from Amsterdam South to Amstelveen and back.
Second Sunday in April Rotterdam Marathon.
April–Sept Alkmaar Cheese Market on Friday mornings.
April 22–24 Groningen: avant-garde jazz festival.
April 28 Flower Parade from Haarlem to Noordwijk.
April 30 Amsterdam: *Koninginnedag* (Queen's Birthday), celebrated by street markets and fireworks.

May
Early May Amsterdam Marathon.
End May Breda: traditional jazz festival, with open-air concerts and street parades.
May 30 Scheveningen: "Flag Day" to mark the opening of the Dutch herring season.

June
June 1–30 Holland Festival. Amsterdam, Rotterdam, The Hague: international arts festival.
June 1–21 Amsterdam: Summer Festival of modern theatre, music, dance and mime.
June 8 Landgraaf: Pink Pop Festival.
Early June Bolsward: Frisian "eleven cities" cycle race, using bicycles instead of the traditional ice skates.
Early June Apeldoorn: "Jazz in the Woods" festival.

Mid-June Scheveningen: International Kite Festival.
Mid-June to mid-July Middleburg: International Festival of new avant-garde music.
End June–end Aug Schagen: West Frisian Folk Market, preceded by processions, etc, on Thursday mornings.
Last week in June Amsterdam: Festival van Verleiding, theatre productions and other events to celebrate Gay Pride Week.

July
Early July Drenthe Four-Day Cycle Event.
July 1–Sept 30 The Hague: International Rose Exhibition.
July–end Aug Hoorn: Traditional market, with folk dancing and old crafts, Wednesday mornings.
July–end Aug Purmerend: cheeese market, Thursday mornings.
Early July The Hague: North Sea Jazz Festival.
End July *Vierdaagse*, Nijmegen: Four-Day Walking Event.

August
Early Aug Sneek Week: international sailing event.
Mid-Aug Scheveningen: International Firework Festival, two displays each evening.
Mid-Aug Brabant Four-Day Cycle Event, starting in Tilburg.
End Aug Zandvoort: International Grand Prix motor-racing event.

September
Mid-Sept Amsterdam: Boulevard of Broken Dreams Arts Festival.

October
Mid-Oct Maastricht: Jazz Festival.

November
Mid-Nov Throughout the country: arrival of St Nicholas.

December
Dec 5 Pakjesavond. Though it tends to be a private affair, this is the day Dutch kids receive their Christmas presents. If you're here on that day and have Dutch friends, it's worth knowing that it's traditional to give a present together with a rude poem you have written caricaturing the recipient.

Directory

ADDRESSES These are written, for example, as Haarlemmerstraat 15 III, meaning the third-floor (fourth-floor) apartment at no. 15 Haarlemmerstraat. The figures 1e or 2e before a street name are an abbreviation for *Eerste* and *Tweede* respectively – first and second streets of the same name. Dutch zip codes can be found in the directory kept at post offices; note that complete codes have a two-letter indicator as well.

AIRPORT TAX Not charged when leaving The Netherlands.

BIKE RENTAL See p.29.

BRING Toiletries, film and English-language books, all of which are fairly expensive in Holland. Also bring antihistamine cream if you react badly to mosquitoes – it can be hard to find in Holland.

CAR PROBLEMS See p.28.

CLOGS You'll see these on sale in all the main tourist centres, usually brightly painted and not really designed for wearing. It's estimated that about three million clogs are still made annually in The Netherlands; interestingly, only about half are for the tourist market, the rest mainly being worn by industrial workers as foot protection. Only a few elderly farmers out in the sticks continue to wear clogs in the traditional way.

CONTRACEPTIVES Condoms are available from a *drogist* or – in Amsterdam – the *Condomerie* (p.91). But to get the pill you need a doctor's prescription – see p.15.

DISABLED VISITORS Though public transport systems tend to have no facilities for disabled passengers, many major museums, concert halls, theatres, churches and public buildings are accessible to visitors in wheelchairs. VVV offices, themselves accessible, can provide lists of those that have ramps and lifts, or where staff are trained to escort disabled visitors. *Netherlands Railways* offers a comprehensive service for disabled travellers, including a timetable in Braille, free escort service, and assistance at all stations. Get more details on ☎030/33 12 53 (Mon–Fri 8.30am–4pm), or from The Netherlands Board of Tourism leaflet, *Holland for the Handicapped*, which also describes hotel and camping facilities throughout the country. There is also a desk in the Schiphol Arrivals Hall (North), open 6am to 11pm, to help disabled people through the airport. Last but not least, paper currency has dots in the corner to indicate its value to the visually impaired.

ELECTRIC CURRENT 220v AC – British equipment needs only a plug adaptor; American apparatus requires a transformer and will need new plugs or an adaptor.

EMERGENCIES Phone ☎06 11. In Amsterdam lesser emergencies can be notified on: **Police** ☎622 22 22; **Ambulance** ☎55 55 555; **Fire** ☎621 21 21.

FLOWERS It doesn't take long to notice the Dutch enthusiasm for flowers and plants of all kinds: windows are often festooned with blooms and greenery, and shops and markets sell sprays and bunches for next to nothing. Flowers are grown year-round, though obviously spring is the best time to come if this is your interest, when the bulbfields (and glasshouses) of North and South Holland are dense with colour – tulips, hyacinths, and narcissi are the main blooms. Later in the year there are rhododendrons and, in Friesland and Groningen, fields of yellow rapeseed; in summer roses appear, while the autumn sees late chrysanthemums. For more on Holland's flowers, pick up the NBT's *Flowers* booklet, and turn to p.127 for the best of the bulbfields. Buying bulbs is easiest by placing an order with a specialist company which will handle the packing and legal paperwork for you.

ISIC CARDS Student ID is useful for mensas, but won't help you gain reduced admission to very much at all, and certainly not museums or mainstream tourist attractions.

LEFT LUGGAGE At all train stations. Where there is no actual office, there will always be lockers, charging either ƒ1 or ƒ2 – depending on size – for 24 hours.

MOSQUITOES These thrive in Holland's watery environment, biting their worst at campsites. An antihistamine cream such as *Phenergan* is the best antidote, although this can be difficult to find in Holland – in which case preventative sticks like *Autan* or *Citronella* are the best idea.

SHOPPING Two stores you'll see all over Holland are *Vroom & Dreesmann* and *HEMA* – department stores that are useful for stocking up on basic supplies such as toiletries, etc. Of the two, *HEMA* is the cheaper, a sort of Dutch Woolworths, many branches of which also have a cheap restaurant that makes a good place for an inexpensive if unexciting budget lunch. Most good bookstores stock at least a few English paperbacks, though at higher prices than in the UK and US; look out also for branches of *De Slegte*, a countrywide chain (with a couple of branches in Belgium) that sells secondhand and discounted books, a good proportion of which will be in English; we've listed addresses in the *Guide*. Among things to buy to take home, cheese is an obvious choice – it's better and there's more variety than at home. Flowers (see above) are also dirt cheap everywhere. You might also try *drop* or Dutch liquorice, which comes in myriad different varieties including salted, unsalted or with honey.

TIME One hour ahead of GMT; six hours ahead of Eastern Standard Time; nine hours ahead of Pacific Standard Time.

TIPPING Don't bother, since restaurants, hotels, taxis, etc, must include a fifteen percent service charge by law. Only if you're somewhere *really* flash is it considered proper to round up the bill to the nearest guilder. In public toilets, it's normal to leave about 25c.

TRAVEL AGENTS *NBBS* is the nationwide student/youth travel organization and the best source of *BIJ* tickets, discount flights for anyone, etc. They have branches in all the main Dutch cities – see our listings for addresses.

WAR CEMETERIES Though it saw less action than either Belgium or Luxembourg, there was fierce fighting in parts of Holland during the last war, notably at Arnhem, where several thousand British and Polish servicemen are remembered at the Oosterbeek cemetery. There are other military cemeteries in the east and south of the country, not least at Margraten, where around eight thousand US soldiers are buried.

WINDMILLS The best place to see windmills is at Kinderdijk near Dordrecht; they're also still very much part of the landscape in the polderlands north of Amsterdam. Some, too, have been moved and reassembled out of harm's way in the open-air museums at Zaanse Schans (Zaandam) and the Netherlands Open-Air Museum just outside Arnhem.

CHAPTER ONE

AMSTERDAM

Amsterdam is a compact, instantly likeable capital: appealing to look at, pleasant to walk around, and with an enticing mix of the provincial and the cosmopolitan. The city has a welcoming attitude toward visitors and a uniquely youthful orientation, shaped by the liberal counter-culture of the last two decades. It's hard not to feel drawn in by the buzz of open-air summer events, by the intimacy of the clubs and bars or by the Dutch facility with languages – English, for example, is spoken by almost everyone.

The city's layout is determined by a cobweb of canals radiating out from a medieval core which, along with planned seventeenth-century extensions further out, provide elegant backdrops for living or wandering. The conventional sights are for the most part low key – the **Anne Frank House** being a notable exception – but Amsterdam has developed a world-class group of museums and galleries. The **Van Gogh Museum** is, for many, reason enough in itself to visit the city; add to it the **Rijksmuseum**, with its collections of medieval and seventeenth-century Dutch paintings, the contemporary and experimental **Stedelijk**, plus hundreds of smaller galleries, and the international quality of the art is evident.

But it's Amsterdam's **population and politics** that constitute its most enduring characteristics. Notorious during the 1960s and 1970s as the heart of radical, "liberated" Europe, the city mellowed only marginally during the Eighties, and despite the inevitable late-Eighties yuppification retains a resilient, laid-back feel. The authorities are trying to play down the counter-culture label and boost Amsterdam's economy by cultivating a businesslike image for the city and a more conventional reputation for the arts, and it's true that battles over urban development plans and squatting rights seem to have stopped lately, although the divide between the Social Democrat city council seems to be growing. Despite that, the key words are tolerance and, as the Dutch say, *gezelligheid* – a hard-to-translate term, roughly meaning "cosiness" – that perhaps best sum up the laid-back intimacy of the city.

Amsterdam has responded to its youth culture with a social and sensible attitude to soft drugs. Entertainment has a similarly innovative edge, exemplified by **multimedia complexes** like the *Melkweg*, whose offerings are at the forefront of contemporary film, dance, drama and music. There are some great **coffee shops**, serving cannabis products and juices instead of alcohol, and the more conventional **bars** range from the traditional, bare-floored brown cafés to new-wave designer haunts. The city's **club** scene is by contrast relatively subdued, and modest by the standards of other capital cities, and the emphasis is more on dancing than posing.

If you intend spending any time in Amsterdam, or want to find out about it in greater detail, get hold of a copy of *The Rough Guide to Amsterdam*.

Arrival, city transport and information

Amsterdam has one international airport, **Schiphol**. This is connected by train with Amsterdam's **Centraal Station**, a fast service leaving every fifteen minutes during the day, hourly at night; the journey takes twenty minutes and costs ƒ5.25 one way. The city has a number of suburban **train stations**, but all major internal and international traffic is handled by Amsterdam Centraal. Arriving here leaves you at the hub of all bus and tram routes and just five minutes' walk from Dam Square. Almost all **buses** arrive at **Centraal Station**, too, except for the cross-channel Hoverspeed *City Sprint* service, which calls at **Stadionplein**, before terminating at **Leidseplein**, linked to the city centre by trams #1, #2 and #5.

> The telephone code for Amsterdam is ☎020

City transport

By European capital standards Amsterdam is small, its public transport excellent and most of the things you might conceivably want to see can be found in the city's compact centre: **getting around** couldn't be easier.

Apart from walking, **trams** – and, to a lesser extent, **buses** – offer the easiest transport alternative: the system is comprehensive and not at all expensive. Your first stop should be the *GVB* (city transport) office in front of Centraal Station (next door to the *VVV*; Mon–Fri 7am–10.30pm, Sat & Sun 8am–10.30pm) where you can pick up a free route map and an English guide to the **ticketing** system.

Tickets, the metro and buses
The ticket system needs explaining. *Dagkaarten* – **day tickets** – are valid for as many days as you need – prices currently start at ƒ11.50 for one day, going up to ƒ22.45 for three, and ƒ3.60 for each additional day. Or you can buy a **strippenkaart**. These are valid nationwide and work on a zonal arrangement whereby you cancel two strips for one zone, three strips for two and so on, when you board the tram or bus (the driver will do it for you on a bus; on trams you're trusted to do it yourself). The most practical *strippenkaart* has fifteen strips (currently ƒ10.75), and can be purchased in advance at any *GVB* office (the others are in the Scheepvaarthuis at the corner of Prins Hendrikkade and Binnenkant, in the Amstel Station, and there is sometimes a temporary office sited outside the Stadsschouwburg on Leidseplein), at a post office, selected tobacconists or at train station ticket counters. There's also a 45-strip card available for ƒ31 – useful if you intend to travel further afield. Otherwise two-, three-, and eight-strip tickets are available from the driver – though they work out considerably more expensive.

You'll rarely need to travel outside the central zone, so most of the time cancelling two strips is sufficient. Additional people can travel on the same *strippenkaart* by cancelling the requisite number of strips. Also, don't forget that the stamp made on the *strippenkaart* is timed and valid for an hour: you don't need to cancel it again if you change trams or buses within that time. If caught without a ticket, you're liable for a ƒ60 fine, due on the spot, so it pays to be honest.

The *strippenkaart* system also works on the city's **metro**, which starts at Centraal Station and connects with the building complexes of Bijlmermeer to the east, and the new **sneltrein** running down to Amstelveen. Both lines are clean, modern and punctual, but can be a bit hairy at night: in any case, apart from a couple of stops in the eastern reaches of the centre, most of the stations are in the outskirts and used mainly by commuters.

All of the above services stop running around 12.30am, when a wide network of **night buses** rolls into action, roughly hourly until 4am from Centraal Station to most parts of the city; the *GVB* offers a leaflet detailing all the routes.

Taxis and cars

Taxis are plentiful but expensive, and found in stands on main city squares (Stationsplein, Dam Square, Leidseplein, etc) or by phoning ☎677 77 77 – you can't hail them. A fun alternative are the **water taxis**, which can be ordered (☎675 09 09) to any place on a canal – ƒ40 for twenty minutes. Taxis aside, it's generally unwise to travel **by car**: parking is either difficult or expensive, and even if you have brought your own car it won't make any difference to the zealous traffic police, who will clamp or tow you whatever the licence plate says. Reclaiming a car from the pound costs at least ƒ320; a clamp is cheaper – you're

**TRAMS, BUSES
AND THE METRO**

only charged for the excess meter time – but you have to present yourself person-ally at the nearest clamp office to get it removed. If you get caught and don't know what to do, call ☎627 58 66.

Bikes

Another possibility, and a practical one, is to go native and opt for a **bicycle**: the city's well-defined network of bicycle lanes (*fietspaden*) means that this can be a remarkably safe way of getting around. If you haven't brought your own, it's possi-ble to rent **a bike** from Centraal Station (*f*7.50 a day, *f*30 a week, plus *f*200 deposit), or from a number of similarly priced bike rental firms scattered around town, most of which ask for smaller deposits: try *Hire-a-Bike*, Pieter Jacobsdwarsstraat 17, off Damstraat (☎625 50 29), *f*12.50 a day plus *f*50 deposit and passport. They also do tandems for *f*25 a day. Lock up your bike at *all times*. Bike theft is rife in Amsterdam, and it's not unusual to see the dismembered parts of bicycles still chained to their railings, victims of sharp-eyed gangs armed with bolt cutters who roam the streets hawking their prizes at suspiciously low prices. Ironically, purchasing a "hot" bike is often the cheapest way to pick one up – and you can always sell it (often at a profit) when the time comes to go home.

Canal trips and city tours

One way of getting oriented is to take a **canal trip** on one of the glass-topped boats that jam the major canals during the summer season. While not exactly riveting, these trips are the best way to see canal houses and have a soporific charm if you're feeling lazy. Of the many to choose from, *P.Kooij* (☎623 38 10) runs hour-long tours for *f*10, which leave from the corner of Rokin and Lange Brugsteeg and have (atypically) a live commentary that's just about bearable. Alternatively, you can take a guided tour of the city centre by **bike**. Run by *Yellow Bike*, N. Z. Voorburgwal 66 (☎620 69 40), these leave from outside their office and cost *f*29 for a three-hour tour, taking in all the main sights and accompanied by entertaining and informed guides. Bikes are supplied, and tours leave daily at 9.30am and 1pm.

There are also plenty of people willing to guide you around by **bus**: the *GVB* offers a seventy-minute tour by "tourist tram", which takes in the main sights of the immediate centre; or operators like *Lindbergh* (the cheapest), Damrak 26 (☎622 27 66), *Keytours*, Dam 19 (☎624 73 10), and *Holland International*, Damrak 7 (☎622 3035), offer three-hour tours with stops and, again, live commentary, for *f*30–40.

Information

The first place to head for information is the **VVV**, the nationwide tourist organiza-tion, either at its main branch outside Centraal Station (May–Sept daily 9am–11pm; Oct–April daily 9am–5pm; ☎06/340 34066), or at Leidseplein 1 (May–Sept daily 9am–9pm; Oct–April Mon–Sat 9am–5pm). Either office can sell you a map, book accommodation for a *f*3.50 fee (plus a *f*4 "deposit" which you reclaim from the hotel) and provide informed answers to most other enquiries.

A useful source of budget information is the **centre in the Sleep-In**, 's-Gravesandstraat 51 (see "Other hostels", p.52). Open July to August daily 9am to noon and 2 to 8pm, the centre is run by *Amsterdam Calling* (☎694 33 69), a group set up to encourage alternative ways of working with tourism, youth and culture. They have a mass of information, all specially aimed at the young/independent traveller.

For information on **what's on**, the best source is the monthly *Time Out Amsterdam* (ƒ4), produced by and similar to the London listings magazine. Otherwise, the *VVV* issues a biweekly listings guide, *What's On In Amsterdam*, which you can either pick up directly from their offices for ƒ2.75, or obtain free from selected hotels, hostels and restaurants. This gives reasonably complete, if uncritical listings for museums, the arts, shopping and restaurants.

Of the many Dutch-language monthly freebies to be found in bars and restaurants, the best is *Agenda*, whose listings have a youthful slant and whose addresses, phone numbers and numerous advertisements for various services could prove invaluable.

Accommodation

Unless you're camping, **accommodation** in Amsterdam is a major expense: even hostels are pricy for what you get, and hotels are among the most expensive in Europe. The city's size means that you'll inevitably end up somewhere central, but you'll still need to search hard to find a bargain.

At peak periods throughout the year (July–Aug, Christmas) it's advisable to reserve ahead of time – rooms can be swallowed up alarmingly quickly, especially during the summer, and you may find it difficult to find somewhere to stay. The *VVV* will make advance bookings and book rooms on the spot for a ƒ3.50 fee, or sell you a comprehensive booklet on hotels in the city for ƒ2.50.

Note that all tram line directions given below are from the Centraal Station.

ACCOMMODATION PRICE CODES

All the **hotels and hostels** detailed in this chapter have been graded according to the following price categories. Note that the prices have been calculated as those for the cheapest double room during high season. For more on accommodation, see p.29.

① Up to ƒ30 per person.	④ ƒ100–140.	⑦ ƒ220–260.
② ƒ30–65.	⑤ ƒ140–180.	⑧ ƒ260 and over.
③ ƒ65–100.	⑥ ƒ180–220.	

Hostels

Most **hostels** expect you to provide your own sleeping bag (bed linen is often available for a small fee), set a nightly curfew and, for security reasons, lock guests out of the dormitories for a short period each day.

Official youth hostels

Stadsdoelen, Kloveniersburgwal 97 (☎624 68 32). Nearer to the station (on the edge of the Red Light district) and with slightly more inviting dorms, but no double rooms. Restaurant serves good-value, though very basic food. ƒ5 extra for non–IYHA members. Tram #4, #9, #16, #24, #25. ②.

AMSTERDAM CITY CENTRE

Het Ij

Dijksgracht

aarthuis

Oosterdok

Montelbaanstoron

PRINS HENDRIKKADE

KATTENBURGERSTRAAT

Maritime Museum

KATTENBURGERGRACHT

ron Kerk

Herengracht

Nieuwe

Vaart

WITTENBURGERGRACHT

OOSTENBURGERGRACHT

gergracht

RSTRAAT

HOOGTEKADIJK

ENTREPOTDOK

Kromhout
Museum

MUIDERSTRAAT

PLANTAGE DOKLAAN

Artis Zoo

hof

PLANTAGE MIDDENLAAN

Keizersgracht

PLANTAGE MUIDERGRACHT

Singelgracht

NIEUWE KERK STRAAT

Prinsengracht

Nieuwe

Achtgracht

Muiderpoort

WEESPERPLEIN

SARPHATISTRAAT

Tropenmuseum

MAURITSKADE

Oosterpark

WIBAUTSTRAAT

0   500 m

Vondel Park, Zandpad 5 (☎683 17 44). For facilities, the better of the two official hostels. It has a bar, restaurant, TV rooms and kitchen for guests' use, and is well located for the summer events in the park. In July and August the hostel is open to IYHA members only; the rest of the year non-members pay ƒ5 extra. Curfew 2am. Tram #1, #2, #5. ②.

Other hostels

Boatel Amstel, Steiger 5, De Ruijterkade (☎626 42 47). The only survivor of a number of barge hotels which used to be moored behind Centraal Station – now closed due to fire risks. This was always the largest and best known, and still provides a cheap and central place to stay. All private rooms have phone and TV; all prices include breakfast. ②–③.

Bob's Youth Hostel, N. Z. Voorburgwal 92 (☎623 00 63). An old favourite of backpackers, this has small, clean dorms, and rates include breakfast in the first-floor coffee shop; the curfew is 3.30am. A short walk from Centraal Station or tram #2, #5, #13, #17. ②.

Eben Haezer, Bloemstraat 179 (☎624 47 17). Don't be put off: though you may be given a booklet on Jesus, and the slogans on the walls may not be the ones you'd put up on yours, this Christian youth hostel isn't evangelical, but simply provides neat, clean dormitories for rock bottom prices – including bed linen and a hearty breakfast. Curfew 1am on weekends; age limit 35 – though this is negotiable. Tram #13, #14, #17. ①.

Kabul, Warmoesstraat 38–42 (☎623 71 58). Doesn't really justify its high rates for beds in grungy dorms, but the singles and doubles are quite reasonable and triples and 4-bed rooms are also available. On the plus side, there's no lockout or curfew, it's an easy walk from the station and the late-opening Kabul bar next door has regular live bands. Breakfast ƒ6 extra. Wheelchair access. ③.

Keizersgracht, Keizersgracht 15 (☎625 13 64). Terrific location close to the station, with singles, doubles and 4-bedded rooms. Spotless rooms, too; breakfast is extra. ② in a quad, but a steep ④ in doubles and singles.

Sleep-In, 's-Gravesandestraat 51 (☎694 74 44). A little way out of the centre but one of the city's cheapest places to stay. Dorms are enormous, facilities include a bar, restaurant and information centre (see "Information", on p.48), there are regular weekly musical and theatre performances and the atmosphere is great. Also, around 500 beds means you're unlikely to be turned away. Open year-round, but closed between noon and 4pm. Weesperplein metro station or tram #6. Low ②.

Hotels

Amsterdam's **hotels** start at around ƒ75 for a double, absolute minimum, and although a filling Dutch breakfast is normally included at all but the most expensive places, many middle-range hotels give the barest value for money. There are exceptions, but don't be afraid to ask to see the room first – and to refuse it if you don't like it. Most places have cheaper off-season prices.

Inexpensive to moderate

De Admiraal, Herengracht 563 (☎626 21 50). Friendly hotel just off Rembrandtsplein. Tram #84. ③.

Asterisk, Den Texstraat 16 (☎626 23 96). Good-value budget hotel on the edge of the city, just across the canal from the old Heineken brewery. Tram #16, #7, #10. ③.

Bema, Concertgebouwplein 19b (☎679 13 96). Very small but a friendly place, handy for concerts and museums. ③.

Beursstraat, Beursstraat 7 (☎626 37 01). Nestling behind Berlage's Stock Exchange, this basic hotel is one of the few to exclude breakfast from its room rates. A short walk from Centraal Station. ②.

Casa Cara, Emmastraat 24 (☎662 31 35). Homely, cheapish hotel 5min from the Concertgebouw and major museums. Tram #2, #16. ③.

Clemens, Raadhuisstraat 39 (☎624 60 89). One of a number of inexpensive hotels that are situated in the Art Nouveau crescent of the Utrecht Building. Clean, neat and good value for money. As Raadhuisstraat is one of the city's busiest streets, you should ask for a room at the back. Tram #13, #14, #17. ③.

Galerij Radhuisstraat 43 (☎624 88 51) One of the Radhuisstraat budget options. Tram #13, #14, #17. ③.

Kitty, Plantage Middenlaan 40 (☎622 68 19). A little bit out from the centre, but decent-sized rooms, including as much breakfast as you can eat. Good value. Tram #7, #9, #14. Get off at the zoo. ③.

Pax, Radhuisstraat 37 (☎624 97 35). Basic city-centre cheapie with fair-sized doubles. Breakfast not included. As with the rest of the hotels along here, ask for a room at the back. Tram #13, #14, #17. ②–③.

Prinsenhof, Prinsengracht 810 (☎623 17 72). Tastefully decorated hotel on one of the main canals. Best rooms at the back. Pleasant enough and friendly. Tram #4.③.

Ronnie, Raadhuisstraat 41 (☎624 28 21). Owned by the American cousins of the *Clemens'* owners, and with equally good prices and facilities. Friendly and helpful, with rooms for 3, 4, and 5 as well as doubles. Tram #13, #14, #17. ③–④.

Van Ostade, Van Ostadestraat 123 (☎679 324 52). Friendly place with a youthful atmosphere that bills itself as a "bicycle hotel", renting bikes and giving information with routes and other advice – recommended. Peacefully situated only a 5-min cycle out of the centre in the appealing Old South district. Bikes ƒ1.80 per day. Tram #24, #25. ③.

Vuillings, P.C. Hoofstraat 78 (☎671 21 09). Small, elegantly located hotel. Tram #2, #3, #5, #12. ③.

Moderate to expensive

Acro, Jan Luykenstraat 44 (☎662 05 26). Excellent modern hotel which has been completely refurbished with stylish rooms and a plush bar and help-yourself restaurant. Well worth the money. Tram #2, #3, #5, #12. ⑤.

Agora, Singel 462 (☎627 22 00). Nicely located, small, amiable hotel near the flower market, with doubles, 3- and 4-bedded rooms. Tram #1, #2, #5. ④.

Canal House, Keizersgracht 148 (☎622 51 82). Magnificently restored seventeenth-century building, centrally located on a principal *grachten*. American family-run with a friendly bar and cosy rooms. Discounts in winter. Tram #13, #14, #17. ⑥.

Continental, Damrak 40–41 (☎622 33 63). A clean hotel on the noisy tourist drag of Damrak, a short walk from Centraal Station. ④.

Estherea, Singel 303–309 (☎624 51 46). Pleasant middle-of-the-road hotel in a converted canal house. Tram #1, #2, #5. ⑧.

Seven Bridges, Reguliersgracht 31 (☎623 13 29). One of the city's most beautiful and best-value hotels both inside and out. Tram #4. ④.

Toren, Keizersgracht 164 (☎622 60 33). Fine example of a seventeenth-century canal house and once the home of a Dutch prime minister. Tram #13, #14, #17. ⑤.

Camping

There are several **campsites** in Amsterdam, most of which are easily accessible by public transport or by car. The *VVV* directs most visitors to the "youth campsites" of *Vliegenbos* and *Zeeburg*, open April to September, while grown-ups and those with trailers or campers are advised to use one of the other sites.

Amsterdamse Bos, Kleine Noorddijk 1, Aalsmeer (☎641 68 68). Many facilities but a pretty long way out. Open April–Oct, and charges ƒ7.60 per person, inclusive of showers, and an additional ƒ2.60 for each tent, motorbike, car, camper or caravan. Yellow bus #171 or #172 and a short walk.

Amsterdam IJsclub, IJsbaanpad 45 (☎62 09 16). An enormous campsite situated near the Olympic Stadium: aside from *Vliegenbos*, the closest to the city centre. Camping shop and canteen. Rates ƒ4.25 per person, ƒ3 per tent, parking ƒ2.50. Tram #16 or #24, night bus #73 or #74.

Gaasper Camping, Loosdrechtsedreef 7 (☎696 73 26). Amsterdam's newest campsite, just on the other side of the Bijlmermeer housing complex, ƒ5 per person, ƒ4.25 per tent, plus a charge for showers (ƒ1.50). Metro to Gaasperplas Station and a 3-min walk; night bus #75.

Vliegenbos, Meeuwenlaan 138 (☎636 88 55). Open April–Sept. A relaxed and friendly site, just a 10-min bus ride from the station. Facilities include a general shop and bike rental. Costs ƒ5.75 a night per person without car, ƒ7 if you're over 30; ƒ3.25 for cars, ƒ2.25 for motorbikes. Hot showers ƒ1.50. Bus #32, from Centraal Station, night bus #77.

Zeeburg, Zuider IJdijk 44a (☎694 44 30). Slightly better equipped than the *Vliegenbos*, in that it has a bar. But more difficult to get to and a little more expensive: ƒ5 per person plus ƒ2.50 per tent, ƒ5 per car, ƒ3 per motorbike, ƒ1.50 for a shower. Tram #3 or #10 to Muiderpoort Station, then bus #37, then a 10-min walk; also served by night bus #76.

The City

Amsterdam is a small city: its centre is compact, its buildings restrained and, although the concentric canal system can initially be confusing, finding your bearings is straightforward. The centre of the city – along with the main canals, the area in which you'll spend most of your time – is the old **medieval core**, which fans south from Centraal Station, taking in the main artery of Damrak, Dam Square and Rokin. This, Amsterdam's commercial heart, boasts the best of its bustling street life and is home to shops, many bars and restaurants and, not least, the infamous **Red Light District**. The area is bordered by the Singel, the first of the **big canals**, on the far side of which curl Herengracht, Keizersgracht and Prinsengracht. These canals are part of a major seventeenth-century urban extension and, with the radial streets of Leidsestraat, Vijzelstraat and Utrechtsestraat, create Amsterdam's distinctive cobweb shape.

Further out, the **Jordaan** grew up as a slum and immigrant quarter and remains the traditional heart of working-class Amsterdam, though these days there is a firm yuppie edge to the area. On the other side of town, the **Jodenhoek** was, as its name suggests, once home to the city's Jewish community. Now it's probably Amsterdam's most visibly changed district and, since the construction of the muziektheater and metro, the principal source of squabbles over the city's future.

Across the Singelgracht, which marks the outer limit of today's centre, lie the largely residential districts of **Amsterdam South**, **West** and **East**, in themselves not of great interest, though with attractions (principally the main museums) that could tempt you out that way.

Stationsplein, Damrak and the Red Light District

This is the heart of the city and where you'll almost certainly arrive. It's a small area, but a varied one, ranging from the vigour of Stationsplein – the city's major traffic junction and home of the *VVV* (tourist) office – to the strategic tourist trap of Damrak and the studied (though real enough) sleaze of the Red Light District, not surprisingly one of Amsterdam's biggest tourist attractions.

Stationsplein and down Damrak

The neo-Renaissance **Centraal Station** is an imposing prelude to the city. When built late in the last century, this was a controversial structure as it obscured the views of the port that brought Amsterdam its wealth. Since then, however, shipping has moved out to more spacious dock areas to the west and east, and the station is now one of Amsterdam's most resonant landmarks and a natural focal point for urban life. Stand here and all of Amsterdam, with its faintly oriental skyline of spires and cupolas, lies before you.

Stationsplein, immediately outside, is a messy open space, but in the summer there's no livelier part of the city, as street performers compete for attention with the careering trams that converge dangerously from all sides. It's without a doubt a promising place to arrive, and with that in mind the municipal authorities are cleaning up the area's image, notably in the southeastern corner, where the once-notorious Zeedijk area has been partly redeveloped.

Just down the street from Zeedijk, the dome of the **St Nicolaaskerk** catches the eye. Despite a dilapidated exterior, it is the city's foremost Catholic church, having replaced the clandestine Amstelkring (see p.57) in 1887. Even if you manage to coordinate your visit with the limited opening hours (April–Sept Tues–Sat 11am–4pm, Sun 10am–3pm; Oct Sat 11am–4pm, Sun 10am–3pm), you'll find that there's not much of note inside – except, on the high altar, the crown of Austro-Hungarian Emperor Maximilian, very much a symbol of the city and one you'll see again and again (on top of the Westerkerk and on much of the city's official literature).

Above all, though, Stationsplein acts as a filter for Amsterdam's newcomers, and from here **Damrak**, an unenticing avenue lined by tacky, over-priced restaurants and the bobbing canal boats of Amsterdam's considerable tourist industry, storms south into the heart of the city. Just past the boats is the Stock Exchange, or **Beurs** (known as the "Beurs van Berlage"), designed at the turn of the century by the leading light of the Dutch modern movement, H. P. Berlage. With its various styles from Romanesque to neo-Renaissance interwoven with a minimum of ornamentation, it is something of a seminal work. Slip inside the entrance on Beursplein and look at the main hall, where exposed ironwork and shallow-arched arcades combine to give a real sense of space. Today it's no longer used as an exchange; the Beurs often hosts visiting theatre groups, classical concerts and exhibitions.

During the prewar years, the **De Bijenkorf** department store building, facing the Beurs and extending as far as Dam Square, was a successful Jewish concern – so much so that during the occupation the authorities, fearing possible altercations with the Jewish staff, forbade German soldiers from shopping on the first floor.

Around the Red Light District

Had you turned left off Damrak before the Beurs, you would have found yourself in the **RED LIGHT DISTRICT**, bordered by the oldest street in the city, Warmoesstraat, and stretching across two canals which marked the edge of medieval Amsterdam.

The **prostitution** here is sadly, but perhaps inevitably, one of the real sights of the city – and one of its most distinctive draws. The upfront nature of the porno industry here makes 42nd Street seem tame by comparison.

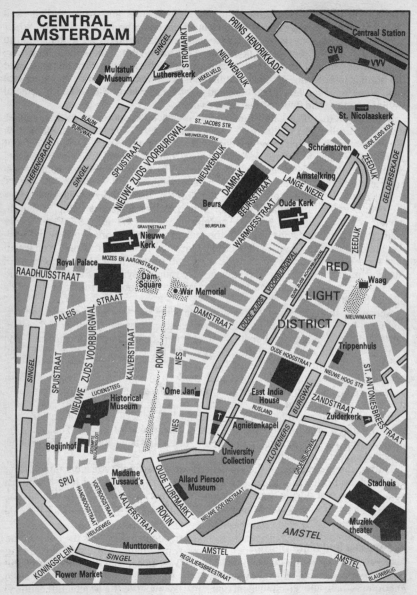

Two canals form the backbone of the area: **Oude Zijds Voorburgwal** and **Oude Zijds Achterburgwal**. These, and the narrow connecting passages, are, most evenings of the year, thronged with people here to discover just how shocking it all is. The nasty edge to the district is, oddly enough, sharper during the daytime, when the pimps hang out in shifty gangs and drug addicts wait anxiously, assessing the chances of scoring their next hit.

Narrow **Warmoesstraat** itself is seedy and uninviting, and a little way up stands the **Oude Kerk**, its precincts offering a reverential peace after the excesses of the Red Light District – though even here some of the houses have the familiar *Kamer te huur* sign and window seat. There's been a church on this site since the late thirteenth century, even before the Dam was built, but most of the present building dates from the fourteenth century.

Having been stripped bare during the Reformation and recently very thoroughly restored, the Oude Kerk is nowadays a survivor rather than an architectural masterpiece. Its handful of interesting features include – apart from a few faded vault paintings – some beautifully carved misericords in the choir, and the memorial tablet of Rembrandt's wife, Saskia van Uylenburg, who is buried here. It costs a guilder to get in and, in summer, another to ascend the tower (summer Mon–Sat 11am–5pm, Sun 1.30–5pm; winter daily 1.30–3pm; ring vestry bell for attention; tower June–Sept Wed–Sat 2–5pm; *f*3.50).

There's little else to stop for along Oude Zijds; only the clandestine **Amstelkring**, at the Zeedijk end of O.Z. Voorburgwal, is of real interest, once the principal Catholic place of worship in the city and now a museum (see p.77). Just past here, **Zeedijk** itself, though much cleaned up, provides evidence of more urban blight; until recently, you had to run the gauntlet of Surinamese heroin dealers trying to fast-talk you into a quick sale while idle groups of policemen looked on. The police claim to have the area under control now – part of the city-wide push to polish up Amsterdam's tarnished reputation as a tourist centre – and certainly this narrow street is considerably less intimidating than it once was. But for the moment there's a long way to go: Zeedijk is still terribly dilapidated, and the heroin dealers – albeit much depleted in number – have moved to the southern end of Zeedijk, near Nieuwmarkt, to shoot up in doorways and hustle passers-by for small change.

For the moment, then, the best thing to do is hurry through. Zeedijk opens out on to **Nieuwmarkt** and the top end of **Geldersekade**, which together form the hub of Amsterdam's tiny Chinese quarter. Nieuwmarkt was once one of Amsterdam's most important markets, first for fish, later for the cloth traders from the adjacent Jewish quarter, and nowadays for antiques on Sunday. During the last war it was surrounded by barbed wire behind which Jews were penned while awaiting deportation. The main focus of the square, the turreted **Waag**, or old **St Antoniespoort**, has played a variety of roles over the years. Originally part of the fortifications that encircled Amsterdam before the seventeenth-century expansion, it later became the civic weighing-house, and for a time was used by a number of the city's guilds, including the Surgeons' – the young Rembrandt's *Anatomy Lesson of Dr. Tulp* was based on the activities here.

Kloveniersburgwal, which leads south from Nieuwmarkt, was the outer of the three eastern canals of sixteenth-century Amsterdam. Although not among Amsterdam's more attractive waterways, it does boast, on the left, one of the city's most impressive canal houses. Built for the Trip family in 1662, and large enough to house the Rijksmuseum collection for most of the nineteenth century, the **Trippenhuis** is a huge, overblown mansion, its Corinthian pilasters and grand frieze providing a suitable reflection of the owners' importance.

Further up the canal, on the corner of Oude Hoogstraat, the red-brick former headquarters of the **Dutch East India Company** is a monumental building, built in 1606 shortly after the founding of the company. It was from here that the Dutch organized and regulated the trading interests in the Far East which made the country so opulent in the seventeenth century. Under the greedy auspices of the East India Company, The Netherlands (especially its most prosperous provinces, Holland and Zeeland) exploited the natural resources of the group of islands now known as Indonesia for several centuries, satisfying the whims of Amsterdam's burghers with shiploads of spices, textiles and exotic woods.

For all that, the building itself is of little interest, occupied these days by offices. It's better to continue on toward the southern end of Kloveniersburgwal, to where the **Oudemanhuispoort** passage leads through to O. Z. Achterburgwal. This was once part of an almshouse for elderly men, but is now filled with second-hand bookstalls and a group of buildings serving Amsterdam University. On O. Z. Achterburgwal you look across to the pretty **Huis op de Drie Grachten**, "House on the Three Canals", on the corner of Grimburgwal, which runs alongside more university buildings. A little way down O. Z. Voorburgwal on the right, through an ornate gateway, is the **Agnietenkapel** (Mon–Fri 9am–5pm; ƒ2.50), also owned by the university and containing exhibitions on academic life through the ages.

At the corner a passage cuts through to **Nes**, a long, narrow street, once home to the philosopher Spinoza; or you can make your way back up Oude Zijds past the **Galerie Mokum**, named after the old Jewish nickname for the city, now in general use. From here it's just a few yards to Rokin and, beyond, Kalverstraat. Alternatively, sink into one of the terrace seats of *'t Gasthuys* café, a popular student haunt and excellent for either a quick drink or a full lunch.

Dam Square to Muntplein

Dam Square gave the city its name: in the thirteenth century the River Amstel was dammed here, and the small fishing village that grew around it became known as "Amstelredam". Boats could sail right into the square and unload their imported grain in the middle of the rapidly growing town, and the later building of Amsterdam's principal church, the Nieuwe Kerk, along with the Royal Palace, formally marked Dam Square as Amsterdam's centre.

Though robbed a little of its dignity by the trams that scuttle across it, the square is still the hub of the city. At its centre there's a **War Memorial**, an unsightly stone tusk filled with soil from each of The Netherlands' provinces and Indonesia. It serves as a gathering place for the square's milling tourists who seem to be wondering if, among the musicians and drug pushers, they've really found the heart of liberated Amsterdam.

Across the square, the **Royal Palace** (daily 12.30–5pm; ƒ5, no museumcards) seems neither Dutch nor palatial – understandably so since it was originally built from imported stone as the city's town hall. At the time of its construction in the mid-seventeenth century, it was the largest town hall in Europe, supported by 13,659 wooden piles driven into the Dam's sandy soil. Inside, the **Citizen's Hall** proclaims the pride and confidence of the Golden Age, with the enthroned personification of Amsterdam looking down at the world and heaven at her feet, the whole sumptuously inlaid in brass and marble. A good-natured and witty symbolism pervades the building: cocks fight above the entrance to the **Court of Petty Affairs**, while Apollo, god of the sun and the arts, brings harmony to the disputes. On a more sober note, death sentences were pronounced at the **High**

Court of Justice at the front of the building and the condemned immediately executed on a scaffold outside.

The building received its royal associations in 1808 when Napoleon's brother Louis commandeered it as the one building fit for an installed king. Lonely and isolated, Louis briefly ruled from here, until forced to acquiesce to Napoleon's autocratic demands. Upon his abdication in 1810 he left behind a sizeable amount of Empire furniture, most of which is exhibited in the rooms he converted.

Vying for importance with the palace is the **Nieuwe Kerk** (March–Dec daily 11am–5pm; *f*6) – despite its name, a fifteenth-century structure rebuilt several times after fires. Though impressive from the outside, the Nieuwe Kerk has long since lost out in rivalries with the Oude Kerk and the Royal Palace (it was forbidden a tower in case it outshone the new town hall), and is now used only for exhibitions, organ concerts and state occasions; Queen Beatrix was crowned here in 1980. The interior is neat and orderly, its sheer Gothic lines only slightly weighed down by seventeenth-century fixtures such as the massive pulpit and organ case. Of the catalogue of household names from Dutch history, Admiral de Ruyter, seventeenth-century Holland's most valiant naval hero, lies in an opulent tomb in the choir, and the poet Vondel, a sort of Dutch Shakespeare, is commemorated by a small urn near the entrance.

Heading south from Dam Square, Damrak Street turns into the broad sweep of Rokin, which follows the old course of the River Amstel. Lined with grandiose nineteenth-century mansions – Amsterdam's Sotheby's is here, and, further down, the elaborate *fin de siècle* interior of the *Maison de la Bonneterie* clothes store – Rokin gives trams running to and from Dam Square their single chance to accelerate in the city; cross with care.

Running parallel with Rokin, **Kalverstraat** has been a commercial centre since it hosted a cattle market in medieval times; now it has declined into a standard European shopping mall, an uninspired strip of monotonous clothes stores differentiated only by the varying strains of disco music they pump out. About halfway down the street, a lopsided and frivolous gateway forms an unexpected entrance to the former municipal orphanage that's now the **Amsterdam Historical Museum** (see p.78). The main way in is by the eye-catching Civil Guard Gallery, just around the corner off Sint Luciensteeg, which leads on to Gedempte Begijnensloot and the **Begijnhof** (see over the page).

Kalverstraat comes to an ignoble end in a stretch of ice-cream parlours and fast-food outlets before reaching **Muntplein**. Originally a mint and part of the old city walls, the **Munttoren** was topped with a spire by Hendrik de Keyser in 1620 and is possibly the most famous of the towers dotting the city, a landmark perfectly designed for postcards when framed by the flowers of the nearby floating Bloemenmarkt (flower market). From here, Reguliersbreestraat turns left toward the gay bars and loud restaurants of Rembrandtsplein, while Vijzelstraat heads straight out to the edge of the Amsterdam crescent.

Nieuwe Zijds Voorburgwal to Spui

Nieuwe Zijds begins with a bottleneck of trams swinging down from the Centraal Station, and one of the first buildings you see is the **Holiday Inn**, built on the site of an old tenement building called Wyers. The 1985 clearance of squatters from Wyers ranks among the most infamous of the decade's anti-squatting campaigns, having involved much protest and some violence throughout the city. The squatters had occupied the building in an attempt to prevent another slice of the city from being handed over to a profit-hungry multinational and converted from residential use. Although widely supported by the people of Amsterdam, they were no match for the economic muscle of the American company, and it wasn't long before the riot police were sent in; construction of the hotel soon followed.

The fate of the **Luthersekerk**, directly west from here on Kattengat, hasn't been much better. Its copper-green dome – which burned down in 1993 and will be undergoing reconstruction until 1994 – gave this area the label of *Koepelkwartier* or Dome Neighbourhood. It's former importance, however, did not prevent it being deconsecrated and turned into a conference centre for the luxury Sonesta Hotel nearby. To the east, **Spuistraat** begins at a fork in N. Z. Voorburgwal, with a small red light area edging around the St Dominicus Kerk. These are the red lights the tourists miss, and the business here has the seamy feel of the real thing.

Things only improve as you move south and approach the Nieuwe Kerk: there's a medieval eccentricity to the streets here, and all seediness vanishes as designer boutiques appear in the old workshops clustered around the church. Walk down the wonderfully named Zwarte Handsteeg (Black Hand Alley) and you're back on Nieuwe Zijds. Just across the road, the former **Post Office** building, now a slick shopping centre, manages to hold its own against the Nieuwe Kerk and Royal Palace. Built in 1899, its whimsical embellishments continue the town's tradition of sticking towers on things – here, as everywhere, purely for the hell of it.

Both Spuistraat and Nieuwe Zijds culminate in **Spui**, a chic corner of town with a mixture of bookstores and packed bars centred around a small, rather cloying statue of a young boy – known as **'t Lieverdje** (Little Darling) – which was a gift to the city from a large cigarette company. Twenty years ago this was the scene of a series of demonstrations organized by the Provos, an anarchist group that grew out of the original squatters' movement. With the alternative culture then at its most militant, the Provos labelled 't Lieverdje a monument to tomorrow's addiction to capitalism and turned up in force every Saturday evening to preach to the Spui's assembled drinkers. When the police arrived to break up these small "happenings", they did little to endear themselves to the public – and much to gain sympathy for the Provos.

Spui's main attraction, though, is neither obvious nor marked. Perhaps those who run the **Begijnhof** want it this way: enclosed on three sides, this small court of buildings is an enclave of tranquillity at once typically Dutch and totally removed from the surrounding streets. Most of the houses are seventeenth century, but one, no. 34, dates from 1475 – the oldest house in Amsterdam, and one built before the city forbade the construction of houses in wood, an essential precaution against fire. *Hofjes* (little courtyards) are found all over the Low Countries. Built by rich individuals or city councils for the poor and elderly, the houses usually face inward around a small court, their backs to the outside world. This sense of retreat suited the women who, without taking formal vows, led a religious life in the *hofjes*, which often had their own chapel. Here the order was known as *Begijnen* (Beguines), and such was its standing in the city community that it was allowed to quietly continue its tradition of worship, even after Catholicism was suppressed in 1587. Mass was inconspicuously celebrated in the concealed **Catholic Church**: the plain and unadorned **English Reformed Church** which takes up one side of the Begijnhof, was handed over to Amsterdam's English community when the Begijns were deprived of their main place of worship, and, like the *hofje* itself, it's a model of prim simplicity. Inside are several old English memorial plaques and pulpit panels designed by the young Piet Mondrian.

The main grachten: from Raadhuisstraat to the Amstel

It's hard to pick out any particular points to head for along the **three main canals**. Most of the houses have been turned into offices or hotels, and there's little of specific interest apart from museums. Rather, the appeal lies in wandering along selected stretches and admiring the gables while taking in the calm of the tree-lined canals, unusual in the centre of a modern European capital. For shops, bars, restaurants and the like, explore the streets connecting the canals.

In the city's expansion in the seventeenth century, the three main waterways, Herengracht, Keizersgracht and Prinsengracht, were set aside for the residences and offices of the richer and more influential Amsterdam merchants, while the radial canals were left for more modest artisans' homes. Even the richest burgher had to conform to a set of stylistic rules when building his house, and taxes were levied according to the width of the properties. This produced the loose conformity you see today: tall, narrow residences, with individualism restricted to heavy decorative gables and sometimes a gablestone to denote name and occupation.

West to Vijzelstraat

Of the three canals, **Herengracht** (Gentlemen's Canal) was the first to be dug, and so attracted the wealthiest merchants and the biggest, most ostentatious houses. The others, **Keizersgracht** (Emperor's Canal) and especially **Prinsengracht** (Prince's Canal), ended up with noticeably smaller houses – though both still hold some of the most sought-after properties in the city. Today, Herengracht remains the city's grandest stretch of water, especially between Leidsestraat and Vijzelstraat, but you may find the older and less pretentious houses and warehouses of Prinsengracht more appealing.

One of the most imposing facades along **Herengracht** is the **Bijbels Museum**, at Herengracht 366 (Tues–Sat 10am–5pm, Sun 1–5pm; *f*3), which occupies a four-gabled, seventeenth-century stone house frilled with tendrils, carved fruit and scrollwork. Further along, **no. 380** is even more ornate, an exact copy of a Loire chateau – stone again, with a main gable embellished with reclining figures and a bay window stuck with cherubs, mythical characters and an abundance of acanthus leaves.

The one mansion you'll notice in your wanderings along **Keizersgracht** is the **Felix Meritis Building** at Keizersgracht 324, a heavy neo-Classical monolith built in the late eighteenth century to house the artistic and scientific activities of the society of the same name. It used to be the headquarters of the Dutch Communist Party; they sold it to the council which now leases it to the *Felix Meritis Foundation*, a centre for experimental and avant garde arts.

On the corner of Keizersgracht and Leidsestraat, the designer department store, *Metz & Co.*, with its corner dome by Gerrit Rietveld, has a top-floor restaurant and tearoom with one of the best views of the city. The **Museum of Torture** at Leidsestraat 27 (daily 10am–7pm; *f*7.50) strikes a very diferent note, with its comprehensive collection of medieval – and more recent – instruments of horror. **Leidsestraat** itself is a long, slender passage across the main canals chiefly given over to airline offices and tourist boards, and to the trams that crash along the narrow thoroughfare, dangerously scattering passers-by. At its southern end the street broadens into **Leidseplein**, hub of Amsterdam's nightlife but by day a none-too-attractive open space littered with sandwich boards advertising the surrounding American burger joints. There's probably a greater concentration of bars, restaurants and clubs here than anywhere else in the city, and the streets extend off the square in a bright jumble of jutting signs and neon lights; around the corner, in a converted dairy, lurks the famous *Melkweg* (p.86). As for the square itself, on summer nights especially it can ignite with an almost carnival-like vibrancy, drinkers spilling out of cafés to see sword-swallowers and fire-eaters do their tricks, while the restaurants join in enthusiastically, placing their tables outside so you can eat without missing the fun. On a good night Leidseplein is Amsterdam at its carefree, exuberant best.

On the far corner, the **Stadsschouwburg** is the city's prime performance space after the muziektheater, while behind, and architecturally much more impressive, is the fairy-castle **American Hotel**. Even if you're not thirsty it's worth a peek inside, the leaded stained glass, shallow brick arches, chandeliers and carefully coordinated furnishings as fine an example of the complete stylistic vision of Art Nouveau as you'll find.

Walking east from here, **Weteringschans** and, running parallel, **Lijnbaansgracht** ring the modern city centre. On the right the **Rijksmuseum** (p.73) looms large across the canal; left, Spiegelgracht and, further on, Nieuwe Spiegelstraat lead into the **Spiegelkwartier**, the focus of the Amsterdam antique trade. It's a small area, but there are around fifty dealers here – none, as you might expect, particularly inexpensive.

Kerkstraat, a narrow street featuring an odd mixture of gay bookshops and art galleries, leads east from here to connect with **Vijzelstraat** at the **ABN Bank Building**, through which the street actually runs. Looking toward Muntplein, the oversized **Nederlandsche Handelsmaatschapij Building** (now also owned by *ABN*) is another bank building totally unsympathetic with its surroundings. Though a much worthier work architecturally than the later ABN bank, it would look more at home in downtown Manhattan than on the banks of a Dutch canal. In the other direction, Vijzelstraat becomes the filled-in **Vijzelgracht**, which culminates in a roundabout at **Weteringplantsoen** and, on its southern side, one of Amsterdam's saddest spots. It was here, on April 3, 1945, that twenty people were shot by the Nazis – an example, in the last few weeks of their power, to anyone who might consider opposing them. An excerpt from a poem by H.M. van Randwijk on the wall recalls the incident with carefully levelled restraint:

> *When to the will of tyrants,*
> *A nation's head is bowed,*
> *It loses more than life and goods—*
> *Its very light goes out.*

In a wholly different vein, the **Heineken Brewery** opposite runs tours from Monday to Friday at 9.30am, 11am, 1pm, 2.30pm and, in summer, at 4.30pm. At two guilders a head these are a must: just be sure to arrive early, since tickets for tours go on sale at 9.30am and are normally gone by 9.45am. Though the brewery recently stopped production and has been turned into a museum, it's still interesting to explore the old plant. Afterward, you are given snacks and free beer, and the atmosphere is convivial – as you'd imagine when there are two hundred people downing as much free beer as they can drink. Whether you have just one, or drink yourself into a stupor, it's a diverting way to get a lunchtime aperitif.

Rembrandtsplein and around

Toward the Amstel, the area cornered by Herengracht's eastern reaches is dominated by **Rembrandtsplein**, a dishevelled bit of greenery fringed with cafés and their terraces. This claims to be a centre of city nightlife, though the square's crowded restaurants are today firmly tourist-targeted; you should expect to pay inflated prices. Rembrandt's pigeon-spattered statue stands in the middle, his back wisely turned against the square's worst excesses, which include live (but deadly) outdoor music. Of the cafés, only the bar of the **Schiller Hotel** at no.26 stands out, with an original Art Deco interior reminiscent of a great ocean liner.

The streets leading north from Rembrandtsplein to the River Amstel are more exciting, containing many of the city's mainstream **gay bars** – accessible to all, and less costly than their upstart neighbours. **Amstelstraat** is the main thoroughfare east, crossing the river at the **Blauwbrug** (Blue Bridge) and affording views across of the new and unimaginative **muziektheater** and **Town Hall** complex. Heading west, **Reguliersbreestraat** links Rembrandtsplein to Muntplein and, among slot-machine arcades and sex shops, houses the **Tuschinski**, the city's most famous cinema, with an interior that's a wonderful example of the Art Deco excesses of the 1920s. Expressionist paintings, coloured marbles and Persian carpets add to a general air of all-pervasive decadence. You can obviously see all this if you're here to watch a film (the Tuschinski shows all the most popular general releases); if you're not, guided tours are laid on during July and August on Sunday and Monday mornings at 10.30am (ƒ5 per person).

To the south of Rembrandtsplein, **Thorbeckeplein** scores points for having a thinner concentration of clog and card shops but is hardly a fitting memorial for Rudolf Thorbecke, a politician whose liberal reforms of the late nineteenth century furthered the city tradition of open-minded tolerance, and whose statue stands a short way from the topless bars and sex shows. **Reguliersgracht** flows south from here, a broad canal of distinctive steep bridges that was to have been filled in at the beginning of the century, but was saved when public outcry rose against the destruction of one of the city's more alluring stretches of water. The three great *grachten* nearby don't contain houses quite as grand as those to the west, but a handful of buildings can be visited: the **Van Loon House** at Keizersgracht 672 and the **Willet-Holthuysen House** at Herengracht 605 are both worthwhile examples of the seventeenth-century patrician canal house, and, best of all, the **Six Collection** at Amstel 218 contains an easily absorbed group of paintings in a remarkably unspoiled mansion – though the current Baron Six, who lives there, discourages visitors. For details, see p.79.

As the canals approach the Amstel, their houses become increasingly residential: even **Kerkstraat** is tamed of its bars and clubs, turning east of Reguliersgracht into a pleasant if unremarkable neighbourhood that lies beside the **Amstelveld**, a small square-cum-football pitch that few visitors happen upon. The **Amstelkerk**, a seventeenth-century, graffiti-covered wooden church with a nineteenth-century Gothic interior, marks the corner, and a Monday **flower market** here adds a splash of colour. **Utrechtsestraat**, the other artery that flows to and from Rembrandtsplein, is probably Amsterdam's most up-and-coming strip and contains most of the area's commercial activity, much of it in the shape of mid- to upper-bracket restaurants. It ends in the concrete wasteland of **Frederiksplein** – more a glorified tram stop than a square, presided over by the massive glass box of the **Netherlands Bank**. Leading off Frederiksplein, Sarphatistraat crosses the wide and windy reaches of the **River Amstel**, whose eastern side is stacked with chunky buildings such as the **Carré Theatre**, built as a circus in the early 1900s, but now more often a space for music and drama. Just beyond, the **Magere Brug** (Skinny Bridge) is (inexplicably) the focus of much attention in the tourist brochures, and hence the most famous of the city's swinging bridges. More worthy of a serious look is the **Amstel Hof**, a large and forbidding former *hofje* that was one of a number of charitable institutions built east of the Amstel after a seventeenth-century decision to extend the major canals eastward toward the new harbour and shipbuilding quarter. Takers for the new land were few, and the city had no option but to offer it to charities at bargain prices.

West from the Dam

Unlike the Jodenhoek, the area west of Amsterdam's immediate centre is one of the city's most untouched neighbourhoods – and one of its loveliest. The Prinsengracht here has a gentle beauty quite unlike its grander rivals, and holds the Anne Frank House as a specific draw; and the Jordaan, just beyond, with its narrow waterways spotted with tiny shops and bars, is as good (and as pretty) a place for idle strolling as you'll find.

The Westerkerk and the Anne Frank House

From behind the Royal Palace, **Raadhuisstraat** leads west across Herengracht and curves around the elegant, nineteenth-century Art Nouveau **Utrecht Building** toward **Westermarkt**. Here, at Westermarkt 6, the seventeenth-century French philosopher René Descartes lived for a short time, happy that the business-oriented character of the city left him able to work and think without being disturbed. As he wrote at the time, "Everybody except me is in business and so absorbed by profit-making I could spend my entire life here without being noticed by a soul".

It's the **Westerkerk** (April–Sept Tues–Sat 10am–4pm; tower *f*3.50), though, which dominates the square, its tower – without question Amsterdam's finest – soaring graciously above the gables of Prinsengracht. The church was designed by Hendrik de Keyser (architect also of the Zuiderkerk and Noorderkerk) as part of the general seventeenth-century enlargement of the city, and was completed in 1631. But while this is probably Amsterdam's most visually appealing church from the outside, there's little within of special note. Rembrandt, who was living nearby when he died, is commemorated by a small memorial in the north aisle. His pauper's grave can no longer be located; indeed, there's a possibility that he's not here at all, since many of the bodies were moved to a cemetery when underground heating was installed. The memorial is, however, close to where Rembrandt's son Titus is buried. During recent excavations, bones have been unearthed which could be those of Titus and even Rembrandt – something which has made the church authorities very excited about the resultant tourist possibilities.

Directly outside the church stands a small, simple statue of **Anne Frank** by the Dutch sculptor Mari Andriessen – a careful and evocative site, since it was just a few steps from here, at Prinsengracht 263, that the young diarist used to listen to the Westertoren bells until they were taken away to be melted down for the Nazi war effort. The story of Anne Frank, her family and friends is well known. Anne's father, Otto, was a well-to-do Jewish businessman who ran a successful spice-trading business and lived in the southern part of the city. The Franks went into hiding in July 1942, along with a Jewish business partner and his family, separated from the eyes of the outside world by a bookcase that doubled as a secret door. As far as everyone else was concerned, they had fled to Switzerland.

One day in the summer of 1944 the Franks were betrayed by a Dutch collaborator: the Gestapo arrived and forced open the bookcase, whereupon the occupants of the annexe were all arrested and quickly sent to Westerbork – the northern Netherlands German labour camp where all Dutch Jews were processed before being moved to Belsen or Auschwitz. Of the eight who had been in the annexe, only Otto Frank survived; Anne and her sister died of typhus within a short time of each other in Belsen, just one week before the German surrender.

Anne Frank's diary was among the few things left behind in the annexe. It was retrieved by one of the people who had helped the Franks and handed to Anne's father on his return from Auschwitz; he later decided to publish it. Since its appearance in 1947, it has been constantly in print, translated into 54 languages, and has sold thirteen million copies worldwide. In 1957 the *Anne Frank Foundation* set up the **Anne Frank House** (Mon–Sat 9am–5pm; Sun 10am–5pm; closed Yom Kippur; ƒ7, no museumcards; ☎626 45 33), one of the most deservedly popular tourist attractions in town; bearing this in mind, the best time to visit is early morning before the crowds arrive.

The rooms the Franks lived in for two years are left much the same as they were during the war, even down to the movie star pin-ups in Anne's bedroom and the marks on the wall recording the children's heights. A number of other rooms offer background detail on the war and occupation, one offering a video biography of Anne, from her frustrated hopes in hiding in the annexe up to her death in 1945, another detailing the gruesome atrocities of Nazism, as well as giving some up-to-date examples of fascism and anti-semitism in Europe which draw pertinent parallels with the war years. Anne Frank was only one of one hundred thousand Dutch Jews who died during that time, but this, her final home, provides one of the most enduring testaments to the horrors of Nazism.

The Jordaan and around

Across the Prinsengracht, between Brouwersgracht in the north and Leidsegracht in the south, **THE JORDAAN** is a likeable and easily explored area of narrow canals, narrower streets and simple, architecturally varied houses. The name is said to come from the French *jardin*, and many of the streets are named after flowers. Falling outside the seventeenth-century concentric-canal plan, the area was not subject to municipal controls, which led to its becoming a centre of property speculation, developing as a series of canals and streets that followed the original polder ditches and rough paths. In contrast to the splendour of the three main *grachten*, the Jordaan became Amsterdam's slum quarter, home of artisans, tradespeople and Jewish or Huguenot refugees who had fled here to escape religious persecution at home. Though tolerated, the immigrants remained distinct minorities and were treated as such, living in what were often cramped and unsanitary quarters. Later, after much rebuilding, the Jordaan became the inner-city enclave of Amsterdam's growing industrial working class – which, in spite of increasing gentrification, it to some extent remains. The last couple of decades have seen the Jordaan gain a reputation as the home of young "alternative" Amsterdam, but there's a core population of residents who retain long-standing roots in the district.

Other than a handful of bars and restaurants, some chic clothes shops and the odd outdoor market, there's nothing very specific to see (though it's a wonderful neighbourhood for a wander) apart from its **hofjes** – seventeenth-century alms-houses for the city's elderly population. There were – and are – *hofjes* all over the city (most famously the Begijnhof, p.60), but there's a concentration in the Jordaan, and if you're passing through, it is worth looking in on a courtyard or two; many of them have real charm. Bear in mind, though, that most are still lived in, and be discreet.

Of those that warrant a specific visit, the **Van Brienen Hofje**, opposite the Noordermarkt at Prinsengracht 89–133, is the grandest, built in 1804, according to the entrance tablet, "for the relief and shelter of those in need". A little way down the canal at Prinsengracht 157–171, **Zon's Hofje** has a leafier, more gentle beauty; and, back in the main grid of the Jordaan, the **Claes Claesz Hofje** on 1e Egelantierdwarsstraat, a much earlier almshouse (built in 1616 for poor widows), is now noisily occupied by students of the Amsterdam Conservatory of Music. For more on *hofjes* – and an account of one of the country's most famous, the Frans Hals Museum in Haarlem – see p.100.

More general wanderings start on **Rozengracht**, the filled-in canal where, at no. 184, Rembrandt once lived – though the house itself has long since disappeared and these days only a plaque marks the spot. Though not the Jordaan proper, the area south of this street is a likeable one, centring on the pretty Lauriergracht and including, at Elandsgracht 109, the **De Looier indoor antique market** – where a leisurely browse may unearth a bargain. North of Rozengracht the Jordaan's streets and canals run off diagonally, bordering Prinsengracht. The main street of the district is **Westerstraat** (where there's a Monday general market), which runs down to join Prinsengracht at **Noordermarkt** and Hendrik de Keyser's **Noorderkerk**. This church, finished in 1623, is probably the architect's least successful creation in Amsterdam; nor is the square particularly attractive, part car park, part children's playground. It's the site of a Monday antiques market and the regular Saturday *Boerenmarkt* (farmers' market) during summer months. The next street over, **Lindengracht**, is home to another Saturday market, this time general. If you're interested in shopping, also check out **Tweede Anjelierdwarsstraat** and **Tweede Tuindwarsstraat** – two streets which hold the bulk of the Jordaan's ever-increasing trendy stores and clothing shops, and some of its liveliest bars and cafés for restorative sipping.

Brouwersgracht, just beyond, is one of Amsterdam's most picturesque and most photographed canals, marking what is in effect the northern boundary of the Jordaan and the beginning of a district loosely known as the **SHIPPING QUARTER**, which centres on the long arteries of **Haarlemmerstraat** and **Haarlemmerdijk**. In the seventeenth century this district was at the cutting edge of Amsterdam's trade: the warehouses along Brouwersgracht provided storage space for the spoils brought back from the high seas, and the building on Haarlemmerstraat at Herenmarkt, the **West Indies House**, was home of the Dutch West Indies Company, which administered much of the business. Today it's a good area for cheap restaurants and off-beat shops: the warehouses have been largely taken over and converted into spacious apartments, and the West Indies Company Building has a courtyard containing an overstated statue of Peter Stuyvesant, governor of New Amsterdam (later named New York), and a swanky restaurant named after the seventeenth-century Dutch naval hero Piet Heijn.

At the far end of Haarlemmerdijk, the **Haarlemmerpoort** is an oversized and very un-Amsterdamlike former gateway to the city. Beyond this you can either walk on to the **Westerpark**, one of the city's smaller and more enticing parks, or duck under the train tracks to the **WESTERN ISLANDS** district, where ships were once unloaded and where there are more rows of gaunt warehouses – an atmospheric area, still largely deserted. Across the Westerkanaal on Zaanstraat and Spaarndammerplantsoen, the **Eigen Haard** housing project is probably the most central example you'll see of the Amsterdam school of architecture that flourished in the early part of this century. Designed by Michael de Klerk, the project attempted to alleviate the previously appalling housing conditions of the city's poor, with rounded corners, turrets and bulging windows and balconies lending individuality to what would otherwise be very plain brick residences.

The Jodenhoek and Eastern Islands

Though there's hardly any visible evidence today, from the sixteenth century onward Amsterdam was the home of Jews escaping persecution throughout Europe. Under the terms of the Union of Utrecht, Jews enjoyed a tolerance and freedom unknown elsewhere, and they arrived in the city to practise the trades of diamond processing, sugar refining and tobacco production – effectively the only ones open to them since the city's guilds excluded Jews from following any of the traditional crafts. This largely impoverished Jewish community lived in one of the least desirable stretches of the city, the old dock areas around Jodenbreestraat, which became known as the **JODENHOEK**. The docks moved east to Kattenburg, Wittenburg and Oostenburg – the **EASTERN ISLANDS**. By the early years of this century Jewish life was commercially and culturally an integral part of the city, the growing demand for diamonds making Jewish expertise invaluable and bringing wealth to the community for the first time.

In the 1930s the community's numbers swelled with Jews who had fled persecution in Germany. In May 1940, however, the Nazis invaded, sealing off the Jodenhoek as a ghetto. Jews were not allowed to use public transport or own a telephone, and were placed under a curfew. Round-ups and deportations continued until the last days of the war: out of a total of eighty thousand Jews in the city, seventy-five thousand were murdered in concentration camps.

After the war the Jodenhoek lay deserted: those who had lived here were dead or deported, and their few possessions were quickly looted. As the need for wood and raw materials grew in postwar shortages, the houses were slowly dismantled and destroyed, a destruction finalized in the 1970s with the completion of the metro that links the city centre to the outer suburbs. Today few people refer to the Jodenhoek by that name, and many Amsterdammers are unaware of its history.

Jodenbreestraat to Plantage Middenlaan

Nieuwmarkt signals the beginning of what was the Jodenhoek, and **St Antoniesbreestraat** leads to its heart, an uncomfortably modernized street whose original old houses were demolished to widen the road for the heavy traffic that the Nieuwmarkt redevelopment would bring. The decorative landmark of Hendrik de Keyser's **Zuiderkerk** (Mon–Wed & Fri noon–5pm, Thurs noon–8pm) is similarly surrounded by new development: undergoing a major reconstruction, its tower is irregularly open in summer months, and it is the best place for an overview of this part of town.

St Antoniesbreestraat runs into **Jodenbreestraat**, once the Jodenhoek's principal market and centre of Jewish activity. After the shipbuilding industry moved
further east, this area (the small islands of Uilenburg and Marken) became the
site of the worst living conditions in the city: it wasn't until 1911 that the area was
declared a health hazard and redeveloped. Jodenbreestraat itself was modernized
and widened in the 1970s and lost much of its character as a result; only when
you reach the **Rembrandt House** at no. 6 (Mon–Sat 10am–5pm, Sun 1–5pm; ƒ5)
do you find any continuity with the past. Rembrandt bought the house at the
height of his fame and popularity, living here for over twenty years and spending
a fortune on furnishings – an expense that contributed to his bankruptcy. The
house itself is disappointing – mostly a reconstruction and with no artefacts from
Rembrandt's life on exhibit – but you can view a great variety of the artist's
engravings here. The biblical illustrations attract the most attention, though the
studies of tramps and vagabonds are more accessible; a good accompanying
exhibit explains Rembrandt's engraving techniques.

Jodenbreestraat runs parallel to its sibling development, the new
Muziektheater and Town Hall on **Waterlooplein**, whose building occasioned
the biggest public dispute the city had seen since the Nieuwmarkt was dug up in
the 1970s to make way for the metro. The Waterlooplein, a marshy, insanitary
area that rapidly became known as the poorest patch of the city, was the first
neighbourhood settled by the Jews. By the late nineteenth century, things had
become so bad that the canals crossing the area were filled in and the shanty
houses razed; the street markets then shifted here from St Antoniesbreestraat
and Jodenbreestraat. The Waterlooplein quickly became Amsterdam's largest
and liveliest market and a link between the Jewish community and the predominantly Gentile one across the Amstel. During the war it became infamous again,
this time as a site for Nazi round-ups; in the 1950s it regained some of its vibrancy
when the city's flea market was established here. Later, when the council
announced the building of a massive new opera complex that would all but fill the
square, opposition was widespread. People believed that it should be turned into
a residential area at best, a popular performance space at least – anything but an
elitist opera house. Attempts to prevent the building failed, but since opening in
1986 the muziektheater has successfully established itself with visitors and
performers alike, and the **flea market** has come back after being moved for a few
years to nearby Valkenburgstraat. If you'd like to explore backstage and get an
idea of the workings of the Muziektheater, guided tours run throughout the year,
except in July (Wed & Sat 4pm; ƒ8.50).

Just behind the Muziektheater, on the corner of Mr Visserplein, is the **Mozes
en Aaron Kerk**, originally a small (clandestine) Catholic church that was rebuilt
in rather glum neo-Classical style in the mid-nineteenth century. The area around
Mr Visserplein, today a busy and dangerous junction for traffic speeding toward
the IJ tunnel, has the most tangible mementoes of the Jewish community. The
brown and bulky **Portuguese Synagogue** (daily except Sat 10am–12.15pm &
1.30–4pm; free) was completed in 1675 by Sephardic Jews who had moved to
Amsterdam from Spain and Portugal to escape the Inquisition, and who prospered here in the seventeenth and eighteenth centuries. When it was completed
the Portuguese Synagogue was the largest in the world: today the Sephardic
community has dwindled to thirty or forty members.

Across the way from the Portuguese Synagogue the **Jewish Historical
Museum** is cleverly housed in a complex of High German synagogues that date

from the late seventeenth century. For many years after the war the buildings lay in ruins, and it's only recently that the museum has moved in. In addition to photos and mementoes from the holocaust, the museum gives a broad introduction to Jewish beliefs and life. For hours and a full description, see p.78.

Between the museum and the Portuguese Synagogue is **J. D. Meijerplein**, where a small statue marks the spot on which, in February 1941, four hundred young Jewish men were arrested and taken to eventual execution at Mauthausen, in reprisal for the killing of a Nazi sympathizer in a street fight between members of the Jewish resistance and the Dutch Nazi party. The arrests sparked off the "February Strike", a general strike led by transport workers and dockers and organized by the outlawed Communist party in protest against the deportations and treatment of the Jews. Although broken by mass arrests after only two days, it was a demonstration of solidarity with the Jews that was unique in occupied Europe and unusual in The Netherlands, where the majority of people had done little to prevent or protest against the actions of the occupying German army.

Leaving Mr Visserplein via Muiderstraat, with the prim **Hortus Botanicus** (botanical gardens) to the right (see p.78), you come to yet another sad relic of the war at Plantage Middenlaan 24. The **Hollandse Schouwburg**, a predominantly Jewish theatre beforc 1940, was the main assembly point for Dutch Jews prior to their deportation to the concentration camps. Inside, there was no daylight and families were jammed together for days in conditions that foreshadowed the camps. The house across the street, now a college for training teachers, was used as a day nursery. Some, possibly hundreds, managed to escape through here, and an exhibition inside extols the memory of those "who saved the children".

Prins Hendrikkade and the Eastern Islands

The broad boulevard that fronts the grey waters of the Oosterdok is **Prins Hendrikkade**, a continuation of the road that leads to Stationsplein in the west and goes on deep into the docks of eastern Amsterdam. In the seventeenth century merchant vessels packed the harbour, carrying the goods that created the city's enormous wealth: today Prins Hendrikkade is a major artery for cars flowing north via the IJ tunnel, and the only ships docked here belong to the police or navy. But the road is lined with buildings that point to its nautical past. The first of these, the squat **Schreierstoren**, was traditionally the place where, in the Middle Ages, tearful women saw their husbands off to sea (the name could be translated as "weepers' tower") – though this is probably more romantic invention than fact. A sixteenth-century inlaid stone records the emotional leave-takings, while another, much more recent tablet recalls the departure of Henry Hudson from here in 1609 – the voyage on which he inadvertently discovered Manhattan. A little further along, the **Scheepvaarthuis** at Prins Hendrikkade 108 is covered inside and out with bas reliefs and other decoration relating the city's maritime history; it's also embellished with slender turrets and expressionistic masonry characteristic of the Amsterdam school of architecture.

Further along still, the wide **Oude Schans** was the main entrance to the old shipbuilding quarter, and the **Montelbaanstoren** tower that stands about halfway down was built in 1512 to protect the merchant fleet. A century later, when the city felt more secure and could afford such luxuries, it was topped with a decorative spire by Hendrik de Keyser, the architect who did much to create Amsterdam's spiky skyline.

The chief pillar of the wealth of the city in the sixteenth century was the **Dutch East India Company**. Its expeditions established links with India, Sri Lanka and the Indonesian islands, and later China and Japan, using the Dutch Republic's large fleet of vessels to rob the Portuguese and Spanish of their trade and the undefended islanders of their wood and spices. Dutch expansionism wasn't purely mercantile: not only had the East India Company been given a trading monopoly in all lands east of the Cape of Good Hope but also unlimited military, judicial and political powers in the countries it administered. Behind the satisfied smiles of the comfortable burghers of the Golden Age was a nightmare of slavery and exploitation.

The twin warehouses from where the East India Company originally started its operations still stand at Prins Hendrikkade 176, but a more accurate picture of the might of the Dutch navy can be found in the **Maritime Museum** on Kattenburgerplein, housed in a fortress-like former arsenal of the seventeenth century (p.79).

As the wealth from the colonies poured in, the old dock area to the southeast around Uilenburg was no longer able to cope, and the East India Company financed a major reclamation of, and expansion into, the marshland to the east of the existing waterfront, forming the three islands of **Kattenburg, Wittenburg** and **Oostenburg**. A shipbuilding industry developed, and in time the Eastern Islands became the home of a large community working in the shipfitting and dockyard industries. The nineteenth century brought the construction of iron ships, and at a wharf at Hoogte Kadijk 147 an old shipyard is now the **Kromhout Museum** (p.78). The museum still patches up ancient boats and offers a slide show that's a useful introduction to the area's history.

In time, the shipyards of the Eastern Islands declined, the working-class neighbourhood shrank and today there's not much evidence of a once-lively community. The **Oosterkerk**, across the water from the Kromhout, now functions as a social and exhibition centre, part of an attempt to restore to this area some of its former identity. South of the Kromhout, it's worth wandering through to the **Entrepot Dok**, a line of old warehouses, each bearing the name of a destination above its door. Recreated as hi-tech offices and apartments, and with weird gurglings coming from the **Artis Zoo** across the way, it seems an odd sort of end for the Eastern Islands' rich maritime tradition.

Keep going down Oostenburgergracht and you'll reach "**De Gooyer**", a windmill that dates from 1814. Once mills were all over Amsterdam, pumping water and grinding grain; today only this old mill remains, now converted into a brewery called 't IJ, though its sails still turn on the first Saturday of the month – wind permitting.

The Outer Limits: South, West and East

Amsterdam is a small city and its residential outer neighbourhoods can be easily reached from the city centre. Of them, the **South** holds most interest, with all the major museums, the Vondelpark (a must on summer Sundays), the raucous "De Pijp" quarter and the 1930s architecture of the New South more than justifying the tram ride. As for the other districts, you'll find a good deal less reason for making the effort. The **West** offers nothing special, aside from the occasional odd park and one lively immigrant quarter; nor does the **East**, although this does have one conceivable target in the Tropical Museum.

The Old South

During the nineteenth century, unable to hold its mushrooming population within the limits of its canals, Amsterdam began to expand, spreading into the neighbourhoods beyond the Singelgracht which now make up the district known as the OLD SOUTH. This large and disparate area includes the leafy residential quarters immediately south of Leidseplein as well as the working-class enclaves further east. The Vondelpark lies at the centre of the former, today the city's most enticing park. Named after the seventeenth-century poet Joost van der Vondel, and funded by local residents, it was landscaped in the latter part of the last century in the English style, with a bandstand and an emphasis on nature rather than on formal gardens. Today it's a regular forum for drama and other performance arts in the summer, and at weekends young Amsterdam flocks here to meet friends, laze by the lake, buy trinkets from the flea markets in the area or listen to music – in June, July and August bands give free concerts here every Sunday at 2pm.

The area to the southeast of the park is one of Amsterdam's better-heeled residential districts, with designer shops and delis along chic P. C. Hooftstraat and Van Baerlestraat, and some of the city's fancier hotels (and plenty of its cheaper ones, too) on their connecting streets. But what this area really means to the visitor is museums, a number of which – the Rijksmuseum, Van Gogh and Stedelijk (p.73–77) – are imposingly grouped around the grassy wedge of Museumplein. This fans back as far as the Concertgebouw at its southern end and is a bare and rather windswept open space.

At the bottom end of Museumplein, on sleek Van Baerlestraat, is the Concertgebouw, completed in 1883 and renowned for its marvellous acoustics and its famed – and much recorded – resident orchestra. The Old South isn't all culture, however, and by no means is it all wealthy either. Walking east from Museumplein, across Hobbemakade, you enter the busy heart of the Old South, known as "De Pijp" (The Pipe) after its long, sombre canyons of brick tenements that went up in the nineteenth century as the city grew out of its canal-girded centre. The population here is dense and overcrowded, much of it made up of immigrants, and De Pijp has always been one of the city's closest-knit communities – and one of its liveliest, with numerous inexpensive Surinamese and Turkish restaurants. It's a cheerful area, its hub the long, slim thoroughfare of Albert Cuypstraat, whose daily general market – which stretches for about a mile between Ferdinand Bolstraat and Van Woustraat – is the largest in the city.

The New South

Aside from the small but pretty Sarphatipark, a few blocks south of the Albert Cuyp, there's little else to detain you in the Old South, and you'd be better off either walking or catching a tram down into the NEW SOUTH – a real contrast to its neighbour and the first properly planned extension to the city since the concentric canals of the seventeenth century. The Dutch architect H. P. Berlage was responsible for the overall plan, but he died before it was started, and the design was largely carried out in the 1930s by two prominent architects of the Amsterdam school, Michael de Klerk and Piet Kramer. Cutbacks in the city's subsidy led them to tone down the more imaginative aspects of the scheme, and most of the buildings are markedly more sober than previous Amsterdam school works (such as the Scheepvarthuis on Prins Hendrikkade). Otherwise they followed Berlage faithfully, sticking to his plan of wide boulevards and crooked side streets, and adding the odd splash of individuality to corners, windows and balconies.

Nowadays the New South is one of Amsterdam's most sought-after addresses. **Apollolaan**, **Stadionweg** and, a little way east, **Churchilllaan** are home to luxury hotels and some of the city's most sumptuous properties, huge idiosyncratic mansions lying far back on the street behind trees and generous gardens. **Beethovenstraat**, main street of the New South, is a fashionable shopping boulevard, with high-priced, slightly staid stores catering for the wealthy residents.

The area achieved a brief period of notoriety in 1969, when John Lennon and Yoko Ono staged their week-long **Bed-In** for peace in the **Amsterdam Hilton** on Apollolaan. The press came from all over; fans crowded outside, hanging on the couple's anti-war proclamations, and the episode was seen as the beginning of John and Yoko's subsequent campaign for peace worldwide. At the opposite end of Beethovenstraat, dense trees and shrubs of the **Beatrixpark** flank the antiseptic surroundings of the adjacent **RAI exhibition centre**: a complex of trade and conference centres built as part of the city's plan to attract more business people – along with their considerable expense accounts. It's of little general appeal (though one hall does sporadically host concerts), but if you're at a loose end you may find one of its many exhibitions interesting. Alternatively, you could visit the excellent **Resistance Museum** at Lekstraat 63 (see p.79). The **Olympic Stadium**, built for the 1928 games, is a useful landmark (for the time being at least – decaying masonry has rendered it dangerous, and it may well be demolished soon). Just north of it is the **Haarlemmermeer Station**, terminus of the summer museum tram which runs several times a day to the Amsterdamse Bos further south, technically outside the city limits in Amstelveen.

The **Amsterdamse Bos** is the city's largest open space, an eight square-kilometre woodland park planted during the 1930s in a mammoth project to utilize the wasted energies of the city's unemployed. If it's out of season or you're not into old trams, take one of the buses (#170, #171, #172) which run directly from Stationsplein. Once there, the best way to get around is to hire a bicycle (March–Oct) from the main entrance on Van Nijenrodeeweg and follow the 43km of path. It's also possible to rent canoes, canal bikes and motor boats. The Bosmuseum, a few kilometres along the Bosbaan from the main entrance, has maps and basic information.

The West

Of all Amsterdam's outer central districts, Amsterdam **WEST** is probably the least appealing, primarily a residential area with only a couple of nondescript parks as possible destinations. There's the **OLD WEST**, whose busy Turkish and Middle Eastern immigrant-based streetlife around De Clerqstraat can be worth checking out if you find yourself in the vicinity: **Kinkerstraat** is a good place to bargain-hunt if you're not after anything fancy, and there's also the vigourous **ten Katestraat market**, about halfway down the street on the right. But outside of this zone, in the districts of Bos en Lommer and Overtoomse Veld, there's little other than the large – but on the whole mediocre – **Rembrandtpark** to draw you out this far.

The East

A cupolaed box splattered with graffiti and topped with a crudely carved pediment, the sturdy **Muiderpoort** marks the boundary between Amsterdam's centre and the beginning of Amsterdam **EAST**. Across the canal the gabled and turreted **Royal Tropen Institute** has a marble-and-stucco entrance hall which you can peek into, though the only part open to visitors is the excellent **Tropenmuseum** around the corner (see p.79).

Behind the Tropen Institute, the **Oosterpark** is a peaceful oblong of green, and a gentle introduction to the area, which extends south and east, a solidly working-class district for the most part, particularly on the far side of Linnaeustraat. There's a high immigrant presence, and housing is still relatively poor, though there's ambitious urban renewal going on, and many of the aging terraced houses have been torn down to make way for new and better-equipped housing projects. As in the Old South, there's an underlying drug problem here, but while you're unlikely to need (or want) to come out here, it's by no means a forbidding district. Two things which may make you decide to visit (apart from the Zeeburg campsite), are the **Dapperstraat market** – a kind of Eastern equivalent to the Albert Cuyp – and, at the end of tram routes #3 and #10, the **Flevopark**, dull in itself but giving access to the IJsselmeer and Dutch countryside right out of Ruisdael.

Amsterdam's museums

Touring the big **museums** of Amsterdam is one of the pleasures of the city, and you should remember that besides the big three – the Rijksmuseum, the Van Gogh and the Stedelijk – there are a large number of specialist galleries, some displaying bizarre oddities, that more than compete in interest. **Opening times**, particularly of state-run museums, tend to follow a pattern: closed on Monday, open from 10am to 5pm Tuesday to Saturday and from 1 to 5pm on Sunday and public holidays. Almost all the museums offer at least basic **information** in English or a written English guide. Entry prices are as listed; kids usually pay half that of the adult admission.

One alternative worth considering if you want to do your museum visiting in a single, condensed trip is the **museumboat**. Running Tuesday through Saturday, this has five stops (Centraal Station, the Anne Frank House, Museumplein, the Jewish Museum and the Maritime Museum), enabling you to get to twenty museums, and departs from each stop every thirty minutes: tickets, valid all day, cost ƒ13, or for ƒ25 a *combi-ticket* allows you to use the boat and get into three museums free.

The Rijksmuseum

Stadhouderskade 42. Tram #7, #10, #16, #24, #25. Tues–Sat 10am–5pm, Sun 1–5pm; ƒ10. For more on Dutch art and artists, see Contexts.

The **RIJKSMUSEUM** is the one museum you shouldn't leave Amsterdam without visiting, if only briefly. Its **seventeenth-century Dutch paintings** constitute far and away the best collection to be found anywhere, with twenty or so Rembrandts alone, as well as copious arrays of works by Steen, Hals, Vermeer and many other Dutch artists of the era – all engagingly displayed with the layperson in mind. There are, too, representative displays of all other pre-twentieth-century periods of Dutch and Flemish painting, along with treasures in the **medieval art** and **Asiatic** sections that are not to be missed. To do justice to the place demands repeated visits; if time is limited, it's best to be content with the core paintings and a few selective forays into other sections.

Paintings of the fifteenth to seventeenth centuries

From the second-floor shop, the eastern wing runs chronologically through the Rijksmuseum's collection of Low Countries paintings. After works from the early **Netherlandish period** begin the classic paintings of the **dutch golden age**: portraits by Hals and Rembrandt, landscapes by Jan van Goyen and Jacob van Ruisdael, the riotous scenes of Jan Steen and the peaceful interiors of Vermeer and Pieter de Hooch. First, though, are some early seventeenth-century works, including **Frans Hals'** expansive *Isaac Massa and His Wife* and more sensational paintings such as **Dirck van Baburen's** *Prometheus in Chains* – a work from the Utrecht School, which used Caravaggio's paintings as its model.

Beyond this are the works of **Rembrandt** and some of his better-known pupils. Perhaps the most striking is the *Portrait of Maria Trip*, but look, too, at Ferdinand Bol's *Portrait of Elizabeth Bas*, Govert Flinck's *Rembrandt as a Shepherd* – interesting if only for its subject – and the *Portrait of Abraham Potter* by **Carel Fabritius**, this last a restrained, skillful work painted by one of Rembrandt's most talented (and shortest-lived) students.

The next rooms take you into the latter half of the seventeenth century and include the carousing peasant paintings of **Jan Steen**. Steen's *Morning Toilet* is full of associations, referring either to pleasures just had or about to be taken, while his *Feast of St Nicholas*, with its squabbling children, makes the festival a celebration of pure greed – much like the drunken gluttony of the *Merry Family* nearby – and the out-of-control ugliness of *After the Drinking Bout* leaves no room for doubt about what Steen thought of all this ribaldry.

It's in the last few rooms, though, that the Dutch interior really comes into its own, with a gentle moralizing that grows ever more subtle. **Vermeer's** *The Letter* reveals a tension between servant and mistress – the lute on the woman's lap was a well-known sexual symbol of the time – and the symbolism in the use of a map behind the *Young Woman Reading a Letter* hints at the far-flung places her loved one is writing from. The paintings of **Pieter de Hooch** are less symbolic, more exercises in lighting, but they're as good a visual guide to the everyday life and habits of the seventeenth-century Dutch bourgeoisie as you'll find.

Mingling with these interior scenes are more paintings by **Hals** and **Rembrandt** – later works, for the most part, from the painters' mature periods. Hals weighs in with a handful of portraits, including the boisterous *Merry Toper*, while Rembrandt – here at his most private and expressive best – is represented by a portrait of his first wife *Saskia*, a couple of his mother and a touching depiction of his cowled son, *Titus*.

A small room off to the side of the last one offers an introduction to the **gallery of honour** and one of the Rijksmuseum's great treasures – Rembrandt's *The Night Watch*, the most famous and most valuable of all the artist's pictures, recently restored after being slashed by a vandal in 1975. The painting is a so-called Civil Guard portrait, named after the bands of militia that grouped together in the sixteenth century to defend the home front during the wars with the Spanish. They later grew into social clubs for local dignitaries – most of whom would commission a group portrait as a mark of prestige. This one, of the Guards of the Kloveniersdoelen in Amsterdam, was erroneously tagged *The Night Watch* in the nineteenth century – a result both of the romanticism of the age and the fact that for years the painting was covered in soot. Though not as subtle as much of the artist's later work, it's an adept piece, full of movement and carefully arranged – these paintings were collections of individual portraits as much as group pictures, and part of the problem in creating one was to include each individual face while simultaneously producing a coherent group scene. The sponsors paid for a prominent position in the painting, and the artist also had to reflect this.

Elsewhere, the Gallery of Honour houses the large-scale works from the museum's collection of Dutch paintings. Some of these are notable only for their size – the selection of naval battles particularly – but a number do stand out, and would in any museum. Two of Rembrandt's better-known pupils crop up here: **Nicholas Maes**, with one of his typically intimate scenes in *Dreaming*, and **Ferdinand Bol**, both in his *Regents of the Nieuwe Zijds Workhouse* and the elegantly composed *Venus and Adonis*. The dashing *Self-portrait* is his too, a rich and successful character leaning on a sleeping cupid. By way of contrast, Rembrandt himself follows with a late *Self-portrait*, caught in mid-shrug as the Apostle Paul, a self-aware and defeated old man. Opposite, *The Staalmeesters* is an example of one of his later commissions, and, as do so many of Rembrandt's later works, it demonstrates his ability to capture a staggering range of subtle expressions. Nearby is *The Jewish Bride*, one of his last pictures, finished in 1665.

Later Dutch painting

To pick up chronologically where the Gallery of Honour left off, it's necessary to move down to the first floor, where the **eighteenth- and nineteenth-century dutch paintings** collection begins. The section is closed until 1995, but in the meantime you'll find most of the paintings mentioned below scattered throughout the main collection. Look out for the works of **Cornelis Troost**, whose eighteenth-century comic scenes earned him the dubiously deserved title of the "Dutch Hogarth". More enduring are the later pictures, notably the pastels of Pierre-Paul Prud'hon and **Jan Ekels'** *The Writer* – small and simple, the lighting and attention to detail imitative of Vermeer.

After this, rooms follow each other haphazardly, with sundry landscapes and portraiture from the lesser nineteenth-century artists. **Jongkind** is the best of the bunch, his murky *River Landscape in France* typical of the Impressionism that was developing in the nineteenth century. The chief proponents of Dutch Impressionism originated from or worked in The Hague, and the handy label of the **Hague School** covers a variety of styles and painters who shared a clarity and sensitivity in their depiction of the Dutch landscape. Of the major Hague School painters, the Rijksmuseum is strongest on the work of the **Maris Brothers** and **Jan Weissenbruch**, whose land- and seascapes, such as *View near the Geestbrug*, hark back to the compositional techniques of van Ruisdael.

While members of the Hague School were creating gentle landscapes, a younger generation of Impressionist painters working in Amsterdam – the **Amsterdam School** – were using a darker palette to capture city scenes. By far the most important picture from this turn-of-the-century group is **G. H. Breitner's** *Singelbrug near Paleisstraat in Amsterdam*, a random moment in the street recorded and framed with photographic dispassion.

Other collections

The collection of **Medieval and Renaissance applied art** on the second floor is perhaps the most impressive other section, filled with jewellery, religious art, woodcarvings and statuary from the Low Countries and northern Europe. There's a massive collection of **fine art** from later centuries, including galleries stuffed from floor to ceiling with **delftware**, furniture, ceramics and textiles from the sixteenth century on: it's mostly dull stuff, with only the **dolls' houses** providing diversion.

The **Dutch history section** focuses on the naval might that brought Holland its wealth, with fearsome **model ships** and galleries filled with relics of Holland's naval and colonial past. Holland's colonial connection with the East means that Asian art can be found in most of the museums' collections, but the **Asian collection** proper holds its most prized treasures: chiefly graceful paintings, ceramics and lacquerwork, and jewellery. Like the eighteenth- and nineteenth-century Dutch paintings, the Asian collection has been dispersed throughout the museum, awaiting the refurbishment of its galleries, due to be completed in 1995.

Rijksmuseum Vincent van Gogh

Paulus Potterstraat 7. Tram #2, #3, #5, #12, #16. Tues–Sat 10am–5pm, Sun 1–5pm; f10.

Vincent van Gogh is arguably the most popular, most reproduced and most talked-about of all modern artists, so it's not surprising that the **RIJKSMUSEUM VINCENT VAN GOGH**, opened in 1973 and comprising the extensive collection of the artist's art-dealer brother Theo, is Amsterdam's top tourist attraction. During the recent celebrations of the hundredth anniversary of his death, the museum was packed for several weeks. Housed in an angular building designed by the aged Gerritt Rietveld, it's a gentle and unassuming introduction to the man and his art – and one which, due both to the quality of the collection and to the building, succeeds superbly well.

The first works go back to the artist's **early years** in southern Holland, where he was born: these are dark and sombre for the most part, like the haunting, flickering light of *The Potato Eaters* – one of van Gogh's best-known paintings. Across the hall, the sobriety of these early works is easily transposed onto the Parisian urban landscape, particularly in his *View of Paris*: but before long, under the sway of fellow painters and, after the bleak countryside of North Brabant and the sheer colour of the city itself, his approach began to change. This is most noticeable in the views of Montmartre windmills, a couple of self-portraits and the pictures from Asnières just outside Paris.

In February 1888, van Gogh moved to **Arles**, inviting Gauguin to join him a little while later. With the change of scenery came a heightened interest in colour and the predominance of yellow as a recurring motif: it's represented most vividly in *The Yellow House*. A canvas from the artist's *Sunflowers* series is justly one of his most lauded works, intensely, almost obsessively rendered in the deepest oranges, golds and ochres he could find.

At the asylum in **St Remy**, where van Gogh committed himself after snipping off part of his ear and offering it to a local prostitute, nature took a more abstract form in his work – trees bent into cruel, sinister shapes, skies coloured purple and yellow, as in the *Garden of St Paul's Hospital*. Van Gogh is at his most expressionistic here, the paint applied thickly, often with a palette knife, especially in the final, tortured paintings done at **Auvers**, including *Undergrowth, The Reaper* or *Wheatfield with Crows*, in which the fields swirl and writhe under black, moving skies. It was only a few weeks after completing this last painting that van Gogh shot and fatally wounded himself.

On the third floor, the museum shows a revolving selection from its vast stock of van Gogh's **drawings**, notebooks and letters, and also affords space to relevant temporary exhibitions. The top floor is used as a **temporary exhibition space** year round, usually showing works loaned from other galleries that illustrate the artistic influences on van Gogh, or his own influence on other artists.

Stedelijk Museum

Paulus Potterstraat 13. Tram #2, #3, #5, #12, #16. Daily 11am–5pm; f7.50.

Despite its reputation as Amsterdam's number one modern art museum, the **STEDELIJK** can be a bit disappointing. True, its temporary exhibitions are often of world renown, and worth catching if you happen to be in town, but the museum is primarily devoted to displays of **contemporary art on loan**. Should you want to see something of its extensive permanent collection (impressively complete from the nineteenth century onward) you'll need to be here in the summer, when the museum's holdings are shown through much of July and August.

Of the museum's **permanent collection**, there's always a good (rotating) scattering on the **second floor**. Briefly and broadly, this starts off with drawings by Picasso, Matisse and their contemporaries, and moves on to paintings by major Impressionists – Manet, Monet, Bonnard – and post-Impressionists: Ensor, van Gogh and Cezanne. Further on, Mondrian holds sway, from the early, muddy-coloured abstractions to the cool, boldly coloured rectangular blocks for which he's most famous. Similarly, Kasimir Malevich is well represented, his dense attempts at Cubism leading to the dynamism and, again, bold primary tones of his "Suprematist" paintings. You may also find a good stock of Marc Chagall's paintings (the museum owns a wide selection), and a number of pictures by American Abstract Expressionists Mark Rothko, Ellsworth Kelly and Barnett Newman. Jean Dubuffet, too, with his swipes at the art establishment, may well have a profile, and you might catch Matisse's large cut-out, *The Parakeet and the Mermaid*.

Two additional large-scale attractions are on the first floor – Karel Appel's *Bar* in the foyer, installed for the opening of the Stedelijk in the 1950s, and the same artist's wild daubings in the museum's restaurant. Look out, too, for Ed Kienholz's model of his local bar in Los Angeles, the *Beanery* (1965), housed in the basement of the museum.

Other museums

Amstelkring Museum

O. Z. Voorburgwal 40. Tram #4, #9, #16, #24, #25, though in easy walking distance of Centraal Station. Mon–Sat 10am–5pm, Sun 1–5pm; f4.50.

In the seventeenth century, Catholics had to confine their worship to the privacy of their own homes – an arrangement which led to the growth of so-called clandestine Catholic churches throughout the city. Known as "Our Dear Lord in the Attic", this is the only one left; it occupies the loft of a wealthy merchant's house, together with those of two smaller houses behind it. The **church** is delightful and the **house** itself has been left beautifully untouched, its original furnishings (reminiscent of interiors by Vermeer or de Hooch) making the Amstelkring a tranquil and still relatively undiscovered escape from the excesses of the nearby Red Light District. One of the city's best and least demanding small museums.

Amsterdam Historical Museum
*Kalverstraat 92. Tram #1, #2, #4, #5, #9, #14, #16, #24, #25. Mon–Fri 10am–
5pm, Sat & Sun 11am–5pm; f6.50; guided tours on Wed and Sat at 2pm and 3pm.*
Housed in the restored seventeenth-century buildings of the Civic Orphanage,
Amsterdam's Historical Museum attempts to survey the city's development with
artefacts, paintings and documents from the thirteenth century onward. Much is
centred around the "Golden Age" of the seventeenth century: a large group of
paintings portrays the city in its heyday, and the good art collection shows how the
wealthy bourgeoisie decorated their homes. Sadly, most of the rest of the museum
is poorly documented and lacks continuity. Still, it's worth seeing for the nineteenth-century paintings and photos and, more notably, the play-it-yourself **carillon** and the **Regents' Chamber**, unchanged since the Regents dispensed civic
charity there three hundred years ago. Immediately outside the museum, the
glassed-in **Civic Guard Gallery** draws passers-by with free glimpses of the large
company portraits – there's a selection from the earliest of the 1540s to the lighter
affairs of the seventeenth century.

Anne Frank House
*Prinsengracht 263. Tram #13, #14, #17. Mon–Sat 9am–5pm, Sun 10am–5pm,
except Yom Kippur; f7, children f3.50; no museumcards.*
See p.64–65.

Hortus Botanicus
*Plantage Middenlaan 2. Tram #7, #9, #14, or metro Waterlooplein. April–Sept
Mon–Fri 9am–5pm, Sat & Sun 11am–5pm; f6.*
Pocket-sized botanical gardens whose six thousand plant species make a wonderfully relaxed break from the rest of central Amsterdam. Worth wandering in for
the sticky pleasures of the hothouses, its terrapins and for the world's oldest (and
probably largest) pot plant. Stop off for coffee and cakes in the orangery.

Jewish Historical Museum
*J. D. Meijerplein 2–4. Metro to Waterlooplein; tram #9, #14. Daily, except Yom
Kippur, 11am–5pm; f7.*
Housed in a former Ashkenazi synagogue complex in the old Jewish quarter of
Amsterdam, the Jewish Museum is one of the most modern and impressive in
western Europe; it won the 1988 European Museum of the Year award. Four
synagogues, built during the seventeenth and eighteenth centuries, have been
restored and linked together as a centre for the study of the history of the Jewish
community that's designed to be of interest to all.

Kromhout Shipyard Museum
Hoogte Kadijk 147. Bus #22, #28. Mon–Fri 10am–4pm; f3.50.
The Kromhout shipyard was one of the few survivors of shipbuilding's decline in
the nineteenth century. It struggled along producing engines and iron ships until
it closed in 1969 and was saved from demolition by becoming a combination of
industrial monument, operating shipyard and museum. Money is still scarce,
which means that little shipbuilding or restoring is going on at the moment, but
the enthusiastic staff and good explanatory background material make this an up-
and-coming place, and a useful adjunct to the Maritime Museum nearby.

Maritime Museum

Kattenburgerplein 1. Bus #22, #28. Tues–Sat 10am–5pm, Sun noon–5pm; f10, children f7.50.

A well-presented display of the country's maritime past in an endless collection of maps, navigational equipment and weapons, though most impressive are the large and intricate **models** of sailing ships and men-of-war that date from the same period as the original vessels. Outside there's a replica of an eighteenth-century Dutch East India trading ship.

Rembrandt House

Jodenbreestraat 4–6. Metro to Nieuwmarkt or Waterlooplein; tram #9, #14. Mon–Sat 10am–5pm, Sun 1–5pm; f5.

See p.68.

Resistance Museum

Lekstraat 63. Tram #4, #12, #25. Tues–Fri 10am–5pm; Sat–Sun 1–5pm; f4.50.

Strikingly installed in a former synagogue, the Resistance Museum charts the rise of the resistance from the German invasion of The Netherlands in May 1940 to the country's liberation in 1945. The museum has a fascinating collection of contemporary material – photos, illegal newsletters, anti-Jewish propaganda and deportation orders. The English guide to the exhibition is essential.

The Six Collection

Amstel 218. Tram #4. Apply first (with passport) at the Rijksmuseum for a note of introduction. This is essential; the house is still lived in and the current owners are extremely protective of their privacy. You most definitely won't get in without the letter. It's a good idea to try and time your visit to coincide with the guided tours on Mon, Wed and Fri at 10am and 11am. Closed public holidays; free.

The Six Collection is deliberately underplayed in the city's tourist brochures, in part because only those with a little knowledge of Dutch art will find it rewarding, and, more importantly, because the current Baron Six, descendant of the seventeenth-century collector and burgomaster, still lives in the elaborately furnished canal house and doesn't encourage visitors – worth bearing in mind if you do come. **Rembrandt** was a friend of the burgomaster, and his *Portrait of Jan Six* is the collection's greatest treasure. Painted in 1654, it's a brilliant work, the impressionistic treatment of the hands subtly focusing attention on the subject's face. The collection – which contains work by Hals, Cuyp and Terbosch – is well explained by the staff, and the whole group of paintings is a must if you have any interest in seventeenth-century painting.

Tropenmuseum

Linnaeusstraat 2. Tram #3, #6, #9, #10, #14. Mon–Fri 10am–5pm, Sat–Sun noon–5pm; f7.50.

As part of the old Colonial Institute (now the less controversially titled Tropical Institute), this museum used to display only artefacts from the Dutch colonies. Since the 1950s, however, when Indonesia was granted independence, it has collected applied arts from all over, and its holdings now cover the world. It makes for an impressively unstuffy exposition of the contemporary life and problems of the developing world – both urban, covering the ever-expanding slum dwellings of cities such as Bombay, and rural, examining such issues as the dangerous wholesale destruction of the world's tropical rainforests. The best sections are those devoted to Africa, India and (not surprisingly) Indonesia, but it's really all worth seeing, even if you have little interest in ethnography. Also look in on the bookshop, which has a good selection of books on Third World subjects.

Van Loon Museum

Keizersgracht 672. Tram #16, #24, #25. Mon only 10am–5pm; f5.

Less grand and more likeable than the nearby Willet-Holthuysen, with a pleasantly down-at-heel interior of peeling stucco and shabby paintwork. Built in 1672, the house's first tenant was the artist Ferdinand Bol; fortunately he didn't suffer the fate of many subsequent owners who seem to have been cursed with a series of bankruptcies and scandals for over two hundred years. The van Loon family bought the house in 1884, bringing with them a collection of family portraits and homey bits and pieces that stretch from 1580 to 1949.

Willet-Holthuysen Museum

Herengracht 605. Tram #4, #9, #14. Mon–Fri 10am–5pm, Sat & Sun 11am–5pm; f5.

Splendidly decorated in Rococo style, this is more museum than home, containing Abraham Willet's collection of glass and ceramics. But, save for the basement, a well-equipped replica of a seventeenth-century kitchen, it's very much look-don't-touch territory. Out back there's an immaculate eighteenth-century garden – worth the price of the admission alone.

> Two other museums housed in buildings that offer a flavour of seventeenth-century Dutch interiors are the Amstelkring (p.77) and the Six Collection (p.79).

Eating

Amsterdam may not be the culinary capital of Europe, but there's a good supply of ethnic restaurants, especially Indonesian and Chinese, and the prices – by big-city standards – are often hard to beat. In addition there are *eetcafés* and bars which serve increasingly adventurous food, quite cheaply, in a relaxed and unpretentious setting – the **bar listings** on p.83 are certainly worth checking: many serve food, and at lunchtime it's possible to fill up extremely cheaply with a bowl of soup or a french bread sandwich.

Mensas

These are Amsterdam's **college cafeterias**, and as such are not frequented so much for the quality of the food as for the prices which, at around f7–10 for a full meal, can hardly be beaten. The food itself isn't bad, filling enough if not especially tasty.

Agora, Roeterstraat 11 (☎525 2699). Open Mon–Fri noon–2pm & 5–7pm.

Atrium, O. Z. Voorburgwal 237 (☎525 3999). Open Mon–Fri noon–2pm and 5–7pm, year round.

Dutch and fish restaurants

Albatros, Westerstraat 264 (☎627 99 32). Family-run restaurant serving some mouth-wateringly imaginative, if rather expensive, fish dishes. A place to splash out and linger over a meal.

De Bak, Prinsengracht 193 (☎625 79 72). Good portions for moderate prices, though lately somewhat of a tourist hangout and with a menu that seems to have shrunk down to spare ribs and not much else.

De Blauwe Hollander, Leidsekruisstraat 28. Long-established Dutch restaurant serving decent food in generous quantities – quite a boon among the tourist-slanted eateries of this part of town.

Claes Claesz, Egelantiersstraat 24–26 (☎625 53 06). Exceptionally friendly Jordaan restaurant that attracts a good mixed crowd and serves excellent Dutch food, though not at all cheaply. Live music most nights. Closed Mon–Wed.

De Eetuin, 2e Eglantiersdwarsstraat 10 (☎623 77 06). Hefty portions of Dutch food, all with a salad from a serve-yourself bar for ƒ15–18. Non-meat eaters can content themselves with the large, if dull, vegetarian plate, or the delicious fish casserole.

Haesje Claes, Spuistraat 275 (☎624 99 98). Dutch cuisine. Extremely popular; go as early as you can manage.

Keuken van 1870, Spuistraat 4 (☎624 99 98). Basic, traditional Dutch cooking. A good deal if money's short.

Moeder's Pot, Vinkenstraat 119 (☎623 76 43). Ultra-cheap Dutch food. Recommended.

Noordzee, Kalverstraat 122 (☎623 73 37). Central Amsterdam branch of a chain that specializes in cheap fish lunches, sandwiches and takeaway fish and chips.

Vegetarian restaurants

Egg Cream, St Jacobstraat 19 (☎623 05 75). Amsterdam's most famous vegetarian restaurant, cheap and atmospheric, though the food isn't always exclusively veggie. Bear in mind the early closing time of 8pm.

Gimsez, Huidenstraat 19 (☎624 97 47). Pleasant and tasty food, though the ambience is a bit clinical and service can be slow. Good lunch specials.

Het Moorden, Frederik Hendrikstraat 115 (☎684 91 15). Housed in what was once a squat and run by the erstwhile squatters, the *Noorden* retains its counter-culture feel. Simple fish and vegetarian meals.

Klaver Koning, Koningstraat 29 (☎626 10 85). Excellent upmarket vegetarian restaurant, with decent wine and a refreshingly un-ascetic atmosphere. But not cheap.

Sisters, Nes 102 (☎626 39 70). A busy vegetarian restaurant serving *dagschotels* and other entrées for around ƒ16, as well as plenty of snack-type items. Open until 9pm.

Ethnic restaurants

Aphrodite, Lange Leidsedwarsstraat 91 (☎622 73 82). Refined Greek cooking in a street where you certainly wouldn't expect it. Fair prices, too.

Beddington's, Roelg Hartstraat 6–8 (☎676 52 01). French–Japanese cuisine: a memorable blend of delicacy and elegance. Subtle flavours and Japanese-inspired presentation.

Bojo, Lange Leidsedwarsstraat 49 (☎626 89 90). Possibly the best-value – if not the best – Indonesian place in town, and open until 6am. Expect to wait for a table, though – we weren't the first to discover it. Highly recommended. The service, though, can be slow.

Burger's Patio, 2e Tuindwarsstraat 12 (☎623 68 54). Moderately priced, young and convivial Italian restaurant. Despite the name, not a burger in sight.

Casa di David, Singel 426 (☎624 50 93). Solid-value Italian place with a sister self-service restaurant at Kalverstraat 180.

Filoxenia, Berenstraat 8 (☎624 42 92). Small, friendly, reasonably priced Greek restaurant.

Hemelse Modder, Oude Wall 9 (☎624 3202). Tasty meat, fish and vegetarian food cooked French/Italian style in an informal atmosphere off the beaten tourist track. Reasonable prices.

Intermezzo, Herenstraat 28 (☎626 01 67). Good French–Dutch cooking at above-average prices, but worth every penny.

De Kikker, Egelantiersstraat 128 (☎627 91 98). Two-tier, top-quality French restaurant that has a downstairs *eetcafé*. Upstairs is only really accessible for the well-dressed, wealthy, committed gourmet.

Koh-I-Noor, Westermarkt 29 (☎623 31 33). One of the city's better Indian restaurants, and not overpriced.

La Cacerola, Weteringstraat 41 (☎626 53 97). Small and secluded Spanish eatery, with likeable if eccentric service. Phone first as opening hours vary.

Lana Thai, Warmoesstraat 10 (☎624 21 79). Among the best Thai restaurants in town, with seating overlooking the water of Damrak. Quality food, chic surroundings but high prices. Closed Tues.

Mamma Mia, 2e Leliedwarsstraat 13 (☎625 82 38). Good selection of pizzas in a pleasant family atmosphere.

Mogul, Rokin 107 (☎624 24 16). Above-average and centrally located restaurant serving Pakistani food.

Pizzeria Mimo, Lange Leidsedwarsstraat 37 (☎622 79 35). Perhaps the best of the dozens of Italian restaurants along this street.

Rose's Cantina, Reguliersdwarsstraat 38 (☎625 97 97). In the heart of trendy Amsterdam, this qualifies as possibly the city's most crowded restaurant. No bookings, and you'll almost definitely have to wait, but it's no hardship to sit at the bar nursing a cocktail and watching the would-be cool bunch – the margaritas should carry a public health warning. The Tex-Mex food is good, too.

Rum Runners, Prinsengracht 277 (☎627 40 79). Caribbean-style bar/restaurant situated in the old Westerkerk hall. Expensive cocktails but well-priced if not always devastatingly tasty food. Summer terrace and live South American music Wed–Sun evening.

Sluizer, Utrechtsestraat 41–43 (☎622 6376). French-oriented food in one of the city's most atmospheric restaurants. The fish restaurant of the same name next door is also worth a splurge, with a choice of 10 market-fresh types of fish served daily.

Tandoor, Leidseplein 19 (☎623 44 15). Doesn't live up to its excellent reputation, but the tandoori dishes are very tasty.

Tempo Doeloe, Utrechtsestraat 75 (☎625 67 18). Reliable place close by Rembrandtsplein. As with all Indonesian restaurants, be guided by the waiter when choosing a *rijstaffel* – some of the dishes are very hot indeed. Not cheap.

To Ouzeri, De Clerqstraat 106 (☎618 1412). Greek *eetcafé* where you can compose your own meal from the many delicious Greek dishes on offer.

Umeno, Agamemnonstraat 27 (☎676 6089). Reasonably priced Japanese restaurants are hard to find, but this one, though down in the residential South, has cooking and prices that make it well worth the journey. Closed Mon; tram #24.

De Vrolijke Abrikoos, Weteringschans 76 (☎624 46 72). Organic or environmentally friendly fish, meat and vegetarian dishes.

Warung Swietie, 1e Sweelinckstraat 1 (☎671 5833). Surinamese/Javanese *eetcafé*. Cheap and cheerful; closed Wed.

Drinking

There are two kinds of Amsterdam **bar**. The traditional, old-style bar or **brown café** (*bruine kroeg*), so named because of the dingy colour of their nicotine-stained walls, and the slick, self-consciously modern **designer bar**, as un-brown as possible and geared to a largely young crowd. Most bars open until around 1am during the week, 2am at weekends, though some don't open until lunchtime, or even about 4pm; reckon on paying roughly *f*2.50 for a small beer.

You can also use bars as a source for **budget eating**: many (often designated *eetcafés*) offer a complete menu, and most will make you a sandwich or bowl of soup; at the very least you can snack on hardboiled eggs from the counter for a guilder or so each.

Inner centre bars

Cul de Sac, O. Z. Achterburgwal 99. Down a long alley in what used to be a seventeenth-century spice warehouse, this is a handy retreat from the Red Light District. Small, quiet and friendly.

Dantzig, Zwanenburgwal 15. Easy going grand-café-style bar, with comfortable chairs, friendly service and a low-key chic atmosphere. Food served at lunchtime and evenings.

De Drie Fleschjes, Gravenstraat 16. Tasting-house for spirits and liqueurs, which would originally have been made on the premises. No beer, and no seats either; its clients tend to be well heeled or well soused (often both).

De Engelbewaarder, Kloveniersburgwal 59. Once the meeting place of Amsterdam's book-ish types, this is still known as the "literary café". Relaxed and informal, it has live jazz on Sunday evenings.

Flying Dutchman, Martelaarsgracht 13. Principal watering-hole of Amsterdam's British expatriate community and not a word of Dutch is to be heard. Usually packed with stoned regulars crowding in to use the pool table or dartboards, or simply to cash in on the *Dutchman*'s reasonably priced large-size beers.

Frascati, Nes 59. Theatre bar, elegantly brown with mirrors and a pink marble bar, popular with a young media-type crowd. Good, too, for both lunchtime and informal evening eating, with full meals, snacks and soups. Recommended.

't Gasthuys, Grimburgwal 7. Convivial brown café packed during the academic year with students from the university across the canal. Features include good food and summer seating outside by the water.

Gollum, Raamsteeg 4. Small, noisy bar with a huge array of different beers. A genial bartender dispenses lists to help you choose.

't IJ, in De Gooyer windmill, Funenkade 7. Situated in the base of an early nineteenth-century windmill, the beers here (called *Natte, Zatte* and *Struis*) are brewed on the premises and are extremely strong. A fun place to drink yourself silly. Open Fri, Sat & Sun 3–8pm.

De Jaren, Nieuwe Doelenstraat 20–22. Enormous bar overlooking the Amstel: three floors, two terraces and as much trendiness as you could ask for. Serves reasonably priced food, too.

Luxembourg, Spui 22–24. Watering-hole frequented by Amsterdam's advertising and media brigade. It's crowded, too. If you can get in, it's actually a very elegant bar with a good (though pricy) selection of snacks. Overlooks the Singel at the back.

't Pakhuis, Voetboogstraat 10. One of a clutch of bars that line this tiny street, an inviting place with food as well as drink.

De Pilsener Club, Begijnensteeg 4. More like someone's living room than a bar – indeed all drinks mysteriously appear from a back room. Photographs on the wall record generations of sociable drinking.

De Pilserij, Gravenstraat 10. Roomy bar behind the Nieuwe Kerk that has a comfortable back room and plays good jazz. Above all, though, you drink here for the bar's authentic nineteenth-century surroundings – little changed, right down to the cash register.

Scheltema, N. Z. Voorburgwal 242. Journalists' bar, now only frequented by more senior newshounds and their occasionally famous interviewees, since all the newspapers that had their headquarters along here moved to the outskirts. Faded turn-of-the-century feel, with a reading table and meals.

De Schutter, Voetboogstraat 13–15. A spacious and likably unkempt upstairs bar that serves well-priced food.

La Strada, N.Z. Voorburgwal 93-95. Exceptionally trendy bar whose interior changes monthly as aspiring – if not always inspiring – local artists are given free rein with the decor.

Outer centre bars

Aas van Bokalen, Keizersgracht 335. Unpretentious local bar, with good food. Great collection of Motown tapes. Very small, so go either early or late.

De Beeiard, Herengracht 90. Light and airy Fifties-style bar for genuine beer aficionados. A very wide selection of draft and bottled beers, and an owner who delights in filling you in on the relative properties of each.

Café Americain, American Hotel, Leidseplein 28–30. A media gathering point for years, the *Americain*'s chief delight is its Art Nouveau decor – coordinated right down to the doorknobs. Not as pricy as you might imagine.

Chris anno 1624, Bloemstraat 42. Proud of itself for being the Jordaan's (and Amsterdam's) oldest bar. Comfortable and homey.

Het Land van Walem, Keizersgracht 449. Walem is one of Amsterdam's nouveau-chic cafés: cool, light and vehemently non-brown. Clientele are stylish in taste and dress, food a kind of hybrid French–Dutch; there's a wide selection of newspapers and magazines that includes some in English. Usually packed.

Het Molenpad, Prinsengracht 653. Cosy and informal brown café and gallery full of bookish types from the public library just along the canal.

Morlang, Keizersgracht 451. Bar/restaurant of the new wave yuppie variety (much like *Walem* next door), serving good food. Live music Tues.

Nol, Westerstraat 109. Probably the epitome of the jolly Jordaan singing bar, a luridly lit dive popular with jovial Jordaan gangsters and ordinary Amsterdammers alike. Open late.

De Prins, Prinsengracht 124. Boisterous student bar, with a wide range of drinks and a well-priced menu that includes fondues. A good place to drink in a great part of town.

De Reiger, Nieuwe Leliestraat 34. The Jordaan's main meeting-place, an old-style café filled with modish Amsterdammers. Affordable food, too.

Schiller, Rembrandtsplein 26. Art Deco bar of the upstairs hotel, authentic in both feel and decor, and though it's suffered something of a decline of late, offering a genteel escape from the tackiness of most of the rest of Rembrandtsplein. Meals are French/Dutch.

De Tuin, 2e Tuindwarsstraat 13. The Jordaan has some marvellously unpretentious bars, and this is one of the best: agreeably unkempt and filled with locals.

Coffee shops and tearooms

There are two types of **coffee shop** in Amsterdam: those whose principle business is the buying, selling and consuming of dope, and the more traditional places that sell neither dope nor alcohol but do serve sandwiches or a light menu for lower prices than in a fully fledged restaurant; some offer pastries or chocolates.

The so-called **"smoking" coffee shops** are easy to identify: pumping out varieties of house or hard rock, brightly lit, with starkly modern furniture and an accent on healthy food, they're about as far from the cosy Dutch *brown café* as it's possible to get – indeed you'll rarely see Amsterdammers in these places; they're usually filled with tourists. Smoking dope is the primary pastime (all sell a range of hash and grass), and most also have video screens, (loud) music and a selection of games from baccarat to pool; they're open roughly from late morning/midday until around midnight.

The growth of "smoking" coffee shops has made "straight" places increasingly defensive, and all of the coffee shops listed as **"non-smoking"** go to great lengths to emphasize that they don't sell dope and that its consumption on the premises is strictly forbidden; some are even considering calling themselves "tearooms" to avoid confusion. Again, if you're not sure, ask.

"Smoking"

The Bulldog, Leidseplein 15; O. Z. Voorburgwal 90; O. Z. Voorburgwal 132; Hekelveld 7; corner of Singel and Brouwersgracht. The biggest and most famous of the coffee-shop chains, and a long way from its poky Red Light District dive origins. The main Leidseplein branch (the "Palace"), housed in a former police station, has a large cocktail bar, coffee shop, juice bar and souvenir shop. It has always had the reputation of being loud and brash, not at all the place for a quiet smoke (though the dope they sell, in neat little brand-labelled bags, is said to be good) and following a violent incident in July 1991 has been closed down by the police for the foreseeable future.

Extase, Oude Hoogstraat 2. Part of a chain that is far less chi-chi than the big cheeses.

Fancy Free, Martelaarsgracht 4; Haarlemmerstraat 64. Slick, pink, plush and commercial, very much in *The Bulldog* mould.

Goa, Kloveniersburgwal 42. A member of the *Extase* chain (see above).

Pie in the Sky, 2e Laurierdwarsstraat 64. Beautiful canal-corner setting, great for outside summer lounging.

Prix d'Ami, Haringpakkersteeg 3. Pleasant, but lacking the character of its rivals.

Rusland, Rusland 16. One of the first Amsterdam coffee shops, and a cramped and vibrant place that's a favourite with both dope fans and tea addicts (43 different kinds). A little worse for a recent extension, but still a cut above the rest.

De Tweede Kamer, Heisteeg 6. One of the few smoking coffee shops frequented by Amsterdammers: traditional decor, friendly atmosphere.

"Non-smoking"

Bâton, Herengracht 82. Convivial coffee shop with a huge array of sandwiches. Handy for cheap lunches in a central location.

J.G. Beune, Haarlemmerdijk 156. Age-old chocolatier with a tearoom attached.

Café Panini, Vijzelgracht 3–5. Coffee shop-cum-restaurant that features good sandwiches and, in the evening, pasta dishes.

De Eenhorn, Warmoesstraat 16. Raw brick walls, oak beams, paintings and classical music. A stark contrast to the surrounding Red Light District.

Granny, 1e van der Helststraat 45. Just off the Albert Cuyp market, with terrific *appelgebak* and *koffie verkeerd*.

Lindsay's Teashop, Kalverstraat 185. An attempt to recreate a little piece of England in the unlikely location of the basement of the American discount bookshop. The food, though, is fine: real English cream teas, with homemade pies and trifles. And it's a refreshing escape from the Kalverstraat shopping mafia.

Studio 2, Singel 504. Pleasantly situated, airy coffee shop that sells a delicious selection of rolls and sandwiches. Recommended.

Nightlife

Amsterdam is not a major cultural centre, by any standards. Its performance spaces are small for the most part, and the city is not a regular stop on the touring circuits of major companies. Rather, it's a gathering spot for fringe performances, and buzzes with places offering a wide – and often inventive – range of affordable entertainment.

The city has a great many **multimedia centres**; programmes everywhere can be varied and unpredictable, so always check "what's on" listings carefully. As far as live music goes, **rock, jazz, salsa** and **Latin American** music are well represented in a number of small bars and clubs. The Concertgebouw assures Amsterdam a high ranking in the **classical music** stakes, and the city has pulled itself up into the big leagues for **dance and opera** with the building of the new muziektheater on the Amstel. As for **theatre**, while there's only one permanent stage for English plays, a number of companies perform regularly in English, and at **cinemas**, foreign-language films are rarely shown without English subtitles.

The largest of Amsterdam's **festivals** is the annual **Holland Festival**, a prestigious and international, if slightly highbrow, series of opera, music, theatre and dance performances held throughout the city.

Information and tickets

The **Uitburo**, in the Stadsschouwburg on the corner of Marnixstraat and Leidseplein (Mon–Sat 10am–6pm, Thurs until 9pm; ☎621 12 11), offers advice on anything remotely cultural, sells tickets and is a good source of **listings magazines** – of which *Time Out Amsterdam* is undoubtedly the best. **Tickets** for most performances can be bought at the Uitburo (ƒ2 booking fee) and VVV offices (no booking fee), or can be reserved by phone from the VVV. You are also able to book your seats, again free of charge, through the *National Bookings Centre* (☎070/320 25 00).

Concert halls and multimedia centres

Beurs van Berlage, Damrak 213 (☎627 04 66). Slap bang in the middle of the city centre, the former stock exchange (a magnificent nineteenth-century building) provides a great backdrop for concerts of all kinds.

Carré Theatre, Amstel 115–125 (☎622 52 25). Hosts all kinds of top international acts: anything from the Peking Circus to rap and Russian folk dance.

Jaap Eden Hall, Radioweg 64 (☎694 98 94). Large concert hall in the east of the city which occasionally stages big-name gigs. Heavy metal bands a favourite. Tram #9.

Meervaart, Osdorpplein 205 (☎610 73 93). A modern multimedia centre on the outskirts of town (tram #1, bus #19, #23) with a varied programme of international music, film, theatre and dance. Film tickets ƒ9, other events ƒ10–25.

Melkweg, Lijnbaansgracht 234a (☎624 17 77). Probably Amsterdam's most famous entertainment spot, and these days one of the city's prime arts centres. Its theatre space serves as an outlet for small, inventive international groups, virtually all of which perform in English, and the concert hall plays host to a broad range of bands. Other features include a fine monthly film programme, weekend discos, a tearoom selling dope and a bar and restaurant. General admission is ƒ5 plus ƒ4 membership (valid one month); otherwise, concerts begin around 10.30pm and admission ranges from ƒ10–25. The *Melkweg* is closed Mon.

Stadsschouwburg, Leidseplein 26 (☎624 23 11). Somewhat overshadowed by the muziektheater but still a significant venue for opera and dance. Tickets from ƒ15.

Live music

Akhnaton, Nieuwezijds Kolk 25 (☎624 33 96). Three-storey youth centre with live music at the weekends and Latin, African and reggae sounds during the week. Starts around 10pm, admission around ƒ15.

Bimhuis, Oude Schans 73–77 (☎623 1361). Excellent jazz auditorium and ultra-modern bar. Concerts Thurs–Sat (ƒ15–25), free jazz sessions Mon & Tues. Live music in the bar on Sunday afternoons at 4pm, also free.

Café Alto, Korte Leidsedwarsstraat 115 (☎626 32 49). Legendary little jazz bar just off Leidseplein. Quality modern jazz every night from 10pm until about 2.30am. Big on atmosphere, though slightly cramped.

Iboya, Korte Leidsewarsstraat 29 (☎623 78 59). Salsa and live jazz.

Joseph Lamm Jazz Club, Van Diemenstraat 242 (☎622 80 86). Traditional jazz centre which encourages dancing. Live music Fri & Sat 9pm–3am, ƒ5; jam sessions Sun 8pm–2am, free.

Korsakoff, Lijnbaansgracht 161 (☎625 7854). A punk hangout, especially for the Wed night bands. Don't come here for a quiet discussion. Free admission.

Latin Club, O. Z. Voorburgwal 254 (☎624 22 70). Salsa/cocktail bar with occasional live bands and a tape selection imported from South America; 2pm–2am (weekends until 3am).

Mulligan's, Amstel 100 (☎622 1330). Boisterous (and often packed) Irish bar with live folk on Fri and Sat evenings.

Paradiso, Weteringschans 6–8 (☎623 73 481). A converted church that features bands ranging from the up-and-coming to well-known names on the brink of stardom. Also hosts classical concerts, lectures and debates. Entrance ƒ12–30, plus ƒ3.50 for a month's membership. The bands usually get started at 9.30pm.

PH 31, Prins Hendriklaan 31 (☎673 68 50). A bare, whitewashed room smack in the middle of the smart Vondelpark neighbourhood that has amply amplified hard-core punk and new wave bands from 11pm on Thurs, jazz and blues sessions from 8.30pm on Sun night and various other sounds during the week. Tram #2.

Rum Runners, Prinsengracht 277 (☎627 40 79). Trendy Caribbean restaurant and cocktail bar in the former hall of the Westerkerk. Live (mainly laid-back Latin American) bands Sun at 10pm.

Soeterijn, Linnaeusstraat (☎568 85 00). Part of the Tropenmuseum, this theatre specializes in the drama, dance, film and music of developing countries. Admission ƒ10–20; political and ethnic films, ƒ10; ethnic dance and theatre, much of it in English, ƒ15. Tram #9, #10, #14.

The String, Nes 98 (☎625 90 15). Folk every evening in a small, centrally located bar.

Contemporary and classical

Concertgebouw, Concertgebouwplein 2 (☎671 83 45). Conducted by Ricardo Chailly, the *Concertgebouw*'s resident orchestra is one of the most dynamic in the world and after a recent facelift the building is looking and sounding better than ever. Free lunchtime concerts Sept–May (doors open 12.15pm, arrive early), and swing/jazz nights from time to time; tickets from ƒ25.

De IJsbreker, Weesperzijde 23 (☎668 18 05). Large, varied programme of international modern, chamber and experimental music. Out of the town centre near the Amstel, a great place to spend a summer afternoon; ƒ10–15. Tram #3, #6, #7, #10.

muziektheater, Amstel 3 (☎625 54 55). Via the Netherlands Opera, which is resident here, Amsterdam's fullest opera programme. Tickets ƒ23–65 and, except for weekends, go quickly. Check out the programme for free lunchtime concerts

Villa Baranka, Prins Hendrikkade 140 (☎627 64 80). New arts forum which aims to create a "salon" in a 6-storey building and which stages (mainly classical) theatre and music, poetry readings and art workshops. Performances both afternoons and evenings, but mainly confined to the weekends; ƒ10–20.

Discos and clubs

Technically, you have to be a member to **get into** some clubs (those that call themselves "societies"), though in practice this can either be waived or inexpensively arranged at the door. Most clubs open around 10pm and close up around 4am or slightly later, but there's no point in arriving before midnight. On the whole – unless stated otherwise – music is basic Top Forty fodder, drink prices normally fifty percent or so more than what you pay in a bar.

Havana Club, Reguliersdwarsstraat 17–19 (☎620 67 88). Recently opened and already very popular with a mixed clientele (gay, yuppie, art crowd). Early disco on weekdays, 4pm–1am (Fri & Sat until 2am), Sun 2pm–1am.

iT, Amstelstraat 24 (☎625 01 11). A massive and spectacular nightspot (mainly for its stunning light show) that's currently the city's number one gay disco, though it's also very popular with non-gays. Admission charge varies, but it's usually around ƒ10: be warned that it can be difficult to get into.

Mazzo, Rozengracht 114 (☎626 75 00). One of the city's hippest discos. Angular bar, video screens and a sharp, image-obsessed crowd. Live music Tues & Wed and also hosts the monthly Gay Dating show. Open every night 11pm–4/5am, admission ƒ7.50, weekends ƒ10 (includes free drink).

Odeon, Singel 460 (☎624 97 11). Two dance floors (the upstairs one only open weekends) and a stylishly elegant interior play host to an invariably yuppie gang. Open Sun–Thurs 10pm–4am, Fri & Sat 10pm–5am; ƒ7.50.

(Op de schaal van) Richter 36, Reguliersdwarsstraat 36 (☎626 15 73). This small, split-level club, supposed to resemble a building after an earthquake, draws in one of the city's most conspicuously chic crowds. Fairly flexible door policy, and host to a TV chat show. Open throughout the week midnight–5am, admission weekdays ƒ7.50, weekends ƒ10.

The Roxy, Singel 465 (☎620 03 54). Housed in an old cinema with varied music – Saturday night is currently the wildest, Wednesday night is gay. Good place to get invited to parties. Thurs–Sun 11pm–5am. Admission ƒ7.50–15, though the door policy is highly selective, and members only are admitted when it's crowded.

Film

The Dutch use subtitles for foreign films (most of which are in English) which means that language isn't a problem. Movies are very rarely dubbed into Dutch: if you want to be sure, look out for the words *Nederlands Gesproken* printed next to the title in the listings; this indicates it's been dubbed. Tickets go for about ƒ13, although *Alfa*, *Bellevue*, *Cinerama* and *De Uitkijk* have considerably reduced prices Monday to Thursday. One cinema – the extravagantly Art Deco *Tuschinski*, Reguliersbreestraat 26 – is worth visiting no matter what's showing; screen one tends to be especially interesting.

Programmes change on Friday: most bars and cafés have a weekly film schedule pinned up; otherwise check the usual listings sources, principally *Time Out*, or failing that the what's-on supplement of Thursday's *Het Parool*, Friday's *Volkskrant*, and *Uitkrant*'s *Filmagenda* section.

Theatre

Surprisingly, for a city that functions so much in English, there's only one resident English-language theatre, the *Stalhouderij*, 1e Bloemdwarrstraat 4 (☎626 22 82), which puts on a mixture of twentieth-century British and American drama alongside the classics. Check out, too, the city theatres and multimedia centres for regular English-language productions and performances by touring groups.

Shopping

You'll find much of what's available in Amsterdam's stores at home – and often more cheaply. Where Amsterdam scores, however, is in some excellent, unusual **speciality shops** (designer clocks, rubber stamps, Indonesian arts, condoms, to name just a few), a handful of good **markets** and its shopping convenience – the city's centre concentrates most of what's interesting within its tight borders.

There are few specific **shopping areas**. But broadly, **Nieuwendijk** and **Kalverstraat** are where you'll find mass-market clothes and mainstream department stores; **Rokin** and **Leidsestraat** are more pricy; the **Jordaan**, west of the centre, is home to more specialized, more adventurous clothes stores; while to the south, **P. C. Hooftstraat**, **Van Baerlestraat** and **Beethovenstraat** play host to designer clothiers, upmarket ceramics stores, confectioners and delicatessens. There's also the **Spiegelkwaartier**, centre of Amsterdam's antiques trade, which cuts through the main canals near the Rijksmuseum. Many of the most interesting and more specialized shops are scattered among the small streets which connect the main canals.

As for **hours**, most shops take Monday morning off, and open the rest of the week from 9am to 6 or 6.30pm, 9am to 5pm on Saturday and close all day Sunday; late opening (till 9pm) is on Thursday. Larger shops accept **payment** by one of the major credit cards, and most shops will accept Eurocheques. None accept travellers' cheques.

Department stores

De Bijenkorf, Dam 1. Dominating the northern corner of Dam Square, this is the city's top shop, a huge bustling place that has an indisputably wide range and little of the snobbishness of a place like Bergdorfs – or even *Metz* (see below).

HEMA, Nieuwendijk 174; Reguliersbreestraat 10. A kind of Dutch Woolworths, but of a better quality: good for stocking up on toiletries and other essentials, and occasional designer delights.

Metz & Co., Keizersgracht 455. By far the city's swishest store, with the accent on Liberty prints, stylish ceramics and designer furniture. If your funds won't stretch quite that far, settle for a cup of coffee in the top floor Rietveld restaurant, which offers great views over the canals. No credit cards.

Vroom & Dreesmann, Kalverstraat 201–221 & 212–224. The main Amsterdam branch of the middle-ground nationwide chain. Again, useful for essentials.

Books, magazines and card shops

Though prices are higher than at home, virtually all Amsterdam bookshops stock at least a small selection of **English-language books**, and in the city centre it's possible to pick up the *International Herald Tribune*, *USA Today* and most English **newspapers** the day they come out; English-language **magazines**, too, are available from newsstands and bookshops.

A la Carte, Utrechtsestraat 110–112. Travel guides and maps.

Allert de Lange, Damrak 62. Perhaps Amsterdam's best bookstore, with a great stock of Penguins, a marvellous travel section and an informed staff.

Art Unlimited, Keizersgracht 510. Enormous card and poster shop. Good for communiqués home that don't involve windmills.

Athenaeum, Spui 14–16. Excellent all-round bookstore, with a more adventurous stock than Doubleday's.

Bruna. A nationwide chain, and a safe bet for popular paperbacks and mainstream newspapers and magazines. Branches all over town; for the nearest, look in the phonebook under *Bruna*.

The English Bookshop, Lauriergracht 71. Exclusively English-language bookstore with a small but quirky collection of titles, many of which you won't find elsewhere.

W. H. Smith, Kalverstraat 152. Dutch branch of the UK high-street chain – a predictable selection but strong on travel and language, and with a useful ordering service. Prices are sometimes cheaper than in regular Dutch bookshops.

Cheap and secondhand clothes

Amsterdam has a fair array of one-off, individually run places, youth-oriented clothes stores and/or **secondhand clothing** stores in the Jordaan, on Nieuwe Hoogstraat (a handful) or along the narrow streets that connect the major canals west of the city centre. The Waterlooplein flea market (see below) is also an excellent hunting ground for second-hand clothes.

The End, Nieuwe Hoogstraat 26. Unspectacular but expensive.

Jojo, Prinsenstraat 11; Huidenstraat 23. Particularly good for trench coats and Fifties jackets.

Lady Day, Hartenstraat 9. Good-quality second-hand clothes at reasonable prices.

Laura Dab, Wolvenstraat 7. Vintage clothes and lots of hats.

Puck, Nieuwe Hoogstraat 1. Vintage second-hand clothes.

Zipper, Huidenstraat 7; Nieuwe Hoogstraat 10. Mainly used clothes selected for style and quality – or so it says on the door. Prices start high.

Markets

Amsterdam's markets are more diverting than its shops. There's a fine central **flea market** on Waterlooplein, vibrant **street markets** such as the Albert Cuyp, emphasizing food and cheap clothing, and smaller **weekly markets** devoted to everything from stamps to flowers.

Albert Cuyp, Mon–Sat 9am–4.30pm. Amsterdam's best-known – and best – general market.

Bloemenmarkt, on the Singel between Muntplein and Koningsplein. Mon–Sat 9am–4.30pm. Plants and flowers, pots and bulbs, sold from stalls on floating barges. Very reasonable.

Boerenmarkt (Noordermarkt). Sat 10am–4pm. Organic produce, handicrafts, chickens, pets and exotic birds.

Lindengracht, Sat 9am–4pm. Weekly general market, good for a taste of Jordaan atmosphere.

De Looier, Elandsgracht 109. Sat–Wed 11am–7pm, Thurs 11am–9pm. Indoor antiques stalls, selling a wide variety of goods.

Nieuwemarkt, May–Sept Sun 10am–5pm. Good quality antiques.

Noordermarkt, Mon 7.30am–1.30pm. Flea market and some antiques.

Waterlooplein, daily 10am–5pm. New and second-hand clothes, antiques, junk, books and bikes. Amsterdam's biggest, best and most enjoyable browse. On Sun 10–5pm there's an antiques market.

Miscellaneous and ethnic

Perhaps more than any other place in Europe, Amsterdam is a great source of shops devoted to one particular product or interest. Here is a selection of favourites:

Condomerie Het Gulden Vlies, Warmoesstraat 141. Condoms of every shape, size and flavour imaginable. All in the best possible taste.

Electric Lady, 2e Leliedwarsstraat. Pungently 1970s collection of psychedelia of all kinds, most of it luminous..

The Head Shop, Kloveniersburgwal 39. What it says.

Jacob Hooij, Kloveniersburgwal 10–12. Homeopathic chemist with an ancient interior and a huge stock of *drop* – Dutch liquorice.

Joes Vliegerwinckel, Nieuwe Hoogstraat 19. Kites, frisbees, etc. Good to visit before visiting the Vondelpark.

Donald E. Jongejans, Noorderkerkstraat 18. Hundreds of glasses frames, none of them new, some of them very ancient. Supplied the glasses for Bertolucci's *The Last Emperor*.

't Klompenhuisje, Nieuwe Hoogstraat 9a. Amsterdam's best and brightest array of clogs.

Posthumus, St Luciensteeg 23–25. Fancy stationery, cards and, best of all, a choice of hundreds of rubber stamps.

't Winkeltje, Prinsengracht 228. Jumble of cheap glassware and crockery, candlesticks, antique tin toys, kitsch souvenirs, old apothecaries jars and flasks. Perfect for browsing.

Listings

Addresses These are written, for example, as Kloveniersburgwal 30 III, which means the third-floor apartment at no. 30 Kloveniersburgwal. The first floor is indicated by h/s (*huis*) after the number. The figures 1e or 2e before a street name are an abbreviation for *Eerste* and *Twwede* respectively – first and second streets of the same name. Dutch postal codes can be found in the directory kept at the post office, or by taking the number in purple on a large-scale *Falkplan* and putting "10" in front (note that the complete codes have a two-letter indicator as well). The canals of Herengracht, Kaizersgracht, Prinsengracht and Singel begin their numbering at the Centraal Station side of town and increase as they progress counter-clockwise.

Airlines *Aer Lingus*, Heiligeweg 14 (☎623 8620); *Air UK*, Schiphol Airport (☎601 06 33); *British Airways*, Stadhouderskade 4 (☎685 22 11); *British Midland* Strawinskylaan 1535 (☎06 022 24 26); *Canadian Pacific*, Stadhouderskade 2 (☎685 17 21); *KLM*, G. Metsustraat 2–6 (☎649 36 33; bookings ☎6747747); *NLM City Hopper*, Schiphol Airport (☎64 92 227); *Qantas*, Stadhouderskade 6 (☎683 80 810); *Transavia*, Schiphol Airport (☎60 46 518); *TWA*, Singel 540-4 (☎26 22 27).

Babysitters *Babysit Centrale Kriterion*, 2e Rozendwarsstraat 24 (☎624 58 48). Long-established agency with a high reputation, using students at least 18 years old. Inexpensive 24-hr service: *f*5–10 per hr, plus an administrative charge depending on the time of day. Book sitters between 5.30 and 7pm.

Banks and bureaux de change Amsterdam **banks** usually offer the best deal for changing money. Hours are Mon–Fri, 9am–4pm, with a few banks open on Thurs 7 – 9pm or Sat morning; all are closed on public holidays. At other times you'll need to go to one of the many **bureaux de change** scattered around town. The most useful of these is *GWK* in the Centraal Station and at Schiphol Airport (both open daily, 24hr). *Change Express* offers inferior rates, but has branches at Leidsestraat 106, Damrak 17 & 86, Kalverstraat 150 and is open daily until midnight. Beware of all other exchange places, some of which have deliberately misleading names like *GKW*. Their rates are usually appalling.

Car rental *Budget*, Overtoom 121 (☎612 60 66) or *Europcar*, Overtoom 51–53 (☎683 21 23), are slightly less expensive than *Hertz* and *Avis*, but the cheapest are such local operators as *Diks*, van Ostadestraat 278–280 (☎66 23 366), whose prices start at around *f*54 a day plus a charge per kilometre over 100km.

Churches Services in English at the *Anglican Church*, Groenburgwal 42 (☎624 88 77), Sun at 10.30am and 7.30pm; the *English Reformed Church*, Begijnhof 48(☎624 96 65), Sun at 10.30am; English Catholic Mass at the church of *St John and Ursula*, Begijnhof (☎622 19 18), on Sun at 12.15pm, May–Aug. For details of other religious services, consult the *VVV*.

Consulates/Embassies *UK*, General Koningslaan 44 (☎676 43 43); *USA*, Museumplein 19 (☎664 56 61/679 03 21).

Gay and Lesbian Amsterdam's **gay scene** focuses around the bars of Kerkstraat, Reguliersdwarstraat, Amstel and Amstelstraat, and Warmoesstraat. Among the best-known gay bars are: *Amstel Taverne*, Amstel 54; *Chez Manfred*, Halvemaansteeg 10; *Eagle*, Warmoesstraat 86; *Open*, Amstelstraat 5. **Women only/lesbian bars** include: *Het Bruine Paard*, Prinsengracht 44; *Saarein*, Elandstraat 119; and *VivrelaVie*, Amstelstraat 7. For more information on gay and lesbian matters, contact COC, Rozenstraat 8 (☎623 1192).

Launderettes *The Clean Brothers* is the best, at Jakob Van Lennepkade 179; Kerkstraat 56; and Rozengracht 59 (daily until 9pm). Other launderettes at: Warmoesstraat 30; Oude Doelenstraat 12; and Herenstraat 24. Otherwise look under *Wassalons* in the Yellow Pages.

Left luggage Centraal Station. Mon–Fri 5am–1am, Sat–Sun 6am–1am; *f*2 per item per day, bikes *f*1.65; lockers *f*3.50 for 72 hrs.

Lost property For items left on trams, buses or metro ☎551 49 11; on trains ☎557 85 44; elsewhere, try your luck at Police Lost Property, Waterlooplein 11 (Mon–Fri 11am–3.30pm; ☎559 8005).

Parking *Parking Prinsengracht*, Prinsengracht 540–542 (☎625 98 52), *f*3 per hour, around *f*20 per day. Others: *De Bijenkorf*, on Beursplein, and *Europarking*, at Marnixstraat 250. There are also underground garages at the muziektheater and Museumplein, and near Centraal Station.

Police Headquarters: Elandsgracht 117 (☎559 91 11); other central stations include Lijnbaansgracht (☎559 23 10); Warmoesstraat 44-46 (☎559 22 10).

Post Office Main offices are at Singel 250 (Mon, Tues, Wed & Fri 9am–6pm, Thurs 9am–8pm, Sat 9am–3pm; ☎556 331) and near the Centraal Station at Oosterdokskade 5 (Mon–Fri 8.30–9pm; Sat 9am–noon). Other central post offices include Keizersgracht 757; Stadhouderskade 41; Kerkstraat 167; in *Vroom & Dreesmann* at Kalverstraat 201, and *Bijenkorf*, Dam 1.

Telephones and faxes Easiest place to make calls is the *Telehouse*, Raadhuisstraat 48–50 (24hr). A discount rate on international calls is in effect between 8pm and 8am. The *Teletalk Centre*, Leidsestraat 101 (daily 10am–midnight), has phone and fax services, as well as photocopying; it also accepts credit cards for all services. Avoid small, privately run "phone first pay later" outfits, which charge exorbitant rates.

Telephone helplines In English: *AIDS Info Line* (☎06 022 2220), Mon–Fri 2–10pm; *Legal Aid* (☎548 2611); *Mental and Social Problems* (☎555 52 09); *Tram, Bus and Metro Information* (☎06/92 92).

Travel agents *NBBS* at Leidsestraat 53 (☎620 50 71); Rokin 38 (☎624 09 89); and Ceintuurbaan 294 (☎679 93 37), is the Amsterdam branch of the nationwide student/youth travel organization and the best source of *BIJ* tickets, discount flights for anyone, etc. Also worth checking out are: *Nouvelles Frontières*, van Baerlestraat 3 (☎66 44 131); *Budget Bus*, Rokin 10 (☎627 51 51); *Budget Air*, Rokin 34 (☎627 12 51).

Women's contacts Amsterdam has an impressive feminist infrastructure: there are support groups, health centres and businesses run by and for women, and there's a good range of bars and discos, a few exclusively for women. Best starting point to find out what's going on in the city is the *Vrouwenhuis*, Nieuwe Herengracht 95 (☎625 20 66; open most days at varying times), an organizing centre for women's activities/cultural events. *Villa Baranka*, Prins Hendrikkade 140 (☎627 64 80) is a cross-cultural art studio with performing art, literature and poetry readings by and for women; and *Xantippe*, Prinsengracht 290 (☎623 58 54), a women's bookshop with a wide selection of feminist titles in English.

travel details

Trains

Amsterdam to: Alkmaar (approx every 15min; 30min); Amersfoort (every 30min; 35min); Apeldoorn (every 30min; 1hr); Arnhem (every 30min; 1hr 10min); Den Bosch (every 30min; 1hr); Den Helder (every 30min; 1hr 10min); Dordrecht (every 30min; 1hr 30min); Eindhoven (every 30min; 1hr 30min); Enkhuizen (every 30min; 55min); Groningen (every 30min; 2hr 20min); Haarlem (every 10min; 15min); The Hague (approx every 15min; 47min); Hoorn (every 30min; 40min); Leeuwarden (hourly; 2hr 25min); Leiden (approx every 15min; 33min); Maastricht (hourly; 2hr 30min); Middelburg (hourly; 2hr 35min); Nijmegen (every 30min; 1hr 30min); Roosendaal (every 30min; 1hr 45min); Rotterdam (every 30min; 1hr 10min); Schiphol (every 10 min; 20min); Utrecht (every 30min; 30min); Vlissingen (hourly; 2hr 45min); Zwolle (hourly; 1hr 20min).

International trains

Amsterdam to: Antwerp (hourly; 2hr 15min); Brussels (hourly; 3hr); Cologne (8 daily; 3hr); London (4 daily; 10–12hr); Paris (5 daily; 6hr).

CHAPTER TWO

NORTH HOLLAND

The province of **North Holland** is one of the country's most explored regions. Though not as densely populated as its sister province to the south, it's still a populous area, and holds some of Holland's prime tourist attractions. The landscape is typically Dutch, the countryside north of Amsterdam for the most part a familiar polder scene of flat fields, cut by trenches and canals, stretching far into the distance, the vast horizons broken occasionally by the odd farmhouse or windmill. Lining most of the western coast are rugged areas of dune and long and broad sandy beaches, while on the other side the coast of the IJsselmeer, formerly the Zuider Zee, is home to old ports turned yachting communities, which sport the vestiges of a glorious past in picturesquely preserved town centres.

As with much of South Holland, and indeed parts of provinces further afield, the majority of North Holland is easily visited by means of day trips from Amsterdam. But to do this would be to only skim the surface of the region. The urban highlight is undoubtedly **Haarlem**, a very easy day trip from Amsterdam but definitely worth treating as an overnight stop. It also gives access to some wild stretches of dune and beach, and one of the country's largest coastal resorts in **Zandvoort. Alkmaar**, too, to the north, is usually visited by day-excursionists from Amsterdam who come to see its rather bogus ceremonial Friday cheese market, but is worth taking in for longer if you're keen to experience small-town provincial Holland. In the eastern part of the province, the villages nearest Amsterdam – **Marken**, **Volendam** and **Edam** – are kitsch places full of tourists in search of clogs and windmills during summer, and probably worth avoiding at any time of year. Further north, towns like **Hoorn** and **Enkhuizen** are of more interest, formerly major Zuider Zee ports, now pretty towns with yacht-filled harbours that again make either a good day trip from Amsterdam, or pleasant stops if you're travelling up to Friesland by car and are in no hurry. In the far north of the province, the island of **Texel** is the most accessible and busiest of the Wadden Sea islands. It's very crowded during summer, but don't be put off by the numbers: with a bit of walking you can find places well off the beaten tourist track – and far away from the hustle of Amsterdam.

ACCOMMODATION PRICE CODES

All the **hotels and hostels** detailed in this chapter have been graded according to the following price categories. Note that the prices have been calculated as those for the cheapest double room during high season. For more on accommodation, see p.29.

① Up to ƒ30 per person.	④ ƒ100–140.	⑦ ƒ220–260.
② ƒ30–65.	⑤ ƒ140–180.	⑧ ƒ260 and over.
③ ƒ65–100.	⑥ ƒ180–220.	

Transport in North Holland is, as ever, by a mixture of train to the main centres and then bus. For moving on, there's a fast road link along the top of the twenty-kilometre-long dike between Enkhuizen and Lelystad, on the reclaimed Flevoland polders. It was completed in 1976, the first stage of a plan to reclaim the enclosed area in the so-called **Markerwaard** scheme. This met considerable opposition when proposed and has now been indefinitely postponed (you'll still see posters and graffiti against the plan in places like Hoorn and Enkhuizen), but the road it spawned is still a useful way of getting to the east of the country without passing through Amsterdam.

Het Gooi: Muiden, Naarden and Hilversum

Most of the province of North Holland is located, logically enough, north of Amsterdam. But the borders of the province also dip down beneath the capital, taking in Schiphol and parts of the bulb-growing areas (covered in the following chapter) and a suburban agglomeration which sprawls east toward Amersfoort. This is known as **Het Gooi**, an area which was mostly devoted to sheep-farming until 1874, when the Amsterdam–Amersfoort railway was built and the wealthy burghers of Amsterdam began to build mansions among the region's lakes, woods and heather. It remains a popular escape for weekending Amsterdammers, though it has to be said the area is hardly essential viewing. If, however, you have time on your hands in Amsterdam and have seen all the more obvious attractions, a couple of low-key towns might draw your attention – not to mention some modern architectural highlights further east.

Muiden and Naarden

The first town you reach, **MUIDEN** is squashed around the Vecht, a river usually crammed with pleasure boats and dinghies sailing out to the IJmeer and beyond to the IJsselmeer. It's the most famous sailing harbour in the Gooi area, not least because the royal yacht, *De Groene Draek*, is often moored here. As well as the harbour, there are a couple of beaches on the IJmeer – Muiderberg and Muiderzand – and, although most of the sightseeing is done by weekend admirals eyeing up each other's boats, the **Muiderslot** (April–Sept Mon–Fri 10am–5pm, Sun 1–5pm; Oct–March Mon–Fri 10am–4pm, Sun 1–4pm; *f*5) provides an extra spark of interest. In the thirteenth century this was the home of Count Floris V, a sort of aristocratic Robin Hood who favoured the common people at the nobles' expense. They replied by kidnapping the count, imprisoning him in his own castle and stabbing him to death. Destroyed and rebuilt in the fourteenth century, Muiderslot's interior is these days a recreation of the period of a slightly more recent occupant, the poet Pieter Hooft. He was chatelain here from 1609 to 1647, a sinecure that allowed him to entertain a group of artistic and literary friends who became known as the Muiden Circle, and included Grotius, Vondel, Huygens and other Amsterdam intellectuals. The obligatory guided tours (April–Sept every 15 min, Oct–March hourly) centre on this clique, in a restoration that is both believable and likable – two things period rooms generally aren't.

From the jetty outside the Muiderslot, boats leave regularly for the fortress island of **Pampus**, a few kilometres out to sea. It was built at the end of the nineteenth century as part of Amsterdam's defence system, but has now fallen into ruin. Otherwise the VVV, Kazernestraat 10 (April–Sept Mon–Fri 10am–5pm, Sat 10am–1pm; ☎02942/61389), will be able to tell you where to rent watersports equipment. If you fancy pottering around in boats, the *Muiden Jachtverhuur Station* (MYCS), Naarderstraat 10 (☎02942/61413), rents out sailing boats, and *Van Deursen* at Herengracht 119 (☎02942/61385) rents rowing boats. Incidentally, if you want to bypass Muiden, and simply spend a day on the beach, you can get to Muiderberg directly from Amsterdam on bus #136.

Look at a postcard of **NAARDEN**, about 10km east, and it seems as if the town was formed by a giant pastry-cutter: the double rings of ramparts and moats, unique in Europe, were engineered between 1675 and 1685 to defend Naarden and the eastern approach to Amsterdam. They were still used in the 1920s, and one of the fortified spurs is now the wonderfully explorable **Fortification Museum** at Westwalstraat 6 (April–Oct Mon–Fri 10am–4.30pm, Sat & Sun noon–5pm; *f*3.50), whose claustrophobic underground passages show how the garrison defended the town for 250 years.

The rest of Naarden's tiny centre is peaceful rather than dull. The small, low houses mostly date from after 1572 when the Spanish sacked the town and massacred the inhabitants, an act designed to warn other settlements in the area against insurrection. Fortunately they spared the late Gothic **Grote Kerk** (June to mid-Sept daily 2–4pm) and its superb vault paintings. Based on drawings by Dürer, these twenty wooden panels were painted between 1510 and 1518 and show an Old Testament story on the south side, paralleled by one from the New Testament on the north. To study the paintings without breaking your neck, borrow a mirror at the entrance. A haul up the Grote Kerk's **tower** (May–Aug hourly tours 1–4pm; *f*3) gives the best view of the fortress island, and, less attractively, of Hilversum's TV tower.

If you've never heard of Jan Amos Komenski, or Comenius, a seventeenth-century polymath and educational theorist, it's unlikely that the **Comenius Museum** at Turfpoortstraat 27 (guided tours only Nov–March Tues–Sun 2–5pm; April–Oct Tues–Sat 10am–5pm, Sun noon–5pm; *f*2.50) will fire your enthusiasm for the man. A religious exile from Moravia (now in the Czech Republic), Comenius lived in Amsterdam and is buried in Naarden. He's a national hero to the Czechs; they donated most of the exhibits in the museum and also constructed his **Mausoleum** in the **Waalse Kapel** on Kloosterstraat – a building permanently on loan to the Czech people. If you want to see it, the museum guide will take you there.

Practicalities

CN bus #136 leaves Amsterdam every half hour from Weesperplein, stopping first at Muiden (travel time 40min) then Naarden (55min). The Naarden VVV is at Adriaan Dortmansplein 1b (May–Sept Mon–Fri 9am–5pm, Sat 10am–4pm, Sun noon–4pm; Oct–April Mon–Fri 9am–5pm, Sat 10am–2pm, closed Sun; ☎02159/42836).

Hilversum

The main town of Het Gooi is **HILVERSUM**, a nineteenth-century commuter suburb for wealthy Amsterdammers, who created a well-heeled smugness that survives to this day. Their villas have been flashily converted into studios for

Dutch broadcasting companies, and behind the neatly trimmed hedges and lace curtains live some of the country's more comfortably off.

One of the villas, the former studio of a radio broadcasting company, has been converted into the **Omroepmuseum**, at Oude Amersfoortseweg 121–131 (Tues–Fri 10am–5pm, Sat & Sun noon–5pm), which has displays and videos on Dutch broadcasting history. The **Het Goois Museum**, Kerkbrink 6 (Tues–Sun 12.30–4.30pm; *f*1.75) details the history of the Gooi, the area around Hilversum. However, the main sight is really the town's **Raadhuis** of 1931, at Dudokpark 1; the work of the Frank Lloyd Wright-influenced architect W.M. Dudok, it's a deceptively simple progression of straw-coloured blocks rising to a clock tower, with long, slender bricks giving a strong horizontal emphasis to the buildings. The interior (open office hours) is worth seeing, designed as a series of lines and boxes, marble walls margined with black like an uncoloured Mondrian painting, all coolly and immaculately proportioned. Dudok also designed the interior decorations, and though some have been altered, his style confidently continues, even down to the ashtrays and lights.

Practicalities

Dudok was Hilversum's principal architect, and both the Goois Museum and **VVV**, near the station at Emmastraat 2 (mid-May to mid-Sept Mon 9.30am–5.30pm, Tues–Fri 9am–5.30pm, Sat 9am–3pm; mid-Sept to mid-May Mon–Fri 9am–5pm, Sat 9am–2pm; ☎035/211651), sell a walking guide to the many other buildings he designed in the town. The *VVV* can also help with **rooms**, though with Amsterdam so close, and connections onto more interesting towns so easy, there's little reason to stay. As usual, you can **rent bikes** most conveniently at Hilversum's train station; alternatively try *Firma Kok*, Koninginnweg 76–78 (closed Sun & Mon; ☎035/24 57 24), *Hunting*, Neuweg 48 (closed Sun; ☎035/21 45 72) or *Bonhof*, Eikbosserweg 126 (closed Sun; ☎035/21 48 51).

Around Hilversum: exploring Het Gooi

Hilversum makes a good base for seeing the best of **Het Gooi** (which you can easily do in a day), and the *VVV* sells an excellent walking and cycling map of the area, *"Wandel- en fietskaart Gooi en Vechtstreek"* (*f*8,50), which, although not in English, details good walking routes as well as the well-signposted *ANWB* "Gooiroute" – a thirty-kilometre-long cycling route that leads across the heather to Laren, then via Blaricum to Huizen on the shore of the Gooimeer, and back via the woods to Hilversum. To get to the route from Hilversum train station, cross the rail line and continue along this road until just after you've crossed a round-about, where you'll find the first "Gooiroute" signpost at a small road to the right.

The most attractive village in Het Gooi proper is **LAREN**, halfway between Hilversum and the Gooimeer, if only because of its excellent **Singer-Museum** of modern art at Oude Drift 1 (Tues–Sat 11am–5pm, Sun noon–5pm; *f*6). A sheep-farming community for centuries, Laren became fashionable with artists in the 1870s, notably those of the Impressionist Hague School, and the surrounding landscape, as well as the village's farmers and weavers, and even the interiors of their farmhouses, all appear in their paintings. In later years Expressionist and Modernist painters also came to the Laren area, and their works were gathered together by the Singers, an American couple who moved from Pittsburgh to

Laren in 1901. The museum, which is based on their collection, opened in 1956 and, as well as paintings by Laren artists, contains works from France and America.

As for the rest of the town, its shady streets and diminutive houses centre around the main square of Brink, which has several pleasant bars and an outdoor pancake restaurant. On one side of Brink the **St Jans Basiliek**, built in 1925, is the starting-point of the St Jans procession, one of the many festivals celebrated in Laren.

If you want to sail or windsurf, head for the small town of **HUIZEN**, situated on the Gooimeer and known for its favourable windsurfing conditions. It has three modern yacht harbours and two beaches – **Zomerkade**, reputedly the most beautiful beach on the IJsselmeer, and **Stichtsebrug**, a little further out, which is better for windsurfing. Boards and sailing boats can be rented from *EHZ* at Kooizand 70 (☎02152/55055). For more information on the area, call into the VVV in the town hall at Graaf Wichman 10 (Mon–Fri 8.30am–5pm; ☎02152/81227).

Haarlem and around

Though only fifteen minutes from Amsterdam by train, **HAARLEM** has a quite different pace and feel from the capital, an easily absorbed city of around 150,000 people that sees itself as a step above its neighbours. If you've any time at all to spare you'd be mad to miss it. The Frans Hals Museum, in the almshouse where the artist spent his last – and for some his most brilliant – years, is worth an afternoon in itself; there are numerous beaches within easy reach, as well as some of the best of the bulbfields (see the following chapter, *South Holland and Utrecht*). In short, if you're tired of the crowds and grime of Amsterdam, Haarlem makes a good alternative base for exploring North Holland, or even the capital itself.

Arrival, information and accommodation

The **train station** is located on the north side of the city, about ten minutes' walk from the centre; **buses** stop right outside. The VVV, attached to the station (April–Sept Mon–Sat 9am–5.30pm; Oct–March Mon–Fri 9am–5.30pm, Sat 10am–4pm; ☎31 90 59), has maps (50c) and can book **private rooms** for a ƒ7 fee, though you'll find more choice in Zandvoort, about twenty minutes away by bus #80 (every 15min/30min from Tempelierstraat) or #81 (every 30min from the train station). The same goes for **hotels**, although Haarlem has a few reasonably priced places worth considering, like the *Carillon*, centrally placed at Grote Markt 27 (☎31 05 91; ③), and the *Waldor*, close to the station at Jansweg 40 (☎31 26 22; ③). There's also a **youth hostel** at Jan Gijzenpad 3 (open March–Oct; ☎37 37 93); bus #2 or #6 runs frequently from the station – a ten-minute journey. **Campers** should either try the campsites among the dunes along Zeeweg out at Bloemendaal-aan-zee (bus #81), though these tend to be open during spring and summer only, or Haarlem's own site, *Camping Haarlem*, at Liewegie 17, which is open all year – to get there take bus #80 from Tempelierstraat.

The Haarlem area telephone code is ☎023

The Town

For a long time the residence of the counts of Holland, Haarlem was sacked by the Spanish under Frederick of Toledo in 1572. There are reminders of this all over the town, since, after a seven-month siege, the revenge exacted by the inconvenienced Frederick was terrible: very nearly the whole population was massacred, including the entire Protestant clergy. Recaptured in 1577 by William the Silent, Haarlem went on to enjoy its greatest prosperity in the seventeenth century, becoming a centre for the arts and home to a flourishing school of painters.

Nowadays, the place retains an air of quiet affluence, with all the picturesque qualities of Amsterdam but little of the sleaze. The core of the city is **Grote Markt**, an open space flanked by a concentration of Gothic and Renaissance architecture, most notably the gabled and balconied **Stadhuis**, at one end. This dates from the fourteenth century, though it has been much rebuilt over the years, the last time in 1630 – a date recorded on the facade. Inside, the main hall is normally left open for visitors during office hours; it's decorated with a few fifteenth-century paintings. At the other end of Grote Markt there's a statue of one **Laurens Coster**, who, Haarlemmers insist, is the true inventor of printing. Legend tells of him cutting a letter "A" from the bark of a tree and dropping it into the sand by accident. Plausible enough, but most authorities seem to agree that Gutenburg was the more likely source of the printed word.

Coster stands in the shadow of the **Grote Kerk of St Bavo** (Mon–Sat 10am–4pm; closes at 3.30pm between Oct & Jan; ƒ2), where he is believed to be buried. If you've been to the Rijksmuseum, the church may seem familiar, at least from the outside, since it was the principal focus of the seventeenth-century painter Berckheyde's many views of this square – only the black-coated burghers are missing. Finished in the early sixteenth century, it dwarfs the surrounding clutter of streets and houses, and serves as a landmark from almost anywhere in the city. Inside, it is breathtakingly high, its beauty enhanced by the bare, white-painted power of the Gothic vaulting. The mighty Christian Müller organ of 1738 is said to have been played by Handel and Mozart and is one of the biggest in the world, with five thousand pipes and razzamatazz Baroque embellishment. (Organ recitals are given every Tues evening between mid-May and mid-Sept.) Beneath the organ, Xaverij's lovely group of draped marble figures represents Poetry and Music, offering thanks to the town, depicted as a patroness of the arts, for her generosity, while in the choir there's a late fifteenth-century painting that the church traditionally (though dubiously) attributes to Geertgen tot Sint Jans, along with memorials to painters Pieter Saenredam and Frans Hals – both of whom are buried here. Outside, at the western end of the church, the **Vishal** and, opposite that, Lieven de Key's profusely decorated **Vleeshal** (the former fish and meat markets) hold regular art exhibitions (Mon–Sat 10am–5pm, Sun 1–5pm; free).

The Frans Hals Museum

Haarlem's chief attraction, the **Frans Hals Museum** at Groot Heiligland 62 (Mon–Sat 10am–5pm, Sun 1–5pm; ƒ6), is just a five-minute stroll from Grote Markt, housed in the Oudemannenhuis almshouse where the aged Hals is supposed to have lived out his last destitute years on public funds. Little is known

HAARLEM

VERSPRONCKWEG

The Bastions

KENNEMER PLEIN

ROZENSTRAAT

VVV

STATIONS PLEIN

Train Station

KRUISWEG

JANSWEG

Kenau Park

LANGE HERENSTRAAT

PARKLAAN

Nieuwegracht

HOOIMARKT

Binnen Spaarne

RIDDERSTRAAT

Kinderhuissingel

KINDERHUIS VEST

NASSAULAAN

KRUISSTRAAT

JANSSTRAAT

BAKENESSER GRACHT

KOUDENHORN

WILHELMINASTRAAT

GROENMARKT

ZIJLSTRAAT

BARTELJORISTRAAT

SMEDESTRAAT

Waalsekerk

Teylers Hofje

RAAKS

Post Office

GEDEMPTE RAAM GRACHT

Stadhuis

GROTEMARKT

Vishal Vleeshal

OUDE GROENMARKT

Grote Kerke of St. Bavo

VROUWESTRAAT

Bakenesserkerk

Teylers Museum

Waag

DAMSTRAAT

KOMMESTRAAT

BOTERMARKT

GIERSTRAAT

GROTE HOUTSTRAAT

ANEGANG

LANGE VEERSTR

GEDEMPTE OUDE GRACHT

KLEIN HEILIGLAND

GROOT HEILIGLAND

KLEINE HOUTSTRAAT

Nieuwe Kerk

NIEUWE RAAMSTRAAD

Frans Hals Museum

RAAM VEST

KAMPER VEST

GASTHUIS VEST

Kampersingel

To Cathedral of St. Bavo

HOUTPLEIN

about Frans Hals. Born in Antwerp, the son of Flemish refugees who settled in Haarlem in the late 1580s, his extant *oeuvre* is relatively small: some two hundred paintings and nothing like the number of sketches and studies left behind by Rembrandt – partly because Hals wasn't fashionable until the nineteenth century, and a lot of his work was lost before it became collectable. His outstanding gift was as a portraitist, showing a sympathy with his subjects and an ability to capture fleeting expression that some say even Rembrandt lacked. Seemingly quick and careless flashes of colour form a coherent whole, leaving us a set of seventeenth-century figures that are curiously alive.

The museum begins with the work of other artists: first a small group of **sixteenth-century works**, the most prominent a triptych by Gerard David, and an early anti-imperialist painting – *West Indian Scene* by Jan Mostaert, in which the naked natives try fruitlessly to defend themselves against the cannon and sword of their invaders. Van Scorel's *Baptism of Christ* and *Knights of Jerusalem* follow, along with works by van Goyen, Brouwer and van Ostade, and a good group of paintings by the **Haarlem mannerists**, including works by Carel van Mander, leading light of the Haarlem School and mentor of many of the other painters represented here. Cornelis Cornelisz van Haarlem best follows van Mander's guidelines: *The Marriage of Peleus and Thetis* was a popular subject at the time, probably because it was interpreted as a warning against discord, appropriate during the long war with Spain – though Cornelisz gives as much attention to the arrangement of elegant nudes as to his subject. The same is true of his *Massacre of the Innocents*, which could refer to the siege of Haarlem just twenty years earlier.

Frans Hals was a pupil of van Mander too, though he seems to have learned little more than the barest rudiments from him. His paintings in the west wing – a set of "Civic Guard" portraits of the companies initially formed to defend the country from the Spanish, later on just local social clubs – established his reputation as a portraitist and earned him a regular income. There was a special skill involved in painting these: for the first time Hals made the group portrait a unified whole instead of a static collection of individual portraits; his figures are carefully arranged, but so cleverly as not to appear contrived. For a time, Hals himself was a member of the Company of Saint George, and in the *Officers of the Militia Company of Saint George* he appears in the top left-hand corner – one of his few self-portraits.

After this, there are numerous scenes of Haarlem by Berckheyde and Saenredam, among others; landscapes by the Ruisdaels and Berchem; and some group portraits by Veerspronck and the elderly Frans Hals. Hals' later paintings are darker, more contemplative works, closer to Rembrandt in their lighting. The *Governors of the Saint Elizabeth Gasthuis*, painted in 1641, is a good example, as are the portraits of the *Regents* and *Regentesses of the Oudemannhuis* itself – perhaps the museum's finest treasures. These were commissioned when Hals was in his eighties, a poor man despite a successful painting career, hounded for money by the town's tradesmen and by the mothers of his illegitimate children, and dependent on the charity of people like those depicted here. Their cold, hard faces stare out of the gloom, the women reproachful, the men only slightly more affable. The character just right of centre in the *Regents* painting has been labelled (and indeed looks) completely drunk, although it is inconceivable that Hals would have depicted him in this condition; it's more likely that he was suffering from some kind of facial paralysis, and his violently cocked hat was simply a popular fashion of the time. There are those who claim Hals had lost his firm touch by the time he painted these pictures, yet the sinister, almost ghostly power of these paintings, facing each other across the room, suggests quite the opposite. Van Gogh's remark that "Frans Hals had no fewer than 27 blacks" suddenly makes perfect sense.

Other galleries hold lesser works by lesser artists. There's a new wing, which houses temporary exhibitions, usually of modern and contemporary artists, and permanent paintings by Israëls, Appel and Jan Sluyters – though lamentably few of the latter. More interesting is the Oudemannhuis itself, a fairly typical *hofje* whose style of low buildings and peaceful courtyards you'll see repeated with slight variations all over town – and indeed the country. Classical concerts are often held here regularly throughout the year except June–August, usually in the afternoon on the third Sunday of each month, though they were stopped in 1993. To find out if they're starting up again, phone ☎31 91 80.

The *hofjes* ... and Haarlem's other sights

As for the rest of town, Haarlem has a greater number of **hofjes** than most Dutch cities – proof of the town's prosperity in the seventeenth century. The VVV can give information on where to find them; most are still inhabited, so you're confined to looking around the courtyard, but the women who sit outside seem used to the occasional visitor and won't throw you out.

Second in the pecking order of Haarlem sights, the **Teylers Museum**, at Spaarne 16 (Tues–Sat 10am–5pm, Sun 1–5pm; *f*6.50), is Holland's oldest museum, founded in 1778 by wealthy local philanthropist Pieter Teyler van der Hulst. This should appeal to scientific and artistic tastes alike, containing everything from fossils, bones and crystals, to weird, H.G. Wells-type technology (including an enormous eighteenth-century electrostatic generator) and sketches and line drawings by Michelangelo, Raphael, Rembrandt and Claude, among others. The drawings are covered for protection from the light, but don't be afraid to pull back the curtains and peek. Look in, too, on the rooms beyond, filled with work by eighteenth- and nineteenth-century Dutch painters, principally Breitner, Israëls, Weissenbruch and, not least, Wijbrand Hendriks, who was the keeper of the art collection here.

Teyler also lent his charity to the **Teyler's Hofje**, a little way east around the bend of the Spaarne at Koudenhorn 64, a solid, late eighteenth-century building that is more monumental in style than the town's other *hofjes*. Nearby, the elegant tower of the **Bakenesser Kerk** forms the other main protrusion on the Haarlem skyline, a late fifteenth-century church which is usually kept closed. Two other sights which may help structure your wanderings are on the opposite side of town. Van Campen's **Nieuwe Kerk** was built – rather unsuccessfully – onto Lieven de Key's bulbed, typically Dutch tower in 1649, though the interior is symmetrical with a soberness that is quite chilling after the soaring heights of the Grote Kerk. Just beyond, and much less self-effacing, the Roman Catholic **Cathedral of St Bavo** (April–Oct Mon–Sat 10am–noon & 2–4.30pm) is one of the largest ecclesiastical structures in Holland, designed by Joseph Cuijpers and built between 1895 and 1906. It's broad and spacious inside, cupolas and turrets crowding around an apse reminiscent of Byzantine churches or mosques, the whole surmounted by a distinctive copper dome.

Eating and drinking

For **lunches and snacks**, try *Café Mephisto*, Grote Markt 29, which is open all day and serves Dutch food for *f*12–20, snacks for much less. *Café 1900*, Barteljorisstraat 10, is also a good place for lunch, a trendy locals' hangout serving drinks and light meals in an impressive turn-of-the-century interior (it also has live music on Sundays); *H. Ferd. Kuipers* is an excellent patisserie and tearoom at Barteljorisstraat 22. In the evening, there's *Alfonso's* Mexican restaurant just behind the Grote Kerk at Oude Groenmarkt 8, which serves Tex-Mex meals for around *f*19; the *Piccolo* restaurant, Riviervischmarkt 1, serves pasta and decent pizzas from *f*10; or try the Indonesian food at *De Lachende Javaen*, on Frankestraat, which serves *rijsttaffels* from *f*32 per person.

Once you've eaten, *Ze Crack*, at the junction of Lange Veerstraat and Kleine Houtstraat, is a dim, smoky **bar** with good music and – unsurprisingly perhaps – lots of English people and beer by the pint if you want it. On the same street, closer to Grote Markt at Lange Veerstraat 9, *'t Ouwe Proef* is more typically Dutch, a *proeflokaal* that also sells beer – lively early evening.

Around Haarlem

You'll find most of interest **west** of Haarlem. Take bus #80 from Tempelierstraat which runs via Bloemendaal-aan-Zee to Zandvoort, or bus #81 from the train station, which runs directly to Zandvoort. The moneyed Haarlem outskirts quickly give way to the thick woodland and rugged dune landscape of the **Kennemerduinen National Park**, which stretches down to the sea. **BLOEMENDAAL-AAN-ZEE** is the rather grandiose name for a group of beachside shacks that house a thriving ice-cream trade, while a little further south, **ZANDVOORT**, an agglomeration of modern and faceless apartment complexes that rise out of the dunes, is a major Dutch seaside resort. As resorts go it's pretty standard – packed and oppressive in summer, depressingly dead in winter. The best reason to visit is the championship motor racing circuit, which provides background noise to everyone's sunbathing. If you come for the beach, and manage to fight your way through the crush to the water, watch out – the sea here is murky and ominously close to the smoky chimneys of **IJMUIDEN** to the north. This is a sprawling, depressing town, with a modern centre spread along the wide North Sea Canal. The part around the enormous sea locks and fishing harbour is of most interest, but the detour isn't really worth making.

A few miles **north** of Haarlem, **SPAARNDAM** is well known for its statue commemorating the boy who saved the country from disaster by sticking his finger in a hole in the dike. This tale has no basis at all in reality and few Dutch people even know it, but it had a sufficient ring of truth for a little-known American writer to weave a story around it, and so create a legend. The monument to the heroic little chap was unveiled in 1950 – more, it seems, as a tribute to the opportunistic Dutch tourist industry than anything else.

Continuing north, the train line cuts up through unrelenting suburbia to **BEVERWIJK**, not much of a place in itself but very much worth a visit if you're staying in either Haarlem or Alkmaar (or even Amsterdam) for its weekend **market** (Sat 7am–5pm, Sun 9am–5pm; *f*4) – a Turkish/Middle Eastern bazaar basically, rather incongruously situated on the outskirts of town in a number of large warehouses on an industrial estate. People come from all over the surrounding area at weekends to buy cheap hi-fi and clothes, leatherwear, Turkish clothes and *rai* cassettes from a huge number of stalls. There are places, too, selling spices, olives, turkish delight and dried fruits, as well as some excellent – and authentic – places to eat, serving up shoarma and thin, crispy Turkish pizzas, spread with minced meat, at tables on which huge pots of chilli and yoghurt are arranged. The market is a fifteen-minute walk from the train station – turn right out of the station, first right under the motorway and first left onto Parallelweg; follow this for 500m or so and turn right onto Buitenlanden. Alternatively jump on a bus bearing the legend Zwartemarkt, which trundles regularly between the station and the market.

North of Amsterdam

The polders immediately north of Amsterdam and the small towns and villages that line the IJsselmeer are almost enforcedly quaint. The area is a favourite for day-trippers from Amsterdam, who arrive here by way of numerous bus excursions from the capital, and parts at least can be packed to the gills during the summer. The meadows and canals of Waterland, immediately north of Amsterdam have a certain charm, especially if you're touring by bicycle, but don't expect anything too pristine if you're heading up to the tourist towns that line the banks of the IJsselmeer.

Zaandam, Zaanse Schans and Purmerend

Most of the trains heading north from Amsterdam pass through the build-up of settlements that spreads north from the banks of the IJ and is known as **ZAANSTAD**. Looking out of the train window, it's arguable that there's no real reason to get off, and you really wouldn't be missing all that much if you didn't. But some people take an hour or so out to visit the central core of Zaanstad, known as **ZAANDAM**, a small, largely modern town that was a popular tourist hangout in the nineteenth century, when it was known as "La Chine d'Hollande" for the faintly oriental appearance of its windmills, canals, masts and row upon row of brightly painted houses. Claude Monet spent some time here in the 1870s, and, despite being suspected of spying and under constant police surveillance, immortalized the place in a series of paintings.

Follow the main street of Gedempte Gracht from the train station for five minutes, turn right down Damstraat, right again and left down Krimp, and you can see something of this former look, the harbour spiked with masts beyond a little grouping of wooden houses. On Krimp itself is Zaandam's main claim to fame, the **Czaar Petershuisje** (Jan–Nov Tues–Fri 10am–5pm, Sat & Sun 1–5pm; Dec Sat & Sun only 1–5pm; *f*1.50), a house in which the Russian Tsar Peter the Great stayed when he came to study shipbuilding here. In those days Zaandam was an important centre for shipbuilding, and the tsar made four visits to the town, the first in 1697 when he arrived incognito and stayed in the simple home of one Gerrit Kist, who had formerly served with him. A tottering wooden structure enclosed within a brick shelter, the house is no more than two rooms really, decorated with a handful of portraits of the benign-looking emperor and the graffiti of tourists that goes back to the mid-nineteenth century. Among the few things to see is the cupboard bed in which Peter is supposed to have slept, together with the calling cards and pennants of various visiting Russian delegations; around the outside of the house is a display on the shipbuilding industry in Zaandam. As Napoleon is supposed to have remarked on visiting the house, "Nothing is too small for great men".

Most visitors to Zaanstad are, however, here to visit **ZAANSE SCHANS** (April–Oct daily 9am–5pm; rest of the year the site is open but the individual museums and exhibitions are not; admission free, but entrance to exhibitions and museums costs 25c–f3.50 apiece), a re-created Dutch village made up of houses, windmills and workshops assembled from all over the country. An energetic, but ultimately rather fake attempt to reproduce a Dutch village as it would have looked at the end of the seventeenth century, it's a pretty enough place, but it gets crammed in summer, and is frankly not worth the bother for its clogmaking displays and pseudo artisans' premises. However, it does represent the closest chance to Amsterdam to see windmills if that's what you're after, some of them working mills grinding mustard and producing oil. Among other specific attractions are a clock museum and period rooms, and you can also take boat trips on the river (April–Sept 10am–5pm). To get to Zaanse Schans from Zaandam, take bus #97; the same bus runs direct from Amsterdam (Marnixstraat) – an hour's trip in all.

Further up the tracks from Zaandam, **PURMEREND** has a once-weekly summer cheese market on Thursday at 11am – a slightly less crowded affair than its counterpart at Alkmaar. That apart, though, there's not much reason to stop. Purmerend is a rather dull suburb of Amsterdam these days, and aside from a local museum, it has little of much interest.

Waterland

Directly north of Amsterdam, just through the city's northern suburbs, **Waterland** is an endless expanse of green peat meadows peppered with pretty villages. Despite its proximity to the city, very few tourists come to visit, making it an ideal – and easy – escape from the capital, especially if you opt to see all, or part, by bike.

A thousand years ago this land was a vast, high fen area with numerous little streams flowing through it and it's only this century that it actually became habitable, due to a combination of drought and the digging of drainage canals by the first settlers – a process which in fact lowered the water level and made it extremely flood prone (although the last major flood here was way back in 1916). Regular floods have created lakes such as the Kinselmeer, though others were drained, leaving enormous green craters in the flat landscape. The Waterland villagers coped matter-of-factly with their flood-prone habitat, and around 1300, when the waterlevel became too high to farm crops, they switched to cattle-breeding and developed a lucrative sideline in commerce and shipping. Between the fourteenth and seventeenth centuries this area was – although it seems inconceivable now – one of the most prosperous parts of Holland, and rich traders built large wooden mansions painted as brightly as possible to show off their wealth. As Amsterdam's power increased, however, the area fell into poverty, only really reviving in the 1950s when wealthy Amsterdammers began to move into the area.

Practicalities

The VVV at Gedempte Gracht 76 in Zaandam (Mon–Fri 9am–5.30pm, Sat 9am–1pm; ☎075/16 22 21) has information on Waterland, as does the VVV in the church tower at Zarken 2 in Monnickendam (July & Aug daily 10am–6pm; rest of the year Mon–Sat 10am–noon & 2–5pm; ☎02995/1998) and the **Rekreatieschap Waterland** at De Erven 2 in Broek-in-Waterland (☎02903/3606).

Though there are **buses** around the region, to get the best out of the area you either need to walk, or switch to a bike or canoe. Bikes can be rented in Amsterdam, Broek and Monnickendam, canoes in Broek, Monnickendam and Oostzaan (near Landsmeer). If you're cycling, it's worth buying a good cycling map, or, more cheaply, getting hold of the VVV's **cycling route** leaflet, available in English and including a map and text on the route, which runs for 38km, and can at a pinch be done in a day. It starts in Amsterdam, skirts the drained Broekermeer, passes through Broek, continues to Zuiderwoude and then runs up to the coast of the IJsselmeer. From here it follows the coast south past the Kinselmeer and back to Amsterdam. There's also a possible diversion through the less interesting west of Waterland, worth considering if you want to visit the nature reserve of Ilperveld.

To reach **Landsmeer** by bus, take bus #91 which runs every half-hour from Amsterdam Centraal Station; for **Broek**, buses #110, #114 and #116 all run every fifteen minutes from Amsterdam CS. Buses #110, #111, #114 and #115 run every ten minutes between Monnickendam and Broek.

Landsmeer

Though **LANDSMEER** is Waterland's largest village, it's a dull, mostly modern place, and there's little point in visiting unless it's to see its museum, or to visit the Iperveld nature reserve or Het Twiske, a recreational area just to the north. The **Waterland Museum**, or, as it is officially known, the *Stichting Museum Grietje Trump*, at Zuideinde 69 (Sun only 2–5pm; *f*2.50), is housed in an original, garishly painted Waterland farmhouse, and filled with a century's worth of everyday paraphernalia. The aged proprietor will tell you about her own childhood in the area, though as she doesn't speak English, you might want to phone ahead (☎020/631 34 55) to make sure her English-speaking son is around.

A couple of kilometres north of Landsmeer, the **Het Twiske** nature reserve, two parts land, one part water, makes a fine place to go **canoeing**. You can rent canoes from *Jachthaven De Roemer* (☎02984/4890), just south of Het Twiske, in the village of **OOSTZAAN** – reckon on paying around *f*40 daily for a single, *f*50 daily for a two-person canoe. For further information on the area, call into the **Visitors' Centre** next door to the canoe rental place (Easter–May & Sept–Oct Mon–Fri 8am–5pm, Sat & Sun 10am–6pm; June–Aug Mon–Fri 10am–9pm, Sat & Sun 10am–7pm; ☎02984/4338).

Just to the east of Het Twiske, the nature reserve of **Ilperveld** is a unique landscape of meadows, marshes and water inhabited by large colonies of birds. It's accessible only by water from Landsmeer, but there are occasional organized excursions (for details call ☎02518/59750).

There are no hotels, pensions or private rooms in Landsmeer, but frankly there's no real need to stay. Should you want to sleep over, however, there is a **campsite**, *Camping Het Rietveen*, at Noordeinde 122a (April–Nov; ☎02908/21468), and there are several **restaurants** in town, including a cheap pizzeria, *Casa di Angelo* on Zuideinde, with pizza from *f*13.

Broek-in-Waterland and Zuiderwoude

BROEK-IN-WATERLAND – at least the part northeast of the highway which bisects the village – is a likeable and surprisingly lively place, full of seventeenth- and eighteenth-century wooden mansions, painted in the so-called *Broeker* grey. It's a nice place to while away an hour or so, though there's not a lot to see or do. The village centres around a lake, **Het Havenrak**, from which a canal flows into town. On the lake by the canal is a seventeenth-century **church** (May–Sept Mon–Sat 10am–5pm; free) with a beautiful stained-glass window in its north aisle, showing the church being destroyed by the Spanish in 1573 and its rebuilding the following century. Otherwise, if you want targets for your wanderings, you could try the oldest house in Broek close by, supposedly painted the same bright pink it was in the fifteenth century; or head for the more conventionally touristy cheese farm, **De Domme Dirk**, at Roomeinde 17 (Mon–Sat 9am–12.30pm & 1.30–5pm; ☎02903/454). If you're still desparate for a bit of Dutch kitsch, there's also a **clog workshop** at Havenrak 21 (daily 8am–6pm; ☎02903/1432).

Three kilometres east of Broek is **ZUIDERWOUDE**, a tiny place consisting of little more than a single street and one café. It's more rustic than Broek, made up of farm buildings, rather than mansions, in which the house, stable and haystock stand in a single row – the last tarred black, the others painted dark green.

There's one **hotel** in Broek, *Hotel Garni De Bedstede*, located in two houses at Laan 22–28 and 36–38 (☎02903/1509; ②–③). The rooms in 36–38 are slightly more comfortable – and expensive. In between these two houses, there's a pension, simply called *No.32* (☎02903/1784; ①–③), with one large dormitory that sleeps up to ten people. If you don't mind staying in the new part of town, there's also *Pension Familie Mentink*, Keerngouw 4–6 (☎02903/1678; ③). About 2km north of Broek there's a basic but clean **campsite**, *Camping De Leek*, on the waterside at OverLekergauw 5 (April–Oct; ☎02903/1500). Further away – about 7km from Broek – there's a more luxurious campsite, *Camping Uitdam*, at Zeedijk 2 on the Markenmeer shore 1km north of the village of Uitdam: (open all year except Jan; ☎02903/1433).

Broek-in-Waterland is not a great place **to eat or drink**, and your best bet is probably the pancake house, *De Witte Swaen*, Dorpstraat 11–13, near Het Havenrak, which serves pancakes from ƒ7.95 and pizza-like pancakes from ƒ15. Other than that, there's one overpriced restaurant and several brown cafés, but none of them are particularly nice. **Bicycles** can be rented at *Wim*, Laan 44, (closed Tues; ☎02903/1462) and canoes from *Waterland*, Van Disweg 4 (☎02903/3209); they charge ƒ25 daily for a single, and ƒ35 daily for a two-person canoe.

Monnickendam

A few kilometres north of Broek, just outside the boundaries of Waterland proper, **MONNICKENDAM** lies just to the right of the main road, nestling up to the edge of the IJsselmeer. Like the towns of West Friesland (see over), it was once one of the most important ports of the old Zuider Zee, but since the closing up of the Asfluitdijk it has found more fame as a watersports centre for enthusiasts from the Dutch capital. Unless you're travelling by car and have time on your hands, there's no particualar reason to join the yachties and windsurfers, although something of the fishy and nautical atmosphere of the place does survive (Monnickendam is known for its smoked fish, especially eels), and the centre is charmingly well preserved – and certainly less crowded than its touristy neighbours Marken and Volendam.

Really the pleasantest way to spend time here is by idling away the hours down by the harbour. On the way, the **Speeltoren**, the tower of the town hall, with its sixteenth-century carillon, is probably the most prominent thing to see, and houses a small **museum** of local bits and bobs (June–Aug Mon–Sat 10am–4pm, Sun 2–4pm; April, May, Sept & Oct Sat 10am–4pm, Sun 2–4pm; free), while the undeniably picturesque nearby **Waag** is now home to a **restaurant** at which you could sample some smoked specialities. There's only one **hotel**, the nicely situated *Lakeland*, Jachthaven 1 (☎02995/3751; ④).

Marken, Volendam and Edam

The majority of visitors heading out of Amsterdam make for the settlements on the banks of the IJsselmeer. **MARKEN** is the first of these, accessible direct from Amsterdam by way of bus #111 from opposite the St Nicolaaskerk – a thirty-minute journey. It's a popular place, a former island in the Zuider Zee that was, until its road connection to the mainland in 1957, largely a closed community, supported by a small fishing industry. At one time its biggest problem was the genetic defects caused by close and constant intermarrying; now it's how to contain the tourists, whose numbers increase yearly. Marken's distinctiveness has in many ways been its downfall; its character – or what remains of it – has been artificially preserved: the harbour is still brightly painted in the local colours, and local costumes and clogs are worn. Recently a series of eel-smoking houses have been converted into the **Marken Museum**, Kerkbuurg 44 (open April–Oct Mon–Sat 10am–4.30pm), devoted to the history of the former island and its fishing industry. Although visitors now supply the income lost when the Zuider Zee was closed off, it turns out to have been a desperate remedy.

Beyond the Marken causeway turn-off, the road follows the dike as far as **VOLENDAM** – accessible direct from Amsterdam on bus #110 or by ferry from Marken, which takes twenty minutes and costs f2 each way (March–Oct every 30–45min). Volendam is a larger village than Marken and retains some semblance of its fishing industry in conjunction with the more lucrative business of tourism – into which it, too, has thrown itself wholeheartedly. This is everyone's picture-book view of Holland: fishermen in baggy trousers sit strategically along the harbour wall and women scurry about picturesquely to piped music, clad in the winged lace caps that form the most significant part of the well-publicized village costume. Stop off if it's lunchtime, when you can snack your way along the waterfront fish stands; otherwise give the place a wide berth.

Further on down the #110 bus route, almost connected to Volendam, you might expect **EDAM** to be just as bad, especially considering its reputation for the red balls of cheese that the Dutch produce for export. In fact, it's a relief after the mob rule of Volendam, a pretty little town that is these days more a suburb of the capital than a major cheese-producer. It has only a fraction of the souvenir shops of its neighbours, and a charm that they have long since lost. The main draw is the **Grote Kerk** (April–Sept daily 2–4.30pm), an enormous building almost totally rebuilt after a fire in 1602, with some remarkable stained glass dating from that time. Damplein, Edam's nominal centre, is home to the eighteenth-century **Raadhuis**, which, although rather plain from the outside, has a superabundance of luxuriant stucco work within. On the other side of Damplein, Edam's oldest brick house, dating from 1530, houses the **Captain's House Museum** (Easter–Sept Mon–Sat 10am–4.30pm, Sun 1.30–4.30pm; f2), famous for its floating cellar, allegedly built by a retired captain who could not bear the thought of sleeping on dry land. Around the corner on Kaasmarkt, in the sixteenth-century **Waag** (daily 10am–5pm), a **cheese market** is held every Wednesday morning between mid-July and mid-August – a tourist-targeted affair much like the one in Alkmaar. The VVV is housed nearby in the Raadhuis (April–Sept Mon–Sat 10am–5pm; Oct–March Mon–Sat 10am–12.30pm; ☎02993/71727) and has free maps of Edam, though not much else.

West Friesland: Hoorn, Enkhuizen and Medemblik

A little way north of Edam, the IJsselmeer shore curves east to form the jutting claw of land that makes up an area known as **West Friesland**, whose two main towns – Hoorn and Enkhuizen – can be visited either as day trips from Amsterdam (both are connected by twice-hourly train) or, more interestingly, as overnight stops on the way across the Afsluitdijk into Friesland proper. West Friesland is these days not actually a part of Friesland at all, but was one of the three Frisian districts recognized by Charlemagne and at one time boasted its own regional council, whose authority extended as far away as Alkmaar and Purmerend. The area clings jealously to its supposedly separate identity from the rest of North Holland, though it's hardly very different – the same flat polder landscapes, punctured by farmhouses and the odd windmill, that you see throughout the rest of the province. However, as long as the Markerwaard is never reclaimed, Hoorn and Enkhuizen are the best and most appealing examples of old Zuider Zee ports you'll find.

Hoorn

HOORN, the ancient capital of West Friesland, "rises from the sea like an enchanted city of the east, with its spires and its harbour tower beautifully unreal". So wrote the English travel writer E.V. Lucas in 1905, and the town is still very much a place you should either arrive at or leave by sea – though you probably won't get the chance to do either. During the seventeenth century this was one of the richest of the Dutch ports, referred to by the poet Vondel as the trumpet and capital of the Zuider Zee, handling the important Baltic trade and that of the Dutch colonies. The Dutch East India Company was run from here, Tasman went off to "discover" Tasmania and New Zealand, and in 1616 William Schouten sailed out to navigate a passage around South America, calling its tip "Cape Hoorn" after his native town. The harbour silted up in the eighteenth century, however, stemming trade and gradually turning Hoorn into one of the so-called "dead cities" of the Zuider Zee – a process completed with the creation of the IJsselmeer.

The Town
Not surprisingly, Hoorn's former glories are hard to detect in what is today a quiet provincial backwater: the harbour is a yacht marina, and the elegant streets and houses, almost entirely surrounded by water, give only the faintest of echoes of the town's balmy seventeenth-century prosperity. The centre is **Rode Steen**,

literally "red stone", an unassuming square that used to hold the town scaffold and now focuses on the swashbuckling statue of **J.P. Coen**, founder of the Dutch East Indies Empire and one of the bright lights of the seventeenth century. Coen was a headstrong and determined leader of the Dutch imperial effort, under whom the Far East colonies were consolidated and rivals, like the English, were fought off. His settling of places like Moluccas and Batavia was something of a personal crusade, and his austere, almost puritanical way of life was in sharp contrast to the wild and unprincipled behaviour of many of his compatriots on the islands.

On one side of Rode Steen stands the early seventeenth-century **Waag**, designed by Hendrik de Keyser and now a smart restaurant. On the other side, and dominating the square, the **Westfries Museum** (Mon–Fri 11am–5pm, Sat & Sun 2–5pm; *f*3.50) is Hoorn's most prominent sight, housed in the elaborately gabled former West Friesland government building, and decorated with the coats of arms of the house of Orange-Nassau, West Friesland and the seven major towns of the region. Inside, the museum re-creates – convincingly – the interiors of the time when Hoorn's power was at its height. Along with any number of unascribed portraits, furniture and ceramics, the walls of the council chamber (room 7) are covered with militia portraits by Jan Rotius, who portrays himself in the painting by the window – he's the figure by the flag on the left – and employs some crafty effects in the other canvases. Walk past the figure in the far right of the central painting and watch his foot change position from left to right as you pass. On the second floor, in room 16, there's a painting of 1632 by Jan van Goyen (*Landscape with a Peasant Cart*) and a wooden fireplace carved with tiny scenes showing a whaling expedition – Hoorn was once a whaling port of some importance. Other items of interest include a view of Hoorn painted in 1622, a room containing portraits of various East India Company dignitaries, including one of the severe Coen, while on the top floor are mock-ups of trades and shops of the time, even a prison cell.

There's not all that much of special interest in the rest of Hoorn, but it's a good place to drift around aimlessly, and the old **harbour** and the canals which lead down to it (follow G. Havensteeg from Rode Steen) are very pretty, the waterfront lined with gabled houses looking out to the stolid **Hoofdtoren**, a defensive gateway from 1532. On the other side of Rode Steen, on Kerkstraat, the **Boterhal**, formerly the St Jans Gasthuis, permanently exhibits works by Hoorn artists. It's a delightful building with a so-called trap-gable, tapering to a single window and built at an angle to the main body. Opposite, the Grote Kerk is a nineteenth-century church since converted into apartments.

Practicalities

Hoorn's **train station** is on the northern edge of town, about ten minutes' walk from the centre and the **VVV**, which occupies the leaning former town hall at Nieuwstraat 23 (Sept–June Mon 1–5pm, Tues–Fri 9.30am–5pm, Sat 10am–4pm; July & Aug Mon 1–6pm, Tues–Sat 9.30am–6pm, Thurs until 9pm); ☎02290/18342). There's a **youth hostel** about 2km out from the centre at Schellinkhouterdijk 1a (☎02290/14256) – take bus #132, #137 or #147 from the train station and get off at the home for stray animals. Otherwise the cheapest **hotels** are *De Magneet*, close to the harbour at Kleine Oost 5–7 (☎02290/15021; ③–④), and, slightly cheaper, *De Posthoorn*, Breed 25–27 (☎02290/14057; ③). As for **eating**, *Sweet Dreams*, at Kerkstraat 1, is a good, cheap place for lunch, and couldn't be more central, with tasty omelettes and Mexican dishes – though it closes at 9pm. *Het Witte Paard*, by the Grote Kerk at Lange Kerkstraat 27, has Dutch food and vegetarian dishes, though it too closes at 9pm. For later on, there's *Isola Bella*, Grote Oost 65, five minutes from Rode Steen, which has pizza and pasta, and there are a number of bars and restaurants grouped around the harbour.

Between May and October, Hoorn is the starting-point of **steam train services** to Medemblik, which run once a day in May, June, September and October (at 11am), and twice a day in July and August (at 10.45am and 2.15pm). They can be a nice way of getting to the town if you have kids – journey time is one hour, tickets cost ƒ11. Outside summer, if you want to get from Hoorn to Medemblik, catch express bus #139, which takes about 25 minutes. For the full picture see "Travel Details".

Enkhuizen

Another "dead city", though much smaller than Hoorn, **ENKHUIZEN**, twenty minutes further east by train, was also an important port during the seventeenth century, with the largest herring fleet in the country. However, it too declined at the end of the seventeenth century, and the town now offers much the same sort of attractions as Hoorn, retaining its broad, mast-spattered harbours and peaceful canals. It also has a genuinely major attraction in the Zuider Zee Museum, which brings busloads of tourists up here during the summer to experience what is a very deliberate attempt to capture the lifestyle that existed here when the town was still a flourishing port – and which was destroyed once and for all with the building of the Afsluitdijk. Enkhuizen is also a good place to visit for its summer ferry connections to Stavoren and Urk across the IJsselmeer.

The Town . . . and the Zuider Zee Museum

A few hundred metres from the two main harbours, **Westerstraat** is Enkhuizen's main spine, a busy pedestrianized street that is home to most of the town's shops and restaurants. At one end, the **Westerkerk** is an early fifteenth-century Gothic church with an odd wooden belfry, added in 1519. A right turn from here leads into a residential part of town, very pretty, with its canals crossed by white-painted footbridges. The other end of Westerstraat is marginally more monumental, zeroing in on the mid-sixteenth-century **Waag** on Kaasmarkt, which houses the **Stedelijk Waagmuseum**, a small local museum with the usual local artefacts (mid-April to mid-Oct Tues–Fri 11am–5pm, Sat & Sun 2–5pm; ƒ1.50). Nearby is the solid, classically styled mid-seventeenth-century **Stadhuis** – behind which the dangerously leaning **Gevangenis** was once the town prison. This is closed to the public, but a peek through its barred windows gives some idea of the bleakness of conditions for the average prisoner in those days, most of the main furnishings still being in place.

Close by here, along the waterfront at Wierdijk 18, the indoor section of the Zuider Zee Museum, the **Binnenmuseum** (daily 10am–5pm; ƒ5, but see Buitenmuseum below), has a collection of fishing vessels and equipment, and Zuider Zee arts and crafts, recently spruced up and displayed in bright, new surroundings. Exhibits include regional costumes and painted furniture from Hindeloopen (see *The North and the Frisian Islands*), an ice-cutting boat from Urk, once charged with the responsibility of keeping the shipping lanes open between the island and the port of Kampen, displays of sail- and rope-making implements – and much else besides.

Most people, however, give the Binnenmuseum a miss and instead make straight for the **Buitenmuseum** on the far side of the harbour (early April to end Oct daily 10am–5pm; ƒ12.50, children ƒ8), where buildings have actually been transported from 39 different locations to form a period portrayal of the vanished way of life around the Zuider Zee in a re-creation of various towns and villages. The only way to get there is by boat, either from the train station or, if you're driving, from the museum parking area by the end of the Lelystad road. The ticket entitles you to either a free boat-trip or free parking. Once there, you can choose to tour the museum by way of the free hourly guided tours, or – rather nicer – simply wander around taking it all in at your own pace.

Close by the ferry wharf there's a series of lime kilns, conspicuous by their tall chimneys, from which a path takes you through the best of the museum's many intriguing corners, beginning with a row of cottages from Monnickendam, nearby which there's an information centre. A number of streets lined with cottages lead off from here, a mock-up of a typical Zuider Zee fishing village basically, with examples of buildings from Urk among other places, their modest, precisely furnished interiors open to visitors and sometimes peopled by characters in traditional dress, hamming it up for the tourists. Further on, a number of buildings sit along and around a central canal. There's a post office from Den Oever; a grocery from Harderwijk; an old laundry, thick with the smell of washing; a chemist and a bakery from Hoorn, the latter selling pastries and chocolate; while a cottage from Hindeloopen doubles up as a restaurant. It all sounds rather kitsch, and in a way it is: there are regular demonstrations of the old ways and crafts, goats and sheep roam the stretches of meadow and the exhibition is mounted in such an earnest way as to almost beg criticism. But the attention to detail is very impressive, and the whole thing is never overdone, with the result that many parts of the museum are genuinely picturesque. Even if you see nothing else in Enkhuizen (and many people don't), you really shouldn't miss it.

Practicalities

Trains to Enkhuizen – the end of the line – stop right on the corner of the harbour, close by the main **bus stops** and **ferry wharves**. There's a VVV office in the train station (Tues–Sat 10am–5pm; April–Oct also open Sun 10am–5pm; ☎02280/13164) which has free maps but can't help with much else. From here it's a five- to ten-minute walk to Westerstraat and the centre of the small town. If you're **staying**, the cheapest place is the wonderful circular dormitory in the *Dromedaris Tower* (☎02280/12076; ①), on Paktuinen in the outer harbour. If you prefer to sleep in privacy, the cheapest **hotel** is *Het Wapen*, conveniently located close to the Zuider Zee museums and the harbours at Breedstraat 59 (☎02280/13434; ④), which has double rooms for around ƒ100 – though apart from camping that's about it on the budget accommodation front. If you are **camping**, there are two sites handily located on the northern side of town: closest is the *Enkhuizer Zand* on the far side of the Zuider Zee Museum at Kooizandweg 4; there's also *De Vest* – follow Vijzelstraat north off Westerstraat, continue down Noorderweg and turn left by the old town ramparts. Both sites are open April to September only.

Restaurants in Enkhuizen tend to be expensive. *Het Shoutwje*, Westerstraat 98, is less pricy than most, but the food is only average; *Holle Bolle Gijs*, on the waterfront of the outer harbour, has decent main meals and especially good-value lunch dishes; while the *Café Dromedaris*, in the Dromedaris tower, serves well-priced food for lunch and dinner.

During summer you can travel on from Enkhuizen **by ferry** to Stavoren, Urk or Medemblik. These leave from behind the train station. Ferries to Stavoren run roughly three times daily; and to Urk and Medemblik twice daily. To Stavoren and Urk, reckon on paying *f*10–12 plus *f*5 or so for a bike. For more, see "Travel Details".

Medemblik, the Wieringermeer Polder . . . and into Friesland

Just a few miles along the coast from Enkhuizen, **MEDEMBLIK** is one of the most ancient towns in Holland, a seat of pagan kings until the seventh century, though there's not a great deal to entice you there nowadays, unless you're madly into yachts. The only sign visible today of Medemblik's ancient beginnings is the **Kasteel Radboud**, named after, but not really connected with, the most famous of the town's kings, a much-restored thirteenth-century fortress that sits by the harbour at Oudevaartsgat 8 (mid-May to mid-Sept Mon–Sat 10am–5pm, Sun 2–5pm; rest of the year Sun only 2–5pm; *f*3). Not much of what's left these days is original, indeed most of it is the result of a nineteenth-century restoration project under the supervision of P.J.H. Cuijpers, but you are allowed in to take a look at a handful of exhibits relating to the fort's former inhabitants and a small exhibition covering the history of the building. The old train station, where the summer steam train draws in, houses the VVV (☎02274/2852), while at Oosterdijk 4 there's **Stoommachine Museum** (Easter–Aug Tues–Sun 9am–6pm; Sept & Oct also open Mon 9am–6pm; *f*4), an assembly of thirty ancient steam engines in a former pumping station. Otherwise most people come to Medemblik to sail: the harbour is busy throughout summer with the masts of visiting and resident yachtspeople.

North of Medemblik, the **Wieringermeer Polder** was the first of the Zuider Zee polders, created in the 1920s when the former island of Wieringen was connected to the mainland and the area behind it reclaimed. During their occupation, and only three weeks before their surrender, the Germans flooded the area, boasting they could return Holland to the sea if they wished. After the war it was drained again, leaving a barren, treeless terrain that had to be totally replanted. Almost forty years later, it's virtually back to normal, a familiar polder landscape of flat, geometric fields, highlighted by farmhouses and church spires, that most people only pass through on their way to Friesland by way of the Afsluitdijk highway.

The sluices on this side of the **Afsluitdijk** are known as the **Stevinsluizen**, after Henry Stevin, the seventeenth-century engineer who first had the idea of reclaiming the Zuider Zee. He was, of course, constrained here by the lack of technology available, but his vision lived on, to be realized by Cornelis Lely in 1932. At the North Holland end, there's a statue of Lely by the modern Dutch sculptor Mari Andriessen, though the engineer died before the dike was completed. Further along, at the point where the barrier was finally closed, there's an observation point on which an inscription reads: "A nation that lives is building for its future".

Alkmaar and around

An hour from Amsterdam by train, **ALKMAAR** is typical of small-town Holland, its pretty, partially canalized centre surrounded by water and offering a low-key, undemanding provincialism which makes a pleasant change after the rigours of the big city. It's also a good base for exploring the nearby dunes and beaches, or even the towns of West Friesland.

Alkmaar is probably best known for its **cheese market**, an ancient affair which these days ranks as one of the most extravagant tourist spectacles in Holland. Cheese has been sold on the main square here since the 1300s, and although no serious buying goes on here now, it's an institution that continues to draw crowds – though nowadays they're primarily tourists. If you do want to see it (it's held every Friday morning, mid-April to mid-Sept), be sure to get there early, as by the 10am opening the crowds are already thick. The ceremony starts with the buyers sniffing, crumbling and finally tasting each cheese, followed by heated bartering. Once a deal has been concluded, the cheeses – golden discs of Gouda mainly, laid out in rows and piles on the square – are borne away on ornamental carriers by four groups of porters for weighing. Payment, tradition has it, takes place in the cafés around the square.

The Town

Even if you've only come for the cheese market, it's a good idea to see something of the rest of the town before you leave. On the main square, the **Waag** was originally a chapel dedicated to the Holy Spirit, but was converted, and given its magnificent east gable, shortly after the town's famous victory against the Spanish in 1573, when its citizens withstood a long siege by Frederick of Toledo – a victory which marked the beginning of the end for the Spaniards. Nowadays the Waag houses the **VVV** (see below) and the **Kaasmuseum** (April–Oct Mon–Thurs & Sat 10am–4pm, Fri 9am–4pm; *f*2), which has displays on the history of cheese and cheese-making equipment and suchlike. Across the other side of the square, the **Biermuseum de Boom**, Houttil 1 (April–Sept Tues–Sat 10am- 4pm, Sun 1–4pm; Oct–March Thurs–Sun 1–4pm; *f*3), is housed in the building of the old De Boom brewery, and has displays tracing the brewing process from the malting to bottling stage, aided by authentic props from this and other breweries the world over. There's lots of technical equipment, enlivened by mannikins and empty bottles from once innumerable Dutch brewers – though few, curiously, from De Boom itself. It's an engaging little museum, lovingly put together by enthusiasts; it also has a top-floor shop in which you can buy a huge range of beers and associated merchandise, as well as a downstairs bar serving some eighty varieties of Dutch beer.

The **Stedelijk Museum** (Tues–Sat 10am–5pm, Sun 1–5pm; *f*2) on the other side of the town centre in Doelenstraat displays pictures and plans of the siege of 1573, along with a *Holy Family* by Honthorst and portraits by Maerten van Heemskerk and Caesar van Everdingen, the latter a local and very minor seventeenth-century figure who worked in the Mannerist style of the Haarlem painters. Close by, at the far end of **Langestraat**, the town's main shopping street, the **St Laurenskerk**, a Gothic church of the later fifteenth century, is worth looking into for its huge organ, commissioned at the suggestion of Constantijn Huygens by Maria Tesselschade, local resident and friend of the Golden Age elite. The case was designed by Jacob van Campen and painted by Caesar van Everdingen. In the apse is the tomb of Count Floris V, penultimate in the line of medieval counts of North Holland, who did much to establish the independence of the towns hereabouts but who was murdered by nobles in 1296. On Langestraat itself the only notable building is the **Stadhuis**, a florid affair, half of which (the eastern side and tower) dates from the early sixteenth century.

Practicalities

Alkmaar's **train station** is about ten minutes' walk west of the centre of town on Stationsstraat; to get to the centre from the station, turn right outside, then left, and follow the road for five minutes to the St Laurenskerk. The **VVV** is five minutes away from here, housed in the Waag on Waagplein (Mon–Wed 9am–5.30pm, Thurs, Fri & Sat 9am–6pm; ☎072/11 42 84), and has **private rooms** to rent. Failing that, *De Nachtegaal* is the cheapest and most central **hotel**, opposite the town hall at Langestraat 100 (☎072/11 28 94; ③), with reasonable double rooms; otherwise, you could try the slightly more expensive *Pension Ida Margaretha*, Kanaaldijk 186 (☎072/61 39 89; ③). If you're **camping**, there's a site (open April–Sept) ten minutes' bus ride northwest of the town centre; take bus #168 or #169 from the train station.

There are quite a few good places to **eat**. *Jelle's Eethuisje*, between Laat and Oude Gracht at Ridderstraat 24, is good for light lunches and cheap evening meals. *Ikan Mas*, one of several restaurants in the old part of town at Fnidsen 101–103, is a decent Indonesian that does a reasonable *rijstaffel*, while *Rose's Cantina*, two doors down, serves Tex-Mex dishes. For splurges, try *Bistro Wladimir* at Waagplein 36, which offers French–Dutch food in an intimate atmosphere.

Drinking, too, is well catered for. There are two groups of bars: one on Waagplein itself, the other on the nearby canal of Verdronken Noord, by the old Vismarkt. Of the former, *De Kaasbeurs*, at Houttil 30, is a busy place during the day but closes in the early evening; *Café Corridor*, virtually next door, is a lively hangout that plays loud music late into the night and has a small dancefloor at the back. On Verdronken Noord, *De Pilaren* is also noisy, though catering for a slightly older crowd; *Café Stapper*, next door, is a good refuge if the music gets too much.

If you just want to have a quick look around Alkmaar after the cheese market, in summer you can take a boat trip around the town, from near the Waag. They run from April to October, last 45 minutes and cost *f*6.

Around Alkmaar – and points north

The seashore close to Alkmaar is the area's best feature and, if the weather is warm, it's a good place to cool off after the crush of the cheese market. Bus #168 runs out to **BERGEN**, a cheerful village that has been something of a retreat for artists since the Expressionist Bergen School of the early twentieth century worked here. There are a number of galleries around the village, including the **KCB** gallery next door to the VVV at Plein 7 (Tues–Sat 11am–5pm, Sun 2–5pm; *f*1), which holds regular exhibitions of work by contemporary Bergen artists, and there's a small collection of older work in the **Sterkenhuis Museum** on Oude Prinsweg (May–Sept Tues–Sat 10am–noon & 3–5pm; July & Aug also 7–9pm; *f*1.50), which also contains documentation on the defeat of the Duke of York here in 1799, along with period rooms and old costumes.

There's a permanent exhibition of Bergen School paintings on display at the **Smithuizen Museum**, Stationsweg 83 (Jan–Oct Fri–Sun 2–6pm; Nov & Dec Fri & Sat only 2–6pm; free), in **HEILOO**, just south of Alkmaar. Heiloo is also important for bulbs, and has a summer exhibition of flowers and plants in its **Hortus Bulborum** – fair compensation if you missed the Keukenhof. If you're interested in bulbs, there's a **museum** devoted to bulb cultivation south of the town in **LIMMEN** at Dusseldorpweg 64, with exhibits on two centuries of bulb-growing in Holland (mid-April to mid-Sept Mon & Tues 9am–noon & 2–5pm, Fri 9am–noon; free).

Bus #168 runs on from Bergen to **BERGEN-AAN-ZEE**, a bleak place in itself but with access to some strikingly untouched dunes and beach. About 3km south, **EGMOND-AAN-ZEE** (also directly accessible from Alkmaar) is a little larger but not much more attractive, though it also has huge expanses of sand. A short way inland across the dunes, in **EGMOND-AAN-DE-HOEF**, you can see the remains of the castle of the counts of North Holland, destroyed in 1574. Egmond is also an entry point of the **Noordhollands Duinreservaat**, an area of woods and dunes that stretches south beyond Castricum and holds a couple of campsites and any number of cycle paths, not to mention the superb beach.

The coast north of Bergen, from **CAMPERDUIN** to **PETTEN**, has no dunes, and the sea is kept at bay by means of a 4.5-kilometre-long **dike** – something you can learn more about at the **"de dijk te kijk"** ("the dike on show") exhibition on Zuiderhazedwarsdijk, outside Petten, on the dike, which has old maps, photos and drawings illustrating the building of the defence (July & Aug Mon–Fri 10am–5pm, Sat & Sun 2–5pm; May, June & Sept Sat & Sun 2–5pm; free).

SCHAGEN, inland from Petten, draws visitors for its summer market, held every Thursday in July and August, when the small town centre is entirely taken over by stands. Twenty minutes further north by train, **DEN HELDER** is a town of around sixty thousand, though it was little more than a fishing village until 1811, when Napoleon, capitalizing on its strategic position at the very tip of North Holland, fortified it as a naval base. It's still the principal home of the Dutch navy, and at weekends during June national fleet days are held here – a chance, should you desire it, to check out a huge proportion of the Dutch navy (for details contact the Den Helder VVV ☎02230/25544). Otherwise there's little interest to the place, its centre an uninspiring muddle of modern architecture prefacing a seedier old quarter down near the harbour. The only real reason to come here is to take one of the plentiful ferries across the water to the island of Texel. If this is what you are doing, take bus #3 direct from the train station to the harbour and miss out the town altogether.

Texel

The largest of the islands of the Wadden Sea – and the easiest to get to – **TEXEL** is a lush, green thumb of land, speckled with small towns and lined on its western side by large areas of dune and extensive beaches. Much of it has actually been reclaimed from the sea, and, until the draining of its main polder on the northeastern side of the island during the nineteenth century, it was shaped quite differently, the dunes providing a backbone to a much less even expanse of farmland. It's an incredibly pretty island, and very diverse – something borne out by the crowds that congregate here during the summer months. When the weather's hot, Texel is far from empty.

Ferries leave for Texel from Den Helder roughly every hour all year round. The journey takes twenty minutes and costs ƒ10.25 per person, plus ƒ45 for a car, ƒ5.10 if you're taking a bicycle across. For further information call ☎02220/19393.

Ferries from the mainland drop you in the middle of nowhere, but there are always buses continuing to **DEN BURG**, the main town – no more than a large village really, but home to the island's principal VVV office, at Emmalaan 66 (Mon–Fri 9am–6pm, Sat 9am–5pm; July & Aug also Sun 4–7pm; ☎02220/14741), where you can book **private accommodation** throughout the island. The cheapest **hotel** in Den Burg is *'t Koogerend*, Kogerstraat 94 (☎02220/13301; ③). There are also two **youth hostels** on either side of Den Burg on the roads to De Koog and Oudeschild – one called *Panorama* at Schansweg 7 (☎02220/15441), the other, *De Eyercoogh*, at Pontweg 106 (☎02220/12907). Both are open April to October only, and can be reached by bus #28 from the ferry jetty. The *Panorama* can also be reached on bus #29, which leaves from the jetty as well. As for sights, there's not much to see in Den Burg beyond a small **museum** of local history, but it is a good place to rent **bikes** – the best way to get around the island: try *F.Zegel*, Parkstraat 16, or *A. Kievit*, Jonkerstraat 2 – and it makes a decent base for seeing the rest of Texel. The VVV has booklets detailing good cycling routes, as well as the best places to view the island's many **bird colonies**, protected in sanctuaries right across Texel (the island is one of the most important breeding grounds in Europe). Though you can see them well enough from a distance, you may want to get closer – in which case you need permission from *StaatsBosBeheer* at Ecomare in De Koog (see opposite).

As regards other villages, a little way southeast of Den Burg, **OUDESCHILD** is worth a quick look for its **Beachcombers Museum** (Mon–Sat 9am–5pm; ƒ5), a

TEXEL

fascinating collection of marine junk recovered from offshore wrecks – everything from aeroplane engines to messages in bottles. Otherwise, in the opposite direction, **DE KOOG**, halfway up the western coast of Texel, is the island's main resort. It's a very crowded place throughout the summer, with campsites galore dotted all over the surrounding area, many restaurants and hotels, as well as a nature centre, **Ecomare**, Ruyslaan 92 (daily 9am–5pm; *f*6), with a small natural history museum and a refuge for lost birds and seals, who you can see being fed at 11am and 3pm. In the southern part of the island, **DEN HOORN** is a tiny village surrounded by bulbfields that's handy for some very remote spots, including a nudist beach to the southwest. North of De Koog, the **De Slufter** nature reserve feels similarly distanced from the modern world, the scrubby dunes meeting massive stretches of sand in an almost frighteningly windswept environment.

travel details

Trains

Alkmaar to: Hoorn (every 30min; 25min).

Amsterdam CS to: Alkmaar (every 30min; 30min); Castricum (every 30min; 30min); Den Helder (every 30min; 1hr); Enkhuizen (every 30min; 55min); Haarlem (every 15min; 15min); Hilversum (every 2hr; 30min); Hoorn (every 30min; 35min); Purmerend (every 30min; 25min); Schagen (every 30min; 55min); Zaandam (every 15min; 10min).

Haarlem to: Alkmaar (every 30min; 25min); Zandvoort (every 30min; 10min).

Hilversum to: Amersfoort (every 30min; 15min); Utrecht (every 20min; 20min).

Buses

Alkmaar to: Bergen (every 15min; 15min); Harlingen (hourly; 1hr 45min); Leeuwarden (hourly; 2hr 15min).

Amsterdam to: Broek-in-Waterland (every 15min; 20min); Edam (every 30min; 40min); Landsmeer (every 30min; 15min); Marken (every 30min; 30min); Muiden (every 30min; 40min); Naarden (every 30min; 55min); Volendam (every 30min; 30min); Zaandam (every 30min; 40min); Zaanse Schans (every 20min; 1hr).

Bergen to: Bergen-an-See (hourly; 10min).

Broek-in-Waterland to: Monnickendam (every 10min; 30min).

Edam to: Hoorn (every 30min; 25min).

Haarlem to: Bloemendaal (every 30min; 15min); Zandvoort (every 15min; 20min).

Hoorn to: Medemblik (every 30min; 35–45min).

Marken to: Monnickendam (every 30min; 15min).

Monnickendam to: Volendam (hourly; 20min).

Muiden to: Naarden (every 30min; 15min).

Ferries

Den Helder to: Texel (hourly; 20min).

Enkhuizen to: Medemblik (mid-April to June, Sept & Oct 1 daily; July & Aug 2 daily; 1hr 15min); Stavoren (May to mid-Sept 3 daily, 1hr 25min); Urk (July and Aug 2 daily; 1hr 30min).

Marken to: Volendam (March–Oct every 30–45min; 30min).

CHAPTER THREE

SOUTH HOLLAND AND UTRECHT

S outh Holland is the most densely populated province of The Netherlands, with a string of towns and cities that make up most of the **Randstad** or rim-town. Careful urban planning has succeeded in stopping this from becoming an amorphous conurbation, however, and each town has a pronounced identity – from the refined tranquillity of **The Hague** to the seedy low-life of **Rotterdam**'s docklands. All the towns are able to offer good museums and galleries, some outstanding, like The Hague's **Mauritshuis**, Leiden's **Van Oudheden museum** and Rotterdam's **Boymans-van Beuningen**. Since it too now forms part of the Randstad, **Utrecht** is included here, again a city rich in galleries.

Historically, South Holland is part of what was once simply **Holland**, the richest and most influential province in the country. Throughout the Golden Age Holland was far and away the most dominant province in the political, social and cultural life of the Republic, overshadowing its neighbours whose economies suffered as a result of Holland's success. There are constant reminders of this pre-eminence in the buildings of this region: elaborate town halls proclaim civic importance and even the usually sombre Calvinist churches allow themselves little excesses – the later windows of Gouda's Janskerk a case in point. Many of the great painters either came from or worked here, too – Rembrandt, Vermeer, Jan Steen – a tradition that continued into the nineteenth century with the paintings of the Hague School. Outside of the coastal strip of cities, the countryside around the ancient port of **Dordrecht** is of most interest, featuring the windmills of the Kinderdijk, the Biesbosch reed forest and, around **Gouda**, the rural charms of the tidy town of **Oudewater**.

Uniformly flat, the countryside in this area is brightened only by the rainbow flashes of bulbfields. Travelling around is never a problem: none of South Holland's towns are more than 20km apart, and they're linked by a fast and efficient rail network.

ACCOMMODATION PRICE CODES

All the **hotels and hostels** detailed in this chapter have been graded according to the following price categories. Note that the prices have been calculated as those for the cheapest double room during high season. For more on accommodation, see p.29.

① Up to ƒ30 per person.
② ƒ30–65.
③ ƒ65–100.
④ ƒ100–140.
⑤ ƒ140–180.
⑥ ƒ180–220.
⑦ ƒ220–260.
⑧ ƒ260 and over.

Leiden and around

The home of Holland's most prestigious university, **LEIDEN** has an academic air. Like Haarlem to the north, you get the feeling it regards itself as separate from, and independent of, Amsterdam – which is fair enough. There's enough here to justify at least a day trip, and the town's energy, derived largely from its students, strongly counters the myth that there's nothing worth experiencing outside the capital. Leiden's museums, too, are varied and comprehensive enough to merit a visit in themselves, though be selective. The town's real charm lies in the peace and prettiness of its gabled streets and canals.

The university was a gift from William the Silent, a reward for Leiden's enduring (like Haarlem and Alkmaar) a year-long siege by the Spanish. The town emerged victorious on October 3, 1574, when William cut through the dykes around the city and sailed in with his fleet for a dramatic eleventh-hour rescue. This event is still commemorated with an annual fair, fireworks and the consumption of two traditional dishes: herring and white bread, which the fleet were supposed to have brought with them, and *hutspot*, or vegetable and potato stew, a cauldron of which was apparently found simmering in the abandoned Spanish camp.

The Leiden area telephone code is ☎071

Arrival, information and accommodation

Leiden's **train and bus stations** are situated on the northwest edge of town, about ten minutes' walk from the centre. The **VVV** is opposite at Stationsplein 210 (Mon–Fri 9am–5.30pm, Sat 9am–4pm; ☎14 68 46); they have maps and various leaflets and can advise on **accommodation** or make **room** bookings in private homes. Other than that, Leiden is fairly short on **hotel** space for a town of its size, and there are no special bargains. You could try *De Ceder*, out beyond the station at Rijnsburgerweg 80 (☎17 59 03; ④); to get there, turn left outside the station and left again under the train tracks; the slightly more expensive *De Doelen*, is better placed at Rapenburg 2 (☎12 05 27; ④). On the whole, though, accommodation is cheaper in the seaside resorts of Katwijk and Noordwijk. Of the two, Katwijk is the more pleasant place to stay, with several hotels and pensions along its seafront Boulevard; try *Het Anker*, at Boulevard 129 (☎01718/1389; ③), or the *Seahorse*, Boulevard 14 (☎01718/15921; ③). The nearest **youth hostel** is in Noordwijk, at Langevelderlaan 45 (☎02523/72920); take bus #60 from opposite the station. If you're **camping**, the closest large site is the *Koningshof* in Rijnsburg, north of Leiden; take bus #40. Otherwise, Noordwijk has several campsites, Katwijk just the one. All are open from March to October.

The Town

Leiden's most appealing quarter is that bordered by Witte Singel and Breestraat, focusing on Rapenburg, a peaceful area of narrow pedestrian streets and canals. At Rapenburg 28 is perhaps the city's best-known attraction, the **Rijksmuseum Van Oudheden** (Tues–Sat 10am–5pm, Sun noon–5pm; *f*3.50), Holland's principal archeological museum, with a huge collection. You can see one of its major exhibits, the *Temple of Taffeh*, for free. Situated in a courtyard in front of the museum entrance, this was a gift from the Egyptian government in gratitude for the Dutch part in the 1960s UNESCO excavations in Abyssinia (Ethiopia), which succeeded in uncovering submerged Nubian monuments. Dating back to the first century AD, the temple was adapted in the fourth century to the worship of Isis, eventually being sanctified as a Christian church 400 years later. The Egyptians placed very firm conditions on their legacy: no one should have to pay to see it, and the temperature and humidity must be carefully regulated, with the lights overhead simulating the passage – and shadow – of the sun.

Inside the museum proper, the first exhibit is the remains of a temple to Nehellania – a goddess of sailors – which was uncovered in Zeeland. Next come classical Greek and Roman sculptures, leading chronologically through Hellenistic works to busts, statues, and friezes of Imperial Rome. The best collection, though, is the Egyptian one, beginning with wall reliefs, statues and sarcophagi from tombs and temples, and continuing in the rooms immediately above with a set of mummies and sarcophagi as complete as you're likely to see outside Egypt. The *Three Figures of Maya*, to name just one exhibit, are exceptionally well preserved. The third floor is specifically Dutch: an archeological history of the country, from prehistoric, Roman and medieval times, that is, perhaps inevitably, less interesting than the rest of the museum.

Further along Rapenburg, at no. 73, the original home of the **university** still stands, part of which is open as a **museum** (Wed–Fri 1–5pm; free) which details its history. Through the courtyard, the **Hortus Botanicus** gardens (Mon–Sat 9am–5pm, Sun 10am–5pm; *f*3.50) are a lovely spot, lushly planted and subtly landscaped across to the Witte Singel canal. Planted in 1587, they are supposedly among the oldest botanical gardens in Europe, a mixture of carefully tended beds of shrubs and hothouses full of tropical foliage. Leave by the exit off to the left, across the canal, where a red door hides a reconstruction of the original garden, the **Clusiustuin** (April–Oct only Mon–Fri 9am–5pm), named after the botanist who first brought tulips to Holland.

Cross Rapenburg from the university museum, and you're in the network of narrow streets constituting the medieval town, converging on a central square and the **Pieterskerk** (daily 1.30–4pm; free), the town's main church. This is deconsecrated now, used occasionally for a Saturday antique market, and it has an empty warehouse-like feel. But among the fixtures that remain are a simple and beautiful Renaissance rood screen in the choir, and a host of memorials to the sundry notables buried here, among them **John Robinson**, leader of the Pilgrim Fathers.

Robinson lived in a house on the site of what is now the **Jan Pesijn Hofje** on Kloksteeg, right by the church. A curate in England at the turn of the seventeenth century, he was suspended from preaching in 1604, later fleeing with his congregation to pursue his Puritan form of worship in the more amenable atmosphere of Calvinist Holland. Settling in Leiden, Robinson acted as pastor to growing numbers, but still found himself at odds with the establishment. In 1620, a hundred of his followers ("The Pilgrim Fathers") sailed via Plymouth for the freedom and abundance of America, though Robinson died before he could join them; he's buried in the church.

If you want to find out more, stroll down to the **Leiden Pilgrim Collection** at Vliet 45 (Mon–Fri 9.30am–4.30pm; free), part of the city archives and a mine of information on Robinson's group during their stay in Leiden. Otherwise, continue east onto **Breestraat**, which marks the edge of Leiden's commercial centre, flanked by the long, ornate Renaissance front of the late sixteenth-century **Stadhuis**, the only part of the building to survive a fire in 1929. Behind, the rivers which cut Leiden into islands converge at the busiest point in town, the site of a vigorous Wednesday and Saturday general **market** which sprawls right over the sequence of bridges into the blandly pedestrian **Haarlemmerstraat** – the town's main shopping street.

The junction of the Oude and Nieuwe Rijn is marked by the mid-seventeenth-century **Waag**, a replacement for a previous Gothic structure, built to a design by Pieter Post and fronted with a naturalistic frieze by Rombout Verhulst. Across the water from here, on the island formed by the fork in the two sections of river, the **Burcht** (daily 10am–11pm; free) is the rather ordinary, graffiti-daubed shell of a twelfth-century fort perched on an ancient mound, the battlements of which you can clamber up for a view of Leiden's roofs and towers. The **Hooglandsekerk** nearby (April–Oct Tues–Sat 11am–4pm, Mon 1–3.30pm; free) is a light, lofty church with a central pillar that features an epitaph to the burgomaster at the time of the 1574 siege, Pieter van der Werff, who became a hero during its final days. When the situation became so desperate that most people were all for giving up, the burgomaster, no doubt remembering the massacre of Haarlem, offered his own body to them as food. His invitation was rejected, but – the story goes – it succeeded in instilling new determination in the flagging citizens.

Across Oude Rijn from here is the **Museum Boerhaave** at Lange Agnietenstraat 10 (Tues–Sat 10am–5pm, Sun noon–5pm; *f*3), named after the seventeenth-century Leiden surgeon, which gives a brief but absorbing guide to scientific and medical developments over the last three centuries, with particular reference to Dutch achievements, including some gruesome surgical implements, pickled brains and suchlike. Five minutes' walk from here, Leiden's municipal museum, housed in the old **Lakenhal** (cloth-hall) at Oude Singel 28–32 (Tues–Fri 10am–5pm, Sat & Sun 1–5pm; *f*5), has a similarly engaging exhibition, with a picture gallery devoted to natives of the town as well as mixed rooms of furniture, tiles, glass and ceramics. It's also the only museum in Leiden to regularly exhibit modern Dutch art. Upstairs, the rooms are grouped around the *Grote Pers* (Grand Press), and look much as they would have when Leiden's cloth trade was at its height – though most have since been decorated with paintings or now house temporary exhibitions. Downstairs are sixteenth-century paintings centring around Lucas van Leyden's *Last Judgment* triptych, plus canvases by Jacob van Swanenburgh, the first teacher of the young Rembrandt, by Rembrandt himself, and associated Leiden painters – among them Jan Lievens (with whom he shared a studio), Gerrit Dou (who initiated the Leiden tradition of small, minutely finished pictures) and the van Mieris brothers. There's also a painting depicting the sixteenth-century siege that shows the heroic van der Werff in full flow.

Around the corner on Molenwerf, the **Molenmuseum de Valk**, 2e Binnenvestgracht 1 (Tues–Sat 10am–5pm, Sun 1–5pm; *f*3), is a restored grain mill, one of twenty that used to surround Leiden. The downstairs rooms are furnished in simple, period style; upstairs a slide show recounts the history of windmills in Holland, while displays detail their development and showcase their tools and grinding apparatus, all immaculately preserved. An absorbing way to spend an hour, and only five minutes' stroll from the station.

There's one other museum between here and the station, the **Rijksmuseum Voor Volkenkunde** at Steenstraat 1 (Tues–Fri 10am–5pm, Sat & Sun 1–5pm; *f*5), the national ethnological museum, which has complete sections on Indonesia and the Dutch colonies, along with reasonable ones on the South Pacific and Far East. However, it gives most other parts of the world a less than thorough showing and is not an essential stop by any means.

Eating and drinking

It's easy to **eat and drink** cheaply in Leiden. The streets around the Pieterskerkhof and the Hoogslandskerk both hold concentrations of bars and restaurants. For lunch, *Noroc*, just off Breestraat on Pieterskerk Choorsteeg, is a pleasant café with a light menu; *Barrera*, opposite the old university building on Rapenburg, is a cosy bar that serves sandwiches; *Annie's Verjaardag*, pleasantly located by the waterside at Hoogstraat 1a, serves main courses from *f*12.50; and *Het Huis de Bijlen*, just off Noordeinde, has daily specials for around *f*10. In the evening, *De Brasserie*, Lange Mare 38, has Dutch food starting at *f*20; *Eethuis de Trommelaar* is a pleasant and reasonably priced vegetarian restaurant at Apothekersdijk 22; *Eethuis de Stoep*, Oude Rijn 1a, has à la carte dishes from *f*15 and cheap three-course menus ranging in price from around *f*25 to *f*50 for a very varied selection of food. With more money, you might try *Bistro Malle Jan*, just off Pieterskerkhof at Nieuwesteeg 11, which serves evening meals from around ƒ20, and includes a vegetarian dish on its menu. If you want something non-Dutch, *Radja Mas*, on Maarsmansteeg, next door to *Vroom & Dreesman* off Breestraat, is a reasonably priced Indonesian restaurant serving main courses starting at under ƒ10 – though it closes early, at 8pm; *Cojico*, at Breestraat 33, is an amiable Mexican restaurant with main dishes for ƒ12–25.

Because of the university Leiden is a good place to buy **books**. *Kooyker*, Breestraat 93, has a marvellous selection of books in English; there's also a decent branch of *De Slegte* at Breestraat 73. Consider also taking a **canal trip** around the city centre. These run from Beestenmarkt during summer and cost ƒ8 per person for a forty-minute tour.

Around Leiden: the bulbfields and the coast

Along with Haarlem to the north, Leiden is the best base for seeing something of the Dutch **bulbfields** which have flourished here since the late sixteenth century, when one Carolus Clusius, a Dutch botanist, brought the first tulip bulb over from Asia Minor and watched it prosper on Holland's sandy soil. Although bulbs are grown in North Holland too, the centre of the Dutch bulb-growing industry is the area around Leiden and up toward Haarlem. The flowers are inevitably a major tourist pull, and one of Holland's most lucrative businesses, supporting some ten thousand growers in what is these days a billion-guilder industry. Obviously spring is the best time to see something of the blooms, when the view from the train – which cuts directly through the main growing areas – can be sufficient in itself, the fields divided into stark geometric blocks of pure colour. With your own transport you can take in the full beauty of the bulbfields by way of special routes marked by hexagonal signposts – local VVVs sell pamphlets listing the best vantage points.

Lisse and the Keukenhof Gardens

Should you want to get closer to the flowers, **LISSE**, halfway between Leiden and Haarlem, is the place to look at the best of the Dutch flower industry, home to the **Keukenhof Gardens** (late March to end of May daily 8am–7.30pm; ƒ14.50), the largest flower gardens in the world. The Keukenhof was set up in 1949, designed by a group of prominent bulb growers to convert people to the joys of growing flowers from bulbs in their own gardens. Literally the "kitchen garden", its site is the former estate of a fifteenth-century countess, who used to grow herbs and vegetables for her dining table here – hence the name. Some seven million flowers are on show for their full flowering period, complemented, in case of especially harsh winters, by 5000 square metres of greenhouses holding indoor displays. You could easily spend a whole day here, swooning among the sheer abundance of it all. There are three restaurants in the 28 hectares of grounds, and well-marked paths take you all the way through the gardens, which hold daffodils, narcissi and hyacinths in April, and tulips from mid-April until the end of May. Special express buses – #54 – run to the Keukenhof from Leiden bus station twice an hour at ten and forty minutes past each hour, every day including Sunday.

If you can't visit in the spring, the **Bulbdistrict Museum**, also in Lisse at Heereweg 219 (Tues–Sun 1–5pm; ƒ2.50), offers the history of the bulb business, dating from the time the first tulip was brought over from Turkey – but it's a poor substitute for the real thing.

THE BRITISH BULBERS: EXPLOITATION AND EXCESS

Behind the dazzling surface of the bulbfields lies the misery of exploitation. Each summer the bulbs need to be packed and labelled and the core of the workforce for this is around five hundred young British men, many of whom come back year after year to work sixteen-hour shifts for wages no Dutch person would look at. Many of the workers are migrant labourers who follow the various harvests throughout Europe, moving on south afterwards for oranges and, later, work in the vineyards. Others simply come for a good time: the beer is cheap in Holland, as are soft drugs, which are plentifully – and legally – available. The "bulbers", as they refer to themselves, line up for work at 7.30am and toil until the late evening packing and labelling tulip and hyacinth bulbs. The rest of the time they spend drinking in the English bars of Hillegom, Haarlem or Leiden, sleeping in makeshift camps outside the bulb warehouses. Not only are the terms and conditions of the job dire, it is also painful work. The dust from tulip bulbs rots the fingers of the packers, leading to a condition known as "bulb finger" – sometimes fingers become infected and swell up. Hyacinth bulbs are even worse: the dust from them lodges in the skin, causing itching – and again – infection. Bulbers are provided with coats and gloves to protect themselves, but the heat in the warehouses is intense, and most simply don't bother with them. There is a bulb-workers union, the *Voedingsbond FNV*, but the British aren't members, and employers break every rule in the book each year when they take them on. Apart from the bulb barons, the Dutch see the British as a bizarre sub-culture during their time here, amazed at their capacities for an excessive intake of booze and dope; the Brits, for their part, are unconcerned, playing up to the role of "the crazy English".

Aalsmeer and more bulbs

You can see the industry in action in **AALSMEER**, 23km north of Leiden toward Amsterdam, whose flower auction, again the largest in the world, is held daily in a building approximately the size of 75 football fields (Mon–Fri 7.30–11am; *f*4). The dealing is fast and furious, and the turnover staggering. In an average year around *f*1.5 billion (about £500 million/$800 million) worth of plants and flowers are traded here, many of which arrive in florist's shops throughout Europe on the same day.

There are other places, too, with bulbs and flowers, though none as spectacular as the Keukenhof, nor as vibrant as the Aalsmeer auction. The **Frans Roozen nurseries** at Vogelenzangseweg 49 in **VOGELENZANG**, a little way south of Haarlem (April–May Mon–Sun 8am–6pm, July–Sept Mon–Fri 9am–5pm; free), have a show greenhouse displaying blooms. **RIJNSBURG**, just north of Leiden, has a flower parade in early August each year, from Rijnsburg to Leiden and Noordwijk. And there's a similar parade from Haarlem to Noordwijk (see below) at the end of April, culminating with a display of the floats in the town.

The coast: Katwijk and Noordwijk

Like all of the towns in this part of Holland, Leiden has easy access to some fine beaches, though the coastal resorts themselves aren't much to write home about, and unless you're keen to swim the only reason for visiting is for their larger – and cheaper – supply of accommodation and campsites. **KATWIJK-AAN-ZEE**, accessible by bus #31, #41 or express bus #35, from the stop opposite the bus station, is the stock Dutch seaside town, less crowded than Zandvoort and without the pretensions of Scheveningen, but pretty dreary nonetheless – although it does preserve some of the features of an old coastal village in the lines of terraced housing that spread out around the seventeenth-century lighthouse. Its expanse of undeveloped sand dune, though, which stretches along the shore south toward The Hague, is an ideal area for secluded sunbathing. Otherwise its main attraction is the **Katwijk Sluices**, just north of the resort area, beside the main bus route. Completed in 1807, these are a series of gates that regulate the flow of the Oude Rijn as it approaches the sea: around high tide, the gates are closed; when they are opened, the pressure of the accumulated water brushes aside the sand deposited at the mouth of the river by the sea – a simple system that finally determined the course of the Oude Rijn, which for centuries had been continually diverted by the sand deposits, turning the surrounding fields into a giant swamp.

NOORDWIJK-AAN-ZEE, some 3km up the coast and reachable on bus #40, #42 or express bus #25, from the same stop, is of even less appeal, not much more than a string of grandiose hotel developments built across the undulating sand dunes behind the coast. However, it again offers some excellent stretches of beach. The one time when it's worth coming to see the town itself is the last weekend in April, when a flower parade from Haarlem arrives and makes an illuminated tour of Noordwijk. The next morning the floats are displayed in the village.

The Hague and Scheveningen

With its urbane atmosphere, **THE HAGUE** is different from any other Dutch city. Since the sixteenth century it's been the political capital and the focus of national institutions, in a country built on civic independence and munificence. Frequently disregarded until the development of central government in the nineteenth century, The Hague's older buildings are a rather subdued and modest collection with little of Amsterdam's flamboyance. Most of the city's canal houses are demurely classical with a powerful sense of sedate prosperity. In 1859 English poet Matthew Arnold wrote: "I never saw a city where the well-to-do classes seemed to have given the whole place so much of their own air of wealth, finished cleanliness, and comfort; but I never saw one, either, in which my heart would so have sunk at the thought of living." Things haven't changed much: today's "well-to-do classes" – mostly diplomats in dark Mercedes and multinational executives – ensure that many of the city's hotels and restaurants are firmly in the expense account category, and the nightlife is similarly packaged. But, away from the mediocrity of wealth, The Hague does have cheaper and livelier bars and restaurants – and even its share of restless adolescents hanging around the pizza joints.

The town may be rather drab, but it does have some excellent museums, principally the famed collection of old Dutch masters at the **Mauritshuis**, and more modern works of art at the **Gemeente Museum**.

Arrival, information and accommodation

The Hague has two **train stations** – Den Haag HS (Hollands Spoor) and Den Haag CS (Centraal Station). Of the two, Den Haag CS is the more convenient, sited five minutes' walk east of the town centre next door to the complex housing the VVV (April–Sept Mon–Sat 9am–9pm, Sun 10am–5pm; Oct–March Mon–Sat

Scheveningen Harbour

NORTH SEA

Pier

Kurhaus

STRANDWEG BOULEVARD

VVV

GEVERS DEYNOOT WEG

GREVERS DEYNOOT WEG

0   100 m

SCHEVENINGEN

Oostduinpark

SCHOKKER WEG

J. PRONK STR.

North Sea Trips

NEPTUNUS STR

STEVIN

BADHUIS STR

BADHUIS WEG

NIEUWE PARK LAAN

DR. LELYKADE

WEG STRAAT

SCHEVENINGSE WEG

BADHUIS KADE

HARING KADE

KANAL WEG

Westbroek Park

WESTDUIN

HARING KADE

DREKER WEG

NIEUWE PARKLAAN

BADHUIS WEG

Nieuwe Scheveningse Bosjes

STATEN LAAN

EISENHOWER LAAN

PROF. B.M. TELDERS WEG

VERHULL WEG KADE

VAN ALKEMADE LAAN

Gemeente Museum

JOHAN DE WITT LAAN

Madurodam Model City

Museon & Omniversum

JOHAN A. GOEKOOP LAAN

SCHEVENINGSE WEG

Scheveningse Bosjes

VERHULL WEG

FERNELL WEG

HUBERTUS VIADUCT

PLESSISLAAN

PRES. KENNEDY LAAN

STADHOUDERS LAAN

WAALSDORPER WEG

JACOB CATS LAAN

HOENSTR

DEDELSTR

Peace Palace

PATIJN LAAN

RAAM WEG

OOSTDUIN LAAN

VAN MEERDERVOORT

Mesdag Museum

PRINS HENDRIK STR

PRINS HENDRIK PLEIN

KONINGINNE GRACHT

JAVA STRAAT

WASSENAARSE WEG

ZEE STRAAT

Panorama Mesdag

FREDERIK STR

PAULOWNA STR

WITTE DE WITH STR PIET HEIN STR

ELAND STRAAT

HOGE WAL

MAURITS

VAN ALKEMADE LAAN

NORDWAL

MAURITS

PARK STRAAT

KONINGS KADE

Palais Noordeinde

NOORD EINDE

J. VOORHOUT

Mermanno-Westreenianum

To Ockenburgh Campsite & Youth Hostel

WEST EINDE DAG

KNEUTERDIJK

Grote Kerk

GROENMARKT

Mauritshuis

Haagse Bosjes

Paleïs Huis ten Bosch

PRINSEGRACHT

Binnenhof

VLAMINGSTR SPUISTR

LANGE POTEN

HERENGRACHT

BEZUIDEN HOUTSE WEG SPUI

GROTE MARKT STR

WAGENSTRAAT

KALVERMARKT

VVV

Den Haag CS Station

PRINS BERNHARD VIADUCT

STATIONS WEG

RIJSWIJKSE PLEIN

WETERING KADE

STATIONS PLEIN

THE HAGUE AND SCHEVENINGEN

Den Haag HS Station

9am–6pm, Sun 10am–5pm; ☎06/34035051 50c per minute), immediately outside the main entrance, and the bus and tram stations. Den Haag HS is 1km to the south, and frequent rail services connect the two. The Hague may be the country's third largest city, but almost everything worth seeing is within easy walking distance of Den Haag CS; if you intend to use the city's buses and trams, the VVV and counters at the train station sell the standard *strippenkaart* and a *dagkaart* – the best bet if you're only here for the day.

Accommodation in The Hague proper is hard to find and often expensive – you might be better off basing yourself in Scheveningen, twenty minutes' ride away by tram (see p.138), where rooms are more plentiful and slightly cheaper. If you do want to stay in town, the best bet is to pay a few guilders and let the VVV arrange somewhere for you to stay – especially as the cheaper pensions are spread out all over the city. Otherwise, there's a cluster of seedy but reasonably priced **hotels** just outside Den Haag HS station – the *Aristo*, Stationsweg 164–166 (☎389 0847; ③); the *Astoria*, Stationsweg 139 (☎384 0401; ③); which charges from *f*85; the *Limburg*, Stationsplein 49 (☎384 0102: ③); and the *Du Commerce*, Stationsplein 64 (☎380 8511; ③). There are also two relatively central pensions: the *Huize Bellevue*, northwest of the centre along Laan Van Meerdervoort, right at Groot Hertoginne, first left on the northern part of Beeklaan at no. 417 (☎360 5552: ③); and the *Minnema*, a short journey north of the centre just east of Koningskade/Raamweg at Dedelstraat 25 (no phone; ③).

The official **youth hostel**, *Ockenburgh*, is at Monsterseweg 4 (☎397 0011; ②), some 10km to the west of the town centre just behind the beach at Kijkduin (bus #122, #123, #124 from Centraal Station). It's attached to a misleadingly named budget hotel (④). This adjoins the best and largest **campsite** in the area, *Camping Ockenburgh*, Wijndaelerweg 25 (open March–Oct; ☎325 2364) – bus #4 from the station. Both the youth hostel and the campsite are about ten minutes' walk from the nearest bus stop; ask the driver to let you off.

> The Hague area telephone code, including Scheveningen, is ☎070

The city centre

Right in the centre, and the oldest part of the city, the **Binnenhof** ("inner court") is the home of Holland's bicameral parliament. Count William II built a castle here in the thirteenth century, and the settlement that grew up around it became known as the "Count's Domain" – *'s Gravenhage*, literally "Count's Hedge" – which is still the city's official name. As the embodiment of central rather than municipal power, the Binnenhof had a chequered history – empty or occupied, feted or ignored – until the nineteenth century when The Hague shared political capital status with Brussels during the uneasy times of the United Kingdom of the Netherlands. Thereafter it became the seat of government, home to an effective legislature. The present rectangular complex is a rather mundane affair, a confusing mixture of shape and style that irritated nineteenth-century Dutch parliamentarians with its obvious lack of prestige, and their modern equivalents, members of the Tweedekamer, have recently moved into a new extension.

The best view is from the front, where a small lake – the **Hof Vijver** (Court Pond) – mirrors the attractive symmetry of the front facade. Behind the lake, the

Binnenhof is a major tourist attraction, but there's precious little to see except the **Ridderzaal** (Hall of the Knights), a slender-turreted structure used for state occasions. It's been a courtroom, market and stable, and so repeatedly replaced and renovated that little of the thirteenth-century original remains. An undramatic guided tour of the Ridderzaal and the chambers of parliament (often closed on Mon & Tues) starts regularly from the information office at Binnenhof 8a (Mon–Sat 10am–4pm, July–Aug also Sun noon–4pm; *f*5).

The Mauritshuis Collection

To the immediate east of the Binnenhof, the **Royal Picture Gallery Mauritshuis**, Korte Vijverberg 8 (Tues–Sat 10am–5pm, Sun 11am–5pm; *f*7.50 paid as you leave the gallery), is located in a magnificent seventeenth-century mansion. Generally considered to be one of the best galleries in Europe, it's famous for its extensive range of Flemish and Dutch paintings from the fifteenth to the eighteenth centuries, based on the collection accumulated by Prince William V of Orange (1748–1806). All the major Dutch artists are represented, and it's well laid out, with multilingual cards in each room providing background notes on all the major canvases. At present the rooms are not numbered, and the policy of the museum is (rather awkwardly) to spread the works of many of the key artists through several rooms, rather than place them together. For further detailed information, there's a free brochure at the entrance, while the museum shop sells an excellent guidebook for *f*25. Alternatively you can join one of the irregular and expensive conducted tours – prices depend on length; ask at reception for times.

The entrance and museum shop are in the **basement** on the east side of the building, together with **Andy Warhol**'s *Queen Beatrix*, a twentieth-century aperitif to the collection above. Heading up the stairs to the **first floor**, walk back toward the old front doors and enter the room on the left, where **Hans Memling**'s *Portrait of a Man* is a typically observant work, right down to the scar on the nose. Close by, **Rogier van der Weyden**'s *The Lamentation of Christ* is a harrowing picture of death and sorrow, Christ's head hanging down toward the earth, surrounded by the faces of the mourners, each with a particular expression of anguish and pain. **Quinten Metsys** was the first major artist to work in Antwerp, where he was made a Master of the Guild in 1519. An influential figure, the focus of his work was the attempt to imbue his religious pictures with spiritual sensitivity, and his *Descent from the Cross* is a fine example – Christ's suffering face under the weight of the Cross contrasted with the grinning, taunting onlookers behind.

Proceeding in a counterclockwise direction, through a series of rooms on either side of the Italianate dining room, exhibits include two giant allegorical canvases by Jan Sanders van Hemessen; Lucas Cranach the Younger's spirited *Man with a Red Beard*; and two works by **Hans Holbein the Younger**, a striking *Portrait of Robert Cheeseman*, where all the materials – the fur collar, the falcon's feathers and the cape – seem to take on the appropriate texture, and his *Portrait of Jane Seymour*, one of several pictures commissioned by Henry VIII, who sent him abroad to paint matrimonial candidates. Holbein's vibrant technique was later to land him in hot water: an over-flattering portrait of Anne of Cleves swayed Henry into an unhappy marriage with his "Flanders' Mare" that was to last only six months.

Malieveld

Koekamp

BEZUIDENHOUTSEWEG

VVV

JULIANA PLEIN

Den Haag
Centraal
Station

KONINGINNEGRACHT

PRINCESSEGRACHT

ZWARTEWEG

Meermanno
-Westreenianum
Museum

NIEUWE UITLEG

KORTE VOORHOUT

CASUARIESTRAAT

BELEIJENBURG

HERENGRACHT

FLUWELEN BURGWAL

VOS IN TUINSTRAAT

LANGE HOUTSTR

LANGE VOORHOUT

KAZERNE STRAAT

TOURNOOIVELD

Historical
Museum

Mauritshuis

DOELENSTR

KORTE VIJVERBERG

Plein

LANGE POTEN

KALVERMARKT

Ridderzaal

Hof Vijver

HOGE NIEUWSTRAAT

LANGE VIJVERBERG

Binnenhof

HOFSTRAAT

SPUI

100 m

0

PARKSTRAAT

GROTE MARKT STRAAT

PALEISSTRAAT

HOFWEG

KNEUTER DIJK

Buitenhof

Gevangenpoort
Museum

Prince
William V
Gallery

SPUISTRAAT

KETTINGSTR

NOORDEINDE

NOORDEINDE

HOOGSTRAAT

GRAVENSTR

VENESTRAAT

WAGENSTRAAT

Paleis
Noordeinde

PAPESTRAAT

OUDE MOLSTRAAT

NIEUWSTRAAT

Paleis
Tuin

NOBELSTRAAT

Oude Stadhuis

PRINSE STRAAT

Groenmarkt

PRINCESSEWAL

Post
Office

Grote Kerk

Kerkplein

**THE HAGUE
CITY CENTRE**

Of a number of paintings by **Adriaen Brouwer**, *Quarrel at a Card Table* and *Inn with Drunken Peasants* are two of the better known, with thick, rough brush-strokes recording contemporary Flemish low-life. Brouwer could approach this subject with some authority, as he spent most of his brief life in either tavern or prison. **Peter Paul Rubens**, the acclaimed painter and diplomat, was a contemporary of Brouwer, though the two could hardly be more dissimilar: Rubens' *Portrait of Isabella Brant*, his first wife, is a typically grand, rather statuesque work, not perhaps as intriguing as *Adam and Eve in Paradise*, a collaboration between Rubens, who painted the figures, and **Jan Brueghel the Elder**, who filled in the dreamlike animals and landscape behind. In the same room are two examples of the work of Rubens' chief assistant, **Anthony van Dyck**, a portrait specialist who found fame at the court of English King Charles I. His *Pieter Stevens of Antwerp* and *Quinton Simons of Antwerp* are good early examples of his tendency to flatter and ennoble that no doubt helped him into the job. Nearby, and again showing the influence of Rubens, is the robust *Adoration of the Shepherds* by Jacob Jordaens.

On the **second-floor** landing, the broad brush-strokes of **Frans Hals'** *Laughing Boy* are far removed from the restrained style he was forced to adopt in his more familiar paintings of the burghers of Haarlem. **Carel Fabritius**, pupil of Rembrandt and (possibly) teacher of Vermeer, was killed in a gunpowder explosion at Delft when he was only 22. Few canvases survive but an exquisite exception is *The Goldfinch*, a curious, almost impressionistic work, with the bird reduced to a blur of colour. One of his Delft contemporaries was Gerard Houckgeest, who specialized in church interiors, like *The Tomb of William of Orange*, a minutely observed study of architectural lines lightened by expanses of white marble.

Off the second-floor landing, on the left at the front of the museum, is the Mauritshuis' most famous painting, **Jan Vermeer's** *View of Delft*, a superb townscape of 1658, with the fine lines of the city drawn beneath a cloudy sky, a patchwork of varying light and shade – though the dispassionate, photographic quality the painting has in reproduction is oddly lacking in the large canvas. In the same room, Gerard Ter Borch's *Lice Hunt* is in striking contrast to Vermeer's detachment, a vignette of seventeenth-century domestic life.

Heading in a counterclockwise direction, other highlights include the busy, stick-like figures of the *Winter Scene* by Hendrik Avercamp, the deaf and dumb artist from Kampen, and Paulus Potter's lifelike *Young Bull*, a massive canvas complete with dung and rather frightening testicles. Best known of the **Rembrandts** is the *Anatomy Lesson of Dr Tulp*, from 1632, the artist's first commission in Amsterdam. The peering pose of the "students" who lean over the corpse solved the problem of emphasis falling on the body rather than the subjects of the portrait, who were in fact members of the surgeons' guild. Hopefully Tulp's skills as an anatomist were better than his medical advice, which included the recommendation that his patients drink fifty cups of tea a day.

Dotted throughout the museum are no fewer than thirteen paintings by **Jan Steen**, including a wonderfully riotous picture carrying the legend "The way you hear it, is the way you sing it" – a parable on the young learning bad habits from the old – and a typically salacious *Girl Eating Oysters*.

The rest of the city centre

A few metres to the west of the Binnenhof, the **Gevangenpoort**, Buitenhof 33 (Prisoner's Gate Museum; Mon–Fri 10am–4pm, April–Sept also Sun 1–5pm; hourly tours only; last tour 4pm; *f*5), was originally part of the city fortifications.

Used as a prison until the nineteenth century, it now contains an array of instruments of torture and punishment centred around its Chamber of Horrors. As well as the guillotine blades, racks and gallows, the old cells are in a good state of preservation – including the *ridderkamer* for the more privileged captive. Here Cornelius de Witt, Burgomaster of Dordrecht, was imprisoned before he and his brother Johan, another staunch Republican and leader of the States of Holland, were dragged out and murdered by an Orangist mob in 1672. The brothers were shot, beheaded and cut into pieces which were then auctioned to the crowd; Johan's tongue is preserved for a macabre posterity in the storerooms of the Gemeente Museum. The Gevangenpoort is understandably popular; join the line about fifteen minutes before each hourly tour to guarantee a place.

Down the street at Buitenhof 35, the **Prince William V Gallery** (Tues–Sun 11am–4pm; *f*2.50 or free with Mauritshuis ticket) has paintings by Rembrandt, Jordaens and Paulus Potter among others, but it's more interesting as a reconstruction of a typical eighteenth-century gallery – or "cabinet" as they were known. The fashion then was to sandwich paintings together in a cramped patchwork from floor to ceiling: but though it's faithful to the period, this makes viewing difficult for eyes trained by spacious modern museums.

A five-minute walk away to the west, and easily the best of The Hague's old churches, St Jacobskerk or the **Grote Kerk** (July & Aug Mon 11am–4pm; free; otherwise closed to the public except when there are exhibitions, usually open Mon–Fri 11am–4pm, Sun 1–5pm) is a hall church with an exhilarating sense of breadth and warmly decorated vaulting. The one thing you can't miss, as it's placed where the high altar should be, is the memorial to the unmemorable Admiral Opdam, who was blown up with his ship during the little-remembered naval battle of Lowestoft in 1665. Keep an eye open for the Renaissance pulpit: similar to the one in Delft's Oude Kerk, it has carved panels framing the apostles in false perspective. For the energetic, the church tower (open on Wed at noon for groups of 8–10 people; ☎365 86 65) provides blustery views over the town.

Back in the centre, **Lange Voorhout** is fringed by an impressive spread of diplomatic mansions and the *Hotel des Indes*, where the ballerina Anna Pavlova died in 1931 and where today you stand the best chance of being flattened by a chauffeur-driven limousine. Just to the east, the **Meermanno-Westreenianum Museum**, Prinsessegracht 30 (Mon–Sat 1–5pm; free), has a small collection of remarkably well-preserved medieval illuminated manuscripts and Bibles; and nearby, the **Hague Historical Museum**, Korte Vijverberg 7 (Tues–Fri 11am–5pm, Sat & Sun 1–5pm; *f*4), mixes local history with temporary exhibitions on topical issues.

To the immediate west of Lange Voorhout, the sixteenth-century **Paleis Noordeinde** (no admission) is one of several royal buildings that lure tourists to this part of town. In 1980, Queen Juliana abdicated in favour of her daughter Beatrix, who proceeded to return the royal residence from the province of Utrecht to The Hague. Despite the queen's attempts to demystify the monarchy, there's no deterring the enthusiasts who fill the expensive "Royal Tours" around the peripheries of the palace and Beatrix's other residence just outside town, the seventeenth-century **Huis ten Bosch** (literally "House in the Woods"; no admission).

Much of the rest of the centre is drab and dreary, an apparently unformulated mixture of the stately old and the brashly new (the giant *Babylon* shopping complex by the Centraal Station wins the ugliness award). During the war years the occupying German forces built a V2 launching site just outside the city: as a result it was almost as thoroughly bombed by the Allies as its neighbour Rotterdam had been by the Luftwaffe.

North of the city centre

Ten minutes' walk north of the centre along Noordeinde, the **Panorama Mesdag**, Zeestraat 65b (Mon–Sat 10am–5pm, Sun noon–5pm; ƒ4), was designed in the late nineteenth century by Hendrik Mesdag, banker turned painter and local citizen become Hague School luminary. His unremarkable seascapes are tinged with an unlikable bourgeois sentimentality, but there's no denying the achievement of his panorama, a depiction of Scheveningen as it would have appeared in 1881. Completed in four months with help from his wife and the young G.H. Breitner, the painting is so naturalistic that it takes a few moments for the skills of lighting and perspective to become apparent. Five minutes' walk from the Panorama at Laan van Meerdervoort 7f is the house Mesdag bought as a home and gallery. At the time it overlooked one of his favourite subjects, the dunes, the inspiration for much of his work, and today contains the **Mesdag Museum** (Tues–Sat 10am–5pm, Sun 1–5pm). His collection includes a number of Hague School paintings which, like his own work, take the seascapes of the nearby coast as their subject. There are also paintings by Corot, Rousseau, Delacroix and Millet, though none of them represents the artists' best achievements. Perhaps the most interesting exhibits are the florid and distinctive paintings of Antonio Mancini, whose oddly disquieting subjects are reminiscent of Klimt.

The Peace Palace

Round the corner from the Mesdag Museum, framing the Carnegieplein, the **Peace Palace** (Mon–Fri hourly guided tours at 10am, 11am, 2pm, 3pm, May–Aug also at 4pm; ƒ5; check with the VVV for times of tours in English) is home to the Court of International Justice, and, for all the wrong reasons, is a monument to the futility of war. Toward the end of the nineteenth century, Tsar Nicholas II called an international conference for the peaceful reconciliation of national problems. The result was the First Hague Peace Conference of 1899 whose purpose was to "help find a lasting peace and, above all, a way of limiting the progressive development of existing arms". This in turn led to the formation of a Permanent Court of Arbitration housed obscurely in The Hague until the American industrialist Andrew Carnegie gave $1.5 million for a new building – the Peace Palace. These honorable aims came to nothing with the mass slaughter of World War I: just as the donations of tapestries, urns, marble and stained glass were arriving from all over the world, so Europe's military commanders were preparing their offensives. Backed by a massive law library, fifteen judges are still in action today, conducting trade matters in English and diplomatic affairs in French. Widely respected and generally considered neutral, their judgments are nevertheless not binding.

The Gemeentemuseum, Museon and Omniversum

North of the Peace Palace, the **Gemeentemuseum**, Stadhouderslaan 41 (Tues–Sun 11am–5pm; ƒ7; bus #4 from Centraal Station), is arguably the best and certainly the most diverse of The Hague's many museums. Designed by H.P. Berlage in the 1930s, it's generally considered to be his masterpiece, although its layout can be confusing, and the labelling is erratic. However, the musical instruments are outstanding – especially the harpsichords and early pianos – and the Islamic ceramics are extraordinary. The collection of modern art is frustrating, but it does attempt to outline the development of Dutch painting through the Romantic, Hague and Expressionist schools to the De Stijl movement. **Mondrian,** most famous member of the De Stijl group, dominates this part of the gallery: the museum has the world's largest collection of his paintings, though much of it consists of (deservedly) unfamiliar early works painted before he evolved the abstraction of form into geometry and pure colour for which he's best known.

Adjoining the Gemeentemuseum is a modern building that houses the **Museon** (Tues–Fri 10am–5pm, Sat & Sun noon–5pm; ƒ5), a sequence of nonspecialist exhibitions of human activities related to the history of the earth. Selfconsciously internationalist, it's aimed at school parties, as is the adjoining **Omniversum** or "Space Theatre" (shows on the hour, Tues–Thurs 11am–4pm, Fri–Sun 11am–9pm; ƒ16). A planetarium in all but name, it possesses all the technical gadgetry you'd expect.

The Madurodam Miniature Town

Halfway between The Hague and Scheveningen, the **Madurodam Miniature Town** (daily March–May 9am–10.30pm; June–Aug 9am–11pm; Sept 9am–9.30pm; Oct–Dec 9am–6pm; closed Jan–Feb; ƒ12.50), reachable on tram #1 or #9, is heavily plugged by the tourist authorities, though its origins are more interesting than the trite and expensive present, a copy of a Dutch town on a 1:25 scale. The original money was put up by a J.M.L. Maduro, who wished to establish a memorial to his son who had distinguished himself during the German invasion of 1940 and died in Dachau concentration camp five years later. There's a memorial to him just by the entrance, and profits from the Miniature Town are used for general Dutch social and cultural activities.

Eating and drinking

For cheap **food**, there's a cluster of places along Herenstraat, off Plein near the Binnenhof, the best of which is the *De Apendans* at no. 13, a no-frills, popular restaurant serving a simple Dutch menu for ƒ17 and up. Other reasonably priced, centrally sited alternatives include good fishy snacks at *Noordzee*, Spuistraat 44; pizzas at *Pinelli*, on the way to the Grote Kerk at Dag. Groenmarkt 31; good quality shoppers' lunches and decent pizzas at *Brasserie Renoir* at the bottom of Noordeinde, no. 2a; vegetarian meals at *De Dageraad*, just east of Lange Voorhout at Hooikade 4; and snacks at the *Bodega De Posthoorn*, Lange Voorhout 39a. Failing that, *Eetcafé Hardans*, Nobelstraat 11b, behind the post office, has plenty of choice for around ƒ15, and *Grand Café Popacatepetl*, Buitenhof 4–5, is a great venue for Mexican full meals or just drinks and tapas. On an expense account you could do worse than sample the seafood delights of the *Oesterbar Saur*, at Lange Voorhout 47–53, or Italian specialities at *La Liguria*, Noordeinde 97.

For **bars**, head for the streets to the immediate east of Lange Voorhout, including the quiet canals around Smidswater and Hooikade, where the *De Landeman* and the *Pompernickel* are at Denneweg 48 and 27. In the other direction, along Papestraat, *Café de Paap*, at no. 32, has bands, currently on Tuesday nights and Sunday afternoons.

Listings

Bikes Can be rented from either of The Hague's train stations for *f*7.50 a day, plus a *f*200 deposit.

Bookshop *Boekhandel Plantijn*, Noordeinde 62. Good for art books.

Car rental *Avis*, Theresiastraat 216 (☎385 0698); *Budget*, Juliana van Stolberglaan 214 (☎382 4386); *Europcar* (at the *Hotel Sofitel*), Koningin Julianaplein 35 (☎385 1708).

Chemists Night services listed in newspapers and at the *VVV*.

Dentist Daily 7am–midnight ☎365 46 46, Sat & Sun ☎397 44 91.

Embassies *Australia*, Carnegielaan 12 (☎310 82 00); *Canada*, Sophialaan 7 (☎361 41 11); *Ireland*, Dr Kuyperstraat 9 (☎363 09 93); *UK*, Lange Voorhout 10 (☎364 58 00); *USA*, Lange Voorhout 102 (☎310 9209).

Gay scene There are several gay bars: try *Boko*, Nieuwe Schoolstraat 2, or *Stairs*, Nieuwe Schoolstraat 11.

Hospital Ambulances ☎06 11; general medical care at night ☎345 5300.

Information A free monthly magazine with details of concerts, theatre performances, special events and entertainments in The Hague and environs is available from the *VVV*.

Jazz records *Jazz Inn*, Groenmarkt 32. A superb jazz record shop.

Markets General: Herman Costerstraat (Mon & Sat 8am–5pm). Food: Markthof, Gedempte Gracht/Spui (Mon 11am–6pm, Tues–Fri 9am–6pm). Antiques, books and curios: Lange Voorhout (mid-May to Sept Thurs & Sun 11am–9pm); Plein (Oct to mid-May Thurs 11am–9pm).

Post office Nobelstraat; Prinsenstraat; Kerkplein (Mon–Fri 8.30am–6.30pm, Thurs also 6.30–8.30pm, Sat 9am–4pm).

The **North Sea Jazz Festival**, held every year in mid-July at the Nederlands Congresgebouw, Churchillplein 10, is The Hague's most prestigious event, attracting international media coverage and many of the world's most famous musicians. Details of performances are available from the *VVV*, who will also reserve accommodation, which is virtually impossible to find after the festival has begun. Various kinds of tickets can be purchased; a *dagkaart*, for example, valid for an entire day, costs *f*75.

Scheveningen

Situated on the coast about 4km from the centre of The Hague, the old fishing port of **SCHEVENINGEN*** has none of its neighbour's businesslike air, enjoying instead its status as Holland's top coastal resort, attracting more than nine million visitors a year to its beach, pier and casino. It's not a particularly attractive place, but it can make a good alternative base if you're keen to see something of The Hague, since, not surprisingly, hotels are cheaper and more plentiful. At certain times of year, too, it's worth a special visit – in mid-June for example, when the town hosts a massive international **kite festival** that takes over the beach and much of the town.

---

* One of the difficulties involved in getting to Scheveningen is pronouncing the name. During World War II, resistance groups tested suspected Nazi infiltrators by getting them to say "Scheveningen" – an impossible feat for Germans, apparently, and not much easier for English-speakers.

Scheveningen was a fashionable resort in the nineteenth century, but faded after the 1920s; it's currently being redeveloped as an all-year resort. The centre of town is called **Scheveningen Bad**, grouped around the massive **Kurhaus** hotel that's the most potent symbol of the town's bygone era. Sadly, it's the only reminder, the rest of the town centre a rather tacky mix of shopping precinct, guesthouses and amusement arcades, both around the hotel and along the busy seafront. Inside, the *Kurhaus* has recently been refurbished and is worth a peek into its main central hall, which looks much as it would have done in the town's heyday, richly frescoed, with mermaids and semi-clad maidens cavorting high above the gathered diners. You can enjoy the atmosphere for the price of a cup of coffee, or attend one of the classical concerts occasionally held here.

The town **museum** at Neptunusstraat 92 (Tues–Sat 10am–5pm; f3) recaptures some of the atmosphere of old Scheveningen, with figures in nineteenth-century costume, dioramas showing the cramped conditions on board the primitive fishing boats, and items such as nets and compasses from the boats themselves. But most people come here for the **beach** – a marvellous strand, though very crowded in summer, and it's hard to be sure about the condition of the water. The **pier** isn't especially impressive either, its appendages packed with the rods of fishermen and various amusements, and you'd do better to either indulge yourself in the **Wave Pool** centre, complete with a sub-tropical climate, whirlpools and waterslides, or stroll north to emptier beaches and dunes in the **Oostduinpark**. Otherwise, a kilometre or so in the opposite direction, Scheveningen's harbour and fishing port still flourish in the more workaday environs of **Scheveningen Haven**: the site of a large container depot and an early morning **fish auction**, by the more northerly of the two docks, at Visafslagweg 1 (Mon–Sat 7–10am) – though this is very much a technical, computerized affair. Boat trips on the **North Sea** (June–Sept daily at 4pm) start from Dr. Lelykade, beside the southern dock.

Practicalities

Trams #1, #7 and #9 run from The Hague CS to Scheveningen, stopping by the *Kurhaus*; from The Hague HS, take tram #8. Tram #1 also connects with Delft. If you're staying in Scheveningen, the **VVV** at Gevers Deynootweg 126 (April–Sept Mon–Sat 9am–9pm, Sun 10am–5pm; Oct–March Mon–Sat 9am–6pm, Sun 10am–5pm; ☎06/3403 5051, 50c per minute) books rooms in private homes (for bookings call ☎350 05 00). Failing that, there are plenty of **hotels**. Try *Martin*, Gevers Deynootweg 23 (☎352 41 45; ③); *Albion* across the road (☎355 79 87; ④); or one of the group on the other side of the *Kurhaus* on the seafront Zeekant, which include the comfortable *Aquarius*, Zeekant 107–110 (☎354 36 84; ④). There's another, smaller hotel, the *Marion*, at Havenkade 3a (☎354 35 01; ②), while other cheap options include the *Meyer*, near the town museum at Stevinstraat 64 (☎355 81 38; ③), the *El Cid*, Badhuisweg 51 (☎354 66 67; ③), and the slightly more pricy *Hage*, closer to the sea at Seinpostduin 23 (☎351 46 96; ③).

As for **eating**, the *Big Bell*, on the seafront next to the *Kurhaus*, is about the cheapest place in the town centre, serving huge portions of Dutch food for under f20; the *Olympiade*, underneath the *Martin* hotel, is a cosy Greek eatery, similarly priced. In Scheveningen Haven there are a couple of decent waterside fish restaurants, both by the outer harbour: the *Havenrestaurant* is simple and inexpensive, the *Mero*, further down toward the sea, is more upmarket and pricier. For evening **drinking**, try the *Kings Arms*, a friendly, mock-English pub outside the *Kurhaus* on Gevers Deyjnootplein.

Delft

DELFT has considerable charm: gabled red-roofed houses stand beside tree-lined canals, and the pastel colours of the brickwork and bridges give the town a faded, placid tranquillity – a tranquillity that from spring onwards is systematically destroyed by tourists. They arrive in their air-conditioned busloads and descend to congest the narrow streets, buy an overpriced piece of gift pottery and photograph the spire of the Nieuwe Kerk. And beneath all the tourists, the gift shops and the tearooms, old Delft itself gets increasingly difficult to find.

Why is Delft so popular? Apart from its prettiness, the obvious answer is **Delftware**, the clunky and monotonous blue-and-white ceramics to which the town gave its name in the seventeenth century. If you've already slogged through the vast collection in Amsterdam's Rijksmuseum it needs no introduction; and

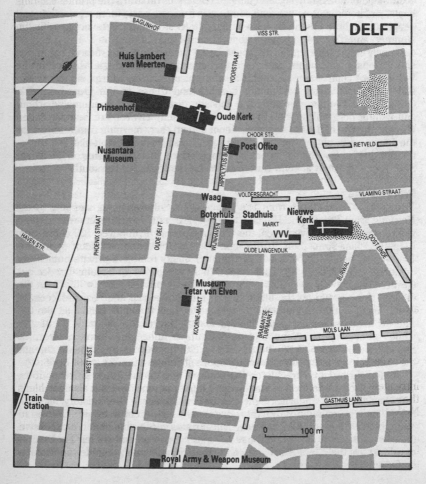

though production of the "real" Delftware is down to a trickle, cheap mass-produced copies have found a profitable niche in today's shops. For those sufficiently interested, *De Porceleyne Fles* at Rotterdamsweg 119, a factory producing Delftware, is open for visits (April–Oct Mon–Sat 9am–5pm, Sun 10am–4pm; Nov–March Mon–Fri 9am–5pm, Sat 10am–5pm; free), and the **Huis Lambert van Meerten Museum** at Oude Delft 199 (Tues–Sat 10am–5pm, Sun 1–5pm; *f*3.50) has a large collection of Delft (and other) tiles.

Another reason for Delft's popularity is the **Vermeer** connection. The artist was born in the town and died here, too – leaving a wife, eleven children and a huge debt to the local baker. He had given the man two pictures as security, and his wife bankrupted herself trying to retrieve them. Only traces remain of the town as depicted in Vermeer's famous *View of Delft*, now in the Mauritshuis in The Hague. You'll find them most easily on foot – it's not a difficult place to explore. The **Markt** is the best place to start, a central point of reference with the Renaissance Stadhuis at one end and the Nieuwe Kerk at the other. Lined with cafés, restaurants and teenagers blaring disco music on ghetto-blasters, it really gets going with the Thursday general market – not, therefore, the ideal day to visit.

The **Nieuwe Kerk** (April–Oct Mon–Sat 9am–5pm; Nov–March Mon–Sat 11am–4pm; *f*2.50) is new only in comparison with the Oude Kerk, as there's been a church on this site since 1381. Most of the original structure, however, was destroyed in the great fire that swept over Delft in 1536, and the remainder in a powder magazine explosion a century later – a disaster, incidentally, which claimed the life of the artist Carel Fabritius, Rembrandt's greatest pupil and (debatably) the teacher of Vermeer. The most striking part of the restoration is in fact the most recent – the 100-metre spire (May to mid-June Tues–Sat 10am–4.30pm; mid-June to Aug Mon–Sat 10am–4.30pm; *f*3.25), replaced in 1872 and from whose summit there's a great view of the town. Unless you're a Dutch monarchist, the church's interior is rather uninspiring: it contains the burial vaults of the Dutch royal family, the most recent addition being Queen Wilhelmina in 1962. Only the mausoleum of William the Silent grabs your attention, an odd hodgepodge of styles concocted by Hendrik de Keyser, architect also of the Stadhuis opposite.

South of the Stadhuis, signs direct you to the **Koornmarkt**, one of the town's most characteristic seventeenth-century streets. At no. 67 is the **Museum Tétar van Elven** (May to mid-Oct Tues–Sat 1–5pm; *f*3), slightly drab in appearance but an authentic restoration of the eighteenth-century patrician house that was the studio and home of Paul Tétar van Elven, a provincial and somewhat forgettable artist/collector. **Wynhaven**, another old canal, leads to Hippolytusbuurt and the Gothic **Oude Kerk** (April–Oct Mon–Sat 10am–5pm; *f*2.50), arguably the town's finest building. Simple and unbuttressed, with an unhealthily leaning tower, it's the result of a succession of churches here from the thirteenth to the seventeenth century; the strong and unornamented vaulting proves interiors don't have to be elaborate to avoid being sombre. The pride of the church is its pulpit of 1548, intricately carved with figures emphasized in false perspective, but also notable is the modern stained glass, depicting and symbolizing the history of The Netherlands – particularly the 1945 liberation – in the north transept. If you're curious about the tombs – including that of Admiral Maarten van Tromp, famed for hoisting a broom at his masthead to "sweep the seas clear of the English" as he sailed up the Medway – take a look at the *Striking Points* pamphlet available at the entrance.

Opposite the Oude Kerk is the former Convent of Saint Agatha or **Prinsenhof** as it came to be known (Tues–Sat 10am–5pm, Sun 1–5pm; June–Aug also Mon 1–5pm; *f*3.50). Housing Delft's municipal art collection (a good group of works including paintings by Aertsen and Honthorst), it has been restored in the style of the late sixteenth century – an era when the building served as the base of **William the Silent** in his Protestant revolt against the Spanish invaders. From here William planned sorties against the imperial Catholic troops of Phillip II, achieving considerable success with his *Watergeuzen* or sea-beggars, a kind of commando-guerrilla unit that initially operated from England. He met his death here at the hands of a French assassin: the bullets that passed through him, made by three pellets welded into one, left their mark on the Prinsenhof walls and can still be seen. Tickets for the Prinsenhof also include admission to the unremarkable **Nusantra** ethnographical museum and the Huis van Meerten tile collection.

Finally, if you have the time, the **Royal Army and Weapon Museum** (Tues–Sat 10am–5pm, Sun 1–5pm; *f*3.50), near the train station, is worth a visit. It has a good display of weaponry, uniforms and military accoutrements – which may sound supremely dull, but isn't, even if you're not an enthusiast. The museum attempts to trace the military history of The Netherlands from the Spanish wars up to the imperialist adventures of the 1950s – which are shown in surprisingly candid detail.

Practicalities

From the train station it's a short walk into town and the VVV at Markt 85 (Mon–Fri 9am–6pm, Sat 11am–3pm; April–Sept also Sun 11am–3pm; ☎015/12 61 00). The cheapest **accommodation** is in the pensions around the station or the Markt; details from the VVV. Otherwise the cheapest hotels are *Les Compagnons*, Markt 61 (☎015/14 01 02; ③), and *De Kok*, Houttuinen 15 (☎015/12 21 25; ③). There's a **campsite**, *De Delftse Hout*, Kortftlaan 5 (bus #60 from the station) which is open from April to October. For **eating**, the *Hotel Monopole*, centrally located on the Markt, is pretty tourist-oriented but has reasonably priced pancakes, *uitsmijters*, light meals and three-course menus; *De Koornbeurs*, close by, is an even cheaper student mensa. *Locus Publicus*, Brabantse Turfmarkt 67, is a popular local hangout, serving a staggering array of beers as well as sandwiches. Try, also, *Café de Wynhaven* on Wynhaven, or *Stadskoffiehuis*, Oude Delft 135, a lunchroom that serves pancakes.

Rotterdam

ROTTERDAM lies at the heart of a maze of rivers and artificial waterways that form the seaward outlet of the rivers Rijn (Rhine) and Maas (Meuse). An important port as early as the fourteenth century, it was one of the major cities of the Dutch Republic, sharing its periods of fortune and decline, until the nineteenth century when it was caught unaware, for the city was ill-prepared for the industrial expansion of the Ruhr, the development of larger ships and the silting up of the Maas. Prosperity returned in a big way with the digging of an entirely new ship canal (the "Nieuwe Waterweg") between 1866 and 1872, and was only brought to a temporary halt during World War II when, without warning, the

Germans bombed the city centre to pieces in 1940 and systematically destroyed the port in 1944.

The postwar period saw the rapid reconstruction of the docks and the town centre, and great efforts were made to keep Rotterdam ahead of its rivals. Consequently, when huge container ships and oil tankers made many port facilities obsolete, the Dutch were equal to the challenge and built an entirely new deep-sea port some 25km to the west of the old town. Completed in 1968, the **Europoort** juts out into the North Sea and can accommodate the largest of ships, contributing to Rotterdam's handling of 300 million tonnes of fuel, grain and materials needed or sold by western Europe each year.

Rapid postwar rebuilding transformed Rotterdam's town centre into a giant covered shopping area, a sterile and formless assembly of concrete and glass. This prospect of docks and shops probably sounds unalluring, but Rotterdam has its moments: in the **Boymans-Van Beuningen Museum** it has one of the best – and most overlooked – galleries in the country, and between the central modernity and dockland sleaze is **Delfshaven**, an old area that survived the bombs. By way of contrast, there's **Oudehaven**. As its name suggests it's an old – in fact the city's oldest – harbour, and was also bombed during the war. However, it's been dazzlingly redeveloped, and is now home to a host of popular bars and cafés. There's not much else, but redevelopment hasn't obliterated Rotterdam's earthy character: the prostitution and dope peddling are for real, not for tourists; if you want to avoid the high spots of the low life, stick to the centre.

> The telephone code for Rotterdam is ☎010

Arrival, information and accommodation

Rotterdam has a large and confusing centre edged by its main rail terminus, **Centraal Station**, that serves as the hub of a useful tram and metro system for the city and its suburbs – though it's a seamy, hostile place late at night. In the station concourse, a sub-office of the **VVV** (Mon–Sat 9am–10pm, Sun 10am–10pm) provides all the usual tourist information, plus a useful city brochure incorporating a street map for ƒ1.50, and free maps of the tram, bus and underground system, divided into zones for the calculation of fares (two sections of a *strippenkaart* or ƒ3 for a single trip in the central zone). The main VVV office, ten minutes' walk away at Coolsingel 67 (Mon–Thurs 9am–5.30pm, Fri 9am–9pm, Sat 9am–5pm; April–Sept also Sun 10am–4pm; ☎06/340 340 65, 50c per minute), offers similar information, concentrating on theatre and concert tickets and more general details on Holland as a whole. Both VVVs operate an **accommodation** booking service and are the best bet for finding somewhere to stay, as Rotterdam's cheaper hotels and pensions are dotted all over the city and are often full in summer. Otherwise, there are a clutch of central, reasonably priced **hotels** and **pensions** a kilometre or so to the southwest of the station. These include the *Rox-Inn*, 's-Gravendijkwal 14 (☎436 61 09; tram #1, #7 or #9; ③); the *Heemraad*, Heemraadssingel 90 (☎477 54 61; tram #1, #7 or #9: ③); and the *Metropole* (☎436 0319; ③). To the immediate north of Centraal Station are the *Bagatelle*, Provenierssingel 26 (☎467 63 48; ②), and the *Holland* (☎465 31 00; ③). For the stouthearted, the **youth hostel** is 3km from the station at Rochussenstraat 107

(☎436 57 63; tram #4 or #6, or metro stop Dijkzigt), and the nearest **campsite** is north of the station at Kanaalweg 84 (☎415 97 72; bus #33). The summer **Sleep In**, Mauritsweg 29b, a five-minute walk south of the station, has very cheap dormitory accommodation.

The City

From Centraal Station, Kruisplein leads south onto Westersingel/Mauritsweg, cutting this part of the city into two sections – to the west is the deteriorated housing of many of the city's migrant workers, and to the east is the **Lijnbaan**, Europe's first pedestrianized shopping precinct, completed in 1953. The Lijnbaan connects into a baffling series of apparently endless shopping areas hemmed in by Weena, Coolsingel, Westblaak and Mauritsweg. To the east of Coolsingel, just off Beursplein, the fifteenth-century **St Laurenskerk** (Grote Kerk; June–Sept Tues–Sat 10am–4pm; Oct–May Thurs noon–2pm; free) has been the object of a clumsy renovation which has left it cold and soulless. Nearby, and marginally more exciting, is the redevelopment of the **Blaak** area with a new central library adjoining a remarkable series of cubist houses, replacing a part of the old city centre destroyed by the bombing. If you're curious, **Kijk-Kubus** (Cube House; Jan & Feb Fri–Sun 11am–5pm; March–Dec Tues–Fri 10am–5pm; June–Sept also open Mon 10am–5pm; *f*2.50), at Overblaak 70, near Blaak train station, is furnished and open to visitors, though there's not much to look at and you're likely to bang your head on a beam or feel dizzy if you peer out of the windows.

Heading west, the **Maritime Museum Prins Hendrik** (Tues–Sun 11am–5pm; *f*6) is situated in the old harbour area beside the Leuvehaven. Apart from an enterprising programme of temporary nautical exhibitions, the outside area has been spruced up for the museum's prime exhibit – an immaculately restored mid-nineteenth-century ironclad, the *Buffel*, complete with communal sinks shaped to match the angle of the bows, a couple of ships' figureheads and a string of luxurious officers' cabins.

Across the boulevard to the north, surrounded by highrise apartment buildings, the **Schielandshuis Museum** (Tues–Sat 10am–5pm, Sun 1–5pm; *f*3.50) is housed in a seventeenth-century mansion at Korte Hoogstraat 31, and has a variety of displays on the history of Rotterdam, incorporating the *Atlas van Stolk* collection of drawings and prints, which includes fascinating sketches of pre-colonial Indonesia. A couple of minutes to the south, the old city docks are enclosed by the Boompjes, a former sea dyke that's now a major freeway, which leads southwest to the **Euromast**, on a rather lonely park corner beside the Nieuwe Maas. This was originally just a drab, grey observation platform thrown up in 1960: the **Spacetower** (March–Oct daily 10am–6pm; Nov–Dec daily 11am–4pm; Jan & Feb Sat & Sun 11am–4pm; *f*13) was added later, its revolving elevator rising on the outside of the 185-metre tower. The view is spectacular, but no less than you'd expect considering the price of entry.

If nothing in the city centre can be called exactly picturesque, **DELFSHAVEN** goes part of the way to make up for it. It's a good 45-minute walk southwest of Centraal Station – fifteen minutes by tram #4 or #6 (direction Schiedam, tram stop Spanjaardstraat), or a couple of minutes on foot from Delfshaven metro. Once the harbour that served Delft, it was from here that the Pilgrim Fathers set sail in 1620, changing to the more reliable *Mayflower* in Plymouth before continuing onward to the New World. Delfshaven was only incorporated into Rotterdam in 1886 and managed to survive World War II virtually intact. Long a neglected area, the town council has recently recognized its tourist potential and has set about conserving and restoring the whole locality as rapidly as possible. Most of the buildings lining the canals are eighteenth- and nineteenth-century warehouses, seen today as "desirable residences" by the upwardly mobile, who are set to turn Delfshaven into a chichi suburb. The **Dubbelde Palmboom**

CENTRAL
ROTTERDAM

Museum, Voorhaven 12 (Tues–Sun 11am–5pm; *f*6), once a jenever distillery, is now an historical museum with a wide-ranging, if unexceptional collection of objects representing work and leisure in the Maas delta. Nearby, the **Zakkendragershuisje**, Voorstraat 13 (Tues–Sat 10am–5pm, Sun 1–5pm; free), was originally the guild room of the Grain Sack Carriers, who decided the allocation of duties by dice. Today, it's a privately owned, fully operational tin foundry, selling a variety of items made in the old moulds.

The Boymans-Van Beuningen Museum

To the northeast of Delfshaven, back toward the centre, the **Boymans-Van Beuningen Museum**, Mathenesserlaan 18–20 (Tues–Sun 11am–5pm; *f*6), is Rotterdam's one great attraction, accessible from Centraal Station by tram #5 or from Eendrachtsplein metro. Amid the enormous collection of paintings, from Flemish Masters to Pop Art, it's impossible not to find something to your liking, though the sheer size of the displays can be overpowering, while the constant rotation of exhibits can make guidebooks confusing. The information desk provides an updated and simplified diagrammatic outline of the museum, but in general terms pre-nineteenth-century paintings are in the old wing, modern paintings in the new wing and both wings are divided into two interconnecting floors.

The entrance to the new wing leads to the modern paintings, best known of which are the **Surrealists**. De rigueur for student bedrooms in the 1970s, it's difficult to appreciate Salvador Dali's *Spain* as anything more than the painting of the poster – not that Dali would have been bothered. Other works by René Magritte, Max Ernst and Giorgio de Chirico provide a representative sample of a movement whose images seem to have lost much of their power. Surrealism was never adopted by Dutch artists, though the Magic Realism of **Carel Willink** has its similarities in the precise, hallucinatory technique he uses to distance and perturb the viewer in *Self Portrait with a Pen*. **Charley Toorop**'s *Three Generations* is also realism with an aim to disconcert – the huge bust of her father, Jan, looms in the background and dominates the painting. Most of the rest of the first floor is devoted to various displays of applied art and design, including a comprehensive range of tiles.

The **Van der Vorm Collection**, housed on the first floor, has paintings from many of Europe's most famous artists, including Monet, Van Gogh, Picasso, Gauguin, Cézanne and Munch, alongside a series of small galleries containing most of the significant artists of the Barbizon and Hague schools, notably **J.H. Weissenbruch**'s *Strandgezicht*, a beautiful gradation of radiant tones.

Adjoining the Vorm Collection, and arranged in roughly chronological order (from Room 1), are the museum's earlier paintings, beginning with an excellent **Flemish and Nederlandish religious art section**, whose sumptuous *Christ in the House of Martha and Mary* by Pieter Aertsen is outstanding. **Hieronymus Bosch**, famed for his nightmarish visions, is represented by four of his more mainstream works. Usually considered a macabre fantasist, Bosch was actually working to the limits of oral and religious tradition, where biblical themes were depicted as iconographical representations, laden with explicit symbols. In his *St Christopher*, the dragon, the hanged bear and the broken pitcher lurk in the background, representations of danger and uncertainty, whereas the Prodigal Son's attitude to the brothel behind him in *The Wanderer* is deliberately ambivalent. Bosch's technique never absorbed the influences of Renaissance Italy, and his figures in the *Marriage Feast at Cana* are static and unbelievable, uncomfortably

SPECIAL INTEREST MUSEUMS

Accessible by bus and tram from Centraal Station, Rotterdam has a number of special interest **museums**, including a collection of rare dolls and mechanical toys dating from 1700 to 1940 at the *Toy-Toy Museum*, east of the city centre at Groene Wetering 41 (Sun & Mon 11am–4pm; ƒ6; tram #3, #7). The *National Museum of Schools*, south of the station at Nieuwe Markt 1a (Tues–Sat 10am–5pm, Sun 11am–5pm; ƒ6; metro Blaak), has six fully furnished classrooms of various periods. The Marine Corps museum, *Mariniersmuseum*, on Wynhaven (Tues–Sat 10am–5pm, Sun 11am–5pm; ƒ2.50; metro Blaak), outlines the history of the brigade from its establishment in 1665. There's African art in the *African Culture Centre*, Eendrachtsweg 41 (Fri–Sun 1–5pm; free; tram #5); the *Trammuseum*, Nieuwe Binnenweg 362 (April–Nov Sat 11am–4pm; free; tram #6), has several interesting old trams; and there are shiny steam trains and engines at the *Steam Depot Museum*, Giessenweg 82 (Sat 10am–5pm; free; bus #38).

arranged around a distorted table. Other works in this section include paintings by **Jan van Scorel**, who was more willing to absorb Italianate styles as in his *Scholar in a Red Cap*; the Bruges artist **Hans Memling**, whose capacity for detail can be seen in his *Two Houses in a Landscape*; **Pieter Brueghel the Elder's** mysterious, hazy *Tower of Babel*; and **Geertgen tot Sint Jans'** beautiful, delicate *Glorification of the Virgin*.

Further on, a small selection of **Dutch Genre** paintings reflects the tastes of the emergent seventeenth-century middle class. The idea was to depict real life situations overlaid with a symbolic moral content. Jan Steen's *Extracting the Stone* or *The Physician's Visit* are good humourous examples, while Gerrit Dou's *The Quack*, ostensibly just a passing scene, is full of small cameos of deception – a boy catching a bird, the trapped hare – that refer back to the quack's sham cures.

Dotted across the museum are a number of **Rembrandts**, including two contrasting canvases: an analytic *Portrait of Alotta Adriaensdr*, her aging illuminated but softened by her white ruff, and a gloomy, indistinct *Blind Tobias and his Wife* painted twenty years later. His intimate *Titus at his Desk* is also in marked contrast to the more formal portrait commissions common to his day. Most of the work of Rembrandt's pupil **Carel Fabritius** was destroyed when he was killed in a Delft gunpowder explosion in 1654; an exception is his *Self-Portrait*, reversing his master's usual technique by lighting the background and placing the subject in shadow.

Waterway excursions

One way of exploring the waterways you can see from the Euromast is on the **Spido cruises** that leave from beside the Willemsplein, to the south of Centraal Station (tram #5 or Leuvehaven metro).

Between April and September tours run every 45 minutes between 9.30am and 3.30pm, less frequently at other times of year, and take an hour and fifteen minutes; prices start at ƒ12 per person. They head off past the wharfs, landings, docks and silos of this, the largest port in the world, though it's most impressive at night, when the illuminated ships and refineries gleam like Spielberg spaceships. In season, there are also longer, less frequent trips to Dordrecht, the windmills of Kinderdijk, the Europoort and the Delta Project (see below), from between *f*20 and *f*42.50 per person. Further details are available from the *VVV*, or the boat operators at Willemsplein (☎413 5400).

The Spido excursion to the series of colossal dams that make up the **Delta Project**, along the seaboard southwest of Rotterdam, only provides the briefest of glances, and it's better to visit by bus, though it'll take you a couple of hours: take the underground to Spijkenisse (30min) and catch bus #104 for Vlissingen (Mon–Sat hourly, Sun every 2hr), which travels along the road that crosses the top of the three dams that restrain the Haringvliet, Grevelingen and Oosterschelde estuaries. For more on the Delta Project and Delta Expo, see *The South*.

Eating and drinking

There are cheap sit-down **meals** (costing between *f*7 and *f*9) at *Eetcafé Van Kampen en de Wit*, on Nieuwe Binnenweg, *Eetcafé Streetlife*, Jonker Franslaan 237, and *De Djoek*, 's Gravendijkwal 100–102. *De Consul*, Westersingel 28, also has a variety of dishes at reasonable prices. *De Eend*, Mauritsweg 28 (5.30–7.30pm), is slightly more expensive. Vegetarians should try *Eetcafé BlaBla*, Piet Heynstraat 35, in Delfshaven, where they serve daily specials for around *f*20 in a nice, if somewhat trendy atmosphere. Other alternatives include excellent Hungarian fare at the *Boris Grill*, Diergaardesingel 93b; Italian food at *Pirandello*, Nieuwe Binnenweg 17b; or the Thai specialities of *Blue Mekong*, Provenierstraat 29a.

If you want to dig out a traditional brown café, try the streets west of Centraal Station, though many have been knocked down and many more are scheduled for modernization. If you have no luck, *Grand Café Dudok*, off Beursplein on Meent, is a good place to drink. *Jazzcafe Dizzy*, 's-Gravendijkwal 127, and the *Harbour Jazzclub*, Delftsestraat 15, have regular **live music**.

Listings

Airport enquiries Rotterdam Airport, Heathrowbaan 4 (☎446 34 55; bus #33).

Bureau de change At most banks (Mon–Fri 9am–4pm). Exchange agency at Centraal Station (Mon–Sat 7.30am–10pm, Sun 9am–10pm).

Car rental *Avis*, Rotterdam Airport (☎415 8842) and Kruisplein 21 (☎433 2233); *Hertz*, Schiekade 986 (☎404 60 88).

Chemists 24hr service details ☎411 0370.

Dental care ☎455 2155.

Football At *Feyenoord* stadium – bus #49 or Stadion train from Centraal Station. Game details from the VVV; most games are on Sundays.

Left Luggage Coin-operated lockers at the train station.

Markets General, including antiques, on Mariniersweg (Tues & Sat 9am–5pm). Stamps, coins and books on Grotekerkplein (Tues & Sat 9.30am–4pm).

Medical assistance ☎411 5504. Ambulance ☎0611.

Police Police Station, Doelwater 2 (☎424 2911).

Post office Coolsingel 42 (Mon 11am–6pm, Tues–Thurs 9am–6pm, Fri 8.30am–8.30pm, Sat 9.30am–3pm); Delftseplein 31 (Mon–Fri 8.30am–6pm).

Taxis *Rotterdam taxi* ☎462 6060; *St Job* ☎425 7000.

Train enquiries Domestic ☎06/9292; international ☎411 7100.

What's on *Rotterdam Punt Uit* is a free monthly magazine on events and entertainments in Rotterdam, available from the VVV.

Gouda and Oudewater

A pretty little place some 25km northeast of Rotterdam, **GOUDA** is almost everything you'd expect of a Dutch country town: a ring of quiet canals that encircle ancient buildings and old docks. More surprisingly, its **Markt**, a ten-minute walk from the train station, is the largest in Holland – a reminder of the town's prominence as a centre of the medieval cloth trade, and later of its success in the manufacture of cheeses and clay pipes.

Gouda's main claim to fame is its **cheese market**, held in the Markt every Thursday morning from June to August. Traditionally, some one thousand local farmers brought their home-produced cheeses here to be weighed, tested and graded for moisture, smell and taste. These details were marked on the cheeses and formed the basis for negotiation between buyer and seller, the exact price set by an elaborate hand clapping system, which itself was based on trust and memory, for deals were never written down. Today, the cheese market is a shadow of its former self, a couple of locals in traditional dress standing outside the Waag, surrounded by modern open-air stands. The promised mixture of food and tradition is mercilessly milked by tour operators, who herd their victims into this rather dreary scene every week – but don't let this put you off a visit, since Gouda's charms are elsewhere.

Finally, if you happen to be in the area in mid-December, it's worth phoning the Gouda VVV to find out exactly when the town will be holding its splendid candlelit pre-Christmas festival. All electric lights are extinguished on the main square, and it is lit up instead by thousands of candles.

The Town

Slap-bang in the middle of the Markt, the **Stadhuis** is an elegant Gothic building dating from 1450, whose facade is fringed by statues of counts and countesses of Burgundy above a tinkling carillon that plays every half-hour. Nearby, on the north side of the square, the **Waag** is a tidy seventeenth-century building, decorated with a detailed relief of cheese weighing, with the remains of the old wooden scales inside. To the south, just off the Markt, **St Janskerk** (March–Oct Mon–Sat 9am–5pm; Nov–Feb Mon–Sat 10am–4pm; f2.50) was built in the sixteenth century and is famous for its magnificent **stained-glass windows**. As well as their intrinsic beauty, the windows show the way religious art changed as Holland moved from a society dominated by the Catholic Church to one dominated by a Calvinist Church. The biblical themes executed by Dirk and Wouter Crabeth between 1555 and 1571, when Holland was still Catholic, have an amazing clarity of detail and richness of colour. Their last work, *Judith Slaying Holofernes* (window no. 6), is perhaps the finest, the story unfolding in intricate perspective. By comparison, the post-Reformation windows, which date from 1572 to 1603, adopt an allegorical and heraldic style typical of a more secular art. *The Relief of Leiden* (window no. 25) shows William the Silent retaking the town from the Spanish, though Delft and its burgomasters take prominence – no doubt because they paid the bill for its construction. All the windows are numbered and a detailed guide is available at the entrance for f3.

By the side of the church, the flamboyant **Lazarus Gate** of 1609 was once part of the town's leper hospital, until it was moved to form the back entrance to the

GOUDA

Train Station

STATIONS-PLEIN

Bus Station

GRAAF FLORISWEG

NOOTHOVEN V. GOORSTR.

VREEBEST

KLEIWEG-PLEIN

KATTEN-SINGEL

BOELEKADE

KEIZERSTR.

REGENTESSE-PLANTSOEN

NIEUWE HAVEN

KLEIWEG

KOLWAN GRACHT

NIEUWSTR.

NIEUWE HAVEN

HOGE GOUWE

LAGE GOUWE

TURFMARKT

TURFMARKT

BLAUWSTR.

HOOGSTR.

NIEUWE MARKT

ACHTER DE WAAG

HOUTMANS GRACHT

MAARSTE.

Stadhuis

VVV

St.-Janskerk

ACHTER DE VISMARKT.

LAGE GOUWE

HOGE GOUWE

DUBBELE BUURT

ACHTER DE KERK

Lazarus Gate

RAAM

Catharina Gasthuis Museum

PEPERSTR.

JERUZALEMSTR.

De Moriaan Museum

Post Office

SPOERINGSTR.

RAAM

Youth Hostel

PEPERSTR.

WESTHAVEN

OOSTHAVEN

VEERSTAL

Toll House

IJSSELKADE

NIEUWEN

VERSTAL

0   100 m

Hollandse Ijssel

Catharina Gasthuis, a hospice till 1910. A likable conglomeration of sixteenth-century rooms and halls, including an old isolation cell for the insane, the interior of the Gasthuis has been turned into the municipal **Stedelijk Museum** (Mon–Sat 10am–5pm, Sun noon–5pm; *f*3.50). The collection incorporates a fine sample of early religious art, notably a large triptych, *Life of Mary*, by Dirk Barendsz and a characteristically austere *Annunciation* by the Bruges artist Pieter Pourbus. Other highlights include a spacious hall, *Het Ruim*, that was once a sort of medieval hostel, but is now dominated by paintings of the Civic Guard, principally two group portraits by Ferdinand Bol; the intricate silver-gilt *Chalice and Eucharist Dish* was presented to the Guard in the early fifteenth century. Two later rooms have a modest selection of Hague and Barbizon School canvases, notably work by Anton Mauve and Charles Daubigny.

Gouda's other museum, **De Moriaan** (Mon–Sat 10am–5pm, Sun noon–5pm; use Stedelijk Museum ticket), is in a cosy old merchant's house at Westhaven 29, with a mixed bag of exhibits from clay pipes to ceramics and tiles. Westhaven itself is a charming jumble of old buildings that head off toward the old toll house and a dilapidated mill beside the Hollandse IJssel river, on the southern edge of the town centre. There's a restored, fully operational **grain mill** (Mon–Sat 9am–5pm; *f*1.50) to the immediate west of the Markt, at Vest 65.

Practicalities

Gouda's **train** and **bus stations** are to the immediate north of the town centre, ten minutes from the VVV, Markt 27 (Mon–Fri 9am–5pm, Sat 10am–4pm; ☎01820/13666), which has a limited supply of private **rooms**, and will ring ahead to make a booking for a small cover charge. Otherwise, the cheapest place in town is an unofficial **youth hostel**, conveniently sited at Westhaven 46 (☎01820/12879; ①). The most reasonably priced **hotel** is the *Het Blauwe Kruis*, Westhaven 4 (☎01820/12677; ③). There are two other, more agreeable hotels in the centre, the reasonably priced *De Utrechtse Dom*, a couple of minutes' walk to the east of St Janskerk at Geuzenstraat 6 (☎01820/2794; ②), and the slightly more expensive *De Keizerskroon*, to the west of Westhaven at Keizerstraat 11 (☎01820/28096; ③).

For **food**, Gouda has literally dozens of cafés and snack bars catering for the hundreds of tourists who day-trip here throughout the season. *Borsalino*, Naalerstraat 4, serves a variety of dishes, including vegetarian options starting at *f*12.75; look out as well for Balkan specialities at the imaginatively named *Balkan*, Markt 10; pancakes at *'t Goudse Winkeltje*, Achter de Kerk 9a; and cheap pizzas at the *Rimini*, Markt 28.

Oudewater

Eleven kilometres east of Gouda and easily accessible by bus, **OUDEWATER** is a compact and delightful little town that holds a unique place in the history of Dutch witchcraft.

It's estimated that over a million people across Europe were burned or otherwise murdered in the widespread **witch-hunts** of the sixteenth century, and not only from fear and superstition: anonymous accusation to the authorities was an easy way of removing an enemy – or even a wife, at a time when there was no divorce. Underlying it all was a virulent misogyny and an accompanying desire to terrorize women into submission. There were three main methods for investigating accusations of witchcraft: in the first, **trial by fire**, the suspect had to walk barefoot over hot cinders or have a hot iron pressed into the back or hands. If the burns blistered, the accused was innocent as witches were supposed to burn less easily than others; naturally, the (variable) temperature of the iron was crucial. **Trial by water** was still more hazardous: dropped into water, if you floated you were a witch, if you sank you were innocent – and probably dead from drowning. The third method, **trial by weight**, presupposed that a witch would have to be unduly light to fly on a broomstick, so many towns – including Oudewater – used the Waag (town weigh-house) to weigh the accused. If the weight didn't accord with a notional figure derived from the height, the woman was burned. The last Dutch woman to be burnt as a witch was a certain Marrigje Ariens, a herbalist from Schoonhaven, whose medical efforts, not untypically, inspired mistrust and subsequent persecution. She died in 1597.

Oudewater's Waag gained its fame from the actions of Charles V (1516–52), who saw a woman accused of witchcraft in a nearby village. The weighmaster, who'd been bribed, stated that the woman weighed only a few pounds, but Charles was dubious and ordered the woman to be weighed again in Oudewater, where the officials proved unbribable, pronouncing a normal weight and acquitting her. The probity of Oudewater's weighmaster impressed Charles, and he granted the town the privilege of issuing certificates, valid throughout the empire, stating that "The accused's weight is in accordance with the natural proportions of the body". Once in possession of the certificate, one could never be brought to trial for witchcraft again. Not surprisingly, thousands of people came from all over Europe for this life-saving piece of paper, and to Oudewater's credit no one was ever condemned.

Oudewater's sixteenth-century Waag has survived, converted into the **Heksenwaag** (witches' weigh house; April–Oct Tues–Sun 10am–5pm; *f*2), a family-run affair, where you can be weighed on the original rope and wood balance. The owners dress up in national costume and issue a certificate in olde-worlde English that states nothing, but does so very prettily. There's not much else to see here, but it's a pleasant little place, whose traditional stepped gables spread out along the River Hollandse IJssel as it twists its way through town.

If you decide to **stay**, the VVV, Markt-Oostzyde 8 (April–Sept Tues–Sat 10.30am–4pm, Sun 1–4pm; Oct–March Tues 10am–noon, Thurs 1.30–3.30pm, Sat 11am–3pm; ☎03486/4636), has details of several private rooms and a pension; there are no hotels.

Dordrecht and around

Some 15km southeast of Rotterdam, the ancient port of **DORDRECHT**, or "Dordt" as it's often called, is a likable town beside one of the busiest waterway junctions in the world, where tankers and containers from the north pass the waterborne traffic of the Maas and Rijn. Eclipsed by the expansion of Rotterdam and left relatively intact by World War II, Dordrecht has been spared the worst excesses of postwar development and preserves a confusion of ancient and dilapidated buildings that stop it from being just another tidy Dutch showpiece. Within easy reach is some of the province's prettiest countryside, including the windmills of the **Kinderdijk** and the **Biesbosch** nature reserve.

Granted a town charter in 1220, Dordrecht was the most important and powerful town in Holland until well into the sixteenth century. One of the first cities to declare against the Habsburgs in 1572, it was the obvious site for the first meeting of the Free Assembly of the Seven Provinces, and for a series of doctrinal conferences that tried to solve a whole range of theological differences among the various Protestant sects. After all, the Protestants may have hated the Catholics, but they also inherited the medieval church's desire for theological debate. In 1618, at the Synod of Dordt, the Remonstrants or Arminians had prolonged arguments with the Calvinists over the definition of predestination, though this must have seemed pretty important stuff compared to the Synod of 1574, when one of the main rulings had required the dismantling of church organs.

From the seventeenth century, Dordrecht lost ground to its great rivals to the north, slipping into comparative insignificance, its economy sustained by trade and shipbuilding.

Arrival, information and accommodation

Well connected by train to all the Randstad's major cities, Dordrecht's adjoining **train** and **bus** stations are a ten-minute walk from the town centre, straight down Stationsweg/Johan de Wittstraat and left at the end along Bagijnhof/Visstraat. A couple of minutes from the station, the **VVV**, Stationsweg 1 (Sept–April Mon–Fri 9am–5.30pm, Sat 9.30am–1pm; May–Aug Mon–Fri 9am–5.30pm, Sat 9am–4.30pm; ☎13 28 00), has a list of **pensions** and **private rooms**, which they will reserve for a cover charge of *f*1.25. There are three central **hotels**: the *Klarenbeek*, near the VVV at Johan de Wittstraat 35 (☎14 41 33; ④); the *Dordrecht*, by the river near the west end of Spuiboulevard at Achterhakkers 12 (☎13 60 11; ⑤); and the excellent *Bellevue*, Boomstraat 37 (☎13 79 00; ⑤), overlooking the Maas from the northern tip of the old town by the Groothoofdspoort. There are cheaper alternatives approximately 4km east of town along Baanhoekweg, the road that forms the northern perimeter of the Biesbosch (bus #4 from the station), in a complex that includes *Budget Hotel De Hollandse Biesbosch* at no. 25 (☎21 21 67; ③), a campsite of the same name (open April–Oct) and a **youth hostel** (☎21 21 67). The most agreeable **campsite**, *De Kleine Rug* (open April–Oct; ☎16 35 55; advance bookings essential in July & Aug), is about 1km south of Baanhoekweg on a sandspit at Loswalweg 1: take bus #5 to Stadspolder, walk fifteen minutes down to the end of Loswalweg and, at the jetty, ring for the boat to take you across. If there's no sign of life, *Camping 't Vissertje*, Loswalweg 3 (open April–Sept; ☎16 27 51), is a reasonable second choice.

The Town

The old part of Dordrecht juts out into the Maas, divided by three concentric waterways that once protected it from attack. From the train station, the second canal is the heart of the town, flowing beside the **Voorstraat**, today's main shopping street. At the junction of Voorstraat and Visstraat, the Groenmarkt spans the canal with a heavy-handed **monument** to the de Witt brothers, Jan and Cornelius, prominent Dutch Republicans who paid for their principles when they were torn to pieces by an Orangist mob in The Hague in 1672. To the right, Voorstraat bends its way northeast, a chaotic mixture of the old, the new, the restored and the decayed, intersected by a series of tiny alleys that once served as the town's docks. Cutting off Voorstraat at Nieuwebrug, the **Wijnhaven** was used by the city's merchants to control the import and export of wine when they held the state monopoly from the fourteenth to the seventeenth centuries.

Straight ahead, the **Groothoofdspoort** was once the main city gate and has a grand facade dating from 1618, pushed up against the *Hotel Bellevue*, with its fine views over the surrounding waterways. The town's innermost canal is just along the waterfront from here, divided into two harbours, home to the cruisers, barges and sailing boats that ply up and down the Maas. Fringed by stately buildings and criss-crossed by rickety footbridges, it's an attractive setting for the **Museum Simon van Gijn**, Nieuwe Haven 29 (Tues–Sat 10am–5pm, Sun 1–5pm; *f*5), whose collection of local memorabilia and period rooms is of some moderate interest, best of all the eighteenth-century Brussels tapestries and a fine Renaissance chimneypiece of 1550, transferred from the old guild house of the arquebusiers.

Near the southwest end of Nieuwe Haven, the **Grote Kerk** (April–Oct Tues–Sat 10.30am–4.30pm, Sun noon–4pm; July & Aug also Mon noon–4pm; Nov &

Dec first & third Sat of the month 2–4pm; free) is visible from all over town, its fourteenth-century **tower** (same times, except Nov–March when it opens Tues–Sun 1–4pm if the weather's fine; *f*2) topped with incongruous seventeenth-century clocks. One of the largest churches in Holland, it was built to emphasize Dordrecht's wealth and importance, but it's heavy and dull, despite its attractive environs, and there's only an elaborately carved choir inside to hold your interest. Climb the tower for a great view over the town and its surrounding waters. From beside the church, Grotekerksbuurt leads to the stolid classicism of the **Stadhuis**, back on the Voorstraat.

The Dordrechts Museum

To the southeast of the town centre, the **Dordrechts Museum**, Museumstraat 40 (Tues–Sat 10am–5pm, Sun 1–5pm; *f*6.25), is a ten-minute walk from the train station: turn right off Johan de Wittstraat on the far side of the first canal as you head into town, and follow the signs. Well presented and clearly labelled, the museum concentrates on the work of local artists, both in its permanent and temporary displays. Highlights of the permanent collection include a couple of finely drawn portraits by Jacob Cuyp, and a whole room devoted to the work of his son, Albert. Born in Dordrecht in 1620, **Albert Cuyp** was influenced by those of his contemporaries who had visited Italy, modulating his work with the soft, yellowish tones of the Mediterranean. Noted for his Italianate landscapes, seascapes and town scenes, his *Resting Riders in a Landscape* is representative of his work, in contrast to the muted tones of traditional Dutch landscape painting, as illustrated by Jan van Goyen's *View of Dordrecht*, the city's bustle restricted to the bottom section of the canvas, beneath a wide sky and flattened horizon.

A student of Rembrandt, Nicolaes Maes first specialized in informal domestic scenes, as in *The Eavesdropper*, turning his skills to portrait painting after his visit to Antwerp in 1670. A good example of his later work is his flattering picture of *Jacob de Witt the Elder*. More curiously, *De Dordtse Vierling* (the Dordt quadruplets) is an odd, unattributed seventeenth-century painting of a dead child and her three swaddled siblings, a simple, moving tribute to a lost daughter; and on the staircase nearby, the massive *Gezicht op Dordt* (View of Dordt) is a masterpiece of minutely observed naturalist detail by Adam Willaertz (1577–1644).

On the second floor, there's a selection of work by the later and lesser Ary Scheffer, who was born in Dordrecht in 1795, but lived in Paris from 1811. His much-reproduced *Mignon Pining for her Native Land* struck a chord in the sentimental hearts of the nineteenth century. Jozef Israels' *Midday Meal at the Inn* and G.H. Breitner's *Lauriergracht 1891* are among a small collection of Amsterdam and Hague School paintings, though the collage style of their Italian associate, Antonio Mancini, is of more immediate appeal.

Eating and drinking

Dordrecht has a couple of excellent **restaurants**, the *Costa d'Oro*, Voorstraat 444, which serves a wide range of tasty Italian dishes from *f*16.50, and the pricier *Crimpert Salm*, Visstraat 5, where you'll pay twice that for imaginative seafood and exquisite daily specials. Alternatives include another decent Italian, *Piccolo Italia*, Voorstraat 259, the expensive but good value *De Troubadour*, Vriesplein 8, the fish dishes of *De Stroper*, Wijnbrug 1, and the snacks and cheaper full meals of *In de*

Klandermuelen, Statenplein 86. For **bars**, try *'t Avontuur*, at Voorstraat 193, or the more staid *De Pul*, on the Spuiplein. There's **live music** at the *Jazz and Folk Club* on the Grote Kerksplein, with a list of future attractions pinned to the door.

Around Dordrecht: the Biesbosch and the Kinderdijk

On November 18, 1421, South Holland's sea defences gave way and the "St Elizabeth Day flood" formed what is now the Hollands Diep sea channel and the **Biesbosch** (reed forest) – an expanse of river, creek, marsh and reed covering around 15 square kilometres to the south and east of Dordrecht. It was a disaster of major proportions, destroying some seventy towns and villages, and early accounts put the death toll at over one hundred thousand. The catastrophe disrupted the whole of the region's economy, breaking up the links between South Holland and Flanders and accelerating the shift in commercial power to the north. Even those hamlets and villages that did survive took generations to recover, subject, as they were, to raids by the wretched refugees of the flood.

Inundated twice daily by the rising tide, the Biesbosch produced a particular **reed culture**, its inhabitants using the plant for every item of daily life, from houses to baskets and boats, selling excess cuttings at the local markets. It was a harsh and gruelling existence that lasted well into the nineteenth century, when the reeds were no longer of much use, replaced by machine-manufactured goods.

Today, the Biesbosch is a nature reserve whose delicate eco-system is threatened by the very scheme that aims to protect the province from further flooding. The Delta Project (see *The South*) dams have controlled the rivers' flow and restricted the tides' strength, forcing the reeds to give ground to other forms of vegetation incompatible with the area's special mixture of bird and plant life. Large areas of reed have disappeared, and no one seems to know how to reconcile the nature reserve's needs with those of the seaboard cities.

The park divides into two main sections, north and south of the Nieuwe Merwede channel, which marks the provincial boundary between South Holland and North Brabant. The undeveloped heart of the nature reserve is the **Brabantse Biesbosch**, the chunk of land to the south, whereas tourist facilities have been carefully confined to the north, on a strip of territory to the immediate east of Dordrecht. Here, the **Bezoekerscentrum De Hollandsche Biesbosch**, Baanhoekweg 53 (Tues–Sun 10am–5pm; March–Nov also Mon noon–5pm; ☎078/21 13 11), accessible by bus #4 from Dordrecht train station, has displays on the flora and fauna of the region, and a beaver observatory. **Boat trips** for the Brabantse Biesbosch leave from the jetty beside the Bezoekerscentrum (July & Aug once daily Mon, Wed, Fri & Sun, twice daily Tues & Sat; Sept & Oct once daily Wed & Sun). Prices vary according to the itinerary, but start at *f*22.50 for the day ("Dagtocht") and at *f*8.50 for a two-hour excursion ("Panoramatocht"). There are similar trips at similar prices from the **Bezoekerscentrum Drimmelen**, Dorpsstraat 14, Drimmelen (Jun–Aug Mon, Wed & Fri 10am–5pm, Sun 11am–5pm; Sept–May Tues–Fri 10am–5pm, Sat 1–5pm, Sun 10am–5pm; ☎01626/82991), on the southern bank of the Amer, about 20km north of Breda – though this cannot readily be reached by public transport from Dordrecht. From Drimmelen, boats leave for the Brabantse Biesbosch (July & Aug Mon–Fri three times daily, Sat & Sun once daily; April–June & Sept Sun only twice daily).

Some of the longer excursions visit the **Biesboschmuseum**, on the southern shore of the Nieuwe Merwede at Spieringsluis 4 (Mon 1–5pm, Tues–Sat 10am–5pm, Sun noon–5pm; *f*2), where there are further details on the ecology of the Biesbosch and the origins of its distinctive reed culture. Further details of boat trips are available at the Dordrecht VVV and direct from both visitors' centres.

The other way of visiting the nature reserve is by **bike**, for rent at standard rates from Dordrecht train station and the VVV, which also sells detailed maps of the district and brochures on suggested cycle routes. The ride from town to the Biesbosch takes about half an hour, via the shuttle passenger boat service that runs from the dock by Kop van 't Land, 5km southeast of the town centre, to a point about 1km northeast of the Biesboschmuseum.

The Kinderdijk

Some 12km north of Dordrecht, the **Kinderdijk** (child's dyke) sits at the end of a long drainage channel which feeds into the River Lek, whose turbulent waters it keeps from flooding the polders around Alblasserdam. Sixteenth-century legend suggests it takes its name from the time when a cradle, complete with cat and kicking baby, was found at the precise spot where the dyke had just held during a particularly bad storm. A mixture of symbols – rebirth, innocence and survival – the story encapsulates the determination and optimism with which the Dutch fought the floods for hundreds of years, and is repeated in many different forms across the whole province.

Today, the Kinderdijk is famous for its picturesque, quintessentially Dutch **windmills**, all eighteen stringing alongside the main channel and its tributary beside the Molenkade for some 3km. Built around 1740 to drive water from the Alblasserwaard polders, the windmills are put into operation every Saturday afternoon in July and August, and one of them is open to visitors from April to September (Mon–Sat 9.30am–5.30pm; *f*2.50). If that hasn't satsified your curiosity, there's also a **mill exhibition centre** at Molenstraat 236 (Tues–Sun 9.30am–5.30pm; *f*5).

Without a car, the easiest way to explore the district from Dordrecht is by **bike**, and if you decide to **stay**, the tiny village of Kinderdijk is to the immediate west of the dyke, on the banks of the Lek. There's just one **hotel**, *Kinderdijk*, West Kinderdijk 361 (☎01859/12425; ③). Advance booking is essential from June to August.

Utrecht

"I groaned with the idea of living all winter in so shocking a place", wrote Boswell in 1763, and **UTRECHT** still promises little as you approach: surrounded by shopping centres and industrial developments, the town only begins to reveal itself in the old area around the Dom Kerk, roughly enclosed by the Oude and Nieuwe Grachts. These distinctive sunken canals date from the fourteenth century, and their brick cellars, used as warehouses when Utrecht was a river port, have been converted to chic cafés and restaurants. Though the liveliest places in town, they don't disguise Utrecht's provincialism: just half an hour from Amsterdam, all the brashness and vitality of the capital is absent, and it's for museums and churches rather than nightlife that the town is enjoyable.

Founded by the Romans in the first century AD, the city of Utrecht became home to a wealthy and powerful medieval bishopric, which controlled the surrounding region under the auspices of the German emperors. In 1527 the bishop sold off his secular rights and shortly afterward the town council enthusiastically joined the revolt against Spain. Indeed, the **Union of Utrecht**, the agreement that formalized the opposition to the Habsburgs, was signed here in 1579. Some two hundred years later the **Treaty of Utrecht** brought to an end some of Louis IV of France's grand imperial ambitions.

> The telephone code for Utrecht is ☎030

Arrival, city transport, information and accommodation

Train and bus stations both lead into the Hoog Catharijne shopping centre, on the edge of the city centre; the main VVV office is at Vredenburg 90 (Mon–Fri 9am–5.30pm, Sat 9am–1.30pm; ☎340 340 85, 50c per minute), a seven-minute walk away. Though the city is compact enough to explore on foot, touring the canals, either by boat or by cycling along towpaths, adds another dimension to a visit. **Cyclists** should apply to *Canal Bikes* on Oude Gracht opposite the former town hall (Sun–Wed 10am–7pm, Thurs–Sat 10am–9pm), whose rental prices include a map of the canal network. If you prefer to go by **boat**, canal trips depart hourly from Oude Gracht at the corner of Lange Viestraat and Potterstraat near the Viebrug (Oct–May daily from 11am–5pm; June–Sept also Tues and Thurs from 6–9pm; ƒ10; ☎72 01 11). If you're keen to visit Utrecht's museums, perhaps the easiest and pleasantest way to do so is by **Museumboot**. There are two of these: one leaves every hour from Oude Gracht – opposite no. 85 – (Mon–Sat noon–4pm; Sun 11am–4pm; ƒ7) and plies along to the Centraal Museum and the National Railway Museum/Catharijne Convent. The other leaves from the Viebrug (daily 10am, 11.30am, 1pm, 2.30pm & 4pm; ƒ11 – gives a 50 percent discount at the museums), which spans Oude Gracht near the main post office, and chugs along to Gaardbrug (for the Speelklok tot Pierement Museum and Dom Tower), to the Centraal Museum/Railway Museum and the Catharijne Convent Museum.

The VVV offers the usual help with **accommodation**. Among the cheaper hotels there's *Van Ooyen*, Dantelaan 117 (☎93 81 90; ③), *Hotel Ouwi*, FC Donderstraat 12 (☎71 63 03; ③), and *Domstad,* Parkstraat 5 (☎31 01 31; ③). The **youth hostel** at Rhijnauwenselaan 14, Bunnik, linked to the train station by bus #40 or #43, is a little far out but beautifully sited in an old country manorhouse; the well-equipped **campsite** at Arienslaan 5 can be reached by a #57 bus from the Centraal Station.

The Town

The focal point of the centre is the **Dom Tower**, at over 110m the highest church tower in the country. It's one of the most beautiful too, its soaring, unbuttressed lines rising to a delicate, octagonal lantern added in 1380. A guided tour (April–Oct Mon–Fri 10am–5pm, Sat 11am–5pm, Sun noon–5pm; Nov–March Sat 11am–

UTRECHT

Railway Museum

NACHTEGAALSTRAAT

MALIE SINGEL

MALIE SINGEL

LEPELENBURG

Servaas Park

Gracht

Stadsbuiten TOLSTEEG SINGEL

NOBELDWARSSTRAAT

NIEUWEGRACHT

NIEUWEGRACHT

LANGE NIEUWSTRAAT

Centraal Museum

NOBELSTRAAT

KROMME NIEUWEGRACHT

St. Pieterskerk

PIETERSKERKHOF

Catherine Convent Museum

St. Nicolaaskerk

DRIFT

ACHTER STR. PETER

KROMME NIEUWE GRACHT

HAMBURGER STR.

ZUILENSTRAAT

St. Catharijnekerk

JANSKERKHOF

Janskerk

LANGE JANS STR.

ACHTER DE DOM

Dom Kerk

KORTE NIEUWSTRAAT

OUDEGRACHT

ROZENDAAL

MINREBROEDER

OUDKERKHOF

DOM PLEIN

Dom Tower

OUDEGRACHT

Stadhuis

SERVET STR.

HAVER STR.

SPRINGWEG

Stadsbuitengracht

CATHARIJNE SINGEL

Post Office

POTTERSTRAAT

VINKENBURG STRAAT

VISMART

CHOORSTR.

STEENWEG

LANGE SMEESTRAAT

LANGE SMEESTRAAT

GEERTEBOL WERK

LANGE VIE STR.

OUDEGRACHT

OUDEGRACHT

Buurkerk and Speelklok tot Pierement Museum

ZADELSTRAAT

LANGE ELIZABETH STR.

VREDENBURG

MARIAPLAATS

CATHARIJNE BAAN

VREDENBURG

VVV

Hoog Catharijne Centre

WILLEMS PLANTSOEN

CATHARIJNE BAAN

MINDER BROEDERS DEILEDUIK

CATHARIJNE SINGEL

Centraal Station VVV

Kruisvaart

200 m

CROESELAAN

0

5pm & Sun noon–5pm; last entry one hour before closing; ƒ3.50) takes you unnervingly near to the top, from where you can see Rotterdam and Amsterdam on a clear day. Only the eastern part of the great cathedral remains, the nave having collapsed (with what must have been an apocalyptic crash) during a storm in 1674. It's worth peering inside (May–Sept daily 10am–5pm; Oct–April Mon–Sat 11am–4pm, Sun 2–4pm; free) to get a sense of the hangar-like space the building once had, and to wander through the **Kloostergang**, the fourteenth-century cloisters that link the cathedral to the chapterhouse. The Kloostertuin, or cloister gardens, are reckoned to be the best place in town to listen to the carillon concerts from the Dom Tower, which you can do from a pleasant tea-house. If bells are not your thing, you might be lucky enough to catch music played on more conventional instruments during the classical concerts that are regularly performed here.

Except for the Dom, Utrecht's churches aren't all that interesting: the oldest is the **St Pieterskerk** (Tues–Fri 11am–4.30pm, Sat 11am–3pm), a shabbily maintained building that's a mixture of Romanesque and Gothic styles with twelfth-century paintings and reliefs. Heading northwest from here to the bend in the Oude Gracht, between the ludicrously grandiose nineteenth-century **Stadhuis**, and the huge, brick Amsterdam School **post office**, is the oldest house in Utrecht, the fourteenth-century **Huis Oudaen** – recently renovated and with a café on the ground floor, the *Proeflokaal*, where you can sample beer brewed in the steam brewery in its basement.

Not far from the Stadhuis are a couple of unusual little museums, well worth checking out. **Den Dubbelden Arend** at Schoutenstraat 13 (Tues & Thurs 10.30 am; guided tours only), is the oldest working bakery in the city; while the **Museum voor het Kruideniersbedrijf** at Hoogt 8 (Tues–Sat 12.30–4.30pm; free) is possibly the world's only museum devoted to groceries – not exactly a vital stop, but something at least to base a walk around. Close by, further down Oude Gracht, the **Buurkerk** was the home of one sister Bertken, who was so ashamed of being the illegitimate daughter of a cathedral priest that she hid away in a small cell here – for 57 years, until her death in 1514. It's now a peculiar location of the **Speelklok tot Pierement Museum** (Tues–Sat 10am–5pm, Sun 1–5pm; ƒ6, children ƒ3), a collection of burping fairground organs and ingenious musical boxes worth an hour of anyone's time.

The city's other museums are a little way from the centre. The national collection of ecclesiastical art, the **Catharijne Convent Museum** (Tues–Fri 10am–5pm, Sat & Sun 11am–5pm; ƒ5), at Nieuwe Gracht 63, has a mass of paintings, manuscripts and church ornaments from the ninth century on, brilliantly exhibited in a complex built around the old convent. This excellent collection of paintings includes work by Geertgen tot Sint Jans, Rembrandt, Hals and, best of all, a luminously beautiful *Virgin and Child* by van Cleve. Part of the convent is the late Gothic **St Catharijnekerk**, whose radiant white interior is enhanced by floral decoration.

Keep walking down along Nieuwe Gracht and you reach Utrecht's other important museum, the **Centraal Museum**, at Agnietenstraat 1 (Tues–Sat 10am–5pm, Sun noon–5pm; ƒ5). Its claim to hold "25,000 curiosities" seems a bit exaggerated, but it does have a good collection of paintings by Utrecht artists of the sixteenth and seventeenth centuries. Van Scorel lived in Utrecht before and after he visited Rome, and he brought the influence of Italian humanism north. His paintings, like the vividly individual portraits of the *Jerusalem Brotherhood*, combine High Renaissance style with native Dutch observation. The central figure in white is van Scorel himself: he made a trip to Jerusalem around 1520, which accounts for his unusually accurate drawing of the city in *Christ's Entry into Jerusalem*. A group of painters influenced by another Italian, Caravaggio, became known as the Utrecht School. Such paintings as Honthorst's *The Procuress* adapt his chiaroscuro technique to genre subjects, and develop an erotic content that would itself influence later genre painters like Jan Steen and Gerrit Dou. Even more skilled and realistic is Terbrugghen's *The Calling of St Matthew*, a beautiful balance of gestures dramatizing the tax collector's summoning by Christ to become one of the apostles.

Gerrit Rietveld, the de Stijl designer, was most famous for his brightly coloured geometrical chairs, displayed in the applied art section. Part of the de Stijl philosophy (see *Contexts*) was that the approach could be used in any area of design, though Rietveld's angular furniture is probably better to look at than to sit on. There are more pieces of his furniture out of town, in the **Schröderhuis** at Prins Hendriklaan 50, accessible on bus #4 from the train station, which he designed and built in 1924 for one Truus Schröder and her three children (organized tours only Wed–Sat 11am–5pm, Sun noon–5pm; *f*9; call first on ☎362310). It's hailed as one of the most influential pieces of modern architecture in Europe, demonstrating the organic union of lines and rectangles that was the hallmark of the de Stijl movement. The ground floor is the most conventional part of the building, since its design had to meet the rigours of the building licence. However, Rietveld was able to let his imagination run riot on the top floor, the actual living space, designing an utterly flexible environment where only the outer walls are solid – indeed the entire top floor can be subdivided in any way you want by simply sliding the temporary walls.

Back in Utrecht, there's one final museum that might detain you: the **Spoorweg (Railway) Museum** (Tues–Sat 10am–5pm, Sun 1–5pm; *f*8.50, children *f*4) at Maliebaanstation – bus #3 from the station – with trains, buses and trams sitting in Utrecht's out-of-use train station: not much information, but enthusiastic attendants.

Eating and drinking

Places to eat group mainly along Oude Gracht, and along Lange Janstraat and Nobelstraat. Along Oude Gracht, among the best are *Tussen Hemel en Aarde*, with mid-priced meals served on the first floor of the medieval *Huis Oudaen* at No. 99, and, further along and slightly cheaper, the mostly vegetarian *De Werfkring*, at No. 123. A really cheap option is to go for a *dagschotel* at *Eetcafé De Baas* at Lijnmarkt 6. Along Lange Janstraat and Nobelstraat, try *Cafe Zeezicht* on Nobelstraat 2, which serves reasonably priced breakfasts, lunches and dinners, to an accompaniment of live music on Tuesday nights. Also check out nearby *Grand Cafe Polman's Huis*, on the corner of Jansdam and Keistraat, if only for its turn-of-the-century interior. *Stadscafee Broers*, on Janskerkhof 9 opposite the St Janskerk, in the same building as *Hotel Pays-Bas*, has a beautiful stained-glass dome inside, and serves good, though not cheap *dagschotels*.

The town's best **bars** cluster around the junction of Oude Gracht and Wed: check out the lively *De Witte Ballons* at Lijnmarkt 10–12, and, around the corner at Oude Gracht 196, the very pleasant *Cafe Belgie*. As for Utrecht's **gay scene**, try *De Wolkenkrabber* at Oude Gracht 47, and the gay and lesbian disco, *De Roze*

Wolk, right underneath. There's also dancing at *Fellini*, in the former prison below the old town hall, on Tues, Fri and Sat from 10.30pm. For alternative movies, try one of Utrechts' many *filmhuizen*, such as *'t Hoogt* on Hoogt 4.

Amersfoort

On the eastern edge of the province of Utrecht, the town of **AMERSFOORT** was first fortified in the eleventh century and received its charter in 1259. Surprisingly, it managed to avoid the attentions of the rival armies during the Revolt of the Netherlands, and some of today's centre dates from the fifteenth century, lying at the heart of a series of twisting canals that once served to protect the town from assault and to speed the import and export of goods. The main square, the Hof, where the market is held on Friday and Saturday, is edged by the giant hulk of the **St Joriskerk**, an unusual, predominantly Gothic edifice finished in 1534. The nave and aisles are of equal height, and only the south porch stops the exterior from resembling an aircraft hangar. Like most churches of the period, it was an enlargement of an earlier building, but here the original Romanesque tower was left inside the later fifteenth-century construction.

A few minutes' walk northeast along Langestraat, the **Kamperbinnenpoort** is a turreted thirteenth-century gate, extensively renovated in the 1930s. From here, north and south of Langestraat, Muurhuizen follows the line of the old city moat, and is named for its **"wallhouses"**, built into the city walls. At the northern end of Muurhuizen, the **Museum Fléhite**, Westsingel 50 (Tues–Fri 10am–5pm, Sat & Sun 2–5pm; *f*2.50), is located in a wallhouse, a fancifully gabled building of neo-Renaissance design. This is the town's main museum, but it's packed with a dreary assortment of items of strictly local interest. The museum also has a bizarre annexe, the chapel and male ward of a medieval hospice, the **St Pieter's-en-Bloklands Gasthuis** (Tues–Fri 10–11.30am & 1.30–5pm, Sat & Sun 2–5pm; apply at the Museum Fléhite). Close by, spanning the canal, is the ridiculously picturesque **Koppelpoort**, a fifteenth-century town gate, which defended Amersfoort's northern approach by dropping down a wooden panel and sealing off the canal.

Back on Westsingel, 500m past the museum, all that remains of Amersfoort's other main church, the **Onze Lieve Vrouwekerk** (also known as Langejan), is the fifteenth-century tower: the rest was accidentally blown up in 1797. The original building was paid for by pilgrims visiting the *Amersfoort Madonna*, a small wooden figure that had been thrown into the town canal by a young girl in 1444. Legend has it that the girl was on her way to enter one of Amersfoort's convents when she became ashamed of her simple figurine, so she decided to throw it away. In the manner of such things, a dream commanded her to retrieve the statuette, which subsequently demonstrated miraculous powers. Part morality play, part miracle, the story fulfilled all the necessary criteria to turn the figure into a revered object, and the town into a major centre of medieval pilgrimage. The final call for secular pilgrims to the town, should, however, be the **Brewery de Drie Ringen**, Kleine Spui 18 (Oct–April Tues–Sat noon–6pm; May–Sept Tues–Sat 11am–6pm; July & Aug also Sun noon–5pm), where you can tour the plant and have a quick taster afterwards.

Practicalities

Amersfoort **train station** is opposite the VVV, Stationsplein 27 (Oct–April Mon–Fri 9am–6pm, Sat 9am–1pm; May–Sept Mon–Fri 9am–6pm, Sat 9am–2pm; ☎033/635 151), which is a good ten-minute walk west of the centre of town, the Hofplein: turn left out of the station building along Stationsstraat and keep going. The VVV has a good supply of private **rooms** and **pensions**, and they'll call ahead to make a booking, though most of their addresses are way out of the town centre. There's only one convenient, reasonably priced **hotel** in Amersfoort, the *De Witte*, just to the southwest of the Onze Lieve Vrouwetoren at Utrechtseweg 2 (☎033/614 142; ④). The closest **campsite**, *De Bokkeduinen*, is about 2km west of the station at Barchman Wuytierslaan 81 (April–Oct; ☎033/619 902), take bus #70 or #72, direction Soest, from the bus stop outside the train station. For **food**, there are a number of snack bars and restaurants on the main shopping street, Langestraat: try the pleasant *Den Grooten Slock*, beside the St Joriskerk; *In Den Kleinen Hap*, at Langestraat 95; or *De Kluif* at Groenmarkt 44.

travel details

Trains

Amersfoort to: Amsterdam CS (every 15min; 35min); Utrecht (every 15min; 20min); Zwolle (every 30min; 35min).

Leiden to: Amsterdam CS (every 30min; 35min); The Hague CS (every 30min; 35min).

The Hague to: Amersfoort (every 20min; 1hr); Delft (every 15min; 12min); Dordrecht (every 30min; 40min); Gouda (every 20min; 20min); Rotterdam (every 15min; 25min); Utrecht (every 20min; 40min).

Rotterdam to: Dordrecht (every 10min; 20min); Gouda (every 20min; 20min); Utrecht (every 20min; 45min).

Utrecht to: Amersfoort (2 an hour; 15min); Arnhem (every 15min; 30min); Leeuwarden (hourly; 2hr); Zwolle (2 an hour; 1hr).

Buses

Gouda to: Oudewater (hourly; 20min).

The Hague to: Katwijk (every 30min; 25min).

Leiden to: Katwijk (every 10min; 25min); Noordwijk (every 30min; 40min).

International trains

Dordrecht to: Antwerp (hourly; 1hr); Brussels (hourly; 1hr 40min).

The Hague HS to: Antwerp (hourly; 1hr 35min); Brussels (hourly; 2hr 15min); Paris (4 daily; 5hr 10min).

Leiden to: Antwerp (hourly; 1hr 50min); Brussels (hourly; 2hr 30min).

Rotterdam CS to: Antwerp (hourly; 1hr 15min); Brussels (hourly; 1hr 55min); Paris (4 daily; 4hr 50min).

CHAPTER FOUR

THE NORTH AND THE FRISIAN ISLANDS

U ntil the opening of the Afsluitdijk in 1932, which bridged the mouth of the Zuider Zee, the **north** of Holland was a relatively remote area, a distinct region of small provincial towns that was far from the mainstream life of the Randstad, further south. Since the completion of the dyke, the gap between north and west Holland has narrowed, and fashion and custom seem almost identical. The main exception is linguistic: Friesland has its own language, more akin to Low German than Dutch, and its citizens are keen to use it.

Three provinces make up the north of the country – **Drenthe**, **Groningen** and **Friesland** – though for a long time the Frisians occupied the entire area. Charlemagne recognized three parts of Friesland: West Frisia, equivalent to today's West Friesland, across the IJsselmeer; Central Frisia (today's Friesland); and East Frisia – now Groningen province. At that time much of the region was prey to inundation by the sea, and houses and sometimes entire settlements would be built on artificial mounds or *terpen* (known as *wierden* in Groningen), which brought them high above the water level. It was a miserable sort of existence, and not surprisingly the Frisians soon got around to building dykes to keep the water out permanently. You can still see what's left of some of the mounds in Friesland, though in large settlements they're usually obscured.

During the Middle Ages the area that is now Friesland proper remained independent of the rest of Holland, asserting its separateness regularly until it was absorbed into the Hapsburg empire by Charles V in 1523. It's still something of a maverick among Dutch provinces, although the landscape is familiar enough – dead flat and very green, dotted with black-and-white cattle and long thatched farmhouses crowned with white gable finials or *uleburden*, in the form of a double-swan motif, that were originally meant to deter evil spirits. Of the towns, **Leeuwarden**, the provincial capital of Friesland, is pleasant, if sedate, with two outstanding museums, one of which has the largest collection of tiles in the world. However, many visitors prefer the west coast of the province, where a chain of small towns prospered during the sixteenth-century trading heyday of the Zuider Zee. Each coastal town has its own distinct charm and character, from the splendid merchant houses of **Harlingen**, to the painted furniture and antique neatness of **Hindeloopen** and the tile manufacturers of **Makkum**. Inland, southwest Friesland is a tangle of lake and canal that's been transformed into one of the busiest water sports areas in the country, centring on the town of **Sneek**.

East of Friesland, the province of Groningen, equivalent to Charlemagne's East Frisia, has comparatively few attractions. Its villages tend to be dull and suburban, and most tourists stick to the university town of **Groningen**, a lively, cosmopolitan

place that makes up for its shortage of historic sights with its busy bars and restaurants and the best nightlife in the north. Off the north coast lie the **Frisian Islands**, a fragmented extension of the sandbank that runs the length of Holland's western coastline. There are five populated Dutch islands in all, four of which are in Friesland (Texel, the fifth, is officially part of the province of North Holland; see *North Holland*). The most westerly two, **Vlieland** and **Terschelling**, are accessible by boat from Harlingen; further east, **Ameland** is reachable by bus and ferry from Leeuwarden, **Schiermonnikoog** by bus and boat from Leeuwarden or Groningen. One of the few areas of the country you have to put any effort into reaching, the islands preserve a rare peace and constitute an important nature area, with thriving colonies of birds and a rich flora and fauna. They're also, inevitably, popular holiday destinations, although the tourists who arrive here each summer are easily absorbed into the miles of beach and wide expanses of dune. Plans to build dykes connecting the islands to the mainland and reclaim the shallows all around were met with such resistance from naturalists and islanders that they have now been abandoned, and there's a strong feeling among the people here that they should remain as distinct from the Dutch mainland as possible.

South of Groningen, **Drenthe** is the most sparsely populated and least visited of the Dutch provinces, and it's not hard to see why. Though the Hondsdrug, the range of low hills that spreads northeast of Emmen towards Groningen, bears traces of settlement dating back to around 2500 BC – the earliest sign of any civilization in Holland – for most of its history Drenthe was little more than peat bog and barren moor, of little military or economic significance.

During the nineteenth century, the face of much of the province was changed by the founding of innumerable peat colonies, whose labourers drained the land and dug the peat to expose the subsoil below. As a result of their work, parts of Drenthe are given over to prosperous farmland, with agriculture the dominant local industry. Drenthe's two main towns are of no special interest and have only a couple of attractions that could conceivably bring you this far off the beaten track: **Assen**, the capital, has the Drents Museum, which has a superb collection of prehistoric finds, and **Emmen** is the best place to see Drenthe's most original feature – its *hunebeds*, or megalithic tombs.

ACCOMMODATION PRICE CODES

All the **hotels and hostels** detailed in this chapter have been graded according to the following price categories. Note that the prices have been calculated as those for the cheapest double room during high season. For more on accommodation, see p.29.

① Up to ƒ30 per person.   ④ ƒ100–140.   ⑦ ƒ220–260.
② ƒ30–65.   ⑤ ƒ140–180.   ⑧ ƒ260 and over.
③ ƒ65–100.   ⑥ ƒ180–220.

Leeuwarden and around

An old market town at the heart of an agricultural district, **LEEUWARDEN** was formed from the amalgamation of three *terpen* that originally stood on an expanse of water known as the Middelzee. Later it was the residence of the powerful Frisian Stadholders, who vied with those of Holland for control of the United

Provinces. These days it's the neat and distinctly cosy capital of Friesland, with an air of provincial prosperity and a smug sense of independence. It lacks the concentrated historic charm of many other Dutch towns, but it has a number of grand buildings and two outstanding museums, not to mention an appealingly compact town centre that is almost entirely surrounded and dissected by water.

The Leeuwarden area telephone code is ☎058

Arrival, information and accommodation

Leeuwarden's **train and bus stations** virtually adjoin each other, five minutes' walk south of the town centre. The VVV at the train station (Mon–Fri 9am–5.45pm, Sat 9am–4pm; ☎13 22 24) publishes a leaflet in English detailing a brick-by-brick walking tour of the centre and has a short list of private **rooms** that covers the whole of Friesland, including the town itself, though last-minute vacancies are rare. The list is pinned to the office door when closed. There are only two reasonably priced **hotels** in town: the *De Pauw*, near the train station at Stationsweg 10 (☎12 36 51; ③), is the best bet for getting a room late at night; the *Hotel 't Anker*, on the north side of the centre at Eewal 69–75 (☎12 52 16; ③), is a good and more central alternative, though it does sometimes get full – book in advance if you can. Otherwise try *Pension Bellevue*, near the Oldehove (see below) at Oldehoofsterkerhof 50 (☎15 53 18; ③). **Camping Kleine Wielen** is about 6km out toward Dokkum, nicely sited by a lake; take bus #20, #51 or #57 from the station.

The Town

If you've swallowed all the tourist office myths about Friesland being a land of historic beauty, rural charm and the like, Leeuwarden is initially a bit of a disappointment, with the southern part of the town centre near the station an indeterminate, rather careless mixture of the old and new. Here, at Zuiderplein 9, the revamped **Frisian Resistance Museum** (Tues–Sat 10am–5pm, Sun 1–5pm; f2.50) is a chronological exhibition tracing the early days of the Nazi invasion, through collaboration and resistance on to the Allied liberation. A variety of photographs, Nazi militaria, Allied propaganda and tragic personal stories illustrate the text, but the emphasis is very much on the local struggle rather than the general war effort.

Heading north, high-rise blocks and shopping centres line Wirdumerdijk into the centre of town at **Waagplein**, a long, narrowing open space cut by a canal and flanked by cafés and large department stores. The **Waag** itself dates from 1598, but it's been converted into a restaurant and bank. Walking west, **Nieuwestad** is Leeuwarden's main shopping street, from where Kleine Kerkstraat, a turn on the right, leads to the **Oldehoofster Kerkhof** – a large square-cum-car park near the old city walls. At the end of the square stands the precariously leaning **Oldehove**. Something of a symbol for the city, this is part of a cathedral started in 1529 but never finished because of subsidence, a lugubrious mass of disproportion that defies all laws of gravity and geometry. To the right stands a statue of the Frisian politician and trade unionist P.J. Troelstra, who looks on impassively, no doubt admonishing the city fathers for their choice of architects. Those brave enough can climb the tower for a couple of guilders (Tues–Sat 10am–4pm).

Along Grote Kerkstraat

Grote Kerkstraat leads east from the square, following the line of the track that connected two of Leeuwarden's original *terpen*, Oldehove and Nijehove. Close by, at Grote Kerkstraat 11, is **Het Princessehof** (Mon–Sat 10am–5pm, Sun 2–5pm; *f*3.50), a house from 1650 that was once the residence of the Stadholder William Friso. It's now a ceramics museum, with the largest collection of tiles in the world, though sadly the layout is confusing and there are no English guidebooks available – though one is promised. If you're really interested in ceramics you could spend days here; if not, be selective, as the sheer quantity of material is overwhelming.

Of the many displays, two are outstanding. The first, through the ornamental arch at the reception desk and up the stairs to the third floor, is the collection of **Chinese, Japanese and Vietnamese ceramics**, which outlines the rise and fall of Far Eastern "china" production. In the sixteenth century Portuguese traders first began to bring back Chinese porcelain for sale in Europe. It proved tremendously popular, and by the seventeenth century the Dutch, among others, had begun to muscle in. Ships crammed with plates and dishes shuttled back and forth to the China coast, where European merchants bargained with local warlords for trade and territorial concessions or "hongs" – hence Hong Kong. The benefits of the trade were inevitably weighted in favour of Western interests, and the Chinese could only watch with dismay as the bottom fell out of the market when European factories began to reproduce their goods. The Dutch soon modified the original, highly stylized designs to more naturalistic patterns with a lighter, plainer effect, with the result that Chinese producers were forced to make desperate attempts to change their designs to fit Western tastes.

The earliest pieces on display in this section date from the sixteenth century, notably several large blue and white plates of naive delicacy, decorated with swirling borders and surrealistic dragons. Although Chinese producers began to work to European designs in the early eighteenth century, it was many years before the general deterioration in manufacture became apparent, and some of the most exquisite examples of Chinaware date from as late as the middle of the eighteenth century – not least those from the Dutch merchantman *Geldermalsen*, which sank in the waters of the South China Sea in 1752 and was salvaged in 1983. Some 150,000 items of cargo were retrieved, and there's a small sample here, including a magnificent dish of bright-blue entwined fish bordered by a design of flowers and stems – in stark contrast to the crude, sad-looking Chinese imitations of Western landscapes and coats of arms across the room.

On the second floor, to the left of the stairs, you'll find another room devoted to the development of **Chinese porcelain** from prehistory onward, with representative examples illustrating major trends. The finest work dates from the Ming Dynasty (1368–1644), with powerful open-mouthed dragons, billowing clouds, and sharply drawn plant tendrils. This room leads to the other section you shouldn't miss, a magnificent array of **Dutch tiles**, with good examples of all the classic designs – soldiers, flowers, ships, etc – framed by uncomplicated borders. Well documented and clearly laid out, the earliest tiles date from the late fifteenth century, the work of Italians based in Antwerp who used a colourful and expensive tin-glazing process. By the seventeenth century, tiles were no longer exclusive to the wealthy, and the demands of a mass market transformed the industry. Popular as a wall covering – the precursor of wallpaper – thousands of identical tiles were churned out by dozens of Dutch factories (there were seven in Friesland alone). The emphasis was on very simple designs, characteristically blue on white, the top end of the market distinguished by extra colours or the size of the design: the more tiles it took to make the "picture", the more expensive the tile.

The collection of **European ceramics and porcelain** slots awkwardly around the other exhibits: best are the Art Deco and Art Nouveau pieces on the second floor, and the modern work in the basement.

Heading east from the museum along Grote Kerkstraat, is the house (no. 212) where **Mata Hari** spent her early years – a native of Leeuwarden whose name has become synonymous with the image of the "femme fatale". A renowned dancer, she was arrested in 1917 by the French on charges of espionage and subsequently shot, though what she actually did remains a matter of some debate. In retrospect it seems likely that she acted as a double agent, gathering information for the Allies while giving snippets to the Germans. Something of a local heroine, her old home has become the **Frisian Literary Museum** (Mon–Fri 9am–12.30pm & 1.30–5pm), a repository for a whole range of Frisian documents, together with a few derisory exhibits on Mata Hari herself. There are plans to enlarge the museum and move it down the street in 1994. Better is the permanent display on P.J. Troelstra, the Frisian socialist politician and poet, who set up the Dutch Social Democratic party in 1890 and was at the head of the Dutch labour movement until 1924.

At the far end of Grote Kerkstraat, the **Grote** or **Jacobijner Kerk** (July–Sept Tues–Fri 2–4pm) has recently undergone a very extensive restoration, though it's still an unremarkable Gothic construction. Another victim of subsidence, the whole place tilts slightly toward the newer south aisle, where some fragmentary remnants of sixteenth-century frescoes are exhibited. In front of the church is a modernistic **memorial** to Leeuwarden's wartime Jewish community, based on the classroom registers of 1942; it's an imaginative and harsh reminder of suffering and persecution.

The Fries Museum and around

South of here, on Turfmarkt, the **Fries Museum** (Tues–Sat 10am–5pm, Sun 1–5pm; *f*3) is one of Holland's best regional museums, founded by a society that was established in the nineteenth century to develop interest in the language and history of Friesland, and with displays that trace the development of Frisian culture from prehistoric times up until the present day.

Just by the entrance, what was once the museum's pride stands demoted: the **portrait of Saskia van Ulenborch**, Rembrandt's wife, has recently been proved to be the work of his studio, rather than by the great man himself. On the first floor, among a chain of period rooms, is an extensive collection of silver. A flourishing Frisian industry throughout the seventeenth and eighteenth centuries, most of the work was commissioned by the local gentry, who were in their turn influenced by the fashions of the Frisian Stadholder and his court. The earliest piece is an elegant drinking horn of 1397, and there are some particularly fine examples of chased silver in Baroque style, where each representation is framed by a fanciful border or transition. This distinctive "Kwabornament" design flourished in Friesland long after it had declined in the rest of Holland. Some of the more curious exhibits here date from the middle of the seventeenth century when it was fashionable to frame exotic objects in silver: a certain Lenert Danckert turned a coconut into a cup, and Minne Sikkes fitted silver handles to a porcelain bowl to create a brandy cup. Most of the later exhibits are ornate, French-style tableware.

On the second floor there's a selection of early majolica, many examples of different sorts of porcelain and a mundane collection of seventeenth-century Frisian painting. Rather more interesting are the rooms devoted to the island of Ameland and the painted furniture of Hindeloopen – rich, gaudy and intense, patterned with tendrils and flowers on a red, green or white background. Most peculiar of all are examples of the bizarre headgear of eighteenth-century Hindeloopen women – large cartwheel-shaped hats known as *Deutsche muts* and (the less specifically Frisian) *oorijzers*, gold or silver helmets that were an elaborate development of the hat clip or brooch. As well as an indication of social standing, a young girl's first *oorijzer* symbolized the transition to womanhood. On the top floor look out for the "Golden Whips", presented as prizes in eighteenth-century horse races.

Opposite the Fries Museum stands one of the most striking buildings in Leeuwarden – the **Kanselarij**, a superb gabled Renaissance structure of 1571, which hosts art exhibitions in the summer. The original plan placed the gable and the corresponding double stairway in the centre of the facade, but they are in fact slightly to the right because the money ran out before the work was finished – making the Kanselarij an early example of public expenditure cuts. Just south of the Fries Museum, at Turfmarkt 48, is the weirdly wonderful 1930s **Utrecht Building**, today containing a restoration workshop. A little way north of Turfmarkt, is the Catholic church of **St Boniface**, a belated apology to an English missionary killed by the pagan Frisians in 754, along with 52 other Christians, at nearby Dokkum. It's a neo-Gothic building of 1894 designed by P.J.H. Cuypers, its ornamented spire imposing itself on what is otherwise a rather flat skyline. The spire was almost totally destroyed in a storm of 1976 and many people wanted to take the opportunity to pull the place down altogether – even to replace it with a supermarket. Fortunately the steeple was replaced at great expense and with such enormous ingenuity that its future seems secure, making it one of the few Cuypers churches left in Holland.

Eating and drinking

One of the best places to **eat** in Leeuwarden is *Eetcafé Spinoza* on Eewal, a youthful, reasonably priced restaurant with a good range of vegetarian dishes; try also the excellent *De Brasserie* at Wirdumerdijk 23, especially good for lunch. Alternatively, *Pizzeria Sardegna*, Grote Hoogstraat 28 (closed Mon), serves an extravagant variety of reasonably priced pizzas, or you can eat Mexican food at the *Yucatan* on St Jacobsstraat. As for Dutch food, *Eetcafé de Linde*, on Groente Markt, has cheapish *dagschotels*, though it closes early, about 9.30pm; *Eetkamer*, on Grote Hoogstraat, has plenty of affordable dishes, as does *De Stadthouder*, on Nieuwestad N.Z. If you want to go more upmarket, *Café He Teven*, at Druifsteeg 57, is the favoured spot for light meals among Leeuwarden's smart young set, followed by a beer at the adjacent *Albert Silberman*.

For **drinking**, the bar of the *Hotel De Pauw*, Stationsweg 10, is quiet and has some delightful old furniture; the *Herberg De Stee*, next door, is busy and boisterous. In the centre of town, the *Spoekepolle*, on St Jacobsstraat, is a students' favourite; the *Fire Palace*, at Nieuwestad N.Z. 49, is a big bar overlooking the canal which doubles as the town's main disco at weekends; *L'Escalier*, on Grote Hoogstraat, is a convivial small bar with dartboards; and there's a series of lively bars on Doelesteeg, most with loud music.

Listings

Boat tours For information on guided boat trips to the Frisian lakes contact the VVV.
Books *Van der Velde*, Nieuwestad 90, has a good stock of English-language titles.
Car rental *Interrent*, Marshallweg 12–14 (☎12 55 55).
Chemist Details of nearest (emergency) chemist from ☎13 52 95.
Emergencies ☎0011.
Left luggage Lockers (*f*3.50 per day) at the station (daily 6am–midnight).
Markets General market on Fri, Wilhelminaplein.
Police Holstmeerweg 1 (☎13 24 23).
Post office Near the Fries Museum, Tweebaksmarkt 25 (Mon–Fri 8.30am–6pm).

Around Leeuwarden: Popta Slot

On the western outskirts of Leeuwarden, the tiny village of **MARSSUM** incorporates **Popta Slot** (April–Sept Mon–Fri guided tours at 11am, 2pm & 3pm; *f*3) – a trim, onion-domed eighteenth-century manor house, which sits prettily behind its ancient moat. Inside is a series of period rooms, furnished in the style of the local gentry. Doctor Popta was an affluent lawyer and farmer who spent some of his excess wealth on the neighbouring **Popta Gasthuis**: neat almshouses cloistered behind an elaborate portal of 1712. Buses #71 and #91 leave Leeuwarden bus station for the ten-minute trip to Marssum approximately every half-hour during the week, every hour on Sundays.

West of Leeuwarden: Franeker, Harlingen and the islands

Seventeen kilometres west of Leeuwarden, **FRANEKER** was the cultural hub of northern Holland until Napoleon closed the university in 1810. Nowadays it's a quiet country town with a spruce old centre of somewhat over-restored old buildings. The train station is five minutes' walk to the southeast of town – follow Stationsweg round to the left and over the bridge, first left over the second bridge onto Zuiderkade and second right along Dijkstraat. Buses from Leeuwarden drop off passengers on Kleijenburg, at the northwest corner of the old town centre.

All the town's key sights are beside or near the main street, **Voorstraat**, a continuation of Dijkstraat, which runs from east to west to end in a park, **Sternse Slotland** – the site of the medieval castle. Near the park at Voorstraat 51, the VVV is housed in the **Waag** of 1657, which also serves as the entrance to the **Museum 't Coopmanshus en Kaatsmuseum** (Tues–Sat 10am–5pm; May–Sept also Sun 1–5pm; *f*2.75) next door, whose ground floor has bits and pieces relating to the university and its obscure alumni. In the old senate room, there is a pile of slim boxes carved to resemble books that contain dried samples of local flora and fauna, the gift of Louis Bonaparte. Upstairs, a couple of rooms are devoted to trophies and pictures of the Frisian game of *kaatsen* – a sort of distant relative of baseball.

Heading east along Voorstraat, past the stolid **Martenahuis** of 1498, the Raadhuisplein branches off to the left, edged by the **Stadhuis** (Mon–Fri 9am–4pm), with its twin gables and octagonal tower – a magnificent mixture of Gothic and Renaissance styles built in 1591. Opposite, at Eise Eisingastraat 3, there's a curious, primitive eighteenth-century **Planetarium** (Tues–Sat 10am–12.30pm & 1.30–5pm; May–Aug Mon same times & Sun 1–5pm; *f*3.50) built by a local woolcomber, Eise Eisinga, in the living room of his house. Born in 1744, Eisinga was something of a prodigy: he taught himself mathematics and astronomy, publishing a weighty arithmetic book at the age of only seventeen. In 1774, the unusual conjunction of Mercury, Venus, Mars and Jupiter under the sign of Aries prompted a local paper to predict the end of the world. There was panic in the countryside, and an appalled Eisinga decided on his life's work, the construction of a planetarium that would dispel superstition by explaining the workings of the cosmos. It took him seven years, almost as long as he had to enjoy it before his distaste for the autocratic Frisian Stadholder caused his imprisonment and exile. His return signalled a change of fortunes. In 1816 he was presented with the order of the Lion of the Netherlands, and, two years later, a royal visit persuaded King Willem I to buy the planetarium for the state, granting Eisinga a free tenancy and a generous annual stipend until his death in 1828.

The planetarium isn't of the familiar domed variety but was built as a false ceiling in the family's living room, a series of rotating dials and clocks indicating the movement of the planets and associated phenomena, from tides to star signs. The whole apparatus is regulated by a clock which is driven by a series of weights hung in a tiny alcove beside the cupboard-bed. Above the face of the main dials, the mechanisms are open for inspection, hundreds of hand-made nails driven into moving slats. A detailed guidebook explains every aspect and every dial.

Finally there's an extraordinarily dull provincial coin collection, the **Munt en Penningkabinet**, at Voorstrat 2a (May–Sept Mon–Fri 1–5pm; ƒ1.50).

Practicalities

Franeker's VVV is at Voorstraat 51 (Tues–Sat 9am–5pm; ☎05170/94613), five minutes' walk northwest of the train station. There are four **hotels** in town, of which the two most central are *De Doelen*, at Breedeplaats 6 (☎05170/92261; ③), and *De Bogt Fen Gune*, on the left turn at the west end of Voorstraat, Vijverstraat 1 (☎05170/92416; ③); *De Bleek*, near the station at Stationsweg 1 (☎05170/92124; ③), and *De Stadsherberg*, on the continuation of Stationsweg at Oude Kaatsveld 8 (☎05170/92686; ③), are not much further out.

The town **campsite** (April–Sept) is a couple of minutes' walk east of the train station down Schurmansingel and across Tzummerweg on J. Stapertlaan. For **food**, try *La Terraz*, Zilverstraat 7 or *De Grillerije* at Groenmarkt 14, good for a sandwich or croissant at lunchtime, or the hotel *De Bogt Fen Gune*. *Grillerije*, Zilverstraat 14, is nice in the evening, though its menu is basically for carnivores; *Amicitia*, Voorstraat 9, is a reasonably priced pizzeria and bar.

Harlingen

Just north of the Afsluitdijk, 30km west of Leeuwarden, **HARLINGEN** is more compelling than Franeker, an ancient and historic port that serves as the ferry terminus for the islands of Terschelling and Vlieland and is something of a centre for traditional Dutch sailing barges, a number of which are usually moored in the harbour. A naval base from the seventeenth century, the town straddles the **Vliestroom** channel, once the easiest way for shipping to pass from the North Sea through the shallows that surround the Frisian islands and on into the Zuider Zee. Before trade moved west, this was Holland's lifeline, where cereals, fish and other foodstuffs were brought in from the Baltic to feed the expanding Dutch cities.

Harlingen has two **train stations**, one on the southern edge of town for trains from Leeuwarden, the other, Harlingen Haven, right next to the docks, handling trains connecting with boats to the islands. From Harlingen Haven the old town spreads east, sandwiched between the pretty Noorderhaven and more functional Zuiderhaven canals, a mass of sixteenth- to eighteenth-century houses that reflect the prosperity and importance of earlier times. However, Harlingen is too busy to be just another cosy tourist town: there's a fishing fleet, a small container depot, a shipbuilding yard and a resurgent ceramics industry. The heart of town is the **Voorstraat**, a long, tree-lined avenue that's home to an elegant eighteenth-century **Stadhuis**, the **VVV** and the **Hannemahuis Museum** at no. 56 (July to mid-Sept Tues–Sat 10am–5pm; mid-Sept to Nov 1 & April–June Mon–Fri 1.30–5pm; *f*2.50). Sited in an eighteenth-century merchant's house, the museum concentrates on the history of the town and includes some interesting displays on shipping and some lovely, locally produced tiles – for once in manageable quantities.

Harlingen was once a tile-making centre, and the industry flourished here until it was undermined by the rise of cheap wallpaper. The last of the old factories closed in 1933, but the demand for traditional crafts has led to something of a recovery, with the opening of new workshops in the Seventies. If you like the look of Dutch tiles, this is a good place to buy. The **Harlinger Aardewerk en Tegelfabriek** at Voorstraat 84 sells an outstanding range of contemporary and traditional styles, if you've got the money – Dutch handicrafts don't come cheap.

Practicalities

Another of Harlingen's specialities is fresh **fish**: dotted all over the centre of town are fish stands, fish restaurants and snack bars. Best is *Veltman's* on the edge of the Noorderhaven at Rommelhaven 2, a combined snack bar and restaurant with a wide range of North Sea delicacies. Alternatives are the excellent *t' Gastronom* next to the VVV, *'t Noordeke* at Noorderhaven 17, which has good-value daily specials, and the hotel restaurants. If you're planning to stay, there are three reasonably priced **hotels** in Harlingen. Try the *Heerenlogement*, on the eastern continuation of Voorstraat at Franekereind 23 (☎05178/15846; ③), the slightly more expensive *Anna Casparii* (☎05178/12065; ③), sited on the canal at Noorderhaven 6, or the *Zeezicht*, by the harbour at Zuiderhaven 1 (☎05178/12536; ④), which, despite its higher rates, isn't in such a nice location. For about half the price, the **VVV** at Voorstraat 34 (Mon–Fri 8.35am–12.30pm & 1.30–6pm, Sat 9am–5pm; ☎05178/17222) has a small stock of **rooms** and **pensions**, though they go fast in the summer. The nearest **campsite**, *De Zeehoeve* (April–Sept), is a twenty-minute walk along the sea dyke to the south of town at Westerzeedijk 45 – follow the signs from Voorstraat.

Terschelling

Of all the Frisian islands, **Terschelling** is the easiest to reach – which is both an attraction and a problem. If you just want a taste of the islands without making too much effort, this is the place to head for; but, if you're looking for tranquillity, Vlieland, Ameland or Schiermonnikoog are a better bet. A major tourist resort in its own right, the town of **WEST TERSCHELLING** is a rather unappealing sprawl of chalets, bungalows and holiday complexes that spreads out from what remains of the old village – a mediocre modernity that belies West Terschelling's past importance as a port and safe anchorage on the edge of the Vliestroom channel, the main shipping lane from the Zuider Zee.

Strategically positioned, West Terschelling boomed throughout the seventeenth century as a ship supply and repair centre, with its own fishing and whaling fleets, paying the price for its prominence when the British razed the town in 1666. The islanders were renowned sailors, much sought after by ships' captains who also needed them as pilots to guide vessels through the treacherous shallows and shifting sandbanks that lay off the Vliestroom. Despite the pilots, shipwrecks were common all along the island's northern and western shores – the VVV sells a sketch of the island marked with all the known disasters. The most famous victim was the *Lutine*, which sank while carrying gold and silver to British troops stationed here during the Napoleonic wars. The remains are still at the bottom of the sea, and only the ship's bell was recovered – now in Lloyd's of London, where it's still rung whenever a big ship goes down.

The best place to bone up on Terschelling's past is the excellent **Museum 't Behouden Huys**, near the ferry terminus at Commandeurstraat 30 (April 1–Oct 31 Mon–Fri 10am–5pm; June 15–Sept 30 also Sat 1–5pm; July 1–Aug 31 also Sun 1–5pm; *f*5). The prime exhibits here include maps of the old coastline illustrating Terschelling's crucial position, various items from the whaling fleet, lots of sepia photos of bearded islanders and a shipwreck diving room. There's also a rather desultory tribute to the local explorer Willem Barents, who hit disaster when pack ice trapped his ship in the Arctic in 1595. Undaunted, he and his crew managed to survive the whole winter on the ice and sailed back in the spring. Barents mounted other, more successful expeditions into the Arctic regions, discovering Spitzbergen and naming the Barents Sea – all in the fruitless search for the northwest passage to China. He died in the Arctic in 1597. If you're extra keen on things aquatic, there's a tiny **Fishing Museum** at the back of a shop on Radhuisstraat (Mon–Fri 2–4pm; *f*1.50) and, just east of town, the **Centre for Nature and Landscape**, Burg Reedekerstraat 11 (April–Oct Mon–Fri 9am–5pm, Sat & Sun 2–5pm; *f*6.50), which contains a decent aquarium.

Throughout the summer West Terschelling is packed with tourists sampling the restaurants and bars that line the main streets, Torenstraat in particular, while others cycle off across the island to the beach at **WEST-AAN-ZEE** where there's a café, *Zilver Meeuw*, and as much empty beach as you're prepared to look for. On a more sombre note, the more northerly of the two cycling routes passes through an odd cemetery in a wood, with a small Commonwealth forces graveyard – as ever the inscriptions make sad reading, with few of the downed bomber crews aged more than 25.

REACHING THE ISLANDS

Ferries leave Harlingen for the crossings (about 1hr 45min) to the islands of Terschelling and Vlieland at least three times daily throughout the summer and twice daily during the winter. The return fares are currently *f*37 to Terschelling and *f*35 to Vlieland, with a supplement of *f*15 for bikes. The ferries dock at West Terschelling and Oost-Vlieland, the islands' main settlements. There's also a fast **hydrofoil** service: from May to September it runs three times a day to Terschelling, twice daily to Vlieland and from September to May twice a day to Terschelling only. The hydrofoil costs an extra *f*7.50 each way, but at around only 45 minutes it's worth it if you're going for a day trip. From May to the end of September there's an additional ferry service connecting Terschelling and Vlieland (*f*17 return, *f*9 one-way).

Visitors' cars are not allowed on Vlieland, but anyway the best way of exploring any of the Frisian islands is by bike. There are rental companies near the ferry terminals on both islands, charging a uniform rate of *f*7 per day, *f*30 per week, for a basic bike – although given the steep, stony hills, it's worth shelling out a few extra guilders for a machine with decent gears.

If you want to stay on the island, **accommodation** is hard to come by in July and August when all the cheaper places tend to be booked up months in advance. At other times you have a wide choice, including a number of decent small **pensions** – try *De Boekanier*, Commandeurstraat 19 (☎05620/2524; ②), or the *De Holland*, Molenstraat 5 (☎05620/2302; ②), both of which are near the ferry terminus. There's a **youth hostel** at Burgmeester Van Heusdenweg 39 (April–Sept; ☎05620/2338), with a **campsite** nearby, the *Dellewal* (☎05620/2305), the nearest of several sites, some 25 minutes east of town along the southern shore.

The **VVV** (Mon–Fri 9am–noon & 2–5.30pm, Sat 11am–noon & 4–5pm; ☎05620/3000), near the ferry port, provides a full list of pensions and **rooms** and operates a booking service (*f*5). They also take bookings for the rest of the island; if you're after a bit of peace and quiet, aim for **pensions** between the villages of Formerum and Oosterend – far enough east to escape most of the crowds. They also offer a variety of **walking tours**, and can give details of cycling routes.

From West Terschelling the other villages stretch out along the southern part of the island, sheltered from winter storms by the sand dunes and occasional patches of forest that lie to the immediate north. The island's **bus** service leaves from right next to the ferry terminus and is excellent, connecting all the villages in a matter of minutes; as an alternative, it's possible to rent **bikes** at a cost of about *f*6 a day from a number of shops down near the harbour and also from the VVV. Quite simply, the further east you go the more attractive the island becomes: the two final settlements, **HOORN** and **OOSTEREND**, are particularly pleasant places within easy reach of empty tracts of beach and the nature reserve **De Boschplaat**, where thousands of waterfowl congregate in the marshy shallows of the southeastern shore. To help protect the birds, De Boschplaat is closed during the breeding season (March 15–Aug 15), although the VVV runs guided tours for bird enthusiasts. Oosterend also has a **café**, *De Boschplaat*, one of the best places to eat on the island, and three **campsites**, including the cosy *'t Wantij*.

Vlieland

The complex pattern of sandbank shallows that lies to the south of **VLIELAND**, just west of Terschelling, helped to make the island one of the most isolated and neglected parts of nineteenth-century Holland. Of minor importance during the great days of the Zuider Zee trade, Vlieland lost one of its two villages to the sea in the eighteenth century, and there was never enough money to have it rebuilt. Tourism has brought wealth to the thousand or so islanders, but it's all very low key: development has been restrained and the island is popular for family holidays – cycling, windsurfing, beaches and country walks. The quietest of the Frisian islands, no cars are allowed, and the only settlement, **OOST-VLIELAND**, is little more than a restaurant-lined main street surrounded by second homes, chalets and bungalows. There's little to see in the village as such, although the plastic globe in the small square is a surprising tribute to Esperanto, and the Armenhuis behind it a particularly attractive seventeenth-century country dwelling. The town's museum, the **Tromps Huys** at Dorpsstraat 99 (Mon–Sat 10am–noon & 2–5pm), has a mundane collection of antiques and Vlieland bygones.

Accommodation is limited, and virtually impossible to find throughout the summer, although the **VVV** (Mon–Fri 9am–5pm; Oct–April also Sat 11am–noon; May–Sept also Sat & Sun 11am–noon & 4–5pm; ☎05621/1357) does its best with the few private **rooms**, and will help groups rent apartments and "dune houses". Vlieland has several pensions and hotels, cheapest of which is the *De Herbergh van Flielant* on the main street at Dorpsstraat 105 (☎05621/1378; ③); you'll find more for around the same price down the road at nos. 11, 61 and 88. The most convenient **campsite**, *De Stortemelk* (☎05621/1225), is sited on the sand dunes behind the beach, about half an hour's walk or a ten-minute bike ride northeast of Oost-Vlieland, at Kampweg 1.

The best way of seeing the island is by bike, though there's also a limited **bus** service that travels along the southern shore from near the ferry terminus. For **excursions**, the VVV run birdwatching expeditions, and private operators organize day-long trips to the northern tip of Texel (*f*15 return) by means of a tractor-like lorry, which crosses the great expanse of sand ("Vliehors") that forms Vlieland's western extremity to connect with a boat.

South of Leeuwarden: Sneek, the lakes, and the IJsselmeer ports

The Leeuwarden–Stavoren train line passes through a series of small Frisian towns with a speed that gainsays their earlier isolation. Until well into the nineteenth century, the lakes, canals and peat diggings **south and east of Sneek** made land communications difficult, and the only significant settlements were built close to the sea or on major waterways. Dependent on water-borne commerce, these communities declined with the collapse of the Zuider Zee trade, but, because of their insularity, some maintained particular artistic and cultural traditions – from the painted furniture and distinctive dialect of Hindeloopen to the style and design of many of Makkum's tiles. Passing through by train, the small settlements resemble what in fact they once were – islands in the shallow marshes. Nowadays, all the tiny old towns are popular holiday destinations, of which Sneek, the centre of a booming pleasure-boat industry, is by far the busiest.

Sneek

Twenty minutes by train from Leeuwarden, **SNEEK** (pronounced "snake") was an important shipbuilding centre as early as the fifteenth century, a prosperous maritime town protected by an extensive system of walls and moats. Clumsy postwar development has robbed the place of most of its charm – its centre has one of the most interminable shopping precincts in western Europe – but there are still some buildings of mild interest.

Sneek's **train** and **bus** stations are five minutes' walk from the old centre, directly east down Stationsstraat. This leads to the scruffy main square, **Martiniplein**, whose ponderous sixteenth-century **Martinikerk** is edged by an old wooden belfry. Around the corner at the end of Grote Kerkstraat, the **Stadhuis**, Marktstraat 15, is all extravagance, from the Rococo facade to the fanciful outside staircase; inside (July–Aug Mon–Fri 2–4pm) there's an indifferent display of ancient weapons in the former guardroom. Heading east along Marktstraat, veer right after the VVV and follow the signs to the nearby **Scheepvart Museum en Oudheidkamer**, Kleinzand 14 (Mon–Sat 10am–5pm; Sun noon–5pm; *f*2), a well-displayed collection of maritime models, paintings, and related miscellany. There's also a room devoted to the Visser family, who made a fortune in the eighteenth century, transporting eels to hungry Londoners. A little further along, at Kleinzand 32, the **Weduwe Joustra** off-licence has an original nineteenth-century interior, worth glancing in for its old barrels and till, even if you decide not to indulge in a bottle of *Beerenburg*, a herb-flavoured gin that's a local speciality. Similarly worth a passing look is **De Tovebal**, an old sweetshop directly south of the Martiniplein at Oude Koemarkt 17. Turn right at the end of Koemarkt and you reach the grandiose **Waterpoort** – all that remains of the seventeenth-century town walls.

Practicalities

If you want to stay in Sneek, the **VVV**, right in the centre of town near the Stadhuis at Marktstraat 18 (Mon–Fri 9am–5pm & Sat 9am–2pm; ☎05150/14096), will arrange private **rooms** for a small fee. The town's cheapest **hotel** is the down-at-heel *Ozinga*, immediately to the south of the Waterpoort at Lemmerweg 8 (☎05150/12216; ③); otherwise try the more expensive *Bonnema*, by the train station at Stationsstraat 64 (☎05150/13175; ④), or *De Wijnberg*, Marktstraat 23 (☎05150/12421; ④). The Sneek **youth hostel** (☎05150/12132; mid-June to mid-Sept) is some 3km southeast of the town centre at Oude Oppenhuizerweg 20 – head east to the end of Kleinzand, turn right down Oppenhuizerweg, and it's the first major road on the left. The nearest **campsite** is *De Domp*, Domp 4 (☎05150/12559; no buses), a couple of kilometres to the northeast of the centre on Sytsingawiersterleane, a right turn off the main road to Leeuwarden. *Camping De Potten*, Paviljoenweg (☎05150/15205; April–Sept), lies some 5km east of town beside the pretty **Sneekemeer**, the nearest of the Frisian lakes, but again there are no buses; taxis can be arranged at the VVV. *De Potten* rents a good range of watersports equipment at reasonable prices.

Sneek has a large number of **restaurants**, few of which have much character: *'t Stoofje*, Oude Koemarkt 11, has cheap, filling Dutch food (including pancakes); *Hinderlooper Kamer*, Oosterdijk 10, is a smart, cheerful bistro with reasonably priced Dutch food; or you could take your pick from any number of places where Leeuwenburg meets Suupmarkt. One of the better places to **drink**, *Amicitia*, is here too, though the other bars have little to distinguish them.

If you want to see more of the lakes, there are **boat trips** leaving from the Oosterkade, over the bridge by the east end of Kleinzand, throughout the summer. Itineraries and prices vary and there's no fixed schedule of sailings: you can do anything from a quick whizz around the town's canals to venturing out into the open sea. Contact the VVV or the boat owners at the dock for up-to-date details.

One word of warning: expect Sneek to be exceptionally busy and accommodation impossible to find during **Sneek Week**, the annual regatta held at the beginning of August, when the flat green expanses around town are thick with the white of slowly moving sails.

Bolsward

Some 10km west of Sneek, **BOLSWARD** (pronounced "Bozwut" in the local dialect) is the archetypal Frisian country town, with tractors on the roads and geese in the streets. Founded in the seventh century, there are only a handful of sights to speak of – the scant ruins of the **Broerekerk**, opposite the VVV, and the **Stadhuis**, at Jongemastraat 2, a magnificent red-brick, stone-trimmed Renaissance edifice of 1613. The facade is topped by a lion holding a coat of arms over the head of a terrified – or surprised – Turk, and below a mass of twisting, curling carved stone frames a series of finely cut cameos, all balanced by an extravagant external staircase. Inside there's a small **museum** of local archeological/historical bits and pieces (April–Nov Mon–Fri 9am–noon & 2–4pm; slightly longer hours in summer). Otherwise, unless you're fanatical about such things, even the dull fifteenth-century **Martinikerk** at Groot Kerkhof (May–Oct 10am–noon & 1.30–5pm) need not detain you.

Buses #90 and #99 connect Sneek train station with Bolsward (Mon–Sat 3 hourly, Sun 1 hourly; 15min), and, should you decide to **stay**, the **VVV**, Broereplein 1 (Mon–Fri 9am–noon & 1.30–5pm; ☎05157/2727), has a handful of private **rooms.** There are two cheap and convenient **hotels**, the *Centraal*, Nieuwmarkt 10 (☎05157/2589; ③), and, a little pricier, *De Wijnberg*, Marktplein 5 (☎05157/2220; ③).

Workum and Makkum

Ten minutes' southwest of Sneek by train, **WORKUM**, a long, straggly town with an attractive main street, has the appearance of a comfortable city suburb, protected by several kilometres of sea defences. In fact, until the early eighteenth century it was a seaport, though nowadays indications of a more adventurous past are confined to the central square, 3km from the train station, with its seventeenth-century **Waag** at Merk 4, which contains a standard nautical-historical collection (March–Oct Tues–Fri 10am–5pm, Mon & Sat 1–5pm; *f*2.50). Immediately behind, the **St Gertrudskerk** (Mon–Sat 11am–5pm), is the largest medieval church in Friesland, and contains a small collection of mostly eighteenth-century odds and ends. Far more absorbing, if you're into religious art, is the **Museum Kerkelijke Kunst** in the neo-Gothic St Werenfridus Kerk at Noard 175 (June–Sept Mon–Sat 10am–5pm; *f*1.50). Just down the road at Noard 6, the likeable **Jopie Huisman Museum** (April–Oct Mon–Sat 10am–5pm; *f*4) is devoted to paintings by a contemporary artist, most of which have an appealingly unpretentious focus on Frisian life.

If you want to **stay over**, the VVV (Mon–Fri 9am–5pm; ☎05151/1300) on the first floor of the Waag, has a limited number of **private rooms**. Alternatively, head for the *Gulden Leeuw*, Merk 2 (☎05151/2341; ③) where the facilities include a decent restaurant.

From Workum train station a minibus service (#102, Mon–Sat every 2–3 hours, no Sun service; 30min) heads south to Hindeloopen (see opposite) or north to the agreeable town of **MAKKUM** – in fact more easily accessible from Bolsward by bus #98 (Mon–Sat hourly, Sun afternoon every 2hr; 20min). Though saved from postcard prettiness by a working harbour, Makkum's popularity as a centre of traditional Dutch ceramics manufacture means it can be overwhelmed by summer tourists. The local product rivals the more famous Delftware in quality, varying from the bright and colourful to more delicate pieces. The VVV (April–Oct Mon–Fri 10am–5pm; summer also Sat 10am–5pm & Sun 1.30–5pm; ☎05158/31422) is sited beneath the **Fries Aardewerkmuseum** (May–Sept Mon–Sat 10am–5pm; Sun 1.30–5pm; *f*2.50), which features, predictably enough, representative samples of local work. If you haven't seen enough tiles here to satisfy your curiosity, there's plenty more, notably in the Tichelaar family **workshops** at Turfmarkt 61 (Mon–Fri 9am–5.30pm, Sat 9am–4pm; *f*3), or you can visit their two shops for free, at Kerkstraat 9 and Plein 10. There are no bargains, though, and most of the modern tiles have either staid traditional motifs or ooze an unappealing domestic cosiness; the vases and larger plates are more exciting but also more expensive.

If you decide to **stay**, the VVV has a few **private rooms**; otherwise try *Hotel de Prins* at Kerkstraat 1 (☎05158/31510; ③), or the more pleasantly located *De Waag*, two minutes around the corner at Markt 13 (☎05158/31447; ③). Both hotels contain basic, low-priced restaurants; or head for *De Maitak* on Markt, which does a good range of sandwiches, pizzas and light lunches.

Hindeloopen

The next stop down the rail line, the village of **HINDELOOPEN** juts into the IJsselmeer twenty minutes' walk west of the train station, its primness extreme even by Dutch standards. Until the seventeenth century Hindeloopen prospered as a Zuider Zee port, concentrating on trade with the Baltic and Amsterdam. A tightly knit community, the combination of rural isolation and trade created a specific culture, with a distinctive dialect – *Hylper*, Frisian with Scandinavian influences – a sumptuous costume and, most famous of all, an elaborate style of painted furniture. Adopting materials imported into Amsterdam by the East India Company, the women of Hindeloopen dressed in a florid combination of colours where dress was a means of personal identification: caps, casques and trinkets indicated marital status and age, and the quality of the print indicated social standing. Other Dutch villages adopted similar practices, but nowhere were the details of social position so precisely drawn. The development of dress turned out to be a corollary of prosperity, for the decline of Hindeloopen quite simply finished it off.

Similarly, the furniture was an ornate mixture of Scandinavian and Oriental styles superimposed on traditional Dutch carpentry. Each item was covered from head to toe with painted tendrils and flowers on a red, green or white background, though again the town's decline resulted in the lapsing of the craft. Tourism has revived local furniture-making, and countless shops now line the main street selling modern versions, though even the smallest items aren't cheap, and the florid style is something of an acquired taste.

Tradition apart, Hindeloopen is a delightful little village pressed against the sea in a tidy jigsaw of old streets and canals, crossed by wooden footbridges; it's popular – and very busy – in summer with yachting types who keep their boats in the huge marina, and windsurfers who benefit from the shallow, sloping beach to the south of the town. There are no particular sights, but the **Church** – a seventeenth-century structure with a medieval tower – has some Royal Air Force graves of airmen who came down in the Zuider Zee, while the small **Schaats Museum**, Kleine Wiede 1 (Mon–Sat 10am–6pm), displays some skating mementoes relating to the great Frisian ice-skating race, "De Friese Elfstedentocht" (see overleaf), as well as plenty of painted Hindeloopen-ware in its out-front shop. You can see original examples of this in the small village museum, the **Hidde Nijland Museum**, next door to the church (March–Oct Mon–Sat 10am–5pm, Sun 1.30–5pm; ƒ3.50), although there's a wider display at the Fries Museum in Leeuwarden.

Hindeloopen's popularity makes finding **accommodation** a problem during the summer season, and the town's only hotel, the *Skipshotel*, Oosterstrand 22 (☎05142/2452; ④), tends to be nearly always full – book well in advance if you want to be sure of getting a room. The **VVV**, located on the main street at no. 26 (summer Mon–Fri 9am–noon & 1–5pm; ☎05142/2550) can organize the odd private **room**, and the only other alternative is the **campsite** a kilometre or so to the south of town near the coast at Westerdijk 9. For **eating**, try the smart *De Gasterie*, just off the harbour at Kalverstraat 13, a lovely place to dine out in the evening, or *De Brabander*, Nieuwe Wiede 7, which has main dishes on offer for under ƒ20 and a wide array of excellent pancakes – a good option for both lunch and dinner. Failing that, the fish stands on the harbour serve sumptuous lunchtime snacks.

THE ELFSTEDENTOCHT

The **Elfstedentocht** is Friesland's biggest spectacle, a gruelling ice-skating marathon around Friesland that dates back to 1890, when one Pim Muller, a local sports journalist, skated his way around the eleven official towns of the province – simply to see whether it was possible. It was, and twenty years later the first official Elfstedentocht or "Eleven Towns Race" was born, contested by 22 skaters. Weather – and ice – permitting, it has taken place regularly ever since, nowadays a major ice-skating event, attracting skaters from all over the world.

The race is organized by the Eleven Towns Association, of which you have to be a member to take part. Perhaps not surprisingly, the current interest in the race means membership is restricted and very difficult to obtain, over-subscribed by around seventeen times at the last count.

The route of the race, which measures about 200km in total, takes in all the main centres of Friesland, starting in the capital, Leeuwarden, at about 5am in the town's Friesland Hall, when the racers sprint, skates in hand, 1500m to the point where they start skating. The first stop after this is Sneek, taking in Hindeloopen and the other old Zuider Zee towns before finishing in Dokkum in the north of the province. The contestants must stop briefly at each town to have their card stamped. These days the event is broadcast live on TV across the country, and the route lined with spectators. Of the seventeen thousand or so who take part in the race, only around three hundred are serious skaters; the rest are there just to see if they can complete the course.

All the skaters need to have all-round fitness. They attempt to skate the whole route, but it's not always possible, and at times – crossing from one canal to another, for example, or avoiding a stretch of thin ice – they have to try something called *kluning*, a Frisian word which basically means walking on dry land in skates: not easy. Casualties are inevitably numerous. Of the ten thousand who took part in 1963, only seventy or so finished, the rest beaten by the fierce winds, extreme cold and snowdrifts along the way. On the last few occasions things have been gentler, around three-quarters of those who started out crossing the finishing line. But competitors still go down with frostbite, and many have to drop out because their sweat turns to ice and clogs up their eyes – a condition only a trip to hospital will put right.

Sloten

Close to the southern coast of Friesland, the main problem with **SLOTEN** is getting there. Of the possible permutations, the easiest option is to take bus #42 (Mon–Fri every half-hour, Sat & Sun hourly; 35min) from Sneek train station to the bus change-over point on the motorway at Spannenburg, where connecting service #41 continues west to Sloten, and #44 runs on to Sloten and Bolsward. Double-check your destination with the driver as there are connecting buses with the same numbers heading east.

The smallest of Friesland's eleven towns, Sloten was ruined by the demise of the Zuider Zee trade, and, robbed of its importance, it became something of a museum-piece. Little more than a main street on either side of a central canal, Heerenval, it's really not worth going out of your way for, although it *is* undeniably charming, even if there are a lot of other people sharing its cobbled alleys, windmill, old locks and decorated gables. There's a small **museum** in the town hall on Heerenval (Tues–Fri 10am–noon & 2–5pm, Sat & Sun 2–5pm) but otherwise nothing at all to see. **Accommodation** is limited to a **campsite**, the *Lemsterpoort*, Jachthaven 3, and the **pension** *'t Brechje* at Voorstreek 110 (☎05143/1298; ②), so call ahead to make sure of a vacancy. The **VVV**, at Heerenwal 57 (☎05143/1583), rarely has rooms to rent. If you're hungry, there are a couple of **restaurants** on the canal by the bridge with outdoor seating that do good light lunches and more expensive evening meals.

Stavoren

At the end of the rail line, **STAVOREN** was also once a prosperous port, but is now an ungainly combination of modern housing and old harbour, from where **ferries** make the crossing to Enkhuizen for connecting trains to Amsterdam (see *North Holland* for rough frequencies and prices). Named after the Frisian god Stavo, Stavoren is a popular boating centre and has a large marina adjoining a **campsite** that in turn is just behind a pleasant sandy beach, some ten minutes' walk south of the train station. The campsite is surrounded by a swampy strip of water, so come equipped with mosquito repellent. The best place to **stay** is the hotel *De Vrouwe van Stavoren*, Havenweg 1 (☎05149/1202; ③), attractively sited by the harbour and surprisingly good value. The **VVV** at the station (June–Aug Mon–Sat 10am–noon & 1.30–5pm; ☎05149/1616) has details of **pensions** and private **rooms**, but you'll probably want to move straight on.

North of Leeuwarden: Dokkum and the islands

Edged by the Lauwersmeer to the east and protected by interlocking sea-dykes to the north, the strip of Friesland between Leeuwarden and the Waddenzee is dotted with tiny agricultural villages that were once separated from each other by swamp and marsh. Sparsely inhabited, the area's first settlers were forced to confine themselves to whatever higher ground was available, the *terpen* which kept the treacherous waters at bay.

DOKKUM, the only significant settlement and one of Friesland's oldest towns, is half an hour by bus from Leeuwarden (#51; Mon–Fri 2 hourly, Sat & Sun hourly). The English missionary Saint Boniface and 52 of his companions were murdered here in 754 while trying to convert the pagan Frisians to Christianity. In part walled and moated, Dokkum has kept its shape as a fortified town, but it's best by the side of the **Het Grootdiep** canal, which cuts the town into two distinct sections. This was the commercial centre of the old town and is marked by a series of ancient gables, including the **Admiralty Building** which serves as the town's mediocre **museum** (April–Sept Mon–Sat 10am–5pm; rest of year Mon–Sat 2–5pm; *f*2.50). There's not much else: a couple of windmills, quiet walks along the old ramparts and all sorts of things named after St Boniface. Give it a couple of hours and move on. If you decide to stay, the **VVV** at Grote Breedstraat 1 (Mon–Fri 9am–5pm; ☎05190/93800) has a supply of private **rooms**, while the cheapest **hotel** is the *Van der Meer*, Woudweg 1 (☎05190/92380; ③). There's not much choice as far as **eating** goes: at lunchtime *De Waag*, at Waagstraat 11, serves a good variety of sandwiches and croissants; in the evening try *Pizzeria Romana*, on Koornmarkt just off the main canal, which has decent pizzas.

Wierum and Moddergat

Of all the tiny hamlets in north Friesland, two of the most interesting are Wierum and neighbouring **Moddergat**. MODDERGAT, the more easterly of the two, spreads out along the road behind the seawall 10km north of Dokkum, merging with the village of **Paesens**. At the western edge of the village, a memorial commemorates the 1893 tragedy when seventeen ships were sunk by a storm with the loss of 83 lives. Opposite, the **'t Fiskerhuske Museum**, Fiskerpad 4–8 (March–Oct Mon–Sat 10am–5pm; *f*2.50) comprises three restored fishermen's cottages with displays on the history and culture of the village and details of the disaster: as such small museums go, it's pretty good. If you're further interested in the locality, the **Agricultural Museum** in the Brink Building at Kleasterwei 2 (April–Oct Tues–Sat 10am–noon & 1–5pm, Sun 1–5pm) gives a round-up of farming and reclamation in the area.

Huddled behind the sea-dyke 5km to the west, **WIERUM** has one main claim to fame, its twelfth-century church with a saddle-roof tower. The **Wadloopcentrum** here organizes guided walks across the mud flats: times vary with conditions and tides; further details from Dokkum VVV.

Readily accessible from Dokkum, Moddergat and Wierum are on the same bus route (#52; Mon–Sat 7 daily, Sun 2 daily). There are a couple of places to **stay**, the pension *Meinsma*, at Meinsmaweg 5 in Moddergat (☎05199/9396; ②), or the pension *Visser* in Wierum (☎05199/9727; ②).

Ameland

Easy to reach from the tiny port of Holwerd, a few kilometres from Wierum, the island of **Ameland** is one of the major tourist resorts of the north Dutch coast, with a population that swells from a mere three thousand to a staggering thirty-five thousand during summer weekends. Boats dock near the main village, **NES**, a tiny place that nestles among the fields behind the dyke. Once a centre of the Dutch whaling industry, Nes has its share of cafés, hotels and tourist shops, though quite a bit of the old village survives. High-rise development has been forbidden, and there's a focus instead on the seventeenth- and eighteenth-century captains'

AMELAND AND SCHIERMONNIKOOG

North Sea

Ameland

Camping Koudenburg
Youth Hostel
Duinoord Campsite
Nes
Ballum
Buren
Hollum

Wadden

To Holwerd

houses, known as **Commandeurshuizen**, which line several of the streets. Perhaps surprisingly, the crowds rarely seem to overwhelm the village, but rather to breathe life into it, which is just as well as there's not a lot to do other than wander the streets and linger in cafés. If it's raining, you might consider the pricy **Natuurcentrum** at Strandweg 38 (Mon–Fri 10am–noon & 1–5pm, Sat 1–5pm; *f*4.25), an aquarium and natural history museum with no information in English.

Nes has a wide range of **accommodation**, but prices do rise dramatically in summer, when many places are full, peaking at high-season weekends. It's advisable to call ahead if you are visiting in July and August. For a small charge, the **VVV** (July & Aug Mon–Sat 9am–5pm & 7–8pm; rest of year Mon–Fri 9am–noon & 2–5pm; ☎05191/42020) will fix you up with a **pension** or private **room** anywhere on the island. Failing that, you could try the centrally sited *Hotel De Jong* at Reeweg 29 (☎05191/42016; ④) or the basic hotel *Bos en Duinzicht*, Strandweg 27 (☎05191/42368; ③). The best-appointed **campsite** is *Duinoord* (☎05191/2070), by the beach about half a mile north of Nes at Jan van Eijckweg 4.

If you prefer some peace and quiet, it's fairly easy to escape the crowds on all but the busiest of days, and **bikes** can be rented at a number of shops in Nes. Ameland is only 2km wide, but it's 25km long, and its entire northern shore is made up of a fine expanse of sand and dune laced by foot and cycle paths. The east end of the island is the most deserted, and you can cycle by the side of the marshy shallows that once made up the whole southern shore before the construction of the sea-dyke. Of the smaller villages that dot the island, the prettiest place to stay is **HOLLUM**, a sedate settlement of old houses and farm buildings west of Nes. If you're an aquatic addict or seriously bored there are a couple of small museums here: the **Sorgdragermuseum** at Herenweg 1 (April–Oct Tues–Fri 9am–12.30pm & 2–4.30pm, Sat, Sun & Mon 2–4.30pm; *f*3), an old *commandeurshuis*, and the **Reddingsmuseum Abraham Fock**, Oranjeweg 18 (same times), devoted to the local lifeboat teams and the horses that used to drag the boats to the sea.

The pension *de Welvaart* here, at Burenlaan 4 (☎05191/54634; ③) is good value and convenient. Alternatives include the **campsite**, *Koudenburg* (☎05191/54367), by the heath to the north at Oosterhemweg 2; and to the west, near the lighthouse and the tip of Ameland, a good **youth hostel** (☎05191/54133; April–Sept), surrounded by sand dune and forest.

REACHING THE ISLANDS

It only takes 35 minutes by bus #66 to get from Leeuwarden to Holwerd, where you can catch the connecting ferry to **Ameland**. Boats leave five or six times daily throughout the year, and nine times daily on summer weekends. The trip takes 45 minutes and costs ƒ14 return. For **Schiermonnikoog**, bus #51 runs from Dokkum (30min) and Leeuwarden (1hr 30min), and bus #63 from Groningen (1hr), for the port of Lauwersoog, where connecting boats make the crossing two to six times daily (ƒ15 return; 45min). There are also combined trips direct from Groningen. Taking your bike over will cost extra. Only residents' cars are allowed on Schiermonnikoog.

If you're heavily laden, a summer island **bus** service runs between the principal villages from three to nine times daily, connecting with ferries. There are a variety of **boat** excursions from Nes, including trips to the islands of Terschelling and Schiermonnikoog, and to the sandbanks to see sea lions – though sadly these have been decimated following a recent pollution-based viral epidemic. Details from the VVV or tour operators in Nes.

Schiermonnikoog

Until the Reformation, **SCHIERMONNIKOOG** belonged to the monastery of Klaarkamp, on the mainland; its name means literally "island of the grey monks". Nothing remains of the monks, however, and these days Schiermonnikoog's only settlement is a prim and busy village bordering on long stretches of muddy beach and sand dune to the north and mud flat and farmland to the south. Schiermonnikoog is the smallest of the Friesian islands, and, once you're clear of the weekend homes that fringe the village, it's a wild, uncultivated place, criss-crossed by cycle paths, and, not surprisingly, a popular spot for day-trippers.

Boats from Lauwersoog dock at the island jetty, some 3km from the village; there's a connecting bus service which drops you off outside the VVV in the centre. It's even possible to walk to the island across the mud flats from Kloosterburen, a distance of about 8km, but this is not feasible without a guide; see overleaf for details.

Accommodation becomes more difficult to find in season, when prices rise sharply, and it's essential to ring ahead. The **VVV** (Mon–Sat 9am–1pm & 2.30–6.30pm; ☎05195/31233) will help by booking private **rooms** and **pensions**. The cheapest **hotel** on the island is the *Zonneweelde* (☎05195/31133; ③), situated in the heart of the village at Langestreek 94. A good second bet is the *Duinzicht* (☎05195/31218; ④), to the north of town on the way to the beach at Badweg 17. Schiermonnikoog's **campsite**, *Seedune* (☎05195/31398), is also to the north, in the woods just east of Badweg at Seeduneweg 1. The **youth hostel** at Knuppeldam 2 (☎05195/31257) is on the east side of the village, fifteen minutes' walk from the VVV.

The *Strandhotel*, about twenty minutes' walk from the VVV, overlooks the beach at the end of Badweg and has **windsurfing** equipment for rent; **bikes** are available from several small shops in the village, and the VVV sells good **maps**. For **food and drink** have a wander along Langestreek and Badweg to the north of the VVV.

Groningen and around

Nominally a fiefdom of the bishops of Utrecht from 1040 until 1536, the city of **GRONINGEN** was once an important centre of trade, in reality an autonomous merchant state ruled by a tightly defined oligarchy, whose power was exercised through the city council or *Raad*. In 1536 Charles V forced the town to submit to his authority, but Groningen was nevertheless still hesitant in its support of the Dutch rebellion against his successors. The dilemma for the city fathers was that, although they stood to gain economically from independence, the majority of the town's citizens were Catholic, deeply suspicious of their Protestant neighbours. In the end, the economic argument won the day, and the town became the capital of the Dutch province of Groningen in 1594.

Virtually destroyed during the Allied liberation in 1945, the city has few sights and is an eclectic jumble of architectures. However, it does benefit from the presence of its large and prestigious university – one in eight of the town's population are students – which gives the place a cosmopolitan and vigorous feel quite unexpected in this part of the country, and keeps prices in its restaurants and bars surprisingly low. This, combined with a couple of good budget places to stay, and its wide range of contemporary arts performances and exhibitions, especially during the academic year, makes Groningen the best urban target in the north Netherlands.

Arrival, information and accommodation

Groningen's **bus** and **train** stations are side by side on the south side of town, ten minutes' walk from the VVV at Ged Kattendiep 6 (Mon–Fri 9am–5.30pm, Sat 10am–4pm; ☎13 97 00). The VVV provides a wide range of services, from tourist information (much of it in English) on the town and province to tickets for visiting bands, theatre groups and orchestras, as listed in their free booklet *Uit in Groningen*. They also have a short list of **private rooms** in both Groningen and the surrounding area, though hardly any are near the city centre.

PEDAL POWER IN GRONINGEN

One of the best things about Groningen is the lack of traffic: almost all the centre is car free, the result of several municipal decisions dating back to the mid-Seventies, when the city was suffering from some of the worst congestion in Europe. In a typically bold and sensible Dutch way, Groningen decided to get rid of a six-lane motorway intersection in its city centre, close most of its roads to cars and spend a fortune on cycle paths and bus lanes.

This paid off. Now 57 percent of Groningeners travel regularly by bike, the highest percentage in the country. The city has become one of the most popular in the Netherlands, and there are demands for even more stringent restrictions on cars. Meanwhile city planners have realized how well they spent their money: the £20 million invested in cycle paths over the last twelve years has brought industries and popularity to the city in a way the usual publicity campaigns would never have managed; and, for every car kept out of the city centre, it's reckoned that almost £200 a year is saved in environmental damage.

> The Groningen area telephone code is ☎050

The cheapest place to stay in town is the *Simplon Jongerenhotel*, north of the centre at Boterdiep 73 (☎135221; ①) with accommodation in dorms. Otherwise, Groningen has three reasonably priced **hotels**, all situated just south of the Grote Markt: the *Garni Friesland* at Kleine Pelsterstraat 4 (☎121307; ③); the *Garni Groningen*, Damsterdiep 94 (☎135435; ④); and the likeable old *Weera*, Gedempte Zuiderdiep 8 (☎129919; ④), with a decent, reasonably priced restaurant. Outside the centre, the *Bastion*, Bornhomstraat 99 (☎414977; ③), is a little smarter yet cheaper. If you're camping, catch bus #2 via Piezerweg from the main square for the ten-minute journey to **Camping Stadspark** (March–Oct).

The Town

The centre of town is **Grote Markt**, a wide open space that was badly damaged by wartime bombing and has been reconstructed with little imagination. At its northeast corner is the tiered tower of the **Martinikerk** (June–Sept Tues–Sat noon–4pm; *f*1), a beacon of architectural sanity in the surrounding shambles. Though the oldest parts of the church go back to 1180, most of it dates from the mid-fifteenth century, the nave being a Gothicized rebuilding undertaken to match the added choir. The vault paintings in the nave are beautifully restored, and in the old choir there are two series of frescoes on the walled-up niches of the

WADLOPEN

Wadlopen, or mud-flat walking, is a popular and strenuous Dutch pastime, and the stretch of coast on the northern edge of the provinces of Friesland and Groningen is one of the best places to do it: twice daily, the receding tide uncovers vast expanses of mud flat beneath the Waddenzee. It is, however, a sport to be taken seriously, and far too dangerous to do without an experienced guide – the depth of the mud is too variable (you have to walk up to thigh-depth in places) and the tides inconsistent. In any case, channels of deep water are left even when the tide has receded, and you need to be aware of the whereabouts of these; the currents, too, can be perilous. The timing of the treks depends on weather and tidal conditions; most start at anything between 6am and 10am. It's important to be properly equipped, not least with adequate clothing. The weather can change rapidly up here, and group leaders request you take or wear walking shorts or a bathing suit, a sweater, a wind jacket, knee-high wool socks, high-top trainers and a complete change of clothes stored in a watertight pack. In recent years *wadlopen* has become extremely popular, and it's advisable to book at least a month in advance between May and August.

Prices of **organized excursions** are not bad, in the region of *f*25–30 a head, and include the cost of the return ferry crossing; the *VVV*s in Dokkum, Leeuwarden and Groningen can provide details, or you could contact one of the *wadlopen* organizations direct: *Dijkstras Wadlopencentrum*, Hoofdstraat 118, Pieterburen (☎05952/8345), has the most multilingual guides; there's also *Stichting Wadlopcentrum Pieterburen*, Hoofdstraat 68, Pieterburen (☎05952/8300), and *Wadlopcentrum Friesland* (☎05912/2100).

clerestory. On the right, a series of eight depicts the story of Christmas, beginning with an *Annunciation* and ending with a portrayal of the young Christ in the temple. On the left, six frescoes complete the cycle with the story of Easter. Also in the choir is a maquette of the city centre as it looked before wartime destruction: fifteen years in the making, it's painstakingly accurate. Adjoining the church is the essentially seventeenth-century **Martinitoren** (April to end Sept daily noon–4.30pm; *f*2). If you've got the energy, it offers a view that is breathtaking in every sense of the word – fainthearts be warned. Behind the church is the lawn of the **Kerkhof**, an ancient piece of common land that's partly enclosed by the **Provinciehuis**, a rather grand neo-Renaissance building of 1915, seat of the provincial government. A little way north of here, the **Natuursmuseum**, St Walburgstraat 9 (daily 10am–5pm), has the usual exhibition on the wildlife, geology and reclamation of the area.

On the opposite side of the Grote Markt, the classical **Stadhuis** dates from 1810, tucked in front of the mid-seventeenth-century **Goudkantoor** (Gold Office); look out for the shell motif above the windows, a characteristic

Groningen decoration. From the southwest corner of the Grote Markt, the far side of Vismarkt is framed by the **Korenbeurs** (Corn Exchange) of 1865. The statues on the facade represent, from left to right, Neptune, Mercurius (god of commerce) and Ceres (goddess of agriculture). Just behind, the **A-kerk** is a fifteenth-century church with a Baroque steeple, attractively restored in tones of yellow, orange and red. The church's full name is the *Onze Lieve Vrouwekerk der A*, the A being a small river which forms the moat encircling the town centre. Immediately to the west along A-Kerkhof N.Z., the **Noordelijk Scheepvaart Museum**, Brugstraat 24 (Tues–Sat 10am–5pm, Sun 1–5pm; *f*3.50), is one of the best-equipped and most comprehensive maritime museums in the country, tracing the history of north Holland shipping from the sixth to the twentieth centuries. Housed in a warren of steep stairs and timber-beamed rooms, each of the museum's twenty displays deals with a different aspect of shipping, including trade with the Indies, the development of peat canals and a series of reconstructed nautical workshops. The museum's particular appeal is its imaginative combination of models and original artefacts, which are themselves a mixture of the personal (seamen's chests; quadrants) and the public (ship figureheads; tile designs of ships). In the same building, the much smaller **Niemeyer Tabaksmuseum** (same times) is devoted to tobacco smoking from 1600 to the present day. Exhibits include a multitude of pipes and an outstanding collection of snuff paraphernalia in all sorts of materials, from crystal and ivory to porcelain and silver. The Niemeyer family built their fortune on the tobacco trade, and here you can see the origins of those familiar blue tobacco packets.

To the northwest of here, down a passage off Zwanestraat, the **Groningen University Museum** (Tue–Fri 2–4pm, Sat & Sun noon–4pm; *f*2) gives a taste of the university's history, with exhibits ranging from scientific equipment to photos of derby-hatted students clowning around at the turn of the century. Further north still, up Nieuwe Kijk in 't Jatstraat 104, the **Geraldus van de Leeuw ethnological museum** (Tues–Fri 10am–4pm, Sat & Sun 1–5pm) has collections from Asia, Africa, the Pacific and South America.

South of here, the excellent collection of the **Groninger Museum** was at the time of writing closed, waiting for its new building, directly opposite the train station, to be completed. By the time you read this it should be open, its freshly-displayed collection taking you through a melange of arts and applied arts relating to Groningen and the locality, from early *terp* culture to the twentieth century. There are displays of local silver and Far Eastern ceramics, notably a two hundred-piece sample of porcelain rescued from the *Geldermalsen*, which sank in the South China Sea in 1572 (see "Leeuwarden"). Of the examples on display, several are still encrusted with accumulated detritus, but others have been cleaned and polished to reveal designs of delicate precision, fine drawings of flowers and stems, and bamboo huts where every stick is distinct.

The museum's collection includes Rubens' energetic *Adoration of the Magi* among a small selection of seventeenth-century works, Isaac Israels' inviting *Hoedenwinkel* from a modest sample of Hague School paintings, and a number of later works by the Expressionists of the Groningen *De Ploeg* association, principally Jan Wiegers, whose *Portrait of Ludwig Kirchner* is typically earnest. An adventurous acquisition policy has also led the museum to dabble in some of the more unusual trends in modern art, like Carel Visser's 1983 collage *Voor Dali* and the bizarre *Can the Bumpsteers while I Park the Chariot* by Henk Tas.

There are also two more specialized museums you might want to see: the **Printing Museum** at Rabenhauptstraat 65 southeast of the train station (Tues–Fri & Sun 1–5pm; *f*4), outlining the history of printing with everything from a nineteenth-century steam-driven printing press to the latest wordprocessors. Lastly, and certainly most weirdly, the **Museum of Anatomy and Embryology**, east of the centre at Oostersingel 69 (Mon–Fri 9am–5pm), is even nastier than you might imagine.

Groningen's final sight is its **train station**: built in 1896 at enormous cost, it was one of the grandest of its day, decorated with the strong colours and symbolic designs of Art Nouveau tiles from the Rozenburg factory in The Hague. The grandeur of much of the building has disappeared under a welter of concrete, glass and plastic suspended ceilings, but the old first- and second-class waiting rooms have survived pretty much intact and were recently refurbished as restaurants. The epitome of high Gothic style, the oak-panelled walls are edged by extravagantly tiled chimney pieces, while a central pillar in each room supports a papier-mâché fluted ceiling. The third-class waiting room is now a travel agency, but a yellow, blue and white tiled diagram of the Dutch rail system still covers one wall.

Eating, drinking and nightlife

Unless you're on an extra-tight budget, in which case the cheapest place to fill up is at the decent *mensa* at Oosterstraat 44 (Mon–Fri noon–1.30pm & 5–7pm), the city's best places to **eat and drink** are concentrated in three loose areas, each only a couple of minutes' walk from the next. Best of the three is the area centred on Poelestraat, where an array of open-air cafés pulls in mainly youthful punters. *Bistengo*, on the western end of the street, is a decent Tex-Mex restaurant with vegetarian specialities; the *pizzeria* next door is slightly cheaper. Around the corner on Peperstraat, *'t Pakhuis* at no. 88 has good Dutch snacks and a lively bar in an atmospheric building. *Andy Warhol*, roughly opposite *'t Pakhuis*, is a cool night café.

Across the canal from Poelestraat, the tiny boisterous *Café Kachel* at Schuittendiep 62 is the best of the town's traditional Dutch bars, while the *Himawari* restaurant at no. 50 has excellent (but pricy) Japanese food. There are also a handful of places worth seeking out to the south of Poelestraat: the elegant *Schimmelpennink Huys*, Oosterstraat 53, with exquisite and reasonably priced daily specials; the Mexican American *Four Roses* at the junction of Oosterstraat and Gedempte Zuiderdiep; and, if you want to get stoned, the *Knarie Bar* at Oosterstraat 69.

A short walk from Poelestraat, there's a flank of outdoor cafés on the south side of the Grote Markt, best of which are the cosy *De Witz* at no. 48, the civilized *De Drie Gezusters* at no. 29, with a great old interior, and the *Café Hooghoudt* in the old Lloyds Insurance building at no. 41; this last also contains a night café serving food until 4am at weekends. Northwest of the Grote Markt, around Zwanestraat, the *Ugly Duck* at no. 28 has fish and Dutch food, including a good-value tourist menu; just to the west, *Soest Dijk*, at Elleboog 6, is pricier and posher; while *Brussels Lof* at A-Kerkstraat 24, is an excellent vegetarian restaurant.

For **live music** try *De Vestibule*, Oosterstraat 24; *Vera*, in the basement below the *mensa*, at Oosterstraat 44; or *Troubadour*, Peperstraat 19. The jazz café *De*

Spieghel at Peperstraat 11 has live jazz (including some reasonably big names) nightly. Most of the more important visiting bands play in the municipal concert hall, the *Stadsschouwburg*, Turfsingel 86; others sometimes perform on July and August Sundays in the **Stadspark**, to be found about 3km southwest of the town centre (bus #2 from the Grote Markt to Peizerweg on the northern edge of the park, but confirm with the driver as routes vary). Good **discos** include *Gdansk*, Poelestraat 53, and the *Palace*, Gelkingestraat 1, which occasionally host live bands. The **cinema** with the most varied programme is the *Filmhuis*, Poelestraat 30. **Listings** of all events are contained in *Groninger Zomer Manifestatie* and *Uit in Groningen*, both available free from the VVV.

Listings

Boat trips Summer trips along the old town moat around the town centre, *f*7.50 for 75min. Times of sailings and bookings at the VVV.

Books A good range of English titles at *Scholtens*, Grote Markt 42.

Car rental From *Interleasing*, Vechtstraat 72 (☎261659).

Emergencies ☎0611.

Left luggage At the train station (daily 8am–noon & 1–5.30pm); also coin-operated lockers in the ticket hall.

Markets General market, including fruit and vegetables, on the Grote Markt (Tues–Sat from 8am), with curios and miscellaneous antiques on Tues, Fri, and Sat.

Police Schweitzerlaan 1 (☎131313).

Post office on Munnekeholm by the A-kerk (Mon–Fri 8.30am–6.30pm, Sat 10am–1pm) or at Stationsweg 10 (Mon–Fri 9am–5pm, Sat 9am–noon).

Travel agent *NBBS*, Brugstraat 15.

Around Groningen

A patchwork of industrial complexes and nondescript villages, the **province of Groningen** has little going for it, and there's nowhere that really warrants an overnight stay. Of possible day trips from Groningen city, the most agreeable is to the village of **UITHUIZEN**, 25km to the north (hourly trains; 35min), where the moated manor house of **Menkemaborg** (April–Sept daily 10am–noon & 1–5pm; Oct–March Tues–Sun 10am–noon & 1–4pm; closed Jan; *f*5) is a marked ten-minute walk from the station. Dating from the fifteenth century and surrounded by formal gardens in the English style, the house has a sturdy compact elegance and is one of the very few mansions, or *borgs*, of the old land-owning families to have survived. The interior consists of a sequence of period rooms furnished in the style of the seventeenth century. For those interested, the **Bevrijdingsmuseum**, Dingeweg 1–3 (April–Sept daily 10am–6pm; *f*6) has an excellent collection dedicated to World War II military artefacts – uniforms, weapons and secret radios, etc.

The trip to Uithuizen can be combined with a guided walk across the coastal **mud flats** (*wadlopen* – see p.188) to the uninhabited sand-spit island of **Rottumeroog**. Guided excursions leave from outside Menkemaborg by bus to the coast, between three and four times monthly from June to September. The cost is *f*25 per person and booking is essential; further details and bookings at Groningen VVV. Without a guide, it's too dangerous to go on the mud flats, but it is easy enough to walk along the enclosing dyke that runs behind the shoreline for the whole length of the province. There's precious little to see as such, but when the weather's clear, the browns, blues and greens of the surrounding land and sea are unusually beautiful. From Uithuizen, it's a good hour's stroll north to the nearest point on the dyke, and you'll need a large-scale map for directions – available from Groningen VVV.

The Lauwersmeer

Some 35km northwest of Groningen, the **Lauwersmeer** is a broken and irregular lake that spreads across the provincial boundary into neighbouring Friesland. Once an arm of the sea, it was turned into a freshwater lake by the construction of the Lauwersoog dam, a controversial Sixties project that was vigorously opposed by local fishermen, who ended up having to move all their tackle to ports on the coast. Spared intensive industrial and agricultural development because of the efforts of conservationists, it's a quiet and peaceful region, increasingly popular with anglers, windsurfers, sailors and cyclists.

The local villages are uniformly dull, however; the most convenient base is **ZOUTKAMP**, near the southeast corner of the lake on the River Reitdiep, accessible by bus from Groningen (#65; hourly; 1hr). Zoutkamp has one **hotel**, the *De Zeearend*, Dorpsplein 1 (☎05956/1647; ③), where rates include breakfast, and a **VVV**, Dorpsplein 1 (June–Aug Mon–Fri 10am–noon & 1.30–4.30pm, Sat 1.30–4.30pm; Sept–May Mon–Fri 10am–noon & 1.30–4pm; ☎05956/1957), which has a limited supply of private **rooms**. These can also be reserved at Groningen VVV.

Situated at the mouth of the lake, some 10km north of Zoutkamp, the desultory port of **LAUWERSOOG** is where **ferries** leave for the fifty-minute trip to the island of Schiermonnikoog (see p.186). It's also the home of **Expo Zee** (April–Sept Tues–Fri 10am–5pm, Sat & Sun 2–5pm; ƒ2.50), 500m south of the harbour, which gives background information on the Lauwersmeer, the Waddenzee and Dutch land reclamation in general. Bus #63 connects Groningen with Lauwersoog and the ferries (5 daily; 1hr).

Fraeylemaborg and Bourtange

There are two other minor attractions in the province. The first, **Fraeylemaborg** (March–Dec Tues–Sun 10am–noon & 1–5pm), is a well-preserved, seventeenth-century moated mansion set within extensive parkland. It lies 21km east of Groningen on the northern edge of the small town of **SLOCHTEREN**, and is accessible on bus #78 or #178 from the town centre.

The second, some 60km southeast of Groningen, is **BOURTANGE**, a superbly restored fortified village which lies close to the German frontier. Founded by William of Orange in 1580 to help protect the eastern approaches to Groningen, Bourtange fell into disrepair during the nineteenth century, only to be entirely refurbished as a tourist attraction in 1964. The design of the village is similar to that of Naarden, outside Amsterdam, and is best appreciated as you walk round the old bastions of the star-shaped fortress. There's a **campsite**, at Vlagtwedderstraat 88, and one **hotel**, *De Staakenborgh*, up the road at no. 33, (☎05993/54216; closed Sept–May; ③). There's also a **VVV** at Marktplein 4 (April–Oct Mon–Fri 9am–noon & 1–5pm, Sat & Sun 1–5pm; Nov–March Mon–Fri 9am–noon; ☎05993/54600).

Drenthe

The sparsely populated province of **DRENTHE** was little more than a flat expanse of empty peat bog, marsh and moor until the early nineteenth century. Its only conspicuous geographical feature is a ridge of low hills that runs northeast for some 50km from Emmen toward Groningen. This ridge, the **Hondsrug**, was high enough to attract prehistoric settlers whose **hunebeds** (megalithic tombs) have become Drenthe's main tourist attraction. There are few others. **Assen**, the provincial capital, is a dull place with a good museum, and **Emmen**, the other major town, can only be recommended as a convenient base for visiting some of the *hunebeds* and three neighbouring open-air folk culture museums.

Governed by the bishops of Utrecht from the eleventh century, Drenthe was incorporated into the Hapsburg empire in 1538. The region sided with the Protestants in the rebellion against Spain, but it had little economic or military muscle and its claim to provincial status was ignored until the days of the Batavian Republic. In the nineteenth century, work began in earnest to convert the province's peat bogs and moors into good farmland. *Veenkulunies* (peat colonies) were established over much of the south and east of Drenthe, where the initial purpose of the labourers was to dig drainage canals (*wiels*) and cut the peat for sale as fuel to the cities. Once cleared of the peat, the land could be used to grow crops, and today the region's farms are some of the most profitable in the country.

Assen and around

Some 16km south of Groningen, **ASSEN** is a possible first stop, though not at all a place that you'd wish to get stuck in. Its train and bus station are about five minutes' walk from the centre of town, moving straight ahead across the main road down Stationsstraat. On the eastern side of the central square, Brink is home to both parts of the **Drents Museum** (Tues–Sun 11am–5pm; July & Aug also Mon 11am–5pm; *f*5), which, spread over a pleasant group of old houses, is the only thing that makes a stop in town worthwhile. Of the buildings, the *Ontvangershuis*, Brink 1, holds no more than a predictable plod of period rooms, but on the second floor of Brink 5 there's an extraordinary assortment of prehistoric bodies, clothes and other artefacts that have been preserved for thousands of years in the surrounding peat bogs. The bodies are the material remains of those early settlers who built the *hunebeds*, and the museum has a modest display dealing with what is known of their customs and culture. There's also the much vaunted *Pesse Canoe*, the oldest water vessel ever found, dating from about 6800 BC and looking its age.

Five kilometres west of the centre of Assen, straight down Torenlaan, is an **Automuseum**, Rode Heklaan 3 (April–Oct daily except Sat 9am–6pm; *f*12), which has a wide selection of antique and vintage cars. To get there take a bus marked *Verkeerspark* from the train station.

Practicalities

Assen's **VVV** is in the town centre at Brink 42 (Mon–Fri 9am–5.30pm, Sat 10am–1pm; June–Aug Sat also until 3pm; ☎05920/14324). The cheapest place to **stay** is the *Christerus* (☎05920/13517; ③), on the way in from the station at Stationsstraat 17. The *De Nieuwe Brink Hotel*, Brink 13, is a reasonable place to **eat**.

South of Assen: Westerburk Concentration Camp

If you have access to your own transport, you might want to visit the **Herinneringscentrum Kamp Westerburk** (April–Sept Mon–Fri 9.30am–5pm, Sat & Sun 1–5pm; *f*3.50) a little way to the south of town, on the road between the villages Amen and Hooghalen. It was here that Dutch Jews were gathered before being transported to the death camps in the east, and, although little remains of the camp itself, the documents and artefacts on display are deeply affecting.

Emmen and around

To all intents and purposes **EMMEN** is a new town, a twentieth-century amalgamation of strip villages that were originally peat colonies. The centre is a modernistic affair, mixing the remnants of the old with boulders, trees and shrubs and a selection of municipal statues that vary enormously in quality.

Emmen is well known for two things: its *hunebeds* and its zoo. The **Zoo** (daily 9am–5pm; *f*17) is right in the middle of town at Hoofdstraat 18 and claims to be one of the most modern zoos in the world. It boasts an imitation of an African savanna, where the animals roam "free", a massive sea lion pool, the biggest in Europe, and a giant, brand-new hippo house. Emmen is also the most convenient place to see *hunebeds*, of which the best is the clearly marked **Emmerdennen Hunebed**, in the woods a kilometre or so east of the station along Boslaan. This is a so-called passage-grave, with a relatively sophisticated entrance surrounded by a ring of standing stones. The other interesting *hunebed* within easy walking distance is the **Schimmer-Es**, a large enclosure containing two burial chambers and a standing stone; to get there follow Hoofdstraat north from the VVV, take a left down Noorderstraat, right along Noordeinde, left along Broekpad, and first right at Langgrafweg – a distance of about 2km. The VVV sells detailed maps of a circular car route along the minor roads to the north of town that covers all the principal remains. A particular highlight is the largest *hunebed* of the lot, 25m long, on the northeast edge of the village of **BORGER**, some 20km from Emmen.

Practicalities

Emmen **train** and **bus** stations adjoin each other, five minutes' walk north of the town centre: head straight down Stationsstraat into Boslaan and turn left down Hoofdstraat, the main drag. The **VVV** (Mon–Fri 9am–5pm, Sat 10am–4pm; ☎05910/13000), in the central Raadhuisplein, will arrange **accommodation** if required. Their list includes **pensions**, **private rooms** and **hotels**. The cheapest pension is the *Centrum* at Sterrenkamp 9 (☎05910/14158; ③), first left after the zoo, heading south; for the same price you could stay in the cheapest hotel, the *Bos en Zon* at Burg Tymesstraat 1 (☎05910/11369; ③), which is immediately behind the train station. For **food**, try the first-floor café of the *Hotel Boerland*, Hoofdstraat 57.

Around Emmen

Approximately 11km east of Emmen, toward the German border, the **Veenmuseumdorp 't Aole Compas** (daily 9am–5pm; *f*10; bus #43 hourly from Emmen station; 30min) is a massive open-air museum-village which traces the history and development of the peat colonies of the moors of southern Groningen and eastern Drenthe. The colonies were established in the nineteenth century, when labour was imported to cut the thick layers of peat that lay all over the moors. Isolated in small communities, and under the thumb of the traders who sold their product and provided their foodstuffs, the colonists were harshly exploited and lived in abject poverty until well into the 1930s. Built around some old interlocking canals, the museum consists of a series of reconstructed villages that span the history of the colonies. It's inevitably a bit folksy, but very popular, with its own small-gauge railway, a canal barge, and working period bakeries, bars and shops. A thorough exploration takes the whole day.

Thirteen kilometres northwest of Emmen, **De Zeven Marken** (April–Oct daily 9am–6pm; f3; bus #21 from Emmen), on the northern edge of the village of **SCHOONOORD**, is another open-air museum concerned with life in Drenthe. The exhibits here concentrate on the end of the nineteenth century and cover a wide range of traditional community activities – from sheep farming to education and carpentry. Seven kilometres to the west, tiny **Orvelte** (May–Sept Mon–Fri 10am–5pm, Sat & Sun 11am–5pm; f8.50) is another village-museum, fully operational and inhabited this time, though certain buildings may be closed at anytime. Owned by a trust which exercises strict control over construction and repair, Orvelte's buildings date from the seventeenth to the nineteenth centuries and include examples of a toll house, a dairy, a farmhouse and a number of craft workshops. Most are open to the public, but you'll need a car to get here.

travel details

Trains

Emmen to: Zwolle (2 hourly; 70min).

Groningen to: Amsterdam (2 hourly; 2hr 20min); Assen (2 hourly; 20min); Leeuwarden (2 hourly; 50min); Zwolle (2 hourly; 70min).

Leeuwarden to: Amsterdam (2 hourly; 2hr 25min); Franeker (every 30min; 15min); Groningen (2 hourly; 50min); Harlingen (every 30min; 25min); Hindeloopen (hourly; 35min); Sneek (hourly; 20min); Stavoren (hourly; 50min); Zwolle (every 30min; 1hr).

Buses

Bolsward to: Makkum (hourly; 20min).

Groningen to: Emmen (hourly; 1hr 10min); Zoutkamp (hourly; 1hr).

Leeuwarden to: Alkmaar (hourly; 2hr 20min); Dokkum (1–2 hourly; 30min); Franeker (hourly; 25min).

Sneek to: Bolsward (3 hourly; 15min).

Buses and connecting ferries

Groningen to: Lauwersoog (*GADO* bus #63: 5 daily; 1hr) for boats to Schiermonnikoog (2–6 daily; 50min).

Leeuwarden to: Holwerd (*FRAM* bus #66: 5–7 daily; 50min) for boats to Ameland (4–8 daily; 45min); Lauwersoog (*FRAM* bus #51: 4–7 daily; 90min) for boats to Schiermonnikoog (2–6 daily; 50min).

Ferries

Harlingen to: Terschelling (2–3 boats daily; 1hr 30min); Vlieland (2–3 daily; 1hr 30min).

Stavoren to: Enkhuizen (May–Sept 3 boats daily; 1hr 20min).

Terschelling to: Vlieland (2–3 boats weekly; 65min).

Vlieland to: Terschelling (2–3 boats weekly; 65min).

International trains

Groningen to: Oldenburg, Germany (2 or 3 daily; 2hr 10 min).

CHAPTER FIVE

OVERIJSSEL, FLEVOLAND AND GELDERLAND

With the eastern provinces of Holland, the flat polder landscapes of the north and west of the country begin to disappear, the countryside growing steadily more undulating as you head toward Germany. Coming from the north, **Overijssel** is the first province you reach, "the land beyond the IJssel", which forms the border with Gelderland to the south. Its more appealing western reaches are a typically Dutch area, in part cut by lakes and waterways around the picturesque water-village of **Giethoorn**, at the heart of a series of towns – **Kampen, Deventer, Zutphen** and the provincial capital of **Zwolle** – which enjoyed a period of immense prosperity during the heyday of the Zuider Zee trade, from the fourteenth to the sixteenth centuries. At the junction of trade routes from Germany in the east, Scandinavia to the north and South Holland in the west, their future seemed secure and all of them were keen to impress their rivals with the splendour of their municipal buildings. The bubble burst in the seventeenth century, when trade moved west and the great merchant cities of South Holland undercut their prices, but today all are well worth a visit for their ancient centres, splendid churches and extravagant defensive portals. Southeast of here, **Twente** is an industrial region of old textile towns that forms the eastern district of the province, near the German frontier. It's one of the least visited parts of the country and with good reason, only **Enschede**, the main town, providing a spark of interest with an excellent local museum.

The boundary separating Overijssel from the reclaimed lands of Holland's twelfth and newest province, **Flevoland**, runs along the old shoreline of the Zuider Zee. Divided into two halves, the drab **Northeast Polder** in the east and the later **Flevoland Polder** to the west, there's not really much to attract the visitor here, except for the fishing village of **Urk**, which was an island until the land reclamation scheme got under way. The provincial capital is **Lelystad**, a pretty dire modern town with one point of interest, the **Nieuw Land** centre, providing background information on the draining of the IJsselmeer.

Gelderland, spreading east from the province of Utrecht to the German frontier, takes its name from the German town of Geldern, its capital until the late fourteenth century. As a province it's a bit of a mixture, varying from the fertile but dull agricultural land of the **Betuwe** (Good Land), which stretches west from Nijmegen as far as Gorinchem, to the more distinctive – and appealing – **Veluwe** (Bad Land), an expanse of heath, woodland and dune that sprawls down from the old Zuider Zee coastline to Arnhem. Infertile and sparsely populated, the Veluwe separated two of medieval Holland's most prosperous regions, the ports of the River IJssel and the cities of the Randstad and today it constitutes one of the most

---

ACCOMMODATION PRICE CODES

All the **hotels and hostels** detailed in this chapter have been graded according to the following price categories. Note that the prices have been calculated as those for the cheapest double room during high season. For more on accommodation, see p.29.

① Up to ƒ30 per person. ④ ƒ100–140. ⑦ ƒ220–260.
② ƒ30–65. ⑤ ƒ140–180. ⑧ ƒ260 and over.
③ ƒ65–100. ⑥ ƒ180–220.

---

popular holiday destinations in the country, strewn with campsites, second homes and bungalow parks. Some people use **Apeldoorn** as a base for the area, but it's a dreary town and if you want to visit the less developed southeastern sector, which has been set aside as the Hoge Veluwe National Park (and its Kröller-Müller Museum with a magnificent array of modern art, including one of the largest collections of Van Goghs in the world), you'd be better off basing yourself in Arnhem itself. **Arnhem** is most famous for its bridge, a key objective in the failed Operation Market Garden of 1944 – Field Marshal Montgomery's audacious attempt to shorten the war by dropping parachute battalions behind enemy lines to secure a string of advance positions across the rivers of southeast Gelderland – which left most of the city centre ruined. But it's a lively, agreeable place and a base for other attractions besides the Veluwe – the Netherlands Open-Air Museum, and, of course, the sites remembering the 1944 battle. The ancient town of **Nijmegen** too, 21km to the south, is a fashionable university city, with a quality contemporary music and arts scene, despite similarly extensive war damage and makes a good, if brief stop before heading south into the province of Limburg or east into Germany.

Northwest Overijssel: Steenwijk, Giethoorn and the lakes

Trains from Leeuwarden slip into the province of Overijssel near the village of **WILLEMSOORD**, in the northernmost corner of the province. The area was no more than empty moorland until the nineteenth century, when the so-called "Society of Charity" established a series of agricultural colonies here to cater for the poor. The Dutch bourgeoisie was as apprehensive of the unemployed pauper as its Victorian counterpart in Britain and the 1900 *Baedeker* noted approvingly that, "the houses are visited almost daily by the superintending officials and the strictest discipline is everywhere observed".

Trains stop at **STEENWIJK**, on the edge of the old moorlands, an unremarkable settlement that's only really useful as a base for exploring the surrounding lakes of western Overijssel. The town has seen more than its fair share of siege and assault, and, as a result, the towering mass of the Grote Kerk is an inconclusive mixture of styles that's suffered repeatedly from war damage. Otherwise, the centre is still roughly circular, following the lines of the original fortifications whose remains can be seen on the south side of town in a chain of steep, moated earth ramparts.

The town's **train** and **bus stations** are five minutes' walk north of the centre; head straight out of the station and follow the road around until you reach the ring road, cross over onto Doelenstraat, take a right at the T-junction and the Markt is in front of you. The VVV, Markt 60 (Mon–Fri 9am–5pm; June–Aug also Thurs until 9pm & Sat 9am–noon; ☎05210/12010), is the place to find out about bus services around the lakes; for up-to-date timetables, ask for the *NWH* bus book, which costs *f*4.95. Steenwijk has one reasonably priced **hotel**, *De Gouden Engel*, at Tukseweg 1 (☎05210/12436; ③), five minutes' walk northwest of the Markt – follow Kerkstraat around into Paardenmarkt and Tukseweg is dead ahead. The VVV also has details of a small number of private **rooms**.

Meppel and Staphorst

South of Steenwijk, the railway tracks from Leeuwarden and Groningen join at **MEPPEL**, a second possible base for travelling on to the lakes, though frankly it's a dull town and its **bus** and **train stations** are a good ten minutes' walk south-east of the centre. The town's VVV is at Kromme Elleboog 2 (Mon–Fri 9am–5pm; July & Aug also Sat 10am–noon; ☎05220/52888). There's one hotel, the *De Poort van Drente*, at Parallelweg 25 (☎05220/51080; ③), and a **youth hostel**, at Leonard Springerlaan 14 (☎05220/51706); it's marked from the train station and takes about five minutes to reach on foot.

Beyond Meppel lie the elongated villages of **STAPHORST** and **ROUVEEN**, tiny squares of brightly shuttered and neatly thatched farmhouses that line some 10km of road in the shadow of the motorway. Despite significant industrial development in the last decade, both these communities still have strong and strict Calvinist traditions: the majority still observe the Sabbath and many continue to wear traditional costume as a matter of course – and do not wish to be photographed. That said, apart from the custom of painting their houses in vicious shades of green and sky blue, Staphorst and Rouveen are undistinguished.

BUSES AROUND THE LAKES

From Steenwijk train station #72 to Giethoorn/Zwartsluis (Mon–Sat hourly, Sun 5 daily; 15/30min); change at Zwartsluis for connecting #71 to Vollenhove (Mon–Sat 2 hourly, Sun 6 daily; 20min); to Blokzijl #75 (Mon–Fri hourly, Sat 5 daily, Sun 3 daily; 20min).

From Meppel train station #73 to Zwartsluis (Mon–Fri 2 hourly, Sat 5 daily, Sun 3 daily; 20min); change at Zwartsluis for Vollenhove, as above.

From Zwolle train station #71 to Zwartsluis & Vollenhove (Mon–Sat 2 hourly, Sun every 2hr; 30/50min); change at Zwartsluis for connecting #72 to Giethoorn and Steenwijk (Mon–Sat hourly, Sun 5 daily; 15/30min).

Giethoorn and the lakes

Meppel and Steenwijk in the east and the old seaports of Vollenhove and Blokzijl in the west, rim an expanse of lake, pond, canal and river that's been formed by centuries of haphazard peat digging. Although it's a favourite holiday spot for watersports enthusiasts, public transport is limited and in any case you really miss the quiet charm of the region if you aren't travelling by **boat**. Fortunately these are available for rent at Giethoorn, in a variety of shapes and sizes, from canoes to motorboats and dinghies. Prices vary, but reckon on ƒ80 per day for a motorboat down to ƒ30 for a canoe. The other alternative is to come on a **boat trip** from Kampen (see p.207). Itineraries vary, but once or twice weekly, from mid-July to mid-August, boats sail from Kampen to Vollenhove, Blokzijl and Giethoorn. Further details from Kampen VVV.

Giethoorn

The best-known and most picturesque lakeland village is **GIETHOORN**, which flanks a series of interlocking canals that lie some 200m east of the minor N334 road from Steenwijk to Zwolle – not to be confused with the modern village of the same name on the main road itself. Bus #72 from Steenwijk station travels right through modern Giethoorn before reaching the VVV beyond. Make sure the driver lets you off at the old village – the bus stop is marked "Ds.T.O. Hylkemaweg", though few of the drivers seem to use the name.

Giethoorn's origins are rather odd. The marshy, infertile land here was given to an obscure sect of flagellants in the thirteenth century by the lord of Vollenhove. Isolated and poor, the colonists were dependent on local peat deposits for their livelihood, though their first digs only unearthed the horns of hundreds of goats who had been the victims of prehistoric flooding, leading to the settlement being named "Geytenhoren" (goats' horns). Nowadays Giethoorn's postcard-prettiness of thatched houses and narrow canals criss-crossed by arching footbridges draws tourists in their hundreds, Dutch and German weekenders swarming into the village throughout summer to jam the busy footpaths and clog the waterways in search of some sort of northern Venice. The high prices and water-borne hubbub are certainly similar, although sadly Giethoorn has little else to offer besides.

If you decide to stay, Giethoorn **VVV**, roughly 2km further along the N334 (June–Aug daily 9am–noon & 1–6pm; April, May & Sept Mon–Sat 10am–noon and 1–5pm; Oct–March Mon–Fri 10am–noon & 1–4pm; ☎05216/1248), has a list of private **rooms** and **pensions** and they'll telephone ahead to make a booking; clarify the exact location before you make a booking, or you could end up walking for miles. Two of the more convenient **hotels** are *'t Centrum* (☎05216/1225; ②) and *De Pergola* (☎05216/132; ②), both beside Giethoorn's central canal, at Ds. Hylkemaweg 39 and 7. Another alternative, is *Hotel Giethoorn* (☎05216/1216; ④), conveniently located next door to the VVV. Accommodation is very tight between June and August. For **eating**, try the *Achterhuis*, on the main canal at no. 43, or *Café Fanfare*, further east at Binnenpad 68, which has cheap daily dishes on its wide-ranging menu.

On the eastern edge of old Giethoorn, **Lake Bovenwijde** has no fewer than seven **campsites** on its western shore. The two nearest ones, at the end of the main canal, are the *Botel Griethoorn*, Binnenpad 47A and *De Kragge*, Binnenpad 113; both are open April to October. Both these campsites and all of the above hotels rent **boats**. **Water taxis** leave from pretty much everywhere and cost about ƒ7 per hour for a trip round the village.

Zwartsluis, Vollenhove and Blokzijl

South of Giethoorn, bus #72 travels the length of the dyke across Lake Belterwijde before cutting down into **ZWARTSLUIS**, once the site of an important fortress at the junction of waterways from Zwolle and Meppel. There's nothing much to the place today, but a couple of minutes' walk east of the bus station, at the bottom of Dawarsstraat, off Handelskade, is a small Jewish **cemetery** with a touching memorial to those locals who died in the concentration camps.

At the bus station on the edge of Zwartsluis passengers change for the journey west to **VOLLENHOVE**, one of the most agreeable little towns in northwest Overijssel. Once a maritime fortification guarding the approach to Zwolle, Vollenhove spreads out east from the Vollenhover Kanaal that marks the path of the old Zuider Zee coastline. Buses stop on Clarenberglaan, a five-minute walk away from the main square (straight up Doelenstraat), where the **Onze lieve Vrouwekerk** is a confusion of towers, spires and gables. The elegant, arcaded **Stadhuis** is attached to the church, and, across Kerkplein, the weathered stone gateposts outside the bank were originally part of the entrance to the **Latin School**. Around the corner from the church is the town's charming ancient **harbour**, a cramped, circular affair encased in steep grass banks.

Vollenhove **VVV** (June–Aug daily 10am–noon & 1.30–5pm; ☎05274/1700), beside the harbour, has details of a couple of private rooms. There's one basic hotel, the *Saantje*, Kerkplein 1(☎05274/1403; ③) and one pension, *De Haare*, Bisschopsstraat 29 (☎05274/3234; ②). The **restaurant** *De Vollenhof*, Kerkplein 12, serves good fish dishes and has a three-course menu; more appealing – and more expensive – is the *Seidel* restaurant in the old Stadhuis at Kerkplein 3. If you can't afford a meal, pop in for a coffee: the decor is delightfully antique.

Some 6km to the north, **BLOKZIJL** is more beguiling still, an orange-pantiled cobweb of narrow alleys and slim canals surrounding a trim little harbour. Formerly a seaport, Blokzijl has scores of restored seventeenth-century houses reflecting is mercantile past and one of the grandest has been converted into the *Hotel Kaatje Bijde Sluis*, Brouwerstraat 20 (☎05272/1833; ⑦), overlooking the main canal. More basic accommodation is available as ever through the **VVV**, Kerkstraat 12 (June–Sept Mon–Sat 9am–6pm & Sun 10am–noon & 1.30–4.30pm; ☎05272/1414), but it's wise to book in advance in season. Camping *De Sas* is on the south edge of town at Zuiderkade 22 (April–Sept).

The town is stuffed with **restaurants**: the *Kaatje Bijde Sluis* hotel (see above) has the finest food for miles around, but it is expensive and its restaurant is closed on Monday and Tuesday. Cheaper choices include the *Vans Ems*, Zeedijk 1, and the *Prins Mauritshuis*, Brouwerstraat 2.

Blokzijl is easily reached in summer by boat from Vollenhove and Zwartshuis, but is a little awkward to reach by bus from Vollenhove: take #71 or #171 heading west and change at **MARKNESSE** to #75 travelling east. Bus #75 (Mon–Fri hourly, Sat 5 daily, Sun 3 daily) connects Blokzijl direct with Steenwijk – the easier approach – and drops you on the north edge of town, five minutes' walk from the harbour. Blokzijk also makes a good base for exploring the surrounding countryside, in particular the **National Park De Weerribben**, a chunk of protected canal and marshland starting about 3km to the northeast of the town. The VVV will suggest cycle routes through the Weerribben, linking up with any of many motorboat trips. The *Bezoekerscentrum*, at Hoogweg 27 (Tues–Fri 10am–5pm, Sat & Sun noon–5pm), on the north edge of the park, has information on the loca flora and fauna.

Bikes can be rented in Blokzijl at *Het Keldertje*, Zuiderstraat 21 (☎05272/1747), at ƒ10 per day. For the less energetic, **boat trips** leave Blokzijl for Vollenhove and Zwartshuis three times daily in July and August, charging ƒ15 per person. The VVV will have the latest details.

Zwolle

The first major rail junction as you come from the north, **ZWOLLE** is the small and compact capital of Overijssel. An ancient town, it achieved passing international fame when Thomas à Kempis settled here in 1399 and throughout the fifteenth century Zwolle prospered as one of the principal towns of the Hanseatic League, its burghers commissioning an extensive programme of public works designed to protect its citizens and impress their rivals. Within the city walls, German textiles were traded for Baltic fish and grain, or more exotic products from Amsterdam, like coffee, tea and tobacco. The boom lasted for some two hundred years, but by the middle of the seventeenth century the success of Amsterdam and the general movement of trade to the west had undermined its economy – a decline reflected in Zwolle's present-day status as a small market town of no particular significance.

Refortified in successive centuries, today's centre is still in the shape of a star fortress, nine roughly triangular earthen bulwarks encircling both the old town and its harbour, whose waters separate a northern sector off from the rest. Prettily moated and still partly walled, Zwolle is engaging, though the surrounding suburbs, by comparison, are an unattractive modern sprawl.

Arrival, information and accommodation

Well connected by train to many of Holland's major cities and by bus to most of Overijssel's tourist attractions, Zwolle's **train** and **bus** stations are some ten minutes' walk south of the centre, a little way from the moat down Stationsweg. If you're intending to travel around the lakes and Flevoland by bus, it's well worth buying timetables from the bus station kiosk (Mon–Fri 8am–6pm).The VVV is at Grote Kerkplein 14 (Mon–Fri 9am–5.30pm, Sat 9am–4pm; ☎038/21 39 00). If you're **staying**, *Hotel Beniers*, Oosterlaan 6 (☎038/21914; ③), is conveniently situated opposite the bus station; the *Cityhotel*, Rode Torenplein 10 (☎038/21 81 82; ③), is just northwest of the Grote Markt at the end of Melkmarkt, while the best bargain for those counting every penny is the no-frills *Sleep Inn* at Rode Torenplein 4 (☎038/22 74 84/22 56 18; ①), although this is run by volunteers and open only in July and August. There's also the excellent, plush *Grand Hotel Wientjes*, Stationsweg 7 (☎038/25 42 54; ⑤), where there are often substantial discounts on offer at weekends. The town's nearest **campsite**, *Camping Agnietenberg*, Haersterveerweg 22 (April–Sept), is by the River Vecht on the northeastern outskirts of town and difficult to reach without a car; take the Meppel bus #40 from Zwolle station and ask for the campsite. You'll be let off on the east side of the bridge across the Vecht on the A28. Immediately east of the bus stop, Ordelseweg goes under the A28 and leads north to the campsite, a distance of about 2km.

The Town

In the centre of the Grote Markt stands the recently restored **Grote Kerk**, dedicated to St Michael, patron saint of the town. If the exterior seems a little plain it's because it's been dogged by ill luck. Its bell tower used to be one of the highest in the country and was struck by lightning three times in 1548, 1606 and 1669.

ZWOLLE

After the third time it was never rebuilt and eventually the bells were sold. Inside, the church has the familiar austerity of Dutch Protestantism, with the choir a bare and dusty forgotten corner and the seats arranged on a central pulpit plan. The pulpit itself is an intricate piece of Renaissance carving by the German Adam Straes, where the grace of Christ is emphasized by the brutal ugliness of the faces of the sinners.

Attached to the church is the **Hoofdwacht** of 1614, an ornately gabled building which once served as a guardhouse. In front was the place of public execution, the remaining inscription "Vigilate et Orate" (Watch and Pray) a stern piece of advice to the crowds who gathered to witness these bloody spectacles. Appropriately, the building later housed the town's main police station.

A little way west, down an alley off the Grote Markt, the primly restored **Onze Lieve Vrouwekerk** (May–Sept Wed–Fri 10am–4pm & Sat 10am–4.30pm; Oct–April Wed–Fri 12.15–3.30pm & Sat 12.30–4.30pm) is a discordant mixture of styles dating from the fifteenth century. Once again, the church has been plagued with difficulties – the original building contractor ran off with an advance payment and the tower was rebuilt after a fire in 1815 with an odd-looking turret on top, giving rise to its nickname "Peperbus" (pepperpot), which you can climb if you wish.

From beside the Grote Kerk, Sassenstraat twists and turns its way southeast toward the old city walls. No. 33, the **Karel V Huis**, is all that's left of the mansion built for the Emperor Charles V in case he decided to pay the town a visit. He never did, but then all the major cities of his empire were obliged to construct similarly grand buildings for his possible convenience. Strangely, the bas-relief medallion of Charles on the gable is dated 1571, thirteen years after his death in 1558. At the end of the Sassenstraat, the massive **Sassenpoort** is a fine example of a fifteenth-century defensive portal, complete with boiling oil and water holes; it gives some idea of just how grand the medieval town must have been.

West of the Grote Markt, at Melkmarkt 41, is the main entrance to the **Provinciaal Overijssels Museum** (Tues–Sat 10am–5pm, Sun 2–5pm; ƒ2.50), which is divided between two houses: the **Drostenhuis** (bailiff's house) on Melkmarkt, a grand sixteenth-century mansion topped with an uncomfortable Rococo pediment and the **Gouden Kroon**, through the garden at the side on Voorstraat. Pride of place in the Drostenhuis goes to the Blokzijl room, a meticulous reconstruction of a wealthy local family's seventeenth-century living quarters. The walnut, leather-upholstered chairs are a good illustration of Dutch furniture making and the mantelpiece holds some examples of Chinese ceramics. There's not much else of note, but of the items displayed on the second floor, there's a bizarre Vollenhove drinking cup in the shape of a bearded man in a doublet and a group of distinctive Art Nouveau Rozenburg vases – all deep strong colours with insects and flowers at the heart of the design – made by the same Hague company that tiled Groningen train station. The Gouden Kroon, around the back, is used for modest temporary exhibitions and houses a tiny natural history museum.

North of the Grote Markt, Roggenstraat and subsequently Vispoortenplas lead to a bridge over what was once the city harbour. On its south side much of the old town wall has been restored, including sections with a covered defensive parapet and a couple of fortified towers – principally the **Wijndragerstoren** (wine-porters' tower), which dates from the fourteenth century.

Eating and drinking

Zwolle isn't a marvellous place to eat. The most imaginative menu in town is offered at the *Poppe*, at Luttekestraat 66 (closed Mon), on the way from the station to the Grote Kerkplein, where they serve dishes with names like "Summer Flowers" and "Autumn Winds"; otherwise, there's *De Sassenpoort*, at Sassenstraat 54 (closed Mon), which offers reasonably priced meals and a three-course set menu; a branch of *Nordzee*, Deizerstraat 23, serving takeaway seafood; or the *Bella Napoli*, Grote Kerkplein 11 – the most appetizing of a number of pizzerias. *Le Clochard*, Bethlehemskerplein 34 (closed Mon), is another place doing a reasonably priced set menu, though it's otherwise fairly pricy. Zwolle is deadly dull at night: the best of the **bars** is perhaps the *Swing Café* at Voorstraat 3, which has regular live music.

Kampen

Just ten minutes from Zwolle by train, the small town of **KAMPEN** strings along the flat flood plain of the IJssel, a bold succession of towers and spires that, together with the other towns along the river, enjoyed a period of real prosperity in the fifteenth century as members of the Hanseatic League. Their success was short lived, however and by the late sixteenth century they were in decline as trade moved west and Amsterdam mopped up what was left by undercutting their merchants. Indeed, the IJssel towns slipped into obscurity just as Amsterdam rose to the full height of its glory.

The Town

Sidelined by history, Kampen nowadays is little more than four roughly parallel streets edging the river, dotted with the remnants of the town's heyday. A bridge from beside the station spans the IJssel, leading directly into the centre. Clearly visible to the right of the bridge is a leaning tower with a bizarre top that resembles a hollowed-out onion, part of the Stadhuis. Just across the street is a second tower, the seventeenth-century **Nieuwe Toren**, which becomes Kampen's main tourist attraction every summer on five consecutive Thursdays, beginning at the end of July, when the **Kampen cow** is pulled up to its top. Insult turned to civic celebration, the cow is a symbol of the stupidity of the inhabitants of Kampen, who are unlucky enough to be the butt of the Dutch equivalent of "Irish jokes". The legend is that when grass began to grow at the top of the tower, local farmers asked if they could graze their cattle up there, without considering how the animals could get up and down. To commemorate this daft request, an animal has been hoisted up the tower every year ever since, though thankfully it's recently been replaced by a stuffed model.

The **Stadhuis** itself (Mon–Thurs 11am–noon & 2–4pm; also May–Sept Sat 2–5pm; ƒ1) is divided into two parts, the **Oude** and **Nieuwe Raadhuis**: the former was built in 1543, the latter added during the eighteenth century. Of the two, it's the old building which has most of interest, namely the *Schepenzaal* or "Magistrates' Hall", a claustrophobic medieval affair with dark-stained walls capped by a superbly preserved barrel-vault roof and a magnificent stone chimneypiece – a grandiloquent, self-assured work carved by Colijn de Nole in tribute to Charles V in 1545, though the chimney's typically Renaissance representations of Justice, Prudence and Strength speak more of municipal pride than imperial glory. To the right, the magistrate's bench is the work of a more obscure local carpenter, a Master Frederik, who didn't get on with de Nole at all. Angry at not getting the more important job of the chimneypiece, his revenge can still be seen on the left-hand pillar, where a minute, malevolent satyr laughs maniacally at the chimney. For further details, pick up the glossy booklet on your way in – entry through the Nieuwe Raadhuis.

From outside the Stadhuis, Oudestraat leads directly south to the **Bovenkerk** (mid-April to mid-Sept Mon & Tues 1–5pm, Wed–Fri 10am–5pm; mid-Sept to early April Mon–Fri 1–4pm; free), a lovely Gothic church with a light, spacious sandstone interior. Generally regarded as one of the most important Dutch medieval churches, its choir – with thirteen radiating chapels – was the work of Rotger of Cologne, a member of the Parler family of masons who worked on

Cologne Cathedral. In the south transept an urn contains the heart of Admiral de Winter, a native of Kampen who fought to rid his country of what he considered to be the yoke of the House of Orange. A staunch Republican, he took part in the successful French invasion of 1795 that created the Batavian Republic; the rest of him lies in the Pantheon in Paris. Beside the church is the earliest of Kampen's three surviving gates, the fourteenth-century **Koornmarktpoort**. The others, the **Cellebroederspoort** and the **Broederpoort**, are of a later, more ornamental design and lie on the west side of town along Ebbingestraat, reached from the Bovenkerk via Schoolstraat.

Practicalities

It takes ten minutes for the twice-hourly train from Zwolle to reach Kampen **station**, five minutes' walk from the town centre. Unfortunately, finding somewhere to **stay** is difficult as the town has only two **hotels** and these are often full in high season. There's the *Van Dijk*, IJsselkade 30 (☎05202/14925; ④) and the *D'Olde Brugge*, IJsselkade 48 (☎05202/12645; ④), neither of which is cheap, although you do get a river view. The nearest **campsite** is the *Seveningen*, some 3km northeast of town at Frieseweg 7 (April–Sept): heading out of Kampen, cross the bridge and turn left; follow the main road around until it crosses the Ganzendiep canal and the campsite is just beyond – watch out for signs. If you're in difficulties, the Kampen **VVV** is on the main street at Botermarkt 5 (Mon–Fri 9am–5pm, Sat 9am–4pm; ☎05202/13500) and has a very short list of **private rooms**.

If you do manage to get fixed up, Kampen makes a good base for **day trips** into Flevoland and the Northeast Polder. Throughout June, July and August **boat trips** leave Kampen to explore the surrounding waterways; there are two- or three-times weekly excursions to Urk, Giethoorn and Enkhuisen. Prices vary according to the itinerary, but the longest trips will only cost about *f*30; up-to-date schedules and bookings are available at the VVV. Alternatively, **bikes** can be rented, as ever, from the train station or from *Potkamp*, Oudestraat 152 (☎05202/13495), for *f*8 a day.

For **food**, there's rather stolid Dutch fare at both hotels, or you can try either the fish and Dutch specialities of *D'Olde Vismark*, IJsselkade 45, or one of Kampen's oriental restaurants, like the popular Chinese *Peking* at Oudestraat 28, or the even busier Indonesian *Kota Radja*, Oudestraat 119.

Elburg

Half an hour from Zwolle by bus, just across the provincial boundary in Gelderland, the tiny coastal town of **ELBURG** once looked out across the Zuider Zee, whose perimeter is now marked by the path of the Veluwemeer as it snakes its way between the mainland and the polders of Flevoland. These days it's one of the most popular day-trip destinations in this part of Holland, awash with visitors throughout the season, here to enjoy the town's seaside flavour and to tour the homeopathic gardens on the outskirts.

Elburg was a successful port with its own fishing fleet from as early as the thirteenth century. However, in 1392 the governor, a certain Arent thoe Boecop, moved the whole town a little inland as a precaution against flooding. Familiar with the latest developments in town planning, Boecop and his overlord, the

Count of Zutphen, laid out the new town in the shape of a grid-iron, encircled by a protective wall and moat. Not all of Elburg's citizens were overly impressed – indeed the street by the museum is still called Ledigestede, literally "Empty Way" – but the basic design, with the notable addition of sixteenth-century ramparts and gun emplacements, survived the decline that set in when the harbour silted up and can still be observed today. Elburg's two main streets are Beekstraat, which forms the north–south axis and Jufferenstraat/Vischpoortstraat, which runs east–west; they intersect at right angles to form the main square, the Vischmarkt and all of Elburg's streets radiate from one or the other.

Buses from Zwolle drop visitors just outside the old town, a couple of minutes' walk from the **Gemeentemuseum**, Jufferenstraat 6 (Sept–May Mon 2–5pm, Tues–Fri 9.30am–noon & 2–5pm; June–Aug Mon–Fri 10am–5pm; *f*2.75), housed in an old convent, with predictable period rooms and objects of local interest. The entry fee covers all three town museums. Heading north across Jufferenstraat, the **St Nicolaaskerk** (Mon 1.30–4.30pm, Tues–Fri 10–11.30am & 1.30–5pm; church free, tower *f*1.50) dominates the landscape, even without its spire, which was destroyed by lightning in 1693. West of the church, down Van Kinsbergenstraat, is the old **Stadhuis**, which once served as Boecop's home. At the end of Van Kinsbergenstraat, turn left into Beekstraat for the town's main square, the Vischmarkt, from where Vischpoortstraat leads straight to the best preserved of the medieval town gates, the **Vischpoort**, a much restored brick rampart tower dating from 1594. Inside there's a modest exhibition on the local fishing industry (mid-June to Aug Mon 2–4.30pm, Tues–Fri 10am–noon & 2–4.30pm; free).

Outside the gate, the pattern of the sixteenth-century defensive works is clear to see – from interior town wall, to dry ditch, to earthen mound and moat. The interior of one of the subterranean artillery **Kazematten** (casements) is open from mid-June to August (Mon 2–4.30pm, Tues–Fri 9.30am–noon & 2–4.30pm). Cramped and poorly ventilated, it's easy to see why the Dutch called such emplacements *Moortkuijl*, literally "Pits of Murder". From the Kazematten it's about an hour's stroll right around the ramparts.

Ten minutes' walk northwest from the Vischpoort – turn right along Havenkade and take the second left – lie the **De Vier Jaargetijden** homeopathic gardens (guided tours only; April–Oct Mon–Fri 9.30am–4pm; June–Aug also Sat 10am–3.30pm; ☎05250/7373), 6 hectares of land that hold a comprehensive collection of homeopathic plants, the life's work of one Alfred Vogel. They form part of a successful business and are in fact Elburg's main tourist attraction. In the summer, free guided tours of two hours' duration begin at the visitors' centre (see below) once every two hours, on the hour, subject to demand and within opening times. It's easy to tag onto any of the groups visiting the gardens, but if you're keen to have the tour in English, call ahead to make arrangements. It's also possible to negotiate a tour in English on the spot, but you may have to wait a couple of hours. The visitors' centre, or **Bezoekerscentrum**, at Industriestraat 15, has a variety of illustrative displays and a mock-up of an old chemist's. However, it's all in Dutch and the surrounding gardens are of far more interest.

Practicalities

Elburg is easily reached from **Zwolle bus station** by service #101 (Mon–Sat every 30min, Sun hourly; 35min). The nearest **train station** is 8km from town at **T HARDE**, on the Zwolle–Amersfoort line, with trains in both directions every half hour; however, bus #123 from 't Harde station to Elburg runs infrequently (Mon–Fri 4 daily, Sat & Sun none; 15min).

Elburg's **VVV** is around the corner from the Gemeentemuseum at Ledige Stede 31 (May–Aug Mon–Fri 9am–5.30pm & Sat 9am–5pm; Sept–April Mon 1.30–5pm, Tues–Fri 9am–12.30pm & 1.30–5pm, Sat 11am–4pm; ☎05250/1520). They have a list of private **rooms** and will phone around to make a booking, but try to get a room in the old centre and come early in high season when accommodation often runs short. There's one **hotel**, *Het Smeede*, Smedestraat 5 (☎05250/4560; ④), off Beekstraat on the southwest side of the centre. The nearest **campsite** is the *Old Putten*, Zuiderzeestraatweg 65 (May–Oct), some 500m east of the VVV; head out of the old town along Zwolseweg and Zuiderzeestraatweg is the first on the right.

Of Elburg's many **restaurants** it's difficult to find any of real note. However, *'t Olde Regthuys*, Beekstraat 33, serves a reasonable range of fish dishes underneath fishing nets and ship models; the *Papillon* bistro, Vischpoortstraat 15, serves some good-quality food; the *'t Scheepje*, Vischpoortstraat 16, is lively and cheap; and the *Beekzicht*, Beekstraat 39 (closed Sun), is fine for pancakes.

For **boat trips**, there are hour-long excursions from Elburg around the Veluwemeer throughout the summer (*f*6 per person). There are also day trips to Urk (July & August 3 weekly) and occasional sailings to Ketelmeer and Harderwijk, among other destinations, which cost around *f*18 per person. The VVV has the latest schedules and will make bookings on your behalf.

The **strip of coast** on both sides of the Veluwemeer around Elburg is popular with Dutch holidaymakers for its watersports, nature reserves and forests. The whole region is dotted with campsites and the best way to explore it all is by **bike**. Cycles are available for rent in Elburg at *Koops*, Beekstraat 1 (☎05250/4461), for about *f*7 a day. The VVV has a comprehensive range of suggested cycle routes.

Flevoland

With the damming of the Zuider Zee and the creation of the IJsselmeer, the coastline north and west of Kampen and Elburg has been transformed, creating two new polder areas, the **Oostelijk and Zuidelijk Flevoland polders**, which form an island of reclaimed land in front of the old shoreline and make up the greater part of Holland's twelfth and newest province – **FLEVOLAND**. To the north, the reclaimed land mass of the **Northeast Polder** forms the rest of the new province, the small towns that mark the line of the old coast – Vollenhove, Blokzijl and Kuinre – cut off from open water and now marking the provincial boundary between Flevoland and Overijssel.

The Northeast Polder

The **Northeast Polder** was the first major piece of land to be reclaimed as part of the Zuider Zee reclamation scheme, which began in earnest with the Zuider Zee Reclamation Act of 1918. The key to the project was the completion of the Afsluitdijk between Den Oever in North Holland and Zurich in Friesland in 1932, which separated the open sea from the Zuider Zee and thereby created the freshwater IJsselmeer lake. The draining of the polder was completed in 1936: drained and dried, it provided 119,000 acres of new agricultural pasture, which the government handed out under an incentive scheme to prospective settlers. The original aims of the project were predominantly agricultural and (unlike later polders) little consideration was given to the needs of the settlers, with the result that most of the Northeast Polder is unimaginably boring (the only town of any size, **Emmeloord**, is like a vast housing development) and it's no surprise that, even with the incentives, there were difficulties in attracting settlers. Also, a number of design faults soon became apparent. Without trees the land was subject to soil erosion and the lack of an encircling waterway meant the surrounding mainland dried out and began to sink – problems that have persisted until the present day.

The Schokland Museum

The Northeast Polder incorporates the former Zuider Zee islands of Urk and Schokland, which in Roman times were actually connected as one island. Schokland, however, was abandoned in the last century because of the threat of flooding and only the church of 1834 has survived, converted into the **Schokland Museum** (April–Sept daily 10am–5pm; Oct–March Tues–Sun 11am–5pm), with displays of all sorts of bits and pieces found during the draining of the polders. From beside the museum, a circular foot and cycle path follows the old shoreline of the island, a distance of about 10km. Bikes can sometimes be rented by the hour from the museum; phone ahead (☎05275/1396) to confirm.

The Schokland Museum is a 400-metre walk south of the minor road between Ens and Nagele/Urk – some 3km west of Ens. Buses drop you off on the stretch of road nearest the museum, but it's an awkward journey without a car: take bus #141 from Zwolle or Kampen station to Ens bus station (Mon–Fri every 30 min, Sun hourly), from where you can either walk or take the connecting #142, which passes Schokland on its way to Urk (Mon–Fri 4 daily, none at weekends; 5min).

Urk

The only place really worth a visit in the Northeast Polder is **URK**, a trim harbour and fishing port that was a reluctant addition to the mainland. Centuries of hardship and isolation bred a tight-knit island fishing community here, with its own distinctive dialect and version of the national costume – aspects that have inevitably become diluted by connection to the mainland. However, the island's earlier independence does to some extent live on, rooted in a fishing industry which marks it out from the surrounding agricultural communities.

The damming of the Zuider Zee posed special problems for the islanders and it's hardly surprising that they opposed the IJsselmeer scheme from the beginning. Some feared that when the Northeast Polder was drained they would simply be overwhelmed by a flood of new settlers, but their biggest concern was that their fishing fleet would lose direct access to the North Sea. After futile negotiations at national level, the islanders decided to take matters into their own hands: the larger ships of the fleet were sent north to fish from ports above the line of the Afsluitdijk, particularly Delfzijl and transport was organized to transfer the catch straight back for sale at the Urk fish auctions. In the meantime, other fishermen decided to continue to fish locally and adapt to the freshwater species of the IJsselmeer. These were not comfortable changes for the islanders and the whole situation deteriorated when the Dutch government passed new legislation banning trawling in the IJsselmeer in 1970. When the inspectors arrived in Urk to enforce the ban, years of resentment exploded in ugly scenes of dockside violence and the government moved fast to sweeten the pill by offering substantial subsidies to compensate those fishermen affected. This arrangement continues today and the focus of conflict has moved to the attempt to impose EC quotas on the catch of the deep-sea fleet.

There's nothing spectacular about Urk – it's neither especially pretty nor particularly picturesque, but its setting is attractive, its waterfront a pleasant mixture of the functional and the ornamental and an appealing series of narrow lanes of tiny terraced houses indicate the extent of the old village. A surprising number of the islanders still wear traditional costume and further examples are on display in the **Museum Het Oude Raadhuis**, Wijk 2, no.2 (April–Sept Mon–Fri 10am–5pm; Oct, Feb & March 10am–1pm; f2.50).

The only convenient way of reaching Urk by **bus** is to take #141 from Kampen and Zwolle (Mon–Sat every 30min, Sun 3 daily after 4pm; 60–80min): ask the driver to drop you off at the stop nearest the centre. From early May to mid-September, Monday to Saturday, **ferries** cross the IJsselmeer between Enkhuizen and Urk two or three times daily and the trip takes around ninety minutes: check with any VVV for times and prices.

Adjoining the museum, Urk **VVV**, Wijk 2, no. 2 (April–June & Sept Mon–Fri 10am–1pm & 2–5pm; July & Aug, Mon–Fri 10am–5pm, Sat 10am–1pm; ☎05277/4040), will help arrange **accommodation** in both private **rooms** and **pensions** There are several cheap pensions near the harbour: *De Kroon*, Wijk 7, no. 54 (☎05277/1216; ②), *De Kaap*, Wijk 1, no. 5 (☎05277/1509; ②) and the unnamed pension of *Mw. J. Bakker* at Wijk 3, no. 76 (☎05277/2363; ③). The nearest **campsite** is *De Vormt*, Vormtweg 9 (April–Sept), in the woods some 4km north of Urk along the coastal road. Finally, Urk is a great place to eat **fresh fish** – *De Kaap* (address above), does good lunch specials and all-you-can-eat deals in the evening and has fine views over the IJsselmeer from its window tables; if you're not hungry enough to take advantage of that, try the *Havenzicht*, Wijk 1, no. 65, or the more expensive *De Zeebodem*, further down at no. 67.

The Flevoland polders

The Dutch learned from their mistakes on the Northeast Polder when, in the 1950s and 1960s, they drained the two polders that make up the western portion of the province of Flevoland, ringing the new land with a water channel to stop the surrounding land drying out and sinking. The Dutch government also tried hard to make these polders attractive: they're fringed by trees and watersports facilities. However, it remains an uphill struggle and people have moved here reluctantly, only persuaded by large financial carrots and very cheap housing. **LELYSTAD**, accessible direct from Kampen on bus #143 (Mon–Sat every half hour, Sun hourly; 55min) or by train from Amsterdam CS (every half hour, 40min), is where most of them end up, a characterless expanse of glass and concrete surrounded by leafy suburbs. The epitome of 1960s and early 1970s urban design, Lelystad is something of a disaster and things may get worse if plans to expand the city to accommodate some hundred thousand by the year 2000 proceed. The new railway link to Amsterdam was completed early in 1990, confirming both Lelystad and the other new town of **ALMERE**, 25km to the west, as commuter suburbs for the capital and home to some of its most poorly paid workers.

Lelystad takes its name from the pioneer engineer who had the original idea for the Zuider Zee scheme and for those with a passing interest in land reclamation there is at least one reason to stop – the **Informatiecentrum Nieuw Land**, at Oostvaardersdijk 1–13 (daily 10am–5pm; *f*3.50). This gives the background on the Zuider Zee plan, with photos, models, films and slides. Most of the information has been translated into English and you get a good idea of what's happened and what's scheduled to happen. The main problem is getting there: from the train and neighbouring bus stations, walk north beside the busy road that runs along the east side of the railway tracks and turn left at the first main intersection – a 1500-metre walk; the information centre is straight ahead across the island at the end of the road, a further 1500m on. If you're travelling by car from Enkhuizen, take the first major right as you come off the dyke and right again at the first island.

The area's other attraction, the **Scheepsarcheologisch Museum** (daily 10am–5pm; *f*1.50), is on the northeastern edge of the polder at tiny **KETELHAVEN**. It's a collection of all sorts of material retrieved as the land was drained. Most of the exhibits come from the extraordinary number of ships that foundered in the treacherous shallows of the Zuider Zee, notably much of the hull of a seventeenth-century merchant ship. Once again, though, you really need a car to get here: the nearest bus stop is some 6km away on the main Dronten–Kampen road. For the determined, take bus #143 from Kampen station and tell the driver where you're going. The bus stop is a couple of hundred metres east of Colijnweg, a right turn that takes you from the main road right into Ketelhaven.

Eastern Overijssel: Twente

Southeast of Zwolle, the flat landscape of western Holland is replaced by the lightly undulating, wooded countryside of **Twente**, an industrial region whose principal towns – **Almelo**, **Hengelo** and **Enschede** – were once dependent on the textile industry. Hit hard by cheap Far Eastern imports, they have been forced to diversify their industrial base with mixed success: the largest town, Enschede, still has around ten-percent unemployment.

Enschede and around

If you visit anywhere in Twente it should really be **ENSCHEDE**, the region's main town. Laid waste by fire in 1862, it has a desultory modern centre that's been refashioned as a large shopping precinct, but it's a lively place, with regular festivals, exhibitions and the like and it has a museum with an excellent collection of Dutch art and some interesting 1930s architecture. All in all it's a worthwhile detour if you're heading east into Germany.

The Town
Five minutes' walk south of the train station, **Langestraat** is Enschede's main street. At its northern end, **Markt** is the town's main square, home to the nineteenth-century **Grote Kerk** (July & Aug Sat 2–4pm) in the middle, with its Romanesque tower and the **St Jacobuskerk** just across the Markt, completed in 1933 on the site of a previous church that burned down in 1862. The severe

rectangular shape of the building is punctured by angular copper-green roofs, huge circular windows and a series of Gothic arches. It's normally kept closed, but you can visit by appointment (☎053/32 07 79) or ask at the VVV. It's worth the trouble, as the church is built in a beautiful domed and cloistered neo-Byzantine style, with some good modern sculpture and stained glass. The **Stadhuis**, a couple of minutes away down Langestraat, was finished in the same year and is also something of an architectural landmark, its brown brick tower topped by four eye-catching blue and gold clocks. No expense was spared in its construction and the interior is richly decorated with mosaics and, again, stained glass.

Fifteen minutes' walk north of the centre at Lasondersingel 129 – over the railway tracks at the crossing beside the station, first right, second left and follow the road to the end – the **Rijksmuseum Twente** (Tues–Fri 10am–5pm, Sat & Sun 1–5pm; *f*3) is housed in a building of the same era, an Art Deco mansion of 1929, the gift to the nation of a family of mill owners, the Van Heeks, who used the profits they made from their workers to build up one of eastern Holland's finest art collections. Clearly laid out and labelled, the museum has three main sections: fifteenth- to nineteenth-century art to the right of the entrance in rooms 1 to 11a; modern art, primarily Dutch with the emphasis on Expressionism, to the left of the entrance in rooms 12 to 21 and 23 to 32 (though many of these rooms are used for temporary exhibitions); and applied art, based on exhibits from the region of Twente, in the rooms at the back of the museum – prehistoric and medieval artefacts, tiles and porcelain, tapestries and a reconstructed farm.

It's the paintings, inevitably, that provide the most interest, especially the Dutch and Flemish sections. Among a fine sample of early religious art are seven brilliant blue and gold fragments from a French hand-illuminated missal; a primitive twelfth-century wood carving of *Christ on Palm Sunday*; a delightful cartoon strip of contemporary life entitled *De Zeven Werken van Barmhartigheid* (The Seven Acts of Charity); and an extraordinary pair of fifteenth-century altar doors by one Tilman van der Burch, where a deep carved relief of a pastoral scene resembles a modern pop-up book. Of later canvases, Hans Holbein's *Portrait of Richard Mabott* is typical of his work, the stark black of the subject's gown offset by the white cross on his chest and the face so finely observed it's possible to make out the line of his stubble. Pieter Bruegel the Younger's *Winter Landscape* is also fastidiously drawn, down to the last twig and contrasts with the more loosely contoured bent figures and threatening clouds of his brother Jan's *Landscape*. Lucas Cranach's studies of a bloated *Frederick Grootmoedige* and the spectacularly ugly *Barbara van Saksen* must have done little for the self-confidence of their subjects. Jan Steen's *The Alchemist* is all scurrilous satire, from the skull on the chimneypiece, to the lizard suspended from the ceiling and the ogre's whispered advice and compares with the bulging breasts and flushed countenance of the woman in his *Flute Player*, where the promise of forthcoming sex is emphasized by the vague outline of tussling lovers on the wall in the background. The modern section, too, has a few highlights – Claude Monet's volatile *Falaises près de Pourville*; a characteristically unsettling canvas by Carel Willink, *The Actress Ank van der Moer*; and examples of the work of less well-known Dutch modernists like Theo Kuypers, Jan Roeland and Emo Verkerk.

From beside the Stadhuis, it's a ten-minute walk southwest to Enschede's **Museum Jannink** (Tues–Fri 10am–5pm, Sat & Sun 1–5pm; *f*1.50), at the junction of Haaksbergerstaat and Industriestraat (head straight down Van Loenshof, turn right at Boulevard 1945 and take the first left), housed in a former mill and devoted to portraying everyday life in Twente from the nineteenth century onward. The most intriguing displays are a series of representative living rooms and a bewildering variety of looms reflecting the development of the textile industry from its origins as a cottage industry to large-scale factory production.

A third museum, the **Natuurmuseum**, De Ruyterlaan 2 (Tues–Sat 10am–5pm, Sun 2–5pm; f2.50), is also worth a peek: there's a vivarium on the second floor, some well-presented fossils on the first floor and a mineralogy section in the basement. To get there, turn right leaving the train station along Stationsplein and then down the first major road on the left – a five-minute walk.

Practicalities

The best place to **stay** in Enschede is the unpretentious *Hotel Chaplin*, right in the centre at Korte Haaksbergerstraat 2 (☎053/31 17 87; ④). Alternatively and somewhat cheaper, both the *Parkhotel*, Hengelosestraat 200 (☎053/32385; ③) and the *Modern*, Parkweg 39 (☎053/323438; ③), are a short walk out of the city centre. The **VVV**, in the centre of town at Oude Markt 31 (Mon 10am–5.30pm, Tues–Fri 9am–5.30pm, Sat 9am–1pm; June–Aug Sat also 1–5pm; ☎053/32 32 00), has details of a limited number of private **rooms**.

For **food**, stick to the streets around the Markt, where the *Atrium* serves up tasty daily specials before 6pm, as does *Eetcafé Sam Sam*, Zuiderhagen 16. Other options include student hangouts like *Chez Eugene* at Walstraat 5 and *Graffity*, Markt 6. *Graffity* is also a stop on the bar-crawlers' circuit of the Markt, other notable ones being *De Kater* and *De Geus*.

Around Enschede: Hengelo, Almelo, Oldenzaal, Ootmarsum and Denekamp

Some 10km northwest of Enschede, **HENGELO** has about eighty thousand inhabitants and is Twente's second town, a grim place whose old centre was destroyed during World War II. **ALMELO**, a further 17km northwest, is the region's third largest town, but this too has few attractions: the only buildings of any real interest are the centrally sited **Waag**, whose stepped gables date, surprisingly enough, from 1914, and, in a park east of the Marktplein, a stately seventeenth-century mansion, the **Huize Almelo** (no entry).

Things pick up a little north of Enschede with **OLDENZAAL**, the most agreeable of Twente's other settlements. Founded by the Franks, it was a medieval city of some importance and it was from here, too, that Overijssel's textile industry began its rapid nineteenth-century expansion, spurred on by the introduction of the power loom by Englishman Thomas Ainsworth. The town's principal sight, the **St Plechelmusbasiliek**, is right in the centre (June–Aug Tues 2–3pm, Wed 2–4pm, Thurs 2–3pm; free), an impressive, essentially Romanesque edifice dating from the thirteenth century. Named after Saint Plechelm, the Irish missionary who brought Christianity here, the interior (visits organized by the VVV) is an exercise in simplicity – strong, sturdy pillars supporting a succession of low semicircular arches. Above, the bell tower is the largest in Europe with a carillon of no less than 46 bells.

Bus #60 leaves Enschede for the twenty-minute trip to Oldenzaal train station every thirty minutes from Monday to Saturday and once hourly on Sunday. The approach by **rail** is less convenient as passengers have to change at Hengelo, where it's a half-hour wait for the right connection. Oldenzaal's **train station** is ten minutes' walk south of the centre – head down Stationsplein, turn right at the end onto Haerstraat, first left along Wilhelminastraat and it's dead ahead – where the **VVV**, Ganzenmarkt 3 (Mon–Fri 9am–5pm, Sat noon–4pm; ☎05410/14023), has information on private **rooms**. There are several **hotels**: try either the *Muller* at Markt 14 (☎05410/12093; ③), or the somewhat cheaper *de Zon*, Bentheimerstraat 1 (☎05410/12413; ③), two minutes from Markt. For **eating**, Markt is lined with **bars** and **restaurants**: try *'t Geveltje* at no. 19, which has cheap daily specials, or the more middle-ranging *Las Carretas* at no. 21.

Oldenzaal is a good base for visiting the wooded countryside that stretches northeast from near the town to the German border. This is a popular holiday area, littered with campsites, summer cottages, and bungalow parks. The village of **OOTMARSUM** (bus #64 from the station hourly; 15min) is noted for its half-timbered houses and quaint Markt.

By comparison, **DENEKAMP** (bus #52 from the station; hourly; 30min) is rather drab, though the elegant classicism of the **Kasteel Singraven**, some 2km west of the centre, partly makes up for it. Details of guided tours around the castle (mid-April to Oct Tues–Fri at 11am, 2pm, 3pm, & 4pm; *f*6) are available from the Denekamp **VVV**, Kerkplein 2 (Mon–Fri 9am–12.30pm & 2–5pm; June–Aug also Sat 1–4pm; ☎05413/51205). While you're up at the castle, look out for the **watermill** on the banks of the river, built in 1448 and still functioning. Don't omit, either, to grab a pancake from the **restaurant** next door – they're outstanding.

Deventer and Zutphen

South of Zwolle, the River IJssel twists its way through flat, fertile farmland as it marks out the boundary between Overijssel and Gelderland. For two hundred years the towns of the lower IJssel, **Deventer** and **Zutphen**, shared with Zwolle and Kampen a period of tremendous prosperity as the junction of trade routes from Germany, the Baltic and Amsterdam. Although both towns suffered grievously during the wars with Spain, the underlying reasons for their subsequent decline were economic – they could do little to stop the movement of trade to the west and could not compete with the great cities of South Holland. By the eighteenth century, they had slipped into provincial insignificance.

Deventer

Twenty minutes by train (every 30min) from Zwolle, **DEVENTER** sits calmly on the banks of the IJssel, an intriguing and – in tourist terms – rather neglected place, whose origins can be traced to the missionary work of the eighth-century Saxon monk, Lebuinus. An influential centre of medieval learning, it was here in the late fourteenth century that Gerrit Groot founded the Brotherhood of Common Life, a semimonastic collective that espoused tolerance and humanism within a philosophy known as *Moderne Devotie* (modern devotion). This progressive creed attracted some of the great minds of the time and Thomas à Kempis and Erasmus both studied here.

The Town

Five minutes from the train station, the centre of town is **Brink**, an elongated marketplace that runs roughly north to south, dividing the old town in two. The **Waag** edges the southern end of the square, a late Gothic edifice that retains an ancient dignity despite something of a rickety appearance. Inside, the **Town Museum** (Tues–Sat 10am–5pm, Sun 2–5pm; *f*3, or *f*5 for a ticket including the Toy Museum as well) has a thin collection of portrait paintings and a few antique bicycles. More intriguing is the large pan that's nailed to the outside of the Waag's western wall. Apparently, the mintmaster's assistant was found making a tidy profit by debasing the town's coins, so he was put in the pan and boiled alive. The bullet holes weren't an attempt to prolong the agony, but the work of idle French soldiers taking, quite literally, "pot shots".

Behind the Waag, the VVV is housed in what was once a sixteenth-century merchant's mansion, *De Drie Haringen* (The Three Herrings), close by which is the **Speelgoed en Blikmuseum** (Toy and Tin Museum; Tues–Sat 10am–5pm, Sun 2–5pm) which specializes in mechanical dolls. Walking west from here, Assenstraat's **window cuts** were completed in the early 1980s by a local artist, J. Limburg. Precise and entertaining, each illustrates a particular proverb or belief: at no. 119 the hedgehog's inscription translates as "Thrift yields big revenues" and at no. 81, on a house called *Gevaarlijke Stoffen* (Dangerous Materials), the totem pole is surrounded by slogans including *E pericolose sporcare* (It is dangerous to pollute). Continuing to the west along Assenstraat and veering left down Grote Poot (Big Leg), the **Lebuinuskerk** (Mon–Sat 11am–5pm; free) is one of the most impressive Gothic buildings in eastern Holland and is an expression of Deventer's fifteenth-century wealth and self-confidence. Carefully symmetrical, the massive nave is supported by seven flying buttresses, trimmed by an ornate stone parapet. The interior has recently been restored and today the expanse of white stone is almost startling, high arched windows and slender pillars reaching up toward a distant timber roof. Below, the church has two magnificent Baroque organs, the delicate remnants of some medieval murals and an eleventh-century crypt with a simple vaulted roof supported by Romanesque, spiral columns.

Back outside, the rear of the Lebuinuskek is joined to the fourteenth-century **Mariakerk**. Services haven't been held here since 1591 and the town council considered demolishing it as early as 1600, but in the event it survived as the town's arsenal and now houses a smart restaurant. Back at Brink, east of the Waag, Rijkmanstraat takes you into the **Bergkwartier**, an area of fairly ancient housing that was tastefully refurbished during the 1960s, one of Holland's first urban renewal projects. Turning left onto Kerksteeg, there's a small piece of iron, the remnants of a ring, embedded in a hole on the right-hand wall. Fearful of marauding Spanish armies, the 1570s were desperate times for the inhabitants of Deventer, and, in their efforts to reinforce the town's defences, iron rings were embedded in the walls of many of the streets so that chains could be hung across them. At the end of Kerksteeg, the **Bergkerk** is fronted by two tall towers dating from the thirteenth century, the differences in the colouring of the brick indicating the stages of construction. From the church, Roggestraat leads downhill to the east side of Brink; opposite is a tiny triangle edged by the **Penninckshuis**, whose florid Renaissance frontage is decorated with statuettes of six virtues. The inscription *Alst Godt behaget beter benyt als beclaget* is smug indeed – "If it pleases God it is better to be envied than to be pitied".

Practicalities

Deventer's **bus** and **train** stations are a five-minute walk north of the town centre – left out of the station and first right straight down Keizerstraat and onto the Brink. For a place of this size, **accommodation** is thin on the ground: there's only one central **hotel**, the grimly modern *Royal*, Brink 94 (☎05700/11880; ③) and one budget place, *Shita*, at Tjoenerstraat 25 (☎05700/26085; ②), a twenty-minute walk from the centre, which charges extra for sheets and blankets. Bookings should be made at the VVV, who will also give you directions on how to get there. The other alternative is the **campsite**, *De Worp* (May–Sept), west of the centre in the fields across the IJssel. A shuttle boat service crosses the river from the landing stage at the bottom of Vispoort and on the other side it's a five-minute walk down the first turn on the right, Langelaan.

Bars and **restaurants** line both sides of Brink: *In de Waagschaal*, no. 77, is a pleasant brown café; there are filling snacks at *Mart's Inn*, Brink 81, delicious Dutch meals at *De Drie Nissen*, Grote Poot 19 and pricy Portuguese fare at *Chez Antoinette*, Roggestraat 8, as well as a varied French and Dutch menu at *La Balance*, no. 72. The local speciality is a sort of honey gingerbread, *Deventer koek* and the best place to try it is the antique cake shop, *Bussink*, at no. 84.

The **VVV**, Brink 55 (Mon–Fri 9am–5pm & Sat 9am–2pm, till 4pm in summer; ☎05700/16200), sells a town guide (*f*3.50) and has details of **boat trips** up the IJssel leaving from the jetty near the Vispoort. A weekly programme throughout July and August includes excursions to Enkhuizen, Urk, Kampen, Zwolle and Zutphen, once or twice a week; prices vary according to the itinerary, but for the longer trips reckon on *f*25–30 per person return.

Zutphen

A sleepy little town some 15km south of Deventer, over in Gelderland, **ZUTPHEN** was founded in the eleventh century as a fortified settlement at the junction of the Berkel and IJssel rivers. It took just one hundred years to become an important port and today's tranquillity belies an illustrious and sometimes torrid past. Attacked and sacked on numerous occasions, the massacre of its citizens by Spanish forces in 1572 became part of Protestant folklore, strengthening their resolve against Catholic cruelty and absolutism. It was also here that Sir Philip Sidney, the English poet, soldier and courtier, met his death while fighting with the Earl of Leicester's forces against the Spanish in 1586. Sir Philip personified the ideal of the Renaissance man and died as he had lived – in style: wounded in the thigh as a consequence of loaning his leg-armour to a friend, he had every reason to feel outraged by his poor luck. Instead, realizing he was about to die, he offered his cup of water to another wounded soldier, uttering the now commonplace phrase "thy need is greater than mine".

The Town

A five-minute walk from the train station, the effective centre of Zutphen is the **Wijnhuis**, a confused building of pillars and platforms that was begun in the seventeenth century and now houses the VVV. All the old town's main streets radiate from here and although there aren't many specific sights, the place does have charm, a jangle of architectural styles within much of the medieval street plan.

Around the corner from the Wijnhuis, Lange Hofstraat cuts down to the **Grote Kerk** of St Walburga (early May to end Sept, normally Mon 2–4pm, Tues–Sat

11am–4pm; guided tours at 11am, 2pm & 3pm; *f*2.50), an indifferent, though immense Gothic church. Inside, the most impressive features are an extravagant brass baptismal font and the remarkable medieval **Library**, sited in the sixteenth-century chapterhouse. Established in 1560, the library has a beautiful low-vaulted ceiling that twists around in a confusion of sharp-edged arches rising above the original wooden reading desks. It has all the feel of a medieval monastery, but it was in fact one of the first Dutch libraries to be built for the general public, a conscious effort by the Protestant authorities to dispel ignorance and superstition. The collection is wonderful, ranging from early illuminated manuscripts to later sixteenth-century works, a selection of which are still chained to the lecterns on which they were once read. There are also two manuscript volumes – one a beauti-ful sixteenth-century illuminated missal, the other an original manuscript attrib-uted to Thomas à Kempis. Curiously, the tiles on one side of the floor are dotted with paw marks, which some contemporaries attributed to the work of the Devil.

Down the alleys east of the church entrance is the fifteenth-century **Drogenapstoren**, one of the old city gates. This is a fine example of a brick rampart tower, taking its name from the time when the town trumpeteer, Thomas Drogenap, lived here.

Heading back toward the Wijnhuis along the Zaadmarkt, you'll come to the **Museum Henriette Polak** at no. 88 (Tues–Fri 11am–5pm, Sat & Sun 1.30–5pm; *f*2.50) which has a modest collection of twentieth-century Dutch paintings, nota-bly *Landschap* by Wim Oepts, a profusion of strong colours, roughly brushed, that manages a clear impression of a Dutch landscape.

Finally, the **Stedelijk Museum** (same times, same ticket), on the other side of town toward the station at Rozengracht 3, is housed in the shell of a thirteenth-century Dominican monastery and has a fairly predictable selection of shards, armour and silver. In the old refectory on the second floor there's an altarpiece from around 1400, originally from the Grote Kerk.

Practicalities

Zutphen's **VVV**, in the Wijnhuis (April–Sept Mon–Fri 9am–5.30pm, Sat 10am–2pm; Oct–March Mon–Fri 9am–5.30pm, Sat 10am–12.30pm; ☎05750/19355), has details of a couple of centrally situated **rooms**, though in July and August it's advisable to arrive early as they disappear fast. There's only one **hotel**, the pension-like *Berkhotel*, straight down the Groenmarkt from the VVV at Marschpoortstraat 19 (☎05750/11135; ③).

As far as **eating** is concerned, there are two good and reasonably priced **restaurants** in Zutphen: *Pizzeria da Enzo*, near the Drogenapstoren at Pelikaanstraat 1a and the *Berkhotel*'s vegetarian café *De Kloostertuin*, Marschpoortstraat 19 (closed Mon). For **bars**, try the lively *'t Winkeltje*, Groenmarkt 34, or the quieter *De Korenbeurs*, Zaadmarkt 84.

Boat trips run north up the IJssel in July and August with occasional excur-sions to Deventer and Apeldoorn. Prices vary according to the route, but a day trip will cost about *f*25. Times of sailing from the VVV.

Around Zutphen: the Achterhoek

Extending some 30km southeast from Zutphen to the German border, the **Achterhoek** (Back Corner) is aptly named, a dozy rural backwater whose towns and villages have little to hold your attention. The easy hills have, however, made it a popular spot for cyclists. Small enough to tour from Zutphen, there are no really noteworthy monuments, with the possible exception of the old frontier settlement of 'S-HEERENBERG, whose tedious, modern centre edges the medieval Raadhuis, church and castle that once belonged to the counts Van de Bergh. Of the three, its castle, the Huis Bergh, that dominates, its impressive red-brick walls bedecked with shutters, rising abruptly above the moat. Its present appearance was acquired in 1912 when an Enschede industrialist, J. H. van Heek, bought the place and had it restored. Guided tours (March to mid-Dec; ☎08346/61281) whisk you round an interior littered with sundry late medieval paintings, statues, prayer books and other paraphernalia installed by Heek.

The quickest way to reach 's-Heerenberg is by train from PRODEM to DOETINCHEM, where you can pick up bus #24 from the train station for the twenty-minute trip (Mon–Fri every 30min, Sat & Sun hourly). In 's-Heerenberg the bus stops outside the VVV (Mon–Fri 9am–5.30pm, Sat 9am–3.30pm, Sun 10am–2.30pm; ☎08346/63131), which has good suggestions for walking and cycling. Bicycles can be rented from *G. Nijland*, Klinkerstraat 36. If you need to **stay over**, try *Burgers Hotel*, Marktstraat 1 (☎08346/61989; ②). *De Molenhoek*, Molenpoortstraat 35, has cheap and filling snacks.

Through the Veluwe: Apeldoorn

Extending west of the River IJssel, the **Veluwe** (literally "Bad Land") of the province of Gelderland is an expanse of heath, woodland and dune edged by Apeldoorn and Amersfoort to the east and west and the Veluwemeer and Arnhem to the north and south. For centuries these infertile lands lay almost deserted, but today they make up Holland's busiest holiday centre, a profusion of campsites, bungalow parks and second homes that extends down to the Hoge Veluwe National Park, a protected zone in the southeast corner that is much the prettiest part and the best place to experience the area – though it's more sensibly seen from Arnhem.

Apeldoorn

The administrative capital of the Veluwe, **APELDOORN** was no more than a village at the turn of the century, but it's grown rapidly to become an extensive garden city, a rather characterless modern place that spreads languidly into the surrounding countryside. However, as one-time home of the Dutch royal family, Apeldoorn is a major tourist centre in its own right, popular with those Dutch senior citizens who like an atmosphere of comfortable, rather snobbish privilege. The only sign of life is the annual jazz festival, the **Jazztival**, held over a weekend in either late May or early June, with jazz musicians performing in the bars and clubs around town. Further details from the VVV.

The Paleis Het Loo

Apeldoorn is most famous for the **Paleis Het Loo** (Tues–Sun 10am–5pm; ƒ10), situated on the northern edge of town and reachable by buses #102 and #104 (about once hourly) from the bus stop around the back of the *Hotel Suisse*, opposite the train station. Designed in 1685 by Daniel Marot for William III and his Queen Mary, shortly before he acceded to the throne of England and Scotland, the palace was later the favourite residence of Queen Wilhelmina, who lived here until her death in 1962. No longer used by the Dutch royal family – they moved out in 1975 – it was opened as a national museum in the early 1980s, illustrating three hundred years of the history of the House of Orange-Nassau. Inside, seven years of repair work have restored an apparently endless sequence of bedrooms, ballrooms, living rooms and reception halls to their former glory, supplemented by displays of all things royal – from costumes and decorations in the West Wing, to documents, medals and gifts in the East Wing and dozens of royal portraits and miscellaneous memorabilia spread across the main body of the palace. You can view the rooms of William and Mary, including their colourful individual bedchambers, as well as the much later study of Queen Wilhelmina. It's an undeniably complete display, but, unless you've a special interest in the House of Orange, not especially diverting. Better are the formal **gardens** (both William and Mary were apparently keen gardeners), a series of precise and neatly bordered flowerbeds of geometric design that are accessible by long walkways ornamented in the Dutch Baroque style, with fountains, urns, statuettes and portals. The other part of the palace, the **Royal Stables** of 1906 (same times), next to the entrance on Amersfoortweg, has displays of some of the old cars and carriages of past monarchs, including a baby carriage that's rigged up against gas attack.

Practicalities

The Apeldoorn **VVV** (Mon–Fri 9am–6pm, Sat 9am–5pm; closes at 1pm out of season; ☎055/78 84 21) adjoins the **train station** and has maps of the town and the surrounding area and (if you need to stay) lists of **rooms** – in season it's advisable to ask them to ring ahead to confirm vacancies. The most reasonably priced **hotel** in or near the town centre is the *Abbekerk*, Canadalaan 26, a ten-minute walk from the centre (☎055/22 24 33; ③). There's also a **youth hostel**, 4km to the west of town at Asselsestraat 330 (☎055/55 31 18; April–Sept), reachable with bus #2 or #4 from beside the train station. The nearest **campsite**, *De Veldekster*, is some 5km southwest of the centre, off Europaweg at Veldekster 25 (bus #110 from the train station).

Apeldoorn's popularity means that cheap **eating** is difficult and you have to fall back on either pizza houses or fast-food joints. For something a little more nutritious, try the centrally sited *Café de Paris*, Raadhuisplein 5, or the Greek restaurant, *Parthenon*, at no. 2.

An easy way to see the countryside around town is by **bike**. Details of suggested routes are available from the VVV and cycles can be rented at *Harleman*, Arnhemseweg 28.

Arnhem and around

Around 20km south of Apeldoorn, on the far side of the heathy Hoge Veluwe National Park, **ARNHEM** was once a wealthy resort, a watering-hole to which the merchants of Amsterdam and Rotterdam would flock to idle away their fortunes. This century it's become better known as the place where thousands of British and Polish troops died in the failed Allied airborne operation of September 1944, codenamed Operation Market Garden. The operation gutted the greater part of the city and most of what you see today is a postwar reconstruction – inevitably not particularly enticing. However, Arnhem is a lively town that makes a good centre for seeing the numerous attractions scattered around its forested outskirts

– the war museums and memorials, the Dutch open-air museum and the Hoge Veluwe Park itself, incorporating the Kröller-Müller Museum and its superb collection of modern art.

Arrival, information and accommodation

Arnhem is a major rail junction, well connected with both Dutch and German cities. The town's **train** and **bus stations**, a couple of minutes' walk from the centre, are next door to the VVV, Stationsplein 45 (Mon–Fri 9am–5.30pm & Sat 9am–4pm; ☎085/42 03 30), which has a good selection of Dutch maps, books on "Operation Market Garden", brochures and up-to-date cultural information. It also operates an **accommodation** booking service – useful in July and August when Arnhem's handful of reasonably priced **pensions** and **hotels** can fill up early. The cheapest double rooms in town are at *Hotel Pension Parkzicht*, Apeldoornsestraat 16 (☎085/42 06 98; ③), ten minutes' walk east from the station: head round the northern edge of Willemsplein onto Jans Buiten Singel; Apeldoornsestraat is at the far end on the left. Other cheap and central places to stay include *Hotel Rembrandt*, Paterstraat 1 (☎085/42 01 53; ③), on the second right off Apeldoornsestraat and the slightly pricier *Hotel Rijnoever*, by the river at Rijnkade 86 (☎085/45 31 94; ③). If money's not too tight, there's the reassuringly comfortable *Hotel Haarhuis* opposite the train station at Stationsplein 1 (☎085/427441; ⑤). If you're on a budget, there's a **youth hostel** some 5km north of town at Diepenbrocklaan 27 (bus #3, direction Cranvelt; ☎085/42 01 14). The nearest **campsite** is *Camping Warnsborn*, northwest of the centre at Bakenbergseweg 257 (☎085/42 34 69; bus #2 direction Heidekamp), although there are many others around the edge of the Hoge Veluwe Park, 5km further north.

If you have problems finding something, there's a good alternative outside the city proper, the *Pension Little Tower*, Vijverlaan 29 (☎085/63 51 76; ③), in the leafy suburb of **VELP** (trains every 30min; 10min), bookable at Arnhem VVV. Untouched by the war, parts of Velp are still much as they were at the turn of the century – comfortable country mansions and landscaped streets and gardens. The *Little Tower* is right in the middle of Velp, ten minutes' walk from the train station and very inexpensive. To get there, turn right along Stationsstraat, left at the main road, first right down Overbeeklaan and first left.

Walking is the best way to **get around** Arnhem town centre, although to see any of the outlying attractions and for some of the accommodation, you'll need at some point to use a **bus**. Arnhem has a rather odd system of trams which describe a figure-of-eight pattern over town. This means there'll often be two buses at the station with the same number and different destinations, so it's important to get the direction as well as the number right.

The Town

Since the war, Arnhem has been something of a place of pilgrimage for English visitors, who flock here every summer to pay their respects to the soldiers who died, or to view the spots immortalized by the battle; only recently have the graves begun to seem distant reminders of an ancient conflict, as World War II veterans age and memories fade. Predictably, the postwar rebuilding has left Arnhem a patchy place with the usual agglomerations of concrete and glass, surrounded by formless empty spaces. Five minutes' walk southeast from the train station, the best part of what's left is the northwest part of town, around the **Korenmarkt**, a small square which escaped much of the destruction and has one or two good facades. The streets which lead off the Korenmarkt are pleasantly animated, full of restaurants and bars, while the **Filmhuis**, at Korenmarkt 42, has an excellent programme of international films and late-night showings.

Arnhem deteriorates as you walk southeast from the Korenmarkt and into the area most badly damaged by the fighting. Here you can find "The Bridge too Far", the **John Frostbrug**, named after the commander of the battalion that defended it for four days. It's just an ordinary modern bridge, but it remains the

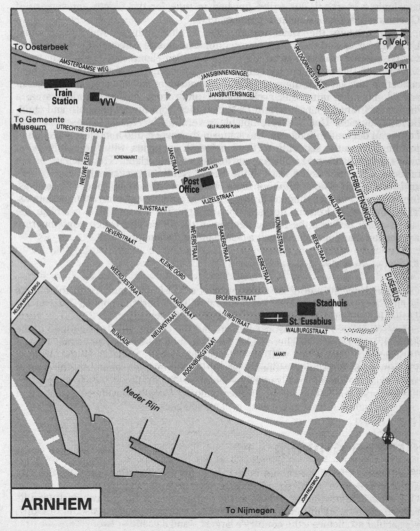

symbol and centre of people's remembrance of the battle, Dutch and British alike. Around its north end you can see the results of the devastation – wide boulevards intersect broad open spaces edged by haphazardly placed tower blocks and car parks. Overlooking this rather desolate spot, at the end of the characterless **Markt**, is the church of **St Eusabius** (mid-June to mid-Sept Tues–Sat noon–4.30pm; ƒ1.50, ƒ2.50 for the tower), with the dainty fifteenth-century **Stadhuis** tucked in behind. The church is a fifteenth- to sixteenth-century structure surmounted by a valiantly attempted but rather obvious replacement tower, which you can climb. Shrouded in scaffolding, the church is in the final stages of a complete overhaul, due to be finished in time for the fiftieth anniversary of Operation Market Garden in September 1994.

From outside the train station, it's a fifteen-minute walk west along Utrechtsestraat and then Utrechtseweg (or take bus #1 direction Oosterbeek) to the **Gemeentemuseum** at no. 87 (Tues–Sat 10am–5pm, Sun 11am–5pm; free), whose speciality is temporary exhibitions of modern Dutch art. The permanent collection, displayed in the main part of the museum and the annexe opposite at no. 74, includes numerous archeological finds from the surrounding area; a display of Chinese, Japanese and Delft ceramics from the seventeenth and eighteenth centuries; Dutch silver, notably several *guild beakers*, whose size and degree of decoration indicated the status of the owner; and a modest selection of paintings from the sixteenth to the nineteenth centuries, with the emphasis on views of the landscape, villages and towns of Gelderland. The nucleus of the modern art section is the work of the **Magic Realists**, particularly Carel Willink and Pyke Koch, whose *Vrouwen in de Straat* is a typically disconcerting canvas, the women's eyes looking out of the picture in a medley of contrasting emotions. The paintings of Renier Lucassen, for example *The Kiss* of 1976, establish the stylistic link between the Magic Realism of the 1930s and Dutch contemporary art, the familiar once again given a disturbing and alienating slant.

Eating and drinking

Cheap and decent **eating** isn't too much of a hassle in Arnhem and the streets around Korenmarkt are best for restaurants, including the popular *Pizzeria Da Leone*, Korenmarkt 1, the excellent *Nola Rae*, Marienburgstraat 2, with its vegetarian specialities (closed Mon), and, around the corner, the Turkish food of the *Mozaik*, Ruiterstraat 43. There's also Mexican food at *Amigo*, Pauwstraat 14, and Tunisian specialities (as well as the occasional belly dancer) at the *Medina*, Pauwstraat 6. Both are reasonably priced. As the evening wears on, the bars in and around Korenmarkt begin to heave with drinkers: *Le Grande Café*, Korenmarkt 16, is one of the livelier options; *Dingo's*, Boyenbeekstraat 28, a couple of minutes' walk to the east, is more laid-back.

Around Arnhem

Most people who visit Arnhem in fact do so for the attractions **outside the city** and certainly you could spend several days here visiting the wartime sites of Operation Market Garden, taking in the countryside of the Veluwe park (and its superb modern art museum), not to mention a huge open-air museum of Dutch vernacular archicture – the country's largest – and a castle or two.

AROUND ARNHEM

Two castles: Doorwerth and Rosendaal

For the most part the banks of the River Rhine near Arnhem are rather dull, though there's an appealing stretch to the west, where you'll find the massive, moated thirteenth-century **Kasteel Doorwerth** (Tues–Fri 10am–5pm, Sat & Sun 1–5pm; ƒ6), carefully reconstructed after war damage. To get there, take bus #6 from the Gemeentemuseum and ask to be dropped at the stop nearest the Kasteel – from where it's a thirty-minute walk along the river. There's an excellent and pricy **restaurant** there too, which for most people is more of an attraction than the collection of stuffed carcasses and old weapons at the **Nederlands Jachtmuseum** (Dutch Hunting Museum; April–Oct Tues–Fri 10am–5pm, Sat & Sun 1–5pm; Nov–March Tues–Sun 1–5pm; ƒ4.50) which occupies the castle.

On the opposite side of Arnhem, lying on the edge of the suburbs of Velp, there's another castle, the **Kasteel Rosendaal** (April–Oct Tue–Sat 10am–5pm,

OPERATION MARKET GARDEN

By September 1944 most of France and much of Belgium had been liberated from Nazi occupation. Fearing that an orthodox campaign would take many months and cost many lives, Field Marshal Montgomery decided that a pencil thrust north through Holland and subsequently east into the Ruhr, around the back of the Siegfried line, offered a good chance of ending the war early. To speed the advance of his land armies, Montgomery needed to cross several major rivers and canals in a corridor of territory stretching from Eindhoven, a few kilometres north of the front, to Arnhem. The plan, **Operation Market Garden**, was to parachute three airborne armies behind enemy lines, each responsible for taking and holding particular bridgeheads until the main army could force their way north to join them. On Sunday September 17, the 1st British Airborne Division parachuted into the fields around Oosterbeek, their prime objective to seize the bridges over the Rhine at Arnhem. Meanwhile, the 101st American Airborne Division was dropped in the area of Veghel to secure the Wilhelmina and Zuid-Willemsvaart canals, and the 82nd was dropped around Grave and Nijmegen, for the crossings over the Maas and the Waal.

All went fairly well with the American landings and, by the night of September 20, sections of the main British army, 30 Corps, had reached the American bridgehead across the River Waal at Nijmegen. However, despite Polish reinforcements, the landings around Arnhem had run into problems. Allied Command had estimated that immediate opposition was unlikely to exceed a force of some three thousand men, but as luck would have it, the entire 2nd SS Panzer Corps was refitting near Arnhem just when the 1st Division landed. Taking the enemy by surprise, 2nd Parachute Battalion, under Lieutenant-Colonel John Frost, did manage to capture the north end of the road bridge across the Rhine, but it proved impossible either to reinforce them or capture the southern end. Surrounded, out-gunned and out-manned, the 2nd Battalion held their position from the 17th to the morning of the 21st, far longer than anybody could have anticipated, a story of extraordinary heroism. There were more heroics elsewhere, for the Polish and British battalions of the rest of the Division had concentrated around the bridgehead at Oosterbeek, which they held at tremendous cost under the command of General Urquhart. Elements of 30 Corps made desperate efforts to join up with them, but by the morning of the 25th it was clear that it was not going to be possible to provide reinforcements in sufficient numbers. Under cover of darkness, a dramatic withdrawal saved 2163 soldiers from an original force of 10,005.

Sun 1–5pm; *f*6; bus #4 direction Velp Zuid) – an attractive mixture of medieval and eighteenth-century architecture, set in its own parkland. Not far away, on the west side of Velp, the **Museum Bronbeek**, Velperweg 147 (daily 9am–5pm; *f*2.50; bus #1 direction Velp), occupies a building gifted to ex-soldiers by William III in 1859. The collection has all sorts of curious relics left over from the Dutch occupation of Surinam and Indonesia.

World War II memorials: Oosterbeek

The area around Arnhem is scattered with the graveyards of thousands of soldiers who died during **Operation Market Garden**. If you're a devotee of battle grounds and battle plans, Arnhem VVV sells specialist books on the campaign and provides details of organized tours. Otherwise, the easiest way to

get some idea of the conflict and its effect on this part of Holland is to visit
OOSTERBEEK, once a small village and now a prosperous suburb of Arnhem (4
trains hourly; 4min).

Following the signs from beside Oosterbeek train station, it's a five-minute
walk east to the **Airborne Cemetery**, a neat, symmetrical tribute to several
hundred paratroopers whose bodies were brought here from the surrounding
fields. It's a quiet, secluded spot; the personal inscriptions on the gravestones are
especially poignant. Ten minutes' walk (or bus #1) south of the station down
Stationsweg, the village proper has spruced lawns and walls dotted with details of
the battle – who held out where and for how long – as the Allied forces were
pinned back within a tighter and tighter perimeter.

The **Airborne Museum** (Mon–Sat 11am–5pm, Sun noon–5pm; ƒ4) is just to
the west of the village centre along Utrechtseweg, reachable direct from Arnhem
on bus #1, housed in the former *Hotel Hartenstein*, where the British forces were
besieged by the Germans for a week before retreating across the river, their
numbers depleted from 10,005 to 2163. With the use of an English commentary,
photographs, dioramas and original military artefacts – from rifles and light artillery to uniforms and personal memorabilia – the museum gives an excellent
outline of the battle and, to a lesser extent, aspects of World War II as it affected
Holland as a whole. The Army Film and Photographic Unit landed with the
British forces, and, perhaps more than anything else, it's their photographs that
stick in the memory – grimly cheerful soldiers hauling in their parachutes, tense
tired faces during the fighting, shattered Dutch villages.

The Nederlands Openluchtmuseum

Immediately north of Arnhem, the **Nederlands Openluchtmuseum** (April–Oct
Mon–Fri 9am–5pm, Sat & Sun 10am–5pm; ƒ10, children ƒ6), reachable by bus #3,
direction Alteveer (every 20min), or direct by special bus #13 (July & Aug only;
every 20min), is a huge collection of Dutch buildings open to public view. One of
the first of its type, the museum was founded in 1912 to try to "present a picture
of the daily life of ordinary people in this country as it was in the past and has
developed in the course of time". Over the years, original and representative
buildings have been taken from all over the country and assembled here in a
large chunk of the Veluwe forest. Where possible, buildings have been placed in
groups that resemble the traditional villages of the different regions of Holland –
from the farmsteads of Friesland to the farming communities of South Holland
and the peat colonies of Drenthe. There are about 120 buildings in all, including
examples of every type of Dutch windmill, most sorts of farmhouse, a variety of
bridges and several working craftshops, demonstrating the traditional skills of
papermaking, milling, baking, brewing and bleaching. Other parts of the museum
incorporate one of the most extensive regional costume exhibitions in the country and a comparatively modest herb garden.

All in all, it's an imaginative attempt to recreate the rural Dutch way of life over
the past two centuries and the museum's own guidebook explains everything
with academic attention to detail – at ƒ10 certainly worth every cent. It recom-
mends three marked routes – red (1hr), green (2hr) and blue (4hr); the green
route, with selected forays into other sections, is perhaps a reasonable
compromise.

The Hoge Veluwe National Park and Rijksmuseum Kröller-Müller

Spreading north from the Open-Air Museum is the **Hoge Veluwe National Park**, an area of sandy heath and thick woodland that was once the private estate of Anton and Helene Kröller-Müller. Born near Essen in 1869, Helene Müller came from a wealthy and influential family whose money was made in the blast-furnace business. She married Anton Kröller of Rotterdam, whose brother ran the Dutch side of their trading interests and the couple's fortunes were secured when the death of her father and his brother's poor health placed Anton at the head of the company at the age of 27. Apart from extending their business empire and supporting the Boers in South Africa, they had a passionate desire to leave a grand bequest to the nation, a mixture of nature and culture which would, she felt, "be an important lesson when showing the inherent refinement of a merchant's family living at the beginning of the century". She collected the art, he the land and in the 1930s ownership of both was transferred to the nation on the condition that a museum was built in the park. The museum opened in 1938 and Helene acted as manager until her death in 1939. Today, the park is one of Gelderland's most popular day-trip destinations, although it's large enough to absorb the crowds quite comfortably on all but the sunniest of summer weekends.

Around the park

The Hoge Veluwe Park has three entrances – one near the village of Otterlo on the northwest perimeter, another near Hoenderloo on the northeast edge and a third to the south at Rijzenburg, near the village of Schaarsbergen, only 10km from Arnhem. The park is open daily (8am–sunset; ƒ6.50), though in September and early October certain areas are off-limits during the rutting season. The entry fee includes the museum, but cars are charged ƒ6 extra.

There are a number of ways to get to the park by **bus**; easiest is to take the museum special from outside Arnhem train station (June–Sept daily except Mon, bus #12 direction Hoge Veluwe; hourly; ƒ6.25 for a return plus ƒ6.50 entry ticket: pay the driver) to the **Bezoekers Centrum** (April–Oct daily 9.30am–5pm; Nov–March Sun 10am–4pm only), in the middle of the park not far from the museum. The centre has information on the park and is the place to pick up one of the white bicycles that are left out for everyone's use at no extra charge – definitely the best way of getting around once you're here, though you should return them to the same place when you've finished. When the bus isn't running, you can either rent a bike at Arnhem train station or take bus #107 (direction Lelystad; hourly; 25min) to the entrance at Otterlo. From here it's a four-kilometre walk east to the visitors' centre, unless you're lucky enough to find a museum bike by the entrance.

Once mobile you can cycle around as you wish, along clearly marked tracks and through stretches of dune and woodland where it's possible to catch sight of some of the park's big game – principally red deer, roe and moufflon (Corsican sheep). By comparison, the park's wild boar keep to themselves. Apart from the Kröller-Müller Museum (see opposite), the only thing to see is the **Jachtslot St Hubertus** (May–Oct Mon–Fri 10–11.30am & 2–4.30pm), some 3km north of the visitors' centre, a hunting lodge and country home built for the Kröller-Müllers by the modernist Dutch architect, H.P. Berlage, in 1920. Dedicated to the patron saint of hunters, it's an impressive Art Deco monument, with lots of plays on the hunting theme. The floor plan – in the shape of branching antlers – is representative of the stag bearing a crucifix that appeared to Saint Hubert, the adopted patron of hunters, while he was hunting and each room of the sumptuous interior symbolizes an episode in the saint's life – all in all a somewhat unusual commission for a committed socialist who wrote so caustically about the *haute bourgeoisie*.

The Rijksmuseum Kröller-Müller

Most people who visit the Hoge Veluwe Park come for the **Rijksmuseum Kröller-Müller** (all year round Tues–Sat 10am–5pm; April–Oct also Sun 11am–5pm; Nov–March 1–5pm), made up of the private art collection of the Kröller-Müllers. It's one of the country's finest museums, a wide cross-section of modern European art from Impressionism to Cubism and beyond, housed in a low-slung building that was built for the collection in 1938 by the Belgian architect Van de Velde. Entry is included in the price of admission to the park (see opposite).

The bulk of the collection is in one long wing, starting with the most recent Dutch painters and working backward. There's a good set of paintings, in particular some revealing *Self-portraits* by Charley Toorop, one of the most skilled and sensitive of twentieth-century Dutch artists. Her father Jan also gets a good showing throughout the museum, from his pointillist studies to later, turn-of-the-century works more reminiscent of Aubrey Beardsley and the Art Nouveau movement. Piet Mondriaan is well represented too, his 1909 *Beach near Domburg* a good example of his more stylized approach to landscape painting, a development from his earlier sombre-coloured scenes in the Dutch tradition. In 1909 he moved to Paris and his contact with Cubism transformed his work, as illustrated by his *Composition* of 1917 – simple flat rectangles of colour with the elimination of the object complete, the epitome of the De Stijl approach. Much admired by Mondriaan and one of the most influential of the Cubists, Fernand Léger's *Soldiers Playing Cards* is typical of his bold, clear lines and tendency toward the monumental. One surprise is an early Picasso, *Portrait of a Woman*, from 1901, a classic post-Impressionist canvas very dissimilar from his more famous works.

The building as a whole gravitates toward the works of **Vincent Van Gogh**, with one of the most complete collections of his work in the world, housed in a large room around a central courtyard and placed in context by accompanying contemporary pictures. The museum owns no fewer than 278 examples of his work and doesn't have the space to show them all at any one time; consequently exhibits are rotated, with the exception of his most important paintings. Of earlier canvases, *The Potato Eaters* and *Head of a Peasant with a Pipe* are outstanding; rough, unsentimental paintings of labourers from around his parents' home in Brabant. From February 1886 till early 1888 Van Gogh lived in Paris, where he came into contact with the Impressionists whose work – and arguments – convinced him of the importance of colour. His penetrating *Self-portrait* is a superb example of his work of this period, the eyes fixed on the observer, the head and background a swirl of grainy colour and streaky brush-strokes. One of his most famous paintings, *Sunflowers*, dates from this period also, an extraordinary work of alternately thick and thin paintwork of dazzling, sharp detail and careful colour.

The move to Arles in 1888 spurred Van Gogh to a frenzy of activity, inspired by the colours and light of the Mediterranean. The joyful *Haystacks in Provence* and *Bridge at Arles*, with its rickety bridge and disturbed circles of water spreading from the washerwomen on the river bank, are from these months, one of the high points of his troubled life. It was short-lived. The novelty of the south wore off, Gauguin's visit was a disaster and Van Gogh's desperate sense of loneliness intensified. At the end of the year he had his first attack of madness – and committed his famous act of self-mutilation. In and out of mental hospital till his suicide in July of the following year, his *Prisoners Exercising* of 1890 is a powerful, sombre painting full of sadness and despair: heads bent, the prisoners walk around in a pointless circle as the walls around them seem to close in.

Finally, outside the museum, behind the main building, there's a **Sculpture Park** (April–Oct Tues–Sun 10am–4.30pm), spaciously laid out with works by Auguste Rodin, Alberto Giacometti, Jacob Epstein and Barbara Hepworth, all appearing at manageable intervals. Noteable is Jean Debuffet's *Jardin d'email*, one of his larger and more elaborate jokes.

Nijmegen

One of the oldest towns in Holland, **NIJMEGEN**, some 20km south of Arnhem, was built on the site of the Roman frontier fortress of *Novio Magus*, from which it derives its name. Situated on the southern bank of the Waal, just to the west of its junction with the Rhine, the town's location has long been strategically important. The Romans used Nijmegen as a buffer against the unruly tribes to the east; Charlemagne, Holy Roman Emperor from 800 to 814, made the town one of the principal seats of his administration, building the Valkhof Palace, an enormous complex of chapels and secular buildings completed in the eighth century. Rebuilt in 1155 by another emperor, Frederick Barbarossa, the complex dominated Nijmegen right up until 1769, when the palace was demolished and the stonework sold; what was left suffered further demolition when the French occupied the town in 1796. More recently, in September 1944, the town's bridges were a key objective of Operation Market Garden (see "Arnhem" p.221) and although they were captured by the Americans, the disaster at Arnhem put the town on the front line for the rest of the war. The results are clear to see: the old town was largely destroyed and has been replaced by a centre reconstructed to a new plan.

The Town

The town centre is **Grote Markt**, a good fifteen-minute walk from the train station, or five minutes by any bus from immediately outside. Much of the Grote Markt survived the shelling and is surprisingly well preserved, in stark contrast to the modern shopping streets across the road. The **Waag**, with its traditional stepped gables and shuttered windows, stands beside a vaulted passage, the **Kerkboog**, which leads through to the peaceful precincts of the much-renovated Gothic **Grote Kerk of St Stephen**. The church is entered around the back to the left, past the attractively carved facade of the old **Latin School** and inside there's some fine Renaissance woodwork. The **tower**, with its vaguely oriental spire, offers a commanding vista over the surrounding countryside (mid-May to mid-June & mid-Aug to Sept Mon–Fri 10am–12.30pm & 1–5pm, Sat 10am–1pm; mid-June to mid-Aug Mon–Fri 10am–5pm, Sat 10am–1pm, Sun 2–5pm; church *f*2, tower *f*1.50). The view over the streets beside and behind the church isn't what it used to be – the huddle of medieval houses that sloped down to the Waal was almost totally destroyed during the war and has been replaced by a hopeful but rather sterile residential imitation.

To Arnhem, Utrecht & Rotterdam

Belvedere

Palace chapel

Chapel

Valkhof Palace

VVV

To Rijksmuseum Kam

SINT JORISSTRAAT

DERGE WALSTRAAT

GERARD NOODTSTRAAT

CANISIUSSINGEL

BERG EN DALSEWEG

KETKENSBOS

HERTOGSTRAAT

DAALSEWEG

BURCHTSTRAAT

MARIENBURGSTRAAT

GROTE STRAAT

Commanderie van St. Jan Museum

Stadhuis

V. BROECKHYSENSTRAAT

ORANJESINGEL

Post Office

Waag

BROERSTRAAT

GROTE MARKT

STIKKE HEZELSTRAAT

BROERSTRAAT PROMENADE

ZIEKERSTRAAT

V. SCHEVIC HAVENSTR.

PRINS BERNHARDSTR.

Kerkboog

Grote Kerk

Latin School

AUGUSTIJNENSTR.

Commanderie van St. Jan Museum

PLEIN 1944

V. WELDERENSTRAAT

HOUTSTRAAT

MOLENSTRAAT

LANGE HEZELSTRAAT

DODDENDAAL

BLOEMERSTRAAT

To Camping de Kwakkenberg

WALSTRAAT

Kronenburger Park

ID BETOUWSTR.

KRONENBURGERSINGEL

KEIZER KAREL PLEIN

SINT ANNA STRAAT

GRAAFSEWEG

GROESBEEKSEWEG

0   200 m

TUNNELWEG

STATIONSPLEIN

NIJMEGEN

Train Station

A few metres away, down toward the river, the **Commanderie van St Jan** is more authentic looking, a reconstruction of a seventeenth-century building that now houses the **Municipal Museum** (Mon–Sat 10am–5pm, Sun 1–5pm; free). Here you'll find a variety of exhibits with a local flavour, including innumerable paintings of Nijmegen and its environs – none particularly distinguished except for Jan van Goyen's *Valkhof Nijmegen*, which used to hang in the town hall. Painted in 1641, it's a large, sombre-toned picture – pastel variations on green and brown – where the Valkhof shimmers above the Waal, almost engulfed by sky and river.

Returning to the Grote Markt, Burchtstraat heads east roughly parallel to the river, past the dull reddish-brown brick of the **Stadhuis**, a square, rather severe edifice with an onion-domed tower, another reconstruction after extensive war damage. A couple of minutes away, in a park beside the east end of Burchtstraat, lie the scanty remains of the **Valkhof Palace** – a ruined fragment of the Romanesque choir of the twelfth-century palace chapel and, just to the west, a sixteen-sided chapel built around 1045, in a similar style to the palatinate church at Charlemagne's capital, Aachen. The smaller chapel (May–Oct Mon–Sat 1–5pm, Sun 2–5pm) is complete, though the atmosphere is somewhat marred by the crowds and piped choral music. These bits and pieces are connected by a footbridge to a **belvedere**, which was originally a seventeenth-century tower built into the city walls; today it's a restaurant and a lookout platform with excellent views over the river.

Some fifteen minutes' walk southeast of the town centre, the **Provinciaal Museum G.M. Kam**, Museum Kamstraat 45 (Tues–Sat 10am–5pm, Sun 1–5pm; *f*3), is the best of Nijmegen's many other museums. Devoted mainly to the history of Roman Nijmegen and founded by the eminent archeologist G.M. Kam, who died in 1922, the museum features his collection alongside other artefacts that have been added more recently; together they form a comprehensive picture of the first Roman settlements. To get there walk east along Burchtstraat and onto Kelfkensbos, which brings you to the island beside the VVV. Heading south off the island, down Mr. Franckenstraat, you reach Mariaplein, where you turn left down Berg en Dalseweg; Museum Kamstraat is the third on the left.

More bizarre, southeast of Nijmegen on the road to Groesbeek, the **Biblical Open-Air Museum**, Profetenlaan 2 (*Heilig Land Stichting*; Easter–Oct daily 9am–5.30pm; *f*8), is accessible by bus #84 (destination Groesbeek; every 30min, 15min), from beside the train station. Ask the driver to indicate your stop on Nijmeegsebaan, from where it's a five-minute walk northeast along Meerwijkselaan to the museum. Here you'll find a series of reconstructions of the ancient Holy Land, including a Galilean fishing village, a complete Palestinian hamlet, a town street lined with Egyptian, Greek, Roman and Jewish houses and, strangely enough, "Bedouin tents of goats' hair as inhabited by the patriarchs". An experience not on any account to be missed.

There's another unusual museum 2km east of here, along Meerwijkselaan – the **Afrika Museum** at Postweg 6, Berg en Dal (April–Oct Mon–Fri 10am–5pm, Sat & Sun 11am–5pm; Nov–March Tues–Fri 10am–5pm, Sat & Sun 1–5pm; *f*5), where there's a purpose-built West African village, a small animal park and a museum full of totems, carved figurines and musical instruments. You can get here on bus #5, which runs every twenty minutes to Berg en Dal, though from the bus stop it's still a twenty-minute walk to the museum.

Practicalities

Nijmegen's **train** and **bus stations** are a good fifteen-minute trudge west of the town centre and the VVV at St Jorisstraat 72 (Mon–Fri 9am–6pm, Sat 10am–4pm; June–Aug also Sun 10am–2pm; ☎080/22 54 40). If you don't like the idea of a walk, take any bus into the centre.

Cheap **accommodation** is pretty thin on the ground in Nijmegen; it's easiest to let the VVV make a booking by phone. Alternatively, there are two **pensions** not far southeast of the train station – the *Catharina*, St Annastraat 64 (☎080/23 12 51; ③) and *Mrs Fortuin's*, Groesbeekseweg 9 (☎080/22 42 98; ③). To reach them head east along one of the southern pair of roads from the station to the Keizer Karelplein; from here St Annastraat is the road heading southeast, with Groesbeekseweg the first turn on the left. The cheaper **hotels** are no more expensive and tend to be more convenient: the *Apollo* is on the street running east off Keizer Karelplein, at Bisschop Hamerstraat 14 (☎080/22 35 94; ③); and the rather seedy *Europa Hotel* (☎080/22 66 45; ③) is between the train station and Grote Markt at Bloemerstraat 65. If you're stuck, the *Atlanta*, right in the centre at Grote Markt 38 (☎080/60 30 00; ④), isn't as pricy as you might imagine, although it can be rather noisy. The nearest **campsite** is *De Kwakkenberg*, Luciaweg 10 (April–Sept), a few kilometres south of town, reachable from the station by bus #5, direction Berg en Dal, every twenty minutes. Ask the driver to drop you off at your stop, which will be on the main road, Kwakkenbergweg; Luciaweg runs roughly parallel, a block to the south.

There are plenty of places to **eat**. *Les Entrees*, Kelfkenbos 30 and *Het Poortwachtershuys*, at Kelfkenbos 57, are two good places, though neither is especially cheap. *Roberto*, Smetiusstraat 7, is a good Italian restaurant. Otherwise, there are several pleasant cafés and bars around the Grote Markt, including *In de Boterwaag*, no. 26, with main courses for around *f*18.

Every inch a fashionable town, Nijmegen attracts some top-name rock **bands**, especially during the academic year. Most perform at the municipal concert hall, the *Stadsschouwburg*, at Van Schaeck Mathonsingel 2, close to the train station; for latest details see the VVV. For **films**, the *Filmcafé*, Hertogstraat 71 (☎080/22 19 05) and the *Filmcentrum*, Marienburg 59 (☎080/22 16 12), have good international programmes and some late-night shows. Between June and August, there are a variety of **boat trips** on the Waal. Prices vary according to the itinerary, but excursions range from an hour's river tour to sailings all the way to Rotterdam (once weekly; *f*52).

travel details

Trains

Apeldoorn to: Amersfoort (every 30min; 25min); Deventer (every 30min; 10min); Zutphen (every 30min; 15min).

Arnhem to: Amsterdam (every 30min; 1hr 10min); Cologne (14 daily; 1hr 50min); Nijmegen (every 30min; 20min); Roosendaal (every 30min; 1hr 45min).

Zutphen to: Arnhem (every 15min; 30min).

Zwolle to: Amersfoort (every 15min; 35–50min); Amsterdam CS (every 30min; 1hr 15min); Arnhem (every 30min; 1hr); Deventer (every 30min; 25min); Emmen (2 hourly; 50min–1hr 10min); Groningen (2 hourly; 1hr 5min); Kampen (2 hourly; 10 min); Leeuwarden (every 30min; 55min); Meppel (every 30min; 15min); Nijmegen (2 hourly;

65–75min); Schiphol (every 30min; 1hr 40min); Steenwijk (2 hourly; 15min); Zutphen (2 hourly; 25–35min).

Buses

Enschede to: Oldenzaal (every 30min; 20min).

Kampen to: Lelystad (*VAD* bus #143 every 30min; 55min); Urk (2 hourly; 60min).

Lelystad to: Enkhuizen (*VAD* bus #150 every 30min; 35min).

Steenwijk to: Giethoorn (*NWH* bus #72 Mon–Sat hourly, Sun 5 daily; 15-30min).

Zwolle to: Elburg (*VAD* bus #101 every 30min; 25min); Urk (*VAD* bus #141; 1hr 20min).

Ferries

Urk to: Enkhuizen (May, June & Sept 2 daily, July & Aug 3 daily; 1hr 30min).

CHAPTER SIX

THE SOUTH

Three widely disparate provinces make up Holland's south: Zeeland, North Brabant and Limburg. **Zeeland** is a scattering of villages and towns whose wealth, survival and sometimes destruction have long depended on the vagaries of the sea. Secured only in 1986, when the dykes and sea walls of the Delta Project were finally completed, once and for all stopping the chance of flooding, at their best – for example in the small wool town of **Veere** or the regional market centre of **Middelburg** – they seem held in suspended animation from a richer past.

As you head across the arc of towns of **North Brabant** the landscape slowly fills out, rolling into a rougher countryside of farmland and forests, unlike the precise rectangles of neighbouring provinces. Though the change is subtle, there's a difference in the people here, too – less formal, less Dutch, and for the most part Catholic, a fact manifest in the magnificent churches of **Breda** and **'s Hertogenbosch**. But it's in solidly Catholic Limburg that a difference in character is really felt.

Continental rather than Dutch, **Limburg** has only been part of Holland since the 1830s, but way before then the presence of Charlemagne's court at Aachen deeply influenced the identity of the region. As Frankish emperor, Charlemagne had a profound effect on early medieval Europe, revitalizing Roman traditions and looking to the south for inspiration in art and architecture. Some of these great buildings remain, like **Maastricht's** St Servaas and most have a wealth of devotional art that comes as a welcome change after the north. What's more, the landscape steepens sharply and you're within sight of Holland's first and only hills.

ZEELAND

Formed by the delta of three great rivers, the Rijn, the Schelde and the Maas, **Zeeland** comprises three main peninsulas, each consisting of a cluster of islands and semi-islands, linked by dykes, which as well as providing protection from flooding, also form the main lines of communication between each chunk of land. The northernmost landmass, Goeree-Overflakkee, is linked by two dams to Schouwen-Duiveland; the southern cluster is known as Noord and Zuid Beveland, with its western tip, traversed by a narrow canal, known as Walcheren.

Before the Delta Project (see p.243) secured the area, silting up and fear of the sea had prevented any large towns developing and Zeeland remains a condensed area of low dunes and nature reserves, popular with holidaymakers escaping the cramped conurbations nearby. Zeeland also has more sun than anywhere else in Holland: the winds blow the clouds away. Getting around isn't a problem, with bus services making up for the lack of north–south train connections, though undoubtedly the best way to see these islands is to **cycle**, using **Middelburg** as a base and radiating out to the surrounding smaller towns.

ACCOMMODATION PRICE CODES

All the **hotels and hostels** detailed in this chapter have been graded according to the following price categories. Note that the prices have been calculated as those for the cheapest double room during high season. For more on accommodation, see p.29.

① Up to ƒ30 per person.	④ ƒ100–140.	⑦ ƒ220–260.
② ƒ30–65.	⑤ ƒ140–180.	⑧ ƒ260 and over.
③ ƒ65–100.	⑥ ƒ180–220.	

Vlissingen (Flushing)

VLISSINGEN is an important ferry terminus, linked to Sheerness in England by twice-daily ferries. The best thing to do on arrival at the bleak ferry port is leave; a bus takes you to the **train station**, from where there are hourly departures to Amsterdam and intermediate stations. There's also a **ferry service**, leaving from outside the train station, to **BRESKENS** on the southern side of the Westerschelde estuary (Mon–Sat 4.50am–11.10pm every 30min, Sun 6.20am–11.10pm hourly, every 30min in July & Aug), from where buses go on to Bruges.

Perhaps significantly, there are no buses from the ferry dock to the centre of town, although bus #56 plies between the train station and the centre. Here you'll find the unremarkable **St Jacobskerk** on Kleine Markt (July & Aug Mon–Sat 10am–noon; ƒ1), the improbably named **Cornelia Quackhofje**, an eighteenth-century almshouse for sailors just north of the Lange Zelke shopping precinct and a **Stedelijk Museum** at Bellamypark 19 (Mon–Fri 10am–5pm, Sat & Sun 1–5pm; ƒ2.50), whose collection includes a room devoted to local naval hero Michiel de Ruyter. Alternatively and rather more fun, you could head for **The Arsenal** (April–Sept daily 11am–8pm; Oct–March Tues–Sun 11am–6pm; ƒ15, children under 12 ƒ10; ✆01184/11472), a new, expensive maritime theme park where you can go on a simulated sea voyage, climb an observation tower and walk on a mocked-up seabed among tanks of sharks. Should you need to stay, the **VVV** at Nieuwendijk 15 (Sept–June Mon–Fri 9am–5pm, Sat 9am–1pm; July & Aug Mon–Sat 9am–6pm, Sun 1–5pm; ✆01184/12345) has a list of **pensions** including the nearby *Pension El Porto*, Nicuwendijk 5 (✆01184/12807; ③).

Middelburg

MIDDELBURG is the largest town in Zeeland and by any reckoning the most likeable. While not crammed with things to see, its streets preserve some snapshots of medieval Holland and a few museums and churches provide targets for your wanderings. Rimmed with the standard shopping precinct, its centre holds a large Thursday market, and, if you can only make it for a day, this is the best time to visit, with local women still wearing traditional costume – to picturesque effect. However Middelburg is best used as a base for exploring the surrounding area, with good regional bus connections and plentiful accommodation.

The telephone code for Middelburg is ✆01180

Arrival, information and accommodation

The **train station** is just a short walk from the centre of town: head straight out across the bridge onto Segeersstraat and Lange Delft and you find yourself on the Markt, where the **VVV** office at Markt 65a (Sept–June Mon–Fri 9am–5pm, Sat 9am–2pm; July & Aug Mon–Sat 9am–6pm; ☎16851) has details of summer events in the city and a list of **private rooms**. Most of Middelburg's **hotels and pensions** are only minutes away from the Markt: the friendly *Wapen van Middelburg* hotel, Pottenmarkt 12–20 (☎14706; ③), is the most central, across the street from the VVV, while other pension options include *De Geere*, Langeviele 51 (☎13083; ②), a particularly good deal as the price includes breakfast; *Huize Orliëns*, Nieuwstraat 23 (☎27529; ③); and *Bij de Abdij*, Bogardstraat 14–16 (☎27135; ③). The nearest **campsite**, *Camping Middelburg*, Koninginnelaan 55 (April–Oct), is about 2km out of town. Head down Zandstraat and Langeviele Weg, south and east of the Koveniersdoelen, or take bus #57 (every 30min) from the station.

The Town

Middelburg owed its early growth to the comparative safety of its situation in the centre of Walcheren. The slight elevation gave the settlement protection from the sea and its position on a bend in the River Arne made it reasonably easy to defend. Though its abbey was founded in 1120, the town's isolation meant that it did not start to develop until the late Middle Ages, when, being at the western end of the Scheldt estuary, it began to get rich off the back of Antwerp, Bruges and Ghent. Conducting its own trade in wool and cloth, it became both the market and administrative centre of the region and some of the town's street names – Houtkaai (Timber Dock), Londense Kaai (London Dock), Korendijk (Grain Dyke) and Bierkaai (Beer Dock) – reveal how various its trade became. Most of Middelburg's most interesting buildings come from this period, though the town's **Stadhuis**, generally agreed to be Zeeland's finest, is a wonderfully eclectic mix of architectural styles. The towering Gothic facade is especially magnificent, dating from the mid-fifteenth century and designed by the Keldermans family from Mechelen. Ranged in niches across the front are 25 statues of the counts and countesses of Holland, starting with Charles V and ending with queens Wilhelmina and Juliana placed above the **Vleeshal**, a former meat hall that now houses changing exhibitions of contemporary art which can be visited on conducted tours. If you're further interested, there are also hour-long tours of the Stadhuis (April–June & Sept–Oct Mon–Fri 10.30am, 11.15am & 1.30–4pm; July & Aug 11am–4pm; check noticeboard for exact times; *f*3) which take in the mayor's office, council chambers and various reception rooms.

The Stadhuis' impressive pinnacled tower was added in 1520, but it's as well to remember that this, along with the Stadhuis itself and much of Middelburg's city centre, is only a reconstruction of the original. On May 17, 1940 the city was practically flattened by German bombing in the same series of raids that destroyed Rotterdam. In 1944, in an attempt to isolate German artillery in Vlissingen, Walcheren's sea defences were breached, which resulted in severe flood damage to Middelburg's already treacherous streets.

Restoration was a long and difficult process, but so successful that you can only occasionally tell that the city's buildings have been patched up. Middelburg's most distinctive tower, that of the **Abdijkerken (Abbey Churches)** on Onderdentoren, collapsed under German bombing, destroying the churches below. Today the abbey complex – really three churches in one – is pretty bare inside, considering that it's been around since the twelfth century. There's a reason for this: Middelburg was an early convert to Protestantism following the uprising against the Spanish and in 1574 William the Silent's troops threw out the Premonstratensian monks and converted the abbey to secular use. The abbey's three churches (May–Nov Mon 10am–noon & 1–5pm; Tues–Fri 10am–5pm; free) were adapted to Protestant worship and most of what can be seen inside dates from the seventeenth century. The **Nieuwe Kerk** has an organ case of 1692 and the **Wandel Kerk** the outrageously triumphalistic tomb of admirals Jan and Cornelis Evertsen, brothers killed fighting in a naval battle against the English in 1666. The **Koor Kerk**, on the eastern side of the tower, retains the oldest decoration, including a Nicolai organ of 1478. Best fun of all is to climb the 207 steps of the tower (April–Oct Mon–Sat 10am–5pm; ƒ2.25), known locally as *Lange Jan* (Long John). As long as the weather is clear, there's a tremendous view from its 91-metre summit across Middelburg and over Walcheren as far as the Zeelandbrug and the eastern Scheldt, giving a good idea of how vulnerable Zeeland is to the sea and estuaries.

At the rear of the abbey, housed in what were once the monks' dormitories, the **Zeeuws Museum** (Zeeland Museum; Tues–Fri 10am–5pm, Sat & Sun 1.30–5pm; April–Oct also open Mon 10am–5pm; ƒ4) holds a mixed bag of collections and finds from the Zeeland area. The museum opens with a tiny but choice collection of twentieth-century painting by Mesdag, Jan and Charley Toorop and other (local) artists. Downstairs, there's a well-documented assembly of Roman and medieval artefacts, including Nehallenia altar stones. Like those in Leiden's Van Oudheden Museum (see *South Holland and Utrecht*), these seem to have been votive offerings, given by sailors in Roman times in thanks for safe passage across the English Channel. Little more is known about the goddess Nehallenia, though it's possible she was also a goddess of flowers, akin to Flora. Elsewhere in the museum are lively tapestries, a cabinet of curiosities and a comprehensive display of local costumes.

East of the abbey, **Damplein** was recently restored to its original breadth by the demolition of a couple of rows of houses. It forms a quieter focus for bars than the Markt and is the site of the **Graanbeurs**, a grain exchange rebuilt in the nineteenth century and today containing some intriguing (and humorous) stone plaques by international artists – a project known as "Podio del Mondo per l'Arte" – as well as the **François Ryckhals Museum**, Dam 71 (April–Oct & Dec Thurs–Sat 1–5pm; ƒ2). The latter is the birthplace of an unmemorable local artist and tells his life story through an exhibit of his paintings.

To the western side of the square, the **Blauwpoort** (also known as the **Gistpoort** or Yeast Gate) forms a decorative entrance to the abbey complex. Built at the beginning of the sixteenth century from blue limestone, it was virtually destroyed in the last war and what you see today is an indifferent renovation.

Directly north of Damplein on Molenwater, **Miniature Walcheren** (April–June & Sept–Oct daily 9.30am–5pm; July & Aug daily 9.30am–8.30pm; ƒ7, children ƒ3.50) has scaled-down models of Walcheren island's best buildings. It's about as enjoyable as you'd imagine, but might entertain kids for an hour or so.

Further east, the distinctive profile of the domed, octagonal **Oostkerk** (July–Aug Thurs 10am–4pm; free) stands high above the surrounding suburbs, near the main road to Veere: built in 1647 to designs by Pieter Post and others, it was one of the first churches in Holland to be built expressly for Protestant use.

While the streets around the Abdijkerken and Stadhuis are the most atmospheric, it's worth walking to the western edge of town to reach the landmark of the **Kloveniersdoelen** at the end of Langeviele. Built in 1607 in exuberant Flemish Renaissance style, this was the home of the city's civic guard, the Arquebusiers, until the end of the eighteenth century later becoming the local headquarters of the East India Company, later still a military hospital. Restored in 1969 (as you might have guessed if you had spotted the weather vane), it's now a recital hall for concerts and is particularly renowned for presenting new and experimental music (there's a festival every year in July; call ☎23650 for details). A short walk north or south of the Kloveniersdoelen, by the edge of Middelburg's old encircling defensive canal, are a couple of eighteenth-century **windmills**: *De Hoop* mill to the south was once a barley peeling mill; *De Seismolen* to the north a cereal mill, though it's not possible to enter either today.

Finally there are two further **minor museums** that might capture your attention if you have an hour or two to spare. The **Ramschip de Schorpioen**, moored off Loskade, opposite the train station (April–Oct daily 10am–5pm; *f*3.50), is one of only three remaining iron ramming ships left in the world, built in France in 1867 and nowadays serves as a floating maritime museum – worth a scramble around if only for the ornate, if cramped, interior. The **Roosevelt Study Centre**, Abdij 9 (Mon–Fri 10am–12.30pm & 1.30–4.30pm), is a centre for the study of twentieth-century American history (one of the largest in Europe) and has a permanent exhibition on presidents Theodore and Franklin Delano Roosevelt and the latter's remarkable wife Eleanor.

Eating and drinking

Vlasmarkt, running northwest of Markt, has Middelburg's best selection of **restaurants**. *La Piccola Italia* at no. 19 offers cheap pizzas; the café-bar *De Lachende Vis* at no. 20 has average-priced *dagschotels* and a good selection of beers – though it closes at 9.30pm. Best of all, *De Mug*, Vlasmarkt 56, has mouthwatering Dutch–French cooking at moderate prices. To tempt you further, there's live jazz here every last Tuesday of the month. If your budget is tight, there are also a couple of excellent shoarma joints around here: *Grill-Room Ramses*, at 45 St Janstraat and *Grillroom Cleopatra* at Vlasmarkt 2. Most other restaurants are situated on or around Markt and many are tourist-geared and pricy for what you get: *De Ploeg*, Markt 55, offers best value. Elsewhere in town, *Surabaya*, Stationstraat 20, is an Indonesian restaurant with reasonably priced *rijsttafels* and *De Kabouterhut*, Oostkerkplein 7–8, a passable creperie. On Thursday and Saturday the market stands supply limitless cheap and tasty snacks, especially fresh fishy things.

Bars and cafés are also concentrated on or around the Markt. *De Herberg*, Pottenmarkt 2a, is the best of a group of places with outdoor seating and the *Café American* on the corner of Plein 1940 is the chosen drinking spot of the town's long-haired stonewashed set and has live (usually hard) rock once a month. Damplein is another good stretch for drinking: the *Rhythm en Blues Kroeg "Bloesbak"* at no. 20 is a rough-and-ready bar with loud taped music; *Café Meccano* at no. 27 has a young, raucous clientele; *Café Solo* at no. 48 is more mainstream, with drinking on its garden terrace in summer; and *Meneer Jansen*, around the corner at Reigerstraat 7, is a small, relaxed bar that attracts an older crowd.

Listings

Car rental *Autoservice Leo van Liere*, Kanaalweg 10–12 (☎27680); *Louisse Auto Bv*, Kalverstraat 1 (☎25851).

Carillon concerts The carillon at Lange Jan plays every 15min and there are year-round concerts on Thurs noon–1pm; May to mid-Sept additional concerts Sat 11am–noon; July & Aug also Thurs 7.30–8.30pm.

Cycling Bike rental from the station or *De Pree Bikerent*, Zusterstraat 10–12 (☎12344). If you intend to cycle around, get hold of a copy of the yellow *Zuid-Holland Fietskaart* from the VVV or any bookshop/newsagent; the VVV also sells detailed maps of Walcheren and Zeeland and a book of twenty cycle routes in the region, *Fietsen in Zeeland*.

Markets General market on the Markt Thurs 8.30am–4pm; flower, produce market Sat 8.30am–4pm. Vismarkt has a flea market on the first Sat of the month 9am–4pm; and an antique and curio market from June to Aug Thurs 9am–4pm.

Police station Achter de Houttuinen 10 (☎88000).

Post office Lange Noordstraat 48.

Ring tilting *Ringrijderij*, a horseback competition where riders try to pick off rings with lances, takes place at the Koepoort city gate near Molenwater on one day in July and one day in Aug, 9am–4pm. Check with the VVV for dates.

Taxis *Taxicentrale*, ☎12600 or 13200; *Blanker*, ☎13900.

East of Middelburg: Goes

GOES, 22km east of Middelburg and the centre of South Beveland, is an undistinguished town only worth stopping at if you're heading this way into North Brabant. Its late Gothic basilica, the **Grote Kerk** (July & Aug Mon–Fri 11am–4pm), has a seventeenth-century organ and there's a **Museum van Noord en Zuid Beveland** at Singelstraat 13 (Tues–Fri 1–5pm, Sat 1–4pm; *f*2) – very much inferior to Middelburg's Zeeuws Museum. Basically, if you're travelling via Goes to Bergen-op-Zoom, there's no need to stop en route.

Veere

Eight kilometres northeast of Middelburg, **VEERE** is a resolutely picturesque little town by the banks of the Veerse Meer. Today it's a centre for all things maritime, its small harbour jammed with yachts and its cafés packed with weekend admirals: but a handful of buildings and a large church point to a time when Veere was rich and quite independent of other, similar towns in Zeeland.

Veere earned its money from an odd Scottish connection: in 1444 Wolfert VI van Borssele, the lord of Veere, married Mary, daughter of James I of Scotland. As part of the dowry, van Borssele was granted a monopoly on trade with Scottish wool merchants; in return, Scottish merchants living in Veere were granted special privileges. A number of their houses still stand, best of which are those on the dock facing the harbour: *Het Lammetje* (The Lamb) and *De Struys* (The Ostrich), dating from the mid-sixteenth century, were combined offices, homes and warehouses for the merchants; they now house the **Museum Schotse Huizen** (April–Oct Mon–Sat 10am–5pm; *f*2), a rather lifeless collection of local costumes, old books, atlases and furniture, along with an exhibit devoted to fishing. Elsewhere there are plenty of Gothic buildings, whose rich decoration leaves you in no doubt that the Scottish wool trade earned a bundle for the sixteenth- and seventeenth-century burghers of Veere: many of the buildings (which are usually step-gabled with distinctive green and white shutters) are embellished with whimsical details that play on the owners' names or their particular line of business. The **Stadhuis** at Markt 5 (June–Sept Mon–Sat noon–5pm; *f*2) is similarly opulent, dating from the 1470s with an out-of-scale, boastful Renaissance tower added a century later. Its facade is decorated with statues of the lords of Veere and their wives (Wolfert VI is third from the left), and, inside, a small museum occupies what was formerly the courtroom, pride of place going to a goblet that once belonged to Maximilian of Burgundy.

Of all Veere's buildings the **Grote Kerk** (May–Oct Mon–Sat 10am–5pm, Sun 2–5pm; *f*2.25) seems to have suffered most: finished in 1560, it was badly damaged by fire a century later and restoration removed much of its decoration. In 1808 invading British troops used the church as a hospital and three years later Napoleon's army converted it into barracks and stables, destroying the stained glass, bricking up the windows and adding five floors in the nave; later, in the nineteenth century, it became a poorhouse. Despite all this damage, the church's blunt 42-metre **tower** (same opening hours and ticket as church; last entrance 4.30pm) adds a glowering presence to the landscape, especially when seen across the misty polder fields. According to the original design, the tower was to have been three times higher, but even as it stands there's a great view from the top, back to the pinnacled skyline of Middelburg and out across the breezy Veerse Meer.

Veere fell from importance with the decline of the wool trade. The opening of the Walcheren Canal in the nineteenth century, linking the town to Middelburg and Vlissingen, gave it a stay of execution, but the construction of the Veersegatdam and Zandkreekdam in the 1950s finally sealed the port to seagoing vessels and simultaneously created a freshwater lake ideal for watersports. The **VVV** office, Oudestraat 28 (Jan–March & Nov–Dec Mon–Sat 1.30–4.30pm; April–June & Sept–Oct Mon–Sat noon–5pm; July & Aug Mon–Sat 10am–5.30pm; ☎01181/1365), can advise on the rental of all types of watercraft and has details of **private rooms**. If you prefer to organize your own accommodation, the cheaper of Veere's two **hotels** is *'t Waepen van Veere* at Markt 23–27 (☎01181/1231; ③). To reach Veere from Middelburg, catch a #33 bus (hourly on weekdays in July & Aug, otherwise every 30min), or rent a bike from Middelburg train station and take either the main road or the circuitous but picturesque routes leaving from the north of the town.

The Delta Project – and the Delta Expo

On February 1, 1953, a combination of an exceptionally high spring tide and powerful northwesterly winds drove the North Sea over the dykes to flood much of Zeeland. The results were catastrophic: 1855 people drowned, 47,000 homes and 500km of dykes were destroyed and some of the country's most fertile agricultural land was ruined by salt water. Towns as far west as Bergen-op-Zoom and

Dordrecht were flooded and Zeeland's road and rail network wrecked. The government's response was immediate and on a massive scale. After patching up the breached dykes, work was begun on the **Delta Project**, one of the largest engineering schemes the world has ever seen and one of phenomenal complexity and expense.

The plan was to ensure the safety of Zeeland by radically shortening and strengthening its coastline. The major estuaries and inlets would be dammed, thus preventing unusually high tides surging inland to breach the thousands of kilometres of small dykes. Where it was impractical to build a dam – such as across the Westerschelde or Nieuwe Waterweg, which would have closed the seaports of Antwerp and Rotterdam respectively – secondary dykes were to be greatly reinforced. New roads across the top of the dams would improve communications to Zeeland and South Holland and the freshwater lakes that formed behind the dams would enable precise control of the water table of the Zeeland islands.

It took thirty years for the full Delta Project to be completed. The smaller, secondary dams – the Veersegat, Haringvliet and Brouwershaven – were completed first, a plan designed to provide protection from high tides as quickly as possible and a process that enabled engineers to learn as they went along. In 1968, work began on the largest dam, intended to close the **Oosterschelde** estuary that forms the outlet of the Maas, Waal and Rijn rivers. It soon ran into intense opposition from environmental groups, who realized the importance of the flora and fauna in and around the Oosterschelde: at low tides, the mud flats and sandbanks were an important breeding ground for birds and the estuary itself formed a nursery for plaice, sole and other North Sea fish. Local fishermen saw their livelihoods in danger: if the Oosterschelde were closed the oyster, mussel and lobster beds would be destroyed and even without taking into account the social problems caused by the loss of jobs in an area dependent on fishing and related industries, the loss to the economy was estimated (then) at ƒ200 million.

The environmental and fishing lobbies argued that strengthening the estuary dykes would provide sufficient protection; the water board and agricultural groups raised the emotive spectre of the 1953 flood. In the end a compromise was reached, with the design of a supremely elegant and intelligent piece of engineering: in 1976 work began on the **Storm Surge Barrier**, a device that would stay open under normal tidal conditions, allowing water to flow in and out of the estuary, but close ahead of unusually high tides.

The Delta Expo

It's on this barrier, completed in 1986, that the fascinating **Delta Expo** (April–Oct daily 10am–5pm; ƒ12 including boat trip; Nov–March Wed–Sun 10am–5pm; ƒ9 without boat trip – as it's too cold) is housed. In spring and summer you can take a boat trip for a close look at the huge computer-controlled sluice gates. Only once you're inside the Expo itself, though, do you get an idea of the scale of the whole project. It's best to start with the film history of the barrier before taking in the exhibition, which is divided into three areas: the historical background of Holland's response to its water problems; the mechanical and scientific developments that enabled it to protect itself; the environmental problems caused by the project and the solutions that have minimized the damage. The Surge Barrier (and the Delta Project as a whole) have been completely successful. Computer simulations are used to predict high tides, though if an unpredicted rise occurs the sluice gates are programmed to close automatically in a matter of minutes. On average, a dangerously high tide occurs once every eighteen months.

Reaching the Delta Expo is easily managed: from Middelburg take the hourly #104 bus from Hof van Tange or allow an hour and a half to cycle; from Rotterdam, take the metro to Spijkenisse and then bus #104.

Brouwershaven and Zierikzee

The Storm Surge Barrier stretches across to the "island" of **Schouwen-Duiveland**. Most of the Dutch tourists who come here head directly west for the 800 hectares acres of beach and dune between **HAAMSTEDE** and **RENESSE**, themselves pretty villages but with only the **Slot Moermond** (tours of garden arranged by Renesse VVV from mid-June to mid-Aug; ☎01116/2120), a castle built for the local lords just north of Renesse, worth breaking your journey for. You can get to Renesse from Middelburg by bus #104 and from Renesse to **BROUWERSHAVEN**, in the middle of Schouwen-Duiveland's northern coast, by bus #134, which runs hourly. Until the building of the Nieuwe Waterweg linked Rotterdam to the coast, Brouwershaven was a busy seaport, with boats able to sail right into the centre of town. Other than the pretty gabled houses flanking the harbour and a few narrow streets around the Markt, the **Stadhuis** is the single thing to see, an attractive Flemish Renaissance building of 1599.

Schouwen-Duiveland's most interesting town, though, lies to the south. **ZIERIKZEE**'s position at the intersection of shipping routes between England, Flanders and Holland led to it becoming an important port in the late Middle Ages. It was also famed for its salt and madder – a root that, when dried and ground, produces a brilliant red dye.

Encircled by a defensive canal and preferably entered by one of two sixteenth-century watergates, Zierikzee's centre is small and easily explored, easier still if you arm yourself with a map from the **VVV** at Havenpark 29 (Oct–April Mon–Fri 10am–5pm, Sat 10am–1pm; May–Sept 9am–5pm, Sat 10am–3pm; ☎01110/12450). A few minutes' walk from the office, the Gothic **'s Gravensteen** building at Mol 25 (April–Oct Mon–Sat 10am–5pm, Sun noon–5pm; *f*2) was once the jail and is today home to a maritime museum. However, the building is far more interesting than the exhibits: the old cells from the prison are pretty authentic and the removal of plaster walls in 1969 uncovered graffiti and drawings by the prisoners. The basements contain torture chambers and iron cage cells built to contain two prisoners.

Zierikzee's **Stadhuis** is easy enough to find – just head for the tall, fussy spire on Meelstraat 6. Inside, the **Gemeentemuseum** (May–Oct Mon–Fri 10am–5pm; *f*2) has collections of silver, costumes and a regional history exhibition. Also worth seeing is the **Monstertoren** (April to mid-Sept Mon–Sat 11am–4pm, Sun noon–4pm; *f*2), a tower designed by the Keldermans family on which work was stopped when it reached 97 of its planned 167m.

If you need to **stay over**, the VVV has details of **private rooms**; alternatives include the *Beddegoed*, Meelstraat 53 (☎01110/15935; ③); or, slightly more expensive, the *Pension Minique*, Driekoningenlaan 5 (☎01110/12323; ③) and the *Van Oppen*, Verrenieuwstraat 11 (☎01110/12288; ③). Heading to or from Goes from Zierikzee on bus #10 you'll pass over the **Zeelandbrug**, a graceful bridge across the Oosterschelde that, at 5022 metres, is the longest in Europe.

NORTH BRABANT

North Brabant, Holland's largest province, stretches from the North Sea to the German border. Originally, it was part of the independent Duchy of Brabant, which was taken over by the Spanish, and, eventually, split in two when its northern towns joined the revolt against Spain. This northern part was ceded to the United Provinces under the terms of the 1648 Treaty of Munster; the southern part formed what today are the Belgian provinces of Brabant and Antwerp.

The **Catholic influence** is still strong in North Brabant: it takes its religious festivals seriously and if you're here in March the boozy **carnivals** (especially in the province's capital, 's Hertogenbosch) are well worth catching – indeed, it's difficult to miss them. Geographically, woodland and heath form most of the natural scenery, the gently undulating arable land a welcome change in a country whose landscape is ruthlessly featureless.

Bergen-op-Zoom

BERGEN-OP-ZOOM is an untidy town, a jumble of buildings old and new that are the consequence of being the butt of various European powers from the sixteenth century onwards. In 1576 Bergen-op-Zoom sided with the United Provinces against the Spanish and as a result was under near-continuous siege until 1622. The French bombarded the city in 1747 and took it again in 1795, though it managed to withstand a British attack in 1814.

The Town

Walk straight out of the train station and you'll soon find yourself on the **Grote Markt**, an insalubrious square-cum-car park, most cheerful during summer when it's decked out with open-air cafés and the like. The **Stadhuis**, on the north side of the square (Mon–Fri 8.30am–12.30pm & 1.30–5.30pm; free), is Bergen's most attractive building, spruced up following a recent renovation and comprising three separate houses: to the left of the gateway an alderman's house of 1397, to the right a merchant's house of 1480 and on the far right a building known as "De Olifant" whose facade dates from 1611. Ask inside the Stadhuis and someone will show you the council chamber and the *Trouwzaal*, the room where marriages take place. All of this is a lot more appealing than the blunt ugliness of the **Grote Kerk**, a uniquely unlucky building that's been destroyed by siege, fire and neglect innumerable times over the last four hundred years. It's due to reopen after the latest of its many restorations in 1995.

To the left of the Stadhuis, Fortuinstraat leads to the **Markiezenhof Museum**, Steenbergsestraat 8 (Sept–May Tues–Sun 2–5pm; June–Aug Tues–Fri 11am–5pm, Sat & Sun 2–5pm; Oct–April Sat 12.30–4.30pm; *f*4), a first-rate presentation of an above average collection that has a little of everything: domestic utensils and samplers from the sixteenth century onward, sumptuous period rooms, architectural drawings, pottery and galleries of modern art. All this is housed in a palace built by Anthonis Keldermans between 1485 and 1522 to a late Gothic style that gives it the feel of an Oxford college. Before reaching the Markiezenhof's main entrance on Steenbergsestraat, you pass the **Galerie Etcetera** (Tues–Sun

2–5pm), an exhibition space for twentieth-century artists, worth dropping in on if you're interested in what's on show.

Of the rest of old Bergen-op-Zoom little remains: at the end of Lievevrouwestraat, near the entrance to the Markiezenhof, the **Gevangenpoort** is practically all that's left of the old city defences, a solid-looking fourteenth-century gatehouse that was later converted to a prison.

CARNAVAL IN BERGEN-OP-ZOOM

In February each year Bergen-op-Zoom hosts one of southern Holland's most vibrant **carnivals**, with virtually every inhabitant joining in its Sunday procession. It's a great time to be in the town if you can manage it, although you shouldn't expect to find any accommodation – the town gets packed; just do as the locals do and party all night.

Practicalities

The **VVV** office is at Beursplein 7 (Mon–Fri 9am–6pm, Sat & Sun 9am–5pm; ☎01640/66000) and offers a walking tour of the town (ƒ6) on Wednesdays from June to August at 2pm and a free map of the centre. Outside Carnaval, it's hard to imagine why you'd want to stay over in Bergen, but if you did the VVV has details of **private rooms** and there are two **pensions**: *De Lantaarn*, Bredastraat 8 (☎01640/36488; ③), between the train station and the town centre and *Pension Het Fort*, Prins Bernhardlaan 98 (☎01640/54973; ③), a fifteen-minute walk from the centre or a short ride on bus #105 from the station. The cheapest **hotel** is the *Old Dutch*, Stationstraat 31 (☎01640/35780; ④). The **youth hostel**, *Klavervelden* (open mid-March to mid-Oct), is 4km out of town at Boslustweg 1; take bus #1 or #2 from the station.

Restaurants are mainly grouped around the Grote Markt and tend to be expensive. Try *Amadeus* at Grote Markt 3, which has a bar next door; or, considerably cheaper, *Stadscafé de Teerkamer* at Grotemarkt 13 which has set-price daily menus. The town's **drinking scene** is not exactly a buzzing one: try *Kunst- en Proeflokaal de Hemel* at Moeregrebstraat 35, just off Steenbergsestraat.

Breda

BREDA is the prettiest town of North Brabant and the most immediately likeable place in all of the south: its centre is compact and eminently strollable, with a magnificent church and a couple of good museums; there's a range of well-priced accommodation, inexpensive restaurants and lively bars; and it's an excellent springboard for exploring central North Brabant. In short, it's an ideal target, whether you're visiting for the day or looking for a base from which to branch out to Zeeland, Dordrecht, 's Hertogenbosch or even Antwerp.

Though there's little evidence of it today, Breda developed as a strategic fortress town and was badly damaged following its capture by the Spanish in 1581. The local counts were scions of the House of Nassau, which in the early sixteenth century married into the House of Orange. The first prince of the Orange-Nassau line was **William the Silent**, who spent much of his life in the town and would probably have been buried here – had Breda not been in the hands of the Spanish at the time of his assassination in Delft. In 1566 William was among the group of Netherlandish nobles who issued the **Compromise of Breda** – an early declaration against Spanish domination of the Low Countries. The town later fell to the Spanish, was retaken by Maurice, William's son, captured once more by the Spanish, but finally ceded to the United Provinces in 1648.

King Charles II of England lived in the town for a while (it was here that he issued his **Declaration of Breda** in 1660, the terms by which he was prepared to accept the throne), as did (though less reliable historically) Oliver Cromwell and Daniel Defoe. Breda was last fought over in 1793, when it was captured by the French, who hung on to it until 1813.

Arrival, information and accommodation

The **VVV** office, Willemstraat 17 (Mon–Fri 9am–6pm, Sat 9am–5pm; ☎076/22 24 44) is straight outside the **train station**, about six minutes' walk from the Grote Markt and the town centre. It offers **guided tours** between mid-July and mid-August (Tues–Sat at 2pm; f5.25) taking in the grounds of the Kasteel as well as the town; it also sells a detailed guide, *Strolling through Breda* (f2). Another pleasant way to see the town is to take a **boat trip** around the moat encircling the town. They leave from Spanjaardsgat between May and October.

Low-priced **hotels** include *Graumans* (☎076/21 62 71; ③), which should be your first choice as it's near the train station at Delpratsingel 14. The others are all too far to reach on foot – take a yellow #130 bus from the station and ask to be dropped off at Duivelsbruglaan, where you'll find the slightly pricy *Aard Ster*, Duivelsbruglaan 92 (☎076/65 16 66; ③) and the cheaper *Donkers*, Duivelsbruglaan 72 (☎076/65 43 32; ③). Up a notch in price, there's the conveniently located *De Klok* at Grote Markt 26–28 (☎076/21 40 82; ④), though it fills quickly in summer and the *Van Ham*, Van Coothplein 23 (☎076/21 52 29; ③). The **campsite**, *Liesbos* (March–Sept), is 8km out of town on the #111 bus route.

The Town

From the train station and VVV, head down Willemstraat and cross the park for the town centre. The **Grote Markt** is the focus of life, site of a general and second-hand **market** every Tuesday and Friday morning, when stands push up against the pocket-Gothic **Grote Kerk** (May–Oct Mon–Sat 10am–5pm, Sun 1–5pm; Nov–April Mon–Fri 10am–noon & 2–5pm; f2; tower open June–Aug Sat 1–5pm; f2.50), whose intimate interior generates a sense of awe you don't usually associate with so small a building, the short nave and high, spacious crossing adding to the illusion of space. Like the majority of Dutch churches, the Grote Kerk had its decorations either removed or obscured after the Reformation, but a few murals have been uncovered and reveal just how colourful the church once was. At the end of the south aisle there's a huge *St Christopher* and other decorations in the south transept embellish the walls and roof bosses. The Grote Kerk's most remarkable feature, though, is the **Mausoleum of Count Engelbrecht II**, a Stadholder and Captain-General of the Netherlands who died in 1504 of tuberculosis – vividly apparent in the drawn features of his intensely realistic face. Four kneeling figures (Caesar, Regulus, Hannibal and Philip of Macedonia)

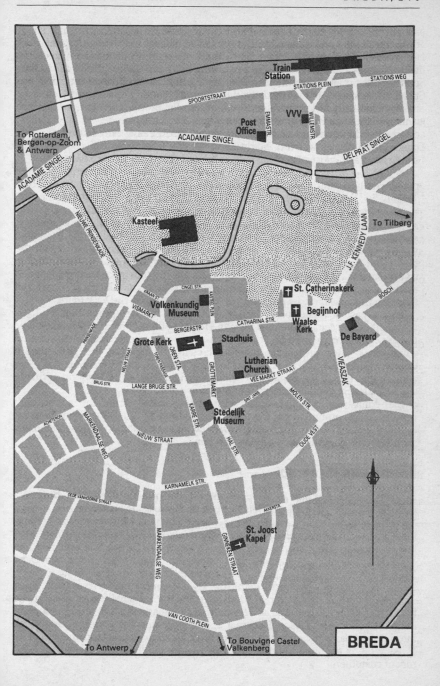

BREDA

support a canopy that carries his armour, so skilfully sculpted that their shoulders sag slightly under the weight. It's believed that the mausoleum was the work of Tomaso Vincidor of Bologna, but whoever created it imbued the mausoleum with grandeur and power without resorting to flamboyance: the result is both eerily realistic and oddly moving. During the French occupation the choir was used as a stable, but fortunately the sixteenth-century misericords, showing rustic and everyday scenes, survived. A couple of the carvings are modern replacements – as you'll guess from their subject matter.

The **Breda Museum** (Wed–Sat 10.30am–5pm, Tues & Sun 1–5pm; ƒ1.50) is close to the church at Grote Markt 19, holding a forgettable collection of ecclesiastical art and oddments, along with exhibits concerning Breda's history.

At the top of Kasteelplein sits the **Kasteel**: too formal to be forbidding and considerably rebuilt since the Compromise of Breda was signed here in 1566. Twenty-five years later the Spanish captured Breda, but it was regained in 1590 thanks to a neat trick by Maurice of Nassau's troops: the Spanish garrison was regularly supplied by barge with peat, so, using the Trojan Horse strategy, seventy troops under Maurice's command hid beneath the peat on the barge and were towed into the castle, jumping out to surprise the Spanish and regain the town. The Spanjaardsgat, an early sixteenth-century watergate with twin defensive bastions that's just west of the Kasteel, is usually (but inaccurately) identified as the spot where this happened. Today the Kasteel is a military academy and there's no admission to its grounds, unless you join one of the VVV tours.

To the east of Kasteelplein on Catherinastraat, the **Begijnhof**, built in 1531, was until quite recently the only *hofje* in Holland still occupied by Beguines (see *Contexts* "Glossaries"). Today it has been given over to elderly women, some of whom look after the dainty nineteenth-century chapel at the rear, the St Catherinakerk and tend the herb garden that was laid out several hundred years ago. To the right of the Begijnhof entrance, incidentally, is the **Walloon Church**, where Pieter Stuyvesant, governor of New York, was married.

Catherinastraat, which is lined with stately houses from the seventeenth century, twists around to **De Beyaard**, Boschstraat 22 (Tues–Fri 10am–5pm, Sat & Sun 1–5pm; ƒ3), a cultural centre with changing exhibitions of contemporary art housed in what was once a lunatic asylum.

Eating and drinking

Breda has a decent range of places to **eat**. For cheap, central food, *Da Attilio* is a pizzeria at Grote Markt 35 and *Willy's Pizza* on Halstraat is handy for snacks. *Bua Gao*, Reigerstraat 20, is a late-closing Thai restaurant with vegetarian options; there's also a late-night disco upstairs. The *Maharajah of India*, Havermarkt 25, has reasonably priced curries; *Het Voske*, Grote Markt 15, is a chic French place; *Pols*, Halstraat 15, is a small and excellent *eetcafé*; and *De Korenbloem*, Ginnekenweg 2b (daily 5–7.30pm), is worth the walk out to the south for its vegetarian food. For down-to-earth **drinking**, try *De Groene Sael*, Havermarkt 8, an unpretentious bar serving draft *Palm* beer and with a small dance floor at the back. Just off the Grote Markt, *Hemeltjelief*, Veemarktstraat 5, also has a good range of beers. *Nickelodeon*, Halstraat 2, is a more upmarket affair, with a swish interior popular with an older crowd; *Café de Bommel*, across the street at Halstraat 3, is *the* place to drink in town, a large and lively café-bar with a good mix of customers.

Tilburg

TILBURG is a faceless and unwelcoming industrial town, its streets a maze of nineteenth-century houses and anonymous modern shopping precinct. Three of its four museums are a stone's throw from the train station and if that's as far as you get into town, you haven't missed much.

Tilburg developed as a textile town, though today most of its mills have closed in the face of cheap competition from India and southeast Asia. The **Nederlands Textielmuseum**, housed in an old mill at Goirkestraat 96 (out of the station, walk west along Spoorlaan, turn right along Gasthuisring and Goirkestraat is the fourth turn on the right; Tues–Fri 10am–5pm, Sat & Sun noon–5pm; ƒ7.50), displays aspects of the industry relating to design and textile arts, with a collection of textile designs by Dutch artists and demonstrations of weaving and spinning, as well as a range of looms and weaving machines from around the world. The shiny new **Scryption**, Spoorlaan 434a (Tues–Fri 10am–5pm, Sat & Sun 1–5pm; ƒ3.50), is a fancy name for a collection of writing implements – everything from lumps of chalk to word processors. Particularly good are the old, intricate typewriters, some of which you can operate yourself. Next door, the **Noordbrabants Natuurmuseum** (Tues–Fri 10am–5pm, Sat & Sun 1–5pm; ƒ5) is basically a load of dead animals and (live) creepy crawlies.

If you do go into town you'll need a map from the **VVV** office at Stadhuisplein 128 (Mon–Fri 9am–5.30pm, Sat 10am–4pm; ☎013/35 11 35) to have any chance of finding the **Poppenmuseum** at Telefoonstraat 13–15 (Sun & Wed 2–4pm; ƒ2.50), a small private collection of dolls. Unless you're mad or desperate there's no earthly reason why you'd want to stay in Tilburg, but, for the record, the least expensive room in town is at the *Het Wapen van Tilburg* hotel, Spoorlaan 362 (☎013/42 26 92; ③).

's Hertogenbosch (Den Bosch)

Capital of North Brabant, **'s HERTOGENBOSCH** is officially known as Den Bosch, the name deriving from the words "the Count's Woods" after the hunting lodge established here by Henry I, Duke of Brabant, in the twelfth century. Hieronymous Bosch lived here all his life, but as the town has only two paintings doubtfully attributed to him, the main draws are its cathedral, a number of museums and, not least, an enjoyable nightlife. Consider staying over for a couple of days.

Arrival, information and accommodation

Den Bosch's centre is a quarter of an hour's walk from the **train station**. The **VVV** office is in "De Mooriaan", Markt 77 (Mon–Fri 9am–5.30pm, Sat 9am–4pm; June–Aug also Sat until 5pm; ☎12 30 71) – worth a stop for its *Wandering around Old Den Bosch* leaflet and to have a quick look at the reproductions of Bosch's greatest works upstairs (Tues–Sun 1–5pm; ƒ2.50).

The telephone code for Den Bosch is ☎073

There are three budget-range **hotels**: the *Terminus* at Stationsplein 19 (☎13 06 66; ③); slightly cheaper, the *Bosch*, Boschdijkstraat 39a (☎13 82 05; ③); and the seedy but friendly *All In* (☎13 40 57; ③), just down the street at Gasselstraat 1, on the corner of Hinthamerpromenade.

If you want to see a lot of the town, but want to save your legs, there are **boat trips** along the city moat. You've a choice between plying along in a traditional open boat (May–Sept Tues–Sun hourly 11am–5pm; ƒ6) from Van Molenstraat (next to *Café van Puffelen*); or a closed boat (May–Sept 12.30pm, 2pm & 3pm daily) from near the Wilhelmina bridge, which also takes in the River Dommel and nearby Ertveld Lake.

The Town

If you were to draw a picture of the archetypal Dutch Markt it would probably look like the one in Den Bosch. It's broad and cobbled, home to the province's largest market on Wednesday and Saturday and is lined with typical seventeenth-century houses. The sixteenth-century **Stadhuis** (Mon–Fri 9am–5pm; free guided tours Tues at 7pm) has a carillon that's played every Wednesday between 10 and 11am and that chimes the half-hour to the accompaniment of a group of mechanical horsemen.

From just about anywhere in the centre of town it's impossible to miss **St Jan's Cathedral** (daily 10am–5pm; restricted entrance during services). Generally regarded as the finest Gothic church in the country, it was built between 1330 and 1530 and has recently undergone a massive restoration. But if Breda's Grote Kerk is Gothic at its most intimate and exhilarating, then St Jan's is Gothic at its most gloomy, the garish stained glass – nineteenth-century or modern – only adding to the sense of dreariness that hangs over the nave. You enter beneath the oldest and least well-preserved part of the cathedral, the western **tower** (open, if you want to climb it, in July & Aug; ƒ2): blunt and brick-clad, it's oddly prominent amid the wild decoration of the rest of the exterior, which includes some nasty-looking creatures scaling the roof – symbols of the forces of evil that attack the church. Inside, there's much of interest. The **Lady Chapel** near the entrance contains a thirteenth-century figure of the Madonna known as *Zoete Lieve Vrouw* (Sweet Dear Lady), famed for its miraculous powers in the Middle Ages and still much venerated today. The brass **font** in the southwest corner was the work of Alard Duhamel, a master mason who worked on the cathedral in the late fifteenth century. It's thought that the stone pinnacle, a weird twisted piece of Gothicism at the eastern end of the nave, was the sample piece that earned him the title of master mason.

Almost filling the west wall of the cathedral is an extravagant **organ case**, assembled in 1602. It was described by a Victorian authority as "certainly the finest in Holland and probably the finest in Europe . . . it would be difficult to conceive a more stately or magnificent design". Equally elaborate, though on a much smaller scale, the south transept holds the **Altar of the Passion**, a retable (a piece placed behind and above the altar to act as a kind of screen) made in Antwerp in around 1500. In the centre is a carved Crucifixion scene, flanked by Christ bearing the Cross on one side and a Lamentation on the other. Though rather difficult to make out, a series of carved scenes of the life of Christ run across the retable, made all the more charming by their attention to period (medieval) costume detail.

'S HERTOGENBOSCH

To Nijmegen
GRAAFSE
MUNTEL BOLWERK
AAWAL DE BOSSCHEPAD
HINTHAMER EINDE
OOSTWAL
MUNTEL WAL
HOFSTAD
KAS TEREN WAL
Zuid Willems Vaart
ST. JACOB STR.
BETHANIE STR.
To Helmond
HEKELLAAN
Zuider Park
PETTELAARSE WEG
HEKELLAAN
PAPENHULST
Het Zwanenbroedershuis
Museum Slager
HINTHAMERSTRAAT
CHOOR STR
ZUID WILLEMS VAART
ST. JOSEPH STR.
TRINITEIT STR
PARADE
NIEUW STRAAT
St. Jan's Cathedral
PEPER STR.
LANGE PUT STR
OUDE DIEZE
HINTHAMERPROMENADE
Post Office
VERWERS STRAAT
WATER STR
ZUIDWAL
De Morian VVV
Stadhuis
Noord-Brabants Museum
OUDERWIJKSTR.
Refugiehuis
Kruithuis
BUKLOEFF PLEIN
TOLBRUG STR.
Markt
HOGE STEEN WEG
SCHAPENMARKT
KEIZER STR.
Paleis van Justice
SPONCUISWAL
Stadsval
Bastion Oranje
JAN HEINS STR
ORTHEN STRAAT
VIS STRAAT
KRUIS STR.
POSTEL STRAAL
De Brabantse Poffer
ST-JORIS STRAAT
St. Catherine Kerk
BUITEN HAVEN
HAVEN SINGEL
SINT JANSSINGEL
Dommel
VAN DER DOES DE WILLEBOIS SINGEL
PARKLAAN
Stadsval
To Utrecht
EMMA PLEIN
KONINGINNEN LAAN
STATIONS WEG
River Dommel
DR. NASSAU
WEST WAL
VUGHTER STRAAT
Train Station
STATIONS PLEIN
KONINGSWEG
MAY WEG
To Tilburg & Eindhoven

Though a few painted sections of the cathedral remain to show it would have been decorated before the Reformation, most works of art that it possessed were destroyed in the iconoclastic fury of 1566. These included several paintings by **Hieronymus Bosch**, who lived in the town all his life: only two works by Bosch remain (in the north transept) and even their authenticity is doubtful. What is more certain is that Bosch belonged to the town's Brotherhood of Our Lady, a society devoted to the veneration of the Virgin and that as a working artist he would have been expected to help adorn the cathedral. Though none of his major works remain in Den Bosch today, there's a collection of his prints in the Noordbrabants Museum (see below).

Opposite the cathedral at Hinthamerstraat 94, the **Zwanenbroedershuis** (Fri 11am–3pm; free) has an intriguing collection of artefacts, liturgical songbooks and music scores that belonged to the Brotherhood of which Bosch was a member. Founded in 1318, there's nothing sinister about the Brotherhood: membership is open to all and its aim is to promote and popularize religious art and music.

South and east of the cathedral, the **Museum Slager**, Choorstraat 16 (Tues–Fri & Sun 2–5pm; free), contains the works of three generations of the Slager family who lived in Den Bosch. The paintings of the family's doyen, P.M. Slager, such as *Veterans of Waterloo*, have the most authority, but some of the other works are competent, encompassing the major trends in European art as they came and went. Over the hundred and thirty years they have been active (the remaining Slager, Tom, lives in France) the Slager family seems to have spent most of its time painting Den Bosch – or their relatives.

A few minutes' walk southwest of the cathedral, the **Noordbrabants Museum**, Verwersstraat 41 (Tues–Fri 10am–5pm, Sat & Sun noon–5pm; *f*5), is housed in an eighteenth-century building that was once the seat of the provincial commissioner and has been enlarged with two new wings. The good-looking collection of local art and artefacts here is uniformly excellent and interesting – unlike many regional museums. It includes drawings and prints by Hieronymus Bosch, works by other medieval painters and assorted early torture equipment. There's also a rare *Schandhuik* or "Cloak of Infamy", a wooden cloak carved with adders and toads, symbols of unchastity. In it, women who had been unfaithful to their husbands were paraded on a cart through the city streets in the seventeenth century.

Just down the road from the museum, the **Refugiehuis** at the end of St Jorisstraat (Mon–Fri 9am–5pm), originally a sixteenth-century safe house for those persecuted for their religious beliefs, is today a commercial crafts centre. St Jorisstraat leads down to the site of the old city walls, which still marks the southern limit of Den Bosch. The **Bastion Oranje** once defended the southern section of the city walls, but, like the walls themselves, it has long gone. Still remaining is a large cannon, **De Boze Griet** (The Devil's Woman), cast in 1511 in Cologne and bearing the German inscription "Brute force I am called, Den Bosch I watch over".

For the rest, the backstreets of Den Bosch are a mass of intriguing facades and buildings. To name just one, the **Kruithuis** at Citadellelaan 7 (Tues–Sat 11am–5pm, Sun 1–5pm; *f*3), northwest of the centre, is an old gunpowder magazine that's been converted into an arts centre, with changing exhibitions of (mostly) contemporary art.

Eating and drinking

Den Bosch's **restaurants** can be pricy: many of those in the centre are geared to expense accounts and are poor value for money. *Da Peppone*, Kerkstraat 77, *Taormina*, Verwersstraat 46 and *Il Brigantino*, Hinthamerstraat 122, are both inexpensive pizzerias. *Bagatelle*, Hinthamerpromenade 29, has well-priced Dutch food. *De Opera*, Hinthamerstraat 115–117, offers a range of wonderful Dutch–French cooking in a relaxed setting: well worth a splurge. *Dry Hamerkens*, Hinthamerstraat 57 (closed Tues), is similarly expensive, though perhaps this is hardly surprising, given that you dine in the neatly elegant ambience of a seven-teenth-century house that looks as if it's fallen out of a Vermeer. More affordably, for lunch, *De Pint*, Hinthamerstraat 76, has soups, salads and sandwiches on the menu as well as full meals. A fairly short distance from the centre of town, *Van Puffelen* at Van Molenstraat 4, is an attractive *eetcafé* above a canal with affordable *dagschotels*.

For **drinking**, it's easy enough to wander up and down Hinthamerstraat or the streets that radiate from the Markt and find somewhere convivial. *Keulse Kar*, Hinthamerstraat 101, is as good a starting point as any, a fairly conservative bar near the cathedral. At Hinthamerstaat 97, *'t Bonte Palet* is a tiny, popular and hence often crowded bar that's good for a swift one as you're working your way along the street. Up a few notches on the trendiness scale, *Café Cordes*, A. de Backer Parade 4 (just southwest of the cathedral), is a stylish, aluminium-clad café-bar that brings in Den Bosch's bright young things. *Café Pavlov*, Kerkstraat 38, is also a popular meeting place for the city's youth. *De Blauwe Druif*, at the corner of Markt and Kolperstraat, is a big, boozy pub that takes off on market days and the bar at 13 Kolperstraat is a friendly place to drink and smoke dope. *Duvelke*, Verwersstraat 55, is a deftly decorated drinking den near the Noordbrabants Museum.

Eindhoven

You might wonder why a town the size of **EINDHOVEN** only merits a page in a guidebook; half an hour there and a few statistics, will tell you why.

In 1890 Eindhoven's population was 4500. In 1990 it was around 197,000. What happened in between was **Philips**, the multinational electrical firm and the name of Eindhoven's benevolent dictator is everywhere – on bus stops, parks, even the stadium of the famous local football team. The town is basically an extended industrial and research plant for the company, and, save for one impressive art gallery, there's no need to come here unless business (or a football game – PSV Eindhoven, basically the Philips company team, are one of Holland's most consistently successful) forces you.

Since the Evoluon, the city's renowned science museum, was closed because of poor attendances, Eindhoven's only real attraction has been the **Van Abbe Museum**, Bilderdijklaan 10 (Tues–Sun 11am–5pm; *f*5), with its collection of modern paintings that includes works by Picasso, Klein, Chagall, Kandinsky and Bacon. To see this, you need to come between June and September: at other times the Van Abbe has changing exhibitions and nothing of the main collection can be seen.

EINDHOVEN

PROF.DR. DORGELOLAAN

JOH.F. KENNEDYLAAN

FELLENOORD

Bus Station

Train Station

VVV

18 SEPTEMBER PLEIN

STATIONSPLEIN

STATIONSWEG

DOMMELSTRAAT

To Philips Stadion

EMMASINGEL

DEMER

HERMANS BOEXSTR.

NIEUWSTR.

VESTDIJK

RAIFFEISEN STRAAT

TRAM STRAAT

MARKTSTR.

MARKT

VRIJSTRAAT

JAN VAN LIESHOUTSTR.

RECHTESTRAAT

HOOGHUIS STRAAT

VESTDIJK

TEN HAGESTR.

KEIZERSGRACHT

KLEINEBERG

BERGSTRAAT

KERKSTRAAT

STRATUMSEIND

SMALLE HAVEN

St. Catharinakerk

GROTEBERG

WAL

WAAGSTRAAT

PARADIJS LAAN

STADHUIS PLEIN

OUDE STADSGRACHT

River Dommel

Stadhuis

River Dommel

STRATUMSEDIJK

Van Abbemuseum

GELDROPSEWEG

HERTOGSTRAAT

BILDERDIJKLAAN

River Dommel

Practicalities

Eindhoven's **VVV** is outside the train station (Mon 10am–5.30pm, Tues–Fri 9am–5.30pm, Sat 9am–4pm; ☎040/44 92 31). It can provide a handy brochure on the city and a list of pensions, of which only *De Swaan*, Wilhelminaplein 5 (☎040/44 89 92; ③), is anywhere near the centre. The only truly central, affordable **hotel** is the *Corso* at Vestdijk 17 (☎040/44 91 31), with doubles at ƒ90. There's a campsite, *Camping Witven* (open all year), 5km outside the city at Rondweg 40 in **VELDHOVEN**; frequent buses run from the station.

As for eating and drinking, Eindhoven's modern streets contain some stylish **bars** that have sprung up over the last few years to assuage the thirst of the town's affluent youth. **Kleine Berg** is the best street to drink your way down, starting at *Artys* at no. 12, whose outdoor seating allows you to people-watch those heading this way. The *Grand Café Berlage* at no. 16, as slick as anything you'll find in Amsterdam, has a good menu, but for a full sit-down meal you might do better at *Eetcafé Bert* at no. 38. *Eetcafé Jez* at no. 34b is trendier and pricier. At no. 26, *Café Troost*'s marble-covered interior attracts local poseurs, but *Café Bommel*, a little further down, is a more old-fashioned traditional bar – and quite a relief if you've bar-hopped your way down the street.

Eindhoven's other strip for drinking is **Stratumseind**, which starts just south of Cuypers' gloomy neo-Gothic **St Catherinakerk**. The *Miller* bar at Stratumseind 51 is usually packed with teenagers; *De Krabbedans* at no. 32 is an arts complex with a pricey bar; *De Bakkerij* at no. 95 is popular with locals and stoners; *La Squale* at no. 35 is a distinctively different bar with changing wall paintings.

Along with Ajax Amsterdam and Feyenoord Rotterdam, Eindhoven's football team, **PSV Eindhoven**, is one of Holland's best. Unfortunately it's renowned for the violence of its fans and famed as the team that sold Ruud Gullitt and Ronald Koeman. Catch games at the **Philips Stadion**, ten minutes' walk west from the train station.

East from Eindhoven: Helmond

HELMOND, on the main train line from Eindhoven to Venray, just about merits a stop for its moated late medieval **Kasteel** (Tues–Fri 10am–5pm, Sat & Sun 2–5pm; ƒ2.50) that contains a museum with a small historical collection and changing exhibitions of art (though wandering around the castle itself is most fun); and a collection of futuristic houses, the **Paalwoningen**, designed by Piet Blom and opened in 1977. Designed to look like Cubist tree-huts, the buildings most resemble a group of tumbling dice – try and get into the small theatre here (box office open Mon–Sat 10am–1pm) to have a look.

LIMBURG

Limburg is Holland's most southerly province, a finger of land that pushes down into Belgium. The north, around **Venlo**, is mostly farmland and woods; the centre, around **Roermond**, dominated by the rivers and canals; and in the south, down to Maastricht, rise Holland's only hills. Like North Brabant it's a deeply Catholic area (if anything even more so) and has been influenced both architecturally and socially by the countries it neighbours.

Venlo, Venray and the National War and Resistance Museum

Only a few kilometres from the Dutch–German border, **VENLO** has been repeatedly destroyed and recaptured throughout its history, particularly during the last war, when most of its ancient buildings were knocked down during the Allied invasion of Europe. As a result the town is short of sights, though the cramped streets of the centre wind medievally around the one architectural highlight, the fancily turreted and onion-domed **Stadhuis**, a much-amended building dating from the sixteenth century. Nearby, along Grote Kerkstraat, is the louring pile of **St Martinuskerk**, rebuilt after bombing in 1944, but still holding a brilliant golden seventeenth-century reredos. From the Stadhuis signs direct you southeast to the **Goltziusmuseum**, Goltziusstraat 21 (Tues–Fri 10am–4.30pm, Sat & Sun 2–5pm; *f*2.50), the city's historical collection. Best exhibit is the nineteenth-century kitchenware, the largest assortment in western Europe. Venlo's other museum, the **Van Bommel-Van Dam**, Deken van Oppensingel 8 (Tues–Fri 10am–4.30pm, Sat & Sun 2–5pm; *f*2.50), has changing exhibitions of the work of contemporary, mostly local artists. From the train station, take the second right off the roundabout and then turn first right.

Venlo's **VVV**, Koninginneplein 2 (Mon–Fri 9am–5.30pm, Sat 9am–4pm; ☎077/ 54 38 00), opposite the train station, hands out glossy leaflets and can help find accommodation. Otherwise try the *Grolsche Quelle*, Eindhovenseweg 3–5 (☎077/ 51 85 60; ③), or the convenient *Stationshotel*, Keulsepoort 16 (☎077/51 82 30; ④). For **eating and drinking**, try the Labierint, in the centre at Houtstraat 2, for snacks and a few samples of their huge range of beers. Otherwise, there are cheap light lunches at the *Delifrance* opposite the Stadhuis.

From beside the train station, bus #83 makes the ten-kilometre trip north up along the Maas to the village of Arcen, home to the **Huis Arcen** (April–late Oct daily 10am–6pm), a trim seventeenth-century moated castle surrounded by a fine series of formal gardens set beside narrow canals and a string of tiny lakes.

Venray and the National War and Resistance Museum

A few minutes by train from Venlo, **VENRAY** is a cosy residential town and a stepping stone to **OVERLOON**, site of the **National War and Resistance Museum**. To reach the museum from Venray, either take hourly bus #97 from the train station or rent a bike, either from the station or from *Kuypers*, Monseigneur Hansen Straat 17a, a ten-minute walk from the station. A fifteen-minute ride through fields of wheat and you're in Overloon (which is actually over the provincial border and back in North Brabant), an affluent little town that was rebuilt following destruction in the last war, when it was the site of a fierce battle in October 1944 in which 2400 men died. The final stages took place in the woods to the east, where hand-to-hand fighting was needed to secure the area and it's on this site that the museum (Sept–May daily 10am–5pm; June–Aug daily 9.30am–6pm; *f*7 plus *f*2 for essential guidebook) now stands, founded with the military hardware that was left behind after the battle. Its purpose is openly didactic: "Not merely a monument for remembrance, it is intended as an admonition and warning, a denouncement of war and violence." This the museum powerfully achieves, with the macabre machinery of war (which includes tanks, rocket launchers, armoured cars, a Bailey bridge and a V1 flying bomb) forming a poignant prelude to the excellent collection of documents and posters. To tour the whole museum takes a couple of hours and it's a moving experience.

Roermond

ROERMOND, the chief town of central Limburg, is an oddity. Except for a few churches and a museum of fairly specialized interest, there's precious little to see here: its nightlife can't hold a candle to that of Maastricht to the south, cultural happenings are few, and, to be honest, it's not one of Holland's prettier towns either. Yet the town has great personality, caused in part by its long adherence to **Catholicism**. In 1579, seven years after William the Silent had captured Roermond from the Spanish, it fell back into their hands without a struggle and remained under the control of the Spanish (or Austrian) Hapsburgs, who actively encouraged Catholic worship, until the town was finally incorporated into the Netherlands in 1839. Reminders of the pre-eminence of the faith are everywhere, most visibly in the innumerable **shrines** to the Virgin built into the sides of houses. Usually high enough off the street to prevent damage, they contain small figures of the Virgin, sometimes decorated with flowers. And it was in Roermond that P.J.H. Cuypers, the architect who crowded the country with Gothic-revival Catholic churches in the nineteenth century, lived and had his workshops. Roermond is also a handy stopover on the way to Maastricht and the south, Aachen, or Düsseldorf and Cologne in Germany and useful as a base for visiting nearby **THORN**.

The telephone code for Roermond is ☎04750

The Town

Walk into town from the train station and you'll come to the **Munsterkerk** (Fri 10am–noon & 2–6pm, Sat 10am–4.30pm; free) on Munsterplein, built in Romanesque style in the thirteenth century, but much altered and gothicized by Cuypers in the nineteenth century. Inside, the chief thing to see is the polychrome thirteenth-century **tomb** of Gerhard III and his wife Margaret of Brabant. From here it's a short walk to the **Markt**, a large sloping square that hit the headlines in May 1990, when two Australian tourists were gunned down by members of the **provisional IRA**, who were under the mistaken belief that they were British soldiers. Its proximity to the German border made Roermond a particularly attractive site for such an action: soldiers often pass through the town en route to their Rhine bases; and fleeing into Germany lessened the likelihood of capture for the assassins, since the Dutch police are not allowed to chase over the border and the minutes taken to alert the German force allowed additional time for a getaway. The town's early eighteenth-century **Stadhuis** stands on the Markt's eastern side, a dull building that's easily overlooked. More noticeable (though not more interesting), **St Christopher's Cathedral** (April–Sept Sat 2–5pm; free) was rebuilt following damage in World War II.

ROERMOND

Making your way down the larger streets leading south from the Markt –
Marktstraat, Neerstraat and Minderbroeders Singel – you'll come across some
later and much more attractive architecture. Wherever you are in town, it's worth

keeping an eye open for Roermond's alluring twentieth-century **facades**: the majority are Art Nouveau, often strongly coloured with heavily moulded vegetal patterns and designs, sometimes with stylized animal heads and grotesque characters.

Roermond's principal architectural claim to fame is celebrated at the **Gemeentelijk Museum**, Andersonweg 2–8 (Tues–Fri 11am–5pm, Sat & Sun 2–5pm; *f*1). **P.J.H. Cuypers** (1827–1921) was Holland's foremost ecclesiastical architect in the nineteenth century, his work paralleling that of the British Gothic revivalist, Augustus Pugin. Almost every large city in the country has a Catholic church by him – those in Eindhoven, Leeuwarden and Hilversum are notable – though his two most famous buildings aren't churches, but the Rijksmuseum and the Centraal Station in Amsterdam. The museum is the building in which Cuypers lived and worked for much of his life and preserves a small private chapel as well as a large extension in which masses of decorative panels, mouldings and fixtures were produced. Other exhibits show his plans and paintings, along with a collection of works by other local artists, chiefly Hendrik Luyten.

Practicalities

Though it looks straightforward enough on the map, Roermond is a confusing place to walk around, its series of wide streets and broad squares irritatingly similar to the unacquainted. Use the Munsterkerk and river as landmarks, consult our map and you shouldn't get lost for too long.

The **VVV** office, Markt 24 (April–Sept Mon–Fri 9am–6pm, Sat 10am–4pm; Oct–March Mon–Fri 9am–5pm, Sat 9am–2pm; ☎33205), is a fair walk from the train station, which makes it worth deciding on accommodation before you arrive. A good range of inexpensive **hotels** includes *De Toerist*, Mariagardestraat 3 (☎18831; ②); and, just a little more expensive, *Fuserhof*, Raadhuisstraat 1 (☎29298; ③) and *De Herberg*, Borgeind 48 (☎51474; ③). Other possibilities include *De Pauw*, Roerkade 1–2 (☎16597; ④), and *Cox*, Maalbroak 102 (☎28946; ④–⑤). Or there's a single **pension**, *Van Eyden*, Burg. Moorenhof 22 (☎20771; ①).

The three main areas to **eat and drink** are those around the Markt, the Munsterkerk and the train station, although *Il Corso*, an excellent value and classily decorated Italian restaurant, is away from all these places at Willem II Singel 16a, the continuation of Godsweerder Singel. On Stationsplein, *Le Journal* and *De Tramhalte*, both at no. 17, are café-bars with inexpensive eats and although it's pricy for dinner, the restaurant of the *De La Station* hotel, Stationsplein 9, is worth checking out for its fixed-price lunches. *Le Chapeau* is a croissanterie ideal for breakfast and snacks, just down from Stationsplein at Hamstraat 54; Jugoslavija, Munsterplein 16, is a better-than-average Balkan restaurant with dishes starting at *f*12. *Tin San* is the best of several Chinese places, just south of the Markt at Varkensmarkt 1; while a little further south, *Marni*, at Schoenmakersstraat 16a (the continuation west of H. Geeststraat), has inexpensive Dutch–French food.

None of the bars in these areas are outstanding and Roermond seems to lack any first-rate watering-holes. Try *Herman's Beer Boetiek*, Schuitenberg 34, for a good range of beers, or *De Boag*, Veldstraat 5, which can get lively. For a more artistic night out, check out the *Orangerie*, a multicultural centre at Kloosterwandplein 12–16.

Thorn

If you do end up staying in Roermond, the village of **THORN** makes for an enjoyable half-day outing. Regular buses link it to the town, but it's more fun to rent a bike from the train station and cycle the 14km through the almost rolling Limburg farmland. If you do cycle, take a map that shows cycle routes – the signs marking the route off the main road are none too good.

Once you get here, it's easy to see why Thorn is a favourite for travel agents' posters. Its houses and farms are all painted white, a tradition for which no one seems to have a credible explanation, but one that distinguishes what would, in any case, be a resolutely picturesque place. The farms intrude right into the village itself, giving Thorn a barnyard friendliness that's increased by its cobblestone streets, the closed-shuttered propriety of its houses and, at the centre, the **Abdijkerk** (March–Oct daily 10am–5pm; Nov–Feb Sat & Sun noon–5pm; *f*2).

The abbey was founded at the end of the tenth century by a powerful count, Ansfried and his wife Hilsondis, as a sort of religious retirement home after Ansfried had finished his tenure as bishop of Utrecht. Under his control the abbey and the land around it was granted the status of an independent principality under the auspices of the Holy Roman Empire and it was in the environs of the abbey that the village developed. The abbey was unusual in having a double cloister that housed both men and women (usually from local noble families), a situation that carried on right up until the French invasion of 1797, after which the principality of Thorn was dissolved, the monks and nuns dispersed and all the abbey buildings save the church destroyed. Most of what can be seen of the church today dates from the fifteenth century, with some tidying up by P.J.H. Cuypers in the nineteenth. The interior decoration, though, is congenially restrained Baroque of the seventeenth century, with some good memorials and side chapels. If you're into the macabre, the crypt under the chancel has a couple of glass coffins containing conclusively dead members of the abbey from the eighteenth century: this and other highlights are described in the notes that you can pick up on entry (in English) for a self-guided walking tour.

Thorn has two small museums worth catching: the good-natured **Radio en Grammofoon Museum** at Hofstraat 10 (mid-April to mid-Oct Tues–Sat 11am–5pm, Sun noon–5pm; *f*2), with ancient radios, record players, telephones and televisions; and the **Poppenmuseum**, Akkerwal 27 (April to mid-Oct daily 11am–6pm; *f*2), packed with dolls, glove puppets, marionettes and old porcelain dolls.

The VVV, Houtstraat 10 (daily 10.30am–4.30pm; ☎04756/2761) can do little more than sell you postcards. Thorn makes a great place to stay if you want to get away from it all: the cheaper of two **hotels** is the *Crasborn*, Houtstraat 10 (☎04756/1281; ④), though the atmospheric *Hostellerie La Ville Blanche*, Hoogstraat 2 (☎04756/2341; ⑤) offers surprisingly affordable luxury. There's also a private **campsite**, reached by turning right halfway down Hofstraat.

Maastricht

MAASTRICHT was jettisoned into the headlines in the early 1990s. Up until then, few people had heard of this provincial Dutch town. Since the signing of the Masstricht treaty, however, in 1992, everyone at least knows its name, even if they couldn't place it on a map.

Don't, however, let Maastricht's Euro-connections put you off visiting. Far from being the bland, concrete Eurocity you might be expecting, it is on the contrary one of the most delightful cities in Holland, quite different in feel to the kitsch waterland centres of the north. Indeed it's obvious why the Eurocrats chose it as the place to sign their united Europe agreement. Outward-looking, vibrant and youthful, situated in the corner of the thin finger of land that reaches down between Belgium and Germany, where three languages and currencies happily coexist, it epitomizes the most positive aspects of European union.

Maastricht is a key industrial centre, with long-established manufacturing companies like Mosa (which produces domestic ceramic products from its plant on the east bank of the river) and Sphinx just north of the city centre, whose name graces toilets nationwide, spearheading Maastricht's prosperity. The town's position in the heart of Europe is also being traded on by the local authorities, keen to draw new money into the region – exemplified in projects like the newly completed MECC conference centre to the south of the city, where the treaty business was conducted.

Maastricht is also one of the oldest towns in the country. The first settlers here were Roman and Maastricht became an important stop on their trade route between Cologne and the coast – the town's name derives from the words *Mosae Trajectum* or "Maas Crossing". The Romans left relatively few obvious traces, but the later legacy of Charlemagne – whose capital was at nearby Aachen – is manifest in two churches that are among the best surviving examples of the Romanesque in the Low Countries.

The Maastricht area telephone code is ☎043

Arrival, information and accommodation

The centre of Maastricht is on the west bank of the river and most of the town spreads out from here toward the Belgian border. You're likely to arrive, however, on the east bank, in the district known as **Wijk**, a sort of extension to the centre that's home to the train and bus stations and is the location of many of the city's hotels. The train station itself is about ten minutes' walk from the St Servaas bridge, which takes you across the river into the centre. All local (ie non-yellow) buses connect with Markt from here, but really, if you have no heavy luggage, it's easy enough to walk. If you're flying direct to Maastricht, the **airport** is north of the city at BEEK, a twenty-minute journey away by bus; take bus #61, which runs every thirty minutes to Markt and the train station, or a taxi – a ƒ25 ride.

For local information, the **VVV** (Mon–Sat 9am–6pm; July & Aug Mon–Sat 9am–7pm, Sun 11am–3pm; ☎25 21 21) is housed just across the river in the Dinghuis, a tall late fifteenth-century building at Kleine Straat 1, at the end of the main shopping street. They have info on the city, decent maps for ƒ1.50 and copies of *Mass en MECC*, a weekly rundown on film, theatre and music events around town. In July and August they organize city tours (in English) currently leaving from the VVV at 12.30pm (ƒ5). **Getting around**, you only really need to use buses to get from the station to the town centre at Markt, or out to St Pietersburg; otherwise it's just as easy to walk everywhere.

For **accommodation**, there's nothing super-cheap. The VVV has **private rooms** and will either book them for you at the usual fee or sell you its list for ƒ1.50. The cheapest pension is in the heart of town, the *Pension Zwets*, Bredestraat 41 (☎21 64 82; ②). Otherwise, of the city's **hotels**, the *De la Guide*, at Stationsstraat 17a (☎21 61 76; ③) and – more comfortably – *De Poshoorn*, Stationsstraat 47 (☎21 73 34; ③), both have doubles from about ƒ90; more upmarket is the *Le Roi*, almost opposite the station at St Maartenslaan 1 (☎25 38 38; ④), which has doubles with private bath for around ƒ125. If you want to stay across the river (though Wijk is quite pleasant and not at all far out), the *La Colombe*, at Markt 30 (☎21 57 74; ③–④), is pleasant and there's also a *Hotelboot* (☎21 90 23; ③), moored on the river on Maasboulevard, not far from the Helpoort. If you're **camping**, the *De Dousberg* site, almost in Belgium on the far western side of town, is open all year, large and well equipped; take bus #8 from the train station and walk for about a kilometre. There's also a **youth hostel** nearby at Dousbergweg 4 (☎43 44 04) – again, bus #8 – and adjoining it a budget hotel (③) which lets private rooms.

The Town

The busiest of Maastricht's squares is the **Markt**, at its most crowded on Wednesday and Friday mornings, when people hop over the nearby borders for the town's cheap general market. At the centre of the square, which is a car park the rest of the time, the **Stadhuis** (Mon–Fri 8.30am–12.30pm & 2–5.30pm; free) of 1664 was designed by Pieter Post, a square, grey limestone building that is a fairly typical slice of mid-seventeenth-century Dutch civic grandeur. Its double staircase was designed so that the rival rulers of Brabant and nearby Liège didn't have to argue about who should go first on the way in. Inside, the building has an imposing main hall, which gives way to a rear octagonal dome supported by heavy arches.

The second of the town's main central squares, **Vrijthof**, is just west of the Markt, a larger, rather grander open space flanked by a couple of churches on one side and a line of cafés on the other, with tables smothering the wide pavement in summer. During the Middle Ages, Vrijthof was the scene of the so-called "Fair of the Holy Relics", a seven-yearly showing of the bones of Saint Servaas, the first bishop of Maastricht, which brought plenty of pilgrims and funds into the town but resulted in such civil disorder that it was eventually banned. The church which holds the relics now, the **St Servaaskerk** (daily 10am–5pm, except Fri 10am–2pm; ƒ3.50), dominates the far side of the square. Dating originally from 950, it's the elaborate amalgamation of an earlier shrine dedicated to Saint Servaas and the site of his burial in 384. Only the crypt remains of the tenth-century church, containing the tomb of the saint himself and the rest is mostly of medieval or later construction. The building looks better than it has done for some time following a recent thorough restoration. Entry is through the mid-thirteenth-century Bergportaal on the south side of the church, into a rich and imposing interior, the round-arched nave supporting freshly painted Gothic vaulting. On the north side of the church, the fifteenth-century Gothic cloister leads into the **treasury** (July & Aug daily 10am–6pm; Dec–March daily 10am–4pm; otherwise daily 10am–5pm; use church entrance ticket), which holds a large collection of reliquaries, goblets and liturgical accessories, including a bust

MAASTRICHT

reliquary of Saint Servaas, decorated with reliefs telling the saint's story, which is carried through the town in Easter processions. There's also a coffin-reliquary of the saint, the so-called "Noodkist", dating from 1160 and bristling with saints, stones and ornate copperwork, as well as a jewelled crucifix from 890 and a twelfth-century Crucifixion in ivory.

The second most prominent building on the square, next door, is Maastricht's main Protestant church, the fourteenth-century **St Janskerk** (Easter to mid-Sept Mon–Sat; f1.50), the baptistery of the church of St Servaas when it was a cathedral and nowadays competing for attention with its high and faded, delicate red fifteenth-century Gothic tower, which you can climb for another f1.50. Inside are some medieval murals, but otherwise a climb up the tower is the church's main appeal. On the south side of the square, the sixteenth-century **Spanish Government House** (guided tours only, every hour, on the hour; Wed 2–5pm; Thurs 10am–1pm & 2–5pm; May–Oct 31 also Sat 10am–1pm; f4.50) has an attractive Renaissance arcade and a number of period rooms furnished in Dutch, French and the more local Liège–Maastricht style. Among various exhibits are statues and figurines, porcelain and applied arts and a handful of seventeenth-century paintings, though none is exactly essential viewing.

The **Bonnefanten Museum** (Tues–Fri 10am–5pm, Sat & Sun 11am–5pm; f5) is more engaging – Maastricht's main city museum, so-called because of its former home in the eighteenth-century convent of the same name, southwest of the city centre and since rehoused in a functional modern structure just off the opposite corner of Vrijthof. Much of the museum is devoted to temporary exhibitions of varying quality, but on the third floor there's a permanent display of artefacts relating to Limburg and Maastricht, as well as a collection of paintings. Of the former, there are lots of archeological finds, many of which date from the Roman era hereabouts, religious statuary and other bits and pieces of limited interest; if you're lucky there'll also be ceramics from the Mosa works on display and a scale model of Maastricht in 1748. Of the museum's art collection, among many indifferent sixteenth-century works are paintings by the Bruegels, van Mander and Bernard van Orley and some canvases from the Italian Renaissance, notably a coolly executed *Mary Adoring Christ* by Filippino Lippi.

Maastricht's other main church, the **Onze Lieve Vrouwe Basiliek**, is a short walk south of Vrijthof, down Bredestraat, in a small, shady square crammed with café tables in summer. It's unusual for its fortified west front, with barely more than one or two slits for windows. First built around the year 1000, it's a solid, dark and eerily devotional place after the bright Protestant churches of the North – or even the relative sterility of the St Servaaskerk. The Gothic vaulting of the nave springs from a Romanesque base, while the galleried choir is a masterpiece of proportion, raised under a high half-dome, with a series of capitals exquisitely decorated with Old Testament scenes. Off the north aisle, the treasury (Easter to mid-Sept Mon–Sat 11am–5pm, Sun 1–5pm; f3.50) holds the usual array of reliquaries and ecclesiastical garments, most notably the dalmatic of Saint Lambert – the evangelical bishop of Maastricht who was murdered at Liège in 705, allegedly by a local noble whom he had rebuked for adultery.

Around the corner from the square, on Plankstraat, on the edge of a district of narrow streets known as the **Stokstraat Kwartier** after its main gallery- and boutique-lined spine, Stokstraat, is the **Museumkelder Derlon** (Sun noon–4pm; free), in the basement of the hotel of the same name. This contains one of the few remnants of Roman Maastricht – the remains of a temple to Jupiter, a well and several layers of pavement, discovered before the building of the present hotel in the mid-1980s. On the other side of Onze Lieve Vrouweplein lies another of Maastricht's most appealing quarters, narrow streets winding out to the remains of the town battlements alongside the fast-flowing River Jeker, which weaves in and out of the various houses and ancient mills. The best surviving part of the walls is the **Helpoort** of 1229, close to a stretch overlooking the river at the end of St Bernadusstraat; and from here you can walk along the top of the walls almost as far as the **Natural History Museum** at De Bosquetplein 6 (Mon–Fri 10am–12.30pm & 1.30–5pm, Sat & Sun 2–5pm; ƒ2.50), where there's a small collection on the geology, flora and fauna of the surrounding area, along with a small, lush garden display. A little way south of here, the **Casemates** in the Waldeck Park (July & Aug tours daily at 2pm; mid-July & mid-Aug also at 12.30pm; ƒ5) are further evidence of Maastricht's once impressive fortifications, a system of galleries created through mining between 1575 and 1825 that were used in times of siege for surprise attacks on the enemy. There used to be many more casemates around the town, but only these survive, making for a fairly drafty way to spend an hour, tours taking you through a small selection of the 10km or so of damp passages. Probably the most interesting thing about them is the fact that the fourth "musketeer", d'Artagnan, was killed here, struck down while engaged in an attack on the town as part of forces allied to Louis XIV in 1673.

Outside the centre: St Pietersberg

There are more dank passageways to explore fifteen minutes' walk from the casemates on the southern outskirts of Maastricht, where the flat-topped hill of **St Pietersberg** rises up to a height of about 110m – a popular picnic spot on warm summer weekends. Again these aren't so much caves as galleries created by quarrying, hollowed out of the soft sandstone, or marl, which makes up the hill – an activity which has been going on here since Roman times. The marl hardens in exposure to the air, so is a much more useful material than might at first be imagined. Of the two cave systems, the **Zonneberg** is probably the better, situated on the far side of the St Pietersberg hill at Casino Slavante (guided tours – not in English – May to mid-Sept Mon–Sat hourly 10.45am–3.45pm, Sun hourly 1.45–3.45pm; mid-Sept to end Sept Sun at 1.30pm; Oct–April Sun at 2.30pm; ƒ5). The caves here were intended to be used as air-raid shelters during the last war and were equipped accordingly, though they were only in fact utilized during the last few days before Maastricht's liberation. There is some evidence of wartime occupation, plus what everyone claims is Napoleon's signature on a graffiti-ridden wall. Also on the walls are recent charcoal drawings, usually illustrating a local story and acting as visual aids for the guides, not to mention the ten varieties of bat that inhabit the dark (and cold) corridors.

The other, more northerly system of caves, the **Grotten Noord** (guided tours Jan–March Wed, Sat & Sun at 2pm; April & May Mon–Sat 12.30pm & 2pm, Sun also at 3.30pm; June, July & Aug daily 12.30pm, 2pm & 3.30pm; Nov & Dec Wed at 2pm, Sat & Sun at 12.30pm & 2pm; ƒ5; tours in English in July & Aug daily at 3pm) is easier to get to (a 15-min walk from the centre of town), but it has less of interest. The entrance is at Chalet Bergrust, on the near side of St Pietersberg close by **Fort St Pieter**, a low brick structure, pentagonal in shape and built in 1702, which nowadays houses a pricy restaurant. You can visit – there are guided tours (July & Aug at 3pm; ƒ5) that leave from the restaurant – but (especially if you've had your fill of fortifications) you'd probably do just as well nursing a drink on the restaurant's terrace, which gives panoramic views over the town and surrounding countryside.

Eating, drinking and nightlife

Eating is never a problem in Maastricht. The city has a huge number of restaurants, covering the spectrum in quality; indeed, in Holland Maastricht is renowned for its good food. At the bottom end of the price scale, on Graanmarkt, just off Onze Lieve Vrouweplein toward the river, *Le Chevalier* is a reasonably priced *eetcafé* where the fare includes omelettes, *uitsmijters* and the like. Nearby, *D'n Blind Genger*, on Koestraat, is only slightly more expensive and has a varied menu and nice atmosphere. *Da Giovanni*, just off Vrijthof on Platielstraat, does a creditable plate of pasta and reasonable pizzas – though, oddly, it doesn't sell beer. *Jansen*, on A.H. Vleeshius, near St Amorsplein, is an *eetcafé* with lots of cheap things to eat, including good salads and vegetarian dishes, although it tends to close up early. With a little more money, *Galerie*, Onze Lieve Vrouweplein 28, is rather self-consciously trendy but has good French–Dutch food. You might also try *L'Escale*, Havenstraat 19, the cheaper arm of the fancy *t'Klaoske*, which does excellent three-course menus and *dagschotels*.

Drinking, too, you're spoiled for choice – there are, apparently, around four hundred bars in Maastricht. Those that line the east side of Vrijthof are packed all day and evening in summer, with outside spaces at a premium. *In den Ouden Vogelstruys*, on the corner of Platielstraat, is one of the nicest, though really any of them make a good place to while away the end of the day sipping a drink – and prices are barely more expensive than anywhere else. Away from Vrijthof, *De Bobbel*, on Wolfstraat just off Onze Lieve Vrouweplein, is a bare-boards bar, lively early evening and serving some well-priced bar snacks. *Falstaff*, on St Amorsplein, just down Platielstraat from Vrijthof, is younger and noisier, playing good music and serving a wide range of beers; it also has outside seating. *Touchdown*, further up Platielstraat, is a good bar with pool and regular live bands, usually playing for free. There are also a few good bars on the Wijk side of the river: *Casjet*, on Corversplein, is one of several close to the St Servaasbrug overlooking the river; *De Gijsbrecht*, toward the station on Wycker Brugstraat, is a very busy bar, packed in the evening and serving cheap meals and snacks during the day.

If you don't want to drink, bear in mind that the *Lumière Filmhuis*, Bogaardenstraat 40b (☎21 40 80), regularly shows interesting **movies**, often English or American and always with Dutch subtitles: details in *Maas en Mecc*.

Listings

Airport Situated north of Maastricht at Beek and connected to the train station and Markt by bus #61, which runs every 30min until about 8pm, then hourly until 10pm – a 20-min ride; otherwise taxis cost about ƒ25. Flight enquiries on ☎66 66 80.

Boat trips Between mid-April and the end of Sept, *Stiphout Cruises* runs hourly cruises down the Maas Mon–Sat 10am–5pm, Sun 1–5pm; ƒ7.50 per person. *Stiphout* also offers (less frequent) trips taking in the St Pietersberg caves (ƒ12) – or even as far as Liège (day trip ƒ27.50). Phone ☎25 41 51 for details.

Books There's a branch of *De Slegte* at Wolfstraat 8, good for second-hand English paperbacks and much else besides. Try also *Bergmans* on Nieuwestraat, off Markt, which has a good selection of new English books.

Bureau de change There's a GWK office at the train station, open every day.

Car rental *Avis*, Spoorweglaan 18 (☎25 23 77); *Hertz*, Wilhelminasingel 32 (☎25 19 71). The major companies also have desks at the airport.

City tours The VVV organizes guided tours, leaving from its office, of the city and its fortifications, usually daily at 2pm between Easter and early Oct, twice daily in July & Aug. They last around 1hr 30min and cost ƒ5 per person. English language tours July & Aug only at 12.30pm.

Post office The main city post office is on Keizer Karelplein, just off the northwest corner of Vrijthof.

Around South Limburg

South Limburg boasts Holland's only true hills and as such is a popular holiday area for the Dutch, many of the villages crammed in summer with walkers from the north taking in the scenery. And this is certainly worth doing, the countryside green and rolling, studded with castles (many of which have been converted to hotels), seamed with river valleys and dotted with the timber-framed houses that are unique to the area. Everywhere is within easy reach of Maastricht and perfectly feasible on day trips, though without a car you shouldn't try and cover too much in one day as public transport connections are patchy. **Valkenburg**, the main resort, is perhaps the easiest place to visit, on the main train line from Maastricht to Aachen, though it is packed throughout the summer. Further east down the train line, **Heerlen** and **Kerkrade** are also easily reached, though neither is any great shakes. To the south of the train line, toward the Belgian border, the countryside is wilder and more impressive, the roads snaking over hills and giving long, expansive views all around. It's not at all a Dutch scene and perhaps not what you came to Holland for. But after the grindingly flat landscapes of the northern provinces, it can be excellent therapy – as numerous hotels, one for every tiny village, testify.

Cadier-en-Keer, Margraten and Gulpen

Five kilometres east of Maastricht, the first stop on the #54 bus route – which eventually goes to Vaals on the German border – **CADIER-EN-KEER** is a small suburb of the city best known for its **Africa Centre** (Mon–Fri 1.30–5pm, Sun 2–5pm; ƒ3), ten minutes' walk off to the left of the main road (follow the signs). Housed in the headquarters of the African Missionaries Society, this contains a small museum of (mainly West) African artefacts, masks, jewellery and statuary arranged by tribe and dating back as far as the thirteenth century – as well as giving details on the contemporary way of life of African peoples.

Bus #54 continues on to **MARGRATEN**, where just before the town proper there's an **American War Cemetery** (daily sunrise–sunset), a peaceful and in some ways moving memorial to over eight thousand American servicemen who died in the Dutch and Belgian campaigns of late 1944 and 1945. Buses stop right outside. The centrepiece is a stone quadrangle recording the names of the soldiers, together with a small visitors' room and a pictorial representation and narrative describing the events in this area leading up to the German surrender – while beyond the quadrangle, the white marble crosses that mark the burial places of the soldiers cover a depressingly huge area.

There's not much else to Margraten, nor is there to **GULPEN**, a few kilometres beyond, a nondescript place though with good bus connections all over South Limburg. The town is known for its *Gulpener* beer, the name of which you see all over the province and indeed the rest of Holland, though that aside the only thing that distinguishes Gulpen is the 161-metre-high **Gulpenberg**, which rises roundly behind the town and is home to a **campsite**. South of Gulpen, the countryside rises higher and makes for a pretty route back to Maastricht, either driving yourself or via the # 57 bus route from Gulpen's bus station, taking in the scenically sited villages of **MECHELEN**, **EPEN** and **SLENAKEN**.

Valkenburg

Set in the gently wooded valley of the River Geul, **VALKENBURG**, ten minutes' east of Maastricht by train, is southern Limburg's major tourist resort, the unloading point for buses full of tourists throughout the summer, with innumerable hotels, restaurants and even a casino. While you wouldn't want to stay here, it's a nice enough place to visit, about as far away from the clogs and canals of the rest of the country as it's possible to get, with a feel more of a Swiss or Austrian alpine resort, its small restaurant-ridden centre sloping up from its fake castle train station to the surrounding green hills, full of grottoes, castles and thermal centres.

Theo Dorrenplein, five minutes' walk from the train station, is the centre of town, fringed with cafés and home to the VVV, from where the main Grote Straat leads up through the pedestrianized old centre through the old **Grendelpoort** arch to **Grendelplein**, which provides a second focus, the streets which lead off going to Valkenburg's main attractions. A great many of these are directed at children – things like bob-sleigh runs, a fairytale wood, a hopeful reconstruction of Rome's catacombs – and even those that aren't are the kind of things kids enjoy.

It's worth a walk up to the **Castle** (April–Oct daily 10am–5pm; *f*2; entrance off Grendelplein), a ruined edifice which overlooks the town from a neatly placed peak above Grote Straat. It was blown up in 1672 on the orders of William III, after he had retrieved it from its French occupiers. Repair and restoration on the castle began in 1921 and continue still, uncovering a series of underground passages that served as an escape route in times of siege. These form part of the **Fluwelengrot** (guided tours only; April–Nov daily 10am–5pm; Dec–March Sat & Sun 11am–4pm; *f*5), further up the road on the left, a series of caves formed – like those of St Pietersberg in Maastricht – by the quarrying of marl, which has been used for much of the building in this area over the years. Tours leave every ten minutes or so in high summer (much less frequently outside this period), but on the whole they're a damp, cold way to spend an hour, the most interesting features the signatures and silhouettes of American soldiers who wintered here from 1944 to 1945 and a clandestine chapel that was used during the late eighteenth-century French occupation.

If you particularly like caves, or can't be bothered to walk around the Fluwelengrot, the **Gemeentegrot** (same times and prices), just off Grendelplein on Cauberg, is similar, but has a train which whips you around its charcoal drawings, memorials to local dignitaries, giant sculptures of dinosaurs and fish hewn out of the rock, and, most engagingly, a weirdly, brightly lit underground lake. The whole tour takes about half an hour and costs a guilder extra. Further up the same road as the Fluwelengrot, on the left, the **Steenkolemijn** (guided tours only April–Oct daily 10am–5pm; Nov–March Sat & Sun at 2pm & 3pm; ƒ8.50) is a reconstruction of a coal mine whose hour-and-a-quarter-long tours include a short film on coal-mining, some fake mine-workings and a small fossil museum. Again, good for the kids but not exactly riveting viewing. If the idea of trudging around dank underground passages doesn't appeal to you, you can ascend to the top of the hill above the castle by way of a **cable car** (July & Aug daily 10am–5pm; rest of the year daily 1–5pm; ƒ4.50 return), five minutes' walk down Berkelstraat from the top of Grote Straat – or you can cut through the passage between the castle and the Fluwelengrot. This, a fairly primitive structure of the kind used for ski lifts, with two-person open cars, takes you up to the **Wilhemina Toren**, where you can enjoy the view from the terrace of the inevitable bar-restaurant.

Practicalities

The VVV at Theo Dorrenplein 5 (Easter–Nov Mon–Fri 9am–6pm, Sat 9am–5pm; Dec–Easter Mon–Fri 9am–5pm, Sat 9am–1pm; ☎04406/13364) has maps and information on all Valkenburg's attractions, as well as lists of **hotels** and **private rooms** if you want to stay. The cheapest is *Hotel de Uitkijk*, Broekhem 68 (☎04406/13589; ③). Bear in mind, though, that, despite the enormous number of rooms here, availability can be a problem in high season. **Camping**, the nearest site is a short walk up Dahlemerweg from Grendelplein on the left. As virtually every other building in Valkenburg is a restaurant, there's little point in listing specific places to **eat**. Suffice to say you can dine cheaply and fairly reasonably at most of the places in the centre – though don't expect haute cuisine.

Heerlen and Kerkrade

HEERLEN, ten minutes further from Valkenburg by train, is quite different, an ugly modern town that sprawls gracelessly over the rolling countryside. But it has one definite attraction in the excellent **Thermen Museum** (Tues–Fri 10am–5pm, Sat & Sun 2–5pm; ƒ3), which incorporates the excavations of a bath complex from the Roman city of Coriovallum here – a key settlement on the Cologne–Boulogne trade route. These have been enclosed in a gleaming hi-tech purpose-built structure, with walkways leading across the ruins and tapes (in English) explaining what's what. An adjacent room displays finds and artefacts from the site, including glasswork from Cologne, shards of pottery, tombstones and coins, all neatly labelled. To get to the museum, follow Saroleastraat from the station as far as Raadhuisplein and turn right.

Fifteen minutes on from Heerlen lies **KERKRADE**, again an unappealing place, but worthy of a visit for its **Abdij van Rolduc** complex, situated on the far side of town, about a twenty minute walk from the station. Originally founded by one Ailbert, a young priest who came here in 1104, this is now almost entirely sixteenth-century, used as a seminary and conference centre, but it does preserve a fine twelfth-century church, a model of simplicity and elegance, with contemporary frescoes and a marvellous mosaic floor. The clover leaf-shaped crypt, dark and mysterious after the church and with pillar capitals carved by Italian craftsmen, contains the relics of Ailbert, brought here from Germany where he died; while next door to the church, a **Mine Museum** describes mining through the ages in the area – appropriate enough in the shadow of the giant slagheaps nearby.

travel details

Trains

Breda to: Dordrecht (every 20min; 20min); 's Hertogenbosch (2 hourly; 35min).

Eindhoven to: Roermond (every 30min; 32min); Venlo (every 30min; 45min).

's Hertogenbosch to: Eindhoven (every 30min; 22min).

Middelburg to: Bergen-op-Zoom (every 30min; 45min); Goes (every 30min; 15min); Roosendaal (every 30min; 55min).

Roermond to: Maastricht (hourly; 30min); Venlo (every 30min; 26min).

Roosendaal to: Breda (every 30min; 18min); Dordrecht (every 30min; 30min).

Tilburg to: Eindhoven (every 30min; 30min); 's Hertogenbosch (every 30min; 15 min).

Vlissingen to: Middelburg (every 30min; 7min).

Buses

Middelburg to: Delta Expo (hourly; 30min); Renesse (hourly; 45min); Veere (hourly; 10min).

Renesse to: Bouwershaven (hourly; 1hr 30min).

Venray to: Overloon (hourly; 10min).

Zierikzee to: Goes (every 30min; 30min).

Ferries

Vlissingen to: Breskens (Mon–Fri every 30min, Sat & Sun hourly; 20min).

International trains

Maastrict to: Bruges (hourly; 2hr 50min); Brussels (hourly; 2hr); Gent (hourly; 2hr 30min); Leuven (hourly; 1hr 30min); Liège (hourly; 30min).

Roosendaal to: Antwerp (every 30min; 30min); Bruges (hourly; 1hr 50min); Brussels (hourly; 40min); Gent (hourly; 1hr 15min); Oostende (hourly; 2hr); Paris (4 daily; 4hr).

PART THREE

BELGIUM AND LUXEMBOURG

HOLLAND

FLANDERS

ANTWERP AND
THE NORTH

WEST
GERMANY

BRUSSELS
AND AROUND

HAINAUT

THE ARDENNES

FRANCE

LUX.
LUXEMBOURG

0   50 km

Introduction

A federal country, with three official languages and an intense regional rivalry, Belgium has a cultural mix and diversity which belie its rather dull reputation among travellers. Luxembourg, too, though known as a tiny refuge of bankers and diplomats, has surprises in store, scenically one of the most beautiful countries in northern Europe, its green, wooded hills rolling down to its strikingly situated capital.

■ The Belgian language divide

Belgium is the land where the French- and German-speaking nations meet, the tensions between the two a consistent historical threat to the prosperity and welfare of its people. Today, the country's population of around ten million is fairly evenly divided between Flemish-speakers (about sixty percent) and Walloons (about forty percent), who speak French as their first language; there are even, in the far east of the country, a few pockets of German-speakers around the city of Eupen. Certainly, Belgium's language problems are not to be taken lightly, reflecting, as they do, deep class and economic divisions. Prosperity has shifted back and forth between the two communities over the centuries: in medieval times Flanders grew rich on its textile trade; later Wallonia developed mining and steel industries. But through the ages the Francophones have always represented the aristocracy, the Flemings the bourgeoisie. The setting-up of the Belgian state in 1830 crystallized the antagonism, with the final arrangements favouring the French-speakers. French became the official language, Flemish was banned in schools (the Belgian Civil Code was only translated into Flemish in 1961), and the industries of Wallonia were dominant. Nowadays, however, Flanders is the industrial powerhouse of Belgium – a fact championed by Flemish nationalist parties like the *Volksunie*, who would also like to see Brussels become a totally Flemish city.

The line between the two cultures – officially called the "language divide" and effectively cutting the country in half, west to east – was drawn in 1962, but in response to increasing acrimony between the two communities the constitution has since been redrawn (in 1982) on a federal basis, with three separate entities – the Flemish North, the Walloon South and Brussels, which is officially bilingual (although its population is eighty percent French-speaking). However, the division between Flemish Flanders and French Wallonia still influences every aspect of working and social life. Schools, political parties, literature, culture – all are segregated along linguistic lines. Neighbours refuse to speak to one another because of the conflict, and stereotypes are deeply ingrained, leading to a set of complex, face-saving rules and regulations which can verge on the absurd. Press conferences, for example, must have questions and answers repeated in both languages, one after the other. Bitterness about the economy, unemployment and the government smoulders within the framework of this linguistic division, and individual neighbourhoods can be paralyzed by language disputes. The communities of Fourons (Voeren), for example, a largely French-speaking collection of villages in Flemish Limburg, known as the *voerstreek*, almost brought down the government in the mid-Eighties when the Francophone mayor, Jose Happart, refused to take the Flemish language exam required of all Flanders officials. He was divested of office several times, and each time stood for mayor again and was re-elected, prompting the prime minister at the time, Wilfred Martens, to offer his own resignation. The Fourons affair was symptomatic of the obstinacy that besets the country to this day. Jose Happart could probably pass that Flemish exam easily, indeed rumour has it that he is fluent in the language. He simply chooses not to submit.

All this said, it would be wrong to assume that Belgium's language differences have yet gone beyond the level of personal animosity and institutionalized mutual suspicion. Belgian language extremists have been imprisoned over the years, but very few, if any, have died in the fight for supremacy. Indeed, some might see a bilingual nation as a positive thing in a Europe where trading – and national – barriers are being increasingly broken down. Suggesting this to a Belgian, however, is useless. He or she will only turn away in disgust.

■ Where to go

There's more to the Flemish–Walloon divide than just language: the North and South of **Belgium** are visually very different places. The **North**, made up of the provinces of West and East Flanders, Antwerp, Limburg and the top half of Brabant, is mainly flat, with a landscape and architecture not unlike Holland. **Antwerp** is the largest city, a big, sprawling, bustling old port with doses of sleaze and high art in roughly equal measure. Further south, in the Flemish heartland of Flanders, are the great Belgian historic cities, **Bruges** and **Ghent** – tourist attractions in themselves, with a stunning concentration of Flemish art and architecture. Bruges especially is the country's biggest tourist pull, and although this inevitably means it gets very crowded, you shouldn't miss it on any account. Beyond lies the Belgian **coast**, which makes valiant attempts to compete with the rest of Europe but is ultimately let down by the crassness of its development and the coldness of the North Sea. Far better to spend time in some of the other inland Flanders towns, not least **Ieper**, formerly and better known as Ypres to the English-speaking world; many veterans and pilgrims come to visit the stark sights of the nearby World War I **battlefields**.

Marking the meeting of the Flemish and Walloon parts of Belgium, **Brussels**, the capital, is central enough to be pretty much unavoidable, a culturally varied city, more exciting and varied than its reputation as bland Euro-capital would suggest. Because Belgium is not a large country, you can also use it as a base for day trips out: Bruges and Ghent are easily feasible, as is the old university city of **Leuven** (Louvain) to the north, or even the cathedral city of **Mechelen**, halfway to Antwerp.

The southern part of Brussels' province, **Brabant**, is French-speaking, and merges into the solely Walloon province of **Hainaut** – rich agricultural country, dotted with ancient cities like **Tournai**, and industrial centres like **Charleroi** and **Mons**. East of here lies Belgium's most scenically rewarding region, the **Ardennes**, spread across the three provinces of **Namur**, **Liège** and **Luxembourg**: an area of deep, wooded valleys, high elevations and heathy plateaux and caverns that, beyond the main tourist resorts, is very wild indeed – by any standards, let alone those of normally tame Belgium. Use either Liège or Luxembourg as a jumping-off point, before heading into the heart of the region at **St-Hubert**, **Han-sur-Lesse** or **La Roche**.

Luxembourg

The Ardennes reach across the Belgian border into the northern part of the **Grand Duchy of Luxembourg**, a high, green, almost Alpine landscape of high hills topped with crumbling castles overlooking rushing rivers. **Vianden**, **Echternach** and **Clervaux** are perhaps the three best of very few centres for touring the countryside – quiet small towns with little life outside the tourist industry. However, the country's status as European nonentity is quite unjust; in fact it packs more scenic highlights into its tight borders than many other, more renowned holiday spots. And while its southern reaches are much more ordinary, **Luxembourg city** at least is worth a stop. Dramatically sited, it's about the closest the country gets to a proper urban environment, although its population of 75,000 people (around a fifth of the Grand Duchy's total) is still tiny by capital city standards.

Getting around

As with Holland, travelling around Belgium **is rarely a problem. Once again, the fact that it's a small country means distances are short, and there's a well-organized – and reasonably priced – train service linking them, supplemented by plentiful buses. Luxembourg, on the other hand, can be problematic for such a tiny country: the train network is not extensive, and bus timetables often demand careful study if you're doing much independent travelling.**

■ Trains

Like Holland, too, the best way of getting around Belgium is by **train**. Run by the *Société National Chemin de Fer de Belgique/Belgische Spoorwegen* (*Belgian Railroads*), denoted by a simple "B" in an oval, the system is comprehensive and efficient, and fares – at least compared to much else in the country – are affordably low, just over F300 for a journey of 100km; indeed you can travel the length of the country for well under F1000.

You can, of course, cut costs further by investing in a **rail pass** – though this is only really worth it if you're going to be doing a lot of travelling. The **Belgian Tourrail pass** gives entitlement to five days' unlimited rail travel within a seventeen-day period for F1980 (F1300 if you're under 26). There is also the so-called Half-Fare Card, which for F550 allows you to purchase first- and second-class tickets at half price during the period of a month, and the **Go Pass**, valid for eight second-class journeys between two stations within six months for one or more people – price F990 for under-25s. Consider also the **Benelux Tourrail Card**, valid for any five days within a month on the Belgian, Dutch and Luxembourg national networks, as well as Luxembourg buses, for F3780 – under-26s F2860. If you're travelling to a town for a specific attraction, you might also consider taking one of *Belgian Railways* organized **excursions**, whereby you pay a price – usually around F200 – that includes a round-trip ticket, entry prices and sometimes a meal.

Belgian Railways publishes lots of **information** on their various offers and services, available in advance from the Belgian Tourist Office branches (see *Basics*). They'll sell you national (F150) and international (F50) timetables, though these are of course also available from train stations inside the country.

In **Luxembourg** the railways are run by *Chemins de Fer de Luxembourg – CFL –* and are not at all as wide-reaching as those in Belgium. There's one main north–south route down the middle of the country to Luxembourg city, but apart from that only a few lines branching out from the capital, and the system is mainly supplemented by buses. There are a number of passes available if you're going to be doing a lot of travelling, giving unlimited train (and bus) travel for periods lasting from one day to a month. The price for a one-day pass is F140, a pack of five one-day tickets F540. These are valid from the first time you use them (you must punch them in the machines provided to record the time) for 24 hours, and as such are much the most flexible kind of pass you can get. Failing that, if you're going to be around for some time, monthly passes, valid for a full

calendar month, cost F1300. Obviously the *Benelux Tourrail Card* is also valid on both trains and *CFL* buses.

■ Buses

As so much of the country is covered by the rail network, **buses** in Belgium (run by *SNCV*, the national bus company) are only really used for travelling short distances, and whenever there are alternatives, the train is generally quicker and not much more expensive. Where you will use buses is to travel around and into the environs of major towns and cities, or in the Botte de Hainaut and some parts of the Ardennes, where the train network is less comprehensive. In most towns the main bus terminal is next door to the train station.

In Luxembourg the reverse is true: because of the sparsity of the rail system, buses are a much more usual way of getting around, many of them run by *Luxembourg Railways* and indeed replacements in many cases for former branch lines. In all cases, the bus services are fully integrated with the trains. Fares are comparable, and it's worth knowing that at weekends and on holidays the price of a one-way and round-trip ticket are the same. There are also a number of passes available if you're doing a lot of travelling; see "Trains" for details.

■ Driving and hitching

In either Belgium or Luxembourg, **driving** is not something that will cause many problems. Both countries are well covered by networks of main roads and (toll-free) motorways, and congestion is normally tolerable outside the major cities.

Rules of the road are much the same as in Holland: you drive on the right, and the speed-limit in residential areas is 60kph, on main roads 90kph and on motorways 120kph. You need an International Driver's Licence in order to drive, available from home motoring organizations for a small charge. In general, fuel costs are broadly the same as the UK, and much higher than those of the US.

There are two national motoring organizations in Belgium: the *Tourist Club Belgique* (*TCB*), rue de la Loi 44, Brussels 1040 (☎02/233 22 11), and the *Royal Automobile Club de Belgique*, rue d'Arlon 53, Brussels 1040 (☎02/287 09 11). In Luxembourg there's the *Automobile Club ACL*, route de Longuly 54, Luxembourg (☎45 00 45). All three organizations have reciprocal arrangements with national motoring organizations worldwide,

and can be called upon in case of **breakdown**. Most major roads in Belgium have phones along the roads. Seat belts in both countries are compulsory, and penalties for drunken driving stiff. Immediate fines are common for some offences, and in Luxembourg it's obligatory to carry at least F600 on you at all times for payment of fines.

Car rental in both countries is quite pricy, from about F13,500 a week with unlimited mileage in Belgium, a little under F10,000 in Luxembourg. As usual it works out cheaper if you book it before you leave home. As in Holland, it is also possible to cut costs greatly by means of special weekend deals and the like.

As for **hitching**, this is easy: the Belgians give lifts to hitchhikers frequently, and the size of the country makes it a perfectly feasible way of getting around. Hitching on motorways is illegal, but the major towns of both countries are well connected by a good network of main roads, so this isn't usually a problem.

■ Cycling

Cycling is something of a national sport in Belgium, and it is also a viable way of getting around, the short distances and largely flat terrain making it a fairly effortless business for the non-enthusiast – and keen cyclists have, in the Ardennes, some ideal and very scenic terrain to indulge their pleasure. Most roads have bicycle lanes (use the outer one where there's a choice), and the *Geocart* maps, detailed in *Basics*, are adequate for route planning; many of the country's tourist offices also have details, and sometimes maps, of recommended cycling routes.

If you haven't brought your own bike, you can **rent** one from around sixty train stations nationwide, returning it to the station of your choice (normally open daily 7am–9pm). Rates are cheap: F150 a day with a valid train ticket, F200 without; for a period of three days or more, the price is F100 a day, and during summer at least, it's advisable to book. No deposits are required. For a list of train stations offering this service, get hold of *Belgian Railways' Train & Vélo (Trein & Fiets)* leaflet, available in advance from the Belgian Tourist Office (again, see *Basics* for details of offices or train stations in Belgium itself.

Whether you have your own, or have rented one from elsewhere, it is possible to take your **bike on the train**; rates are F160 per journey.

In Luxembourg you can rent bikes at local offices throughout the country for around F250 a day; local tourist offices have details of locations where they're not mentioned in *the Guide*. Bear in mind also that you can take your bike on trains anywhere in Luxembourg for F20 or so a machine. The Luxembourg Tourist Office issues a booklet showing possible cycling routes.

Accommodation

In Belgium and Luxembourg, accommodation is one of the major expenses you will incur: hotels, even the roughest places, are never cheap, and hostels only provide an alternative in the larger cities and resorts.

■ Hotels and private rooms

Hotels in Belgium and Luxembourg are roughly classified according to cost: prices range from an absolute minimum of around F1000 for a double room in the cheapest one-star establishment to between F5000 and F8000 in the big city luxury hotels, though prices vary according to the tourist interest-rating of the town. In cheaper establishments breakfast isn't always included in the price, in which case you should add on F200 or so to the cost of the room – or, cheaper and better, use the nearest café.

In summer you'd be well advised to reserve rooms in advance, especially in the larger cities and Ardennes resorts. You can either do this by phoning direct – we've given phone numbers throughout the *Guide* – or by using the free *Belgian Tourist Reservations* service (*BTR*), boulevard Anspach 111, B-1000 Brussels (☎02/513 74 84; fax 513 92 77), through which you can book rooms nationwide. Reservations can also be made through most tourist offices, again for free, though they'll often charge a deposit which will be deducted from your final bill. For a full list of approved hotels throughout the country, with details of prices and facilities, pick up the Belgian Tourist Office's guide before leaving, especially as it can be difficult to find a copy once in Belgium. The Luxembourg Tourist Office also has a booklet of approved hotels, with prices, which is again worth getting hold of before you leave – though it is possible to pick it up once there.

Private accommodation is sometimes a slightly cheaper alternative. Many towns have a limited supply of rooms in private homes which local tourist offices will book for you at no charge.

On average, reckon on spending about F1000 a night on a double room – and expect them to sometimes be inconveniently situated.

■ Hostels, sleep-ins, student rooms

Belgium has around thirty official IYHF **youth hostels**, rather oddly run by two separate organizations, one for Flanders, another for Wallonia. Each operates a similar number of hostels, though they are rather different in many ways, the Flanders hostels large, ruthlessly organized affairs often used by large parties, while those in Wallonia are smaller and more informal. Most of

---

HOTEL PRICE CODES

All the establishments we have listed in Belgium and Luxembourg have been **graded** according to the following categories. These will sometimes correspond to the categories laid down by the tourist authorities in each country, who grade hotels rigorously. Above all, though, as in Holland, they are a guide to price, and they give no indication of the facilities you might expect other than the broad outlines we give below.

Please note that the **prices** we give are for the cheapest double room – ie without private bath, etc – during high season. Note also that they refer throughout the *Guide* to the lowest prices available at a particular establishment. Many hotels in Belgium and Luxembourg have a wide range of rooms, and it's possible that in some places, on some occasions, the only rooms available will in fact be a grade higher than the one we have given.

① **Up to F1000**. Hostel accommodation, either a private establishment or official youth hostel – where the charges will in fact always be much cheaper, normally less than F500 a night in fact. Most hostels also have some form of private accommodation – single-, double- and triple-bedded rooms – and these normally fall into the next category up pricewise. You may also find private rooms that fall into this category, although they just as often fall into the next.

② **F1000–1500**. This category includes either private rooms or the most basic one-star or ungraded hotel, normally without any kind of private facilities in any of the rooms beyond a washbasin, or, sometimes, a shower. Expect decor, etc, to be fairly grim, at least in the big city locations.

③ **F1500–2000**. This is the category that probably comes most often recommended in this guide, consisting mainly of ordinary one-star hotels, sporting a mixture of pleasant enough but rockbottom rooms with no private facilities and usually a selection of slightly more upscale choices with basic private facilities.

④ **F2000–2500**. Again this grade comes up fairly frequently in *the Guide*, basically one- merging into two-star hotels, a little more comfortable than the previous grouping, and with the emphasis on rooms with private facilities – though there may be a handful of cheaper rooms on offer too.

⑤ **F2500–3000**. Standard two-star hotel accommodation, where facilities will almost always be private and you will often have the use of a phone and TV, though rarely any kind of room service.

⑥ **F3000–4000**. Three-star hotels that always have private bath, etc, along with phone, TV, perhaps a minibar, and occasionally room service – although often there won't be a hugely discernible difference between these places and the previous category.

⑦ **F4000–5000**. Four-star hotels, and all the attendant facilities you would expect – private bathroom, minibar, phone and TV, room service – perhaps a gym, swimming pool or sauna.

⑧ **Over F5000**. As with Holland, we've included this category to take in especially decent four-and five-star establishments, with second-to-none service and facilities, along with really special places – notable either for their location, their building, perhaps even their history. They're not places to spend every night of your trip, unless money is no object, but they may be ones in which to indulge yourself on a special occasion.

the hostels charge a flat rate per person to members of around F335 for a bed in a dormitory, more in major centres like Ostend, where you can expect to pay around F400, and Brussels, where the rates are F380–620. Breakfast is usually included at hostels in Flanders, and not in Wallonia, where it costs about F80; charges are levied for sleeping bag rental in both regions – normally around F90. Many hostels in both Flanders and Wallonia also offer lunch and dinner, at around F150 for lunch, F250 or so for dinner.

If you're planning on staying at a lot of hostels, it's a good idea to join your home youth hostelling organization before you leave (see opposite for details) – the prices above will be considerably higher if you're not a member, and annual membership fees are on the whole low.

During the summer at least, you should book in advance wherever possible, since many hostels can be booked up. We've detailed many of the hostels, with phone numbers, in the *Guide*, but for a complete list contact either your home hostelling organization before you leave or one of the Belgian youth hostel organizations direct: the *Vlaamse Jeugdherbergcentrale*, Van Stralenstraat 40, B-Antwerp 2060 (☎03/232 72 18); or the *Les Auberges de la Jeunesse de Wallonie*, rue Van Oost 52, Brussels 1030 (☎02/215 31 00). The Belgian Tourist Office's *Budget Holidays* leaflet also has details of official youth hostels.

Some of the larger cities – Antwerp and Brussels, for example – have a number of **unofficial youth hostels** in addition to the IYHF establishments. These normally cost F400–500 for a dormitory bed and are often just as comfortable; they also have the advantage of being open to non-IYHF members. You'll also come across places known as **Sleep-ins**, which, as in Holland, offer dormitory accommodation for rock-bottom prices – sometimes as low as F200 per person. Where they exist, we've given details in the *Guide*. Finally, you might also find some cities offering **student accommodation** during the summer holidays – in Ghent, for example, where the university opens up its dorms to travellers at very cheap rates. Again we've given details, where relevant, in the *Guide*.

Luxembourg has about a dozen youth hostels, all members of the *Auberges de la Jeunesse de Luxembourg* (*AJL*), place d'Armes 18, Luxembourg (☎22 55 88). Rates for IYHF members are F300–380 per person for a dorm bed, F350–440 if you're over 26. Breakfast is usually about F80 extra,

lunch F110, evening meals F230. There are no other unofficial youth hostels in Luxembourg.

■ **Campsites, farms, gîtes, apartments**

Considering the cost of other forms of accommodation, **camping** is well worth considering in both Belgium and Luxembourg. There are around four hundred sites in **Belgium**, mostly well equipped and listed, with details of facilities, in the Belgian Tourist Office's *Camping* leaflet. Many are close to main roads for the convenience of drivers, and are classified on a one- to four-star coding. The vast majority of sites are one-star establishments, for which you should expect to pay F30–70 per person per night, plus about F40 for a tent, F40 or so for a car or motorcycle. **Luxembourg** has a little over one hundred campgrounds, all detailed in the free booklet available from the national tourist board. Prices again vary, but are usually between F50 and F100 per person, plus F30–60 for a tent, sometimes including hot showers. During peak season it can, in both countries, be a good idea to reserve ahead if you have a car and large tent or trailer; phone numbers are listed in the free directories, and in Luxembourg there's also a special telephone number you can use if you're having difficulty finding somewhere – ☎48 11 99, between 11am and 7.30pm daily.

As for other alternatives, in Luxembourg there's the option of taking an **apartment**. These are also listed in a booklet available from the national tourist board, and it's unusual to rent them for less than a week. In Belgium there are also so-called **farm holidays**, whereby you stay on a farm for a small amount and help out with work that needs doing. Prices vary from province to province and depend partly on the amount of work you are expected to undertake. Advance arrangements are essential. Both countries also offer **gîte d'etapes** – hostels really, situated in relatively remote parts of the country and accommodating between thirty and one hundred people in each establishment. Reckon on about F150 per person per night. Again, the Belgian Tourist Office's *Budget Holidays* leaflet has details of these and of farm holidays. The Luxembourg Tourist Office publishes a leaflet showing *gîte* locations and prices, or you can contact the *Gîtes d'Etapes Luxembourgeois*, rue Michel Welter 29, L-2730 Luxembourg (☎23 698).

Costs, money and banks

Belgium and Luxembourg are, by a narrow margin, the most expensive of the Low Countries. Of the two, Belgium is cheaper, but in both prices for almost everything are above what you will be used to paying at home. A notable exception is beer, which is dirt cheap, especially in Luxembourg. Travel, also, if only because both countries are so small, isn't a major expense.

Those camping or staying in hostel accommodation and cooking for themselves should be able to manage on around £25/$35 a day. Staying in hotels, eating out in restaurants most nights and drinking in bars, you'll get through at least £50/$75 a day – in Luxembourg it might be more.

■ Money and banks

The **currency** in both Belgium and Luxembourg is the franc, normally written as "F" or "BF" and "FLux." The Belgian and Luxembourg franc are actually separate currencies, but they are virtually interchangeable: they have the same rate of exchange against all other currencies, but although Belgian francs are legal tender in Luxembourg, the reverse isn't true in Belgium. Also, it is advisable to change all spare

Luxembourg francs into Belgian notes before you leave for home, since this is the more acceptable currency in foreign banks. Both currencies divide into 100 centimes, and come in **coins** worth 1, 5, 20 and 50 francs, and **notes** worth 50, 100, 500, 1000 and 5000 francs. At the time of writing the exchange rate was around F50 to the pound sterling , F35 or so to the US dollar.

Banks are the best places to change money. In Belgium they are open Monday–Friday 9am–noon and 2–4pm, in Luxembourg 9am–noon and 12.30–4.30pm; some banks also open on Saturday mornings. You can also change money in larger cities at train stations, some hotels and bureaux de change, though the rates are generally less favourable, and if you have a Eurocheque card with a PIN number you can use the *MISTERCASH* dispensers in Brussels and elsewhere. The major **credit cards** – *Mastercard, Visa, American Express, Diner's Club* – are accepted widely in shops, hotels and restaurants. You can also get cash advances on these from some high street banks, though there is usually a F6000 minimum.

Communications

Mail and phones in Belgium and Luxembourg are very efficient. Unlike Holland, however, English newspapers are seldom available on the day of publication.

■ Mail

Post offices in Belgium and Luxembourg are plentiful: in Belgium they are open Monday–Friday 9am–noon and 2–5pm, and in Luxembourg Monday–Friday 8am–noon and 1.30–5pm. Some post offices open Saturday mornings too, and in larger centres like Brussels and Luxembourg city the main offices do not shut at lunchtime. **Postage** costs F14 for a postcard, the same for a letter under 20g inside Europe, and F25 to countries outside. Mail to the US takes 5–7 days, within Europe 2–3 days. **Mail boxes**, painted red in Belgium and yellow in Luxembourg, are, as in Holland, attached to walls.

■ Phones

Both countries have reliable phone systems. Public phones are the usual Continental kind, where you deposit the money before you make your call. In both countries phones take F5, F20 and sometimes F50 coins, and in Belgium there are also public phones that take cards – available from newsagents, post offices and train stations for F100 or F500. Area phone codes for Belgium are given in the *Guide*; you'll notice, however, that Luxembourg is small enough to not need any kind of area coding system – everywhere in the country simply has a five-digit number.

If **calling abroad**, remember that some post offices have booths where you can make your call and settle up afterward. You can also, of course, make calls from your hotel, though as usual this is much more expensive than any other method.

■ Media

The only **American newspapers** available in both Belgium and Luxembourg are *USA Today* and the trusty *International Herald Tribune*; the latter is published in Paris. Otherwise **British**

newspapers are widely available, though normally a day later than published. Train station bookstands in the large cities are a good bet; expect to pay about F50.

As for the **domestic Belgian press**, the major newspapers in Wallonia are the influential, independent *Le Soir*, the left-of-centre *Journal et Independance*, the liberal *Dernière Heure* and the right-wing *Libre Belgique*. In Flanders you'll see the leftish *De Morgen*, *Het Volk*, which is the paper of the Christian Democrats, and the right-leaning *De Standaard* and *Het Laatste Nieuws*. There's also an **English-language weekly magazine**, the Brussels-based *Bulletin* (F70), catering to the sizable ex-pat community here. Though inevitably oriented toward the capital, it's worth buying wherever you are in Belgium for its entertainments and TV listings, and slices of Belgian news in English. It also carries a fair-sized classified section – useful if you've just arrived for an extended stay and are looking for an apartment or even work. In **Luxembourg**, the highest circulation newspaper is the *Luxemburger Wort*. There's also an English-language weekly, the *News Digest*, though this is very dry and not really worth the bother.

British TV and radio stations can, as in Holland, be picked up in Belgium and Luxembourg on the same frequencies. You'll find BBC Radio 4 on 1500m long wave, the World Service on 463m medium wave and short wave frequencies between 24m and 75m at various times throughout the day. BBC1 and BBC2 television channels can also be found, though more so in Belgium than in Luxembourg, as well as the usual pan-European cable and satellite channels – Sky, Superchannel, Eurosport and the rest (see *Holland Practicalities* for details of these). You can also, in most parts of both countries, pick up all the Dutch and German stations, and sometimes those from France and Italy too.

Food and drink

The attitude to food in Belgium and Luxembourg is quite different from that in Holland. Belgian cuisine is held in high regard worldwide, and in Europe at least is regarded as second only to French in quality. The food of Luxembourg isn't as appealing or as varied, but you can still eat out well in much of the country, albeit at high

INTERNATIONAL DIALLING CODES		
USA and Canada	☎001	
UK	☎0044	
Ireland	☎00353	
Australia	☎0061	
New Zealand	☎0064	
USEFUL NUMBERS	**Belg**	**Lux**
Operator calls	☎997	☎0010
Information	☎1307	☎017
International information	☎1304	☎016
Emergencies	☎100/101	☎012
International reverse-charge calls	☎1324	☎0010

prices. As for drink, beer is one of the real delights of Belgium, and Luxembourg produces some very drinkable white wines along its side of the Moselle.

■ Food

Southern Belgian cuisine is not unlike French, retaining the fondness for rich sauces and ingredients that the latter has to some extent lost of late. In Flanders the food is more akin to that of Holland, plainer and simpler on the whole, though here too there are many interesting traditional dishes. For such a small country there's a surprising amount of regional variation, but it's generally true to say that pork, beef, game, fish and seafood, especially mussels, are staple items, often cooked with butter, cream and herbs, or sometimes beer – which is, after all, the Belgian national drink. Soups are common: hearty affairs, especially in the south and Ardennes, where it's usual to be served a huge tureen from which you can help yourself – a meal in itself. The Ardennes is also known for its cured ham (similar to Italian Parma ham) and, of course, its pâté, made from pork, beef, liver and kidney – though it often takes a particular name from an additional ingredient, for example *pâté de faisan* (pheasant) or *pâté de lièvre* (hare). As you might expect, game (*gibiers*) features heavily on most Ardennes menus.

Among common **Belgian dishes** you'll come across are *waterzooi*, a Flanders stew consisting of chicken or fish boiled with fresh vegetables; *truite à l'Ardennaise* – trout cooked in a wine sauce; *carbonnades de porc Bruxelloise* – pork with a tarragon and tomato sauce; *carbonnades à la Flamande* – cubes of beef marinated in beer and cooked with herbs and onions; *fricassée Liègeois* – basically, fried eggs, bacon and sausage or blood pudding; and *konijn met pruimen* – rabbit with prunes. An Antwerp speciality is *paling in 't groen*, eel braised in a white sauce with herbs; *fricadelles à la bière*, or meatballs in beer, is a Brabant delicacy. Among many salads you'll find are *salade de Liège*, made from beans and potatoes, and *salade wallonie*, a warm salad of lettuce, fried potatoes and bacon bits.

Luxembourg cuisine is similar to that of Belgium, but, as you might expect, it has more Germanic influences, with sausages and sauerkraut featuring on menus, as well as pork, game and river fish. Favourite dishes include smoked pork with beans, liver dumplings with sauerkraut and potatoes, and *tripe à la Luxembourgoise*.

Breakfast, snacks and desserts

In most parts of Belgium and Luxembourg you'll **start the day** in routine Continental fashion with a cup of coffee and a roll or croissant, the sumptuous affairs served in Holland never having caught on this far south. Coffee, however, is often served Dutch-fashion, with a small tub of evaporated rather than fresh milk.

Later in the day, the most obvious **snack** is *frites* – served everywhere in Belgium from *friture* stands or parked vans, with salt or mayonnaise, or, as in Holland, with more exotic dressings. Mussels, cooked in a variety of ways, with chips, is virtually the Belgian national dish, and makes a good fast lunch in cafeterias. On the coast you'll see stands selling all kinds of fish delicacies, as in Holland. Other street vendors, especially in the north, sell various sorts of sausage (*worst*), especially black pudding (*bloedworst*); and everywhere there are stands selling waffles (*gaufres*), served up steaming hot with jam and honey. There are also, of course, the usual multinational burger joints, of which the indigenous *Quick* chain is a reasonable approximation.

As for cakes and sweets, Belgium is known best for its **chocolate**. Each Belgian, apparently, eats 12.5kg of chocolate annually, and chocolates are the favoured gift when visiting friends. The big Belgian chocolatiers, *Godiva* and *Leonidas*, have stores in the main towns and cities, and their *pralines* – filled with cream, liqueurs or *ganache* (a fine dark chocolate) – and *truffles*, made of chocolate, butter, cream and sugar, are almost worth the trip alone, especially bearing in mind the prices, which are less than half what you would pay at home. Of the two *Leonidas* is the cheaper outlet – reckon on spending around F200 for 500g of their chocolates. Regular chocolate by the bar (*Côte d'Or* is one of the major manufacturers) is also delicious. Apart from chocolate, look out for *speculaas*, a specialty of the northern part of the country (and also found in Holland) – a rich spiced cake that was originally baked in the form of saints and religious figures but now comes in all shapes and sizes.

Sit-down food

At the cheaper end of the **sit-down meal** scale, many **bars** serve food, at least at lunchtimes, and there are normally a host of **cafeterias** around serving up basic dishes, omelettes, fricassees, soups, chicken or steak with chips and suchlike. Nothing comes cheap, but the quality will

FRENCH FOOD AND DRINK TERMS

Basics

Beurre	Butter	*Oeufs*	Eggs
Chaud	Hot	*Pain (complet)*	Bread
Dessert	Dessert	*Poisson*	Fish
Fromage	Cheese	*Poivre*	Pepper
Froid	Cold	*Salade*	Salad
Fruit	Fruit	*Sel*	Salt
Hors d''oeuvre	Starters	*Sucre*	Sugar
Legumes	Vegetables	*Viande*	Meat

Typical snacks

Un sandwich/une baguette . . .	A sandwich . . .	*brouillés*	scrambled eggs
		Omelette . . .	Omelette . . .
jambon	with ham	*nature*	plain
fromage	with cheese	*au fromage*	with cheese
saucisson	with sausage	*Salade de . . .*	Salad of
à l'ail	with garlic	*tomates*	tomatoes
au poivre	with pepper	*concombres*	cucumbers
Croque-monsieur	Grilled cheese and ham sandwich	*Crêpes*	Pancakes
		au sucre	with sugar
Oeufs . . .	Eggs . . .	*au citron*	with lemon
au plat	fried eggs	*au miel*	with honey
à la coque	boiled eggs	*à la confiture*	with jam
durs	hard-boiled eggs		

Soups and starters

Assiette anglaise	Plate of cold meats	*Bouillon*	Broth or stock
		Consommé	Clear soup
Bisque	Shellfish soup	*Crudités*	Raw vegetables with dressing
Bouillabaisse	Fish soup from Marseilles	*Potage*	Thick soup, usually vegetable

Meat and poultry

Agneau	Lamb	*Hamburger*	Hamburger
Bifteck	Steak	*Jambon*	Ham
Boeuf	Beef	*Lard*	Bacon
Canard	Duck	*Porc*	Pork
Cheval	Horsemeat	*Poulet*	Chicken
Dindon	Turkey	*Saucisse*	Sausage
Foie	Liver	*Veau*	Veal

Fish

Anchois	Anchovies	*Maquereau*	Mackerel
Anguilles	Eels	*Morue*	Cod
Carrelet	Plaice	*Moules*	Mussels
Cervettes roses	Prawns	*Saumon*	Salmon
Escargots	Snails	*Sole*	Sole
Hareng	Herring	*Truite*	Trout
Lotte de mer	Monkfish		

Terms

A point	Medium	Mijoté	Stewed
Au four	Baked	Pané	Breaded
Bien cuit	Well-done	Rôti	Roast
Bouilli	Boiled	Saignant	Rare
Frit/friture	Fried/deep fried	Sauté	Lightly cooked in butter
Fumé	Smoked	Tourte	Tart or pie
Grillé	Grilled		
Hollandaise	Egg yolk, butter and vinegar sauce, often served with fish		

Vegetables

Ail	Garlic	Laitue	Lettuce
Asperges	Asparagus	Oignons	Onions
Carottes	Carrots	Petits pois	Peas
Champignon	Mushrooms	Poireau	Leek
Choufleur	Cauliflower	Pommes (de terre)	Potatoes
Concombre	Cucumber	Riz	Rice
Genièvre	Juniper		

Sweets and desserts

Crème fraiche	Sour cream	Madeleine	Small, shell-shaped sponge cake
Crêpes	Pancakes		
Crêpes suzettes	Thin pancakes with orange juice and liqueur	Parfait	Frozen mousse, sometimes ice cream
Frappé	Iced	Petits fours	Bite-sized cakes or pastries
Glace	Ice cream		

Fruit and nuts

Amandes	Almonds	Noisette	Hazelnut
Ananas	Pineapple	Pamplemousse	Grapefruit
Cacahouète	Peanut	Poire	Pear
Cérises	Cherries	Pomme	Apple
Citron	Lemon	Prune	Plum
Fraises	Strawberries	Pruneau	Prune
Framboises	Raspberries	Raisins	Grapes
Marrons	Chestnuts		

Drinks

Bière	Beer	Tea	Thé
Café	Coffee	Vin...	Wine...
Eaux de vie	Spirits distilled from various fruits	rouge	red
		blanc	white
Jenever	Dutch/Flemish gin	brut	very dry
Lait	Milk	sec	dry
Orange/citron pressé	Fresh orange/lemon juice	demi-sec	sweet
		doux	very sweet

For a list of Dutch food and drink terms – detailing the words and phrases you need when travelling in the Flemish-speaking north of Belgium – see p.36–37.

regularly be excellent, even with the most humble dishes, and portions are usually enormous. In bars, basic restaurants and cafeterias, you can expect to pay about F200 on average for an omelette or something similar; a more substantial meat-and-chips affair might cost F300–400. Most bars and cafeterias that serve food normally have a *plat du jour* on offer too, usually for around F300, often including a starter and a dessert.

Though there's often a thin dividing line between the two as regards the food, **restaurants** are not surprisingly more expensive than bars; they will also probably only be open during the evening. Even in the cheapest restaurant, a main course will rarely cost under F400, and it's likely that prices for most things will be more like F500–700, especially in Luxembourg, where things are that much more expensive.

As for **other cuisines**, in the larger cities there is a huge variety, especially in Brussels, where the authenticity of the ethnic restaurants is one of the city's strengths. However, in country areas of both Belgium and Luxembourg choice is much more limited. Traditional Belgian (and Luxembourgeois) food is fairly meat-based, which means **vegetarians** are in for a difficult time, especially if they want to sample the local specialties – though this is considerably easier if you eat fish. Vegetarian restaurants exist, but are much rarer than in Holland. In the cities, **Italian** and **French** are the most widespread available cuisines aside from Belgian and Luxembourgeois, and restaurants are invariably of good quality. Among less often found alternatives are **Turkish** and **Greek** restaurants (good in Brussels particularly); **Balkan** restaurants appear here and there but are generally overpriced. Of far eastern options, **Vietnamese** restaurants are more common in Belgium than in Britain; **Chinese** restaurants are also fairly widespread; while Luxembourg's sizable Portuguese minority has spawned a higher than average quota of **Portuguese** eateries. There are also a fair few **African** and **North African** restaurants, in Belgium at least – worth sampling, if not cheap.

■ Drink

The price of food in both Belgium and Luxembourg is more than compensated for by the cost of **drinking**, especially if you like beer, which is always good and comes in numerous varieties. There's a bar on almost every corner in both countries: most serve at least twenty types of beer,

and in some beer lists run into the hundreds. Usually they're cosy, unpretentious places, the walls, as in Holland, stained brown by tobacco smoke; they're normally frequented by locals and sometimes serve simple food.

Beer

Beer has been a passion in Belgium since the Middle Ages, when monks did much of the brewing; later the brewers' guilds were founded and became among the most influential institutions in the region. Today there are up to five hundred different kinds of beer in Belgium, many brewed by small family breweries, some still produced by monasteries. Most of these are of the lager – or pilsener – type, but it would be wrong to assume this is all that's on offer.

In both Belgium and Luxembourg, ask for a *bière* in a **bar** and you'll be served a roughly cup-sized glass, larger than in Holland, of whatever the bar has on tap. The most common beers you'll see in Belgium are the Leuven-based *Stella Artois*, *Jupiler* from Liège (the country's biggest-selling beer) and *Maes*. In Luxembourg the most widespread brands are *Diekirch* (the largest domestic brewer), the Luxembourg-based *Mousel* and *Bofferding*. **Bar prices** don't vary much: in Belgium you'll pay around F45 for a glass of beer in all but the swankiest places; in Luxembourg count on F40 or so – about the only thing that is cheaper in Luxembourg than Belgium. For speciality bottled beers like *Duvel* and *Chimay* (see below) you'll pay around F90. As for buying **beer in a supermarket**, you can buy large, 75cl bottles of pilsener beer for about F30; six-packs of 25cl bottles go for about F90. Speciality beers cost upwards of F35 for a 33cl bottle.

In addition to the ordinary draft pilsener beers, there are any number of **speciality beers**, usually served by the bottle but occasionally on draft. These are often regionally based but many are available everywhere. They are usually strong and should be drunk (and sometimes poured) with care – those in the bottle sometimes carry sediment at the bottom. The most famous speciality beer in perhaps the whole of Belgium is *lambic* – the generic title for beer brewed in the Brussels area which is fermented by contact with the yeast naturally available in the air and matured in oak casks. *Lindemans* is one of the best-known producers, but there's also the *Cantillon* museum-brewery in Anderlecht, which brews genuine *lambic* beers. A blend of old and young lambic beers is known as *gueuze*, a cidery concoction sold in all Brussels bars. Of other pilsener brands, *Duvel* stands out: the name means "devil," which is an appropriate tag for a brew that's not far short of the strength of wine – though you wouldn't know it from the taste. Belgium also has plenty of dark beers or ales. *De Koninck*, brewed in Antwerp, is like an English bitter but smoother, with a yeasty taste; *Mort Subite* (literally "sudden death") is, despite the name, not especially strong, actually named after a bar in Brussels. Try also some of the beers traditionally (and still) brewed by Belgium's five Trappist monasteries, strong, top-fermented ales that are usually over six percent alcohol by volume. The best known – and most widely available – is *Chimay*, brewed at the biggest of the country's monastery breweries in Hainaut. Other examples are *Orval*, from the southern province of Luxembourg, a fruitier brew recognizable by its distinctive bowling-pin shaped bottle; *Westmalle*, from north of Antwerp – a rich, sweet malty brew; and there are smaller breweries at Rochefort in Namur and at the monastery of St Sixtus in Westvleteren near Ieper. The Rochefort beer is a dark, chocolatey and immensely satisfying brew; St Sixtus is said to be the strongest beer in the country, over ten percent alcohol by volume.

Besides these there are some other, rather odd brews. *Hoegaarden*, for example, is a so-called "white beer" (*witbier* or *bière blanche*) – actually cloudy rather than white, and drunk in summer, sometimes with lemon. There's also the more commonly drunk *kriek*, which is an *lambic* beer with cherries added during the final fermentation, producing a refreshing, not-too-sweet brew that comes in champagne-style bottles or on tap. *Lindemans*, the well-known *lambic* producer, make *kriek*, but with cherry juice these days rather than the real thing; only *Cantillon* of Anderlecht and the *Liefmans* brewery in Oudenaarde use actual cherries. You'll also come across beers flavoured with other fruits – raspberries (*framboise*), peaches, even grapes; look out also for *faro*, a delicious lambic beer, given a distinctive and refreshing flavour by adding candy sugar.

Wine and spirits

The presence of **wine** in Belgium is obviously much overshadowed by the beer, but it is widely available, at about F120 a bottle from the supermarket, F250 or so for a half litre in a restaurant. French wines are the most commonly drunk, although **Luxembourg** is, in a small way, a wine producer, and its white wines, produced from vines grown along the north bank of the Moselle – which forms the border between Luxembourg and Germany – are very drinkable, not unlike those of Germany, but drier and fruitier than those of France. They also produce some very palatable sparkling wines. As with beer, Luxembourger wines are relatively cheap to buy in shops: the sparkling, *methode champenoise* varieties go for under F250 a bottle (try the *St Martin* brand, which is excellent and dry); ordinary white wine costs about F150.

Unlike Holland, there's no one national Belgian **spirit**, but all the usual kinds are available, at about F60 a glass in a bar. You will also find jenever in most bars, especially in Limburg where it is made. In Luxembourg spirits are cheaper than elsewhere in Europe – a fact reflected by a thriving cross-border trade from France and Germany. You'll also come across home-produced bottles of *eau de vie* – distilled from various fruits and around fifty percent alcohol by volume.

Museums, churches and castles

Like Holland, Belgium, and to a lesser extent Luxembourg, are strong on museums and galleries. The legacy of Flemish art is apparent in a good many decent galleries, and the strong Belgian sense of regionalism has spawned a number of museums devoted to specific provinces.

■ Museums

Most **museums** in Belgium are open, with variations, Tuesday to Saturday from 9am to 4pm, and sometimes on Sunday; Monday is a common closing day. However, travelling outside the April–September period, expect a lot of places to be closed unless they're of really prime touristic importance; a number of museums don't actually open until Easter or May 1, closing up again in the middle or end of September. Displays vary, and are normally of better quality in the historic north Belgian towns, where there are usually at least a handful of Flemish paintings on show, and other trinkets from the era of medieval prosperity. In both countries, most towns of any size at all have some kind of local display, which you can normally miss with a clear conscience – exceptions again being the major Flemish towns, and places like Liège with its important Walloon museums.

■ Churches and castles

Churches in Belgium and Luxembourg are normally different places from those in Holland: Catholicism is the main religion, with the result that places of worship are not the cold, unadorned buildings you find to the north – though most of the great churches of Flanders have little decoration, dating from the ransackings of Flemish Protestants. Churches which are interesting touristically are normally open all day, at least during the summer, only closing for a couple of hours at lunchtime (often noon–2pm). Otherwise you'll only be able to enter during mass.

Southern Belgium and Luxembourg are also blessed with a wealth of **castles and chateaux**, usually perched in isolated – and nowadays picturesque – locations, that can be difficult to reach without a car. Luxembourg, especially, has a dense concentration – some almost entirely ruined now but worth visiting for the views, others sumptuously restored in period fashion. During the summer, hours are generally all day every day for the most interesting sites, though again outside the April–September period you can expect many places to be closed.

Festivals & annual events

Both Belgium and Luxembourg are big on festivals and annual events – everything from religious processions to carnivals to more contemporary-based jazz binges and

the like. Apart from the obvious exception of carnivals, most events, as in Holland, take place in summer. As always, the national tourist offices at home, and offices within Belgium and Luxembourg, can supply details of exact dates, which tend to change from year to year. For more on the events themselves, see the appropriate entry in the *Guide*.

The best annual fun is probably to be had at the many (mainly Belgian) annual **carnivals**, held in February and early March. One of the most renowned of these is held at Binche, in Hainaut, when there's a procession involving some 1500 dancers – or *Gilles* – alone. There are also carnivals in Ostend and Aalst, in Eupen, with events lasting over the weekend before Shrove Tuesday and culminating with *Rosenmontag* on the Monday – a pageant of costumed groups and floats through the town centre – and, most uniquely, in Stavelot, where the so-called "Blancs Mousis" take to the streets.

Both countries have a number of **religion-inspired festivals**, which are among the most intriguing events you're likely to come across. The Brussels *Ommegang* is the best known, a largely secular event these days, held on the first Thursday in July, that nominally commemorates the arrival by boat of a miraculous statue of the Virgin Mary from Antwerp in the fourteenth century. If you want to see anything on the Grand Place, however, where most of the action is, you have to reserve months in advance, and you might be better off visiting the town of Veurne in Flanders for its annual Processions of the Penitents, on the last Sunday in July, where cross-bearers dressed in sack cloth process through the town – a slightly macabre sight. Other religious events include the Procession of the Holy Blood in Bruges, when a shrine brought back from the Holy Land during the Crusades that supposedly contains the blood of Christ is carried solemnly through the streets; and the procession of dancers in memory of St Willibord that winds its way through the streets of Echternach in Luxembourg.

More secular events include the *Meiboom*, held in Brussels on August 9, Ieper's Cat Festival in May, with floats and costumes on a cat theme, and any number of folklore events and fairs. There are also a number of annual sporting occasions, not least the Ieper 24-hour car rally and the Grand Prix at the circuit near Spa.

FESTIVALS DIARY

January

Jan–May Luxembourg international festival of opera and ballet.

February

Early Feb Binche Carnival.

Weekend before Shrove Tuesday Eupen Carnival, climaxing with the *Rosenmontag* procession and festivities on the Monday.

Last weekend Carnivals in Aalst, Vianden.

End Feb to end March Luxembourg City Carnival.

March

Early March Ostend Carnival.

Early March *Buergsonndeg* or "Bonfire Day" all over Luxembourg.

Mid-Lent Stavelot Carnival Parade with the famous "Blancs Mousis".

Last Sun *Bretzelsonndeg* ("Pretzel Day"), markets, processions and displays of folk art in the Luxembourg Moselle towns.

Last Sun Petange Carnival (Luxembourg).

April

Easter weekend Leuven International Folklore Festival.

End April Ghent Flower Show.

May

Early May Bruges: Procession of the Holy Blood

Second Sun Ieper Cat Festival.

Mid-May *Octave*, Luxembourg city, an annual pilgrimage culminating in front of the cathedral.

End May Mechelen Handswijk Procession.

Whit Tuesday Echternach Dancing Procession to commemorate St Willibord.

June

Second Sun Tournai Day of the Four Processions, notably a carnival parade and the traditional procession of the Knight of the Tower.

June 23 Luxembourg National Day.

Last weekend Ieper 24-hour car rally.

June–Sept Knokke-Heist Cartoon Festival.

June–Sept Mechelen Carillon concerts at St Rombout's tower, every Mon, Sat and Sun.

July

July weekends and first week of Aug Middlekerke Folklore Festival.

July and Aug Wiltz International Music Festival.

Early July Brussels Ommegang.

Early July Schoten Folklore Festival.

Early July Torhout-Wecher Rock Festival.

Third weekend Diekirch Beer Festival.

End July Veurne Penitents Procession.

End July Eeklo Hot Air Balloon Festival.

August

Aug 9 Brussels *Meiboom*.

Mid-Aug Leuven *Marktrock* Rock Festival.

Mid-Aug Liège Outremeuse Folklore Festival.

End Aug Lochristi Begonia Festival.

End Aug Blankenberge Flower Procession.

End Aug to early Sept Luxembourg: *Schueberfouer*, a former shepherds' market that's now the capital's largest funfair.

Aug–Sept Ghent Festival of Flanders – concerts, etc, held in the ancient buildings of the medieval town centre.

Aug–Oct Wine festivals in the Moselle Valley.

September

Early Sept Dendermonde International Jazz Festival.

First weekend Kortirjk Golden River City Jazz Festival.

Second weekend Grevenmacher wine and grape festival, with processions, wine-tasting and fireworks.

Second Sun Mechelen horticultural and floral pageant.

Second Sun Tournai Procession of the Plague, to remember an epidemic of 1090.

End Sept Nivelles 16km procession from St Gertrude's tower out through the countryside and back again.

October

Early Oct Vianden Walnut Market.

November

Nov 1 Diest Pilgrimage to All Saints Hill, accompanied by the offering of ex-votos, etc.

Nov 10 Vianden: *Miertchen* or "St Martin's Fire" celebrating the end of the harvest.

Nov 11 Eupen St Martin's Procession through the town, with Roman legionaries and children bearing candles, finishing with a bonfire.

December

Dec 6 Arrival of St Nicholas, celebrated by processions and the giving of sweets to children.

Directory

AIRPORT TAX Not charged when leaving either Belgium or Luxembourg.

BIKE HIRE See p.280.

CAR PROBLEMS See p.277.

CONTRACEPTIVES Condoms are available from chemists (*pharmacie* in French, *apotheek* in Flemish), though for the pill you need a presciption.

DISABLED VISITORS Unlike Holland, access for the physically disabled is rarely considered in either Belgium or Luxembourg – lifts and ramps are few, and steep steps and rough sidewalks are common. The trains, too, unlike Dutch railways, make few concessions.

ELECTRIC CURRENT 220v AC.

EMERGENCIES Belgium: Ambulance/fire brigade ☎100; police ☎101. In Luxembourg the emergency number is ☎012, which can also get you details of late-opening chemists, doctors, dentists, etc.

LEFT LUGGAGE Major train stations have luggage offices (normally open daily 6am–midnight); smaller stations have coin-operated lockers, taking F20 and F50 pieces.

SHOPPING Both countries have a number of things worth buying to take home. In Belgium, chocolates are obviously a major enticement. Beer, too, providing you're up to carrying it, is worth a raid on a supermarket on the way to the airport. The same goes for Luxembourg, where beer is equally affordable; it's also worth buying wine in stores rather than duty-free, since the home-produced stuff is cheap and good, particularly the sparkling variety.

TIME One hour ahead of GMT; normally six hours ahead of Eastern Standard Time, nine hours ahead of Pacific Standard Time.

TIPPING As in Holland, there's no necessity to tip, although it's common to bring the bill up to the nearest ten francs or so in restaurants and cabs. In public toilets, such as they exist, it's usual to leave F5–10.

TRAVEL AGENTS *Wasteels*, *Acotra* and *JEST* are three organizations with branches in both countries that are good places for discount flights, *BIJ* tickets, student cards, etc. Where relevant, we've given addresses in the *Guide*.

WAR CEMETERIES There are a number of war cemeteries in Belgium and Luxembourg, from both world wars. Most, of course, are centred on the World War I battlefields around Ieper. There are others, from World War II, in the Ardennes region, from the heavy fighting there in late 1944.

CHAPTER SEVEN

BRUSSELS AND AROUND

Wherever else you go in Belgium, it's likely that at some point you'll wind up in **Brussels**. The city is the major air gateway for the country; it's on the main routes heading inland from the Channel ports via the Flemish art towns; and it's also a convenient stop on the railway line between France and Holland. As such Brussels is somewhat hard to avoid. However, despite the city's reputation as a dull, faceless centre of commerce and diplomacy, full of dark-suited diplomats and dubious businessmen, you could do, worse than stop here for a while. It has architecture and museums to rank with the best of Europe's capitals, a well-preserved medieval centre, and a vibrant, energetic streetlife and nightscene, especially in its immigrant quarters. It's also small enough to be easily absorbed over a few long days.

It's true to say that since Brussels became home of the European Commission in 1959, parts of it have been sacrificed to a grey district of commerce and government. And it's also true that at times the old centre can feel like a tailor-made playground for tourists and ex-pats. But the most striking aspect of the city is the sharp contrast between the contrived internationalism of the centre and EC zone, and the vital, authentic foreignness of the non-indigenous quarters. This is something that the city's compact nature only heightens: in five minutes you can walk from a designer shopping mall into an African ghetto, or from a depressed slum quarter to a self-regarding square of antique shops and exclusive cafés.

Brussels is, and always has been, a fragmented place. Indeed, the city's historic class divisions are embodied in its very layout. Since the eleventh century, monarchs, aristocrats and the wealthy have lived in the **Upper Town**, shopkeepers and workers in the **Lower Town** – a distinction which is still in part true. In addition to this, the French–Flemish language disputes which have plagued the region for so long continue here in full and concentrated force – so much so that the capital has been officially bilingual since 1962, and by law all road signs, street names and virtually all published information must be in both languages. Nowadays the city is even more diverse, with communities of European bureaucrats, diplomats and business people, and immigrants from North Africa, Turkey, the Mediterranean and Zaire constituting a quarter of the population.

ACCOMMODATION PRICE CODES

All the **hotels and hostels** detailed in this chapter have been graded according to the following price categories. Note that the prices have been calculated as those for the cheapest double room during high season. For more on accommodation, see p.280.

① Up to F1000 per person.

② F1000–1500.

③ F1500–2000.

④ F2000–2500.

⑤ F2500–3000.

⑥ F3000–4000.

⑦ F4000–5000.

⑧ F5000 and over.

Each of these communities leads a very separate, distinct existence, something which only increases the allure of the city, not least in the number and variety of affordable ethnic **restaurants**. Without these, Brussels would still be a good place to eat: its gastronomic reputation rivals that of Paris, and though traditional meals in homegrown restaurants are rarely cheap, there is great-value food to be had in many of the **bars**. The bars themselves are sumptuous, basic, traditional or trendy, and one of the capital's real pleasures.

As the capital of a country where the cost of living is high, prices in Brussels are no joke. But although it's no place to get gripped by a consumer frenzy, numerous antique and contemporary art galleries, some wonderful markets, a host of chocolatiers and shops devoted solely to comic books make **window-shopping** a joy.

The capital is also a feasible base for visiting a number of attractions in **the countryside around,** and – not least because Belgium is such a small country – even farther afield. Close by, and easily accessible on public transit from central Brussels, are the battlefield of **Waterloo** and the intriguing **Museum of Central Africa** at **Tervuren.** You might also consider making trips farther afield, to **Leuven,** or Ghent or Mechelen – all of which can be easily seen in a day out from the capital.

BRUSSELS

BRUSSELS takes its name from Broekzele, or "village of the marsh," the community which grew up on the wide, shallow River Senne in the sixth century around a chapel founded by St Géry, roughly on the site of the current place St Géry. By 979 the dukes of Lower Lotharingia had built a fortress on the island, and a community of soldiers and merchants soon grew up around it, the village benefiting from its position on the trade route between Cologne and the (in those days) more developed towns of Bruges and Ghent. As the village's wealth increased, the marsh was drained and houses were built, the centre moving to the more easily defended hill where the Upper Town now stands. Before long the town fell under the control of the dukes of Brabant, who granted it its first charter in 1229 and controlled things here, on and off, for around two hundred years. In the early fifteenth century, marriage merged the interests of the Duchy of Brabant with that of Burgundy, which in turn fell under Hapsburg and later Spanish rule.

Under the Spanish, the town flourished and grew, eventually becoming capital of the Spanish Netherlands and enjoying a period of comparative calm until 1695, when Louis XIV, keen to incorporate the area into France, bombarded Brussels for 36 hours, leaving it devastated, especially around the Grand Place. The Treaty of Utrecht in 1713 left what is now Belgium under Hapsburg rule, during which time the city once again enjoyed peace, the Hapsburgs building most of the monumental buildings of the Upper Town. From 1815 until 1830, Brussels took turns with The Hague as capital of the new United Kingdom of The Netherlands, after which time, with the establishment of Belgian independence, it became the capital of the new Belgian state.

The nineteenth century was a period of modernization and expansion, the city being established under Burgomaster Anspach and King Leopold II with all the attributes of a modern European capital. The ring boulevards were built; the free university was founded; the Senne – which by then had become an open sewer – was covered over in the city centre; and many slum areas were cleared and grand buildings erected, culminating in the golden jubilee exhibition which celebrated the founding of the Belgian state in the newly inaugurated Parc de Cinquantenaire. Since World War II modernization has proceeded inexorably, the city's elevation in status over the past couple of decades to so-called "capital of Europe" – by way of its appointment as HQ of both NATO and the EEC – instigating many major development projects, not least the new metro system.

The Brussels area telephone code is ☎02

Arrival

Brussels has three main **train stations** – Gare Centrale, Gare du Nord, and Gare du Midi, each a few minutes apart – and most national and international trains stop at all three. A notable exception is the train from Milan via Switzerland, which stops only at Midi and Nord. **Gare Centrale** is, as its name suggests, the most central of the three, a five-minute walk from the Grand Place; **Gare du Nord** lies in a sleazy red-light district just north of the main ring road; and **Gare du Midi** in a depressed immigrant area to the south of the city centre. The Gare du Nord and Gare du Midi are linked by pre-metro tramline #3, which runs straight through the heart of the city centre. If you're heading straight to the Grand Place from Nord or Midi, simply take pre-metro tramline #3 to Bourse – a couple of minutes' walk from the Grand Place. Solo women arriving late at night at either Nord or Midi would be wise to take a taxi to their hotel or hostel. Gare Centrale is on metro line #1 and is best reached from the other two stations by simply jumping on the next available main line train.

Arriving by **bus** from Britain, *Hoverspeed* buses drop you off at place de la Bourse, *Eurolines* at place de Brouckère. Belgium's comprehensive rail network means that it's unlikely that you'll arrive in the city by long-distance domestic bus, but if you do, Gare du Nord is the main terminal.

Coming by air, you'll land at **National Airport** in Zaventem, 13km northeast of the city centre. There's a tourist information desk in the arrivals hall, open throughout the year (Mon–Fri 8am–9pm, Sat & Sun 8am–8pm; ☎722 30 00) which has information on accommodation and transport, sells tickets for the metro/bus/tram network and can make hotel reservations in Brussels (or indeed anywhere else in Belgium). The service is free – you just pay a percentage of the room rate in advance. There is also a branch of *Acotra* (open daily 7am–11pm; ☎720 35 47), which will book you a bed or room in a hostel. There are several bureaux de change too (daily 7am–9pm).

From the airport, trains run every twenty minutes to the Gare du Nord and the Gare Centrale, with one train an hour going on to Midi. The journey time to Gare Centrale is about eighteen minutes; the cost is F80 one way, and tickets can be bought from the train information kiosk (daily 6.40am–10pm) before you go through customs, or from the ticket office in the station. The trains run from around 6am until 11.45pm; after that you'll need to take a taxi into the city centre – reckon on paying around F1500 for the trip.

Information

Aside from the office at the airport, there are two **tourist information offices** in Brussels, both located in the centre of town.

The main one, the **TIB** (Tourist Information Brussels) in the hôtel de ville on the Grand Place (June–Sept daily 9am–6pm; Oct–April Mon–Sat 9am–6pm; ☎513 89 40), handles information on the city only. It has a range of handouts, free public transit maps, can sell you a city guide with a map, and make hotel reservations. The map is adequate for the city centre, but if you want to explore areas outside the ring, it's advisable to get the *Falkplan* map of the city, which includes a street directory, before leaving Britain. The TIB also has a theatre and concert booking office, open daily between 11am and 5pm, which charges a F25 booking fee.

The **National Tourist Office**, nearby at rue Marche aux Herbes 61 (June–Sept Mon–Fri 9am–7pm, Sat & Sun 9am–1pm & 2–7pm; April, May & Oct Mon–Fri 9am–6pm, Sat & Sun 9am–1pm & 2–6pm; rest of the year Mon–Fri 9am–6pm, Sat 9am–1pm & 2–6pm, Sun 1pm–5pm; ☎504 03 90), has information on the whole country and also makes hotel reservations.The **Acotra** office at rue de la Madeleine 51 (Mon–Sat 10am–6pm; ☎512 70 78) books accommodation in youth hostels. The best English-language source of **what's on listings** is the weekly *The Bulletin* (F70); the weekly pull-out in the newspaper *Le Soir* is also useful – it comes out every Thursday, but is available throughout the week at TIB.

City transport

To get around the city centre, within the ring of boulevards, the easiest thing to do is **walk**: you'll end up seeing more and appreciating the transition between the different neighbourhoods. To get from one side of the centre to the other, or to reach some of the more widely dispersed attractions, you'll need to use **public transport**. Operated by *STIB* (☎515 20 00), the urban system runs on a mixture of bus, tram and metro lines and covers the city comprehensively. It's a user-friendly network, with the times of arrival and all stopping points displayed on metro platforms and at bus and tram stops. The metro system consists of two underground train lines: line #1 (red) running west–east through the centre, and splitting into two branches at either end, and line #2 (orange) circling the centre. There are also two underground tram, or "pre-metro" lines, of which line #3 is the most useful, running from the Gare du Nord, through de Brouckère and Bourse, to the Gare du Midi.

Tickets are fairly cheap by any standards. A single ticket costs F50, a strip of five F220, and a strip of ten F290, available either from tram or bus drivers, the tourist offices, metro kiosks, the STIB information offices in the Porte de Namur, Midi and Rogier stations, or from selected newspaper stores. Single tickets can also be obtained from automatic machines at most stations. A go-as-you-please *carte*, for F200, allows for 24 hours of travel on public transport. You're trusted to stamp tickets yourself in the machines provided, after which it is valid for an hour, during which you can get on and off as many trams, metros and buses as you like. The system is wide open to abuse, as once your ticket has been validated you are free to pass through barriers at metro stations and to get on buses and trams without showing the ticket. Fines on the spot, however, are heavy – F1000, or double that if you don't have it on you. Finally, remember that doors on metros and some trams and buses have to be opened manually. **Route maps** are available free from the tourist office and from information kiosks at Porte de Namur and Rogier and Midi metro stations. Services run from 6am until midnight, after which there's a very sporadic **night bus** service – often just one between midnight and around 3am. Women on their own should avoid the metro late at night, especially around Midi and Nord.

Taxis don't cruise the city but can be picked up from the stands spread around the city – notably on Bourse, Brouckère, Grand Sablon and Porte de Namur, at the train stations and outside swanky hotels. Prices start at around F100. When you can't find one, phone ☎511 22 44, 513 62 00, 349 49 49 or 647 22 22.

BRUSSELS: METRO

Line 1
Line 2
Line 3
Line 5

Zeekanaal

Bruxelles Canal Maritime

Heysel / Heizel
Brugman
Stuyvenbergh
Bockstael
Pannenhuis
Belgica
Simonis
Ossegem / Ossegem
Beekkant
Gare de l'Ouest / Weststation
Jacques Brel
Aumale
St-Guido / St-Guidon
Veeweyde

Etangs Noir / Zwarte Vivers
Cte. de Flandre / Grf. V. Vlaanderen
Ste. Catherine / St. Katelijne

Canal de Charleroi
Kanaal van Charleroi: naar Brussel

Gare du Nord / Noordstation
Rogier
Botanique / Kruidtuin
Madou
Kunst-Wet / Arts-Loi
Luxembourg / Luxemburg
Pte. de Namur / Naamsepoort
Louise / Louiza
Hotel des Monnaies / Munthof
Halleport / Porte de Hal
Gare du Midi / Zuidstation
Lemonnier
Anneessens
Bourse / Beurs
De Brouckere
Gare Centrale / Central Station
Parc / Park

Maelbeek / Maalbeek
Schuman
Merode
Thieffry
Petillon
Hanker
Delta
Beaulieu

Diamant
Georges-Henri
Joseph Charlotte
Montgomery
Boileau
Demey
Herrmann-Debroux

Roodebeek
Tomberg
Gribaumont

Stokkel / Stockel
Kraainem
Alma
Vandervelde

In addition to the STIB network are **local trains**, run by Belgian railways, which connect different parts of the inner city and the outskirts, though unless you're living and working in the city, you're unlikely to need to use them. Supplementing these are the **SNCV buses** (☎526 28 28) which run (mainly) from the Gare du Nord and place Rouppe (just off boulevard Lemonnier) to the suburbs of greater Brussels. A few run to other Belgian cities but they can take up to four times longer than the train. They are all listed on the back of the route map.

Guided tours

If you're only around for a short while or just want to get your bearings, it might be a good idea to take an **organized tour**. There are, of course, the regular two-to three-hour **bus tours** in a variety of languages which take in all the sights but really give little opportunity to see anything for very long. Reckon on paying around F700 for a three-hour tour with *De Boeck*, rue de la Colline 8 (☎513 77 44), the most centrally situated company, with whom you can book through the TIB, who also run their own tours. Less conventionally, a company known as *Chatterbus*, rue de Thuyas 12 (☎673 18 35) offers options of **walking tours** of central Brussels and **bus tours of the less obvious sights**, together with **beer-tasting evenings**. Another organization, *ARAU* (Atelier de Recherche et d'Action Urbaines), rue du Midi 2 (☎513 47 61), an architectural action group, also runs good introductions to the city, taking in its architectural specialties (such as Art Nouveau) and the more undiscovered attractions – parks and squares, 1930s Art Deco, industrial archeology – although unfortunately the commentary is usually only in French. Most of these tours are scheduled from March through November – although *Chatterbus* conducts its beer-tasting nights sporadically throughout the winter – and booking in advance is normally essential. Most tours cost around F500 per person; call direct for full details and schedules.

Accommodation

Brussels has no shortage of **places to stay**, but given the number of people passing through the city, finding a room can be hard, particularly in spring and summer – to be sure of a bed, it's best to reserve at least your first night. The tourist offices in the Grand Place and on rue Marché aux Herbes can provide a list of hotels and book hotel rooms, taking a percentage of the room rate as a (refundable) deposit. The *Acotra* office, rue de la Madeleine 51 (☎512 85 07/512 55 40), will book rooms in youth hostels for free, though again you'd be better off doing it yourself well in advance.

Hostels

Bruegel, rue de St Esprit 2 (☎511 04 36). Located just behind Notre Dame de la Chapelle, this is an official IYHF hostel. Housed in a new building, it has identical prices to the *Brel* (see below), though also the disadvantage of shared showers. It is, however, pretty central – close to the Sablon, the Musée des Beaux Arts and the Upper Town. Bus #20 from Midi or bus #48 from Porte de Halle.

CHAB (Centre de'Hébergement de l'Agglomeration de Bruxelles), rue Traversière 8 (☎217 01 58). A rambling, spacious hostel with a good reputation and slightly lower prices than the official youth hostels, though it can seem chaotic. Bike rental F150 a day (F1000 deposit), luggage lockers and laundry facilities. Sinks in all rooms, but shared showers and toilets. Meals are basic, but there's a reasonably priced restaurant across the road. Sleep-in beds (own sleeping bag obligatory) cost F240, dorm beds F290, triples or quads F370, doubles F440, singles F540. All prices include breakfast. Sheet rental F70. Open until 2am, rooms closed 10am–3pm. Metro Botanique.

Jacques Brel, rue de la Sablonnière 30 (☎218 01 87). An official IYHF hostel – modern, comfortable and with a hotel-like atmosphere. Facilities include showers in every room, bar, restaurant and meeting room. Beds in 6 to 12-bed dorms F340, triples or quads F385, doubles F460, singles F560. No access to rooms between 10am and 3pm; 1am curfew. Prices include breakfast, sheets can be rented for F100; temporary membership of the IYHF costs F80. Metro stops Madou, Botanique.

Maison Internationale, chaussée de Wavre 205 (☎648 97 87). An unofficial hostel, and for cleanliness, privacy and conscientious management the best value-for-money in Brussels. Singles F340 per person, doubles F290 (sheets F60 extra). There are no dormitories; showers and toilets are shared, but there are sinks in every room. Handy for the chaussée d'Ixelles shopping district.

Sleep Well, rue du Damier 23 (☎218 50 50). A long-established city centre private hostel, still located just off rue Neuve, 5 minutes' walk from the Gare du Nord, although it has recently moved around the corner from its original position on rue de la Blanchisserie. Still among the lowest prices in Brussels, with summer rates ranging from F295 in a dorm to F490 per head for a double room. Hopefully its new building will have a better reputation for comfort and cleanliness than its predecessor. Metro Rogier.

Hotels

Albert Premier, place Rogier 20 (☎217 21 25). Fairly recently renovated hotel, very handy for the Gare du Nord. ⑥.

Arenberg, rue d'Assaut 15 (☎511 07 70). One of the best situated of the pricier city centre hotels, just around the corner from the Galeries St Hubert, with well-appointed double rooms with TV and sumptuous breakfasts. ⑧.

Bosquet, rue Bosquet 70 (☎538 52 30). Ultra low-priced double rooms, including breakfast, although the standard is basic to say the least. Worth experiencing only if you're on the tightest of budgets. Metro Hotel des Monnaies. ②.

De Boeck, rue Veydt 40 (☎537 40 33). Pleasant hotel in a pretty neighbourhood close to avenue Louise. Double rooms have toilet, sink and shower. Breakfast included. Metro Louise. ③.

Du Congrès, rue du Congrès 42–44 (☎217 18 90). A little shabby, but within walking distance of both the main business and tourist areas. Often used by the European Commission for visiting guests. Breakfast included. Metro Madou. ⑤.

Derby, avenue de Tervuren 24 (☎733 08 19). On the edge of the Parc du Cinquantenaire, with large, somewhat rundown rooms (all have shower or bath). Metro Merode. ③.

George V, rue 't Kint 23 (☎513 50 93). A ramshackle period hotel in a quiet neighbourhood a 5-minute walk to the west of Bourse. Breakfast included. Metro Bourse. ③.

Madou, rue du Congrès 45 (☎218 83 75). A *fin-de-siècle* hotel under friendly management, in which the rooms vary from the simple to the seedily splendid, and all have shower and toilet. Breakfast extra – F150. Book well ahead. Metro Madou. ③.

Osborne, rue Bosquet 67 (☎537 92 51). A mishmash of rooms in an 1860s town house just off avenue Toison d'Or, a short walk from avenue Louise. Breakfast included. Two minutes' walk from metro Munthof. ②.

Rembrandt, rue de la Concorde 42 (☎512 71 39). Popular and pleasant small hotel in the peaceful residential neighbourhood just off avenue Louise. A good option if you don't want to be right in the middle of the hum of the city centre. ④.

Sabina, rue du Nord 78 (☎218 26 37). Spruce, pretty rooms, in a wonderful turn-of-the-century house with a beamed and panelled breakfast room. Prices are low for what you get. A 2-minute walk from metro Madou, in a relatively safe, commercial district of town. ③.

Vendôme, boulevard Adolphe Max 98 (☎218 00 70). A medium-range hotel very conveniently located between places Rogier and de Brouckère, with comfortable rooms, some of which have minibars. Good place to stay if you want to pamper yourself. ⑥.

Windsor, place Rouppe 13 (☎511 20 14). Strikingly clean and cheerful rooms in a decent if rather characterless location. Breakfast included. Metro Anneessens. ③.

Camping

Although there are a number of **campsites** in the Greater Brussels area, only two make feasible bases for the city. One, the *Grimbergen*, is near the Atomium, at Veldkantstraat 46 in Grimbergen (☎269 25 97). Take bus #G from Gare du Nord to the terminal, after which it's roughly a ten-minute walk. The other, the *Paul Rosmant*, is east of the city, at Warandenberg 52, in Wezembeek–Oppem (☎782 10 09). To get there, take the metro to Kraainem (line #1B), and from there bus #30 to place St Pierre. Failing that, it's not much more difficult or time-consuming to escape the sway of the big city, and to go farther afield to Leuven, Villers-la-Ville or one of the smaller towns in Flanders or Antwerp province. See the appropriate chapters for details.

The City

The centre of Brussels sits neatly within the rough pentagon of boulevards that enclose it, a "petit ring" which follows the course of the fourteenth-century city walls, running from place Rogier in the north round to Porte de Halle in the south. The city centre divides in turn into the **Upper and Lower Towns**, the neighbourhoods generally becoming more expensive the higher you go. By far the greater part of the city centre is occupied by the **Lower Town**, which is slung between rue Royale in the east (running from the Jardin Botanique to the Palace Royale), and the north–south central boulevard – slicing through the city from place Rogier to the Gare du Midi – variously named Adolphe Max, Anspach and Lemonnier. Just east of this main thoroughfare, the medieval core of Brussels zeroes in on the Grand Place – the unquestionable centre of Brussels and perhaps the finest preserved city square in Europe, a focus for both tourists and residents. In the Lower Town, keep your position in relation to the Grand Place in your mind and you won't go far wrong. South of the Grand Place the busy centre fades into the old working-class streets of the Marolles district and Gare du Midi – now a depressed, and predominantly immigrant, area. To the north is the rather sleazy rue Neuve, a pedestrianized main street that's home to Brussels' mainstream stores and department stores, leading up to the place Rogier and the tawdry area around the Gare du Nord. It's here that a rather sad red-light district lurks, spilling into the side streets off Adolphe Max, where neon signs advertise peep shows and "sexy girls." West of these streets, however, is an appealingly workaday district, centring on the church of St Catherine, with many fish restaurants along the (now dry) docks.

The *haute de la ville*, or **Upper Town**, is quite different in feel from the rest of the city centre, a self-consciously planned, more monumental quarter, with

statuesque buildings lining wide, classically imposed boulevards and squares. Appropriately, it's the home of the Belgian parliament and government departments, some of the major museums, the swishest shops (around place Louise) and the massive Palais de Justice, which lords it over the rest of the city, commanding views that on clear days reach as far as the Atomium and the park at Laeken, way north of the city centre.

There's much of interest, too, in the **outer boroughs** that radiate from the **petit ring**. From the Palais de Justice, avenue Louise stretches southeast, a fashionable strand that leads into the **St Gilles** neighbourhood and the concentration of houses of the Art Nouveau architect, Victor Horta. There is more Art Nouveau, a good art gallery and some excellent bars and shops in the adjacent quarter, **Ixelles**, leading down to the city's most popular park, the Bois de la Cambre, and the bucolic expanses of the Forêt de Soignes. North of Ixelles, **Etterbeek** is home to the EC and European Parliament buildings, and the rather dull Parc de Cinquantenaire. **St Josse**, beyond, is home to the city's Turkish community, and somewhere you're most likely to go at night to eat. North of the centre, there's **Laeken**, city residence of the Belgian royal family but visited more for the Atomium, a rather monstrous leftover from the 1958 World's Fair; west lies the suburb of **Anderlecht** – with its famous soccer team, the fascinating Gueuze brewery and the Erasmus house.

The Lower Town

The **LOWER TOWN** is the commercial heart of Brussels, a bustling quarter that's home to the major stores, hotels and restaurants. The Grand Place is the centre, although its modern-day rival, place de Brouckère, a little way north, also serves as a major focus, at least for city centre traffic, as do the nearby place de la Monnaie and the seedy place Rogier on the edge of the ring road.

The Grand Place

The obvious place to begin any tour of Brussels is the **Grand Place**, where the magnificently gilded facades of Baroque guildhouses and the elaborate Gothic Hôtel de Ville create a splendid arena for goggling tourists and gin-and-tonic-slugging businessmen. In the sidewalk cafés, and in the maze of narrow cobblestone streets to the north of the square, you'll hear more British, American and German spoken than French or Flemish, and the whole area is almost overwhelmingly geared to tourists and ex-pats. That said, the square is stunning, and there's no better place to get a taste of Brussels' past – and its Eurocapital present.

For centuries the Grand Place was the town's main market place. Now there's just a small daily flower market and a rather mournful caged bird market on Sunday mornings. Originally an area of marsh, it was drained in the twelfth century, and in the thirteenth century covered markets for bread, meat and cloth were erected. Evidence that the market developed beyond the boundaries of the square is obvious from the names of the narrow streets that tangle around it, rues du Beurre, des Bouchers, Marché aux Herbes, Poulets and Fromages all combining to evoke an image of medieval bustle. On the square itself, the city's merchant guilds built themselves headquarters, cementing the Grand Place's role as commercial hub of the city.

In the fifteenth century, with the building of the splendid Gothic town hall, the square took on a civic and political function as well, with the ruling dukes descending from their Upper Town residences to meet the people or show off in tournaments. Official decrees and pronouncements were read here, and public executions took place. The majority of those executed were Protestants, rebelling at the oppressive Catholic regime of Philip II, who in 1567 sent the duke of Alva and an army of twelve thousand to quash the dissenters. Thousands fled from the town, and a period of severe famine ensued, during which a contemporary source described "the poor wrestling with the dogs for the blood and entrails of slaughtered cows and sheep."

Of the square's medieval buildings only the Hôtel de Ville and one guildhouse survive, due to a 36-hour bombardment of the city by the French in 1695, which destroyed four thousand houses and virtually the whole of the Grand Place. Unperturbed, the city's guildsmen swiftly had their headquarters rebuilt, adopting a distinctive and flamboyant Baroque style, making the square more ornate and more imposing than ever. The **Hôtel de Ville** still dominates the proceedings, its splendour little diminished by the scaffolding that currently encases the elegant 330-foot spire. You'll probably be content to take in the intricacies of its pinnacle and statue encrusted facade from a pavement café, but if you're interested to see inside there are guided tours (April–Sept Tues–Fri 9.30am–12.15pm & 1.45–5pm, Sun 10am–noon & 2–4pm; Oct–March Tues–Fri 9.30am–12.15pm & 1.45–4pm, Sun 10am–noon & 2–4pm; F75). These take in various official rooms, most dazzling of which is the sixteenth-century council chamber, decorated with gilt moulding, faded tapestries and an oak floor inlaid with ebony. On a more contemporary note, take a look at the electronic interpreting system, installed to facilitate discussion between French and Flemish speaking councillors. You'll also see the Gallery of the Spanish Kings, with its amazingly sharp and clear full-length portraits, painted between 1715 and 1718 after the monarchs were all dead.

But the the real glory of the Grand Place lies in the **guildhouses**, their slender, gilded facades swirling with exuberant, self-publicizing carvings, and sculptures, pompously promoting the aims and practices of the guildsmen. Each house has a name, usually derived from one of the statues, symbols or architectural quirks decorating its facade. Some of the most spectacular line the western side of the square. At no. 7, the **Maison du Renard** was the house of the haberdashers' guild: on the ground floor cute cherubs in bas relief play at haberdashery, while a gilded fox, after which the house is named, squats above the door; up on the third storey a statue of Justice flanked by statues symbolizing the four continents suggests the guild's designs on world markets – an aim to which St Nicholas, patron saint of merchants, glinting above, clearly gives his blessing. Next door, at no. 6, is the **Maison du Cornet**, headquarters of the boatsmen's guild, a fanciful creation of 1697 whose top storey resembles the stern of a ship. Adjoining it, the **Maison de la Louve** is one of the few guildhouses to have survived the French bombardment, its elegant pilastered facade fronting the former home of the archers' guild, studded with pious representations of concepts like Peace and Discord, together with a pediment relief of Apollo firing at a python. The three lower storeys of the **Maison de Sac**, next door, also escaped; the headquarters of the carpenters and coopers, the upper stories were appropriately designed by a cabinet-maker, and feature pilasters and caryatids which resemble the ornate legs of Baroque furniture. At the end of the row is the

Roi d'Espagne, headquarters of the guild of bakers and now housing the most famous of the square's bars. The house is named after the bust of Charles V on the facade, flanked by a Moorish and an Indian prisoner, symbolizing his mastery of a vast empire. Balanced on the balustrade are allegorical statues of Energy, Fire, Water, Wind, Wheat and Prudence, presumably meant to represent the elements necessary for baking the ideal loaf.

Most of the northern side of the Place is taken up by the sturdy neo-Gothic **Maison du Roi**, a reconstruction of a sixteenth-century Gothic building commissioned by Charles V. It now houses the **Musée de la Ville de Bruxelles** (Mon–Thurs 10am–12.30pm & 1.30–5pm, Sat & Sun 10am–1pm, closed Fri; F80) which painlessly summarizes the history of Brussels. On the ground floor are sculptural fragments from the Hôtel de Ville and Pieter Bruegel's *Wedding Procession*, but it's the second floor which is most interesting, with maps and 3D models of the city at various points in its development. The third floor houses the Manneken Pis' vast wardrobe, four hundred sickeningly saccharine costumes ranging from Mickey Mouse to a maharaja, all of them gifts from various visiting dignitaries.

Just beyond the Maison du Roi is **Le Pigeon** (no. 26), where Victor Hugo lived during his exile from France; he was expelled for his support of the French insurrection of 1848. On the opposite side of the square, **Le Cygne** (no. 9), once housed a bar where an equally famous exile, Karl Marx, was to meet up with Engels. It was in Brussels in February 1848 that they wrote the Communist Manifesto, only to be deported as political undesirables the following month. Appropriately enough, the Belgian Labour Party was founded here in 1885, though ironically the building now shelters one of the city's most exclusive restaurants. Next door, the **Maison des Brasseurs** (no. 10) is the only house still to be owned by its original guild – the brewers' – and it houses a small **Brewery Museum** (April–Oct Mon–Fri 10am–noon & 2–5pm, Sat 10am–noon; Nov–March Mon–Fri 10am–noon & 2–5pm; F100) in the cellar. Here you can sit over a free beer, look at various ancient bits of brewing paraphernalia, and listen to a self-congratulatory commentary in which beer figures as a health-giving, friendship-promoting panacea for the world's problems. On the other side of Le Cygne is the **Maison d'Etoile**, a nineteenth-century rebuilding of the medieval home of the city magistrate. In rue Charles Buls, around the corner, the exploits of one Everard 't Serclaes are commemorated: in 1356 the francophile count of Flanders attempted to seize power from the duke of Brabant, occupied the magistrate's house, and flew his standard from the roof. 't Serclaes scaled the building, replaced Flanders' standard with that of the duke of Brabant, and went on to lead the recapturing of the city, events represented in bas relief above a reclining statue of 't Serclaes. His arm is polished smooth from the long-standing superstition that good luck will come to those who stroke it.

Around the Grand Place

Rue Charles Buls takes you to rue des Brasseurs, scene of a bizarre incident in 1873 when the French Symbolist poet Paul Verlaine shot his fellow poet and lover Arthur Rimbaud, earning himself a six-month prison sentence. There's still a slightly offbeat feel to the quarter, totally at odds with the respectable tourism of the Grand Place, with gutsy bars and cheap Greek eateries running up to rue des Eperonniers and the Galerie Agora, both of which are good hunting grounds for second-hand and alternative clothes.

Rue de la Violette, in contrast, leads down to two of the city's most hyped tourist attractions. The **Musée de Costume et de la Dentelle**, at rue de la Violette 6 (Tues, Thurs & Fri 10am–12.30pm & 1.30–5pm, Sat & Sun 2–4.30pm; closed Mon & Wed; F80) is worth a visit, even if you have no interest in the subject, with some fine examples of antique and contemporary lace. Lace became an important local product in the seventeenth century, and by the eighteenth century, when the industry reached its peak, the city had reputedly ten thousand lacemakers, all of them women. The lace made here was renowned for the intricacy of the designs and was in demand worldwide, bought by the rich to embellish their clothes. Nowadays lace is still made in Brussels, though on a much smaller scale, and it's still very expensive – especially from any of the shops around the Grand Place.

At the foot of rue de la Violette, rue de l'Etuve runs along to the **Manneken Pis**, a diminutive statue of a little boy pissing – normally concealed behind hoards of camera-clicking tourists – that's supposed to embody the "irreverent spirit" of the city (or so visitors are told). Jerome Duquesnoy cast the original statue in the 1600s, but it was stolen several times, notably by a French convict in 1817, who broke it into pieces. The thief and the smashed Manneken were apprehended, the former publicly branded on the Grand Place and sentenced to a life of forced labour, while the fragments were used to create the mould in which the present-day Manneken was cast. It is kitsch culture at its most extreme, and you wouldn't be missing much if you bypassed it altogether.

North of the Grand Place, the quarter hinging on **rue des Bouchers** is the city centre's restaurant ghetto, the narrow cobblestone streets transformed at night into fairy-lit tunnels where restaurants vie for custom with elaborate displays of dull-eyed fish and glistening seafood. There's a feverish atmosphere here, of hard selling and high spending, as street musicians and street vendors attempt to distract Amex-armed tourists and expense-account businesspeople from the serious task of selecting an eatery. Although it's worth seeing what Brussels' role as Eurocapital has done for the city centre, you're unlikely to want to hang around for long.

Things are slightly more subdued in the nearby **Galeries St Hubert**, bisected by rue des Bouchers – one of Europe's first shopping arcades. It consists of three glass-vaulted galleries – du Roi, de la Reine and des Princes – which, with their refined boutiques, exclusive restaurants and cafés, a theatre and cinema, still retain an aura of sophistication.

The Bourse and around

Walking out of the Grand Place along rue du Beurre, the tiny Gothic church of **St Nicholas** stands incongruously hemmed in by touristy shops. The outer shell is in fact a 1950s reconstruction, but the occasionally open interior (try Sundays) retains a fourteenth-century choir and a painting of the *Virgin and Child* attributed to Rubens. Beyond rises the **Bourse**, the grandiose home of the city's stock exchange, a neo-Classical structure of 1873 caked with fruit, fronds, languishing nudes and frolicking putti – details most effortlessly absorbed from a pavement table at the Art Nouveau *Falstaff* café alongside. **Place de la Bourse** itself is little more than an unsightly, heavily trafficked pause along boulevard Anspach, over-endowed with familiar fast-food outlets.

The streets on the other side of the boulevard have more appeal, where **place St Géry** stands at the core of a tangle of semi-gentrified streets. The nineteenth-

CENTRAL BRUSSELS

century covered market on the square has been recently renovated, prompting a face lift for the rest of the area: tall terraces of decayed houses are being returned to their former glory, and the occasional designer boutique or bar is already open in anticipation of the new tenants.

For a taste of what place St Géry was like in its heyday, head north to the neighbourly bustle of **place St Catherine**'s daily market. It's held outside the church of **St Catherine**, a blackened, eroded nineteenth-century replacement for a Baroque church, of which only the creamy, curvy tower remains. Go inside if it's open, ignoring the piped muzak and digital display flashing Christ's message, to see a fourteenth-century Black Madonna, chucked into the Senne by Protestants, but fished out while floating on a fortuitous clod of peat.

The **river**, however, is no longer viewable here. By the nineteenth century it had become intolerably polluted – in the words of the Brussels writer, Lemonnier, "the dumping ground, not only of industry, but also of the houses lining the river: it was not unusual to see the ballooned stomach of a dog mixed pêle mêle with its own litter...." After an outbreak of cholera in 1866, which killed nearly 3500 people, the river was piped underground and paved over. Some of the docks were also filled in (notably Quai aux Briques and parallel Quai aux Bois à Brûler), but, lined with small nineteenth-century buildings, they still have a bank-side feel – an impression heightened in the early morning when the streets are choked with lories bearing loads of fish for the fish restaurants and fishsellers. It's a refreshingly workaday scene after the razz of the streets around the Grand Place. Set back from the docks is another peaceful spot, the triangular **place de Béguinage**, dominated by the supple, billowing Baroque facade of **St Jean de la Béguinage**, a church so decayed that it has a falling rocks sign pasted to its front door. The interior echoes with the flapping and cooing of pigeons, providing an eerie soundtrack as you wander along a nave studded with the chubby faces of curly headed angels to a mock-rustic pulpit resembling a grotesque treehouse.

North of the Grand Place

Farther north from the Grand Place, beyond the rue des Bouchers quarter, **place de la Monnaie** is home to the **Theatre de la Monnaie**, Brussels' opera house, a neo-Classical structure built in 1819 and with an interior added in 1856 to a design by Poelaert, the architect of the Palais de Justice. The square itself is otherwise uninteresting (though in summer it's a site for live bands), its fringe of modern buildings, notably the huge sprouting **centre Monnaie**, housing offices, shops and the main city post office. On the far side, the central **boulevard Anspach** opens out at **place de Brouckère**, Brussels' modern centre, a busy traffic-choked junction surrounded by advertising hoardings.

From place de la Monnaie, **rue Neuve** forges north, a gaudy pedestrianized shopping street meeting the inner ring at the junction of **place Rogier**, beyond which lie the Gare du Nord and the seedy red-light area. Stop instead about a third of the way up rue Neuve, at **place des Martyrs**, a cool, rational square imposed on the city by the Hapsburgs that is nowadays one of its most haunting sights, a forlorn open space that's these days a magnet for the down-and-out – the cracks between the cobblestones are encrusted with glass shards, the fountain no longer flows and many of the windows are smashed and boarded up. Work has actually recently begun to spruce the place up, and many of the buildings are as a result cocooned in scaffolding; however, looking at the state of some of them, you wonder if it might already be too late. The square's position over an underground shrine to the 445 rebels against Dutch rule, who died in the Belgian revolution of 1830, only adds to the desolate mood.

Beyond the square, narrow lanes trace their medieval route past soulless modernistic monoliths up to rue des Sables, where, at no. 20, the city's only surviving Horta-designed department store, the **Magasins Waucquez**, was recently restored after lying empty for sixteen years and now houses the **Centre Belge de la Bande Dessinée** (Tues–Sun 10am–6pm; F150), devoted to the history of the Belgian comic strip. It's worth visiting for the building alone, a wonderfully airy, summery construction, with light flooding through the stained glass that surrounds the central courtyard; even if you're not interested in comics, the *Horta Brasserie* especially (see p.324), with its exposed girders and slender, silvered Corinthian columns, is attraction enough. As for the museum, it has displays tracing the techiques and development of the comic strip until 1960, focusing on a wide range of Belgian cartoonists, past and present, and with specific sections on animation, and – of course – Hergé, complete with a model of Tin Tin's space rocket and other artefacts from the stories. Sadly, labelling is in French and Flemish only, but explanations in English are said to be on the way.

The South: the Marolles and Midi

There's little of interest along the series of dead straight boulevards that run down to the **Gare du Midi**, which can be reached direct by metro from Bourse. The area around the station is home to the city's many North African and Greek immigrants, a severely depressed and at times seedy quarter with an uneasy undertow by day and sometimes overtly threatening at night. There's a closed, ghettoized feel to the streets and in many of the cheap cafés and bars: the exceptions are listed on pp.323–7 under "Eating and drinking." The best time to go is on a Sunday morning, when a vibrant souk-like **market** is held under the station's rail arches (see "Shops and markets").

If you'd rather avoid Midi, you could instead take bus #48 from Bourse to **Notre Dame de la Chapelle**, a clumsy, sprawling Gothic structure, grimy with weather and pollution and newly open after a much-needed restoration. The city's oldest church, built between 1210 and 1300, its main claim to fame is the tomb of Pieter Bruegel the Elder in the third chapel of the south aisle (he's supposed to have lived and died around the corner at rue Haute 132).

Rue Haute and parallel rue Blaes form the double spine of the **Quartier Marolles**, stacked on the slopes below the Palais de Justice. An earthy neighbourhood of run-down housing and cheap, basic restaurants, shops and bars, it's one of the few places in the city where you can still hear older people using the traditional dialect, "Brusselse Sproek" or "Marollien." A brand of Flemish which has, over the centuries, been influenced by the languages of the city's overlords, it is now in danger of dying out, and local people have set up an academy to preserve it, supported by such powerful figures as Jacques Delors. They propose that all newcomers to Brussels should learn one hundred words of the dialect. It's a colourful, earthy language; you could make a start with *dikenek*, "big mouth," *schieve lavabo*, "idiot" (literally "a twisted toilet") or *fieu* – "son of a bitch."

The Marolles neighbourhood grew up in the seventeenth century as a centre for artisans working on the nearby mansions of Sablon, and remained a thriving working-class district until the 1870s, when the paving over of the Senne led to the riverside factories closing down and moving out to the suburbs. The workers and their families followed, abandoning Marolles to the old and poor. Today, gentrification is creeping into the district, and along rues Haute and Blaes there are dilapidated houses in the process of restoration and the occasional swanky restaurant or antique shop sprouting up alongside a basic bar or cheap clothes shop. **Place du Jeu de Balle**, though, is much as it ever was, the heart of Marolles and scene of the city's best flea market (see "Shops and markets"), a shabby square surrounded by basic bars and on Sunday morning completely taken over by the market, which spreads into the adjacent streets – notably rue des Renards. If you're here on a Sunday you'd be mad to miss it, pile after pile of rusty junk alongside muddles of eccentric bric-a-brac that have everything from a chipped buddha, a rococo angel or African idol, to horn-rimmed glasses, a top hat or a pair of antlers.

The Upper Town

The division between Lower and Upper Town is in part a blurred one, the slopes to the **UPPER TOWN** rising only minutes from the Grand Place itself. The gentle slope is home to the city's cathedral and the so-called Mont des Arts, whose rigorous layout is little preparation for the exuberant neo-Classicism along the rue Royale and rue de la Regence, which make up the Upper Town's formal spine. Though heavily trafficked, the wide avenues and grand architecture of what was once the aristocratic quarter lend a dignified feel that's markedly different from the bustle of the Lower Town. It is, however, very much a part of town to visit and then leave, not very neighbourly or residential. Climb up and admire the views and the museum collections, and then descend back into the maelstrom below – or push on into the outer boroughs.

The Cathedral and lower slopes

Climbing the steep slope above rue Marché aux Herbes, rue de Montagne leads up to the city's **Cathedral** (daily 7am–6pm), a Brabant-Gothic building which occupies a commanding position just below the topmost ridge, though sadly it's becoming jostled by modern buildings. Begun in 1220, the cathedral is dedicated jointly to St Michel and St Gudule, the patron and patroness of Brussels – though it's more often known as the church of St Gudule. It was severely damaged during the Restoration and – like so much else in the city – by the French shelling a century later. Napoleon later tentatively restored the building, and another major restoration is in progress now. Flooded with light from the clerestory windows, it's a fine church, though the present restoration means that the choir, the earliest example of the style in the Low Countries, is boarded off. There is, however, some superb sixteenth-century stained glass in the transepts – panegyrics to the Hapsburgs designed by Bernard van Orley.

South of the cathedral is the **Gare Centrale**, a bleak Art Deco creation by Victor Horta, who was also responsible for the drab **Palais des Beaux Arts** just above. A complete contrast with his flamboyant earlier works, it has only one storey, apparently so as to avoid blocking the monarch's view from his palace. It holds a theatre, concert hall, numerous exhibitions and the **Musée du Cinema**, which shows old and silent movies every night, and has displays on the history of film to browse around between screenings – details from the usual sources (see above).

Beyond is the so-called **Mont des Arts**, a collection of severe geometric buildings devoted to a variety of arts-related activities, instituted in 1934 as a memorial to King Albert and built in the late Fifties and early Sixties. They flank a broad flight of steps which link the upper and lower towns, emerging at the foot of rue Coudenberg, which climbs up to place Royale.

Place Royale, the Palais du Roi and the Parc de Bruxelles

Imperiously neo-Classical, **place Royale** forms a fitting climax to rue Royale, the dead-straight backbone of the Upper Town which runs all the way to the Turkish suburb of St Josse. Ostentatious mansions built for the city's aristocrats flank the equally ostentatious church of **St Jacques Coudenberg**, a fanciful version of a Roman temple with a colourfully frescoed pediment. In the centre of the square, posing above a sea of jammed traffic, is a dashing equestrian statue of Saint Godfrey, a Belgian-born Crusader who became Jerusalem's first Christian king.

Around the corner, the **Palais du Roi** is something of an anticlimax, a sombre downbeat 1904 conversion of some eighteenth-century town houses, fronted by bored guards, unkempt hedges and trams rattling across the cobblestone place de Palais. The Belgian dynasty is relatively young, founded in 1831. The second of its five kings, Leopold II, was responsible for gracing Brussels with such pompous monuments as the Palais de Justice, the Cinquantenaire arcades and the mock-medieval prison of St Gilles, partially financed by his private income from the Congo, which was his personal property. His successor, Leopold III, was one of Europe's least popular monarchs. His first wife died in a suspicious car crash, and he nearly lost his kingdom by remarrying (anathema in a Catholic country); later on, during the German occupation, he remained in the country rather than face exile, fuelling rumours that he was a Nazi collaborator. His supporters maintained that he prevented thousands of Belgians from being deported, and in 1950, in a referendum which showed a clear French/Flemish split, the country (or rather, the French-speaking majority) voted to retain the monarchy and Leopold returned. Perhaps fortunately for Belgium, he abdicated in 1951 in favour of his son, the present King Baudouin, who hit the news in April 1990 by standing down for a day so that an abortion bill (which he as a Catholic had refused to sign) could be passed.

Although this is their official residence, the current Belgian royal family has, not surprisingly, elected to live elsewhere (in Laeken) and the palace is open to the public during August. Sumptuous rooms, and tapestries designed by Goya, make a visit worthwhile – which is more than can be said for the displays in the palace annexe, **Hôtel Bellevue** (daily except Fri 10am–5pm; free) – furniture, porcelain and glass mainly, along with an odd array of eighteenth- and nineteenth-century heart-shaped brooches, pendants, perfume bottles and *ex votos*, the collection of an eminent local cardiologist. A third royal exhibition, the **Musée de la Dynastie** (daily except Fri 10am–4pm; F50), on the third floor of the Hôtel Bellevue, charts the brief history of the Belgian royal family, and will thrill only ardent monarchists.

Opposite the Palais, the **Parc de Bruxelles** is the most central of the city's parks, along whose dusty, tree-shaded avenues businesspeople, civil servants and office workers stroll at lunchtime, or race to catch the metro in the evenings. Surrounded by trees with branches tortured to form continuous parallel lines, and dotted with classical statues, it's a dreary, vacuous place, and somewhere you're only likely to want to pause briefly.

The Musées Royaux des Beaux Arts

Facing the place Royale, the **MUSÉES ROYAUX DES BEAUX ARTS** comprise two museums, one displaying modern art, the other older works – the two linked by a passageway. Together they make up Belgium's most satisfying, all-round collection of fine art, with marvellous collections of work by Bruegel, Rubens and the Belgian surrealist painters.

Both galleries are large, and to do them justice you should see them in separate visits. Finding your way around the larger of the two collections, **Musée d'Art Ancien**, is made easy by following the colour-coded routes: the **blue route** takes in paintings of the fifteenth and sixteenth centuries, including Bruegel; the **brown route** concentrates primarily on paintings of the seventeenth and eighteenth centuries, with the collection of Rubens (for which the museum is internationally famous) as the highlight; the **yellow route** is devoted to nineteenth-century works, notably the paintings and sculptures of workers by the social realist Constantin Meunier. The second collection, the **Musée d'Art Moderne**, is laid out on eight subterranean levels, a stimulating collection of works by twentieth-century artists, most of them Belgian, though a handful of French Impressionists, a couple of Chagalls and a Francis Bacon provide more familiar moments.

MUSÉE D'ART ANCIEN

Tues–Sun 10am–noon & 1–5pm; free

It's best to start a visit to the **Musée d'Art Ancien** with the **blue route,** which begins with the **Flemish primitives**. Rooms 11 and 12 hold several delicately realistic paintings by Rogier van der Weyden, city painter to Brussels in the fifteenth century, and room 13 *Justice of Otto* by his contemporary Dieric Bouts, a powerful work of deep characterization and almost photographic realism. Room 14 has some plain, commonsense portraits by Hans Memling and the Master of the St Lucy Legend's *Virgin Mary and Mary Magdalen*, full of strange medieval symbols, and room 17 a *Temptation of St Anthony* by Hieronymous Bosch, painted in the nightmarishly fantastic style that would later so influence Pieter Bruegel the Elder. Room 18 holds works by Cranch, including the sharply observed nudes of *Venus* and *Adam and Eve*, among others. Later rooms hold work by Gerard David, Joos van Cleve and Quentin Matsys, including a marvellous *Virgin and Child* by the latter, and Jan Mostaert's wonderfully busy *Passion*, full of faces and incidents.

The museum's collection of works by the **Bruegel** family, notably Pieter the Elder, is in rooms 31–34. The influence of Bosch is seen most clearly in the *Fall of the Rebel Angels* hanging in the first room, which had actually been attributed to Bosch until Bruegel's signature was discovered hidden under the frame. However, it's for his distinctive use of contemporary life in the treatment of religious and mythical scenes that Bruegel is rightly famed, and there are some wonderful examples here. *The Census at Bethlehem* and the *Massacre of the Innocents* are particularly absorbing, with the traditionally momentous events happening, almost incidentally, among the bustle of everyday life. There are almost identical versions by both Pieter the Elder and Pieter the Younger. The gallery also holds what is possibly Bruegel the Elder's most haunting work, *The Fall of Icarus*, whose mood is perfectly captured by Auden in his poem *Musée des Beaux Arts*:

...In Bruegel's Icarus, *for instance: how everything turns away*
Quite leisurely from the disaster; the ploughman may
Have heard the splash, the forsaken cry,
But for him it was not an important failure; the sun shone
As it had to on the white legs disappearing into the green
Water; and the expensive delicate ship that must have seen
Something amazing, a boy falling out of the sky,
Had somewhere to get and sailed calmly on.

The **brown route** concentrates on work of the seventeenth and eighteenth centuries, notably some glorious canvases by Rubens, stunning refutations of the popular misconception that he painted nothing but flabby nude women. *Landscape with the Chase of Atlanta* in room 52 is a case in point, a brilliant evocation of the depth, light and shade of a forest; *Studies of a Negro's Head* is likewise wonderfully observed, a preparation for the black magus in the *Adoration of the Magi* next door in room 62. This is a luminous work, with the light reflected from the sheen of skin and fabric. In the same room *The Climb to Calvary* is an intensely physical painting, capturing the confusion, agony and strain as Christ struggles on hands and knees under the weight of the Cross up the hill.

The **yellow route** of nineteenth-century works is the gallery's dullest, largely devoted to derivative city- and landscapes, portraits, forgettable canvases by Belgian Impressionists and some rather disagreeable symbolist paintings. Most worth seeing are the paintings and sculptures of workers by the Belgian social realist Constantin Meunier in room 79.

MUSÉE D'ART MODERNE
Tues–Sun 10am–1pm & 2–5pm; free

Revamped in the Eighties, the **Musée d'Art Moderne**, accessible by escalator from the Ancien collection, is the city's most innovative museum, a startlingly varied collection of modern art and sculpture, laid out on eight semicircular subterranean floors. As a gallery it's both enjoyable and challenging. Level 1 is devoted to temporary exhibitions of contemporary art, and levels 2 and 3 are largely reception areas; of the rest, levels 4, 6 and 8 are the most interesting.

The fourth level is as good a place to start as any, with a handful of works by Bonnard, Gauguin and Matisse, a Dufy *View of Marseille*, and two fanciful paintings by Chagall – including the endearingly eccentric *The Frog that Wanted to Make Itself as Big as a Bull*. Undoubted highlights, however, are the series of solitary women by James Ensor, and Leon Spillaert's evocations of intense loneliness, from virtually monochromatic beaches to empty rooms and train cars.

Level 6 is devoted to Expressionists, Cubists and Surrealists, of which the last are by far the most enthralling. There's a fine Dali, *The Temptation of St Anthony*, a hallucinatory work in which spindly legged elephants tempt the saint with fleshy women; and a couple of de Chirico's paintings of dressmakers' dummies. Of the Belgian Surrealists, Paul Delvaux, one of whose less provocative works graces the Bourse metro station, is represented by such diverse paintings as the oddly erotic *Pygmalion*, a *Crucifixion* in which all the figures are skeletons, and *La voix publique*, in which a tram approaches a reclining nude. Even more elusive is the gallery's small collection of paintings by Magritte – perplexing works, whose weird, almost photographically realized images and bizarre juxtapositions aim firmly to disconcert.

There are some equally unsettling works down on level 8, most of them by living artists. The undoubted highlight is Francis Bacon's *Pope with Owls*, but the rest of the collection is always a surprise, ranging from the wacky psychedelic sculpture of a fluorescent flower by Bailleux, to the swirling abstracts of Pierre Alechinsky.

Rue de la Regence and the Sablon neighbourhood

From the Beaux Arts it's a short walk along rue de la Regence to the **place du Petit Sablon**, a rectangular area off to the left which was formerly a horse market. It was laid out as a park in 1890, surrounded by a wrought-iron fence decorated with 48 statues representing the medieval guilds. At one end a fountain decorated with larger statues recounts the story of counts Egmont and Hoorn, beheaded on the Grand Place for their opposition to Spanish tyranny in the 1500s. Count Egmont is further remembered by the **Palais d'Egmont** on the other side of the square. This was originally built in 1548 for Françoise of Luxembourg, mother of the executed count; it was rebuilt in 1750 and again in the 1890s, and it was the palace where in 1972 Britain signed the treaty that admitted it to the EC. On the other corner of the park, back on rue de la Regence, is the **Musée Instrumental du Conservatoire Royal de Musique** (Tues–Sat 2.30–4.30pm, Sun 10.30am– 12.30pm; free). Although at present there is room to show only a fraction of its five thousand exhibits, the long process of preparing a new home in a mansion on place Royale has begun, though this is not likely to be ready for another few years. What you can see of the collection today bodes well for the new museum – exquisitely inlaid and painted keyboard instruments, strings ranging from the unwieldy viola da gambas to miniviolins designed to be slipped into the pockets of street musicians. There's also a display devoted to Adolphe Sax, the Belgian-born inventor of the saxophone (see "Dinant", *The Ardennes*), which includes some of his wilder contraptions, like the oddly contorted saxhorn.

On the other side of the street, the fifteenth-century church of **Notre Dame du Sablon** began life as a chapel for the medieval guild of archers. But after a statue of Mary with powers of healing was brought by boat from Antwerp to the chapel, it became a centre of pilgrimage and a proper church was built to accommodate its visitors. The statue of Mary no longer exists, but a wooden carving of a boat over the entrance, and a stained-glass boat in the west window, commemorate its legendary translation, and the occasion of its arrival is still celebrated annually in July by the Ommegang procession (see "Listings").

If you can track down the sacristan (he's available most weekday mornings and weekend afternoons) he will take you around the church (for the price of a donation) and into the black and white marble chapel containing the tomb of the Tour et Taxis family (who founded the Belgian postal system), dominated by a Baroque set piece showing Life and Time fighting a tug-of-war. Considerably more interesting are the spandrels along the aisles, carved with different figures and animals, and the grotesque tomb of one Claude Bouton, chamberlain of Charles V, at the back of the church, which features a graphically realistic skeleton.

Behind the church, the **place du Grand Sablon**, a sloping wedge of cobblestones surrounded by artisans' houses, is centre of one of the city's wealthiest districts, and is busiest at weekends, when a high-priced antique market clusters below the church. Most of the shops on Sablon and the surrounding streets are devoted to antiques and art, and you could easily spend an hour or so window-browsing from one to another – a cheaper pursuit, at any rate, than eating or drinking in one of Sablon's pavement cafés.

From the square follow rue de la Regence up the hill to **place Poelaert**, named after the architect who designed the immense **Palais de Justice** behind, a great Greco-Roman wedding cake of a building, dwarfing everything around, not least the poor Marolles quarter below. Built in 1883, it's actually larger than St Peter's in Rome; you may recognize it from the TV pictures of the Heysel stadium trial, which took place here. It's possible to wander into the main hall of the building, though really it's the size alone that is impressive.

A stone's throw from the Palais de Justice, **place Louise**, a chaotic traffic junction on the inner ringroad, dominated by fast-food restaurants and flashing ad hoardings, provides an unlikely setting for the discreet emporia of *Hermés*, *Gucci*, *Chanel* and the like. They herald the start of the city's most exclusive shopping district – an area of designer boutiques, jewellers and glossy shopping malls where the air is spiked with the scents of expensive French perfumes.

Rue Royale, the Jardin Botanique and St Josse

It's a long, dreary walk up rue Royale to the Jardin Botanique and the St Josse district. The only real landmark on the way is the 154-foot-high **Colonne de Congrès**, erected in 1850 to commemorate the country's first national parliament, with a blue eternal flame at its base burning to honour Belgium's dead of the two world wars. It dominates a vast, bleak belvedere, flanked by the blank glass and concrete city administration buildings and offering a singularly unflattering view of the city.

The main reason for heading this way is to eat cheaply, or to visit the cultural centre housed in the impressive greenhouses of the **Jardin Botanique**, something you're most likely to do in the evening for a concert or play, as the gardens themselves are exposed to the noise and fumes of traffic whipping along the petit ring. **ST JOSSE**, too, is somewhere you'll probably want to go only at night, the main attraction being its numerous (and cheap) Turkish restaurants. It's a compelling, uncompromisingly foreign neighbourhood, where men while away their days and nights over glasses of tea in cafés and head-scarved women emerge only during the day to shop. The vast, domed and severely dilapidated **Eglise de St Marie**, standing at the head of rue Royale, is the quarter's landmark, but life centres on **chausée de Haecht**, joining rue Royale just beyond the Botanique metro station, packed with restaurants, snack bars and the odd shop-selling fruit and veg, Turkish videos, and gimcrackery.

Outside the Petit Ring: the parks and outer boroughs

Brussels by no means ends with the petit ring. The city burst beyond its ancient boundaries back in the last century, and there's a lot worth seeing in the **districts which lie outside the centre**. Admittedly you won't miss much if you don't visit the self-glorifying monuments and turgid museums of the Parc de Cinquantenaire, or the concrete jungle around the EC buildings. But the boroughs of Ixelles and St Gilles are a different matter – animated neighbourhoods holding the best of the city's Art Nouveau architecture and some of its most congenial nightspots.

East of the Ring: Parc Léopold, the EEC and Parc du Cinquantenaire

East of the inner ringroad, the **QUARTIER LÉOPOLD** is possibly the most visited part of Brussels outside the centre. Taking its name from the late nineteenth-century king of Belgium, who laid out much of the area with large boulevards, monuments and statues, it's home to two of the capital's largest parks, museums and, of course, the European Community – in the form of the huge, winged **Berlaymont** building on rue de la Loi, home to the European Commission until a couple of years back when it was closed for renovation and the bureacrats had to move around the corner. The European Community institutions inevitably colour much of the neighbourhood, not least in their relentless growth: at present much is no more than a vast construction site, as numerous structures go up to house the ever-burgeoning numbers of paper-pushers needed to run the ever-growing community. Off the main road behind the Belaymont building, along rue Archimède, there is an island of peace amongst all the activity, a small stretch of nineteenth-century urban planning, starting with **Square Ambiorix**, at the top. This garden square is now largely overshadowed by modern buildings, although you shouldn't miss the superb wrought iron and windows of no. 11, one of the city's most ornate examples of the Art Nouveau style. Below, at the foot of avenue Palmerston, are three wonderfully subtle **houses** by Brussels' most innovative Art Nouveau architect, Victor Horta, overlooking the artificial lake of **place Marie Louise**. From here, rue de Taciturne will take you to rue de la Loi, from where you can cut across the building site to Parc Léopold.

Parc Léopold (metro Luxembourg or Maalbeek) is the more pleasant of the quarter's two parks, a hilly enclave landscaped around a lake, holding within its borders the **Institut des Sciences Naturelles** (Tues–Sat 9.30am–4.45pm, Sun 9.30am–6pm; F120), the city's rather old-fashioned natural history collection. It's a good place for kids on a rainy day, with a great army of dinosaurs on the first floor, a vivarium with some vicious-looking scorpions and a Mexican orange-kneed tarantula, and scores of stuffed animals. Upstairs are some striking displays of tropical shells, and in the midnight-blue room, the immense white skeleton of a *Balaenoptera musculus*.

Just outside the park gates, at rue Vautier 62, the **Musée Antoine Wiertz** (Tues–Sun 10am–noon & 1–5pm; closes at 4pm Nov–March; free) is devoted to the works of arguably the city's most disagreeable nineteenth-century artist. Once immensely voguish – so much so that Thomas Hardy in *Tess of the d'Urbervilles* could write of "the staring and ghastly attitudes of a Wiertz museum" – Antoine Wiertz painted vast religious and mythological canvases, featuring gory hells and coy nudes, and displayed a penchant for such nasty subjects as *The Burnt Child*, *The Thoughts and Visions of a Severed Head* and *Premature Burial*.

Farther to the east, located just beyond the Berlaymont complex and accessible by metro to Merode, lies the much larger **Parc du Cinquantenaire**, laid out for an exhibition to mark the golden anniversary of the Belgian state in 1880. It's a far-from-peaceful place these days, with a stream of traffic surging up its middle, and its grounds home to trade fairs, yearly car shows and occasional military exercises. But you might want to come out here to visit some of Brussels' largest museums, housing collections of art and applied art, not to mention weapons and cars.

The museums are in the Palais de Cinquantenaire, a vast edifice at the eastern end, with an entrance guarded by the mammoth **Cinquantenaire Arch**, topped by a bronze four-horse chariot, built by Charles Girault in 1905. The **Musée Royal d'Art et d'Histoire**, in the south wing of the palace (Tues–Fri 9.30am–5pm, Sat & Sun 10am–5pm; free; ☎741 72 11), is made up of a maddening (and badly labelled) maze of pottery, carvings, furniture, tapestries, glassware and lacework from all over the world – at its best in the opulent Belgian sections, less engaging in the ancient civilizations sections. There is, in any case, almost too much to take in in its entirety, and the various sections are being rearranged right now – best to phone first to see what's open, and what's located where. There are enormous galleries of mostly run-of-the-mill Greek, Egyptian and Roman artefacts, enough to soon become monotonous, although it's mildly diverting to spot the wobbles on the slap-dash Corinthian pottery or to see mummies of a jackal, crocodile and falcon; there's also a pretty impressive partially reconstructed Syrian synagogue, with some well-preserved mosaics. The European applied arts sections have more immediacy, much of them devoted to Belgian clocks, silver and brasswork. There are reliefs of fourteenth-century knights in chain mail, exhibits of Brussels tapestries, woven between 1427 and 1521, and some fabulously animated wooden relief altarpieces – one notable object displays the saga of Saint George's tortures from the chapel of Notre Dame in Leuven. An adjacent display, complete with wax dummy workmen, explains the process of carving a small altarpiece.

Also in the south wing of the palace is **Autoworld** (daily 10am–6pm, until 5pm Oct–March; F150) – a good, if expensive, place to take the kids, although its extensive displays of vintage cars, motorcycles, fire engines, even an ice-cream truck from Glasgow, should appeal to anyone, tracing the history of the car as a stylesetter, military machine and economic indicator. In the north wing of the palace, the **Musée Royal de l'Armee et d'Histoire Militaire** (Tues–Sun 9am–noon & 1–4.45pm; free) has collections detailing the history of the Belgian army from the eighteenth century to the present day by means of weapons, uniforms and paintings. Most spectacular are the galleries devoted to armoured cars, artillery and military aircraft, though it's far from required viewing unless you're a war buff.

The Horta houses

Victor Horta, who died in 1947, is perhaps Belgium's most famous architect, a well-known champion of the Art Nouveau movement who spent much of his life in Brussels, dotting the city with some marvellous small-scale examples of his work, some of the best of which lie on the fringes of Ixelles and St Gilles.

The **Musée Victor Horta** at rue Américain 25 (Tues–Sun 2–5.30pm; weekdays F100, weekends F200), accessible by tram #92 from place Louise, was built, along with the studio next door, between 1898 and 1901, and served as his home until 1919. From the outside, the house is quite modest, a dark, narrow terraced-house with a fluid facade and almost casually knotted and twisted ironwork. But it is for his interiors that Horta is noted, and the inside is a sunny sensuous dwelling, with all the architect's familiar trademarks – wide, bright rooms spiralling around a superbly worked staircase, wrought iron, stained glass, sculpture and ornate furniture and panelling made from several different types of wood. He designed everything for his houses from the blue prints to the wallpaper, and he never used a straight line or a sharp angle where he could use a curve instead. His use of light was also revolutionary, often filtering through from above, atrium-like, using skylights and as many windows as possible.

The delight Horta took in his work is clear, especially when employed on private houses, but sadly there's not much of this early period left in Brussels, and much of his work has been neglected or destroyed; indeed he actually destroyed many of the drawings he had made for his earlier works himself. That said, there are a couple of other Horta creations nearby, though access is possible only through *ARAU*. (See "Guided tours".)

Somewhere you *can* go inside is the Horta-designed patisserie, *Bardat*, rue Bailli 75, a five-minute walk from the museum, a pretty pastel confection of stained glass and gilt-framed mirrors, and a fitting stage for the elaborate cakes and pastries. From here a left turn up rue Faider takes you past another fine Art Nouveau house (no. 83) with ironwork foliage tracing the windows, and faint frescoes of languishing pre-Raphaelite women. Around the corner, the **Tassel House** at rue Paul Emile Jansen 6, is the building that first placed Horta at the forefront of the Art Nouveau movement. The sinuous facade is appealing enough, with clawed columns, stained-glass and curvaceous ironwork, but it was again with the interior that Horta really made his mark, an uncompromising fantasy featuring a flamboyant wrought-iron staircase and walls covered with linear decoration. It's also a striking example of the way in which Horta tailor-made his houses to suit the particular needs of clients. In this case it was built for an amateur photographer and includes a studio and projection room. Continuing along rue Paul Emile Jansen you hit avenue Louise, with, at no. 224, the **Hôtel Solvay** – reckoned to be Horta's masterpiece, and, like the museum, containing most of the original furniture and fittings. The 33-year-old Horta was given complete freedom and unlimited funds by the Solvay family (they made a fortune in soft drinks) to design this opulent town house. He commissioned an artist to paint a scene from the Solvay's summer cottage on the first staircase landing, choosing the dominant colours himself.

St Gilles

ST GILLES is the most intriguing of the inner boroughs, stretching from the refinement of avenue Louise in the east, to the solidly immigrant quarters toward the Gare du Midi. Here, a tense multiracialism, brought about by generations of political and economic refugees from the Mediterranean and North Africa, contrasts sharply with the bland internationalism of the centre, and you begin to absorb something of the city's grim undertow.

The district's most distinctive landmark is an ersatz medieval castle on avenue Ducpetiaux (bus #54 from Porte de Namur), which houses a **prison**. By night it's floodlit; by day sad clusters of women huddle outside the gates waiting to visit relatives, a disturbing proportion of them veiled, giving some notion of the problems facing Brussels' non-European communities. Ironically, the prison building only increases the picturesqueness of the surrounding streets, whose turn-of-the-century and Art Nouveau houses are numbered among the city's trendiest residences.

Facing the prison at the foot of avenue Jef Lambeaux is the **Hôtel Communal de St Gilles**, the showy, pseudo-Renaissance seat of local government which dominates the **Barrière de St Gilles**, a seven-road junction that until the middle of the last century was the site of a toll gate at which taxes were levied on all merchandise passing into the city. It is here that St Gilles begins to slip down the social scale, the cafés getting cheaper, the shops tackier and the general feel of the streets more depressed. If you want to halt here, you could do worse than blow it on a sauna and Turkish bath at the turn-of-the-century **St Gilles' Baths**, just off avenue du Parc at rue de la Perche 38 (daily 8am–6pm; Tues & Fri for women, Mon, Thurs & Sat for men; ☎539 06 15).

Pressing on down the chausée de Waterloo, past the daily morning market of the **Parvis de St Gilles**, you reach **rue Vanderschrick**, a tall terrace of elaborate, if slightly run-down Art Nouveau houses, the farthest of which now houses the chic café *Porteuse d'Eau*; see "Bars and cafés." This, however, is the only sign of gentrification in the neighbourhood, and continuing along the street, you penetrate farther into the poor, immigrant heartland of the city. As an outsider, you are bound to feel intrusive, even more so if you decide to eat in one of the cheap Spanish, Portuguese and Greek restaurants around the soulless **place de Bethlehem**. Rather than hanging around, walk on along the chausée de Forest, named for the rather dismal **Parc de Forest** at its head. Far nicer is the **Parc Duden**, just beyond, whose elegant towering trees make it perhaps the loveliest of the city's open spaces – an ideal escape or picnicking spot. Bus #48 will take you back to Bourse and the city centre.

Ixelles

IXELLES lies southwest of the petit ring, with the chausée d'Ixelles as its axis. Traditionally an immigrant quarter, and the favoured hangout of arty and Bohemian types, there are now the inevitable pockets of yuppification, a handful of designer stores, and a growing number of chic bars and restaurants joining the more congenial studenty and ethnic haunts. Less intimidating than either St Josse or the Marolles, Ixelles' greatest appeal remains its nightlife, but its shops, a couple of museums and the sprinkling of Art Nouveau houses around the pretty Ixelles lakes make for an interesting, and tourist-free, daytime wander.

At first sight, the beginning of the chausée d'Ixelles looks like any other of the city's shopping streets, and things don't get really interesting until you step into the Galerie d'Ixelles. In sharp contrast to the designer boutiques in the Galerie Toison d'Or across the road, this is the shopping and social centre of Ixelles' Zairean community, packed with tiny shops selling batik cloths, and cheap, cramped snack bars playing African music. Though the neighboring side streets are a great source of night action, there's little to detain you by day until you reach rue J. van Volsem, with Ixelles' **Musée des Beaux Arts** at no. 71 (Tues–Fri 1–7.30pm, Sat & Sun 10am–5pm; free). This holds a modest but palatable collection of mostly French and Belgian modern artists – a couple of Magrittes, including the disturbing *Face of a Genius*, a luminescent *Cannes 1923* by Dufy, an Ixelles street scene by Delvaux, and some dark, lonely canvases by Spillaert. There's also a room containing a series of signed posters by Toulouse-Lautrec, and a powerful *Head of an Italian Woman* by Constantin Meunier, with the years of wisdom and resignation written in the lines of her face.

If you liked Meunier, and have already seen his sculptures and paintings in the Musée d'Art Ancien, it's worth visiting the **Musée Constantin Meunier**, rue de l'Abbaye 59, housed in the artist's old studio on the other side of avenue Louise from the Ixelles lakes, the **Etangs d'Ixelles**, at the foot of the chausée (Tues–Sun 10am–noon & 1–5pm; free). Whether the artist appeals or not, the benches by the two lakes are a restful place to picnic, after which you could wander along avenue Général de Gaulle, to see more of Brussels' Art Nouveau houses.

Farther south, you could also head for the **Bois de la Cambre**, unpleasantly crisscrossed by the main commuter access roads in its upper reaches, but opening out around a lake in the centre. It's Brussels' most popular park, bustling with joggers, dog-walkers, families and lovers at weekends, and is part of the vast **Forêt de Soignes** – through which, if you've the stamina, you could walk the 13km to Tervuren (see pp. 333–4).

North of the Ring: Laeken

To the north of the ringroad, **LAEKEN** (tram #92 from rue Royale or pre-metro #52 from anywhere along line #3) is the royal suburb of Brussels, home of the Belgian royal family – who occupy a large out-of-bounds estate not far from the train station – and a large public **park** close by, laid out in the nineteenth century by Leopold II. Leopold brought a **Chinese Pavilion** here from the Paris World's Fair of 1900, with the intention of transforming it into a fancy restaurant. The restaurant never materialized, and the pavilion now houses a collection of Chinese porcelain (Tues–Sun 9.30am–12.30pm & 1.30–4.30pm; free) – though this is less interesting than the building itself, decorated on the outside with bas-reliefs of comic faces, or indeed the **Japanese Tower** opposite, also brought back from the World's Fair (daily except Mon 10am–4.45pm; free).There are also other monuments dotted around, including a fountain that's a replica of Giambologna's on Piazza Nettuno in Bologna, and a **planetarium**.

However, the park is perhaps best known for the **Atomium** (metro Heysel), an imposing model of a molecule built for the 1958 World's Fair in Brussels, which has since become something of a symbol of the city. It contains a museum – an unremarkable display on the peaceful uses of atomic energy – and a restaurant within its metallic spheres, but the main sensation is the disorienting feeling of traveling from sphere to sphere by escalator. Unfortunately, grey weather often obscures the view from the top sphere, around 110m above the ground, and if you're short of money you may want to save the rather high entrance fee by simply viewing the structure from the outside – at its base there's a scale model of Europe, complete with Channel Tunnel and TGV.

West of the Ring: Anderlecht, Koekelberg and around

It's little surprise that the suburb of **ANDERLECHT**, famous only for its soccer team, is little visited by foreigners. It's a dull, grimy quarter, starting at Midi station and bisected by the city's bleak canal, and were it not for a couple of museums, there'd be little point in going. Make an effort, at least, however, to see the **Musée Gueuze**, rue Gheude 56 (June to mid-Oct Mon–Fri 8.30am–4.30pm, Sat 9.30am–1pm; Jan–May & mid-Oct to Dec Sat only 10am–6pm Sat 10am–12.30pm; F70), ten minutes' walk from Midi station. It's a mustily evocative working brewery, still brewing Gueuze according to the traditional methods. Although there are guided tours on Saturdays at 11am, 2pm and 3.30pm, it's probably more fun to go around alone, using the excellent English-language leaflet. The beer is made only of wheat, malted barley and hops, is allowed to ferment naturally, reacting with natural yeasts peculiar to the Brussels air, and is bottled for two years before it is ready to drink. The result is unique, as you can find out at the tasting at the end of the tour.

Rather than trekking through Anderlecht, head back toward Midi, and catch tram #103 to place de la Vaillance, dominated by the lacily carved spire of the late fifteenth-century church of **St Pierre**. Across from the church is the mellow red-brick **Maison d'Erasme**, rue du Chapitre 31 (daily except Tues & Fri 10am–noon & 2–5pm; F20), the house where the humanist philosopher died. Though it contains none of Erasmus' actual belongings, it does have a display of portraits of the man by Holbein, Dürer and others, together with a collection of ancient editions of his writings, some of which include censors' marks. There's also a mould of the philosopher's skull and seals made with two of his signet rings ("concedo nulli"). Get hold of the guidebook giving the full lowdown, and try and time your visit to coincide with one of the occasional Renaissance music concerts that are held here.

North of here, in the adjoining borough of **KOEKELBERG**, the **Basilique Nationale Sacre Coeur** (metro Simonis) is another of Brussels' Art Nouveau attractions, a huge church (140m long with a 90-metre-tall dome), decorated sumptuously inside with marble and stained glass. Begun in 1905 and still unfinished, it was originally supposed to have six towers but has since been modified; it's dedicated to all those who have died in wars on behalf of their country (Easter–Oct daily 8am–7pm; rest of the year daily 8am–5pm; free; visits to the gallery F30, terrace F50).

Eating and drinking

Although it's never cheap, Brussels can be a great (and great-value) city in which to **eat**. There's a huge variety of restaurants, and even the most touristy places serve reasonable food for acceptable prices; and the city is among Europe's best for sampling a wide range of different ethnic cuisines. As usual many bars serve food, often just spaghetti, sandwiches and *croque monsieurs*, but some have wider ranging menus, taking in traditional Brussels fare. You can also eat excellent fish and seafood, especially in the old fish market district on quais aux Briques and aux Bois à Brûler, although this can cost considerably more. There is also a good range of food and restaurants outside the petit ring, especially in the ethnic districts – the Turkish restaurants of St Josse, and the Greek restaurants around the Gare du Midi, are very good value, and the city's Spanish, Vietnamese, Japanese, even Buddhist vegetarian restaurants, are also worth investigating.

For **fast food**, aside from the multinational burger and pizza chains, there are plenty of *frites* stands and kebab places around the Grand Place, notably on rue Marché aux Fromages and at the beginning of rue des Bouchers. There are carts around place Ste Catherine selling hot mussels and *caricoles*, a poor man's version of escargot. Pitta is also popular, stuffed with a wide range of fillings – though vegetarian ones are rare – along with the more substantial thin Turkish pizzas, or *pide*, topped with combinations of cheese, ground meat or even a fried egg, sold at any number of restaurants along the chausée de Haecht and rue Méridien. For picnics, try the city's street markets or the Italian delis around place Ste Catherine.

Restaurants

L'Auberge des Chapeliers, rue des Chapeliers 1–3. Specializes in mussels prepared in a variety of ways and in soups.

Le Canard à Trois Pattes, rue des Bouchers 5. Despite the touristy location, this place serves excellent omelettes and *gratins* (vegetable-meat-cheese casseroles) at low prices.

Casa Rafael, rue des Tanneurs 144. Simple but comfortable neighbourhood restaurant in the Marolles quarter, with steaks and brochettes, and deep-fried anchovies.

Chez Léon, rue des Bouchers 18–22. Touristy but good-value restaurant near the Grand Place serving traditional Belgian fare. Most famous for its mussels dishes. Open daily noon–midnight.

Chez Mille et Alice, rue de Flandre 101. Unpretentious neighbourhood restaurant where you can get a mountain of mussels and a large plate of chips for F360.

La Grande Porte, rue Notre–Seigneur 9. Long, narrow, cosy and crowded seventeenth-century *estaminet*, whose walls are plastered with old posters and photos. The food is good, hearty and traditional, and you're quite free to just go for a drink. Be warned, though, that it can get very crowded, in which case the food can be slow to arrive.

Hoa Binh, rue Marché aux Fromages 18. Abundant, spicy Vietnamese dishes in a casual atmosphere.

Horta Brasserie, rue des Sables 20. The café of the recently opened *Centre Belge de la Bande Dessinée* (see p.311). Classy food, including smoked salmon, good salads and a generally inventive menu in a summery Art Nouveau setting.

Iberia, rue de Flandre 8. Spanish restaurant at the place Ste Catherine end of rue de Flandre that does great paella.

Jacques, quai aux Briques 44. A long-established and extremely popular fish restaurant –the *cabillaud de poche* is highly recommended. Expect a sedate, middle-aged clientele at lunch-time, and a more raucous, international crowd in the evenings. Reservations always necessary.

't Kelderke, Grand Place 15. Boisterous cellar restaurant right on the Grand Place that has a wide and reasonably priced menu but is best known for its excellent *carbonades à la Flamande*. Bear in mind that you can't make reservations and you may have to stand in line for a table. Now with a next door *estaminet* to wind up at after your meal for a drink and some music.

Le Paon Royale, rue Vieux Marché aux Grains 6. Popular bar in the place Ste Catherine locale that serves good, hearty Belgian grub for low prices – and supplements this with a fine array of Belgian speciality beers. A good choice for both lunch especially, with *plats du jour* running around F250.

Le Perroquet, rue de Minimes 58. Chic café-bar on a street of private art galleries and antique shops. Imaginative range of stuffed pitta and salads, and a superb selection of tarts. Closed Sat & Sun lunchtimes.

Le Portugal, rue de Flandre 118. Good-value Portuguese restaurant that serves an excellent array of fish and seafood dishes for F300–400.

Le Pré Salé, rue de Flandre 16. Friendly, old-fashioned neighbourhood restaurant just off place Ste Catherine, and providing a nice alternative to the swankier eateries of the district. Great mussels, fish dishes and Belgian specialities. Daily specials and a fixed-price – F950 – menu.

Shamrock, rue Jules van Praet 29. A decent Indian restaurant centrally situated close by the Bourse. Perhaps the city centre's best Indian option, although the service can be uneven.

't Spinnekopke, place du Jardin aux Fleurs 1. Ancient restaurant and bar that serves many traditional Bruxellois dishes cooked in beer – the owner has published a book of beer recipes. It's also one of the few places to serve beers from the Cantillon brewery in Anderlecht.

Stekkerlapatte, rue des Prêtres 6. Situated on the far side of the Palais de Justice, this is a wonderful old brasserie, popular with a youngish crowd, that serves main meals for around F500. Usually very crowded; great atmosphere.

La Strada, rue de la Colline 15. Good-value pizza and pasta just off the Grand Place. The food is actually better quality than you might expect from the ultra-central location.

Yamato, rue Francart 11. Excellent, if basic Japanese café-style restaurant where you eat from a central, circular counter – no tables. Fine and eminently affordable authentic Japanese food. Closed Sun & Mon.

Outside the Petit Ring

Amadeus, rue Veydt 13, Ixelles. Trendy wine bar in the one-time studio of Auguste Rodin that serves a good Sunday morning breakfast for F550.

Athanas, rue de l'Argonne 20, St Gilles. Cheap, popular Greek restaurant in the dodgy quarter around Gare du Midi, serving large portions of standard taverna fare. Plats du jour for around F200.

Carrefour St Gilles, avenue de Parc 1, St Gilles. Unassuming but comfortable restaurant/café on the Barrière de St Gilles. Convenient place to stop for lunch while exploring the area.

La Forestière, rue de Rollebeek. The most reasonable place to eat lunch in the Sablon area, with seats outside on an exclusive pedestrianized street of designer shops.

De Hoef, rue Edith Cavell 218, Uccle. One of the best-value restaurants in town for committed carnivores. Belgian grilled meat dishes a speciality.

La Juqutha, rue de Moscou 32, St Gilles. Middle Eastern restaurant that serves a marvellous couscous for under F500.

Le Paradoxe, chausée d'Ixelles 329, Ixelles. Buddhist-run wholefood restaurant and tearoom, with a preciously ascetic feel, and an eclectic programme of live music on most Fri & Sat evenings. Menus are on offer for under F400, plats de jour for around F300, and in any case it's a peaceful place to retreat during the day for a herbal tea and toast. Open Mon–Sat, noon–2pm, 7–10pm.

Quartier Latin, boulevard Général Jacques 212, Ixelles. Relaxed, studenty hangout serving excellent Vietnamese food. Dim sum a speciality.

Sahbaz, chausée de Haecht 102, Schaerbeek. Reckoned to be among the city's best Turkish restaurants. The prices, however, are low, and the atmosphere very friendly.

Trave Negra, rue Th. Verhaegen 9, St Gilles. Excellent, quiet and simple Portuguese restaurant. Very welcoming, too.

Tsampa, rue de Livourne 109, Ixelles. Congenial Buddhist vegetarian restaurant up near avenue Louise, with menus for around F750, plats du jour for F350 or so. Open noon–2pm & 7–10pm, closed Sat & Sun evenings.

Bars and cafés

Drinking in Brussels, as in the rest of the country, is a joy. The city has an enormous variety of **bars and cafés** – sumptuous Art Nouveau cafés; traditional bars with ceilings stained brown by a century's smoke; bars whose walls are plastered with sepia photographs and ancient beer ads; speciality beer bars with literally hundreds of different varieties of ale; and, of course, more modern hangouts. Many of the centrally located places, especially those considered particularly typical, are frequented by tourists and ex-pats, but outside the centre, and even tucked away off the Grand Place, there are places which remain refreshingly local. A number serve meals as well as snacks, often far better value than eating in a restaurant. Bars also stay open late – most until 2 or 3am, some until dawn.

A la Becasse, rue Tabora 1. Spartan, old-fashioned bar not far from the Grand Place that is one of the few remaing venues for sampling *lambic*, along with simple bar snacks.

Le Belgica, rue Marché au Charbon 32. Fashionable bar patronized by politicoes and intellectual types.

Au Bon Vieux Temps, rue du Marché aux Herbes 12. Cosy old place tucked down an alley a minute's walk from the Grand Place, with stained-glass windows, tile-inlaid tables and a seventeenth-century chimney piece.

Au Brasseur, rue des Brasseurs, just off Grand Place. Unpretentious place ideal for late-night drinks – it often stays open until first light. The beer is cheap, and you can usually find a table.

Le Cercueil, rue dés Harengs 10–12. Funereal concept bar just off the Grand Place, where the tables are coffins, the only light UV, and the music alternates between Gregorian chant and Chopin's Funeral March. Expensive, though, and a little tacky. Open daily 11am–3am, until dawn on Fri & Sat.

Chez Richard, rue de Minimes 4. Irish bar that's a favoured hangout of the younger EC crowd. Sometimes intimate in feel, other times crazy.

Cirio, rue de la Bourse 18. One of Brussels' oldest bars, sumptuously decorated in *fin-de-siècle* style. Once frequented, they say, by Jacques Brel.

DNA, rue Plattesteen 18. Young, lively hangout for the studenty and street-credible. Don't expect to find a seat after 10pm, and expect to have your conversation drowned out by Madonna and The Cure. Open weekdays noon–3am, weekends 3pm–3am.

't Dolle Mol, rue des Eperonniers 52. Predominantly Flemish-speaking bar, with a cliquey clientele. Music ranges from manic punk to kitsch music-hall, and everyone sits looking thoroughly miserable. Open daily 11am–1am, 3am at weekends.

Falstaff, rue Henri Maus 17–23. Art Nouveau café next to the Bourse, attracting a mixed bag of tourists, fashionable young things, Eurocrats and the bourgeois Bruxellois. Full of atmosphere, and so crowded in the evenings that you're unlikely to find a seat. Inexpensive beer and sandwiches and well-priced full meals – plats du jour F300. Open daily 9am–3am.

La Fleur en Papier Doré, rue des Alexiens 53. Cluttered, cosy locals' bar, with walls covered with doodles and poems, that was once the chosen drinking place of René Magritte. The novelist Hugo Claus apparently held his second wedding reception here.

Greenwich, rue des Chartreux 7. Brussels' traditional chess café, and with a peace that makes it an ideal place to retreat from the pace of the city.

A l'Image de Notre-Dame, rue du Marché aux Herbes 6. A welcoming, if extremely quiet, bar at the end of a long alley, decorated like an old Dutch kitchen.

Interférences, rue de la Tête d'Or 1. Video bar which gets lively in the evening with a mainly young crowd. Many different kinds of videos, and handily situated just off the Grand Place.

La Lunette, place de la Monnaie 3. An unspectacular bar in itself, but handy for the rue Neuve shopping district. Known for the huge bucket-size stemmed dishes – *lunettes* – in which it serves its beer.

Café Métropole, place de Brouckère 31. Sumptuously ritzy *fin-de-siècle* café, belonging to an equally opulent hotel. Astonishingly many people prefer to sit outside, for a view of flashing ads and zipping traffic. If you've got cash to spare, indulge in a brunch of smoked salmon or caviare.

A la Mort Subite, rue Montagne aux Herbes Potagères7. Twenties bar that loaned its name to a widely available bottled beer. A long, narrow room with nicotine-stained walls and mirrors, a thirtysomethingish clientele and an animated atmosphere. Snacks served, or just order a plate of cheese cubes to accompany your beer. Open daily 9am–1am.

Pitt's Bar, rue des Minimes 53. Business drinkers at lunchtime, rather yuppie at night. They serve tapas and pasta. Open weekdays 11am–2am, evenings only Sat & Sun.

Les Postiers, rue Fossé aux Loups 14. Old-established and unpretentious bar neatly placed close to place de la Monnaie and serving basic snacks and light meals.

Roi d'Espagne, Grand Place 1. Supremely touristy bar in a seventeenth-century guildhouse. Worth wandering inside for a look, if only to view the collection of inflated animal bladders suspended from the ceiling, but don't bother staying for a drink. Open daily until 1am.

Au Soleil, rue Marché au Charbon 86. Popular bar with a wide choice of beers, crowded every night until late with a young, self-consciously trendy crowd.

Stella au Grand Place, rue de la Colline, corner Grand Place. Unassuming bar, with prices to match, tucked into a corner of the Grand Place and, amazingly, totally ignored by tourists.

Toone, petite rue des Bouchers 21. Largely undiscovered bar belonging to the Toone puppet theatre, just off the Grand Place. Two small rooms with old posters on rough plaster walls, a reasonably priced beer list, a modest selection of snacks, and a soundtrack of classical and jazz, make it the centre's most congenial bar.

Vossegat Nord, boulevard Adolphe Max 54. Strange old café with a predominantly aged clientele who sit surrounded by stuffed foxes while drinking dark, syrupy *Vossegat* beer, served with cubes of cheese. Open daily 9am–midnight.

Outside the Petit Ring

L'Aiglon, place Houwert 2. Small African bar in St Josse playing loud reggae and African music. Open daily until dawn.

L'Amor Fou, chaussée d'Ixelles 185, Ixelles. Studiously alternative bar in which tequila, mezcal and pepper vodka feature among the accessorizing drinks; there's also good, reasonably priced food (spinach quiche, spaghetti with basil) and occasional live music.

Conways, avenue de la Toison d'Or 10. American bar full of men on the make, especially on Thurs nights when drinks are half price for women – though if you're in a mixed group this can, of course, be turned to your advantage.

The Drum, avenue d'Audhergem 10. Long-established British bar that has recently moved its premises around the corner. Still a favourite with its almost entirely English-speaking clientele, who enjoy its pints, dartboard and Brit food.

James Joyce, rue Archimède 34. Cliquey and sometimes boisterous hangout for the ex-pat Irish, within staggering distance of the EC building. Worth braving on Tues at 8.30pm if you like Irish folk music.

Kitty O'Shea's, boulevard Charlemagne 42. Large ex-pat bar right opposite the Berlaymont building. Serves Irish food, draught Guinness and the like.

Moeder Lambic, rue de Savoie 68, St Gilles. Over 1000 beers available, including 500 Belgian varieties, and not at all expensive. Open weekdays 11am–4am, weekends 4pm–4am.

Papa Joe's, rue Archimède 55. One of several British-style pubs on this street, popular with Berlaymont *stagières*.

La Porteuse d'Eau, avenue Jean Volders 48a, St Gilles. The last in a row of ornate Art Nouveau houses near the Parvis de St Gilles, and one of the few signs of gentrification in this run-down quarter of the barrière. The food is not cheap, but it's worth the price of a beer to see the swanky interior.

Rick's Café Américain, avenue Louise 344. Situated in a ritzy part of the city, this bar-restaurant has been a gathering-place of resident English-speakers for close to 30 years. The bar can get lively, and there's a full menu available, though it's most famous for its ribs.

SiSiSi, chausée de Charleroi 174A, St Gilles. Youthful bar worth the journey for its splendid range of salads and stuffed pittas. Open daily 9am–midnight.

Stoemelings, place de Londres 7, Ixelles. Small, modern and congenial bar with a good range of Belgian beers and excellent food, including gargantuan portions of inexpensive spaghetti and lasagne, as well as sandwiches.

De Ultieme Hallucinatie, rue Royale 316. Fanciful Art Nouveau bar done up like an old Twenties train car. A youngish crowd sinking a good choice of beers, reasonably priced drinks and food – omelettes, lasagne, etc. There's also an extremely sumptuous restaurant in front. Sun–Mon 11am–3am, Sat 4pm–4am. Live music on Fri from 10.30pm.

L'Ultime Atome, rue St Boniface 14, Ixelles. Congenial café. Good range of beers, superb food and a youngish clientele. Food – at lunchtime & 7pm–12.30am – ranges from pasta and elaborate salads to more exotic fare, such as ravioli with artichokes and *osso bucco*.

Nightlife: music, clubs, film and theatre

As far as **nightlife** goes, you may be happy to while away the evenings in one of the city's bars or restaurants – there are plenty in which you can drink until sunrise. However, although it's not as lively at night as some European cities, Brussels is also a good place to catch **live bands**: the city is – with Antwerp – a regular stop on the European tours of major and up-and-coming artists. On a more local level, the music bars around place Fernand Cocq and the lower end of the chausée d'Ixelles are great for Friday/Saturday night bar hopping.

Clubs and discos are rather less impressive, but they are sometimes free – although at least one, overpriced drink is usually obligatory.

There is also a thriving **classical concert scene** – notably the recently established *Ars Musica* festival of contemporary music held annually in March, and the prestigious four-yearly *Concours Musical Reine Elisabeth*, competition for piano, violin and composition, which numbers among its prize-winners Vladimir Ashkenazy, David Oistrach and Gidon Kremer.

For **listings** of concerts and events, check *The Bulletin* or the Thursday pull-out section of *Le Soir*. **Tickets** for most things are available from *FNAC* in City 2, or from the booking office at *TIB* on the Grand Place.

Concert halls and performance venues

Ancienne Belgique, boulevard Anspach 114 (☎512 59 86). The main venue for local and international indie bands. Also showcases jazz and folk.

Le Botanique, rue Royale 236 (☎217 63 86). Housed in the 150-year-old conservatory of the Jardin Botanique – includes an art gallery, two theatres, and a small cinema. Occasional concerts, and some good, mostly contemporary theatre.

Forest National, avenue du Globe 36 (☎347 03 55). Brussels' main arena for big-name international concerts, holding around 6000 people. Recent gigs included Adeva, Tears for Fears and Bowie.

Palais des Beaux Arts, rue Ravenstein 23 (☎507 82 00). With a concert hall holding around 2000, as well as some smaller theatres, the Palais is used for anything from contemporary dance to Tom Jones.

RTBF/BRT, place Flagey 18 (☎737 28 45). Home of the French (RTBF) and Flemish (BRT) radio and TV symphony orchestras, with concerts almost every Fri & Sat.

Live music bars and clubs

Le Bierodrome, place Ferdinand Cocq 21 (☎512 04 56). Smoky jazz bar whose live gigs (mostly Fri, Sat & Sun from 10.30pm) attract a mixed, comfortably unpretentious crowd. On other evenings, it's just a nice place to drink.

Blues Corner, rue des Chapeliers 12 (☎512 92 74). No-frills bar with local bands playing most nights – you'll be able to hear from outside whether it's worth going in. Occasional touring American and British bands.

Do Brasil, rue de la Caserne 88 (☎513 50 28). Brazilian music and food Tues–Sat.

Machado, rue des Chapeliers 14 (☎513 36 91). Jazz and Latin concerts till dawn, just off the Grand Place. Closed Mon.

Sounds, rue de la Tulipe 28 (☎512 92 50). Seedy, smoky American-oriented bar, serving up a noisy blend of R & B.

Travers, rue Traversière 11. (☎218 40 86). Informal jazz club with an impressive reputation for showcasing up-and-coming Belgian musicians.

Clubs and discos

Le Garage, rue Duquesnoy 16. One of the longest-running and best of the capital's large clubs for dancers, playing a frenetic mix of House, Techno and New Beat. Fairly touristy.

Le Mirano Continental, chaussée de Louvain 38. The club of the posturing media crowd, with a door policy that favours anyone who looks like a model.

Vaudeville, rue de la Montagne 14 (☎514 12 60). Weekends-only clubs housed in an old theatre right in the centre of town that attracts a very mixed crowd.

Film and theatre

About half the films shown in Brussels' cinemas are in English with French and Flemish subtitles (coded VO, *version originale*). *The Bulletin* publishes comprehensive listings of the week's films – the best night to go is Monday, when entry is half price. Although most screens are devoted to the big US box-office hits, programmes at the **Actor's Studio**, petit rue des Bouchers 16, and the **Arenberg/Galeries**, Galerie de la Reine 26, are more adventurous, often showing foreign films. Failing that, the **Musée du Cinema**, rue Baron Horta 9, shows a nightly selection of silent films and old talkies for just F80. There's also an annual **Film Festival** in January at the Palais du Congrès on the Mont des Arts, highlight of which is the "Tremplin" or Springboard section, which features international films favoured by critics but not yet taken on by Belgian distributors.

Obviously most of Brussels' **theatre** is staged in French or Flemish, although the various amateur American, British, and Irish theatre groups frequently put on high-quality productions. More famously, there's the **Toone Puppet Theatre**, at rue des Bouchers 21 (☎511 71 37/513 54 86), which has been around for over twenty years in this location putting on puppet plays in the Bruxellois dialect. It's run by one Jose Gael, the seventh in a long line of puppet masters dating back to the 1830s. He revived the theater in the Sixties and now stages performances at 8.30pm from Wednesday to Saturday.

Shops and markets

Brussels compares pretty well with most other European capital cities for **shopping**. However, although the range and variety will suit most tastes, prices for certain things are considerably higher than those you might be used to at home, including the goods sold in British chains like *Marks & Spencer*, the *Body Shop* and *WH Smith* – so beware of running out of underwear, hair gel or reading matter.

Mainstream shopping: clothes and the Galeries

The main central shopping street is **rue Neuve**, which runs from place de la Monnaie to place Rogier and is home to most of the leading chains, including *Marks & Spencer*, although this is indistinguishable – apart from the prices – from its branches in Britain. At the top end, **City 2** is the ultimate in glossy, sanitized shopping malls, with cinemas, restaurants, department stores and boutiques – and, most usefully, a large supermarket.

For **clothes and accessories**, **chaussée d'Ixelles** is another mid-market shopping street, and also merits a visit for the African shops in the **Galerie d'Ixelles**, and for the cluster of designer shops in its lower reaches, beyond place Fernand Cocq. *Sous Sol*, chaussée d'Ixelles 196, has an unusual range of designer jewellery, *Z'Art*, across the road at no. 223, trendy accessories; *Luxiol*, at no. 221, sells wooden toys and contemporary and Art Deco-style jewellery. In the centre of town, just off the Grand Place, **Galerie Agora** has more mainstream fashions – jeans, leather jackets and the like – while, beyond, the trendily refurbished **St Géry market** is hoping to cash in on the tourist trade when it opens. Apart from the conservative boutiques of the **Galeries St Hubert**, the more upscale clothes stores are mostly concentrated in the upper town, on and around place Louise, Porte de Namur, and avenue Louise. Indoor galleries include **Galerie Louise**, which holds a mixture of middle-range clothes stores and top-flight designers, and the slightly more adventurous **Galeries Toison d'Or**, a little farther along.

Books and magazines

WH Smith at boulevard Adolphe Max 71–75 is not surprisingly one of the best places in town to buy **English-language books and magazines**. Other English-language bookshops include *House of Paperbacks*, chaussée de Waterloo 813, in the suburb of Uccle, and the *Strathmore Bookshop* at rue St Lambert 131 in Woluwe St Lambert.

There are a number of **alternative and second-hand clothes shops** on rue des Eperonniers. There is also a cluster of young Belgian names on rue Dansaert. You can pick up period clothes (and some amazing accessories) at the Jeu de Balle flea market (see below); *Leo Ellébas Boutique*, on the corner of rue Tanneurs and rue Ghislaine, sells mostly 1950s and 1960s clothes. Off avenue Louise, *La Boutique*, rue de Stassaert 114, has second-hand designer clothes for women (the men's branch is a few doors away). Finally, *Genevieve's Pearls*, just off the Grand Place at rue des Harengs 2, is a wonderful source of costume and antique jewellery.

Art, antiques, bric-a-brac and markets

Though prices are predictably prohibitive, the window displays, and – if you've the nerve – the interiors of the numerous **private galleries** selling contemporary art, antiques and archeological, oriental and African artifacts, can be as fascinating as any museum. Most lie on and around **place du Grand Sablon** – where there's an expensive **antiques market** every weekend – in the swanky shopping mall, **Jardin de Sablon**, and on rues Ernest Allard, Minimes, Watteau and Jansens; there are also a few places on rue de la Madeleine and rue St Jean. Less exclusive, and more affordable, is the **Jeu de Balle flea market** in the Marolles quarter, held every morning, but at its best at weekends, where the eccentric muddle of colonial spoils, quirky odds and ends and domestic and eccelesiastical bric-a-brac give an impression of a century's bourgeois fads and fashions. Perhaps more useful, if you've just moved to Brussels and have an apartment to furnish, is the junk **Marché aux Jeunes**, held on the first Sunday of the month (7am–1pm) at place St Lambert in the suburb of Woluwe St Lambert, or the similar **Marché Daily** on place Dailly in Schaarbeek held on Tuesdays from 8am until 1pm.

As for the city's many **other markets**, the largest and most colourful is the one held every Sunday morning at the **Gare du Midi**, a bazaar-like affair, with traders crammed under the railway bridge and spilling out into the surrounding streets. Stands sell pitta, olives, *Rai* tapes, spices, herbs and pulses, among the more familiar fruit, vegetables and cheap clothes.

Specialities: lace, chocolate, comics

If you like **lace**, you'll pick up far nicer pieces at Jeu de Balle than in any of the much-hyped handmade lace shops on and around the Grand Place, where you could pay F650 for a souvenir handkerchief. The other Bruxellois speciality, **chocolate**, is another matter – delicious, and at far lower prices than you'll pay at home. Leonidas is, as ever, the cheapest outlet; it has a central branch at Boulevard Anspach 46, not far from the Bourse; *Neuhaus* in the Galerie de la Reine, and *Corné* in the Galerie du Roi, are also good. **Wittamer**, place du Grand Sablon 12–13, is Brussels' most famous patisserie and chocolate shop, established in 1910 and still run by the Wittamer family, and still peddling gorgeous if pricy pastries, cakes and chocolates.Try also to visit the Belgian speciality shop, *Dandoy*, rue au Beurre 31, where they do marvellous *speculaas*.

Hergé, creator of Tin Tin, was a Belgian, and the cult of the **comic strip** or *bande dessinée* continues to flourish in the capital. As well as the latest publications, there are shops selling second-hand comic books, notably the excellent bookshop of the *centre Belge de la Bande Dessinée* on rue des Sables. *Multi BD*, boulevard Anspach 126, on the corner of rue Plattesteen, sells second-hand as well as new comics, as does *Jonas*, place Fernand Cocq 4. *Espace BD*, place Fernand Cocq 2 is also worth a browse. Just off the Grand Place there's a whole shop dedicated to **Hergé's quiffed hero**: *La Boutique de Tin Tin*, rue de la Colline 13, which has Tin Tin books, postcards, stationery, figurines, T-shirts and sweaters.

Listings

Airlines *Aer Lingus*, 91 avenue Louise (☎537 24 10); *British Airways*, centre Rogier, ninth floor (☎217 74 00); *KLM*, rue des Princes 8 (☎217 63 00); *Luxair*, avenue Louise 104 (☎646 03 70); *Sabena*, rue Cardinal Mercier 35 (☎511 90 30 or 723 60 10).

Airport enquiries ☎277 294 00 (reservations); ☎272 307 23 (flight information).

American Express place Louise 2 (Mon–Fri 9am–5pm, Sat 9am–noon; ☎512 17 40).

Baby sitters ☎647 23 85.

Bureaux de change Outside bank hours you can change money and travellers' cheques at offices at the Gare du Nord and Gare du Midi (daily 7am–11pm) and the Gare Centrale (daily 8am–9pm), though none of these places give cash advances on credit cards. Otherwise there's *Paul Laloy*, rue de la Montagne 6 (Mon–Fri 9am–6pm, Sat 10am–6pm; June–Sept also Sun 11am–1pm); *Thomas Cook*, Grand Place 4 (Mon–Fri 9am–7pm, Sat & Sun 10am–6pm); and *Best Change*, rue de la Colline 2 (daily 9am–8pm). There are also bureaux de change at the airport. Remember, too, that a few central banks also open on Sat morning, and if you have a Eurocheque card with a PIN number, you can use the numerous *MISTERCASH* dispensers scattered throughout the city.

Car rental *Avis*, rue Américaine 145, Ixelles (☎537 12 80, airport arrivals ☎720 09 44); *Europcar*, avenue Louise 235 (☎640 94 00), rue St Denis 117 (☎344 91 47) and airport arrivals (☎721 05 92); *Hertz*, boulevard Lemonnier 8 (☎513 28 86, airport arrivals ☎720 60 44).

Chemists Outside normal working hours, all chemists display a list of open alternatives outside. Weekend rotas are also listed in the Sat newspapers.

Dental problems Call ☎426 10 26 or 428 58 88, weekends and evenings after 9pm.

Embassies *Australia*, avenue des Arts 52 (☎213 05 00); *Canada*, avenue de Telvuren 2 (☎735 60 40); *Ireland*, rue du Luxembourg 19 (☎513 66 33); *New Zealand*, boulevard de Regent 47–48 (☎512 10 40); *UK*, rue Joseph II 28, Etterbeek (☎217 90 00)); *USA*, boulevard de Regent 27 (☎513 38 30).

Emergencies Police ☎101; ambulance/fire brigade ☎100. For young people, there's also *SOS-Jeunes*, rue Mercelis 27 (☎512 90 20), open 24hr to deal with emotional and other problems.

English-speaking Brussels If you've recently come to Brussels to live, there are a number of social groups all advertising in *The Bulletin*: of them, *Fringe* is the least stiff and formal. Amateur dramatics is also a big part of the ex-pat scene: if you're at all into acting or doing backstage work, check out the amateur dramatic groups listed in *The Bulletin*, most of whom put on a wide range of plays. See also our listings of American and English bars, and visit the *British Council* office and library at rue Joseph II, Etterbeek (☎219 36 00).

Festivals Brussels has a number of festivals and annual events worth timing a visit around. Best known is the *Ommegang*, a religious procession from Grand Sablon to the Grand Place that began in the fourteenth century as a religious event, celebrating the arrival by boat of a statue of the Virgin from Antwerp (see p.316). The celebration became increasingly secular – an excuse for the nobility, guilds and civic bigwigs to parade their finery, reaching a peak in 1549, when it was witnessed by Charles V. Today's Ommegang, which finishes up with a dance on the Grand Place, is so popular that it is now held twice annually on the first Tues and Thurs of July; if you want a ticket for the finale, you'll need to reserve (at the TIB on the Grand Place) at least six months ahead. Another fun annual event is the more modest *Planting of the Meiboom*, which takes place every August 9 – a procession from rue des Sables to the Grand Place, which involves much boozing, food and general partying. The story goes that in 1213 a wedding party was celebrating outside the city gates when they were attacked by a street gang from Leuven. They were beaten off (with the help of a group of archers, who just happened to be passing by), and in thanks, the local duke gave them permission to plant a maypole (Meiboom) on the eve of their Patron Saints' feastday. Other events include the *Foire du Midi*, which takes place every year from mid-July to the end of Aug around the Porte de Hal – good for sampling local food and beer – and the biannual *flower carpet*, in mid-Aug, when the entire Grand Place is covered with an intricate design made entirely of begonias.

Football Brussels has several teams, of which *Anderlecht* are by far the best known and most consistent, regularly among the contenders for the Belgian league championship. Their stadium is the Vanden Stock, at avenue Theo Verbeeck 2 (☎522 94 00), reachable by taking tram #103 or bus #46, #74 or #76. The more infamous Heysel stadium, out on avenue de Marathon in Laeken (☎478 93 00), is the home of the rather less impressive *Racing Jet de Bruxelles* – a second-division team since their demotion a couple of years back. To see them, take tram #81, or the metro to Heysel.

Gay and lesbian life For the most up-to-date information on the Brussels gay scene, phone the Gay/Lesbian Line on ☎233 25 02 (daily 9am–9pm). Brussels' gay men meet up in a number of city centre bars, among which the following are centrally situated – *Le Why Not?*, rue des Riches Claires 7, *Tels Quels*, rue Marché au Charbon 81, and *Big Noise*, rue Marché au Charbon 41. There is less of a lesbian scene, but the *Capricorne*, rue d'Anderlecht 8 (off place Fontainas), is a long-established lesbian disco, which attracts a crowd spanning the ages (men admitted, too). It's open at weekends only. *Madam*, Galerie du Roi 25, is about the only truly lesbian bar in town.

Hospital For medical assistance call ☎479 18 18 or 648 80 00, day or night.

Infor-Jeunes rue du Marché aux Herbes 27 (☎512 32 74). An information centre for young people new to the city, giving advice on accommodation, the law and other matters; it's open Mon–Fri 10am–6pm, Sat 10am–1pm.

Laundromat *Salon Lavoir*, rue Haute 5, around the corner from the Bruegel youth hostel.

Lost property For articles lost on public transport, call ☎515 23 94; on a train ☎219 28 80; on a plane ☎720 91 13.

Post office The main central post office is upstairs in the centre Monnaie building at the bottom end of place de Brouckère (Mon–Sat 9am–5pm). There's also a 24-hr post office at the Gare du Midi.

Swimming pools rue du Chevreuil 28 (☎511 24 68).

Telephones boulevard de l'Impératrice 17 (daily 8am–10pm).

Train enquiries ☎219 26 40; *Netherlands Railways*, boulevard de l'Empereur 66 (☎512 83 45).

Travel agents *Acotra*, rue de la Madeleine 51 (☎512 85 07 or 512 55 40); *Europabus*, place de Brouckère 50 (☎217 00 25); *Nouvelles Frontières*, rue de la Violette 21 (☎511 80 13).

Women's contacts The English-speaking *Women's Organization for Equality* (WOE), rue Blanche 29, off avenue Louise (☎538 47 73), holds public meetings on the third Wed of the month, at 8pm. There's a cafeteria on the premises, *Les Dames Blanches* (Mon, Tues & Fri 11am–6pm, Wed & Thurs 11am–10pm), which serves cheap plats du jour. *Artemys*, Galerie Bortier, rue St Jean 8–10, is Brussels' only feminist bookstore, and stocks a large number of books in English; it has a women's tearoom upstairs.

AROUND BRUSSELS: TERVUREN, WATERLOO AND LEUVEN

The bilingual city of Brussels constitutes one-third of the federation which these days makes up Belgium, and lies at the centre of the province of **Brabant**, which is divided more or less equally between French-speakers and Flemings. Much of the province is covered in other chapters, but there are one or two high spots close to the city which are worth getting out to see if you're here for a few days. The battlefield at **Waterloo** is the most popular attraction, though perhaps more interesting is the Central African museum in the quiet suburb of **Tervuren**. Farther afield, the old university city of **Leuven** is worth a day trip, too, though it can also be seen on the way to places farther out.

Tervuren

Avenue de Tervuren leads out of Brussels toward the suburb of **TERVUREN**, lined with embassies and mansions in its upper reaches, and then delving through the wooded areas of the northern Forêt de Soignes, a route most easily covered by tram #44 from place Montgomery. The main attraction of Tervuren, aside from the mere pleasure of escaping the city for a couple of hours, is the **Musée Royal de L'Afrique Centrale** (mid-March to mid-Oct daily except Mon 9am–5.30pm; rest of the year daily except Mon 10am–4.30pm; F50), a short walk along the main road from the tram terminal – housed in a grandiose custom-built pile constructed on the orders of King Leopold II early this century. Leopold owned the Belgian Congo himself, its income making him one of the country's richest men, and it was he who sent the explorer Stanley there (of Livingstone fame) on a five-year fact-finding mission. In 1908, one year before the museum opened, the Belgian government took over the colony, replacing Leopold's chaotic, extraordinarily cruel regime with a marginally more liberal state bureaucracy. The country gained independence as Zaire only in 1960. The museum was Leopold's own idea, a blatantly colonialist and racist enterprise which treats the Africans as a naive and primitive people, and the Belgians as their paternalistic benefactors. However, the collection is undeniably rich, and should not be missed. Displays are devoted to many aspects of Congolese life, from export crops like coffee, cocoa and seed oils, to masks, idols, musical instruments, weapons and an impressive array of dope pipes. The museum's grounds are also worth a stroll, with the formal gardens, fetchingly set around a series of geometric lakes, flanked by wanderable woods. Afterward, if you've not brought a picnic, head for *Il Paradiso* behind the museum parking lot, which serves reasonably priced and authentic Italian pizza – so popular you're unlikely to find a table on Sunday.

Waterloo

About 18km south of Brussels, accessible by orange bus #W from place Rouppe, **WATERLOO** has a resonance far beyond its size. Today, a bland small town with a large American community and a glut of fast-food outlets, it was here on June 18, 1815 that Wellington masterminded the battle which put an end to the imperial ambitions of Napoleon, and so changed the course of European history. The battlefield not surprisingly gets lots of visitors, although frankly it doesn't really live up to expectations, and unless you're especially interested in the battle, there's little reason to go – unless it's to see an annual re-enactment by a local historical society in June.

Actually, the battle is still something of a bone of contention between the French-speakers and Flemings hereabouts. Broadly speaking, French-speakers fought for Napoleon, while the Flemings fought on the side of Wellington, and the souvenir shops and monuments that have gone up in years since have divided along linguistic lines – the shops that sell Napoleonic souvenirs are unlikely to be run by Flemish-speakers; the sights that honour the British will not have been erected by Walloons.

The best starting point if you do visit is the *Name* inn in the centre of town. It was here that Wellington slept the night before the battle and Gordon, Wellington's aide-de-camp, was brought to die. It now houses the **Musée Wellington**, chaussée de Bruxelles 147 (April to mid-Nov 9.30am–6.30pm; mid-Nov to end March 10.30am–5pm; F70), detailing the events of the battle with plans and models, the assorted personal effects of Wellington, Gordon and Napoleon, and a display of amputating instruments – the need for which becomes clearer in the small **chapel** across the street, where a plaque reads "Here is buried the leg of the illustrious, brave and valiant Count Uxbridge." "I say, I've lost my leg," Uxbridge is reported to have said, to which Wellington replied "By God sir, so you have!" In fact, although Uxbridge's leg was initially buried here it was returned to London when he died to join the rest of his body; as a consolation his artificial leg was donated to the museum.

The Waterloo **tourist office** (April to mid-Nov daily 9.30am–6.30pm; mid-Nov to March daily 10.30am–5pm ☎02/354 99 10), next door to the Musée Wellington, has a pamphlet suggesting walking tours in and around the town, though you'd be better off picking up orange bus #W again and heading down to the **battlefield** itself – a totally flat landscape of fields punctuated by the odd clump of trees. The best vantage point is from the hundred-metre-high **Butte de Lion**, built by local women with soil from the battlefield to mark the spot where Holland's Prince William of Orange – later King William II of the Netherlands – was wounded. It's a commanding monument, a regal 28-ton lion atop a stout column, up which it's possible to climb – some 226 steps (April–Oct 9.30am–6.30pm; Nov–March 10.30am–4pm; F40). Nearby, a rotunda-like building holds an enormous panoramic circular **painting** of the battle, 110m in circumference, the work of the French artist Louis Demoulin, naturalistically depicting the French cavalry charge on the opposing forces (Mon–Fri 9.30am–6pm, Sat & Sun 9.30am–6.30pm; F70). Afterward, you could take a look at the **Musée de Cires** (April–Oct daily 9am–6.30pm; Nov–March Sat & Sun only 10am–4.45pm; F60), which has wax figures of the leading characters, and shows a 1936 film of the proceedings.

Napoleon spent the eve of the battle at **Le Caillou**, a white brick farmhouse about 3km down the road from the Butte de Lion, and you can visit this, too (April–Oct daily except Mon 10.30am–6pm; Nov–March daily except Mon 1.30–5pm; F40). The mementoes here, including Napoleon's army cot, death mask and the skeleton of a dead soldier (just one of the thirty-nine thousand who died), are basically a memorial to the emperor, as well as doing something to bring home the chill reality of battle.

Leuven

Less than half an hour away by train, **LEUVEN** provides an equally easy day trip from Brussels. It's home to Belgium's oldest university, and has a fine Gothic square and student atmosphere that combine to give an impression of a relaxed, low-key provincial town. Apart from an extraordinary Gothic town hall and a handful of churches, there's not a great deal to see – the city centre is for the most part an undistinguished tangle of streets lined with modern shops and snack bars. Indeed it's something of a miracle that any of Leuven's ancient buildings have survived at all: in World War I some 1500 houses were destroyed, and the university library and main church gutted, only to suffer further damage in the last war, too. The atmosphere of the town, also, can appear an odd one, with an acute disjunction between town and gown that only begins to reveal itself if you stay a while.

The history of the **University**, founded in 1425, isn't a particularly happy one. By the early sixteenth century it rated among Europe's most prestigious educational establishments: the cartographer Mercator was a student at Leuven, and Erasmus worked here, founding the *Collegium Trilingue* for the study of Hebrew, Latin and Greek, as the basis of a liberal (rather than Catholic) education. However, in response to the rise of Lutheranism, the authorities insisted on strict Catholic orthodoxy, and drove Erasmus into exile. In 1797 the French completely suppressed the university, and, after the defeat of Napoleon, when Belgium fell under Dutch rule, William I replaced it with a Philosophical College – one of many blatantly anti-Catholic measures which fuelled the Belgian revolution. Re-established after the revolution, as a bilingual Catholic institution, it became a hotbed of Flemish Catholicism, and for much of this century French and Flemish speakers here were locked into a sometimes violent nationalist dispute. In 1970 it was decided to found a separate, French-speaking university at Louvain-la-Neuve, just south of Brussels, and today Leuven has been re-established as a power base of Flemish thinking, wielding considerable influence over the country's political and economic thought.

LEUVEN

Arrival, information and accommodation

It's a ten- to fifteen-minute walk from the train station, down Bondgenotenlaan, to the Grote Markt, but you could also take bus #5 or #10. Leuven's **tourist office** is just off the Grote Markt at Naamesestraat 1a (Mon–Fri 9am–5pm, Sat 10am–5pm; March–Oct also Sun 10am–5pm; ☎016/21 15 39), which has maps, what's-on information and a useful booklet on the town listing all hotels and restaurants as well as sights and museums. There are some reasonable **hotels** directly opposite the station, either side of Bondgenotenlaan – the *Industrie*, Martelarenplein 7 (☎016/22 13 49; ③), and the marginally more expensive *Royale*, Martelarenplein 6 (☎016/22 12 52; ③), both of which have plain, clean and basic rooms. There's also the *Mille Colonnes*, Martelarenplein 5 (☎016/22 86 21), which has similarly neat and simple doubles if the other two are full, and is ever-so-slightly cheaper.

Alternatively, the *Majestic* is a little more central at Bondgenotenlaan 20 (☎016/22 43 65; ②), 100m from Fochplein, as well as being probably the town's cheapest option; it also boasts a wonderful period dining room. The closest **campsite** is the *Boudewijn*, east of town on Diestsesteenweg (May–Sept).

The Town

The centre of town is marked by two adjacent squares – **Fochplein** (buses from the station drop you off here), a road junction basically, whose one remarkable feature is the **Font Sapienza**, a wittily cynical fountain of a student literally being brainwashed by the book he is reading, and the wedge-shaped **Grote Markt**. The latter is Leuven's architectural high spot, dominated by two magnificent fifteenth-century Gothic buidings – the St Pieterskerk and the Stadhuis. The **Stadhuis**, or town hall, is the more flamboyant of the two buildings, an extraordinarily light, lacy structure, studded with statues and tracery and crowned by soaring pinnacles. The statues, representing everything from important citizens, artists and nobles, to virtues, vices and municipal institutions, actually date from the nineteenth century: until then, the lavishly carved niches stood empty for lack of money. More appealing than these are the exuberant, sometimes grotesque medieval figures protruding from the niche bases.

After the lavishness of the exterior, the inside of the Stadhuis is something of an anticlimax, with guided tours (Mon–Fri 11am & 3pm; Sat, Sun & hols 3pm; F20) taking you through a succession of heavily elaborate rooms, some of which are incongruously decked out in the fancy French styles of Louis XIV and XV. Even the Gothic hall upstairs is a disappointment, featuring a neo-Gothic chimneypiece and nineteenth-century portraits of people involved in the building of the Stadhuis, including the Leuven artist, Dieric Bouts. The basement – accessible by a separate entrance on Naamsestraat – holds a **Brasserie Museum** (Easter–Oct Tues–Sat 10am–noon & 2–5pm, Sun 2–5pm; F50, ticket includes Vandekelen Martens museum), which holds a singularly unremarkable collection of brewing equipment.

There are few surviving works by Bouts, who worked for most of his life in Leuven, and had considerable influence on fifteenth-century German painting. His figures tend to be rather stiff and bony, but his use of colour is masterful, as you can see in two tryptychs housed in the late Gothic **St Pieterskerk** across the road, whose ambulatory holds a **Museum of Religious Art** (mid-March to mid-Oct Mon–Sat 10am–noon & 2–5pm, Sun 2–5pm; rest of year Tues–Sat 10am–noon & 2–5pm). Of the paintings, the *Last Supper* is of most interest, showing Christ and his disciples in a Flemish dining room, with the (half-built) Stadhuis just visible through the left-hand window. Look also for a copy of Rogier van der Weyden's marvellous *Descent from the Cross*, now in Madrid, which is said to have influenced Bouts' work, and the shrine and paintings in chapels 8 and 9, dedicated to one St (Proud) Margareth, patron of serving girls. A thirteenth-century servant, she witnessed the murder of her employers, was abducted by the murderers, and then killed for refusing to marry one of them. The paintings in the second chapel, by Pieter Vrhagen, retell her story.

From the ambulatory there is access to the **crypt**, uncovered by World War II bomb damage, and still retaining some faint eleventh-century graffiti scratched on the pillars. Have a peek, too, at the immense eighteenth-century **pulpit**, a weighty wooden confection carved with foliage and animals, and showing Saint Norbert being thrown off his horse by lightning – a brush with death that prompted his conversion.

There are more paintings in the **Museum Vandekelen Martens**, east of Fochplein at Savoyestraat 6 (Tues–Sat 10am–noon & 2–5pm, Sun 2–5pm; F50, ticket includes Brasserie museum), an eclectic collection that takes in everything from Japanese porcelain to stained glass. It's badly labelled, where they appear at all, but its array of art exhibits includes work by Quentin Matsys, Cornelis de Vos, Pieter Aertsen and others, as well as polychromatic medieval and Renaissance sculpture.

South of the museum, **Oude Markt** is the lively core of Leuven's student scene, a large cobblestone rectangle surrounded by bars in gabled houses. It's the site of a bustling market on Fridays. Above Oude Markt, Naamsestraat leads south past the supple Baroque facade of the Jesuit **St Michielskerk**, restored after wartime damage, to the **Groot Begijnhof**, a sixteenth-century enclave of mellow red-brick houses, once home to around three hundred *begijns*. In 1962 the Begijnhof was bought by the university and painstakingly restored as student residences. Even now during the day, when the students are out, a wonderfully tranquil, timeless atmosphere pervades.

Eating and drinking

Due to its status as both a student and a tourist town, **eating and drinking** are not at all a problem in Leuven. There are lots of fast-food and sandwich places for lunches on the run, and a great many restaurants where you can get a reasonable meal for a reasonable price, not to mention any number of cosy bars to while away an hour or two with a drink. *Domus*, a little way down Tiensestraat on the right, walking from Fochplein, is a large timbered bar of the brewery of the same name, and as such makes a good place to drink and eat, with a good selection of lunchtime meals and snacks, and a predictably accomplished beer list. Further down the same street, *De Kruimel*, Tiensestraat 92, is a good venue for both lunchtime and evening eating, with a menu that includes regular Belgian food, as well as pizza, pasta and the like. Almost opposite, *Universum*, on the corner of Tiensestraat and Hooverplein, is a big old barnlike bar around the corner from the university that is normally stuffed with students; it also has a limited selection of food – soup, spaghetti, omelettes, etc. On Oude Markt, there is a large selection of bars and cafés, and *Pizzeria il Fornello*, at no. 37, has good and low-priced pizza and pasta dishes; *Ascoli*, nearby at Muntstraat 17, also has decent Italian food – at lower prices than its decor might suggest. Vegetarians should try the food at *Lukemieke*, Vlamingenstraat 55 (Mon–Fri only noon–2pm & 6–8.30pm), behind the St Donatuspark.

Just to **drink**, the best place to head for is Oude Markt. *Bagatelle*, *Café Allee* and *De Kroeg*, on the western side, are all lively places, popular with students. A little way out from the immediate centre, the *Cambridge*, at the corner of Parkstraat and Naamsestraat, is another student hangout, a small and unpretentious bar that does simple food.

travel details

Trains

All trains stop at Midi, Centrale and Nord unless otherwise indicated.

From Brussels to Amsterdam (hourly; 3hr); Antwerp (3 hourly; 40min); Basle, from Brussels Midi & Nord (5 daily; 7hr 30min); Bruges (hourly; 1hr); Charleroi (hourly; 50min); Ghent (hourly; 40min); Liège (hourly; 1hr 20min); Leuven (every 30 min; 30min); Luxembourg, from Brussels Midi & Nord (5 daily; 2hr 30min); Maastricht (hourly; 2hr); Metz, from Brussels Midi & Nord (5 daily; 3hr 45min); Mons (hourly; 55min); Ostende (hourly 1hr 23min); Paris, from Brussels Midi & Nord (10 daily; 3hr); Rotterdam (hourly; 2hr); Strasbourg, from Brussels Midi & Nord, (5 daily; 5hr).

CHAPTER EIGHT

FLANDERS

T he Flemish-speaking provinces of **East** and **West Flanders** spread out from the North Sea coast as far as Antwerp to the east and Kortrijk to the south. As early as the thirteenth century, Flanders was one of the most prosperous areas of Europe, with an advanced, integrated economy dependent on the cloth trade. By the sixteenth century, the region was in decline as trade slipped north toward Holland, and England's cloth manufacturers began to undermine Flanders' economic base. The speed of the collapse was accelerated by religious conflict, for the great Flemish towns were by inclination Protestant, their kings and queens Catholic, and once Hapsburg domination was assured, thousands of weavers, merchants and skilled artisans poured north to escape religious persecution. The ultimate economic price was the closure of the Scheldt at the insistence of the Dutch in 1648. Thereafter, Flanders sank into poverty and decay, a static and traditional society where nearly every aspect of life was controlled by decree, and only three percent of the population could read or write. As Voltaire quipped:

> *In this sad place wherein I stay,*
> *Ignorance, torpidity,*
> *And boredom hold their lasting sway,*
> *With unconcerned stupidity;*
> *A land where old obedience sits,*
> *Well filled with faith, devoid of wits.*

The Flemish peasantry of the seventeenth and eighteenth centuries saw their lands crossed and recrossed by the armies of the great powers, a region where the relative fortunes of dynasties and nations were decided. Only with Belgian independence did the situation begin to change: the towns started to industrialize, tariffs protected the cloth industry, Zeebrugge was built and Ostend was modernized, all in a flurry of activity that shook the land from its centuries-old torpor. Today, despite the devastating dislocation of World War I and the occupation of World War II, Flanders has emerged prosperous, its citizens maintaining a distinctive cultural and linguistic identity that's become a powerful political force in opposition to their Walloon neighbours.

ACCOMMODATION PRICE CODES

All the **hotels and hostels** detailed in this chapter have been graded according to the following price categories. Note that the prices have been calculated as those for the cheapest double room during high season. For more on accommodation, see p.280.

① Up to F1000 per person.	③ F1500–2000.	⑥ F3000–4000.
	④ F2000–2500.	⑦ F4000–5000.
② F1000–1500.	⑤ F2500–3000.	⑧ F5000 and over.

With the exception of the range of low hills around Ronse and the sea dunes along the coast, Flanders is unrelentingly flat and frankly rather dreary. However, there are many reminders of its medieval greatness, readily accessible by means of a comprehensive public transport network. The ancient cloth cities of **Bruges** and less well-known **Ghent** both hold marvellous collections of early Flemish art; and, of the smaller towns, **Oudenaarde** has a delightful Stadhuis and is famed for its tapestries, and **Kortrijk** and **Veurne** are pleasant old places worth stopping off at on the way south into France. There is also, of course, the legacy of World War I. The trenches extended from the North Sea coast, close to Westende, as far as Switzerland, cutting across West Flanders via Dijksmuide and Ieper, and many of the key engagements of the war were fought here. Every year hundreds of visitors head for **Nieuwpoort** and more particularly **Ieper** (formerly Ypres) to see the numerous cemeteries and monuments around these towns – sad reminders of what proved to be a desperately futile conflict.

Not far from the battlefields, the Belgian coast is beach territory, an almost continuous stretch of golden sand that every summer is filled by thousands of tourists. An excellent **tram** service connects all the major resorts, and although a lot of the development has been crass, cosy **De Haan** has kept much of its turn-of-the-century charm, and **Knokke** has all the pretensions of a sophisticated resort. The largest town on the coast is **Ostend**, a lively, working seaport and resort crammed with bars and restaurants full of travellers waiting for the ferries to England.

The coast

Much of the 70km or so of Belgian **coast** groans under an ugly covering of apartment blocks, bungalow settlements, and caravan parks, obscuring a landscape that was largely untouched until the nineteenth century, the beach backing onto a line of sand dunes on which nothing grew except rushes and stunted Lombardy poplars. Behind them, a narrow strip of undulating ground ("Ter Streep"), seldom more than a kilometre or so in width and covered with moss and bushes, connected the barren sand hills with the cultivated farms of the Flemish plain. The dunes were always an inadequate protection against the sea, and the inhabitants here were building dykes as early as the tenth century, an arrangement formalized two hundred years later when Count Baldwin IX of Flanders appointed guardians charged with the duty of constructing defensive works. Despite these efforts, life on the coast remained precarious, and most people chose to live inland; indeed, when Belgium achieved independence in 1830, there were only two coastal settlements of any size – **Ostend**, a small fortified town with an antiquated harbour, and **Nieuwpoort**, in a state of what was thought to be terminal decay.

It was Leopold I, the first king of the Belgians, who began the transformation of the coast, assisted by the development of the country's rail system. In 1834 he chose Ostend as a royal residence, had the town modernized and connected it by train to Brussels. Fashionable by royal approval and now readily accessible, the coast was soon dotted with resorts, and the number of seaside visitors rose meteorically. The next king carried on the work of his father, building a light railway along the shore and completing the chain of massive sea walls that extend from one end of the coast to the other. Barring the extraordinary, the Belgian coastline seemed safe at last.

Ostend

The 1900 *Baedeker* travel guide distinguished **OSTEND** as "One of the most fashionable and cosmopolitan watering places in Europe". The gloss is, however, long gone, the town's aristocratic visitors have moved on to more exotic climes, and Ostend is now among Belgium's largest ports and the main ferry terminus for boats to the south coast of England. It's also the pivot of the region's public transport system, including the fast, frequent and efficient trams that run behind the beach to Knokke-Heist in the east and De Panne in the west.

The old fishing village of Ostend was given a town charter in the thirteenth century, in recognition of its growing importance as a port for trade across the Channel. Flanked by an empty expanse of sand dune, it remained the only important harbour along this stretch of the coast until the construction of Zeebrugge in the nineteenth century. Like so many other towns in the Spanish Netherlands, it was attacked and besieged time and again, winning the admiration of Protestant Europe in resisting the Spaniards during a desperate siege that lasted from 1601 to 1604. Later, convinced of the wholesome qualities of sea air and determined to impress other European rulers with their sophistication, Belgium's first kings, Leopold I and II, turned Ostend into a chi-chi resort, demolishing the town walls and dotting the outskirts with prestigious buildings and parks – some of which were destroyed during World War II, when the town was a prime bombing target.

Arrival – and transport along the coast

Ostend's **ferry terminus** at Montgomerydok is next to the **train station**, a couple of minutes' walk from the centre of town – you couldn't wish for a more convenient setup if you're heading straight through. The station's **information office** (Mon–Fri 7am–7pm, Sat & Sun 8am–7pm) has comprehensive details of international train times. For destinations along the coast, **trams** leave from beside the train station and head east to Knokke-Heist and west to De Panne, putting all the Belgian resorts within easy striking distance. Winter services in both directions depart every half-hour, in summer every ten minutes. Fares are relatively inexpensive – Ostend to De Panne, for instance, costs F145; you can also buy tickets for unlimited tram travel, valid either one day (F290), three days (F490) or five days (F840). If you are moving on immediately, **car rental** is available from *Avis*, Visserskaai 8 (☎059/70 07 89), *Europcar*, Vindictivelaan 6 (☎059/80 29 21), and *Hertz*, Slijkensesteenweg 7 (☎059/32 34 98).

Information and accommodation

If you decide to stay in Ostend, there is a small **tourist kiosk** just outside the station (July–Aug 10am–12.30pm & 2–6pm) and a main **tourist office** a few minutes' away on Monacoplein (June–Sept Mon–Sat 9am–7pm & Sun 10am–7pm; Oct–May Mon–Sat 10am–6pm & Sun 11am–6pm; ☎059/70 11 99). They will help you find **accommodation** in one of many hotels and guesthouses. One of the livelier and more convenient areas to stay is in the series of side streets sandwiched between Albert 1 Promenade, the casino and Langestraat. There are several hotels on Louisastraat, with cheap and basic options including the *Mayfair* at no. 18 (☎059/70 20 68; ②) and the slightly more expensive *Empire* at no. 31 (☎059/70 42 59; ②). Moving up a notch, there's the *Marion* at no. 19 (☎059/70 09 28; ③), and, on nearby Hofstraat, a couple of three-star places – the *Glenmore* at no. 25 (☎059/70 20 22; ④) and the *Pacific* at no. 11 (☎059/70 15 07; ④). The **youth hostel** is

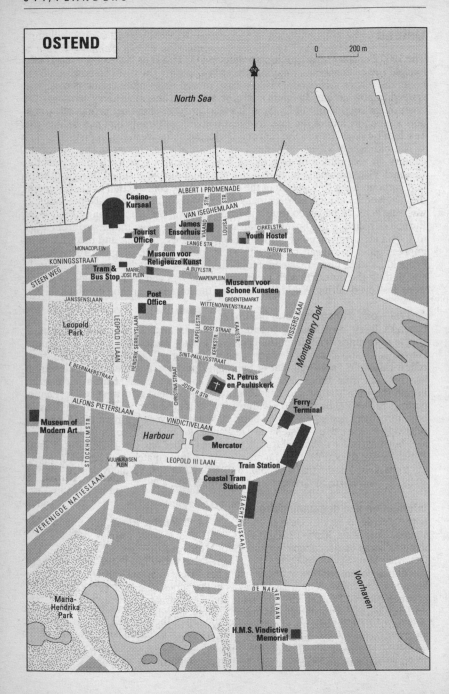

OSTEND

0   200 m

North Sea

Casino-Kursaal

ALBERT I PROMENADE

VAN ISEGHEMLAAN

James Ensorhuis

Tourist Office

VIAAND STR.

LOUISA STR.

CIRKELSTR.

Youth Hostel

NIEUWSTR.

LANGE STR.

MONACOPLEIN

KONINGSSTRAAT

Museum voor Religieuze Kunst

A.BUYLSTR.

Tram & Bus Stop

MARIE JOSE PLEIN

WAPENPLEIN

STEEN WEG

Museum voor Schone Kunsten

GROENTEMARKT

JANSSENSLAAN

Post Office

WITTENONNENSTRAAT

KAPELLSTR.

OOST STRAAT

KAAISTR.

Leopold Park

LEOPOLD II LAAN

HENDRIK SERRUYSLAAN

KERKSTR.

VISSERS KAAI

SINT-PAULUSSTRAAT

Montgomery Dok

E. BEERNAERSTRAAT

CHRISTINA STRAAT

JOSEF II STR.

St. Petrus en Pauluskerk

ALFONS PIETERSLAAN

Ferry Terminal

VINDICTIVELAAN

Museum of Modern Art

STOCKHOLMSTR.

Harbour

Mercator

VUURKRUISEN PLEIN

LEOPOLD III LAAN

Train Station

VERENIGDE NATIESLAAN

Coastal Tram Station

SLACHTHUISKAAI

Maria-Hendrika Park

DE NAE...ER LAAN

Voorhaven

H.M.S. Vindictive Memorial

spick, span and handily placed at Langestraat 82 (☎059/80 52 97; ①), although it's often full in summer. The nearest **campsite** is *Ostend Camping-Coppin* at Nieuwpoortsesteenweg 514 (☎059/70 55 73), just behind the beach several kilometres to the west of town (take the De Panne tram).

The Town

There's precious little left of medieval Ostend, and today's town centre spreads out from beside the train station – a series of narrow, straight streets edged by the beach to the north, Leopold II Laan, the site of the old walls, to the west, and the marina, the former harbour, to the south. Across the Visserskaai from the station, **St Petrus en St Pieterkerk** looks old but in fact dates from the early twentieth century. Next to the church, the last remnant of its predecessor is a massive sixteenth-century tower with a canopied, morbid shrine of the Crucifixion at its base. From here, Kerkstraat leads to the main square, **Wapenplein**, where the **Museum voor Schone Kunsten** (daily except Tues 10am–noon & 2–5pm; F50) is divided into two sections. There are modest temporary exhibitions of local history in the **Museum De Plate** on the second floor, and several well-displayed rooms of nineteenth- and twentieth-century paintings on the third. Apart from the harsh surrealism of Paul Delvaux's *De Ijzertijd*, star billing goes to the canvases of James Ensor, who was born in Ostend in 1860, son of an English father and Flemish mother. Barely noticed until the 1920s, Ensor spent nearly all his 89 years working in his home town, and is nowadays considered a pioneer of Expressionism. His first paintings were rather sombre portraits and landscapes, but in the early 1880s he switched to brilliantly contrasting colours, most familiar in his *Self-portrait of the Artist in a Flowered Hat*, a deliberate variation on Rubens' famous self-portraits. Less well known is *Portrait of a Dead Mother*, a fine, rather fierce example of his preoccupation with the grim and macabre.

A couple of minutes' walk north of the Wapenplein, the **James Ensorhuis**, Vlaanderenstraat 27 (June–Sept daily except Tues 10am–noon & 2–5pm; F50), was the artist's first home and has been restored to something like its former state. On the ground floor there's the old shell and souvenir shop of his uncle and aunt, and up above are the painter's living room and studio, though none of the works on display is original. James Ensor is further remembered immediately to the west of Wapenplein, in the **Museum voor Religieuze Kunst**, St Sebastiaanstraat 41 (July–Sept daily except Mon & Tues 3–6pm; free), sited in a disused chapel, which has several more paintings by the artist along with a mundane collection of eighteenth- and nineteenth-century religious pictures and sculpture. Just to the north of St Sebastiaanstraat, the **Casino-Kursaal** (gaming daily from 3pm) was built in 1953 as a successor to the first casino of 1852. Most of the town's classical concerts are performed here, and one of the gambling rooms is decorated with murals by Paul Delvaux.

On either side of the casino is Ostend's main attraction, a strip of sandy **beach** which extends east to the harbour and west as far as De Panne. On summer days thousands drive into the town to soak up the sun, swim and amble along the seafront **Promenade**, which runs along the top of the sea wall. Part sea defence and part royal ostentation, the Promenade was once the main route from the town centre to the Wellington racecourse 2km to the west, an intentionally grand walkway designed to please the pretensions of Leopold II, whose imperial statue still stands in the middle of a long line of stone columns that now adjoin the **Thermae Palace Hotel**. Built in the 1930s, this is similarly regal, although it spoils the lines of the original walkway.

Heading east from the casino, Albert I Promenade leads into the Visserskaai, where the **Aquarium** (April–Sept daily 10am–noon & 2–5pm; F50), housed in the former shrimp market on the east side of the street, holds a series of displays on North Sea fish, crustacea, flora and fauna. To the south, in the marina, the sailing ship **Mercator** (May–Sept daily 9am–noon & 1–6pm; July & Aug daily 9am–7pm; Oct–March 10am–noon & 1–4pm; F75) is the old training vessel of the Belgian merchant navy, converted into a marine museum holding an enormous collection of items accumulated during her worldwide voyages.

A few minutes' walk south of the train station, in a sunken garden at the end of Westkaai, is the prow of the **HMS Vindictive**. On the night of May 9, 1918, the British made a desperate attempt to block Ostend's harbour. The sacrificial ships were crewed by volunteers, and the *Vindictive* was successfully sunk at the port entrance. After the war the bow was retrieved and kept as a memorial to the sailors who lost their lives. This was one of the most audacious operations of the war, but tragically it was based on false intelligence: German submarines hardly ever used the harbour.

Eating and drinking

The sheer variety of places to **eat** in Ostend is almost daunting. Along Visserskaai (where there are scores of seafood stalls) and through the central city streets are innumerable snack bars, coffee houses and restaurants. Many of them serve some pretty mediocre stuff, although all offer good plates of mussels and french fries. Two of the better restaurants are on the seafront near the station – the pricy *Lusitania*, Visserskaai 35, and the *Marina*, Albert I Promenade 2.

East of Ostend

Trams leave from beside Ostend train station for the journey east to Knokke-Heist every ten minutes in summer and every thirty minutes in winter. Clearing the town's drearyy suburbs, they shoot through a series of tourist developments that disfigure the sand dunes as far as **DE HAAN**, an oasis of restraint amid the predominant high-rise construction, which has never been allowed here. Established at the end of the nineteenth century, De Haan was carefully conceived as an exclusive seaside village in a rustic Gothic Revival style – *style Normand*. The building plots were irregularly dispersed between the tram station and the sea around a pattern of winding streets reminiscent of – and influenced by – contemporaneous English suburbs like Liverpool's Sefton Park. The only formality was provided by a central circus around a casino (demolished in 1929). De Haan has survived pretty much intact, a welcome relief from the surrounding ugliness, and, flanked by empty sand dunes, it's now a popular family resort, with a good beach and pleasant seafront cafés.

The **tourist office** (April to mid-Sept daily 9am–12.30pm & 2–6pm; ☎059/23 34 47) is next to the tram stop named De Haan Aan Zee and they have a small cachet of private **rooms**. There are no fewer than 21 **hotels** in or near the village centre, including the convenient, reasonably priced *Des Brasseurs* (☎059/23 52 94; ①), and the *Belle Vue* (☎059/23 34 39; ②), which has singles at Koninklijk Plein 1 and doubles at Koninklijk Plein 5; both are only a couple of minutes' walk from the tram stop toward the sea. In the opposite direction, there's the *Bouquet de France*, Wenduinesteenweg 11 (☎059/23 45 93; ③), a left turn off Stationsstraat, five minutes' walk south of the tram stop. *Camping 54* is the nearest of a chain of **campsites**, a further five minutes along Wenduinesteenweg at no. 67. The resort's best hotel, *Auberge des Rois*, at the west end of Zeedijk (☎059/23 34 13; ⑤) overlooks the sea. There are **café-restaurants** at regular intervals all along the seafront, and, nearby at Leopoldlaan 18, the *Auteuil*, which serves excellent mussels.

Blankenberge

Nine kilometres east of De Haan, **BLANKENBERGE** is one of the busiest places on the coast, but it has precious little to recommend it. Hopelessly overcrowded during the summer, it's the archetypal seaside town, with a Victorian pier, a tiled Art Deco casino and dozens of boarding houses and fast-food bars pumping out high-energy singalongs. The **tourist office** (Easter to mid-Sept daily 9am–9pm; mid-Sept to Easter Mon–Sat 9am–12.30pm & 2–6pm, Sun 9am–12.30pm; ☎050/41 22 27) is at the end of the main street, next to the tram stop on Leopoldplein.

Zeebrugge

In 1895 work began on a brand new seaport and harbour next to the tiny village of **ZEEBRUGGE**, a few kilometres beyond Blankenberge. The key to the project was a crescent-shaped mole some 2.5km long and 100m wide that was built up from the shore, protecting incoming and out-going shipping from the vagaries of the North Sea. Connected to the rail and canal systems, the harbour was an ambitious attempt to improve Belgium's coastal facilities and provide easy access to the sea from Bruges via the Boudewijnkanaal. Completed in 1907, it was a great commercial success, although two world wars badly damaged its prospects. During World War I, the Allies were convinced that Zeebrugge was a German submarine base, and, in conjunction with the assault on Ostend, attempted to obstruct the harbour in April 1918. Block ships, crewed by volunteers, were taken to strategic positions and sunk with heavy casualties and only partial success. There's a **monument** to the dead sailors and a map of the action at the base of the mole, restored after it was destroyed during the German occupation. World War II saw the same job done rather more proficiently, but it didn't stop further bombing raids and the demolition of the port by the retreating Germans in 1944. The last of the block ships (the *Thetis*) was finally cleared and the harbour reopened in 1957.

Spreading out along the coast among the series of giant docks, Zeebrugge divides into sections, each with its own tram stop. On the west side, a couple of minutes' walk from Zeebrugge Pier tram stop, is the small beach resort. There's nothing much to come here for, but, pushed up against the base of the mole to the east and edged by sand dunes to the west, it's a surprisingly pleasant place to stay if you're catching an early ferry. If you can afford it, the *Maritime* is an agreeable seaside hotel, at Zeedijk 6 (☎050/54 40 66; ⑤). The **tourist office** (July–Aug daily 10am–1pm & 2–6pm) is in a small kiosk on the sea front and can provide up-to-date details of the irregular **bus** service to Bruges train station (#791, 2 daily, 6 in July & Aug; 30min) and of **ferries** to England. *P&O* operates services to Felixstowe from their office about 500m along the mole; *North Sea Ferries* has sailings to Hull from the terminus building another 500m to the north. Tickets are only available direct from the ferry operators on the mole.

THE ZEEBRUGGE DISASTER

On Friday March 6, 1987, the 7pm ferry from Zeebrugge to Dover sank shortly after departure in the icy waters of the harbour, in sight of land. The boat, Townsend Thoresen's *Herald of Free Enterprise*, was a drive-on, drive-off car ferry with an open car deck that filled with water once the ship left its moorings because the bow doors had not been closed. The crew made a desperate last-minute effort to close the doors, but it was too late, and within minutes the ship keeled over, drowning and crushing over 150 people. The cause of the disaster was obvious enough, though the reasons for it have been variously attributed to poor communications between bridge and deck, human error and crew fatigue as a result of the tight schedule of sailings. The biggest controversy has been around the underlying limitations of this sort of open-deck car ferry, and many have argued that if the ferries were fitted with bulkheads on the car decks then they would be far safer. However, the ferry companies themselves remain unconvinced, not least because bulkheads decrease capacity and therefore profits.

A twenty-minute walk east of the beach resort, or a couple of minutes from tram stop Vaart, Zeebrugge **train station** (for Bruges, hourly; 15min) is surrounded by several blocks of terraced houses that were built for harbour workers at the start of this century. The ferry companies run a free bus service from the station to coincide with sailings. A further 1km to the east, the third and oldest part of Zeebrugge fans out north from the tram line to the original fishing harbour, now part of the general dock complex.

Knokke-Heist

Generally regarded as Belgium's most sophisticated resort, **KNOKKE-HEIST** is the collective name for five villages whose individual identities have disappeared in a sprawling development that stretches for some 6km along the coast almost up to the Dutch frontier. Jam-packed in summer, the sophistication is hard to pick out among the confusion of high-rise apartment blocks and expensive second homes hidden away in their leafy, exclusive suburbs. To increase its popularity, a lot of effort goes into planning Knokke-Heist's varied special events programme, notably an annual **sandcastle-building competition** and the **International Cartoon Festival**, with eight hundred entries selected by an international panel shown every year in the **Humourhall**, just to the west of Duinbergen, south of the tram line. Up-to-date details on all events are available from the tourist office.

The most pleasant part of this giant resort is at the east end around **KNOKKE**, which is well connected to Ostend by **tram** and to Bruges by **bus** (#788 every 30min; 70min) and **train** (2 hourly; 15min). Tram, train and bus stations are grouped together at the south end of the long and featureless main street, the Lippenslaan, an inconvenient 2km south of the seafront, where the **tourist office**, Zeedijk 660 (Mon–Fri 10am–noon & 2–5.30pm; July & Aug daily 10am–1pm & 2–7pm; ☎050/60 16 16), will phone around to make a booking in any of the resort's **hotels**. In Knokke, the cheapest choice is *Prince's* at Lippenslaan 171 (☎050/60 11 11; ③) although if you can afford it, splash out on one of the seaview hotels, like the Art Deco *Majestic*, Zeedijk 697 (☎050/61 11 44; ⑥). The nearest **campsite**, *Camping Nr.1* (April–Nov), is 3km to the west at Duinbergenlaan 17, the road heading north from Duinbergen train station.

Knokke itself has all the usual attractions of a busy beach resort, including an excellent range of sporting facilities, but it's distinguished by its desire to cater for the rich, who congregate in the expensive boutiques and private art galleries where many of the big names of modern Dutch art come to exhibit and sell their work. Along the seafront, a few minutes' walk west of Knokke tourist office, is the centre of all the cultural activity: the sumptuous **Casino** (gambling daily from 3pm), which has an international reputation for its exhibitions of modern art and is decorated with canvases by Paul Delvaux in the lobby and René Magritte's *Le Domaine Enchanté* in the gaming room.

Heading east along the sea dyke from Knokke, past the wealthy adjoining resort of **HET ZOUTE**, it's about 4km to the start of the **Het Zwin** nature reserve (Easter–Sept daily 9am–7pm; Oct–Easter daily except Wed 9am–5pm; closed Nov–Easter; F140), a 150-hectare expanse of salt marsh that extends to the Dutch border. Strange as it seems today, this quiet area was once one of the busiest waterways in the world, connecting Bruges with the North Sea until the River Zwin silted up in the sixteenth century. In 1340, it was also the site of one of the largest naval engagements of the century, when Edward III of England sailed up the estuary with his Flemish allies to destroy a French fleet gathered for a projected invasion of England. Nowadays it's simply a beautiful spot, with some unusual flora and fauna nourished by a combination of the river and occasional sea flooding. Two-hour guided visits take place every Sunday and on Thursdays during the summer; ring the warden for times and to make a booking (☎050/60 70 86). Tours begin at the Het Zwin office (and restaurant). Don't come without rubber boots. You'll need a map to reach the reserve on foot – available free from Knokke tourist office. There are two obvious routes – the first is straight along the shoreline, following the sea dyke until the end, before threading your way inland; the second – also the motorists' route – is to follow Kustlaan, a block behind the seafront, and turn right down Bronlaan, which leads into Ooievaarslaan. During the summer, there's also a special **bus service** connecting Knokke train station with Het Zwin, via Knokke town centre and Het Zoute. Incidentally, if you want to **cycle** there, you can rent bikes at the train station.

West of Ostend

West of Ostend, the tram skirts the sand dunes of a long and almost entirely undeveloped stretch of coast, until it rattles into **MIDDELKERKE**, the first of a sequence of undistinguished seaside resorts of apartments and villas that crowd the western reaches of the Belgian coast. The tram line cuts inland to round the estuary of the River Ijzer (Yser) at the small town of **NIEUWPOORT** (tram stop Nieuwpoort Stad) – not to be confused with the crass high-rise development of **NIEUWPOORT-AAN-ZEE** just up the road. Nieuwpoort hasn't had much luck. Founded in the twelfth century, it was besieged nine times in the following six hundred years, but this was nothing compared to its misfortune in World War I. In 1914, the first German campaign reached the Ijzer before the Belgians opened the sluices along the Noordvaart canal, just to the south of the town. The water stopped the invaders in their tracks and permanently separated the armies, but it also put Nieuwpoort on the front line, where it remained for the rest of the war. Every day volunteers had to abandon the safety of their bunkers to operate the ring of sluice gates near the town centre – without this the water would either have drained away or risen to flood the Belgian trenches. Across the bridge near the tram stop, you can still see the ring of sluice gates, dotted with war memorials to the hundreds of men who died.

Four years of shelling reduced the town to a ruin, and what you see now is the result of a meticulous restoration that lasted well into the 1920s. There's nothing remarkable, and the town is only worth a brief visit, though the neo-Renaissance **Stadhuis** and the adjoining **Halle** in the Marktplein give some indication of more prosperous days. The **tourist office** (Mon–Fri 8am–noon & 1.30–5pm; April–Sept also Sat 8am–noon; ☎058/23 55 94), Marktplein 7, has a list of cheap private **rooms**. The nearest **campsite** is southeast of town at Brugsesteenweg 49; take P. Dezwartelaan at the island on the town side of the bridge, first left across the canal, and first right. In July and August, five-hour **boat trips** (daily at 2pm; return F500, one way F350) leave from the landing on P. Dezwartelaan for the journey south along the Ijzer to Dijksmuide, following the path of the front line of World War I. There's also a twice-weekly excursion to Veurne. Further details from the tourist office or the *De Sluiswachter* café at P. Dezwartelaan 9.

De Panne

Some 7km west of Nieuwpoort, **OOSTDUINKERKE-BAD** has a particularly fine beach, from which local fishermen used to ride into the sea on horseback to sweep the ocean for shrimp. It's still done, but these days more usually for the benefit of tourists. Further west, **DE PANNE**, 2km from the French frontier, is now one of the largest settlements on the Belgian coast, though as late as the 1880s it was a tiny fishing village of low white cottages, nestling in a slight wooded hollow ("panne") from which it takes its name. Most of the villagers had their own fishing boats and a plot of land surrounded by trees and hedges. The peace and quiet ended with the arrival of surveyors and architects who reinforced the sea dyke, and laid out paths and roads in preparation for the rapid construction of lines of villas and holiday homes. However, with the exception of the buildings on the seafront, the contours of the land were respected and the houses of much of today's resort perch prettily among the dunes to the south of the beach.

Equipped with all the usual amenities of a seaside town, De Panne tends to be overcrowded in season, and its centre is distinctly unprepossessing. There's a **tourist information kiosk** (April–Sept daily 10am–noon & 2–6pm; ☎058/42 18 19) on the promenade by the beach (tram stop Dijk), and a main office in the **Gemeentehuis** (Mon–Fri 9am–noon & 1.30–5.30pm; ☎058/42 16 17), five to ten minutes' walk south from the kiosk along Zeelaan to no. 21. Both offices have lists of **private rooms** and will phone around to find vacancies, providing they aren't too busy. Alternatively, there's a cluster of **hotels** along Nieuwpoortlaan, one block south of the seafront near its junction with Zeelaan. These include *L'Avenue*, no. 56 (☎058/41 13 70; ④) where rates include breakfast, and the cheaper *Phoebus*, no. 48 (☎058/41 11 73; ②); nearby is *Le Gai Sejour*, at no. 42 (☎058/41 13 03; ⑤), and the cheaper *Des Princes*, at no. 46 (☎058/41 10 91; ③).

There's little to see as such in De Panne, though the rather grand **Monument** at the west end of Zeedijk marks the spot where King Leopold first set foot on Belgian soil in 1831. Otherwise, the town achieved ephemeral fame in World War I, when it was part of the tiny triangle of Belgian territory that the German army failed to occupy, becoming the home of King Albert's government from 1914 to 1918. Some thirty years later, the retreating British army managed to reach the beaches between De Panne and Dunkirk, 15km to the west, just in time for the miraculous evacuation back to England.

The sand dunes southwest of De Panne form the **Westhoek Nature Reserve**, an expanse of wild, unspoiled coastline crisscrossed by marked footpaths. The tourist office sells detailed maps and illustrated guides of local flora and fauna. Otherwise, if you're **heading for Veurne** (see below), 6km inland, it's a good 25-minute walk south from the beach – head down Zeelaan and keep going – to De Panne train station, where trains make the ten-minute journey hourly; if you don't want to walk, buses leave for the station from near the junction of Nieuwpoortlaan and Zeeland every half-hour.

Veurne

Founded in the ninth century, **VEURNE** was part of a chain of fortresses built to defend Flanders from the raids of the Vikings, but without much success. By the eleventh century, Veurne had become a small market town, but all that changed when Robert II of Flanders returned from the Crusades in 1099 with a piece of the True Cross. His ship was caught in a gale, and in desperation he vowed to offer the relic to the first church he saw if he survived. The church was St Walburga at Veurne, and the annual procession that commemorated the gift made the town an important centre of medieval pilgrimage for some three hundred years. These days Veurne is one of the most popular day-trip destinations in West Flanders, a neat and sleepy backwater whose one real attraction is its Grote Markt, one of the best-preserved town squares in Belgium.

The Town

All the main town sights are on or around the **Grote Markt**. At the northwest corner, the **Stadhuis** is a mixture of Gothic and Renaissance styles built between 1596 and 1612, with a fine blue and gold decorated stone loggia projecting from the original brick facade. Inside, a **museum** (April–Sept guided tours 4 times daily; F40) displays items of unexceptional interest, the best of which are a set of leather wall coverings made in Cordoba. The Stadhuis connects with the more austere classicism of the **Gerechtshof**, with its symmetrical pillars and rectangular windows, which once housed the offices of the Inquisition. The attached tiered **belfry** remains closed to visitors, although you can visit the church of **St Walburga** behind (Easter–Sept daily 10am–noon & 3–6pm), the objective of the medieval pilgrimages, an enormous buttressed and gargoyled affair with weather-beaten brick walls dating from the thirteenth century.

On the northeast corner of the Grote Markt, at the end of Ooststraat, the **Spaans Paviljoen** (Spanish Pavilion) was built as the town hall in the middle of the fifteenth century, but takes its name from its later adaptation as the officers' quarters of the Hapsburg garrison. It's a self-confident building, whose long windows and fluted parapet contrast with the Flemish shutters and gables of the **Vleeshuis** standing directly opposite. On the south side of the square, the seventeenth-century **Hoge Wacht** originally served as the quarters of the town watch. Immediately to the east, just off the Grote Markt, the Appelmarkt is edged by **St Niklaaskerk**, whose thirteenth-century detached **tower** (mid-June to mid-Sept 10am–noon & 2–5pm; F30) gives spectacular views of the countryside around.

THE PENITENTS' PROCESSION

In 1650 a young soldier named Mannaert was on garrison duty in Veurne when he was persuaded to commit a mortal sin by his best friend. After he had received the consecrated wafer during Communion, he took it out of his mouth, wrapped it in a cloth, and returned to his lodgings where he fried it over a fire, under the delusion that by reducing it to powder he would make himself invulnerable to injury. The news got out, and he was later arrested, tried and executed, his friend suffering the same fate a few weeks later. Fearful of the consequences of this sacrilege in their town, the people of Veurne resolved that something must be done, deciding on a procession to commemorate the Passion of Christ. This survives as the **Penitents' Procession** (*Boetprocessie*), held on the last Sunday in July – an odd and distinctly macabre reminder of a remote past. Trailing through the streets, the leading figures dress in the brown cowls of the Capuchins and carry wooden crosses that weigh anything up to 50kg.

Practicalities

Buses to Veurne drop passengers a couple of minutes' walk from the Grote Markt; the town **train station** is a ten-minute stroll to the east of the centre – right out of the station building, first left along Stationsstraat and over the canal straight down Ooststraat. **Accommodation** is a problem. The **tourist office**, Grote Markt 29 (Easter–Sept daily 10am–noon & 1.30–5.30pm; Oct–Easter Mon–Fri 10am–noon & 2–4pm; ☎058/31 21 54), has details of a couple of private **rooms**, but they're often full. The only alternative is the town's one **hotel**, the three-star *Croonhof*, at Noordstraat 9 (☎058/31 31 28; ④). Call ahead in summer to make sure of a bed. For **food**, the Grote Markt is lined with snack bars and restaurants: try *De Kroon*, at no. 8 (closed Thurs), where you can sample the local delicacy, *potjesvlees* – veal, chicken and rabbit pies, washed down with the Trappist ale of nearby Westvleteren; a good second choice is *De Vette Os*, Zuidstraat 1 (closed Thurs). In July and August, **carillon concerts** are performed in the belfry of the Gerechtshof every Wednesday morning (10.30–11.30am) and Sunday evening (8–9pm). **Boat trips** leave from the dock beside the train station for Nieuwpoort once daily in July and August (F170 single, F220 return); exact times from the tourist office.

Around Veurne: Beauvoorde, Lo and Dijksmuide

Veurne is the capital of the **Veurne-Ambacht**, an agricultural region of quiet and unremarkable villages that stretches south and west of the town, sandwiched between the French border and the River Ijzer. The best way to see it is by bike (cycles can be rented at Veurne train station): maps of cycle routes are available from the tourist office. The region's prime attraction is the Renaissance castle of **Beauvoorde** (June–Sept daily except Mon, guided tours at 2, 3 & 4pm; F50; no buses), accessible from the turn marked some 7km south of Veurne on the main road to Ieper – follow the road west for about 3km into the village of **WULVERINGEM**, and it's a block north at Wulveringemstraat 10. Built in the early seventeenth century, the castle's angular gables sit prettily behind a narrow moat, and the interior has displays of ceramics, silverware and glass.

The most pleasant village in the district is **LO**, 12km southeast of Veurne, on the bus route between Ieper and Veurne (7 daily; 30min). It was here that Julius Caesar is supposed to have tethered his horse to a yew by the Westpoort on his way across Gaul. Less apocryphally, the village once prospered under the patronage of its Augustinian abbey, founded in the twelfth century and suppressed by the French at the time of the Revolution. Only the dovecote of the abbey survives, but Lo is a classically picturesque village, with a neat whitewashed church, gabled town hall, wooden windmill and the fragmentary remains of an old stone gate, the Westpoort. If you want to stay over, there is just one **hotel**, the *Stadhuis*, Markt 1 (☎058/28 80 16; ②).

Ten minutes from Veurne, the hourly train to Ghent passes the **Ijzertoren**, a massive, sombre war memorial that dominates the western approaches to the small town of **DIKSMUIDE**, which was so extensively shelled in World War I that by 1918 its location could only be identified from a map. It owed its obliteration to its position immediately east of the River Ijzer, which formed the front line from October 1914. Rebuilt, the town is of little appeal, but for a closer look at the memorial and the adjacent **peace museum** (Easter to June & Sept to mid-Nov Mon–Fri 9am–12.30pm & 1.30–5pm, Sat & Sun from 10am; July & Aug daily 9am–7pm; F60), follow the signs for the fifteen-minute walk from the town centre. Not far away is the **Dodengang**, a careful reconstruction of an especially dangerous slice of trench, stuck close to the River Ijzer (April to Sept daily 9am–5pm; F50).

Ieper (Ypres)

Easily reached by train from Kortrijk, and by bus from Veurne, **IEPER** (YPRES) is another Flemish town that prospered from the medieval cloth trade, its thirteenth-century population of two hundred thousand sharing economic control of the region with their rivals in Ghent and Bruges. The most precariously sited of the great Flemish cities, Ypres, as it was then known, was too near the French frontier for comfort, and too strategically important to be ignored by any of the armies whose campaigns crisscrossed the town's environs with depressing frequency. The city governors kept disaster at bay by reinforcing their defences and switching alliances whenever necessary, fighting against the French at the Battle of the Golden Spurs in 1302, and with them forty years later at Roosebeke, where the popular Ghentish leader, Philip van Artevelde, was killed.

The first major misjudgement came in 1383 when Henry Spencer, bishop of Norwich, landed at Calais under the pretext of supporting the armies of Pope Urban VI, who occupied the Vatican, against his rival Clement VII, who was installed in Avignon. The burghers of Ghent and Bruges flocked to Spencer's standard, and the allies had little difficulty in agreeing on an attack against Ypres, which had decided to champion Clement and trust the French for support. The ensuing siege lasted for two months before a French army appeared to save the day, and all of Ypres celebrated the victory. In fact, the town was ruined, its trade never recovered, and, unable to challenge its two main competitors again, many of the weavers migrated. The process of depopulation proved irreversible, and by the sixteenth century the town had shrunk to a mere five thousand inhabitants.

In World War I, the first German thrust of 1914 left a bulge in the Allied line to the immediate east of Ypres, and for the next four years a series of futile offensives attempted to use the bulge – or **Salient** – as a base to break through the enemy's front line. This had disastrous consequences for Ypres, which served as the Allied communications centre. Comfortably within the range of German artillery, the whole population was evacuated in 1915, and by the end of the war Ypres had literally been shelled to smithereens. The town was rebuilt in the 1920s and 1930s, its most prominent medieval buildings, the cloth hall and cathedral, being carefully reconstructed from the originals. The end result, however, can't help but seem a little antiseptic – old-style edifices but with no signs of decay or erosion.

The Town

A monument to the power and wealth of the medieval guilds, the **Lakenhalle**, on the **Grote Markt**, was built in the thirteenth century alongside the River Ieperlee, which now flows underground. Too long to be pretty and too square to be elegant, it's nothing special to look at, but it was meant to be practical. No fewer than 58 doors gave access from the street to the old selling halls, while boats sailed in and out of the gate on the west wing under the watchful eyes of its

THE YPRES SALIENT

World War I was a catastrophe for Ieper. But it was entirely accidental. When the German army launched the war in the west by invading Belgium, they were following the principles – if not the details – laid down by a chief of the German General Staff, Alfred von Schlieffen, who had died just eight years before. The idea was simple: to avoid fighting a war on two fronts, the German army would outflank the French and capture Paris by attacking through Belgium, well before the Russians had assembled on the eastern frontier. It didn't work, with the result that there were two lines of opposing trenches that stretched from the North Sea to Switzerland. No one knew quite what to do, but attention focused on the two main bulges – or salients – in the line, one at Ieper, the other at Verdun, on the Franco-German frontier just to the south of Luxembourg. To the Allied generals, the bulge at Ieper – the **Ypres Salient** – was a good place to break through the German lines and roll up their front from the north; to the Germans it represented an ideal opportunity to break the deadlock by attacking the enemy from several sides at the same time. No one disagreed with these ideas because contemporary military doctrine on both sides taught that the best way to win a war was to destroy the enemy's strongest forces first. In retrospect this may seem strange, but the generals of the day were schooled in cavalry tactics, where a charge that broke the enemy's key formations was guaranteed to spread disorder and confusion among the rest, paving the way for victory. The consequence of this tactical similitude was that the salients attracted armies like magnets, even though technological changes had shifted the balance of war in favour of defence – machine guns were more efficient, barbed wire more effective, and, most important of all, the railways could shift defensive reserves far faster than an advancing army could march. Another problem was supply. Great efforts had been made to raise vast armies but they couldn't be fed off the land, and once they advanced much beyond the reach of the railways, the supply problems were enormous. As historian A.J.P. Taylor put it, "Defence was mechanized; attack was not".

Seemingly incapable of rethinking military strategy, the generals had no answer to the stalemate except an amazing profligacy with people's lives. Their tactical innovations were limited, and two of the new techniques – gas attack and a heavy prelimimassive square belfry. During winter, wool was stored on the upper floor and cats were brought in to keep the mice down. The cats may have had a good time in winter, but they couldn't have relished the prospect of spring when they were thrown out of the windows to a hostile crowd below as part of the **Kattestoet** or Cats' Death festival, the cruel slaughter intended to symbolize the killing of evil spirits. The festival ran right up until 1817, and was revived in 1938, when the cats were replaced by cloth imitations, and it's since become Ieper's main shindig, held on the second Sunday in May. Every third year, the festival merges into the parade of cats, a large-scale celebration of all things feline, complete with processions, dancers and bands, and some of the biggest models and puppets imaginable.

The east end of the cloth hall is attached to the old **Stadhuis**, whose flamboyant Renaissance facade rises above an elegant arcaded gallery. Inside, on the second floor, the **Salient Museum** (April to mid-Nov daily 9.30am–noon & 1.30–5.30pm; F30) outlines the course and effects of World War I on Ieper. Though a little self-conscious in its efforts to remain neutral, it is, at times, powerful stuff. There's a modest collection of personal memorabilia including the pipe,

nary bombardment – actually made matters worse. The shells forewarned the enemy of an offensive and churned the trenches into a giant muddy quagmire where men, horses and machinery simply sunk without trace; the gas was as dangerous to the advancing soldiers as the retiring enemy. Tanks could have broken the impasse, but their development was never a high priority.

Naturally enough, the soldiers of all the armies involved lost confidence in their generals, and by 1917 – despite the court martials and the firing squads – the sheer futility of the endless round of failed offensives made desertion commonplace and threatened to bring mass mutiny to the western front. It is true that few of the military commanders of the day showed much understanding of how to break the deadlock, and they have been bitterly criticized for their failures. However, some of the blame must be apportioned to the politicians who demanded assault rather than defence, and continued to call for a general "victory" even after it had become obvious that each useless attack cost literally thousands of lives. Every government concerned had believed that a clear victor would emerge by Christmas 1914, and none of them was able to adjust to the new situation – there were no moves for a negotiated settlement, because no one was quite sure what they would settle for – a lack of clarity that contrasted starkly with the jingoistic sentiments stirred up to help sustain the conflict, which demanded victory or at least military success. In this context, how could a general recommend a defensive strategy or a politician propose a compromise? Those who did were dismissed.

This was the background to the four years of war that raged in and around the Ypres salient. There were four major battles. The first, in October and November of 1914, settled the lines of the bulge as both armies tried to outflank each other; the second was a German attack in the following spring that moved the trenches a couple of miles west. The third, launched by British Empire soldiers in July 1917, was even more futile, thousands of men dying for an advance of only a few kilometres. It's frequently called the Battle of Passchendaele, but Lloyd George more accurately referred to it as the "battle of the mud", a disaster that cost 250,000 British lives. The fourth and final battle, in April 1918, was another German attack inspired by Ludendorff's desire to break the British army. Instead it broke his own and led to the Armistice of November 11.

IEPER

binoculars, ink pot, boots and revolver of one Major John Tucket; a number of helmets and rifles; and a pristine "Princess Mary" gift box, one of thousands sent out to British troops for Christmas 1914. Along the walls, some excellent photographs trace the development of the war from the packed British cavalry formations in Ieper on October 13, 1914, to smiling soldiers digging trenches, the pathetic casualties of a gas attack, flyblown corpses in the mud and panoramas of a destroyed Flemish countryside.

Around the back of the cloth hall, the **St Maartens Kathedraal**, built in 1930, is a copy of the thirteenth-century Gothic original, given over to a variety of memorials to the soldiers of World War I. The rose window above the west door is a fine tribute to King Albert I, its yellow, red and blue stained glass the gift of the British armed forces. A few metres northwest, at the near end of Elverdingestraat, the **St George's English Memorial Church** was finished in 1929, a further celebration of military sacrifice, with a font cover dedicated to Sir John French, commander-in-chief of the British army from 1914 to 1915.

A few minutes' walk away, on the far side of the Grote Markt, the **Menin Gate** war memorial was built on the site of the old Menenpoort that served as the main route for British soldiers heading for the front. It's a simple, brooding monument, towering over the edge of the town, its walls covered with the names of those fifty thousand British and Commonwealth troops who died in the Ypres Salient but have no grave. The simple inscription above the lists of dead has none of the arrogance of the victor but rather a sense of great loss, although the futile waste of human life is no less striking, reminiscent of Siegfried Sassoon's comment on the memorial:

Was ever an immolation so belied
As these intolerably nameless names?
Well might the Dead who struggled in slime
Rise and deride this sepulchre of crime.

The Last Post is sounded beneath the gate every evening at about 8pm. Oddly enough, the seventeenth-century town ramparts on either side of the Menin Gate were well enough constructed to survive World War I intact – the vaults even served as some of the safest bunkers on the front.

Practicalities

Ieper's **train** and **bus stations** stand on the western edge of the town centre, a ten-minute walk from the Grote Markt, straight down G. de Stuersstraat. The **tourist office** on the Grote Markt (April–Sept daily 9.30am–5.30pm; Oct–March Mon–Sat 9am–4.30pm, Sun 11am–4pm; ☎057/20 07 24) has good town maps and details of suggested car and cycle routes around the battlefields, cemeteries and monuments that dot the countryside to the east of town, marking the shifting perimeters of the Salient.

As regards **accommodation**, there are no pensions or private rooms, and almost all of Ieper's **hotels** are on or very near the Grote Markt. These include the pleasant *'t Zweerd*, at no. 2 (☎057/20 04 75; ②); the *Old Tom*, no. 8 (☎057/20 15 41; ③); and the *Sultan*, at no. 33 (☎057/20 01 93; ④), as well as the *Hostellerie St Nicolas*, G. de Stuersstraat 6 (☎057/20 06 22; ③). For **food**, the Grote Markt is lined with cafés and restaurants, and the hotels themselves offer some of the best food in town: try the reasonably priced *'t Zweerd*, or the cosy restaurant of the *Hostellerie St Nicolas*. The centrally located *Ter Posterie*, Rijselstraat 57, is also worth a visit for its regional snacks and choice of 140 beers.

Around Ieper: Poperinge and the battlefields

It's surprisingly difficult to find anything within the old **World War I Salient**, east of Ieper, which gives any real impression of the scale and nature of the conflict.

The exception – and it's hardly spectacular – is the **Sanctuary Wood Museum** (daily 10am–7pm; F70), 6km southeast of town, marked off the Ieper–Menen road, near the Canadian memorial on "Hill 62". Inside, the museum holds a ragbag of shells, rifles, bayonets, billycans, and incidental artefacts. Outside, things have been left much as they were the day the war ended, with some primitive zigzags of sand-bagged trench, shell craters and a few shattered trees that give an idea – but not much – of what it was like. If you haven't got your own transport, taking a taxi is the easiest way to get here.

The museum is included in the '14–'18 Route, a seventy-kilometre marked car or bike trip around the northeast section of the Ypres Salient, detailed in a brochure sold by Ieper tourist office. The route passes through the villages of Poelkapelle, Passendale and Zonnebeke, around which the dips and sloping ridges signify what were then vitally important vantage points, many of which cost thousands of lives to capture. However, it's difficult to imagine what it was actually like, and the most resonant reminders of the blood letting are the British cemeteries, immaculately maintained by the Commonwealth War Graves Commission. Each cemetery has a Cross of Sacrifice in white Portland stone, and the graves line up at precisely spaced intervals. Every headstone bears the individual's name, rank, serial number, age, date of decease, and the badge of the branch of the military or corps, or a national emblem, plus an appropriate religious symbol and, at the base, an inscription chosen by relatives. The largest cemetery, Tyne Cot, 2km northeast of Zonnebeke on the road to Passendale (Passchendaele), contains 11,924 graves and a memorial to a further 35,000 whose bodies were never found. Some 10km west of Ieper, at the centre of a hopgrowing area of undulating hills topped by trim, circular woods, POPERINGE was a forward base for soldiers heading in and out of the Ypres Salient. It was here that the Reverend Philip Clayton opened the *Everyman's Club* at Talbot House, Gasthuisstraat 43, where everyone, regardless of rank, was able to come and rest or seek spiritual help. Clayton went on to found Toc H, the worldwide Christian fellowship that took its name from the army signallers' code for Talbot House. The original building is still run as a charity and offers simple, reasonable accommodation – though little remains to remind you of its history.

Kortrijk and around

From Ieper, hourly trains slip south to Comines past a string of spruce war cemeteries around the village of ZILLEBEKE, scene of some of the most bloody fighting of World War I. COMINES is a French-speaking town at the centre of a tiny enclave of the province of Hainaut, a sliver of land backing onto the River Leie, the frontier with France. From here, trains travel on to MENEN, the terminus of the infamous "Menin" road from Ypres, which cut across the Front for almost the entire war, crowded with marching armies at night and swept by shrapnel all day.

Just 7km from the French border, KORTRIJK (Courtrai) is the largest town and main rail junction in this part of West Flanders, tracing its origins to a Roman settlement named *Cortracum*. In the Middle Ages, its fortunes paralleled those of Ypres, but although it became an important centre of the cloth trade, it was far too near France for comfort. Time and again Kortrijk was embroiled in the wars that swept across Flanders, right up to the two German occupations of this century.

The Town

Heavily bombed during World War II, the Grote Markt, at the centre of Kortrijk, is an architecturally incoherent mixture of bits of the old and a lot of the new, surrounding the forlorn, turreted Belfort – all that remains of the medieval cloth hall. The rather grand war memorial at its base is still tended with much care and attention. At the northwest corner of the Grote Markt, the **Stadhuis** (Mon–Fri 9am–noon & 2–5pm; free) is a sedate edifice with modern statues of the counts of Flanders on the facade, above and beside two lines of ugly windows. Inside, there are two fine sixteenth-century chimneypieces: one in the old Aldermen's Hall (*Schepenzaal*) on the ground floor, a delicate, intricate work decorated with coats of arms and carvings of the archdukes of Spain; the other, in the first-floor Council Chamber, a more didactic work, ornamented by three rows of precise statuettes, representing, from top to bottom, the virtues, the vices, and the punishments of hell.

Opposite, by the southeast corner of the Grote Markt, the giant tower of **St Maartenskerk** (usually 8am–noon & 2–5pm; free) is swathed in scaffolding, its fifteenth-century white-stone exterior slowly reappearing from beneath the accumulated grime. The main body of the church is worth a peek for a look at the gilded stone tabernacle, the work of Hendrik Maes in 1585. Immediately to the north, the **Begijnhof**, founded in 1238 by Joanna of Constantinople, preserves the cosy informality of its seventeenth-century houses, overlooked from Groeningestraat, a couple of minutes away, by the **Onze Lieve Vrouwekerk** (normally 10am–noon & 2–6pm). This pushes into the street, a muscular grey structure that once doubled as part of the city's fortifications. In July 1302, the nave of the church was crammed with hundreds of spurs, ripped off the feet of dead and dying French knights – the pathetic remains of the army Philip the Fair had sent to avenge the slaughter of the Bruges Matins earlier that year – at what has become known as the Battle of the Golden Spurs. The two armies, Philip's heavily armoured cavalry and the lightly armed Flemish weavers, had met outside Kortrijk on marshy ground, which the Flemings had disguised with brushwood. Despising their lowly-born adversaries, the French knights made no reconnaissance and fell into the trap, milling around in the mud like cumbersome dinosaurs. They were massacred, victims of their own arrogance, and the battle was a military landmark, the first time an amateur civilian army had defeated professional mail-clad knights. The spurs disappeared long ago and today much of the inside of the church is in a predictable Baroque style, though the Counts' Chapel has an unusual series of rather crude late medieval portraits painted into the wall niches. Nearby, van Dyck's *Raising of the Cross* was one of the artist's last paintings before he went to England.

From the church, an alley cuts through to the River Leie, where the squat twin towers, the **Broeltorens**, are all that remains of the old town walls. On the other side of the bridge, the **Stedelijk Museum**, Broelkaai 6 (Tues–Sun 10am–noon & 2–5pm; free), houses a good selection of locally made lace and damask, a fine sample of eighteenth-century Delftware, and several paintings by a local sixteenth-century artist, Roelandt Savery. His favourite subjects were religious and mythical – a romantic classicism appreciated by his mainly German patrons and represented here by vivid variations on these themes.

Practicalities

The town's **train station** is a five-minute walk south of the Grote Markt; take the second road from the right out of Stationsplein. Before you reach the Grote Markt, the **tourist office** at Schouwburgplein 14 (Mon–Fri 8.30am–5pm; July–Aug also Sat 9.30am–12.30pm & 1.30–4pm, Sun 9.30am–12.30pm; mid-April to mid-Oct also Sat 10am–4pm; July & Aug only, Sun 10am–4pm ☎056/23 93 71) has an **accommodation** list (including a couple of cheap private rooms) and will make bookings on your behalf at no extra charge. Otherwise, there are a couple of convenient, if rather pricy, hotels – the *Groeninge*, near the Onze Lieve Vrouwekerk at Groeningestraat 1a (☎056/22 60 00; ⑥) and the *'t Belfort*, Grote Markt 53 (☎056/22 15 63; ⑤). If you seriously want to splash out, head for the classy *Damies*, Grote Markt 41 (☎056/22 15 47; ⑦).There's a **youth hostel** fifteen minutes' walk north of the station at Passionistenlaan 1a (☎056/20 14 42).

For **food**, try the vegetarian restaurant *Nektar* at St Jansstraat 17 (closed Sun), as well as several good snack bars on the Grote Markt, including the *Kantate* at no. 8, and *Al Garda da Franco*, a pizzeria, at no. 9. There's also tasty food at *Evergreens*, Onze Lieve Vrouwstraat 48, and, more expensively, the *Hotel Damien*'s swish restaurant.

Oudenaarde and around

Some 25km east across the Flanders plain from Kortrijk, the small town of **OUDENAARDE**, literally "old landing place", hugs the banks of the River Scheldt as it twists its way toward Ghent, 30km to the north. Granted a charter in 1193, the town concentrated on cloth manufacture until the late fourteenth century, when its weavers switched to tapestry-making, an industry that made its burghers rich and the town famous, the best products the prized possessions of the kings of France and Spain. Oudenaarde was a key military objective during the religious and dynastic wars of the sixteenth to the eighteenth centuries; time and again it was attacked and besieged, perhaps most famously in July 1708 when the Duke of Marlborough came to the rescue and won a spectacular victory here against the French in the War of the Spanish Succession. With the demise of the tapestry industry in the middle of the eighteenth century, the town became an insignificant backwater, a stagnant place in one of the poorest districts of Flanders. In the last few years, things have improved considerably due to its skilful use of regional development funds, and today's town provides an interesting and pleasant day out.

The Town

Heading into Oudenaarde along Stationsstraat, the middle of the **Tacambaroplein** is taken up by a romantic war memorial that commemorates those who were daft or unscrupulous enough to volunteer to go to Mexico and fight for Maximilian, son-in-law of Leopold I. Unwanted and unloved, Maximilian was imposed on the Mexicans by a French army provided by Napoleon III, who wished to take advantage of the American Civil War to develop a western empire. It was all too fanciful and the occupation rapidly turned into a fiasco. Maximilian paid for the adventure with his life in 1867 and few of his soldiers made the return trip.

The Markt: Stadhuis and Halle
Further south, the wide open space of the **Markt** is edged by the **Stadhuis**, one of the finest examples of Flamboyant Gothic in the country. An exquisite creation of around 1525, its elegantly symmetrical facade spreads out on either side of the

THE OUDENAARDE TAPESTRY INDUSTRY

Tapestry manufacture in Oudenaarde began in the middle of the fifteenth century, an embryonic industry that soon came to be based on a dual system of workshop and outworker, the one with paid employees, the other with payment by results. From the beginning, the town authorities took a keen interest in the business, ensuring its success by a rigorous system of quality control that soon gave the town an international reputation for consistently well-made tapestries. The other side of this interventionist policy was less palatable: wages were kept down and the Guild of the Masters cleverly took over the running of the Guild of Weavers in 1501. To make matters worse, tapestries were by definition a luxury item, and workers were hardly ever able to accumulate enough capital to buy either their own looms or even raw materials.

The first great period of Oudenaarde tapestry-making lasted until the middle of the sixteenth century, when religious conflict overwhelmed the town, its Protestant-inclined weavers coming into direct conflict with their Catholic masters, and many of them migrated north to the rival workshops of Antwerp and Ghent. In 1582 Oudenaarde was finally incorporated into the Spanish Netherlands, precipitating a revival of tapestry production which entered its second great period, with a clearly defined luxury market based around the king and queen of Spain, who were keen to support the industry and passed draconian laws banning the movement of weavers. Later, however, French occupation and the shrinking of the Spanish market led to the contraction of production, and the industry only carried on in much diminished form until 1772.

The technique applied to the production of tapestries was a cross between embroidery and ordinary weaving. It consisted of interlacing a wool weft above and below the strings of a vertical linen "chain", a process similar to weaving. However, the weaver had to stop to change colour, requiring as many shuttles for the weft as he had colours, as in embroidery. The appearance of a tapestry was entirely determined by the weft, the design taken from a painting to which the weaver made constant reference. Standard-size Oudenaarde tapestries took six months to make and were produced exclusively for the very wealthy, the most important of whom would, on occasion, insist on the use of gold and silver thread and the employment of the most famous artists of the day for the preparatory painting – Rubens, Jacob Jordaens and David Teniers all had tapestry commissions. There were only two significant types of tapestry: **decorative**, principally *verdures*, showing scenes of foliage in an almost abstract way (the Oudenaarde speciality), and **pictorial** – usually variations on the same basic themes, particularly rural life, knights, hunting parties and religious scenes. Over the centuries, changes in style were strictly limited, though the early part of the seventeenth century saw an increased use of elaborate woven borders, an appreciation of perspective and the use of a far brighter, more varied range of colours – the consequences of changes in the work of the painters. Oudenaarde tapestries are normally in yellow, brown, pale blue and shades of green, with an occasional splash of red.

extravagant tiers, balconies and parapets of a slender central tower, topped by the gilded figure of a knight, *Hanske de Krijger* (Little John the Warrior). Underneath the knight, the cupola is in the shape of a crown, a theme reinforced by the two groups of cherubs on the triangular windows below, who lovingly clutch at the royal insignia. To the rear of the Stadhuis, the dour and gloomy exterior of the adjoining Romanesque **Lakenhalle** dates from the thirteenth century.

Inside the Stadhuis (Mon–Fri 8.30am–noon & 1.30–5pm; F60) a magnficent oak **doorway** forms the entrance to the old Alderman's Hall. A stylistically influential piece of 1531, the work of a certain Paulwel Vander Schelden, it consists of an intricate sequence of carvings, surmounted by miniature cherubs who frolic above three coats of arms and a 28-panel door, each rectangle a master-piece of precise execution. Of the paintings, the most distinguished are those by Adriaen Brouwer, a native of Oudenaarde, represented by five typically ogre-like representations of the five senses. Beyond, in the Lakenhalle, is a brilliant collec-tion of tapestries, notably the seventeenth-century *verdure, Landscape with Two Pheasants,* with a distant castle framed by an intricate design of trees and plants, whist the early eighteenth-century *verdure, Return from Market,* features trees in shades of blue and green, edged by sky and bare earth – a composition directly reminiscent of Dutch landscape painters.

The rest of the centre

Immediately southwest of the Markt, a couple of minutes' walk from the Stadhuis, the **St Walburgakerk** (visits by prior arrangement with the tourist office) is a decaying mass of masonry desperately in need of restoration, its powerful tower starting to crack and lean precariously. Inside there's a monu-ment to four Catholic priests who in 1572 were thrown into the Scheldt from the windows of Oudenaarde's castle (since demolished). Across the road opposite the church, a group of ancient mansions follow the bend in what was once the line of the town wall, leading around toward the southern end of the Markt, where Burg, and subsequently Kasteelstraat, head south to the river past a trim seventeenth-century **portal**, the entrance to the old Begijnhof. On the first left turn over the bridge, near the end of Kasteelstraat, the **Huis de Lalaing**, Bourgondiestraat 9 (Mon–Fri 9am–noon & 1.15–5pm, Sat 9.30–11.30am; free) is the site of the municipal tapestry repair workshops and museum (Museum van Wandtapijten).

Practicalities

A fifteen-minute walk north of the town centre down Nederstraat and Stationsstraat, the Gothic **train station**, with its chandelier in the hallway and coat of arms on the facade, stands in the shadow of the new fast line from Brussels, whose concrete bridges and raised track look down on this side of town. The **tourist office**, in the Stadhuis (Mon–Fri 8.30am–noon & 1.30–5.30pm, Sat & Sun 10am–noon & 2–5pm; ☎055/31 72 51), has an **accommodation** list, but there are no private rooms and only four central **hotels**. The cheapest is the *Tijl*, Stationsstraat 62 (☎055/3184 88; ②). Otherwise head for the pleasant *De Zalm*, on the northwest corner of the Markt at Hoogstraat 4 (☎055/31 13 14; ④), or *La Pomme d'Or*, nearby at Markt 62 (☎055/31 19 00; ⑤). The nearest **camp-site** is in the holiday complex *Vlaamse Ardennen*, some 2km west of the station: walk north over the train tracks beside the station building, away from town and along Beverestraat; turn left down Kortrijkstraat and it's at no. 342.

For **food**, the restaurant of the *De Zalm* hotel (closed Sun & Mon) serves excellent, affordable meals, as does that of the pricier *La Pomme d'Or*. As ever, the Grote Markt is lined with cafés and bars: try the tasty snacks of the *De Cridts* at no. 58.

Around Oudenaarde: Ronse

Some 15km south of Oudenaarde, the flattened fields of the Flanders plain give way to a ridge of low hills that make up the southwest corner of the province of East Flanders. From high points on some of the hills dotted around the road southeast from Kerkhove there are good views to north and west, but the sobriquet **Vlaamse Ardennen** (Flemish Ardennes), used by local tourist offices, is desperately optimistic.

In the middle of these hills lies the tiny textile town of **RONSE**, whose main claim to fame is the **St Hermeskerk**, a late Gothic edifice near the main town square, a five-minute walk from the train station. The church takes its name from a Roman martyr, Hermes, who was recognized for his skills as an exorcist. His relics were presented to Ronse during the ninth century and became the object of pilgrimages, the "possessed" dragged here from all over the Low Countries in the hope of a miraculous cure. Today, the rusted iron rings in a bench near the altar are reminders of the times when those considered insane were chained up waiting for exorcism, while the reliquary of St Hermes is in the chapel on the south side of the choir.

Bruges and around

"Somewhere within the dingy casing lay the ancient city", wrote Graham Greene of **BRUGES**, "like a notorious jewel, too stared at, talked of, trafficked over". And it's true that Bruges' (justified) reputation as one of the most perfectly preserved medieval cities in western Europe has made it the most popular tourist destination in Belgium, packed with visitors throughout the summer season. Inevitably, the crowds tend to overwhelm the town, but you would be mad to come to Flanders and miss the place: its museums, to name just one attraction, hold some of the country's finest collections of Flemish art; and its intimate, winding streets, woven around a pattern of narrow canals and lined with gorgeous ancient buildings, live up to even the most inflated tourist hype. See it out of season, or in the early morning before the hordes have descended, and it can be memorable.

> The Bruges area telephone code is ☎050

Some history

Bruges originated from a ninth-century fortress built by the warlike first count of Flanders, Baldwin Iron Arm, designed to defend the Flemish coast from Norman attack. The settlement prospered, and by the fourteenth century it shared effective control of the cloth trade with its two great rivals, Ghent and Ypres, turning high-quality English wool into thousands of items of clothing that were exported all over the known world. It was an immensely profitable business that made the city a centre of international trade: at its height, the town was a key member of – and showcase for – the products of the Hanseatic League, the most powerful economic alliance in medieval Europe. Through the harbours and docks of Bruges, Flemish cloth and Hansa goods were exchanged for hogs from

BRUGES

500 m

0

To the Youth Hostel

BARON RUZETTELAAN

BUITEN KAZERNEVEST

BUITEN GENTPOORTVEST

BUITEN KATELIJNEVEST

BUITEN SONINGEST

COUPURE

COUPURE

Koningin
Astridpark

NIEUWE GENTWEG

OUDE GENTWEG

KATELIJNE STRAAT

KATELIJNEVEST

Minnewater
Park

Minnewater

KRUISVEST

BUITEN BEGIJNENVEST

Tourist
Office

Brugge Vrije

Vismarkt

Post
Office

Stadhuis

Groeningemuseum

Brangwijnmuseum

Gruuthuse
museum

Halle en
Belfort

PHILIPSTOCKSTRAAT

HOOGSTR

BURG

BREIDEL-STR.

BRIDEL-STR.

BUR. GEESTE

KOLLETTRAAT

BLINDE

ENTLE

WOLLESTRAAT

MALLESTRAAT

MARKT

NIEUWSTRAAT

DIJVER

O. L.
Vrouwkerk

MARIA STRAAT

WALPLEIN

St-Jans Hospital

Memlingmuseum

STEENSTRAAT

SINT AMANDSSTR

HEILIGE GEESTER

ST. JAKOBSSTR.

GELDMUNTSTR

ZUIDZANDSTRAAT

GEERWIJN

EIERMARKT

WESTMEERS

OOSTMEERS

KORTE VULGERE

EZELSTRAAT

Sint-Salvator
Kathedraal

Begijnhof

MAGDALEEN

HENDRIK CONSCIENCELAAN

KONING ALBERTLAAN

STATIONSPLEIN

Railway
Station

Bus Station

HOFFIJZER LAAN

NIEUWE GENTWEG

SINGEL

To Camping
St. Michiel

Denmark, spices from Venice, hides from Ireland, wax from Russia, gold and silver from Poland and furs from Bulgaria. The business of these foreign traders was protected by no fewer than 21 consulates, and the city developed a wide range of support services, including banking, money-changing, maritime insurance and an elementary shipping code, known as the *Roles de Damme*.

Despite – or perhaps because of – this lucrative state of affairs, Bruges was dogged by war. Its weavers and merchants were dependent on the goodwill of the kings of England for the proper functioning of the wool trade, but their feudal overlords, the counts of Flanders and their successors the dukes of Burgundy, were vassals of the king of France. Although some of the dukes and counts were strong enough to defy their king, most felt obliged to obey his orders and thus take his side against the English when the two countries were at war. This conflict of interests was compounded by the designs the French kings had on the independence of Bruges itself, leading to a series of disturbances in the city, the most famous of which, at the beginning of the fourteenth century, took place when Philip the Fair of France attempted to incorporate the towns of west Flanders into his kingdom. He and his wife, Joanna of Navarre, held a grand reception in Bruges, but both clearly felt uneasy in the face of the city's splendour: "I thought", said Joanna, "that I alone was Queen; but here in this place I have six hundred rivals". Their misgivings were confirmed a few weeks later when the town's guildsmen flatly refused to pay a new round of taxes. Enraged, Philip dispatched an army to restore order and garrison the town, but at dawn on Friday, May 18, 1302, a rebellious force of Flemings crept into the city and massacred Philip's sleepy army – an occasion later known as the **Bruges Matins**. Anyone who couldn't correctly pronounce the Flemish shibboleth *schild en vriend* ("shield and friend") was put to the sword.

By the end of the fifteenth century, Bruges was in decline, partly because of a general recession in the cloth trade, but principally because of the silting of the River Zwin – the city's trading lifeline. By the 1490s, the stretch of water between Sluis and Damme was only navigable by smaller ships, and by the 1530s the town's sea trade had collapsed completely. Bruges simply withered away, its houses deserted, its canals empty and its money shifted north with the merchants.

Georges Rodenbach's novel *Bruges-la-Morte* alerted wealthy nineteenth-century Europeans to its aged, quiet charms, and Bruges – frozen in time – escaped damage in both world wars to emerge a perfect tourist attraction.

Arrival, information and accommodation

Bruges **train station** adjoins the **bus station** about 2km southwest of the town centre. At the station, there's an **information desk** and **hotel booking** service (Mon–Fri 7am–7pm; March–Sept also Sat 8.30am–6.30pm, closes 5.30pm in winter; July & Aug Sun 8.30am–6.30pm, closes 5.30pm rest of the year; ☎38 24 06), which will make bookings on your behalf at no charge, though they do require a deposit of F400 – deducted from your final bill. If the twenty-minute walk into town doesn't appeal to you, most of the local buses that leave from outside the station building head into the Markt, bang in the centre, where the **tourist office**, a couple of minutes' walk from the Markt at Burg 11 (April–Sept Mon–Fri 9.30am–6.30pm, Sat & Sun 10am–noon & 2–6.30pm; Oct–March Mon–

Fri 9.30am–5pm, Sat 9.30am–12.45pm & 2–5.45pm; ☎44 86 86), provides a similar accommodation service and currency exchange, and has useful maps for F20, suggestions for cycle trips in the surrounding countryside, and a useful, compli-mentary *Agenda Brugge*, which contains details of all current events and perfor-mances. Local bus timetables are displayed on the walls near the entrance.

Hostels

There are several conveniently situated **unofficial youth hostels** with dormitory beds at F300–400 per person per night, most of which also have a limited supply of smaller rooms at about F1000 for a double per night. These include the *Bauhaus International Youth Hotel*, fifteen minutes' walk east of the Burg at Langestraat 135 (☎34 10 93); *Kilroy's Garden*, west of the Markt at Singel 12 (☎38 93 82); and *Bruno's Passage*, on the same side of town at Dweersstraat 26 (☎34 02 32). There's an **official youth hostel** 2km south of the centre at Baron Ruzettelaan 143 (☎35 26 79) – bus #2 goes right there. The nearest **campsite**, *St Michiel*, is near the motorway 3km southwest of the train station at Tillegemstraat 55 (☎38 08 19): take bus #7 and get off at the junction of St Michielslaan and Rijselstraat; head west from here along Jagerstraat and take the left turn under the motorway, which brings you onto Tillegemstraat.

Hotels

Bruges has over one hundred **hotels** and a smattering of **pensions**, but still can't accommodate all its visitors. If you're arriving in late July or August, make sure you get here in the morning, before all the rooms have gone. There's a cluster of cheap, fairly basic hotels west of the town centre around the square called 't Zand, but this is the dreariest part of Bruges and you're better off paying a little more to stay near the two central squares, Markt and Burg. Accommodation is generally of a high standard, though prices are higher in Bruges than the rest of the country. Also, you shouldn't put too much store by the hotel foyers: hoteliers are wont to deck them out grandly, often in contrast to the spartan rooms beyond.

Aarendshuis, Hoogstraat 18, (☎33 78 89). Spacious doubles in a handsome old mansion east of Burg. Ask for a room at the back, as Hoogstraat can be noisy. ④

Adornes, St Annarei 26 (☎34 13 36). Comfortable rooms in a nicely located hotel at the junc-tion of 2 canals. ⑤

Bourgoensch Hof, Wollestraat 39 (☎33 16 45). Accommodation in a lavishly renovated medieval building backing onto the canal behind the Burg. ⑥; rooms overlooking the canal ⑦–⑧.

Cordbeanier, Cordbeaniersstraat 16 (☎33 90 51). Agreeable hotel on a side street a couple of minutes north of the Burg. ④.

Europ, Augustijnenrei 18 (☎33 79 75). A grand, canal-side eighteenth-century villa 5 minutes' walk north of the Burg. ⑥.

Het Geesterlijk Hof, Heilige-Geeststraat 2 (☎34 25 94). Pleasant, well-cared for pension in the shadow of the Kathedraal St Salvador. No single rooms. ③.

't Keizershof, Oostmeers 126 (☎33 87 28). Simple rooms in a modern brown brick building on the way from the train station and the centre. ②.

Lybeer, Korte Vuldersstraat 31 (☎33 43 55). Cramped tenement with poky rooms just off 't Zand. ③.

Relai Oud Huis Amsterdam, Spiegelrei 3 (☎34 18 10). Magnficent, tastefully furnished hotel in an eighteenth-century mansion overlooking the Spiegelrei canal. ⑦.

't Roosterhuys, 't Zand 13 (☎33 30 35). Clean and basic hotel in a good central location. ③.

't Speelsmanshuys, 't Zand 3 (☎33 95 52). Frugal rooms popular with mosquitos from the canal alongside. ③.

The city centre

In 1896 Arnold Bennett moaned "The difference between Bruges and other cities is that in the latter you look about for the picturesque, while in Bruges, assailed on every side by the picturesque, you look curiously for the unpicturesque, and don't find it easily". Perhaps so, but a fair slice of Bruges is not quite what it seems, the pretty little bridge beside the Onze Lieve Vrouwekerk is nineteenth century; the carved wood facades behind the Halle are from the 1950s; and the Beguines are Benedictine nuns in habits. Bruges has spent time and money preserving its image, and although the bulk of the buildings are genuine enough, sometimes it can resemble nothing so much as a medieval theme park.

The Markt

A twenty-minute walk northeast of the main train and bus stations, the older sections of Bruges fan out from two interlocking central squares, the Markt and the Burg. The **Markt**, edged on three sides by rows of gabled buildings, is the larger of the two, an impressive open space, although something of a cross between a traffic junction and a car park. On the south side, the **Belfry** (April– Sept daily 9.30am–5pm; Oct–March daily 9.30am–12.30pm & 1.30–5pm; F100), built in the thirteenth century when the town was at its richest and most extravagant, is a potent symbol of civic pride and municipal independence, its distinctive octagonal lantern visible for miles across the surrounding polders. Inside, the belfry staircase passes the room where the town charters were locked for safe keeping and an eighteenth-century carillon, before emerging onto the roof. It's well worth the haul up for the view, especially in the late afternoon when the warm colours of the town are at their deepest. At the foot of the belfry, the **Halle** is a much restored edifice dating from the thirteenth century, its style and structure modelled on the Lakenhalle at Ieper. In the middle, a rectangular courtyard is overlooked by a line of long galleries and was the location of the town's principal market, its cobblestone space once crammed with merchants and their wares.

A few metres away, at the centre of the Markt, there's a late nineteenth-century **monument** to the leaders of the Bruges Matins, Peter de Coninck of the Guild of Weavers and John Breidel, dean of the Guild of Butchers. Standing close together, they clutch the hilt of the same sword, their faces turned to the west in slightly absurd poses of heroic determination. There's no other building of note in the Markt, but the *Craenenburg* café, on the corner of St Amandsstraat at

Markt 16, is built on the site of the medieval mansion in which the Hapsburg heir, Archduke Maximilian, was imprisoned by the burghers of Bruges for three months in 1488. The reason for the argument was the archduke's efforts to limit the city's privileges, but whatever the justice of their cause, the burghers made a big mistake. Maximilian became emperor in 1493, and although he never actually attacked the town, he never forgave its people either, doing his best to push trade north to their great rival, Antwerp.

The Burg

From beside the neo-Gothic post office on the Markt, Breidelstraat leads through to the **Burg**, whose southern half is fringed by the city's finest group of buildings. One of the best of these is the **Heilig Bloed Basiliek** (Basilica of the Holy Blood; April–Sept daily 9.30am–noon & 2–6pm; Oct–March daily 10am–noon & 2–4pm; free) on the right, named after the holy relic that found its way here in 1150. The church divides into two parts. Tucked away in a corner, the **Lower Chapel** is a shadowy, crypt-like affair, originally built at the beginning of the twelfth century to house another relic, that of Saint Basil, one of the great figures of the early Greek Church. The chapel's heavy, simple Romanesque lines are decorated with just one carved relief, set above an interior doorway – a representation of the baptism of Basil, a strange giant bird depicting the Holy Spirit, plunging into a pool of water. Next door, approached by a wide staircase, the **Upper Chapel** was built at the same time but has been renovated so frequently that it's impossible to make out the original structure, while the inside has been spoiled by excessively rich nineteenth-century decoration. In a side chapel, the rock crystal phial of the Holy Blood is stored within a grandiose silver **tabernacle**, the gift of the archdukes of Spain in 1611. One of the holiest relics in medieval Europe, the phial purports to contain a few drops of blood and water washed from the body of Christ by Joseph of Arimathea. It was the gift of Diederik d'Alsace, a Flemish knight who distinguished himself by his bravery during the Second Crusade and was given the phial by a grateful patriarch of Jerusalem. After several weeks in Bruges, the relic was found to be dry, but soon after it proceeded to liquefy every Friday at 6pm until 1325, a miracle attested by all sorts of church dignitaries, including Pope Clement V. The Holy Blood is still venerated in the Upper Chapel on Fridays at 6pm, and despite modern scepticism, reverence for it remains strong, not least on Ascension Day when it is carried through the town in a colourful but solemn procession, the *Helig-Bloedprocessie*.

The tiny **Treasury** (April–Sept 9.30am–noon & 2–6pm; Oct–March 10am–noon & 2–4pm; F40) is home to an extravagant gold and silver reliquary that holds the Holy Blood during the procession. Near the entrance, the faded strands of a seventeenth-century, locally woven tapestry depict Saint Augustine's funeral, the sea of helmeted heads and pikes that surround the monks and abbots very much a Catholic view of a muscular state supporting a holy Church.

Just to the left of the basilica, the **Stadhuis** has a beautiful, turreted sandstone facade, a much-copied exterior that dates from 1376 – though its sequence of statues (of the counts and countesses of Flanders) is a 1960s replacement of one destroyed by the occupying French army in 1792. Inside on the second floor, the Gothic Hall of 1400 (April–Sept daily 9.30am–5pm; Oct–March daily 9.30am–noon & 2–5pm; F60) was the magnificent setting for the first meeting of the States General in 1464. The ceiling has been restored in a vibrant mixture of maroon, dark brown, black and gold, dripping pendant arches like decorated stalactites.

The ribs of the arches converge in twelve tiny circular vault-keys, picturing scenes from the New Testament, while below they're supported by sixteen gilded corbels, representing the months and elements. The paintings around the walls were commissioned in 1895 to illustrate the history of the town, and an adjoining room has a modest display of incidental artefacts, including coins, seals and information on the modernization of the town's harbour facilities at the turn of the century.

Next door to the Stadhuis, the **Oude Griffie** (no admission) was built to house the municipal records office in 1537, its elegant facade decorated with Renaissance columns and friezes superimposed on the Gothic lines of the gables below. To the immediate left, the **Bruges Vrije Museum** (Tues–Sun 10am–noon & 1.30–5pm; F20) has just one exhibit, an enormous marble and oak **chimneypiece** located in the province's old Schepenzaal (Magistrates' Hall), the only room to have survived from the original fifteenth-century palace. A fine example of Renaissance carving, the chimneypiece was completed in 1531 under the direction of Lancelot Blondeel, to celebrate the defeat of the French at Pavia in 1525 and the advantageous Treaty of Cambrai that followed. A paean of praise to the Hapsburgs, the work is dominated by figures of the Emperor Charles V and his Austrian and Spanish relatives, each person identified by the diagram in front of the chimneypiece, although the most outstanding features are the three large codpieces. Adjoining the Bruges Vrije, the drab courtyard complex of the **Gerechtshof** (Law Courts) dates from 1722 and houses the tourist office, while just north of here the new *Holiday Inn* stands on the site of the Cathedral of St Donatian, destroyed by the French at the end of the eighteenth century.

Along the Dijver

From the arch beside the Oude Griffie, Blinde Ezelstraat (Blind Donkey Street) leads south across the canal to the eighteenth-century Doric colonnades of the **Vismarkt**, beyond which the huddle of picturesque houses that make up the **Huidevettersplaat** hold some of the most popular drinking and eating places in town. Nearby, the **Dijver** begins by the bridge at the bottom of Wollestraat, which is overseen by a statue of the patron saint of bridges, **Saint John Nepomuk**, who is reputed to have been thrown into a Bohemian river for refusing to reveal the confessional secrets of the consort of King Wenceslas IV. From here, the Dijver – scene of a busy weekend flea market – tracks along the canal as far as Nieuwestraat, passing opposite the path to the first of the city's main museums, the Groeninge.

The Groeninge Museum

The **Groeninge Museum** at Dijver 12 (April–Sept daily 9.30am–5pm; Oct–March daily except Tues 9.30am–12.30pm & 2–5pm; F130) houses the city's art collection, a superb sample of Flemish paintings from the fourteenth to the twentieth centuries. The exhibits are well displayed in a series of small, connecting rooms, and although they are only labelled in Flemish, further information is available in the multilingual pamphlets on sale at the reception desk; there are also clear plans of the place laid out by the entrance. The Groeninge doesn't have enough room to display all its paintings at one time, so lesser works are rotated, though the kernel of the collection, the early paintings in rooms 1–6, remains fairly constant.

The museum's best section is without question the one holding **early Flemish paintings**, among which there are several by Jan van Eyck, who lived and worked in Bruges from 1430 until his death eleven years later. Arguably the greatest of the early Flemish masters, he was a key figure in the development of oil painting, modulating its tones to create paintings of extraordinary clarity and realism, good examples being the fine miniature *Portrait of Margareta van Eyck* and the *Madonna with Canon George van der Paele*, a glowing and richly analytical work with three figures surrounding the Madonna: the kneeling canon, Saint George, his patron saint, and Saint Donatian, to whom he is being presented. Though the work is full of symbolic minutiae it's the luminous, fastidious detail that impresses; to those who saw it in the fifteenth century the portraiture must have seemed miraculous, the Virgin as real as the palpably human canon. In St George's armour you can just make out the reflection of a man, presumably van Eyck himself, observing the scene, a similar statement of presence to the mirror reflection in his famous *Arnolfini Marriage* in London's National Gallery.

Nearby, there are two fascinating matching panels of *The Legend of St Ursula*, completed in the middle of the fifteenth century by an unknown artist known as the "Master of the Ursula Legend". The panels were probably inspired by the discovery in Cologne a couple of centuries earlier of the supposed bones of the nuns massacred with St Ursula – a medieval sensation that would certainly have been known about in Bruges. Look also at the *Judgement of Cambyses*, a painting by Gerard David on two oak panels that was hung in the town hall by the city burghers as a sort of public apology for the imprisonment of Archduke Maximilian here in 1488. The painting is based on a story told of the Persian court by Herodotus, and in the first panel the corrupt judge, Sisamnes, is sentenced to be flayed alive; in the gruesome second panel the judgement is carried out by the king's servants, who apply themselves to the task with a clinical detachment. Nearby, the *Baptism of Christ* is a later work by the same artist, depicting a boyish, partly bearded Christ as part of the Holy Trinity, which forms the symmetrical heart of the painting.

There's also work by Hieronymus Bosch, his *Last Judgement*, a trio of oak panels crammed with mysterious beasts, microscopic mutants and scenes of awful cruelty – men boiled in a pit or cut in half by a giant knife. It looks like unbridled fantasy, but the fact is that the scenes were read as symbols, each tiny cameo understood as a sort of strip cartoon of legend, proverb and tradition. Indeed Bosch's religious orthodoxy is confirmed by the appeal his work had for that most Catholic of Spanish kings, Philip II.

There's more grim symbolism in Jan Provost's striking *The Miser and Death*, the merchant with his money on one panel, trying desperately to pass a promissory note to the grinning skeleton on the next. Other highlights include the riotous violence of the unattributed *Scenes of the Legend of St George*; the *Moreel Triptych* by Hans Memling, where the general formality of the scene is offset by some gentle individual acts – the priest stroking the fawn, the knight's hand on a neighbouring shoulder; and two paintings in imitation of lost works by Rogier van der Weyden, a tiny *Portrait of Philip the Good*, the sombre cloak balanced by the brightness of the hatpin and necklace, and the almost impudent smile of the baby Christ in *St Luke painting the Virgin*.

The museum's selection of **seventeenth-century paintings** is far more modest, though there's a delightfully naturalistic *Peasant Lawyer* after Pieter

A combination ticket for Bruges' central museums, the Groeninge, Brangwyn, Gruuthuse and Memling, is available from any of the four and costs F350.

Brueghel the Younger; a couple of muted riverscapes by Jan van Goyen; and a *Country Scene* by Aelbert Cuyp. The **modern paintings**, too, aren't exactly engaging, but look out for Jean Delville's enormous and weird *De Godmens*, a repulsive, though compelling picture of writhing bodies striving for Christ's salvation; the harsh surrealism of Paul Delvaux's *Serenity*; a lively *Birdspark* painted in 1918 by James Ensor; and the charcoal on paper *Angelus* by Constant Permeke – a typically dark and earthy representation of Belgian peasant life dated 1934.

The Brangwyn and Gruuthuse museums
Further along Dijver, at no. 17, the **Gruuthuse Museum** (April–Sept daily 9.30am–5pm; Oct–March daily except Tues 9.30am–12.30pm & 2–5pm; F130) occupies a rambling fifteenth-century mansion, a fine example of civil Gothic architecture which takes its name from the owners' historical right to tax the *gruut*, the fermented barley used in brewing beer. The mansion's ancient beams and chimneypieces frame a varied collection of fine and applied art, well laid out in a series of clearly numbered rooms. The exhibits are only labelled in Flemish, but, if you're feeling flush, a detailed guidebook is available at the reception desk for F595. Of the range of material on display, there are good samples of old Flemish lace, musical instruments, sixteenth- and seventeenth-century pictorial tapestries, and many different types of furniture. Most intriguing of all is an oak-panelled chapel of 1472, which juts out from the second floor of the museum to overlook the high altar of the cathedral next door. A curiously intimate room, the low, rounded ceiling is partly decorated with simple floral tracery, its corbels cut in the form of tiny angels.

Almost next door, the **Brangwyn Museum**, Dijver 16 (same times; F80), has a dull display of paintings, plates, pots and pewter, but is worth visiting if you're interested in the work of Sir Frank Brangwyn, a Welsh artist born in Bruges who donated this sample of his work to the town in 1936. A specialist in giant murals (the best of which are in the Royal Exchange and Lloyd's Registry in London), there's a large collection of his moody etchings, studies and paintings here.

The Onze Lieve Vrouwekerk
Also on the Dijver, next door to the Gruuthuse, the **Onze Lieve Vrouwekerk** (April–Sept Mon–Sat 10–11.30am & 2.30–5pm, Sun 2.30–5pm; Oct–March Mon–Sat 10–11.30am & 2.30–4.30pm, Sun 2.30–4.30pm; free) is a massive shambles of a building of different dates and different styles, whose bleak spire is the tallest in Holland and Belgium. Of the accumulated treasures inside, the most famous is a delicate marble *Madonna and Child* by Michelangelo, an early work which seems sadly out of place at the centre of an eighteenth-century altar, beneath the cold stone walls of the south aisle. Brought from Tuscany by a Flemish merchant living in Bruges, it was the only work to leave Italy during the artist's lifetime and had a significant influence on the painters working here at the beginning of the sixteenth century.

There's a small charge to enter the choir and ambulatory, where the **mauso-leums** of Charles the Bold and his daughter Mary of Burgundy are fine illustrations of Renaissance carving, the panels decorated with coats of arms connected by the most intricate of floral designs. On top, the royal figures are enhanced by tiny details which give a sense of familiarity, from the helmet and gloves placed gracefully by the side of Charles to the pair of dogs by Mary's feet. The earth beneath the mausoleums has been dug up and a couple of mirrors now reveal the original frescoes, painted on the tomb walls at the start of the sixteenth century. Both Mary and Charles died in unfortunate circumstances, she after a riding accident in 1482, when she was only 25, Charles during the siege of Nancy in 1477 – indeed there is some argument as to whether this is the body of Charles at all, since identification was, apparently, difficult. The body was buried in Nancy, but eighty years later Charles V had it exhumed for a more suitable burial in Bruges.

St Jans Hospitaal: the Memling Collection

Opposite the entrance to Onze Lieve Vrouwekerk, **St Jans Hospitaal** is a six hundred-year-old complex used as an infirmary until the nineteenth century. Towards the rear, the main body of the hospital has been turned into the sleek exhibition and visitors' centre of **Oude St-Jan** (daily 10am–6pm); to the front there's a well-preserved seventeenth-century dispensary as well as a number of partly furnished meeting rooms and old wards. Next door, the old hospital church now houses the small but important **Hans Memling** collection (April–Sept daily 9.30am–5pm; Oct–March daily except Wed 9.30am–12.30pm & 2–5pm; F130).

Born near Frankfurt in 1433, Hans Memling spent most of his working life in Bruges, where he was taught by Rogier van der Weyden – whose themes he often borrowed. Of the six works on display, the *Mystical Marriage of St Catherine* forms the middle panel of an altarpiece painted for the hospital church between 1475 and 1479. Graceful and warmly coloured, its gently formal symmetry is in the Eyckian realist tradition. Memling's figures here – and elsewhere – bear grave and pious faces, and have a velvet-like quality that greatly appealed to the city's burghers. Indeed, their enthusiasm made Memling a rich man – in 1480 he was listed among the town's major moneylenders. Nearby, the *Reliquary of St Ursula* is an unusual and lovely piece of work, a miniature wooden Gothic church painted with the story of St Ursula and the eleven thousand martyred virgins. Memling accepted the rather unpopular theory that the number of virgins had been erroneously multiplied by a thousand somewhere along the line, and his six panels show Ursula and ten companions on their way to Rome, only to be massacred by Huns as they passed through Germany. It's the mass of incidental detail that makes the reliquary so enchanting – the tiny ships, figures and churches in the background exhaustively depicting the late medieval world.

The Kathedraal St Salvator

Just to the north of the entrance to St Jans Hospitaal, Heilige Geeststraat heads northwest to the **Kathedraal St Salvator** (currently closed for renovation, but usually open April–Sept Mon–Sat 10am–noon & 2–5pm, Sun 3–5pm, closed Wed; Oct–March Mon–Sat 2–5pm, closed Wed; free, museum F40), a replacement for the city-centre cathedral that was destroyed by the French in the eighteenth century. Its spartan, undecorated interior is similar to that of the Onze Lieve Vrouwekerk, though its graceful Gothic proportions are more appealing. The thirteenth-century choir is the oldest part of the interior, worth a quick glance for its stalls, whose misericords are decorated with delightful scenes of everyday life. Many of the city-centre cathedral's treasures were moved here following its destruction, some of which are on display in the cathedral **museum**, notably a vividly realistic triptych by Dieric Bouts and Hugo van der Goes entitled *The Martyrdom of St Hippolytus.*

South of the city centre

From outside the Onze Lieve Vrouwekerk, Mariastraat runs south past turns marked to the **Begijnhof** (daily 9am–6pm), a rough circle of whitewashed houses that surround a tidy green. The best time to visit is in spring, when a carpet of daffodils springs up between the wispy elms, creating one of the most photographed sights in Bruges. The streets around the Begijnhof have kept their seventeenth-century design, but the simple terraced houses now contain dozens of restaurants and bars. To the immediate south of the Begijnhof, the picturesque **Minnewater** is another popular spot, edged by a fifteenth-century lock gate, a reminder of the lake's earlier use as a town harbour.

North and east of the city centre

A five-minute walk northeast of the belfry, **Jan van Eyckplein** stands at the western edge of a canal that once ran as far as the Markt. This was at one time Bruges' busiest harbour, with the trade missions of some 21 countries and towns spread out around the Spiegelrei; today the series of uncrowded streets in the vicinity of the Spiegelrei canal and around nearby St Annarei are some of the most charming in Bruges, classically picturesque terraces dating from the town's golden age, enriched by the grandest of eighteenth-century mansions. The square itself is edged by the elegant facade of the fourteenth-century **Poorters Loge**, where the most powerful of the town's merchants met, opposite the slim fifteenth-century **Tolhuis**, decorated with the coat of arms of the dukes of Luxembourg, who levied tolls here. Next door is the tiny old **guild house** of the stevedores. Further afield, to the east, the **Jeruzalemkerk**, on Balstraat (Mon–Sat 10am–noon & 2–6pm; free), is not the grandest but is perhaps the most likable of the town's churches, built by the Adornes family in the fifteenth century as a copy of the church of the Holy Sepulchre in Jerusalem. Anselm Adornes, son of the church's founder, was executed in Scotland for spying, but his heart was returned to Bruges and buried here. You can see his portrait in the windows of the church, which was until very recently still owned by his descendants. A few metres to the north, the **Kantcentrum** (Lace Centre; same times) is situated in the almshouses sponsored by the same family. Inside, there's a modest display of different sorts of traditional Belgian lace and a couple of workshops. The **Museum voor Volkskunde** (April–Sept daily 9.30am–5pm; Oct–March daily except Tues 9.30am–12.30pm & 2–5pm; F80), around the corner at Rolweg 40, has more lace, some period interiors, and a miscellany of everyday objects.

Still further east, the **Schuttersgild St Sebastian**, Carmersstraat 174 (Archers' Guild house; Mon, Wed, Fri & Sat 10am–noon & 2–5pm; F40), dates from the middle of the sixteenth century and has records of the guild alongside precious gold and silver trophies. The **De Potterie Museum**, at the northeastern end of Potterierei (April–Sept daily 9.30am–noon & 12.45–5pm; Oct–March daily except Wed 9.30am–12.30pm & 2–5pm; F60), consists of a chapel and a small museum in an old people's home. The main highlights are some delightful fifteenth- and sixteenth-century pictorial tapestries hung in the chapel aisles.

Eating

Most of the restaurants in Bruges are aimed at tourists and tend to be pricy, although, if you avoid the plusher bistros, there are still lots of places dotted around the centre of town where you can get good, filling, reasonably priced meals. In particular, there are cheap meals on offer at most of the youth accommodations, best of which are those served up by the *Bauhaus International Youth Hotel*, Langestraat 135. For **snacks**, the fish shops that line the Vismarkt are a good bet, with delicious prepared specialities for around F200; the *Selfi* cafeteria, Steenstraat 58, is another good alternative for cheap eats.

Central, Markt 30 (☎33 18 05). One of the most popular of the many café-restaurants lining the Markt.

Taverne Curiosa, Vlamingstraat 22 (☎34 23 34). Lively bar-restaurant serving light snacks along with more substantial meals. Good smoked fish and regional specialities, and a wide-ranging beer menu to wash it down.

La Dentellière, Wijngaardstraat (☎33 18 98). The most agreeable of the somewhat over-priced restaurants around the Minnewater. Specializes in regional dishes and steaks.

Koffieboontje, Hallestraat 4 (☎33 80 27). Unpretentious hotel restaurant serving good veggie snacks.

Malpertuus, Eiermarkt 9 (☎33 30 38). Generally excellent restaurant that cooks up a fine *waterzooi*. Closed Thurs.

't Mozarthuys, Huidenvettersplein 1 (☎33 45 30). Inevitably crowded centrally-located pasta restaurant with outside tables in summer. Closed Mon.

Raspoetin, St Amandsstraat 6, off the Markt (☎33 30 36). Intimate family-run restaurant serving a superb range of regional Belgian and French cuisine at reasonable prices. Closed Tues.

Staminée de Garre, De Garre 1 (☎34 10 29). Down an alley off Breidelstraat between the Markt and the Burg, this delightful cosy café-bar has a good range of Belgian beers and delicious filling snacks and sandwiches.

Hotel de Tassche, Oude Burg 11 (☎33 03 19). Plush, expensive restaurant specializing in steaks.

't Traptje, Wollestraat 39 (☎33 89 18). Excellent, if expensive Flemish cuisine in a restaurant overlooking the main canal.

De Visscherie, Vismarkt 8 (☎33 02 12). Extremely expensive seafood restaurant, not least because the ethos is minimalist, and you may leave with your tastebuds more satisfied than your stomach. Closed Tues.

Zen, Beenhouwersstraat 117, a 10min walk west of the Markt (☎33 67 02). Reasonably priced vegetarian food, though it closes early – at 8.30pm. Closed Sun.

Drinking

Most visitors to Bruges **drink** where they eat, but there are lots of decent bars in and around the town centre and it would be a shame not to try one or two. The *Uilenspiegel* hotel bar, at the city centre end of Langestraat, is a lovely place for an early evening tipple, with its terrace overlooking the canal. *'t Brugs Beertje*, Kemelstraat 5, is also worth a few hours of your time, a friendly speciality beer café that claims a stock of three hundred ales. If you're fed up with beer, head for *'t Dreupelhuisje* (closed Tues) further along Kemelstraat at no. 19, which specializes in genevers and advocaats. Across the street, *De Hobbit*, at no. 8 (closed Mon & Tues) has live music, as does *De Verste Endenacht*, Hoogstraat 71. Finally, there's a lively, convivial bar at the *Bauhaus* youth hostel.

Listings

Bike rental Available at standard rates from the train station, or for F250 a day and F850 a week from *Popelier*, Hallestraat 14 (☎34 32 62), or the *Koffieboontje* hotel, Hallestraat 4 (☎33 80 27).

Books A good range of English titles at *De Reyghere*, Markt 12.

Bureaux de change Outside banking hours you can change money at the station (April–Oct Mon 9am–noon & 1–3pm, Wed & Thurs 8am–12.30pm & 2–6pm, Fri 7am–7pm, Sat 10.30am–3pm, closed Tues).

Hospital St Franciscus-Xavieriuskliniek, Spaanse Loskaai (☎33 98 01).

Left luggage At the station, daily 5am–midnight.

Markets General markets on the Burg (Wed 7am–1pm) and on 't Zand (Sat 7am–1pm). Flea markets along Dijver (Sat & Sun afternoons from March to Oct).

Medical emergencies ☎100. Weekend doctors (Fri 8pm–Mon 8am) ☎81 38 99.

Music Details of concerts and performances in *Agenda Brugge*, free from the tourist office.

Police ☎101.

Post office Markt 5 (Mon–Fri 9am–5pm, Sat 9am–noon).

Public transport Train details on ☎38 23 82; bus details on ☎35 31 43.

Taxis From the Markt (☎33 44 44) and Stationsplein (☎38 46 60).

Around Bruges: Damme

Originally Bruges' main port, the trim village of **DAMME**, 7km northeast of the town, was once a hectic, fortified harbour. It stood on the banks of the River Zwin, which gave direct access to the sea until it silted up in the late fifteenth century, and at its height had a population of ten thousand. It was the site of the marriage of Charles the Bold and Margaret of York, and the scene of a famous naval engagement on June 24, 1340. In the summer of that year, a French fleet assembled in the estuary of the Zwin to prepare for an invasion of England. To combat the threat, the English king, Edward III, sailed across the Channel and attacked at dawn. Although they were outnumbered three to one, Edward's fleet won an extraordinary victory, his bowmen causing chaos by showering the French ships with arrows at what was (for them) a safe distance. A foretaste of the Battle of Crecy, there was so little left of the French force that no one dared tell King Philip of France, until finally the court jester took matters into his own hands: "Oh! The English cowards! They had not the courage to jump into the sea as our noble Frenchmen did". Philip's reply is not recorded.

Today Damme spreads out prettily beside the canal, its one main street, Kerkstraat, edged by what remains of the medieval town. Funded by a special tax on barrels of herrings, the fifteenth-century **Stadhuis** has an elegant, symmetrical facade balanced by the graceful lines of its exterior stairway. Just down the street, the **Museum St Jans Hospitaal** (April–Sept Tues–Sat 10am–noon & 2–6pm, Sun 11am–noon & 2–6pm; Oct–March Sat & Sun only 2–5.30pm; F30) contains a number of partly furnished period rooms, while a couple of minutes further south there's an early thirteenth-century church tower, ruined in part and detached from the nave of the **Onze Lieve Vrouwekerk** (daily 10am–noon & 2.30–5.30pm) – a wide, high Gothic church that has been beautifully restored.

The best way to get to Damme from Bruges is by **boat** along the poplar-lined canal from Noorwegse Kaai (April–Sept 5 times daily each way; one-way fare F130, return F190). The mundane alternative is by **bus**, either #799 (Sept–June

Mon–Sat 2 or 3 daily; 25min) or #788 (July & Aug; every 2hr), which both leave from 't Zand, near the town centre. It's also a very pleasant and not overlong **cycle ride**. If you decide to **stay**, there are about a dozen private houses that offer double **rooms** (②); just follow the signs on Kerkstraat. Otherwise, Damme has one good **hotel**, the *De Gulden Kogge*, by the canal at Damse Vaart Zuid 12 (☎35 42 17; ③), although it's usually necessary to reserve ahead in summer. Damme's **tourist office**, in the Stadhuis (May–Sept Mon–Fri 9am–noon & 2–6pm; Sat & Sun 10am–noon & 2–6pm, Oct–April Mon–Fri 9am–noon & 2–5pm; Sat & Sun 2–5pm ☎35 33 19), will help you find a bed if you're in difficulties. As for **food**, Kerkstraat is lined with expensive **restaurants**, mainly aimed at the town's many day-trippers. One of the best is *Bij Lamme Goedzak*, Kerkstraat 13. If your budget won't stretch to its prices, head for *'t Uylkotje*, Kerkstraat 44, which has good bar snacks and fifty types of beer.

Ghent and around

The seat of the Counts of Flanders and the largest town in western Europe during the thirteenth and fourteenth centuries, **GHENT** was at the heart of the Flemish cloth trade. By 1350, the city boasted a population of fifty thousand, of whom no fewer than five thousand were directly involved in the industry, a prodigious concentration of labour in a predominantly rural Europe. Like Bruges, Ghent prospered throughout the Middle Ages, but it also suffered from the endemic disputes between the nobles (who supported France) and the cloth-reliant citizens (to whom friendship with England was vital).

The relative decline of the cloth trade in the early sixteenth century did little to ease the underlying tension, the people of Ghent still resentful of their ruling class, from whom they were now separated by language – French against Flemish – and religion – Catholic against Protestant. Adapting to the new economic situation, the town's merchants switched from industry to trade, exporting surplus grain from France, only to find their efforts frustrated by another long series of wars. The catalyst for insurrection was taxation: long before the Revolt of the Netherlands Ghent's citizens found it hard to stomach the financial dictates of their kings, and time and again they rose in revolt and were punished. In 1540 the Holy Roman Emperor Charles V lost patience and stormed the town, abolishing its privileges, filling in the moat and building a new secure castle at the city's expense. Later, captured by Philip II's armies in 1584, Ghent was too far south to be included in the United Provinces and was reluctantly pressed into the Spanish Netherlands. Many of its citizens fled north, and those who didn't may well have regretted their decision when the Dutch forced the Hapsburgs to close the Scheldt as the price of peace in 1648.

In the centuries that followed, Ghent slipped into a slow decline from which it emerged during the industrial boom of the nineteenth century. In optimistic mood, the medieval merchants had built the city's walls a fair distance from the town centre to allow Ghent to expand. But the expected growth never took place, and the empty districts ended up choked with factories whose belching chimneys encrusted the old city with soot and grime. Ghent did, however, become a major

The Ghent area telephone code is ☎091

BOAT TRIPS

Between April and early November **boat trips** around Ghent's inner waterways depart from the Korenlei and Graslei daily between 10am and 7pm. Trips last 35 minutes, cost F130, and leave roughly once every 15 minutes, though the wait can be longer as they'll only go when reasonably full.

There are also other excursions which leave from the Ketelbrug, behind the Recollettenlei (Law Courts), at the west end of Zonnestraat. They include trips on the Lys (June–Aug 3 or 4 times weekly 1.30–6.30pm; F250) and day trips to Bruges (July Thurs 9am–8pm; F450) – though this isn't as good a deal as it sounds: food and drink are expensive, and long sections of the canal are too deep to see over the banks. If you're after countryside, the excursion to the village of St Martens (mid-July to mid-Aug 3 times weekly; 3–6pm; F220) is far better. Further details from the tourist office, or from *Benelux Rederij*, Recollettenlei 10 (☎224 32 33)

---

economic force and its entrepreneurial mayor, Emille Braun, brought the Great Exhibition here in 1913. More recently, Ghent has struggled to maintain its economic success, mounting a concerted campaign to attract new business into the area. It's a larger, more sprawling and less immediately picturesque city than Bruges, which may be to its advantage; it has also benefitted from a comprehensive cleaning and restoration programme that has been taking place over the last decade. Certainly if you're put off by the tourists or tweeness of Bruges, or you simply can't find a room, it's a good alternative base, a city full of character.

Arrival, information and city transport

Ghent has three **train stations**, but the one you're most likely to use is **St Pieters**, which adjoins the main **bus station**, some 2km south of the city centre. From outside the train station, **trams** #1, #10, #11 and #12 connect with the centre every few minutes, passing along Nederkouter and continuing through to the central square of Korenmarkt. A couple of minutes' walk east of the Korenmarkt, the **tourist office**, in the crypt of the Stadhuis (April–Oct daily 9.30am–6pm; Nov–March daily 9.30am–4.30pm; ☎224 15 55), has a comprehensive range of information, including a full list of **accommodation**, which it will book on your behalf for a refundable deposit of F2000.

The best way of seeing the sights is on foot, but Ghent is a large city and you may find you have to use a **tram** or **bus** at some point. This is easy enough: standard one-way fares cost F40, and a ten-journey *Rittenkaart* F230. One-way tickets can be bought direct from the driver; *Rittenkaarts* are sold at shops and kiosks all over town and at the **kiosk** by the tram stop on the Korenmarkt (Mon–Fri 7am–7pm, Sat 9.30am–4.30pm), which also has maps of the transport system (the *Netplan* – F50). The 24-hour pass is available from the tourist office.

Accommodation

Although a lot of Ghent's **accommodation** is at the expensive end of the market, there is also a variety of cheap alternatives, though you'll be lucky to get anything at all during the city's main festival – a boozy affair held in mid- to late July. There's an excellent new youth hostel in the city centre, *De Draeke*, a couple of minutes' walk north of the Korenmarkt at St Widostraat 1 (☎233 70 30; ①). Alternatively, between mid-July and the end of September, over one thousand **student rooms** are let to visitors for F500 per person per night including breakfast. The rooms are dotted around the south of town in a number of complexes; ask at the tourist office for further details or enquire direct at *Home Vermeylen*, Stalhof 6 (☎22 09 11).

Ghent's cheapest **hotels** are clustered around the train station, but you really miss the atmosphere of the town around here, and would do better to head for the youth hostel. If this is not your style, consider splashing out on a city-centre hotel.

Those **camping** should proceed to *Camping Blaarmeersen*, Zuiderlaan 12 (☎21 53 99; March to mid-Oct), at the water sports centre to the west of town. Buses #51, #52 and #53 run direct from Ghent St Pieters station.

Hotels

Adoma, St-Denijslaan 19 (☎222 65 50). Cheap and slightly seedy hotel behind Ghent St Pieters station. ②.

Alfa Flanders, Kon. Albertlaan 121 (☎222 60 65). Comfortable modern hotel north of the station near the River Leie. Huge doubles and discounts when trade is slack. ⑧.

Arcade, Nederkouter 24 (☎225 07 07). Clean, quiet and efficiently run hotel. ⑥.

Carlton, Kon Astridlaan 138 (☎222 88 36). Standard modern hotel near the train station. Discounts in summer. ⑥.

Chamade, Blankenbergestraat 2 (☎220 15 15). Standard 3-star accommodation. ⑥.

Erasmus, Poel 25 (☎224 21 95). Easily the most charming hotel in Ghent. Family run, and tastefully decorated with rooms furnished with antiques. ⑥.

Flandria, Barrestraat 3 (☎223 06 26). A good medium-price choice closer to the city centre than the train station options, and a not a huge amount more expensive. ⑤.

Gravensteen, Jan Breydelstraat 35 (☎225 11 50). Small, conducive hotel in a Baroque mansion overlooking the Castle of the Counts. ⑥.

Novotel, Goudenleeuwplein 5 (☎224 22 30). Attractive modern hotel bang in the middle of the town centre. Outdoor swimming pool. ⑦.

Trianon, St-Denijslaan 203 (☎221 39 44). Cheap, tatty doubles behind the station. ②.

The City

The shape and structure of today's **city centre** reflects Ghent's ancient class and linguistic divide. The streets to the south of the Korenmarkt tend to be straight and wide, lined with elegant old mansions, the former habitations of the wealthier, French-speaking classes, while, to the north, Flemish Ghent is all twisting alleys and low brick houses. They meet at the somewhat confusing sequence of large squares that surrounds the town's principal buildings, spreading out to the immediate east of Korenmarkt.

St Baaf's Cathedral

The best place to start an exploration of the city centre is the mainly Gothic **St Baaf's Cathedral**, squeezed into the eastern corner of St Baafsplein (April–Sept Mon–Sat 9.30am–noon & 2–6pm, Sun 1–6pm; Oct–March Mon–Sat 10am–noon & 2.30–4pm, Sun 2–5pm; free). St Baaf's mighty nave, begun in the fifteenth century, is supported by tall, slender columns that give the whole interior a cheerful sense of lightness, though the seventeenth-century marble screens spoil the effect by darkening the choir. In a small ambulatory chapel is the cathedral's –

GHENT

To
Dampoort Railway
Station (100 m)

STIERSTRAAT

DAMPOORTSTR.

HAGELANDKKAAI

SCHOOLKAAI

Sint
Baafsabdij

DE
VIGNE-PL.

GRANDMANAAT

Leie

BRUGKAAI

NIEUW

GEBR. V. EYCKSTR.

VOLMOLENSTR.

STEENDAM

NIEUWPOORT

BRABANTDAM

VLAANDERENSTRAAT

BRABANTDAM

KROMME-OTTOGRACHT

NEDERPOLDER

St.-Baaf's
Cathedral

LIMBURGSTRAAT

KORTEDAGSTG.

LEIE

GRAUWPOORT

OUDBURG

Mad Meg

SINT
JACOBS

VRIJDAGMARKT

Toreken

Stadhuis &
Tourist Office

Lakenhalle

MAGELEINSTR

ZONNESTR.

KOUTER

PATERSHOL

Museum voor
Volkskunde

Gravensteen

GELDMUNT

ST.-VEERLE
PLEIN

HOOGPOORT

GOUDEN-
LEEUWPL.

St.-
Niklaas

KOREN-
MARKT

VOLDERSTRAAT

VELDSTRAAT

LÉ STEENSTR.

JAN BREYDELSTRAAT

Museum voor
Sierkunst

City Boat Trips

KORENLEI

GRASLEI

LEIE

Post
Office

AJUINLEI

Ketelbrug

LINDENLEI

LEVEKAAI

GEWAD

BRADERIISTRAAT

St.-Michielsbrug

LEPENSTR.

PRINSENHOF

Museum of Industrial
Archaeology & Textiles

RAMEN

HOOGSTRAAT

OUDE HOUTLEI

Rabot

RABOTSTRAAT

THÉRESIANENSTRAAT

COUPURE RECHTS

COUPURE

COUPURE LINKS

COUPURE RECHTS

COUPURE

COUPURE LINKS

MARTELAARSL

MAGELEINSTR

LANGE VIOLETTESTRAAT

BELLEVUESTRAAT

HUBERT FRERE-ORBANLAAN

ZUIDPARKLAAN

TENTOONSTELLING

ST-LIEVENSLAAN

FRANKLIN ROOSEVELTLAAN

OPPERSCHELDE

ST-PIETERSNIEUWS

200 m

C TADELLAAN

STALHOF

ST-PIETERSNIEUWSTRAAT

OVERPOORTSTRAAT

Museum voor
Schone Kunsten

KATTENBERG

NEDERKOUTER

KORTRIJKSEPOORTSTRAAT

LEIE

CH. DE KERCHOVELAAN

CLAUSLAAN

COUPURE RECHTS

LINKS

Bijlokemuseum

IJZERLAAN

COUPURE LINKS

COUPURE

GODSHUIZENLAAN

KORTRIJKSESTEENWEG

GR. BRITTANNIELAAN

KON. ASTRIDLAAN

KON. ELISABETHLN.

KON MARIA
HENDRIKAPLEIN

St-Pieters Railway Station

LEIE

Post Office

Trams

Bus
Station

KONING ALBERTLAAN

and Ghent's – greatest treasure, an **altarpiece** known as *The Adoration of the Mystic Lamb*, a seminal work of the early fifteenth century, though of dubious authorship. Since the discovery of a Latin verse on its frame in the nineteenth century, academics have been arguing about who actually painted the masterpiece. The inscription reads that Hubert van Eyck "than whom none was greater" began, and Jan van Eyck "second in art" completed the work, but as almost nothing is known of Hubert, some art historians doubt his existence. They argue that the citizens of Ghent invented "Hubert" to counter Jan's fame in the rival city of Bruges. No one knows for sure, but what is certain is that in their manipulation of the technique of oil painting the artists were able to capture a needle-sharp realism which must have seemed revolutionary to their contemporaries.

Certainly it's a complex work, an explanation of which (with its rich structure and symbolism) could fill volumes. The cover screens display a beautiful Annunciation scene with the archangel Gabriel's wings reaching up to the timbered ceiling of a Flemish house, the streets of a town visible through the windows. In a brilliant coup of lighting, the frames of the shutters throw their shadows into the room, emphasizing the reality of the apparition. Below, the donor and his wife kneel piously alongside statues of the saints. But the restrained exterior painting is but a foretaste of what's within, a stunning visionary interior that was only revealed when the shutters were opened on Sundays and feast days. On the upper level sit God the Father, the Virgin and John the Baptist in gleaming clarity; on the left is a group of singing angels who strain to read their music. (Van Mander, writing in the sixteenth century, thought they were so artfully painted you could discern the different pitches of their voices.) In the lower panel the lamb, the symbol of Christ's sacrifice, is approached by bishops, saintly virgins and Old and New Testament figures in a heavenly paradise – "the first evolved landscape in European painting" thought Kenneth Clarke, seen as a sort of idealized Low Countries. Look closely and you can see the cathedrals of Bruges, Utrecht and Maastricht surrounded by flora so fastidiously detailed they have been used in college reference books.

Tucked away in the small chapel, it's actually remarkable that the altarpiece has survived at all. Not surprisingly, the Calvinists wanted to destroy it; Philip II of Spain tried to acquire it; the Emperor Joseph II disapproved of the painting so violently that he replaced the nude Adam and Eve with a clothed version of 1784 (exhibited today just inside the church entrance); while a few years later the Germans stole and hid it in an Austrian salt mine until the end of World War II. It'll cost you F50 to see the altarpiece, and you'd be crazy to miss it.

Compared to the altarpiece, the cathedral's **crypt** (F50) is a bit of an anticlimax. Dating from the twelfth century, it preserves features of the earlier Romanesque church of St John, along with murals painted between 1480 and 1540 but only rediscovered in 1936. Full of religious bric-a-brac, one or two of the reliquaries are worth a second look, but the prime exhibit is Justus van Gent's fifteenth-century **triptych**, *The Crucifixion of Christ* – with the crucified Christ flanked on the right by Moses and the bronze serpent that cured poisoned Israelites on sight, and on the left by Moses purifying the waters of Mara with wood.

Around the cathedral

Just west of St Baaf's, the fifteenth-century **Lakenhalle** or Cloth Hall is little more than an empty shell with a dismal restaurant in the basement. The first-floor entrance leads to the adjoining **Belfry,** a much amended edifice dating from the fourteenth century. Once a storehouse of civic documents, today the interior is a rather bare, dusty ruin. A glass-sided lift climbs up to the roof for excellent views over the city centre (daily every 30min, 10am–4.30pm; F100).

Access to the **Stadhuis** across the street is limited (April–Oct Mon–Fri afternoons, guided tours only; F60), and of the series of halls open to the public, the most interesting is the *Pacificatiezaal*, the site of the signing of the Pacification of Ghent in 1576. This was an agreement which momentarily bound north and south Flanders together against the Hapsburgs, with the promise of religious freedom. The tiled floor is, curiously enough, designed in the form of a sort of maze. Outside, the entrance to the tourist office is framed by a section of facade whose severity is a good example of post-Reformation architecture, in stark contrast to the wild, curling patterns of the section to the immediate north, carved in the Flamboyant Gothic style at the turn of the sixteenth century. Designed by Rombout Keldermans, each ornate niche holds a statuette – detailed carvings of the powerful and famous in characteristic poses, including Keldermans himself rubbing his chin and studying his plans for the Stadhuis. This architectural contrast reflects Ghent's relative decline: the money ran out when the wool trade collapsed, and the city couldn't afford to finish Keldermans' design.

The last of this central cluster of buildings is **St Niklaaskerk**, an architectural hybrid dating from the thirteenth century. Once again it's the shape and structure that please the eye most, though the giant-sized Baroque high altar is no mean piece, with its remarkable representation of *God the Father* glowering down into the church surrounded by a flock of cherubic angels. Dodging the trams of the Korenmarkt and heading west, you pass the main **post office building**, whose carved heads represent the kings who came to Ghent for the Great Exhibition of 1913. A few yards away, the St Michielsbrug bridge overlooks the city's oldest harbour, the **Tussen Bruggen** (Between the Bridges), where **boats** leave for trips around the neighbouring canals roughly once every fifteen minutes throughout the summer months (35min; F135 – see above). The **Korenlei**, the western side of the harbour, is home to a series of stolid merchants' houses dating from the eighteenth century; the **Graslei**, opposite, has the squat, gabled guild- and warehouses of the town's boatmen and grainweighers. Some of these are particularly fine examples of late medieval design, specifically no. 14, the *Gildehuis van de Vrije Schippers* (Free Boatmen), whose golden sandstone is decorated with badly weathered scenes of boatmen weighing anchor and a delicate galleon. The nearby tiny *Tolhuisje* was built 150 years later, a delightful example of Flemish Renaissance architecture.

's Gravensteen

A few minutes' walk north of Graslei, the **'s Gravensteen** (daily Oct–March 9am–5pm; April–Sept 9am–6pm; F80), or Castle of the Counts, looks sinister enough to be in a Bosch painting. Cold and cruel, its dark walls and angular turrets were built in 1180 as much to intimidate the town's unruly citizens as to protect them. Considering the castle has been used for all sorts of purposes (it was even a textile mill in the nineteenth century), it's survived remarkably intact, its gateway a deep-arched tunnel leading to the courtyard, framed by protective battlements complete with ancient wooden flaps, arrow slits and holes for boiling oil and water. In the middle of the courtyard stand the castle's two main buildings, the dungeon on the right and the Count's Residence on the left, riddled with narrow, interconnected staircases set within the thickness of the walls. A self-explanatory, numbered tour guides visitors through this labyrinth, and highlights include an assembly room with a magnificent stone fireplace, a gruesome collection of instruments of torture with a few illustrations of their use, and a couple of particularly dank oubliettes.

The rest of the centre

On the opposite side of the square from the castle entrance, at the junction of the two main canals, is the extravagant facade of the old **Vismarkt,** dominated by a grand relief of Neptune. Beyond, the market itself is in a terrible state, scheduled for restoration but for the moment used as a car park. Crossing the bridge immediately to the west, turn first left for the **Museum voor Sierkunst,** Jan Breydelstraat 5 (Tues–Sun 9.30am–5pm; F80), which has a pleasant sequence of period rooms interspersed with displays that concentrate on comparative furniture design. Back at the top of Breydelstraat, cross over and follow Gewad, turning right down Braderijstraat for the **Lievekaai,** Ghent's second oldest harbour, by the side of the canal to Bruges. Closed and partly filled in during the nineteenth century, the Lievekaai originally extended right up to the front of the old merchants' houses that now flank what remains of the waterway from behind a cobbled pavement. To the northwest, a mixture of tumbledown and renovated seventeenth- and eighteenth-century properties line the sides of the canal as far as the **Rabot,** a fortified medieval sluice that today marks the end of the canal. The Rabot was crucial to the defence of old Ghent: the water level behind the sluice was higher than the water level outside, and in emergencies the gates could be opened and the surrounding fields flooded, keeping the enemy at a safe distance.

Retracing your steps to the 's Gravensteen and continuing east across St Veerleplein onto the Kraanlei, you'll come to one of Ghent's better museums, the **Museum voor Volkskunde,** Kraanlei 65 (April–Oct daily 9am–12.30pm & 1.30–5.30pm; Nov–March Tues–Sun 10am–noon & 1.30–5pm; F50). Housed in a series of restored almshouses surrounding a central courtyard, this is made up of a delightful chain of period rooms depicting local life and work in the eighteenth and nineteenth centuries. A good detailed guide is available at reception (F30), and the reconstructed grocery and cooper's workshop are especially interesting. The most curious exhibits are the two wooden "goliaths" in the church: of obscure origin, goliaths are a common feature of Belgian street processions and festivals.

Behind the Kraanlei are the lanes and alleys of the **Patershol,** a web of terraced houses dating from the seventeenth century. Once the heart of the old Flemish working-class city, this thriving residential quarter had, by the 1970s, become a slum threatened with demolition. The area was preserved and a process of gentrification began that has crowded the streets with good bars and expensive bistros. The process isn't complete, and the fringes of the Patershol remain a ragbag of decay and restoration, including the old **Carmelite Monastery** on Vrouwebroerstraat, which is a good example of how things used to be – a rotting ruin that was, until recently, a squat.

Back on the Kraanlei, a modern canal walkway opposite the Folklore Museum has replaced part of the original towpath and heads off northeast past gabled facades and nineteenth-century textile factories to re-emerge at the eastern end of the Patershol. Alternatively, the bridge adjacent to the start of the walkway leads into the **Vrijdagmarkt**, the old political centre of Ghent and the site of public meetings and executions. By the bridge, there's a fifteenth-century cannon that proved more dangerous to the gunners than the enemy: the most powerful siege gun of its day, the cannon, named *Mad Meg (Dulle Griet)* after Bruegel's painting, cracked its barrel the first time it was fired. The slim turret at the other end of the square, the **Toreken**, was once the Tanners' Guild House. Adjoining the Vrijdagmarkt is the crowded **Bij St Jacobs**, with Steendam heading off east, sprinkled with antique shops.

East of the centre

East of the Bij St Jacobs, Ghent's eighteenth- and nineteenth-century industrial suburbs stretch out toward the Dampoort train station. A mishmash of terrace, factory, and canal, these suburbs were spawned by the sea canals that were dug to replace the obsolete, narrow waterways of the city centre. Right next to the station, the large water-filled hole on **Oktrooiplein** is the link between the old and the new systems. One of the area's more interesting parts is sandwiched between the River Leie and the railway tracks just north of Gandastraat, on and opposite **Stierstraat** – housing that dates from the very earliest days of the Industrial Revolution, including courtyard dwellings and a dilapidated row of urban houses incorporating some of the features of the rural workers' cottages that they were beginning to replace. Nearby, at the west end of Gandastraat, are the scant remains of the church of **St Baafsabdij** (Tues–Sun 9.30am–5pm; F80), the birthplace of John of Gaunt and the site of a small lapidary **museum** in the thirteenth-century refectory.

South of the centre

Ghent's main shopping street, **Veldstraat**, leads south from the city centre parallel with the course of the river to a couple more of Ghent's top-flight museums. The first, the **Bijlokemuseum** at Godhuizenlaan 2 (Tues–Sun 9.30am–5pm; F80), isn't especially remarkable, and the labelling of the exhibits – mainly art and applied art pertaining to the Ghent region – is chaotic. But the old abbey buildings in which the museum is housed are packed with all sorts of bygones, from collections of guild pennants and processional banners to masonic tackle, porcelain, pottery, keys and costumes. Amongst the period rooms, the guilds' meeting room is splendid. There's also an extensive collection of military hardware, including dozens of the halberds and pikes favoured by the weaver-armies of Flanders, and a rare example of a *goedenday* (literally "good-day"). This is, in fact, a primitive fourteenth-century weapon, a long pole with a short spike at one end, which was designed to stab the enemy's Adam's apple, a part of the body poorly protected by armour. In response, the French bobbed their heads down to protect their necks, a nodding motion which the Flemish interpreted as a greeting, hence the name of the weapon.

Ten minutes' walk away to the southeast, the **Museum voor Schone Kunsten** (same times and price), on the edge of the park at Nicolaas de Liemaeckereplein 3, is poorly laid out too. There are two main collections here, a fairly small display of modern art concentrated on the first floor and in the rooms to the left of the entrance, and older masters on the ground floor to the right. Of the latter (which is the more interesting part), highlights include a fourteenth-century *Head of Christ* and a finely detailed, unattributed panel of a triptych, *The Taking of Jerusalem by Titus*. Nearby are Bosch's *Carrying of the Cross*, showing

Christ mocked by some of the most grotesque and deformed characters Bosch ever painted, and the smaller, less well-known *St Jerome at Prayer*. There's also work by Pieter Bruegel the Younger, who inherited his father's interest in the landscape and those who worked and lived on it, as seen in his *Wedding Feast* and *Peasant Wedding*. Later paintings include several canvases by Jacob Jordaens, the *Men's Heads* and *Mythological Scene* mimicking the robust romanticism of his friend Rubens – who is poorly represented by several sketches for proposed paintings in Antwerp and Brussels. Rather better are Anthony van Dyck's muscularly romantic *Jupiter and Antione*, and an earnest Frans Hals simply entitled *Elderly Lady*.

Eating and drinking

Ghent is as good a place to eat as any other Belgian city, although the centre is mainly given over these days to restaurants and snack bars that are primarily aimed at the tourist trade – meaning low prices but often questionable quality. Use these between sights during the day for refuelling, and in the evening head up to trendy Patershol, where there's a mushrooming of ethnic restaurants and trendy bars.

Restaurants

Aroma, Donkersteeg 9, off Goudenleeuwplein. Centrally situated café that serves light lunches and pastries. A good sightseeing stop-off.

Buddhasbelly, Hoogpoort (☎225 17 32). Interesting veggie fare, though open limited hours. Mon–Sat noon–2pm & 6–9pm .

Camelia, Zeugsteeg 7 (☎25 08 49). This is a chic restaurant specializing in French and Belgian food. Closed Sun & Mon.

La Compostela, St Veereplein 3–4 (☎225 09 02). Spanish restaurant, with occasional flamenco performances at its next-door bar.

Djerba, Oudburg 19. Decent restaurant that serves Tunisian specialities. Good for a bit of light relief from Belgian staples.

De Hel, Kraanlei 81 (☎224 32 40). Decent Franco-Belgian fare, behind an extravagant facade decorated with Classical-style red stone reliefs. Closed Mon.

Overpoort, Overpoortstraat. Down near the Museum voor Schone Kunsten, this is Ghent's university cafeteria, serving the cheapest sit-down meals in town. ISIC cards sometimes requested.

Pascalino, Botermarkt 11 (☎225 36 57). Cheap snacks and meals until late, in a convenient location opposite the Stadhuis.

Progres, Korenmarkt 10 (☎225 17 16). Good, basic fare, in an extremely central location. Always busy.

Rococco, Corduwanierstraat. Informal restaurant-bar in a grand eighteenth-century house, serving reasonably priced light meals.

Bars

't Dreupelkot, Groentenmarkt 12, Bar specializing in genever, next door to the more famous *Het Waterhuis* – see below.

't Galgenhuisje, Groentenmarkt. Tiny bar opposite *Het Waterhuis* that serves something like 80 different beers.

Ludwig, Hoogpoort 37. A sedate bar housed in a Renaissance drawing room.

De Tap en de Tepel, Gewad. Dark, mysterious bar, whose name translates as "the tap and nipple".

Tolhuisje Tavern, Graslei XX. Cosy café in the centre of town that's always packed.

De Trolle Kelder, Bij St Jacobs 17. Huge selection of beers in an ancient merchants' house, with trolls of all descriptions stuffed in the window.

Het Waterhuis, Groentenmarkt 9. Over 100 types of beer in a pleasant bar near the castle. Be sure to try *Stropken*, (literally "noose"), a delicious local brew, named after the times in 1453 when Philip the Good compelled the city burghers to parade outside the town gate with ropes around their necks.

De Witte Leeuw, Graslei 6. Inevitably packed bar in a former guildhouse.

Listings

Airport There's a regular bus service (5 times daily) from Ghent St Pieters train station and from outside the *Sabena* office, Kouter 151 (Mon–Fri 8.30am–6pm; ☎225 60 99), to the city's nearest airport, Brussels Nationaal. Price F400.

Bookshop *Fnac* at Veldstraat 88, close to the junction with Zonnerstraat, has the best selection of English titles.

Bureaux de change The two most central banks are *Generale*, Belfortstraat 41, and *Driege*, St-Baafsplein 12. Outside banking hours use the office at St Pieters station, open until 6pm on Thurs and Fri, and on Sat 9.30am–2pm.

Car Rental *Avis*, Kortrijksesteenweg 676 (☎22 00 53); *Europcar*, Einde Were 312 (☎226 81 26); *Garage Gantois*, Kortrijksesteenweg 200 (☎22 10 22).

Curios *The Fallen Angel*, Jan Breydelstraat 29, has a wide selection of bygones – well worth a look.

Festivals Ghent's main festivals are the Flanders Spring Fair in late March/early April, the *Gentse Feesten* or town fair (held in mid- to late July for 10 days, always including July 21), the Patershol celebrations in mid-Aug, and the Flanders Music Festival at the end of Aug.

Left luggage Office at Ghent St Pieters station (6am–midnight); lockers in the station concourse.

Markets There's a flower market daily on the Kouter, although Sun is best (7am–1pm), and a fruit and veg market on Groenenmarkt Mon–Fri in the morning, all day on Sat. There are also flea markets ("prondelmarkt") on Beverhoutplein (Sat & Sun 7am–noon) and Bij St Jacobs (Fri 7am–1pm).

Police ☎101.

Post office Main post office at Korenmarkt 16 (Mon–Fri 9am–6pm, Sat 9am–noon).

Swimming There are public swimming pools at Peerstraat 1 (Mon 10am–noon, Tues–Fri 8am–noon & 2–6.30pm, Sat 9am–noon & 2–6.30pm, Sun 9am–noon).

Taxi *V-Tax*, Overpoortstraat 38 (☎225 25 25).

Telephones Keizer Karelstraat 1 (Mon–Thurs 8am–4pm, Fri 8am–6pm).

Train enquiries ☎2282 44 44 (daily 7am–9pm).

Travel agents *Divantoura*, Bagattenstraat 176 (☎223 00 69).

Around Ghent

The flat and dreary countryside that encircles Ghent and its untidy suburbs is without much interest, except for the moated and turreted castle of **Laarne** (July & Aug daily 2–5.30pm; Easter–June & Sept–Oct daily except Mon & Fri 2–5.30pm; F100), which lies some 12km east of the city. Founded in the twelfth century, most of today's building is medieval, a picturesque mixture of towers and steeples that hides a magnificent collection of old silver and several beautifully preserved Brussels tapestries. The castle is accessible by bus #688 from St Pieters bus station (every 1–2hr; 30min).

East of Ghent: St Niklaas, Dendermonde and Aalst

To the northeast of Ghent lies the agricultural region of the **Waasland**, its sand and clay soils sandwiched between the Dutch border to the north, the Ghent–Terneuzen canal to the west, and the River Scheldt to the east. Once an isolated area of swamp and undrained forest, the lands of the Waasland were first cultivated by pioneering religious communities who cleared the trees and built the dykes. The soil was poor and conditions were hard until Ghent's demand for wool encouraged local landowners to introduce the sheep that produced the district's first cash crop and provided some degree of prosperity. Today, the area is popular with tourists seeking the quiet of the countryside.

St Niklaas

Some 40km east of Ghent, **ST NIKLAAS** is the only settlement of any size in the Waasland, an unremarkable town whose principal feature is its Grote Markt, the largest in Belgium. It's edged by a motley combination of old and new buildings, including an attractive **Stadhuis** from the nineteenth century, and the seventeenth-century **St Niklaaskerk**, which has a later Baroque interior. The only real surprise in town is the tiny old castle, **Kasteel Walburg** (no admission), a couple of minutes from the tourist office on Walburgstraat. Built of reddish brick in the middle of the sixteenth century, the castle is in the Flemish Renaissance style and was clearly made for comfort rather than defence. Part of an attractively wooded city park and encircled by a slender moat, it's classically picturesque – or at least it will be when the repairs are finished.

The municipal **museum** (Tues–Sat 2–5pm, Sun 10am–5pm; F30 ticket valid for both town museums), back towards the train station at Zamanstraat 49, consists of a predictable display of local artefacts saved from mediocrity by a wing dedicated to the maps, atlases and a couple of globes made by the Flemish cartographer Mercator, who was born in the neighbouring village of Rupelmonde in 1512. It's Mercator's projection of the spherical surface of the world onto a two-dimensional map that is now accepted as the usual view of the earth's surface, and it was originally an invaluable aid to navigation – though the view it gives of the world is to some extent a misleading one, distorting the relative size of the continents at the expense of the southern hemisphere: Europe simply isn't that big and neither is Greenland, while the surface area of Africa is in fact much larger. The other "trick" is the layout, with the colonizing nations of Europe at the centre of the world.

Continuing up Zamanstraat, the first junction brings you to Regentiestraat, and, at no. 65 in the "Exlibris Centrum", St Nikolaas' other museum, the **Barbers' Museum** (*Barbierama*; Tues–Sat 2–5pm, Sun 10am–5pm) – an original and varied presentation that features some early electrical hairdressing appliances that look like sci-fi props from early *Flash Gordon* movies.

Practicalities

If you decide to stay in St Niklaas, the **tourist office**, Grote Markt 45 (Mon–Fri 8am–5pm; June–Aug also Sat & Sun 10am–4pm; ☎03/777 26 81), will provide a list of **campsites** and **hotels** in the town and surrounding area. There's one cheap and central **hotel**: *De Arend*, in the centre at Onze Lieve Vrouweplein 8 (☎03/777 11 73; ②). The tourist office also has details of cycle tours and walks in the Waasland.

Dendermonde

Southeast of Ghent, the River Scheldt twists its way across the industrial heartland of east Flanders, its towns home to the host of factories that sprang up in the nineteenth century as Belgium was transformed from a predominantly agricultural society to – briefly – the fourth greatest industrial power in the world. Some 25km from Ghent, **DENDERMONDE**, at the confluence of the rivers Scheldt and Dender, shared in the industrial boom, just as previously its strategic location had seen it suffer its share of siege and assault. Badly damaged by the Germans in 1914, today's town centre is rather drab, but there are several medieval buildings of note spread out around the trim **Stadhuis**, whose fourteenth-century shape and structure were restored in the 1920s. Nearby, the turreted **Vleeshalle** has a somewhat sombre facade dating from 1460, and to the rear, Kerkstraat leads west to the stolid **Onze Lieve Vrouwekerk**, housing the town's prime exhibits: a *Crucifixion* and *Adoration of the Shepherds* by Anthony van Dyck – two early canvases that are typical of the painter's Romantic approach.

Dendermonde is, however, best known for its **carnival**, an extraordinary attempt to re-enact the medieval story of the *Steed Bayard* – a medieval tale of knights and honour, loyalty and friendship, dynastic quarrels and disputes. Picaresque in form, the story doesn't seem to make much sense – though the whole thing revolves around the trials and tribulations of the horse, represented by a giant fabricated model, and its masters, the four brothers who perch on top. The clearest part of the story is the end, where the redoubtable steed repeatedly breaks free from the millstones tied around its neck and refuses to drown. The third time he comes to the surface, one of his masters walks away, unable to stand and watch the agonies of his horse any longer. The horse assumes he's been abandoned, cries out and only then does he drown. The carnival is held every few years at the end of May, but there are plans to make it an annual event. Further details are available at most Belgian tourist offices.

Dendermonde's **tourist office** is in the Stadhuis (Mon–Fri 8.30am–noon & 1–5pm; May–Sept also Sat & Sun 10am–noon & 1.30–4.30pm; ☎052/21 39 56) and if you're staying over, can advise on accommodation.

Aalst

About 20km south of Dendermonde, the ancient town of **AALST** was first fortified in the eleventh century and became a settlement of some importance as a seat of the counts of Flanders, at the point where the Bruges to Cologne trade route crossed the River Dender. Later on Aalst became a key industrial centre, producing beer and textiles, as well as some of the worst slum and factory conditions in the country. Cleaned up in the 1950s, the town has one outstanding building, the fifteenth-century **Belfry**, a slender, balconied turret that rises elegantly from the Grote Markt, adorned by the statues of a knight and an armed citizen, symbols of municipal power and individual freedom. The belfry is attached to the **Schepenhuis** (Aldermen's House), a somewhat incoherent jangle of odds and ends shoved together over the centuries, with a delicate flamboyant Gothic **gallery** pushing out into the square from the main body of the building. Inside the belfry there's a small town **museum** (Mon–Fri 10am–noon & 2–5pm), commemorating the work of a local nineteenth-century radical Catholic priest, Adolf Daens, who campaigned to improve the pay and conditions of local workers. It's a modest collection, but an engaging one, sepia photographs illustrating the work of the priest, the organization of a local Catholic-led trade union, and the harsh poverty of the period.

Just to the east of the Grote Markt lurks the massive hulk of the **St Martinuskerk** (normally daily 8am–noon & 2–6pm), a gloomy church that hides Aalst's only famous painting, the clumsily named *St Roch Receiving from Christ the Gift of Healing Victims of the Plague* by Rubens. Commissioned by the guild of beer brewers and hop growers in 1623, the painting has faded quite badly, but it's still possible to make out the artist's fluent, exuberant lines, displayed within the original carved wooden frame. Close by, an ornate **Tabernacle** fills out the space between two of the church's arches, an extravagant mixture of columns and statuettes in several different sorts of marble, the work of Jeroom du Quesnoy in 1604.

Aalst **tourist office** (Oct–May Mon–Fri 10am–noon & 1–5pm; June–Sept Mon–Fri 10am–noon & 2–6pm, Sat 2–6pm, Sun 10am–12.30pm & 2–6pm; ☎053/ 73 21 11) at Grote Markt 3, has maps of the town and can help with accommodation. The town has one reasonably priced **hotel**, the *De Lange Muur*, near the station at Stationsplein 13 (☎053/77 37 46; ③).

travel details

Trains

Bruges to: Brussels (every 20min; 65min); Ghent (every 20min; 25min); Ostend (every 20min; 15min).

Ghent to: Aalst (every 20min; 25min); Antwerp Centraal (every 30min; 45min); De Panne (1 hourly; 80min); Dendermonde (every 30min; 30min); Kortrijk (every 30min; 30min); Mechelen (every 30min; 65min); Oudenaarde (1 hourly; 35min); St Niklaas (every 30min; 25min); Veurne (1 hourly; 70min); .

Ieper to: Kortrijk (hourly; 30min).

Kortrijk to: Ghent (every 30min; 25min); Ieper (hourly; 30min); Lille (France) (hourly; 30min); Oudenaarde (hourly; 20min).

Ostend to: Bruges (every 20min; 15min); Brussels (every 15min; 80min); Ghent (every 20min; 40min).

Veurne to: De Panne (hourly; 10min); Dijksmuide (hourly; 10min); Ghent (hourly; 70min).

Buses

Ieper to: Lo (7 daily; 33min); Veurne (7 daily; 60min).

Ostend to: Nieuwpoort (Mon–Sat 8 daily, Sun 3 daily; 35min); Veurne (Mon–Sat 8 daily, Sun 3 daily; 75min).

Veurne to: Ieper (7 daily; 1hr); Nieuwpoort (Mon–Sat 8 daily, Sun 3 daily; 40min); Ostend (Mon–Sat 8 daily, Sun 3 daily; 75min).

Trams

Ostend to: De Panne (every 10min in summer & 30min in winter; 1hr 4min); Knokke (same frequency; 1hr).

CHAPTER NINE

ANTWERP AND THE NORTH

T he Flemish-speaking provinces of Antwerp and Limburg form the north-eastern rim of Belgium, stretching from the city of Antwerp in the west to the River Maas in the east, which forms the border with Holland. It's dull countryside on the whole, heralding the flat landscapes of Holland further north, and the main attraction of the region is inevitably **Antwerp** – a large and ancient port that is definitely worth a stopover of at least a couple of days. It's a sprawling and intriguing place, the international centre of the diamond trade and in part still a seedy dock city; it also has many reminders of its sixteenth-century golden age, before it was upstaged by Amsterdam as the prime commercial centre of the region, from splendid medieval churches and guild houses to as fine a set of museums as you'll find anywhere in the Low Countries – Rubens spent most of his career in the city and produced many of his finest works here. Outside of the city, **Antwerp province** has two other ancient towns that are worth a visit – the old centre of **Lier** and the ecclesiastical capital of the country, **Mechelen.**

The province of **Limburg** to the east is, unlike Antwerp, seldom visited by tourists, and to be honest its low-key mixture of small industrial towns and tranquil farmland doesn't have terrific appeal. The capital, **Hasselt,** is of no special interest, but it does have a bustling, lively centre; and the nearby **Bokrijk** estate holds one of the best open-air museums in the country, primarily dedicated to the rural traditions of Flemish Belgium. Of the smaller towns, **Tongeren,** on the edge of the linguistic divide, is most worth a visit, a pretty market town dominated by its giant Grote Kerk. Just to the west is **Sint Truiden,** from which buses run to the village of **Zoutleeuw** over the border in Flemish Brabant, with its spectacular fourteenth-century church – the only one in Belgium that managed to entirely avoid the depredations of Protestants, iconoclasts and invading armies.

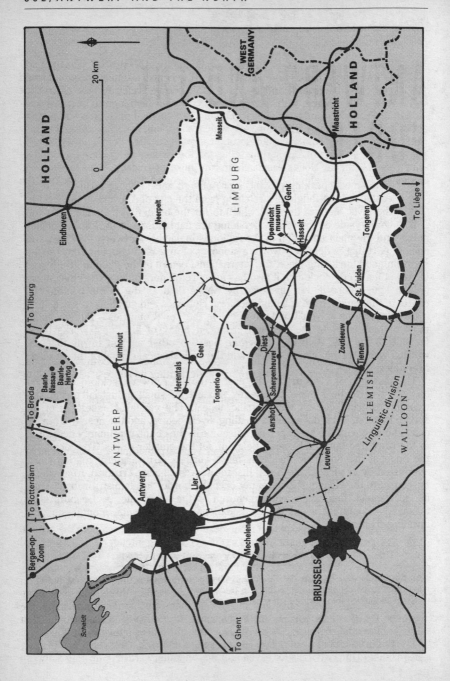

Antwerp

About 30km north of Brussels, Belgium's second city, **ANTWERP**, fans out care-lessly from the east bank of the Scheldt, its gritty centre a rough polygon formed by its enclosing boulevards and the river. Most people prefer it to the capital: it's a hectic, likeable place, with a denser concentration of things to see, not least some fine churches and a varied selection of distinguished museums – reminders of its auspicious past as the centre of a wide trading empire. It has a more clearly defined character, too, less a dull location of political life, more a lively cultural centre, with a colourful, spirited nightlife. On the surface it's not a wealthy city – the area around the docks especially is run down and seedy – but its diamond industry (centred behind the dusty facades around Centraal Station) is the world's largest. On a less contemporary note there is also the enormous legacy of Pieter Paul Rubens, some of whose finest works adorn Antwerp's many galleries and churches.

Some history

Antwerp wasn't originally much sought after: although it occupied a prime river site, it was too far east to be important in the cloth trade and too far west to be on the major trade routes connecting Germany and Holland. But a general move-ment of trade to the west, and in particular the decline of Bruges, toward the end of the fifteenth century, led to its rapid rise from obscurity: within 25 years, many of the great trading families of western Europe had moved their headquarters here, the tiny old fortified settlement becoming overwhelmed by a deluge of splendid new mansions and churches, docks and harbours. Frustrated with the turbulent burghers of Ghent and Bruges, the Emperor Maximilian and his successor Charles V patronized Antwerp, underwriting its success as the leading port of their expanding empire.

Antwerp's golden age lasted for less than one hundred years, prematurely stifled by Charles V's son Philip II, who inherited the Spanish part of the empire and the Low Countries in 1555. Fanatically Catholic, Philip viewed the Reformist stirrings of his Flemish-speaking subjects with horror, encouraging the Inquisition to send thousands to the gallows. Antwerp seethed with discontent, its population swollen by religious refugees. The spark was the *Ommegang* of August 18, 1566, when priests carted the image of the Virgin through the city's streets, insisting that all should bend the knee as it passed. The parade was peaceful enough, but afterwards, with the battle cry of "Long live the beggars", the Protestant guildsmen of Antwerp smashed the inside of the cathedral to pieces – the most extreme example of the "iconoclastic fury" that was sweeping the region. Philip responded by sending in an army of occupation, intended to overawe and intimidate from a brand new citadel on the south side of town. Nine years later, it was this same garrison that sat unpaid and underfed in its fortress, surrounded by the wealth of the "heretical" city. Philip's mercenaries mutinied, and at dawn on November 4, 1576, they stormed Antwerp, running riot for three long days, plun-dering Antwerp's public buildings and private mansions, and slaughtering some eight thousand of its citizens in the "Spanish fury". It was a catastrophe that finished the city's commercial supremacy, and more disasters were to follow. In 1577, Philip's soldiers were driven out, but they were back eight years later, laying siege outside the city walls for seven months, and afterwards confirming Antwerp as part of the Spanish Netherlands. Under the terms of the capitulation, Protestants had two years to leave town, and a flood of skilled workers poured north to the relative safety of Holland, further weakening the city's economy.

In the early sixteenth century there was a modest recovery, but the Dutch now controlled the seaways of the Scheldt and were determined that no neighbouring Catholic-controlled port would threaten their trade – in 1648, under the Treaty of Münster, they closed the river to all non-Dutch shipping. Antwerp was ruined, and remained so until the French arrived in 1797, when Napoleon declared it to be "little better than a heap of ruins . . . scarcely like a European city". The French rebuilt the docks and revived the city, and Antwerp later became independent Belgium's largest port, a position it has maintained until the present day.

> The Antwerp area telephone code is ☎03

Arrival, information and city transport

Antwerp has two main **train stations**, Berchem and Centraal. Some domestic and international trains stop at Berchem 4km south of the town, but the majority halt at Centraal – far more more conveniently placed on the edge of the city centre about 2km east of the Grote Markt. Connections between the two stations are frequent and fast (10 hourly; 3min). Inside the **Centraal Station** complex, a *Belgian Railways* **information office** (Mon–Sat 8am–10pm, Sun 9am–5pm; ☎233 70 15) has international and domestic timetables along with details of special bargains and fares. Most long-distance **buses** arrive at the bus station on Franklin Rooseveltplaats, a five-minute walk northwest of Centraal Station. The **information kiosk** here (Mon–Fri 7am–7pm, Sat 9am–4pm) deals with bus services throughout the province of Antwerp.

Antwerp's tiny **airport** is in the suburb of **DEURNE**, about 6km east of the city centre, connected by regular *Sabena* buses to the airline's office close to Centraal Station at Appelmansstraat 12. The one-way fare is F250. Failing that, ordinary city bus #16 leaves from the main road straight ahead of the airport building hourly (9am–6pm) for Pelikaanstraat, also by Antwerp Centraal. Taxis to Antwerp Centraal cost about F400.

Antwerp's **tourist office** is in the city centre at Grote Markt 15 (April–Oct Mon–Sat 9am–8pm, Sun 9am–5pm; Nov–March Mon–Sat 9am–6pm, Sun 9am–5pm; ☎232 01 03), and has a comprehensive range of information on the city and its sights, including a map of the city, its transport system and its suburbs for F10, and leaflets detailing where to see the works of Rubens for F30.

A useful **tram** and **bus** system serves the city and its suburbs from a number of points around Centraal Station, especially from bus stops along Pelikaanstraat and in Koningin Astridplein. Tram services from Centraal Station to the city centre (#2 or #15 to Groenplaats) go underground. A city transport **information office** (Mon–Fri 8am–12.30pm & 1.30–4pm, Sat 9am–12.30pm) in the "Diamant" underground station beside Antwerp Centraal, sells tickets and has free maps of the city transport system (*Netplan*). A standard one-way fare costs F40, and an eight-strip *Rittenkaart* F185. There's also a 24-hour unlimited travel tourist card, which despite a discount price of F50 in 1993 (Antwerp's European City of Culture year), will now cost you around F150.

BOAT TRIPS

There are a number of **boat trips** that can be made in and around Antwerp. Cruises down the **Scheldt** leave from the landing beside the Steen fortress from May to September. Hour-long trips cost F230 (May & June daily every hour from 11am–4pm), ninety-minute trips F280 (July & Aug daily every 45min, 11am–4pm). Tours also take in the city's port area, leaving from dock 13 (by Londenbrug at the end of Italielei on the left-hand side) and costing F375 per person for the two-and-a-half-hour trip (May–Aug daily at 10am & 2.30pm; Sept Sat 2.30pm & Sun 10.30am & 2.30pm only). A special bus leaves for dock 13 from beside the Steen fortress thirty minutes before each departure, costing an extra F40.

Day-long excursions to **Bruges** are also possible via Zeebrugge. They leave from beside the Steen once or twice monthly in June, July and August, departing at 8.30am and returning by 9.30pm. The fare is F1950 per person and advance booking is essential.

Further information, including details of extra summer season sailings to other cities in Flanders, can be had from the tourist office or the operators themselves, *Flandria*, located on Steenplein (☎231 31 00).

Accommodation

Antwerp has the range of hotels you'd expect of Belgium's second city, as well as a number of both unofficial and official youth hostels, so accommodation is not usually a problem. The range of cheap hotels isn't especially expensive, although most of them are clustered around Centraal Station, where – late at night – you should exercise caution, particularly if travelling alone. The tourist office has an extensive **accommodation** list and will make bookings on your behalf at no cost, charging only a F200 deposit that is subtracted from your final bill. Their list covers all grades of accommodation – from dormitory-style beds to executive suites – but excludes the dodgier-looking places around the station. It's not that they're particularly dangerous – Antwerp is not a heavy city – just sometimes unpleasantly seedy.

Hostels

International Seamen's House, Falconrui 21 (☎232 16 09). Accommodation in doubles, a 10minwalk north of the Grote Markt. Despite the name, it's open to landlubbers and females as well as mariners. ③.

New International Youth Hotel, Provinciestraat 256 (☎230 05 22). Cheap beds in dorms, and good-value doubles a 10min walk from Centraal Station. To get here head south down Pelikaanstraat, turn left along Plantin en Moretuslei, and take the second right. Dorm ①, private rooms ②.

Scoutel Jeugdverblifcentrum, Stoomstraat 3–7 (☎226 46 06). Doubles and triples in a youth hotel 5min walk from Centraal Station. Be sure to check in before 8pm as it fills up fast. ②.

Youth Hostel, Eric Sasselaan 2 (☎238 02 73). About 3km south of the centre. Tram #2 from Centraal Station, direction Hoboken. ①.

Hotels

Alfa Empire, Appelmansstraat 31 (☎231 47 55). Enormous, sumptuous and well-equipped rooms with TV close to Centraal Station. ⑧.

Steen National
Maritime Museum

Sint
Paulskerk

Vleehuis
Museum

Tourist
Office

GROTE MARKT

Cathedral

Groen
Plaats

Plantin Moretus
Museum

Post Office

Schelde

Museum of
Contemporary Art

Museum Voor
Schone Kunsten

ANTWERP

PAARDENMARKT

VEKESTRAAT

VENUSSTRAAT

ROODESTRAAT

ITALIELEI

OLIJFTAKSTR

ROTTERDAMSTR

ST.ELISABETHSTR

BLINDERSTR

PRINSSTRAAT

P.VAN HOBOKENSTR

OOSEN MARKT

HOLLANDSTR

VAN ARTEVELDESTR

VAN WESEBEKESTRAAT

VAN SCHOONHOVENSTRAAT

DAMBRUGGERSTRAAT

Rockox House

olus

meus

KEIZERSTRAAT

KIP DORP

ST JACOBS MARKT

PIJLSTR

VAN STRALENSTR

DOSSINSTR

LANGE NIEUWE STRAAT

✝ **St.Jacobskerk**

Bourse

JEZUSSTR

FRANLIN
ROOSEVELT
PLAATS

GEMEENTESTRAAT

KONINGIN
ASTRIDPLEIN

CARNOTSTRAAT

MEIR

MEIR

**Post
Office**

FRANKRIJKEI

DE KEYSERLEI

STATIESTR

ANNEESSENSSTRAAT

KISSENSSTRAAT

**Rubens'
House**

OODENSTR

Wapper

QUELLINSTRAAT

APPELMANSSTRAAT

VESTINGSTRAAT

Train Station

DIE

er van den
gh Museum
JBERGSTRAAT

MEISTRAAT

OUDE VAARTPLAATS

**Provinciaal
Diamant
Museum**

PELIKAANSTRAAT

Zoo

PLOEGSTR

agdenhuis

LEOPOLDSTRAAT

FRANKRIJKLEI

RUBENSLEI

VAN BREESTRAAT

LANG HERENTALSESTRAAT

QUINTIN MATSYSLEI

STOOMSTRAAT

SIMONSTRAAT

LANG KIEVILSTR

VAN IMMERSEELSTR

ORT

MECHELSE STEENWEG

Stadspark

JACOB JACOBSSTR

PLANTIN EN
MORETUSTEI

VAN EYCK LEI

PLANTIN EN MORETUSLEI

LANGE LEEMSTRAAT

CHARLOTTA LEI

BELGIE LEI

PROVINCIESTRAAT

MERCATORSTRAAT

0   200 m

MECHELSE STEENWEG

ST.JOZEFSTR

LANGE LEEMSTRAAT

TR

**To the Campsite
& Youth Hostel**

**Ridder Smidt Van
Gelder Museum**

Arcade, Meistraat 39 (☎231 88 30). Standard-issue modern hotel, in a decent location behind the Rubenshuis. ⑥.

Billiard Palace, Konigen Astridplein 40 (☎233 44 55). Rather grim cheapie in the station area . ②–③.

Cammerpoorte, Nationalestraat 38 (☎231 97 36). Convenient, comfortable and very centrally located hotel. Reserve ahead in summer, though. ⑤.

Eden, Lange Herentalsestraat 25 (☎233 06 08). Standard, moderately comfortable hotel in the station area. ⑥.

Monico, Konigen Astridplein 34 (☎225 00 93). Basic hotel next to a strip joint in the station district. ②–③.

Terminus, Franklin Rooseveltsplaats 9 (☎231 47 95). About 5min walk from the station. Noisy. ③.

Tourist, Pelikaanstraat 20 (☎232 58 70). Another cheap option near the station – OK if you're staying a night or two. ③.

Villa Mozart, Handschoenmarkt 3 (☎231 30 31). Delightfully plush hotel in a great location in the old centre. ⑧.

Campsites

Vogelzang, Vogelzanglaan behind the Bouwcentrum (☎238 57 17). Antwerp's closest campsite (April–Sept) is reachable by way of tram #2 from Centraal Station, direction Hoboken.

The city centre

The centre of Antwerp is the **Grote Markt**, at the heart of which stands the **Brabo Fountain**, a haphazard pile of roughly sculpted rocks surmounted by a bronze of Silvius Brabo, depicted flinging the hand of the giant Antigonus into the Scheldt. Legend says that Antigonus extracted tolls from all passing ships, cutting off the arms of those who refused to pay. He was eventually beaten by the valiant Brabo, who tore off his hand and threw it into the river, giving rise to the name of the city, whch means literally "hand-throw". There are more realistic theories to explain the city's name, but this is the most colourful, and it certainly reflects Antwerp's early success at freeing the river from the innumerable taxes levied on shipping by neighbouring landowners.

The north side of the Grote Markt is lined with daintily restored **Guild Houses**, their sixteenth-century facades decorated with appropriate reliefs and topped by finely cast gilded figures basking in the afterglow of the city's Renaissance lustre. No. 5, the **House of the Crossbowmen**, with its figures of St George and the dragon, is the tallest and most distinctive, and it stands next door to the *Coopers' House*, with its barrel motifs. They are overshadowed, though, by the **Stadhuis**, completed in 1566 to an innovative design by Cornelis Floris (Mon, Tues, Wed & Fri 9am–3pm, Sat noon–4pm; F30; guided tours only; entry from a side door on the right on Zilversmidstraat from Mon–Fri; from Suikerrui, on the left, on Sat). The building's pagoda-like roof gives it a faintly oriental appearance, but apart from the central gable it's quite plain, with a long pilastered facade of short and rather shallow Doric and Ionic columns, which, along with the windows, lend a simple elegance, in contrast to the purely decorative gable (there's no roof behind it) – added at a time when a tower would have been considered old-fashioned. The niches at the top contribute to the self-congratulatory aspect of the building, with statues of Justice and Wisdom proclaiming virtues the city burghers reckoned they had in plenty. Inside, by way of the Zilversmidstraat entrance, the staircase of the high main hall used to be an open courtyard and was only covered in the late nineteenth century, accounting for the monumental gallery on all four sides. The paintings which take the place of windows represent aspects of commerce and the arts – a balance which Antwerp has long been conscious of, and is now anxious to preserve. Among the other rooms you can see are the Leys Room, named after Baron Hendrik Leys, who painted the frescoes in the 1860s, and the Wedding Room, which has a chimneypiece from the original town hall, decorated with two caryatids by Floris himself, who was also a master sculptor.

The Onze Lieve Vrouwe Cathedral

Leaving the Grote Markt by its southeast corner, the triangular **Handschoenmarkt** is bordered by more handsome old facades, its tiny stone well adorned with an iron canopy bearing the legend "It was love connubial taught the smith to paint" – a reference to the fifteenth-century painter Quentin Matsys, who learned his craft in order to successfully woo the daughter of a local artist (at the time marriage was discouraged between families of different guilds). The Handschoenmarkt is the most westerly of a sequence of somewhat confusing pedestrianized squares that occupy the area around the **Onze Lieve Vrouwe Cathedral** (Mon–Fri 10am–5pm, Sat 10am–3pm, Sun 1–4pm; F60), one of the finest Gothic churches in Belgium, mostly the work of Jan and Pieter Appelmans in the middle of the fifteenth century. A forceful and self-confident structure, the cathedral dominated the skyline of medieval Antwerp with a graceful spire that was finally completed in 1518. Long a source of fascination to travellers, William Beckford, fresh from spending a million pounds on his own house in Wiltshire at the start of the nineteenth century, was still impressed enough to write that he "longed to ascend it that instant, to stretch myself out upon its summit and calculate, from so sublime an elevation, the influence of the planets". Over the centuries the building weathered badly, and in 1969 a long-term restoration project began with the roof and nave. The last stage, the renovation of the choir and ambulatory, was finally completed in May 1993.

The triple-aisled nave is breathtaking, if only because of its sense of space, an impression that's reinforced by the bright, light stonework revealed by the restoration. A fire of 1533, the Iconoclastic Fury of 1566, and the fact that the church briefly became Protestant later that century, have ensured that no Gothic decoration remains, and what you see today are a number of subsequent Baroque embellishments, notably four early paintings by Rubens. Of these, the *Descent from the Cross*, just to the right of the central crossing, is without doubt the most beautiful, a triptych painted after the artist's return from Italy that displays an uncharacteristically restrained and moving realism, derived from Caravaggio. Christ languishes in the centre in glowing white, surrounded by mourners or figures who are tenderly struggling to lower him. As was normal, with commissions pouring in from everywhere, students in Rubens' studio worked on the painting, among them the young van Dyck, who repaired the face of the Virgin and the arm of Mary Magdalen. His work was so masterful that Rubens is supposed to have declared it an improvement on his own, though this story appears to originate from Van Dyck himself. Oddly enough, the painting was commissioned by the Guild of Arquebusiers, who asked for a picture of St Christopher, their patron saint; Rubens' painting was not at all what they had in mind, and they promptly threatened him with legal action unless he added a picture of the saint to the wings.

A second painting, the *Assumption*, hangs over the high altar, a swirling Baroque scene, full of cherubs and luxuriant drapery, painted in 1625, while on the left-hand side of the central crossing, there's a second triptych, *The Raising of the Cross* which, painted in 1610, is the earliest of the four, a grandiloquent Baroque canvas full of muscular soldiers and saints. On the right-hand side of the ambulatory, there's the cathedral's fourth Rubens, the *Resurrection*, painted in 1612 for the tomb of his friend, the printer Jan Moretus, showing a strident, militaristic Christ carrying a red, furled banner. A free leaflet with a diagram of the church and a numbered list of exhibits is available at the entrance. However, the only other highlight is Maarten de Vos' *Marriage at Cana*, hung near the *Descent from the Cross*, a typically mannered work completed toward the end of the artist's life in 1597.

Groenplaats, Vrijdagmarkt and the Plantin-Moretus Museum

Behind the cathedral is **Groenplaats**, a dreary open square that was once the town graveyard and now holds an uninspired statue of Rubens. From here, it takes a couple of minutes to thread your way west to **Vrijdagmarkt**, where the **Plantin-Moretus Museum** (Tues–Sun 10am–5pm; F75) is housed in the old mansion of the printer Christopher Plantin, who rose to fame and fortune here in the second half of the sixteenth century. Born in Tours in 1514, Plantin moved to Antwerp when he was 34 to set up a small bookbinding business, but in 1555 he was forced to give up all heavy work when, in a case of mistaken identity, he was wounded by revellers returning from the carnival. Paid to keep quiet about his injuries, Plantin used the money to start a printing business. He was phenomenally successful, his fortune assured when Philip II granted him the monopoly of printing missals and breviaries for the whole of the Spanish Empire. On Plantin's death, the business passed to his talented son-in-law, Jan Moerentorf, who changed his name, in accordance with the fashion of the day, to Moretus; he in turn was succeeded by his son Balthasar, a close friend of Rubens. The family donated their mansion to the city in 1876.

From the entrance, a clearly labelled route takes visitors through most of the rooms of the house, set around a compact central courtyard. The mansion is worth seeing in itself, and the museum as a whole provides a marvellous insight into how Plantin and his offspring conducted their business. A detailed booklet is on sale at reception, and highlights include several well-preserved pictorial tapestries in room 1; a delightful seventeenth-century bookshop, equipped with a list of prohibited books, the *Librorium Prohibitorum*, along with a money-balance to help identify clipped and debased coins in room 4; and the old print room, with seven ancient presses, in room 14; not to mention dozens of intriguing, precise woodcuts and copper plates in room 27, the best of an enormous number that were used by several centuries of print workers. There are also a number of examples of the work of Christopher Plantin, including the *Biblia Polyglotta*, an annotated, five-language text produced on vellum for King Philip II in 1572, as well as sketches by Rubens, who occasionally worked for the family as an illustrator, and a portrait of *Seneca* by the same artist.

Down to the waterfront and the National Maritime Museum

Head east across Vrijdagmarkt from the museum, turn left and left again, and the first turn on the right is **Pelgrimsstraat**, which has one of the best views of the cathedral, a tumble of sloping, uneven roofs set against the majestic lines of the church behind. A restored sixteenth-century merchant's house at no. 15, **De Pelgrom**, has been converted into a restaurant, but has a tiny, privately owned museum upstairs, decked out with some period furniture (Sat & Sun 11.30am–7pm; F60). On the same street, by no. 6, an ancient alley called the **Vlaeykensgang** (Pie Lane) twists its way down to **Oude Koornmarkt**, a surviving fragment of the honeycomb of narrow streets that made up medieval Antwerp. From the end of the alley, Oude Koornmarkt and subsequently Suikkerui lead west to the banks of the Scheldt, clearly separated from the town since Napoleon razed the riverside slums and constructed proper wharves in the early 1800s. Jutting out into the river close to the end of Suikkerui, the scant remains of the Steen fortress are approached past a great statue of giant **Lange Wapper**, a somewhat confusing local folklore figure – part practical joker, part peeping Tom – who, despite a fondness for children, exploited his height by spying into people's bedrooms.

The **Steen** marks the site of the ninth-century fortification from which the rest of the town spread, later the location of an impressive medieval stronghold, successively reinforced and remodelled to keep the turbulent guildsmen of Antwerp in check. The gatehouse and front section are all that have survived, and today they house the **National Maritime Museum** (Tues–Sun 10am–5pm; F75), whose cramped rooms feature exhibits illustrating a whole range of shipping activity from inland navigation to life on the waterfront and shipbuilding. Clearly laid out and labelled, with multilingual details on all the major displays, the museum is a delight, an appealing mixture of the personal and the public. The high points include some charming British scrimshaw and whale tooth engraving in room 1, an intriguing fifth-century nautical totem in the form of a snake's head in room 3, and several fine model ships in room 9. You should also look out for a model of the Italianate barge that was built for Napoleon's second visit to Antwerp, and peek into the old council chamber, decorated by two large canvases of the docks in the seventeenth century. Behind the Steen, the museum has an open-air section with a long line of tugs and barges packed in under a rickety corrugated roof.

The Vleeshuis

Crossing Jordaenskaai from beside the Steen, it's a couple of minutes' walk east along Vleeshuisstraat to the tall, turreted gables of the **Vleeshuis** (Tues–Sun 10am–5pm; F75), built for the Guild of Butchers in 1503. With its alternating layers of red brick and stonework, the outside has often been compared to rashers of bacon, but it's still an impressive building, the suitably grand headquarters of one of the most powerful of the medieval guilds. It was here in 1585, with the Spanish army approaching, that the butchers made the fateful decision to oppose the opening of the dykes along the Scheldt – a defensive ploy strongly recommended by William the Silent because it would have made it impossible for the Spaniards to mount a blockade of the river from its banks. However, the butchers were more worried about the safety of their flocks which grazed the threatened meadows, and so sent a deputation to the city magistrates to object. The magistrates yielded, and the consequences were disastrous – the Spaniards were able to close the Scheldt and force the town to surrender, a defeat that placed Antwerp firmly within the Spanish Netherlands.

Today, the enormous brick halls of the interior are used to display a large but rather incoherent collection of applied arts, in particular several fine fifteenth-century wood carvings on the ground floor and a curious set of seventeenth- to eighteenth-century musical instruments on the uppermost level. The exhibits are labelled exclusively in Flemish although an English guide is available for F30, but it's the setting rather than the displays that pleases most.

North to the St Pauluskerk and the Falconplein

The streets around the Vleeshuis were badly damaged by wartime bombing, leaving a string of bare, open spaces edged by some of the worst of the city's slums. The whole area is gradually being rebuilt, but progress is slow and many of the crumbling rows of houses have yet to be restored, though most of the gaps have been filled by solid modern houses whose pinkish stone facades imitate the style of what went before. Cosy and respectable, these new buildings are in stark contrast to the dilapidated **red light area** all around, a sequence of seedy little streets with sporadic tattoo parlours and bored faces at the windows. It's a soulless district, a sure sign that you're approaching Antwerp's tough dockland area just to the north.

From the entrance to the Vleeshuis, it's a couple of minutes' walk north along Vleeshouwersstraat to Veemarkt, where an extravagant Baroque portal leads through to the precincts of the **St Pauluskerk** (May–Sept daily 2–5pm; Oct–April daily 10am–noon F50), a dignified late Gothic church of 1571. The most prominent feature of the interior is the extraordinary wood carving of the confessionals and choir stalls, their snake-like, almost arabesque pillars the work of P. Verbrugghen the Elder in the mid-seventeenth century. Rubens' *Disputation on the Holy Sacrament*, an early work of 1609, hangs in an altar in the south transept, opposite a long series of paintings that lines the north aisle, including another Rubens (the *Scourging* of 1617), and works by van Dyck and Jordaens – though they're not at their best in the gloomy church light. Outside, near the entranceway, the **Calvaryberg** is an artificial grotto of 1697–1747 that clings to the buttresses of the south transept, eerily adorned with statues of Christ and other figures in a rather tawdry representation of the Crucifixion. Writing in the nineteenth century, the traveller Charles Tennant described it as "exhibiting a more striking instance of religious fanaticism than good taste", and he wasn't far wrong.

Five minutes northeast of the church, Klapdorp leads to **Paardenmarkt** and **Falconplein**, at the heart of a solid working-class district just to the south of the docks. A far cry from the tourist trimmings of Grote Markt, it's here that Slav and Jewish minorities have set up their textile and domestic appliance shops, advertising their goods in Cyrillic script for the benefit of those Russian sailors whose ships are in port.

South to the Huis Rockox Museum and Hendrik Conscienceplein

From Falconplein, Mutsaertstraat leads south to Keizerstraat, where the **Huis Rockox Museum** at no. 12 (Tues–Sun 10am–5pm; free) is housed in the splendidly restored seventeenth-century town house of Nicolaas Rockox, friend and patron of Rubens. Inside, a sequence of rooms has been crammed with period furnishings and art work, based on an inventory taken after the owner's death in 1640. Of particular interest is Pieter Bruegel the Younger's *Netherlandish Proverbs*, one of several canvases he did on the subject. It's a mass of finely drawn detail, frenetically mixing the observed and imagined.

Close to the western end of Keizerstraat, **Hendrik Conscienceplein** takes its name from a local nineteenth-century novelist whose work concentrated on the life of the traditional Flemish peasantry. One of the most agreeable places in central Antwerp, the square is fringed by the church of **St Carolus Borromeus** (Mon, Wed & Thurs 8.30am–12.15pm, Tues 9.30am–12.15pm & 6–7pm, Fri 8.30am–12.15pm & 4.15–7pm, Sat 9.30am–12.15pm & 3–7pm, Sun 9.30am–12.45pm; F20), whose finely contrived facade is claimed to have been based on designs by Rubens. Much of the interior was destroyed by fire at the beginning of the eighteenth century, but on the right of the entrance, the so-called Lady's Chapel survived, its streaky, coloured marble a key feature of the original church, here serving as a background for a series of tiny pictures.

From Hendrik Conscienceplein, walk west to the end of Wijngaardstraat, where a left and then a right turn takes you into the series of tiny squares that front the northern side of the cathedral. Here, the **Het Elfde Gebod** (The Eleventh Commandment) is one of the most unusual bars in the city, jam-packed with a bizarre assortment of religious statues – see below.

South of the city centre

South of Groenplaats spread Antwerp's older residential areas, bounded by the Amerikalei and Britselei boulevards, which mark part of the course of a circle of city fortifications finished in the early years of this century. Enormously expensive and supposedly impregnable, the design was a disaster, depending on a series of raised gun emplacements that were sitting targets for the German artillery in September 1914. The Allies had expected Antwerp to hold out for months, but in the event the city surrendered after a two-week siege, forcing Churchill and his party of marines into a hurried evacuation just two days after their arrival.

The Mayer van den Bergh Museum

Five minutes' walk southeast of Groenplaats, the delightful **Mayer van den Bergh Museum**, at Lange Gasthuisstraat 19 (Tues–Sun 10am–5pm; F75), consists of the private art collection of the wealthy merchant family of the same name, given to the city in 1920. Very much a connoisseur's collection, there are fine examples of many different branches of applied arts, from tapestries to ceramics, silver, illuminated manuscripts and furniture, all crowded into a reconstruction of a sixteenth-century town house. There are also a number of excellent paintings, including a *Crucifixion* triptych by Quentin Matsys in room 4, the unidentified donors painted on the wings alongside a curious picture of one of the family's patron saints, Mary of Egypt – a repentant prostitute who spent her last years in the desert miraculously sustained by three little loaves. Room 6 holds an early fourteenth-century carving of *St John on the Breast of Jesus*, and two tiny panels from a fifteenth-century polyptych that once decorated a fanciful travelling altar, the rest of which is on display in the United States. On each panel, the formality of the religious scene is in contrast to the informality of the detail – Saint Christopher crosses a stream full of fish and Joseph cuts up his socks for use as swaddling clothes for the infant Jesus. The next room holds another picture of *St Christopher*, the work of Jan Mostaert, its bold tones influenced by his long stay in Italy, while room 9 is home to the museum's best-known work, Bruegel's *Dulle Griet* or "Mad Meg", one of his most Bosch-like paintings, a rather misogynistic allegory in which a woman, loaded down with possessions, stalks the gates of hell, a surrealist landscape of monsters and pervasive horror. The title refers to the archetypal shrewish woman, who, according to Flemish proverb "could plunder in front of hell and remain unscathed". Nearby, Bruegel's *Twelve Proverbs* is a less intense vision of the world, a sequence of miniatures illustrating popular Flemish aphorisms.

The Maagdenhuis

Down the street from the van den Bergh Museum, the **Maagdenhuis**, at Lange Gasthuisstraat 33 (Mon & Wed–Fri 10am–5pm, Sat & Sun 1–5pm; F50), was formerly a foundling hospital for children of the poor but is now occupied by the city's social security offices and a small museum. Founded in the middle of the sixteenth century, the refuge was run on the strictest of lines, its complex rules enforced by draconian punishments. At the same time, those children who were left here were fed and taught a skill, and desperate parents felt that they could at least retrieve their children if their circumstances improved. To make sure their offspring could be identified, they were left with tokens, usually irregularly cut playing cards or images of saints – one part left with the child, the other kept by the parent. If the city fathers didn't actually encourage this practice, they certainly accepted it, and several buildings even had specially carved alcoves on their facades where foundlings could be left under shelter, sure to be discovered in the morning.

Entrance to the museum is through an ornamental archway decorated with figures representing some of the first girls to be admitted to the hospital set beside a tidy classroom scene, so finely chiselled that you can make out the tiny bookshelves. Inside, six first-floor rooms, a chapel and a courtyard display a varied but modest collection of art include a touching *Portrait of an Orphan Girl* by Cornelius de Vos, an overpowering *Descent from the Cross* by Jordaens and an Italianate *Adoration of the Shepherds* by Jan van Scorel. There's also an assembly of some fifty colourful, late medieval porridge bowls, the largest collection of its sort in Belgium, and a sealed certificate confirming the election of Charles V as Holy Roman Emperor in 1519. The exhibits are labelled exclusively in Flemish, but an English guidebook is available at reception for F30.

The Museum voor Schone Kunsten

Fifteen minutes' walk southwest of the Maagdenhuis (tram #8 from Groenplaats), the **Museum voor Schone Kunsten** (Tues–Sun 10am–5pm; free) occupies an immense neo-Classical edifice. It's normally free, though charges are sometimes made for temporary exhibitions. Of the permanent collection, downstairs displays relatively modern works, while upstairs shows older pieces, from Flemish Primitives to seventeenth-century masters. Everything is a little mixed up, including most of the signs, and it's difficult to plan a chronological route, but the larger rooms in the middle concentrate on Rubens, whilst the corridors on either side – eight galleries in each – begin with the earlier works, and move, in haphazrd fashion, up to the seventeenth century.

The **early Flemish** section isn't as comprehensive as you might expect from a major museum, but the collection includes two fine works by Jan van Eyck, a *Madonna at the Fountain* and a tiny *St Barbara*, where the usual symbol of the saint's imprisonment, a miniature tower held in the palm of her hand, has been replaced by a palm and prayer book, to represent her faith and self-sacrifice.

Behind, a full-scale Gothic tower looms over her, a more powerful indication of her imprisonment. Hans Memling's *Portrait of Giovanni de Candida* and his *Angels Singing and Playing Instruments* are not among his most distinguished works, but they have a finely textured quality for which he is famous, while the angels are clearly copies of figures that had already appeared in his *Reliquary of St Ursula*, kept in Bruges. Rogier van der Weyden's *Triptych of the Seven Sacraments* was painted for the Bishop of Tournai in 1445, its inventive frame merging with the lines of the Gothic architecture inside; his *Portrait of Philippe de Croy* blends a dark background into the lines of his subject's cloak, a simple technique to emphasize the shape of the nobleman's angular face and his slender hands. Elsewhere, Jean Fouquet, the most influential French artist of the fifteenth century, has one canvas on display, a *Madonna and Child*, with remarkable, orange-red Latex-like angels surrounding a chubby Jesus who looks away from a pale, bared breast. Look out also for Quentin Matsys's triptych of the *Lamentation*. Commissioned for the carpenter's chapel of Antwerp Cathedral in 1511, it's a profound and moving work, a dishevelled Christ pressed tightly into the foreground by crowds of mocking, twisted faces.

Rubens has two large rooms to himself, in which one very large canvas stands out: the *Adoration of the Magi*, a beautifully free and very human work, painted in 1624. Rubens apparently finished it in a fortnight, no doubt with the help of his studio, the major figures of which – van Dyck and Jordaens – are represented in the room that follows, the latter by an especially skilled *Last Supper*.

Highlights of a small group of **Dutch paintings** from the late sixteenth and seventeenth centuries include Frans Hals' prim *Fisher Boy*; two genre paintings by Joachim Beuckelaer, *The Fish Market* and *The Vegetable Market*; and, fittingly placed in the same room, on the left-hand side, raucous scenes of peasant life by Adriaen Brouwer and David Teniers. Born in Flanders, apprenticed to Frans Hals in Haarlem, and very much influenced by Bruegel, Brouwer bridges the gap between Flemish and Dutch art. When he was imprisoned in 1633, the prison baker, Joos van Craesbeeck, became his pupil, and his pictures are here too, sometimes excelling even Brouwer in their violence.

The museum also has a comprehensive collection of **modern Belgian art**, supplemented by a smattering of works by well-known foreign artists. However, there's not enough room to show all the collection at any one time, and an ambitious exhibition programme means that paintings are regularly rotated, so it's difficult to give precise directions. Even so, you should be able to see the work of James Ensor, whose subdued, conservative beginnings, such as *Afternoon at Ostend*, 1881, contrast with his piercing later works – *Skeletons Fighting for the Body of a Hanged Man*. Also likely to be on show are paintings by Paul Delvaux, whose *Red Bow* shows a classical city in the process of disintegration, and the Impressionistic Rik Wouters – the latter's *Woman Ironing* a sensitive picture of his wife completed in 1912.

East of the city centre

From the northeast corner of Groenplaats, Eiermarkt curves round to **Meir**, Antwerp's main shopping street, which connects the centre of town with Centraal Station, some fifteen minutes' walk to the east. At the start of Meir, near its junction with St Katelijnevest, the short Twaalfmaandenstraat ends in the **Beurs** (Mon–Fri 7.30am–7pm; free), the recently restored late nineteenth-century stock exchange, built as a rough copy of the medieval original which was burned to the ground in 1868. Gloomy and deserted, it's still a splendid extravagance, a high, glass-paned roof supported by spindly iron beams above the coats of arms of the maritime nations, with walls showing a giant map of the world.

The Rubenshuis

Back on the Meir, it's a five-minute walk east to Wapper, a mundane pedestrianized square, where the **Rubenshuis** at no. 9 (Tues–Sun 10am–5pm; F75) attracts tourists in droves. Arguably the greatest northern Baroque painter, and certainly Antwerp's most celebrated, his house was only acquired by the town in 1937, by which time it was little more than a shell. Skilfully restored, it opened as a museum in 1946. It's not so much a house as a mansion, splitting into two parts – on the left the traditional, gabled Flemish house, and on the right the classical Italian studio, where Rubens worked, taught and entertained the artistic and cultural elite of Europe. He had an enviably successful career, spending the first eight years of the seventeenth century studying the Renaissance masters in Italy, and settling in this house in 1608. Soon after, he painted the Antwerp Cathedral series and his fame spread, both as a painter and diplomat, working for Charles I in England, and receiving commissions from all over Europe.

Unfortunately, there are only one or two of his more undistinguished paintings here, and very little to represent the works of those other artists he collected so avidly throughout his life. The restoration of the rooms is convincing though, and a clearly arrowed tour twists its way through a pleasant series of domestic interiors, neatly panelled and attractively furnished. In contrast to the cramped living quarters, the spacious **art gallery** was where Rubens once displayed his favourite pictures to his friends, in a scene comparable to that portrayed in Willem van Haecht's *The Gallery of Cornelis van der Geest*, which is now on display here in the main gallery, a suitable illustration of Rubens' grand lifestyle. Behind the house, the garden is laid out in the formal style of his day, as it appears in Rubens' *Amid Honeysuckle*, now in Munich. The Baroque portico might also be familiar from the artist's Medici series, on display in the Louvre.

The St Jacobskerk

Rubens died in 1640 and was buried in the **St Jacobskerk**, just to the north of the Wapper at Lange Nieuwstraat 73 (April–Oct Mon–Sat 2–5pm; Nov–March Mon–Sat 9am–noon; F50). Very much the church of the Antwerp nobles, who lined up to be interred in its vaults and chapels, the church is a Gothic structure begun in 1491 but not finally finished until 1659, a delay that means much of its Gothic splendour is hidden by an over-decorous Baroque interior, the soaring heights of the nave broken and flattened by the heavy black altars. Seven chapels radiate out from the ambulatory, including the **Rubens Chapel**, directly behind the high altar, where the artist and his immediate family are buried beneath a tombstone in the floor whose lengthy Latin inscription gives details of his life. The chapel's altar was the gift of Helene Fourment, Rubens' second wife, and shows one of his last works, *Our Lady Surrounded by Saints*, in which he painted himself as Saint George, his wives as Martha and Mary, and his father as St Jerome. It's as if he knew this was to be his epitaph; indeed, he is said to have asked for his burial chapel to be adorned with nothing more than a painting of the Virgin Mary with Jesus in her arms, encircled by various saints.

The rest of the church is crammed with the chapels and tombs of the rich and powerful, who kept the city's artists busy with a string of commissions destined to hang above their earthly remains. Most is only of moderate interest, but the chapel next to the tomb of Rubens is worth a peek for its clumsily titled *St Carolus Borromeus Pleading with the Virgin on Behalf of those Stricken by the Plague*, completed by Jacob Jordaens in 1655. It's a dark, gaudy canvas, not without its ironies: Borromeus, (better known as Carlo Borromeo) Archbishop of Milan, was an ardent reactionary and leader of the Counter Reformation, while the artist was a committed Protestant. In the north aisle of the nave, there's the chapel of the Rockox family (see above) who are pictured on the panels of the triptych above the altar by Jan Sanders, and in the chapel at the far end of the south aisle, a flamboyant *St George and the Dragon* by van Dyck.

East to Centraal Station

Meir heads east from the Rubenshuis past its junction with Jezusstraat, where the carved relief on the building on the corner is a tribute to **Lodewijk van Berckem**, who introduced the skill of diamond-cutting to the city in 1476. From here, Leystraat, a continuation of Meir, is lined by a sweeping facade ending in a pair of high, turreted gables, whose gilt figures and cupolas formed the impressive main entrance to the nineteenth-century town. Straight ahead, the magnificent neo-Baroque **Centraal Station** was finished in 1905, a confusion of spires and balconies, glass domes and classical pillars designed by Louis Delacenserie, who had made his reputation as a restorer of Gothic buildings in Bruges. It's an extraordinary edifice, a well-considered blend of earlier architectural styles and fashions – particularly the Gothic lines of the main body of the building and the ticket hall, which has all the darkened mystery of a medieval church – yet displaying all the self-confidence of the new age of industrial progress. Sadly, the station was also the victim of one of the greatest cock-ups in Belgium: the construction of the underground tram tunnels by its side disturbed the water table so that the oak pillars supporting the station dried out, threatening it with collapse. The repairs took years and cost millions of francs, but the building has finally been restored to its full glory.

Immediately behind the station, Antwerp's **Zoo**, just off Koningin Astridplein (winter daily 9am–4.45pm; summer daily 9am–6.30pm; F370), is a fairly standard zoo, incorporating a dolphinarium (winter 11.30–3pm; summer at 2pm, 4pm & 5pm) and a planetarium (Sun & Wed at 2pm) – good for those with kids in tow, but otherwise probably not worth the money.

The Diamond District

The discreetly shabby streets just to the southwest of Centraal Station are home to the largest **diamond** market in the world. Behind these indifferent facades precious stones pour in from every continent to be cut or re-cut, polished and sold. There's no show of wealth, no grand bazaar, and no tax collector could ever keep track of the myriad deals that make the business hum.

The diamond trade is largely controlled by Orthodox Jews, many of whom arrived here from Eastern Europe toward the end of the nineteenth century, and are often the only obvious sign that the business exists at all. They make most of their money by acting as middlemen in a chain that starts in South Africa, where eighty percent of the world's diamond production is mined. As a form of price-fixing, the rate of production and the speed of distribution are strictly controlled by an all-powerful South African cartel led by the *De Beers* company, which organizes ten "showings" in London every year. Guests are there by invitation only, and although the quality of the assortment of diamonds in each lot is controlled by the producers, if potential purchasers fail to buy on three occasions they aren't invited again.

In the heart of the diamond district, the bright, modern **Provinciaal Diamantmuseum** at Lange Herentalsestraat 31 (daily 10am–5pm; free) deals with the geology, history, mining and cutting of diamonds in a series of clearly labelled displays. The photographs of early prospectors and examples of most of the major types of diamond are of particular interest, but it's all a bit of a public relations job, glossing over, for example, the lucrative trade in stolen gems, mine conditions in South Africa itself, or the devious way the former Soviet Union sold their thousands of diamonds without lowering the price fixed by *De Beers*. Every Saturday (2–5pm) there are diamond cutting demonstrations.

Antwerp's other museums

Though none is essential by any means, Antwerp has a number of other, more **specialist museums** that are either shrines of arcane interest or good places to shelter on rainy afternoons. The following is a more or less comprehensive round-up.

Middelheim Open-Air Staturary Museum, Middelheim Park, 5km south of the centre (Tues–Sun 10am–5pm; free). Has over 300 exhibits, including pieces by Henry Moore and Auguste Rodin.

Museum van Hedendaagse Kunst, Leuvenstraat 16–30 (Tues–Sun 10am–5pm; F100). Museum of contemporary art mounting large-scale, ambitious, avant-garde exhibitions: *Anti-art*, *Metalanguage* and the like.

Provinciaal Fotografiemuseum, Waalse Kaai 47 (Tues–Sun 10am–5pm; free). Mixes displays of all sorts of old photographic equipment with modern exhibitions of different photographic techniques. Labelling and guidebook in Flemish only.

Provinciaal Sterckshof Museum, Hooftvunderlei 160, Deurne (closed until May 1994, but was open March–Oct Tues–Thurs, Sat & Sun 10am–5pm). Period rooms and a large collection of silver.

Ridder Smidt van Gelder Museum, Belgielei 91 (visits are by prior arrangement only; phone ☎239 06 52). A collection of art and applied art donated to the city by an aristocratic patron of the same name. The Japanese and Chinese porcelain is especially fine.

Volkskundemuseum, Gildekamersstraat 2–6 (Tues–Sun 10am–5pm; F75). Folklore museum that provides a survey of Flemish popular life, with a particular emphasis on puppets and devotional objects.

Eating and drinking

Antwerp is a wonderful and inexpensive place to **eat**, full of informal café-restaurants, which excel at combining traditional Flemish techniques and dishes with Mediterranean, French and vegetarian cuisines. There are places serving decent food all over the city centre, and you don't pay much of a premium at places on or around Grote Markt.

For **lunches on the run**, there's a baker a few doors down Hoogstraat on the right selling sandwiches etc, a *frites* place almost opposite at Hoogstraat 1, as well as plenty of kebab and falafel places along Oude Koornmarkt.

Antwerp is also a fine place to **drink**. There are loads of bars in the city centre, notably those on Groenplaats, whose terraces make a nice place to watch the world go by in summer. The favourite local tipple, incidentally, is *De Koninck*, drunk by the *bolleke*, or small stemmed glass.

Restaurants

Brasseurs, 53 Britselei (☎237 69 01). Informal French-style brasserie. Lip-smacking sauces. Closed Sun.

Den Yzeren Pot, 12 Hendrik Conscienceplein (no phone). Excellent food with an ethno-vegetarian slant.

De Peerdestal, Wijngaardstraat 8, just west of Hendrik Conscienceplein (☎231 95 03). Undistinguished, touristy place, but *the* place to try horse-meat.

Facade, 18 Hendrik Conscienceplein (☎233 59 31). Funky atmosphere, good music and great food, influenced by just about everything. Vegetarian, meat and fish dishes.

Falafel Beny, Lange Herentalsestraat (☎234 26 32). Popular and cheap vegetarian café-restaurant.

Hippodroom, L. de Waelplein 10, near the Schone Kunsten Museum (☎238 89 36). Wide-ranging Flemish dishes and more. You can eat outside in the garden in summer. Closed Sun.

Metalurgie, Pieter Potstraat 1 (☎232 34 10). Menus on old pieces of steel, and the interiors a cross between a train and a steelworks. Good food, and a lively crowd.

Pizzeria Tony, Suikerrui, on the corner of Grote Markt (☎233 31 81). Decent, swiftly served pasta and pizza.

Popof, Oude Koornmarkt 18 (☎232 00 38). The best pies, desserts and gateaux in town. Closed Sun.

La Terrazza, Wisselstraat 2 (☎232 66 58). High quality, moderatately priced Italian restaurant at the northeast corner of Grote Markt.

Trattoria dal Dottore, Tabaksvest 93 (☎232 70 10). Despite its glum appearance, this is an excellent Italian restaurant. Try anything – especially the *Pizza Reginald* named in honour of a Flemish comedian who comes here regularly.

Viskeuken, Korte Koepoortstraat 10 on the corner of Kaaskrui and Melkmarkt (☎233 08 66). Wonderful, unpretentious fish restaurant, good for both lunch and dinner.

Bars

Bierland, Korte Nieuwestraat 28. Large city-centre speciality beer bar that claims to stock over 400 types of beer.

Den Billekletser, Hoogstraat 22. Chess, music, a youngish clientele and light meals and snacks at lunchtime.

De Cluyse, Oude Koornmarkt 26. Civilized bar housed in a wonderful thirteenth-century cellar. Rather staid, but good for a quiet drink.

De Duifkens, Graanmarkt, behind the Bourla Theatre. Old-style Antwerp café-bar that is popular with actors.

Het Elfde Gebod, Torfbrug 10, on the north side of the cathedral. Worth visiting for its interior alone – filled with a huge variety of ancient statues.

Den Engel, Grote Markt (northwest corner). Pleasantly-located bar, right on the main square in one of the guildhouses, which attracts a mixture of business people and refugees from the red light area.

L'Entropot du Congo, Vlaamse Kaai. An old warehouse outside the city centre that has been transformed into a café patronized by art students.

De Grote Witte Arend, Reyndersstraat 18. Pleasant old place set around a peaceful courtyard. Serves food.

Kulminator, Vleminckveld 32–34. Long-established bar that serves a very wide range of different beers, a 5min walk west of the centre.

Pavane, General Belliardstraat 17. Candlelit old wine-cellar – good for both a drink or its veggie snacks.

De Pelgrom, Pelgrimsstraat 15. Crowded cellar bar right in the centre of town that's usually full of Antwerp's young and boisterous.

Café Pelikaan, off Kaasrui, on the north side of the cathedral. Nicely situated but otherwise unspectacular bar that's normally full of locals.

Swingcafé, Suikkerrui. Good jazz and good beer in this lively, popular central haunt, and open well into the early hours.

De Volle Mann, Koornmarkt 7. Lively, noisy and youthful bar off main square. Always busy.

Wuzli Puzli, at the foot of the cathedral, close to *Het Elfde Gebod*. Good music and a fine collection of spirits.

Listings

Airlines *KLM* 13–15 second floor, Deurne Airport (☎239 79 79); *Sabena*, Appelmansstraat 12 (☎231 68 25).

Airport enquiries ☎218 12 11.

Bikes Can be rented at Centraal Station; standard rates.

Books English books are available from *Standaard*, Huidevetterstraat 57, and *Fnac*, Groenplaats 31.

Bureaux de change Outside bank hours there's an office at Centraal Station (daily 8.15am–10pm).

Buses and trams City transport enquiries at Teniersplaats in tram station Opera (Mon–Fri 8am–6pm, Sat 9am–noon) and at tram station Diamant, by Centraal Station (Mon–Fri 8am–12.30pm & 1.30–4pm, Sat 9am–12.30pm). Details of bus services in the province of Antwerp from the kiosk on Franklin Rooseveltplaats (Mon–Fri 7am–7pm, Sat 9am–4pm).

Car rental *All-Car-Rent*, Mechelsesteenweg 141 (☎230 81 00); *Avis*, Plantin en Moretuslei 62 (☎218 94 96), and at the airport (☎218 94 96); *Hertz*, Mechelsesteenweg 43 (☎233 29 92), and at the airport (☎230 16 41).

Chemists Details of 24-hr chemists are available from the tourist office and in weekend copies of local newspapers.

Cinema Good programmes at *Cartoons*, Kaastraat 4–6 (☎231 78 00).

Consulates *Ireland*, Rudolfstraat 30 (☎237 69 94); *UK*, Korte Klarenstraat 9 (☎232 69 40); *USA*, Rubens Centre, Nationalestraat 5 (☎225 00 71).

Doctors List of 24-hr doctors' service from the tourist office.

Emergencies Police ☎101; fire/ambulance ☎100.

Gay scene There's a small group of gay bars behind Centraal Station in Van Schoonhovenstraat and Dambruggestraat.

Hospital 24-hr service, St Elizabeth Hospital, Leopoldstraat 26 (☎234 41 11).

Left luggage Office (daily 6am–midnight) and coin-operated lockers at Centraal Station.

Lost property Police, Oudaan 5. Train, Centraal Station. City bus and trams, Grote Hondstraat 58 (Mon–Fri 8.30am–4pm).

Markets Second-hand goods, including some great bargains if your Flemish is up to haggling, Wed and Fri mornings on Vrijdagmarkt. General and bric-a-brac market, along with flowers, plants and birds, Sun mornings on Theatreplein. During the summer there are Sat antique and jumble markets on both Theatreplein and Lijnwaadmarkt, near the cathedral.

Post office Main office at Groenplaats 42 (Mon–Fri 9am–6pm; Sat 9am–noon).

Telephones International direct dialling and operator-connected calls at Jezusstraat 1 (daily 8am–8pm).

Train enquiries Centraal Station (Mon–Sat 8am–10pm, Sun 9am–5pm; ☎233 39 15).

Travel agents *JEST*, St-Katelijnevest 68 (☎232 38 71), is good for discount flights, student cards, etc.

North and east of Antwerp: the Kempen

North of Antwerp the flat, sandy moorlands of the **Kempen** stretch east as far as the River Maas: a once barren wasteland, punctuated by tracts of acid heath, bog and deciduous woodland, and dotted with the poorest of agricultural communities, its more hospitable parts were first cultivated and planted with pine by pioneering Cistercian monks in the twelfth century. The monks helped develop and sustain a strong regional identity and dialect, though today the area's towns and villages are drab and suburban, formless modern settlements with little to attract the visitor. The principal exception is **Geel**, with a couple of interesting medieval relics and a strong sense of its own long and unusual history.

Herentals and Geel

Some 20km east of Antwerp, dreary **HERENTALS** became the principal town of the Kempen in the fourteenth century and made a living by supplying Antwerp's brewers with fresh water by barge along the River Nete. Industrialized toward the end of the nineteenth century, the only building of any real interest is the medieval **St Waldetrudiskerk**, home to an intricate retable carved by Pasquier Borremans in the sixteenth century.

Seven kilometres to the east of Herentals, **GEEL** has an international reputation for its treatment of the psychiatric ill, who have been cared for within the community here for hundreds of years, though the system only came under orthodox medical control in the middle of the nineteenth century. The system has its origins in the tragedy of Saint Dimpna, a thirteenth-century Irish princess who fled her home and went into hiding near Geel as a result of her father's incestuous advances. The king managed to track her down and beheaded her, an act that could only have been committed, it was felt at the time, by a lunatic, and Dimpna's tomb became a centre of pilgrimage for those seeking a cure for madness. The **St Dimpnakerk** (Fri 10am–noon & 1–7pm, Sun 4–6pm), five minutes' walk east of the Markt along Nieuwstraat, supposedly marks the spot where she was interred, its striped fourteenth-century brickwork home to several fine examples of medieval craftsmanship. Framed by the slender pillars of the nave, these include a typically intricate mausoleum by Cornelis Floris (the architect of Antwerp's town hall) and several fine retables, one illustrating the Passion, the other the story of St Dimpna, carved with extraordinary attention to detail during the fourteenth and fifteenth centuries. Opposite the entrance to the church, the **Dimpna en Gasthuismuseum**, Gasthuisstraat 3 (April–Sept Wed, Thurs & Sun 2–5.30pm; F30), has a modest display of various aspects of local history.

Practicalities

Geel **tourist office** (Mon–Fri 9am–3.30pm; May to mid-Sept also Sat & Sun 10am–3pm; ☎014/57 09 55), in the town centre at Markt 1, has a list of private **rooms**, which they'll book for you at no charge. The *Sportwarande*, Markt 91 (☎014/58 80 19; ③), is the only conveniently situated **hotel**. As far as **eating** goes, try the prim and proper restaurant *Het Lam*, Markt 53, or *Taverne Toerist*, Markt 93, for cheaper snacks and meals.

Tongerlo Abbey

From Geel bus station, buses every 30 minutes make the fifteen-minute trip south to a bus stop that's a five-minute walk from the low brown buildings of **Tongerlo Abbey**. Founded in 1130, the abbey played a key role in the district's agricultural development until it was forcibly dissolved by the French in 1796. Re-established in 1840, it's become a flourishing farmstead once again, a hive of activity where the **Da Vinci Museum** (May–Sept Mon–Thurs & Sat 2–5pm) houses a copy of the great man's *Last Supper* by his pupil, a certain Andrea del Solario.

Turnhout

Readily accessible by train from Herentals and bus from Geel, **TURNHOUT** is typical of the industrialized towns of the northern Kempen, a careless, untidy sprawl fanning out into the surrounding countryside. The only conceivable object of interest is the **St Pieterskerk**, a giant, originally medieval brown-stone edifice that towers over the Grote Markt, its interior attractively Baroque in style. There's also a tiny **Museum van de Speelkaart** close by at Begijnenstraat 28, with an exhibition of playing cards through the ages – the product the town is famous for. Turnhout's **tourist office** is in the Stadhuis at Grote Markt 1 (Mon–Fri 9am–noon & 1.30–3.30pm ☎014/41 89 41). The best place to grab a bite to **eat** is the *Theatrecafé*, in an old theatre on the east side of the Grote Markt.

South of Antwerp: Lier and Mechelen

South and west of the city of Antwerp, the boundary between the provinces of East Flanders and Antwerp follows the line of the Scheldt as it meanders its way to the tiny villages just to the east of Dendermonde; here it meets the northern edge of the province of Brabant, whose boundary heads east, cutting between Mechelen and Brussels. Crisscrossed by rivers and canals, this western sector of the province of Antwerp is densely populated, a string of industrial townships dotted around the ancient cities of **Mechelen** and **Lier**.

Lier

Seventeen kilometres southeast of Antwerp, **LIER** has an air of suburban comfort, appropriate for what is basically the prosperous outskirts of a big city. Founded in the eighth century, Lier has always lived in the shadow of its larger neighbour, though Felix Timmermans, one of Belgium's best-known Flemish writers, did add a certain sparkle when he lived here from 1886 to 1947. The sparkle was needed – other Belgians once referred to Lier's citizens as "sheepheads", a reference to their reputation for stubbornness and stupidity.

The Town

Lier spreads out from a large, rectangular **Grote Markt**, encircled and bisected by waterways that mark the course of its old harbours and moats. At the centre of Grote Markt, the turreted fourteenth-century **Belfry** is incongruously attached to the classically elegant **Stadhuis**, built to replace the medieval cloth hall in 1740.

The **Municipal Museum Wuyts** (April–Oct daily except Wed & Fri 10am–noon & 1.30–5.30pm; Nov–March Sun only 10am–noon; F40; combined ticket with Opsomerhuis F60) is just off the northwest corner of the Grote Markt at Florent van Cauwenberghstraat 14. Its collection of paintings is surprisingly varied and includes several works by David Teniers the Younger, who made a small fortune from his realistically earthy peasant scenes, as represented by *The Alchemist* and *The Jealous Woman*. There's also a cruelly drawn *Brawling Peasants* by Jan Steen and a pious portrait of *St Theresa* by Rubens, as well as several works by the Bruegels: Pieter the Older and his two sons, Jan and Pieter the Younger. The most distinguished of their canvases here is the second Pieter's *Flemish Proverbs* (*Vlaamse Spreekwoorden*), illustrating over eighty proverbs satirizing every vice and foolery imaginable. There are explanations below each picture in Flemish, but most – like the man pissing against the moon – are self-explanatory. There's also a laughable, pseudo-religious painting by local artist Isidore Opsomer (see below) entitled *Christ Preaches to Lier*. A list of all the exhibits is available from reception, though only in Flemish.

From the southwest corner of the Grote Markt, Eikelstraat leads to the **Gevangenenpoort**, a strongly fortified medieval gate which served as the town's prison for many years. Opposite, the curious **Zimmertoren** (winter 9am–noon & 2–4pm; summer 9am–noon & 1–7pm in summer; F50) is an old section of the ramparts that now houses the remarkable clocks and astronomic studio of one Lodewijk Zimmer (1888–1970). A wealthy city merchant, Zimmer made his clocks and dials in a determined effort to dispel superstition and show his fellow townspeople how the cosmos worked. An exercise in mathematical and pictorial precision, Zimmer's *Centenary Clock* coordinates the phases of the moon, the zodiac, the tides of Lier and just about everything else you can think of, with a similar bevy of rotating dials in the studio above. The *Wonder Clock*, in the pavilion next door, is just as detailed and was exhibited at the World Fairs of Brussels and New York in the 1930s. A detailed guide explaining the internal works of the clocks and the meaning of all the dials is available in English for F40.

From beside the Zimmertoren, Schapekoppenstraat leads southwest to a sidegate into the **Begijnhof**, a mixture of cosy cottages and cramped terraced houses that edges toward the site of the old city walls. Founded in the thirteenth century, most of the surviving buildings date from the seventeenth century, including an elegant Baroque church whose proud, curving lines are badly in need of restoration.

Immediately southeast of the Zimmertoren, a narrow road crosses over an arm of the River Nete as it gracefully slices Lier into two. To the left, **Werf** was once the main city dock; to the right the **Timmermans-Opsomerhuis** (April–Oct daily except Wed & Fri 10am–noon & 1.30–5.30pm; Nov–March Sun only 10am–noon & 1.30–4.30pm; F40) celebrates the town's two most famous inhabitants, the writer Felix Timmermans and the painter Isidore Opsomer. Timmermans and Opsomer were good friends and thought of themselves as leading artistic custodians of Flemish culture, the one writing of traditional village life, most memorably in the earthy humour of his *Pallieter*; the other proud of his sea- and townscapes and of his influence on contemporary Belgian painters. Inside, the spacious rooms of the first floor contain a comprehensive selection of Opsomer's work, including a whole batch of heavy, rather pretentious portraits and, of more immediate appeal, a number of rural scenes, such as the Expressionistic *Middelburg*. An adjoining room is devoted to the work of their friend, the sculptor Lodewijk van Boeckel, whose old forge is surrounded by examples of his intricate, profoundly black – and somewhat aggressive – ironwork. Upstairs, there's a collection of writings by Timmermans, supplemented by several first editions together with general details of his life and times, all in Flemish.

Heading northeast along the Werf from here, the third turn on the right, Rechtestraat, leads to the **St Gummaruskerk** (Easter–Sept daily 9am–noon & 2–5pm; Oct–Easter daily 9am–noon & 2–4pm; free), which takes its name from a courtier of King Pepin of France, who settled in Lier as a hermit in the middle of the eighth century. Built in Flamboyant Gothic style in the fifteenth century, and painstakingly restored in the 1980s, the immense buttresses of the church, surmounted by a tiered and parapeted tower, dominate the surrounding streets. On the inside, chunky pillars rise up to support a vaulted roof, whose simplicity contrasts with the swirling, twisting embellishments of the **rood-loft** below, a decoration which frames a passionate bas-relief cartoon strip of Calvary and the Resurrection. Behind, the high altar is topped by a second fine carving, a wooden altarpiece of the fourteenth century whose inside panels are alive with a mass of finely observed detail, from the folds of the bed linen to the pile of kindling underneath Abraham's son. The church's **stained-glass windows** are reckoned to be some of the finest in Belgium, the five elongated windows above the high altar presented to the town by the Emperor Maximilian in 1516, a stately contrast to the more intimate themes and finely balanced yellows, reds, and blues of the windows overlooking the first section of the left-hand side of the choir, partly the work of Rombout Keldermans in 1475.

Practicalities

It takes just fifteen minutes for the train (every 30min) from Antwerp Centraal to reach Lier **train station**, which adjoins the **bus station**, ten minutes' walk north of Grote Markt; veer left out of the train station building, turn right at the main road and carry straight on. The **tourist office**, in the basement on the south side of the Stadhuis in the Grote Markt (Mon–Fri 9am–noon & 2–5pm; Easter–Oct also Sat & Sun same times; ☎03/489 11 11), can provide town maps (F30) and make **accommodation** bookings for free, although the options are limited. There's only one **hotel**, the trim *Handelshof* (☎03/480 03 10; ⑤) and just a handful of **private rooms** (②), most of them stuck out on Antwerpsesteenweg, a couple of kilometres northeast of the centre. For **food**, most day-trippers stick to the mundane snacks of the series of bars and restaurants in front of the Zimmertoren – the *Delfin* at no. 6 and the *Pallieter* at no. 11, are your best bets. Alternatively, *De Werf*, Werf 16, serves a wider range of meals, while at *Caves*, on nearby G. Timmermansplein, you can eat good food on a canalside terrace, or indulge in their wide range of ales.

Mechelen

Home of the Primate of Belgium and the country's ecclesiastical capital, **MECHELEN** was converted to Christianity by the itinerant eighth-century evangelist Saint Rombout. By the thirteenth century it had become one of the more powerful cities of medieval Flanders and entered a brief golden age when the Burgundian prince, Charles the Bold, decided to base his administration here in 1473. Impetuous and intemperate, Charles used the wealth of the Flemish towns

Begijnhof

Klein Begijnhof

St. Katelijne

Museum Hof van Busleyden

VAN HOEYSTR.

GOSWIN DE STASSARTSTRAAT

LANGE HEERGRACHT

Refuge of the Abbey of St. Truiden

ST. KATELIJNESTRAAT

KLAPGAT

St. Jan

BEST

FREDERIK DE MERODESTRAAT

WOLLMARKT

0   100 m

St. Rombout Cathedral

St. Pieter en Paulus

VEEMARKT.

Place of Margaret of Austria

Post Office

GROTE MARKT

BEFFERSTR.

Stadhuis

Tourist Office

Lakenhalle

Schepenhuis

HAVERWERT

IJZERENLEEN

BRUUL

De Zalm Museum

GOUDENSTR.

HOOGBRUG

River Dijle

ZOUTWERF

LANGE SCHIPSTRAAT

BRUUL

LEEMARKT

ONZE LIEVE VROUWSTRAAT

KORENMARKT

OLV Over de Dijle

HOOGSTRAAT

GR. VON EGMONTSTRAAT

Brusselpoort

MECHELEN

To Railway & Bus Station

to fund a series of campaigns that ended with his death on the battlefield in 1477. His widow, Margaret of York, and his son's regent, the remarkable Margaret of Austria, stayed in Mechelen and formed one of the most famous courts of the day. Artists and scholars were drawn here from all over Flanders, attracted by the Renaissance pomp and ceremony, with enormous feasts in fancy clothes in fancy buildings – a glamorous facade that camouflaged a serious political motive. Surrounded by wealthy, independent merchants and powerful, well-organized guilds, the dukes and duchesses of Burgundy realized that they had to impress and overawe as a condition of their survival.

Margaret of Austria died in 1530, the capital moved to Brussels and Mechelen was never quite the same. The *Baedeker* of 1900 described the town as a "dull place . . . totally destitute of the brisk traffic which enlivens most of the principal Belgian towns". Things aren't so bad today, but considering Mechelen's proximity to Antwerp and Brussels, it has a surprisingly provincial atmosphere supplemented by a modest range of sights that make for an enjoyable day out from either of its neighbours.

The Town

The centre of town is, as ever, **Grote Markt**, marked by a mundane statue of Margaret of Austria and flanked on the eastern side by the **Stadhuis**, whose bizarre and incoherent appearance was partly her responsibility. In 1526, she had the left-hand side of the original building demolished and replaced by what you see today, an ornate arched loggia backing onto a fluted, angular facade, to a design by Rombout Keldermans. The plan was to demolish and rebuild the rest of the building in stages, but after her death in 1530 the work was simply abandoned, leaving Keldermans' extravagance firmly glued to the plain stonework and the simple gables of the fourteenth-century section on the right. The interior of the later section (occasional opening; ask at the tourist office) is just as confused as the exterior, though there are a couple of interesting paintings – principally Coussaert's *A Sitting of the Parliament of Charles the Bold* and a fine sixteenth-century tapestry of the *Battle of Tunis*.

A little way west of the Grote Markt, the **Cathedral of St Rombout** (April–Sept daily 9am–noon & 2–6pm; Oct–March daily 9am–noon & 2–4pm; free) dominates the centre of Mechelen just as it was originally supposed to. A gigantic, buttressed church attached to a great square tower, work began with the draining of the surrounding marshes in 1217, though the money ran out before the tower was built, and the initial design had to be put on ice for over two hundred years. In 1451, the pope provided the extra funds when he put St Rombout on a list of specified churches where pilgrims could seek absolution for their sins without visiting Rome. Pilgrims and money rolled into Mechelen, and the present tower was completed by 1546. The problem today is that the structure is literally breaking up as it sinks unevenly into its foundations. A long-term effort to hold the church together began in 1963 and is still far from finished, encasing the building in almost permanent scaffolding.

Entry to the cathedral is around the back off Wollemarkt. Inside, the thirteenth-century nave has all the cloistered elegance of the Brabantine Gothic style, although the original lines are spoiled by an unfortunate series of seventeenth-century statues of the apostles. Between the arches lurks an extraordinary Baroque **pulpit**, a playful mass of twisted and curled oak dotted with carefully camouflaged animal carvings. To the right of the entrance, a chapel contains the tomb of Cardinal Mercier of Mechelen and a plaque, presented by the Church of England, commemorating his part in coordinating the Mechelen Conversations. These ran from 1921 up to the time of his death in 1926 and investigated the possibility of reuniting the two churches – although in Belgium Mercier is more often remembered for his staunch opposition to the German occupation of World War I. His pastoral letters, notably "Patriotism and Endurance", proclaimed loyalty to the Belgian king, paid tribute to the soldiers at the front and condemned the invasion as illegal and un-Christian.

The most distinguished painting in the church is in the south transept, where Van Dyck's muscular *Crucifixion* stands above a tidy eighteenth-century altar. Close by, the nine chapels of the **ambulatory** are rather dreary, with the exception of the Chapel of the Relics, dedicated to a group of monks and priests who were slaughtered by Protestants near Dordrecht in 1572. Their supposed remains are stored in a number of gilt caskets, surrounded by the coats of arms of the Knights of the Golden Fleece, a Burgundian order established by Philip the Good in 1430. The elaborate doors at the rear of the high altar hide the remains of St Rombout himself, and are opened on major religious festivals only, when the reliquary is paraded around the town centre. Incidentally, many of the columns in and around the ambulatory are made of wood painted as marble, a trompe l'oeil technique for which Mechelen was famous.

Attached to the church, the cathedral tower contains Belgium's finest **carillon**, a fifteenth-century affair of 49 bells. There are concerts throughout the year, and regular performances on Monday evenings between June and mid-September at 8.30pm. Guided tours of the tower leave from outside the tourist office regularly throughout the summer.

From the cathedral entrance, Wollemarkt leads north into Goswin de Stassartstraat, where the **Refuge of the Abbey of St Truiden** (no entry) sits prettily by an old weed-choked canal, its picturesque gables once home to the destitute. Opposite, an alley called Klapgat leads to the weathered sandstone of the church of **St Jan** (Sat & Sun 3–3.30pm), worth a visit for the beautiful setting it provides for an altar triptych by Rubens, painted in 1619. A fine example of the artist's use of variegated lighting, the central panel depicts the *Adoration of the Magi*, with Rubens' first wife portrayed as the Virgin.

A few metres further east along St Jansstraat, Mechelen's **Carillon School** (no entry) is one of the most prestigious institutions of its sort in the world, attracting students from as far away as Japan and helping the town to sustain its international reputation for carillon playing. Next door, the **Museum Hof van Busleyden** (daily except Tues 10am–noon & 2–5pm; F50) is housed in a splendid early sixteenth-century mansion, built in high Gothic style with Renaissance touches for Hieronymus Busleyden, a prominent member of Margaret's court. It's a confusing, poorly organized affair, but a reorganization and English guidebook are promised. The collection includes a display of miscellaneous bells, a room devoted to Mechelen's guilds, and a whole range of local artefacts dating from the Gallo-Roman period. There's also an interestng assortment of mostly unattributed paintings, including a seventeenth-century picture of the Groot Begijnhof supplemented by 46 miniatures of the Beguines at work, along with a graphic series of sixteen panels portraying the multiple sufferings of St Victor, painted for a local convent in around 1510.

The grotesque wooden doll by the museum entrance is **Op Signoorke**, whose festival is held every year on the second Sunday in September. Once a generalized symbol of male irresponsibility, the doll and its forebears had a variety of names – *vuilen bras* (unfaithful drunkard), *sotscop* (fool) and *vuilen bruidegom* (disloyal bridegroom) – until the events of 1775 redefined its identity. Every year it was customary for the dummy to be paraded through the streets and tossed up and down in a sheet. In 1775, however, a young man from Antwerp attempted to steal the doll and was badly beaten, as the people of Mechelen were convinced he was part of an Antwerp plot to rob them of their cherished mascot. The two cities were already great commercial rivals, and the incident soured relations even further. Indeed, when news of the beating reached Antwerp, there was sporadic rioting and calls for the city burghers to take some sort of revenge. Refusing to be intimidated, the people of Mechelen derisively renamed the doll after their old nickname for the people of Antwerp – "Op Signoorke", from "Signor", a reference to that city's favoured status under earlier Spanish kings. Today, although the doll has kept its nickname, the intense rivalry between the two cities has disappeared, and the festival is just a good excuse for a long drinking session.

From opposite the Carillon School, Biest leads southeast to the Veemarkt where the church of **St Pieter en St Paulus** (May–Sept Mon–Fri 9am–noon & 2.30–7pm, Sat & Sun 9am–noon & 2.30–5pm; Oct–April daily 9am–noon) was built for the Jesuits in the seventeenth century. The interior has a huge oak pulpit that pays tribute to the order's missionary work, carved in 1701 by Hendrik Verbruggen, with a globe near its base attached to representations of the four continents that were known at the time.

There's not much else, but if you've the inclination, the **Begijnhof** is to the northwest of town and provides a pleasant stroll, while to the south of the Grote Markt some intriguing sixteenth-century **facades** overlook the River Dijle from the Haverwerf. The most striking is the Devil's House, presumably named after the pagan-looking satyrs that adorn the windows. From here, it's a couple of minutes' walk southeast to the **Onze Lieve Vrouw over de Dijle**, on Onze Lieve Vrouwestraat (May, June & Sept Sat 2–6pm; July & Aug also Wed 2–5pm), begun in the fifteenth century, but only completed two hundred years later. Inside, Rubens' exquisite *Miraculous Draught of Fishes* was a triptych painted for the Fishmongers' Guild in 1618, the year when the artist confided to a friend "I am so overburdened with public and private tasks, and already committed for the future, that for the next few years I cannot even be master of my own person". Five minutes' walk away, on the southern edge of town, the **Brusselpoort** is the only survivor of Mechelen's twelve fourteenth-century gates.

Practicalities

Mechelen's **train** and adjoining **bus stations** are about fifteen minutes' walk south of the town centre, straight ahead down Hendrik Consciensestraat. The **tourist office**, in the Stadhuis on the east side of the Grote Markt (April–Sept Mon–Fri 8am–6pm, Sat & Sun 9.30am–5pm; Oct–March Mon–Fri 8am–5pm, Sat 10am–5pm; ☎015/29 76 55), has a handful of private **rooms**, which they will book on your behalf at no extra charge. Alternatively, the town has several centrally located **hotels**, of which the cheapest is the *Claes*, on the south side of town at Onze Lieve Vrouwestraat 51 (☎015/41 28 66; closed Dec–March; ④). For a convenient alternative, try the *Egmont*, near the station at Oude Brusselstraat 50 (☎015/42 13 99; ⑤–⑥).

There are plenty of **places to eat** around Grote Markt and along the main streets that lead off to the south – principally Bruul and Ijzerenleen. If money's tight, the café of the *INNO* department store on Bruul is the cheapest place in town, but more enjoyable are two moderately priced Spanish restaurants, *La Riera*, Veemarkt 24 (great paella), and the *Madrid*, overlooking the Dilje at Lange Schipstraat 4 (closed Tues). There are also excellent and cheap seafood delicacies at the *De Gouden Vis*, by the River Dilje, off Ijzerenleen on Nauwstraat. *Den Stillen*, Nauwstraat 9, is easily the best bar in town, with snacks, a canalside terrace and over three hundred beers to choose from. Otherwise try the bars on Grote Markt, or the lively *Lord Nelson* and *Arms of York* on Wollemarkt. Mechelen, incidentally, is well known for its beers, including *Toison d'Or* and *Gouden Carolus* – as recommended by Emperor Charles V.

Around Mechelen: Fort Breendonk
About 11km west of Mechelen, signposted off the main Antwerp–Brussels road just south of **WILLEBROEK**, **Fort Breendonk** (daily 10am–4pm; F75) was a Gestapo headquarters during World War II. Built as part of the circle of fortifications that ringed early twentieth-century Antwerp, it was established as a National Memorial in 1947, a tribute to the men and women who died or suffered in its dark, dank tunnels and cells. As you might expect, it's a powerful, disturbing place to visit, with a clearly marked tour taking you through the SS tribunal room, poignantly graffitied cells and the Bunker (or Torture Room). It also includes a museum dealing with prison life and the growth of Fascism.

Hasselt and around

The capital of the province of Limburg, **HASSELT** is a busy, modern town that acts as the administrative centre for the surrounding industrial region. A pleasant but unremarkable place, the roughly circular city centre fans out from a series of small interlocking squares, with surprisingly few buildings to indicate its medieval foundation. To compensate for this lack of appeal and to attract foreign investment, the local authority has spent millions of francs on lavish and imaginative prestige projects, from an excellent range of indoor and outdoor sports facilities to a massive culture complex that aims to draw some of the world's finest artists. But perhaps more than anything else, Hasselt is associated with the open-air museum of Bokrijk which lies some 8km east of town – an extraordinarily comprehensive reconstruction of traditional Belgian village life.

The Town

In Hasselt itself, there's nothing special to look at, although the **Gerechtshof** on Havermarkt, just off Grote Markt, is housed in the town's one surprise – a trim Art Deco building, whose flamboyant interior of brown tiles, statuettes and lamps is in pristine condition. There are four modest municipal **museums** each charging F80 for entry, or you can buy a combined ticket from the tourist office for F120. Of them, the **Nationaal Jenevermuseum**, north from the Grote Markt down Hoogstraat/Demerstraat at Witte Nonnenstraat 19 (Tues–Fri 10am–5pm, Sat & Sun 2–6pm; closed Jan), is probably the most interesting, sited in a restored nineteenth-century distillery and detailing the history of local jenever production, with a free drink included in the ticket price. The **Stadsmuseum**, nearby at Thonissenlaan 73 (same times, but closed until 1995), has displays on the history of fashion from 1830 to the present, while the **Stellingwerff-Waerdenhof Museum**, five minutes east of the Grote Markt at Maastrichterstraat 85 (same times), has some interesting Art Nouveau ceramics and possesses the oldest surviving monstrance in the world. Dating from 1297, it's reputed to bleed if subjected to sacrilege. Lastly, the **Beiaardmuseum** (June–Sept Sat & Sun 2–6pm; July & Aug also Tues–Fri 10am–5pm), in the tower of the St Quintinus cathedral on Vismarkt, covers the development and workings of carillons.

Practicalities

Ten minutes' walk east of the adjoining **train** and **bus stations** – along Stationsplein and keep straight ahead – the Hasselt **tourist office** is right in the centre of town at Lombaardstraat 3 (Mon–Fri 9am–5pm; also April–Oct Sat 10am–4pm; ☎011/23 95 40) and has free maps and information. There are no private rooms in town, and the cheapest place to **stay** is the *Hotel Schoofs*, by the train station at Stationsplein 7 (☎011/22 31 88; ②). Otherwise, there's the handy *Hotel Pax*, Grote Markt 16 (☎011/22 38 75; ④). **Eating** in Hasselt is easy: there are numerous cheap bars and restaurants on and around Grote Markt and Botermarkt and adjoining Zuivelmarkt. The popular *Majestic*, Grote Markt 2, is a good place for snacks; the *Martenshuys*, Zuivelmarkt 18, serves both light meals and more substantial dishes. The *De Karakol*, Zuivelmarkt 16 (closed Mon), is a more expensive restaurant, with a varied menu including vegetarian dishes. The *De Levensboom*, a couple of minutes' walk south of the Grote Markt at Leopoldplein 44 (closed Mon), is entirely vegetarian.

The Bokrijk Park and Museum

The **Open-Air Museum of Bokrijk** (Openluchtmuseum; April–Sept daily 10am–6pm; Oct daily 9am–5pm; F200) is one of the best of its type in the country, a series of reconstructed buildings and villages from various parts of Flemish Belgium spread out within an enormous park of rolling fields and forest. Each village has been meticulously restructured, each building thoroughly researched, and although the emphasis is still largely on rural life, it's a bias partly balanced by the reconstruction of a small medieval cityscape in one corner of the park. Perhaps inevitably it gives a rather idealized picture, and certainly the assembled artefacts sometimes feel out of context and rather antiseptic. But the museum is tremendously popular and some of the individual displays outstanding. An excellent English guidebook provides a wealth of detail about every exhibit, and the whole museum is clearly labelled and directions well marked.

The museum's collection is divided into five sections, each with its own colour code. The most extensive range of buildings is in the **yellow** sector, where there are a number of Kempen farmhouses, from the long gables of a building from Helchteren to a series of compound (all-inclusive) farms that come from all over the provinces of Antwerp and Limburg. Other highlights include a lovely half-timbered blacksmith's workshop from the village of Neeroeteren, a bakehouse from Oostmalle, a fully operational oil-press from Ellikom, an entire eleventh-century church from Erpekom and a peat-storage barn from Kalmthout. One particular curiosity is the skittle-alley and pall-mall. Throughout the Middle Ages, skittles was a popular pastime among all social classes, played in tavern and monastery alike. The original game had nine targets arranged in a diamond pattern until some time in the sixteenth century, when it was banned because the pattern was associated with gambling, and replaced by the more familiar ten-skittle game. Pall-mall, where heavy balls are driven through an iron ring with a mallet, was popular throughout Europe in the seventeenth and eighteenth centuries, but is now confined to some of the more remote villages of Limburg.

The open-air museum occupies most of the western half of the **Bokrijk estate**, whose other marked attractions include a herb garden, a fine arboretum with over three thousand identified shrubs and trees, an animal park, a nature reserve, and a rose garden. These spread out east of the museum section from beside the park's administrative building, the nineteenth-century **Kasteel Bokrijk**, which adjoins an information centre. The park is open daily during daylight hours throughout the year and entrance is free.

Practicalities

There are two easy ways of reaching Bokrijk from Hasselt: **buses** #1 and #46 leave from the bus station every twenty minutes and pass the museum entrance (F50); **trains** leave hourly, take ten minutes, cost much the same and drop you off a five-minute walk from the gates. For **food**, the *St Gummarus* restaurant, straight ahead of the main entrance, serves reasonable food at affordable rates. If you want to **stay** near here, camping is not allowed in the Bokrijk estate, but there is a **youth hostel** (☎011/35 62 20; closed Nov–Feb), reachable through the park some 2km north of Bokrijk train station – just follow the signs from the information centre.

Diest

Some 20km west of Hasselt, the small and ancient town of **DIEST** lies just south of the River Demer, its cramped but leafy centre still partly surrounded by the remnants of the town's once mighty fortifications, built to guard the eastern approaches to Brussels.

Its centre, **Grote Markt**, a fifteen-minute walk from the train station toward the southern end of the old town, is a wide-open, irregularly shaped area, edged by trim seventeenth- and eighteenth-century facades. The spartan Stadhuis houses the municipal **museum** (April–Oct daily 10am–noon & 2–5pm; free), hidden away in the old vaulted cellars, whose prime exhibits are some seventeenth-century silver suits of armour and a fearful, anonymous *Last Judgment* from about 1430. More interesting is the **Begijnhof**, a five-minute walk along Koning Albertstraat, and one of the best preserved in this part of Belgium, founded in the thirteenth century and retaining much of its medieval shape and atmosphere. The main entrance at the far end of Begijnenstraat – a continuation of Koning Albertstraat – is marked by an extravagant Baroque portal with a niche framing a statue of the Virgin above a text that reads "Come in my garden, my sister and bride". Nearby, the weathered fourteenth-century Gothic chapel has an elegant Rococo interior.

The Begijnhof also harbours **Gasthof 1618**, on Kerkstraat, a restaurant, adorned with all sorts of bric-a-brac ranging from pikes and swords to holy statues, that serves excellent, traditional Flemish food at high prices. While you're here, either of the local brews – *Gildebier* or *Diesterse* – is worth tasting, or you can try old-fashioned sweets made in the traditional way at the "museum" on Engelen Conventstraat (July & Aug daily 2–5pm; otherwise Sat & Sun only).

For devotees of nineteenth-century municipal fortifications, the **Schaffensepoort,** five minutes east of the station, is a dramatic defile through concentric lines of ramparts and across the River Demer. Heavy, studded oak gates indicate an enthusiasm for defence that was superseded by the development of more effective artillery.

Practicalities

Diest **tourist office,** next to the museum in the Stadhuis basement on the Grote Markt (Mon–Sat 10am–noon & 1–5pm; ☎013/31 21 21), has free town maps and – although it's unlikely you'll want to stay – a list of local **hotels,** the cheapest convenient choice being the *De Fransche Croon,* just south of the Grote Markt at Leuvensestraat 26 (☎013/31 45 40; ⑤). There's also a **youth hostel** at St Jansstraat 2 (☎013/31 37 21), ten minutes' walk east of the Grote Markt, overlooking the city park – take Berchmansstraat/Botermarkt from the Grote Markt, turn left along Wolvenstraat, keep going until the park at the end, then turn right. For **eating,** try the solid snacks of the *Old Tom,* Grote Markt 15; the *Pergolesi,* nearby at no. 28; or the Flemish food of *Gasthuis 1618* (see previous page).

Genk

About 15km east of Hasselt, approaching the Dutch frontier, the gritty industrial town of **GENK** was a tiny, inconsequential village until the discovery of coal and the development of the Limburg coalfield at the start of the century. Bolstered by the mines, its economy – and the region – prospered until the 1960s, when the enforced contraction of coalmining led to periods of intense labour unrest and steep rises in unemployment, both in Genk and in the surrounding pit villages. This situation has been complicated by the composition of the workforce, which, in contrast to British mines, includes a high percentage of immigrant workers. Desperate efforts have been made to diversify the local economy, notably with the establishment of a giant Ford car factory, but right-wing pressures for various forms of repatriation have been strong.

South of Hasselt: Tongeren and St Truiden

South of Hasselt, the Kempen opens out into the **Haspengouw,** a fertile expanse of gently undulating land that fills out the southern part of the province of Limburg, its soils especially suited to fruit growing. Frankly, the scenery is rather dreary, though blossom time shows it at its best, and the area's tiny towns and villages spread carelessly along the sides of the roads without much charm or style. Even so, the ancient towns of **St Truiden** and more particularly **Tongeren** are well worth a visit for their wide range of historic monuments.

Tongeren

Twenty kilometres southeast of Hasselt, tiny **TONGEREN** is the oldest town in Belgium, built on the site of a Roman camp on the important route to Cologne. Destroyed by the Franks and razed by the Vikings, its early history was plagued by misfortune, though it became a prosperous dependency of the bishops of

Liège during the Middle Ages. Nowadays, it's a small market town with an old-fashioned, rural appearance on the border of Belgium's language divide.

Five minutes' walk west of the train station, the haughty statue of Ambiorix, in the Grote Markt, is supposed to commemorate a local chieftain who defeated the Romans here in 54 BC – a "noble savage" inspired more by mid-nineteenth-century Belgian nationalism than historical accuracy. Directly opposite, the **Onze Lieve Vrouwekerk** (daily 9am–noon & 2–5pm) towers over the city centre, with an impressive, symmetrical elegance that belies its piecemeal construction: it's the eleventh- to sixteenth-century outcome of an original fourth-century foundation that was the first church to be dedicated to the Virgin north of the Alps. Still very much in use, the dark tomb-like interior has preserved the feel of Catholic mystery with a bedecked, medieval, walnut statue of "Our Lady of Tongeren" in the north transept, surrounded by candles and overhung by a gaudy canopy. In the choir, an intricately carved retable shows scenes from the life of the Virgin, and just outside are the well-preserved columns of the medieval cloister. The church **treasury** (same times; F20) is full of reliquaries, monstrances and reliquary shrines from as early as the tenth century. Bones and bits of body poke out at you from every corner, but best are a beautiful sixth-century Merovingian buckle, a pious and passive *Head of Christ* and an eleventh-century *Shrine of the Martyrs of Trier*.

On the right-hand side of the church, a small section of the second **Roman city wall** has been carefully excavated, though unfortunately it's underground and access is by a short flight of steps more reminiscent of a urinal than an archeological site. Nearby, on the southern side of the Grote Markt, the eighteenth-century **Stadhuis** houses an unremarkable municipal **museum** (daily 10am–noon & 2–4.30pm; F30), whose exhibits illustrate the town's history. Tongeren's main museum, the **Gallo-Romeins** (Tues–Sat 9am–noon & 2–5pm, Sun 2–5pm; F20), is a couple of minutes' walk east of here along Groendreef, at Kielenstraat 15, and features a miscellany of prehistoric and Roman bric-a-brac that's really only of interest to the specialist. The **Moerenpoort** (May–Aug Sat & Sun 10am–4pm) was one of Tongeren's six medieval gates and is now home to a small military museum.

Practicalities

Tongeren's **train** and adjoining **bus stations** are five minutes' walk east of the Grote Markt, along Stationslaan and Maastrichterstraat. For **accommodation**, the town's **tourist office**, in the Stadhuis (May–Sept Mon–Fri 8am–noon & 1–4.30pm, Sat & Sun 10am–noon & 2–5pm; Oct–April Mon–Fri 9am–noon & 1–4.30pm; ☎012/23 29 61), has the details of a handful of private **rooms**, for about F1100 for a double per night, and will call ahead to make a booking. There are also three conveniently situated **hotels**, of which the *Chemin de Fer*, at Stationslaan 44 (☎012/23 31 05), with doubles for F1000, and *Lido*, Grote Markt 19 (☎012/23 19 48), which charges F1900, are cheapest. There's a **camping** complex, *Pliniusbron*, a twenty-minute walk north of the Grote Markt; take St Truiderstraat west from the Grote Markt, turn right down Beukenbergweg, the third road along, and keep straight down past the eighteenth-century Castle Betho. For **food**, *'t Vrijthof*, by the Onze Lieve Vrouwekerk at Graanmarkt 5, serves excellent fish dishes, the *Du Phare*, Grote Markt 21, is good for snacks, and the *Etna*, Grote Markt 23, serves cheap pizzas.

St Truiden

Around 20km west of Tongeren, the small market town of **SINT TRUIDEN** grew up around an abbey founded by St Trudo in the seventh century and is today surrounded by the orchards of the Haspengouw. Known for the variety, if not the excellence, of its ancient churches, St Truiden is only of moderate interest, but it is the best place to catch the bus to the spectacular church at the village of Zoutleeuw.

The town's Grote Markt is edged by an elegant eighteenth-century **Stadhuis**, attached to an older **Belfry** – the middle of three sturdy towers that push against each other on the east side of the square. On the right, the spire of the **Onze Lieve Vrouwekerk** has had a particularly chequered history: built in the eleventh century, it's been dogged by misfortune and in 1668 gave everyone a shock when it simply dropped off; it wasn't replaced for two hundred years. On the left, the untidy, truncated **Abdijtoren** dates from the eleventh century, a massive remnant of the original religious complex that once dominated the medieval town. The abbey has been replaced by a dull and forbidding seminary that spreads out from the tower, though the ornate **gateway** does break the monotony – a carved relief showing the cruel, misogynistic legend attached to the abbey's foundation. The story goes that every time Saint Trudo tried to build a church, it was pulled down by an interfering woman. Not to be thwarted, Trudo prayed fervently and the woman was stricken with paralysis.

The pick of St Truiden's many other churches are **St Gangulfus**, just west of the Grote Markt down Diesterstraat (daily 9am–5pm), and **St Pieters** (same times), south along Naamsesteenweg. Extensively renovated and built in the eleventh and twelfth centuries respectively, both these churches are classically Romanesque mixtures of cubic and square forms. For its period, the ribless cross-vaulting of St Pieters was experimental; the architect balanced the risk by deciding not to put windows in the upper walls.

Practicalities

St Truiden's **tourist office**, in the Stadhuis (Mon–Sat 8am–noon & 1–5pm; April–Sept also Sun 10.30am–12.30pm & 1.30–4.30pm; ☎011/68 68 72), has brochures with details of cycle routes in the countryside around the town, but no private rooms. The **hotel** *Cicindria*, just north of the Grote Markt at Abdijstraat 6 (☎011/68 13 44; ④), is probably the best place to stay. The coffee bar *Rimini*, Grote Markt 40, serves good, cheap **snacks**. Buses for Zoutleeuw leave beside the train station (Mon–Fri 2 hourly 8am–6pm; Sat & Sun once every 2 hours).

Eastern Brabant: Zoutleeuw and Tienen

Just inside the eastern boundary of the province of Brabant, the tiny village of **ZOUTLEEUW**, well connected by bus to both St Truiden, 7km to the east, and Tienen, 15km west, was prosperous from the thirteenth to the fifteenth centuries, though it's been in economic decline ever since. Its rambling, irregularly turreted and towered church, **St Leonardus** (April–Sept daily except Mon 2–5pm; F30), has a magnificently intact pre-Reformation interior that's among the most impressive in the country. Clearly labelled in English, it's crammed with the accumulated treasures – paintings, statues, sculptures – of several hundred years, its dark and mysterious nave and chapels redolent of medieval superstition. There's a wrought-iron, sixteenth-century double-sided image of the Virgin high in the nave, a fifteenth-century wooden cross hanging in the choir arch, an intricate altar and retable of St Anna, and, in the south transept, a fifteenth-century chapel dedicated to St Leonard, whose life is outlined in a gorgeous, naive altarpiece by Arnold de Maeler. Pride of place goes to the huge stone tabernacle carved in almost miraculous perspective by Cornelis Floris, architect of Antwerp's town hall, between 1550 and 1552. Opposite the church, the sixteenth-century **Stadhuis** was designed by Rombout Keldermans and now houses the **tourist office** (April–Sept Tues–Sat 10am–noon & 1–4pm, Sun 1–5pm; Oct–March Tues–Fri 2–4pm; ☎011/78 12 88).

Tienen

The sugar-beet centre of Belgium, the undistinguished town of **TIENEN** spirals out from a pleasant, open main square that's fringed by a tidy nineteenth-century **Stadhuis** and the solemn late medieval bulk of the church of **Onze Lieve den Poel**. The interior of the church is predictably Baroque, but it's unusual in that it has no nave. Directly behind the Stadhuis and up on the hill, the church of **St Germanus** is a ninth-century foundation that's been repeatedly rebuilt and reshaped. The western facade is imposing, and inside there are some particularly theatrical statues dating from the sixteenth and seventeenth centuries. The *Au Nouveau Monde hotel*, opposite the station at 4e Lancierslaan 75 (☎016/81 43 21; ③), is a convenient place to **stay**, should you want to. The **tourist office** is in the Stadhuis (☎016/81 61 37).

travel details

Trains

Antwerp to: Amsterdam (hourly; 2hr 15min); Bruges (hourly; 1hr 10min); Brussels (every 20 min; 40min) for Brussels–Paris (7 daily; 3hr); Diest (every 30 min; 50min); Geel (hourly; 40min); Hasselt (every 30 min; 70min); Lier (every 30 min; 15min); Mechelen (every 20 min; 20min).

Diest to: Leuven (hourly; 45min).

Hasselt to: Bokrijk (hourly; 15min); Diest (every 30 min; 15min); Liège (hourly; 55min); St Truiden (1 or 2 hourly; 15min); Tongeren (hourly; 20min).

Tienen to: Brussels (hourly; 40min).

Tongeren to: Hasselt (hourly; 20min); Liège (hourly; 30min).

Turnhout to: Herentals (hourly; 15min).

Buses

Geel to: Turnhout (every 30 min; 40min).

St Truiden to: Zoutleeuw (Mon–Fri every 30 min, Sat & Sun 1 every 2hr; 10min).

Tienen to: Zoutleeuw (Mon–Fri every 30 min, Sat & Sun 1 every 2 hours; 20min).

CHAPTER TEN

HAINAUT

Southwest of Brussels, the central portion of Wallonia is given over mainly to the province of **Hainaut**, a rolling agricultural area in its western reaches, but in the east, between Mons and Charleroi, home to one of Belgium's most concentrated belts of industry. The highlight of Hainaut is **Tournai** in the western part of the province, close to the French border. Once part of France, it's a relaxing, rather genteel place, with a number of decent museums and the finest Romanesque–Gothic cathedral in the country. East of

Tournai, **Mons** and the industrial and engineering city of **Charleroi** – the provincial capital – are less interesting, although you may have to use one or the other as a base for seeing some of Hainaut's more scattered attractions, especially if you're travelling by public transport. Mons is sited just to the east of the coal-mining area of the **Borinage** and is home to a fine Gothic church and a couple of interesting museums covering the town's role in both world wars. Within easy striking distance there are several castles and stately homes, of which **Beloeil** is the grandest, while the countryside around Charleroi holds several abbeys, notably that of **Villers-la-Ville** – outstanding in size if nothing else. To the north, **Soignies** and **Nivelles**, the latter the principal town of French-speaking Brabant, contain superb examples of religious Romanesque architecture, though otherwise they're nothing special. South of Charleroi, the **Botte de Hainaut** is actually an extension of the Ardennes, so named for its position jutting deep into France from Hainaut's southeastern corner and growing hillier and more beautiful the further southwest you go. Half of the "boot" is officially Namur province, but for touring purposes it's included here. **Chimay**, the main town, merits a visit for its castle and charming old centre; **Couvin**, a little way east, is also quite picturesque and has more plentiful accommodation. Outside of Couvin or Chimay you'll more often than not need a tent – and definitely a car.

ACCOMMODATION PRICE CODES

All the **hotels and hostels** detailed in this chapter have been graded according to the following price categories. Note that the prices have been calculated as those for the cheapest double room during high season. For more on accommodation, see p.280.

① Up to F1000 per person.	③ F1500–2000.	⑥ F3000–4000.
② F1000–1500.	④ F2000–2500.	⑦ F4000–5000.
	⑤ F2500–3000.	⑧ F5000 and over.

Tournai

TOURNAI is the nearest equivalent that southern Belgium has to the Flemish "art towns" of Flanders and the north: prosperous and bourgeois, it's a pleasant and relaxing place to spend a couple of days. Along with Tongeren it's the oldest town in Belgium: Clovis, the Merovingian king, was born here in 465 and made it the capital of his kingdom; later it became the first capital of the Frankish kingdom, remaining in French hands for a large part of its history, and staying loyal to France during the Hundred Years War. Tournai fell into the hands of the French kings in 1187, was incorporated in the Netherlands in 1521 and retaken by Louis XIV in 1667, who left his mark on the physiognomy of the town with a number of striking buildings, some of which survive, mostly along quai Notre-Dame and rue St-Nicholas. Louis was also responsible for the construction of the dockside walls and houses that flank parts of the river. Sadly much of Tournai's beautifully preserved old centre was destroyed by Allied bombing, but the town does *feel* old, and its cathedral is renowned as perhaps the finest in the country.

To Mont-St.Aubert

BOULEVARD DELWART

BOULEVARD EISENHOWER

River des Trous

PONT DES TROUS

River Escaut

QUAI ST.LINE

Bus
Station

BOULEVARD DES NERVIENS

Train
Station

RUE DU CHATEAU

Tour Henry VIII
(Musée d'Armes)

AVENUE LERAY

Pl.
Crombez

Ste.Marie
Madeleine

St.Nicolas

QUAI DUMON

RUE DU SONDART

RUE BEYAERT

PONT DE

RUE ROYALE

RUE ST.JACQUES

RUE DU CYGNE

QUAI NOTRE DAME

RUE DUBUCQUERELLE

RUE CHILDERIC

Chap.de
l'Athenée

St.Jacques

RUE DES CARMES

Musée d'Historie
et d'Archeologie

RUE PERQUE

RUE DE LYSER

RUE DE L'HOPITAL

RUE DU MARCHE POISSON

RUE DE MONNEL

RUE DE PONT

RUE DU QUESNOY

PLACE
CLOVIS

St.Brice

RUE ST.BRICE

St.Quentin

RUE DES MAUX

RUE CURE N.D.

QUAI ST.BRICE

River Escaut

To Camping
de L'Orient 750m

PLACE DE
L'EVECHE

GRAND
PLACE

PLACE
ST-PIERRE

QUAI VIFOUIN

Halle de Daps

Cathedral

RUE ST.GEORGES

Belfry

RUE DES CHAPELIERS

Tourist
Office

RUE DES PUITS L'EAU

RUE DES CLAIRSSES

RUE TÊTE D'OR

RUE ST.JEAN

Maison
Tournaisienne

RUE ST.MARTIN

PL.R.
ASTRID

QUAI TAILLE PIERRES

Musée de la
Tapisserie

BLVD BARA

Youth
Hostel

RUE STE.CATHERINE

Musée des
Beaux Arts

Hôtel
de Ville

Parc
Communal

RUE DES JESUITES

BLVD. LALAING

RUE DU CHAMBGET

RUE DE LA JUSTICE

AVE DES ETATS-UNIS

0   200 m

BLVD. DU ROI ALBERT

TOURNAI

Arrival, information and accommodation

Tournai's **train station** is located on the northern edge of the town about 400m from the river – five to ten minutes' walk from the centre. The **tourist office** is at rue du Vieux Marché-aux-Poteries 14, right opposite the belfry (Mon–Fri 9am–7pm, Sat & Sun 10am–1pm & 3–6pm; ☎069/22 20 45). It has a list of **hotels**, the cheapest of which are on or around the Grande Place. *Aux Armes de Tournai*, five minutes beyond the Grande Place on place de Lille 24, the square at the end of rue des Maux and rue Dorez (☎069/22 67 23; ②–③), is probably the best of the budget choices; alternatively, try the similarly priced *Tour St-Georges*, behind the Halle de Draps at rue St Georges 2 (☎069/22 53 00; ②–③). A notch up in price, curly gabled *L'Europe*, at Grande Place 36 (☎069/ 22 40 67; ③–④), is perhaps the best-sited of Tournai's hotels, and has a restaurant, as does the pricier *Cathédrale*, on place St-Pierre (☎069/21 50 77; ⑤). There's a very handily located **youth hostel** towards the end of rue St-Martin at no. 64, right by the Beaux Arts museum, open April to September (☎069/21 61 36). The nearest **campsite** is *Camping de l'Orient* (☎069/22 26 35), about 500m east of the ring road along rue Vieux Chemin de Mons.

The Town

The town centre is split down the middle by the River Escaut (Scheldt) and girdled by a ring road that follows the course of the old city ramparts. Most things of interest are on the southern side of the river, grouped around or within easy walking distance of the main hub, the sprawling, roughly triangular **Grande Place**. The main sight, the **Cathédrale**, is just east of here.

The Cathédrale Notre-Dame

Dominating the skyline with its distinctive five towers is Tournai's Romanesque **Cathédrale Notre-Dame** (April–Oct daily 9am–noon & 2–6pm; Nov–March daily 2–4.30pm; free), built with the wealth of the flourishing wool and stone trades out of the local slate-coloured Tournai marble – a stone which led to a school of architecture and sculpture developing here whose influence was felt throughout the Scheldt valley. The present structure is the third church on this site, most of it completed in the latter half of the twelfth century – though the choir was reconstructed in the middle of the thirteenth. Apart from the spired towers, the most unusual feature of the exterior is the west facade on place de l'Evêche, which has three tiers of sculptures dating from the fourteenth to seventeenth centuries, though they are currently shrouded in scaffolding, the subject of a major restoration. Assuming you can see them, the oldest, along the bottom, carved from local stone, narrate scenes from the story of Adam and Eve among other Old Testament themes. Around the corner, the northern Porte Mantile sports earlier sculpture, much of which is contemporary with the church – slightly decrepit morality scenes of Virtue fighting Vice, Avarice, and Satan and the like.

The entrance is on the south side, the choir and nave unexpectedly almost the same length. The nave is part of the original structure, erected in 1171, as are the intricately carved capitals, but the vaulted roof is eighteenth century. The choir was the first manifestation of the Gothic style in Belgium (where it appeared later than in France), and its too-slender columns had to be reinforced later at the base – the whole still leans slightly to one side due to the unstable soil beneath. Communication galleries run along the inside, evidence of a Norman influence, while in front of the choir the Renaissance rood screen is a flamboyant marble extravaganza by Cornelis Floris. The ample and majestic late twelfth-century transepts are probably the most impressive – and most beautiful – feature of the cathedral. Apsed and aisled to a very unusual plan, they impart a lovely diffuse light through the many windows, some of which (in the south transept) hold superb sixteenth-century stained glass by Arnoult de Nimegue, depicting semi-mythical scenes from far back in Tournai's history. The side chapels of the north transept have a number of twelfth-century wall paintings, a pock-marked cartoon strip of figures set against a beautiful blue background that shows a clear Byzantine influence in both style and form, while, to the left of the entrance, a chapel holds a melodramatic *Crucifixion* by Jordaens. Take a look, too, at Rubens' characteristically bold *Souls in Purgatory*, which hangs, newly restored, in the north aisle of the choir.

Be sure to see the **Treasury** before you leave (F30), which houses two important gilt reliquaries: the Romanesque–Gothic *châsse de Notre-Dame* (1207) by Nicolas de Verdun, with its fluidly carved robes and expressive faces, and medallions on the top evoking the life of Christ; and the *châsse de St Eleuthère* (1247), the first bishop of Tournai – a richer and more ostentatious but less elegant work. There is also a Byzantine Cross, Quinten Matsys' early sixteenth-century *Ecce Homo*, showing Christ surrounded by monstrous faces, as well as a tapestry sewn in Arras showing the lives of St Piat and St Eleuthère. Dated to the end of the fourteenth century, it's apparently the only Arras tapestry of the period which can be certified as authentic. You can see a selection of the cathedral's treasures carried around the town each year in the *Procession de Notre-Dame* – held on the second Sunday in September.

Across the way from the cathedral, virtually on the corner of the Grande Place, the **Belfry** is the oldest such structure in Belgium, its lower portion dating from 1200. The bottom level held a prison cell, while higher up there's a minuscule balcony from which public proclamations were made, and above that, a carillon, dating from the sixteenth to the nineteenth centuries. You can normally go inside and climb to the top for a view over the town , though at the time of writing it was undergoing a substantial restoration.

Around the Grande Place

A few steps west of the Belfry, on the Grande Place itself, the fine seventeenth-century **Halle aux Draps** maintains its original sombre grey facade, although the inside has been rebuilt after destruction in the wartime bombing. A few metres away, back toward the belfry, an alley leads to the **Musée de Folklore**, housed in the so-called **Maison Tournaisienne** (daily except Tues 10am–noon & 2–5.30pm; F50), and holding several floors detailing old Tournai trades and daily life in the mid-nineteenth century – although its reconstructions of various workshops and domestic rooms are not terribly spectacular. The highlight is a reconstruction of the cloister on the second floor, where there's a cell dotted with pathetic tokens left by impoverished parents, who were forced to leave their children here. Particularly affecting are the letters cut in half in the vain hope that they would be rejoined at a later date – something which rarely happened.

On the northwest side of the Grande Place, the rock-solid, fortress-like church of **St-Quentin** is also impressive from the outside, another building with its original (thirteenth-century) facade, but it has a disappointing, partially rebuilt interior. Continuing north, the church of **St-Jacques** is more interesting, with a twelfth-century tower and slightly later nave. Just up from here, behind a discreet brown door, the combined **Musée d'Histoire et d'Archéologie**, rue des Carmes 8 (same times; free), contains – as well as an attached prehistorical section – rooms devoted to the development of Tournai sculpture, a modest collection of pewterware and a good sample of porcelain from the town's own factory, which produced mostly Chinese-influenced work.

In the opposite direction, just south of the Grande Place on place Reine Astrid, the **Musée de la Tapisserie** (same times; free) features old tapestries on the first floor and modern works above. Tournai was among the most important pictorial tapestry centres in Belgium in the fifteenth and sixteenth centuries, producing characteristically huge works, juxtaposing many characters and several episodes of history, and leaving no empty space – a stylized design without borders. Major themes included history, heraldry and mythology, and although several of the best surviving Tournai tapestries are in Brussels, there are one or two good examples here, not least the tapestry of *Hercules* – an excellent and still richly coloured instance of the tendency to cram the picture with life and wry observation. Around the corner, cut through the gardens to the eighteenth-century **Hôtel de Ville**, part of which now houses a small **natural history museum** (same times; free); it was renovated following a hefty bombardment during the last war. Behind, the **Musée des Beaux Arts** (daily 10am–noon and 2–5.30pm, closed Tues; F50) is housed in a spacious and symmetrical late-Twenties building by Victor Horta, and has a well-displayed collection of mainly Belgian painting from the Flemish primitives to the twentieth century. There's work by Roger van der Weyden, a native of Tournai, including a precise triptych, paintings by Pieter Breughel the Younger and Jan Gossaert, and some big, fleshy pieces by Jordaens. One room holds the work of one L. Galliat, a nineteenth-century artist, two of whose vast historical canvases – of the *Plague in Tournai* and the *Coronation of Charles V* – virtually cover a whole wall. There are also a number of works by French Impressionists – among which Manet's romantic *Argenteuil* and the swirling colours of Monet's *Marine* stand out.

Along the river

The only remaining part of Tournai's old city ramparts is the thirteenth-century **Pont des Trous**, on the northern edge of the centre. Otherwise many of the buildings along the river show a clear French influence, especially those left from the time of Louis XIV, although curiously enough the town was also English for five years from 1513 to 1518, after Henry VIII seized it in a war against France. All that remains of the citadel he built is a tower, near the station side, known as the **Tour Henri VIII** – basically a cylindrical keep, with walls over 6m wide and a conical brick-vaulted roof, located in some public gardens. Nowadays it's home to Tournai's **Musée d'Armes** (same times; F50) with a display on the Belgian Resistance. On the same side of the river there are two restored **Romanesque houses** (1172–1200) in rue St-Brice – said to be the oldest examples of bourgeois dwellings in western Europe. Sadly you can't go inside, though their precarious, leaning appearance is convincing enough.

Eating and drinking

There are plenty of places for an affordable **snack or meal** in central Tournai. The slightly dour *A La Bancloque*, just down from the belfry at rue des Chapeliers 46, has delicious crepes, while, next door to the tourist office, the *Bistro de la Cathèdrale*, rue Vieux Marché aux Poteries 15, has excellent daily specials for around F400, and is *the* place to try the local speciality, *lapin à la Tournaissienne* (rabbit cooked in beer); The *Petit Bedon*, rue des Maux 6, near the St Quentin church, is a good place for fish – menus start at F600 – and, close by, the *Carillon*, Grande Place 64, has nice food if you don't mind spending a touch more. *Le Verdi*, rue de l'Yser 2, a minute from the Grande Place, is a simple Italian place, with decent and well-priced pasta dishes and pizzas cooked in a wood-fired oven .

If all you want is a **drink**, the *Tavern de l'Aigle*, just along from the Halle aux Draps on the Grande Place, is as good a place as any, as is the faded *Quai des Brumes* on place St Pierre. There are a few good bars, too, down by the riverside – *Au Scaldis*, and *Le Belize* on quai Notre-Dame, *Le Petit Boudon* on Quai Marché aux Poissons, and, a little further along, at quai Tailles-Pierres 3, *La Cave à Bières* has an excellent selection of regional beers (and does food), but sadly its opening times are limited (evenings only Thurs–Sun, plus Sun lunchtimes).

Out of Tournai: Mont-St-Aubert and Antoing

There's not much to see around Tournai, but the countryside around the hamlet of **MONT-ST-AUBERT**, 7km out of town, is nice for gentle hikes, though you really need a car to get there. Otherwise, take bus #U from outside the train station to **KAIN**, from where it's a fifteen-minute walk uphill. Helpfully, suggested walks are marked on a board near the village church. Beware on summer weekends, though, when Mont–St–Aubert and environs can be packed with escaping townies.

Otherwise the only real thing to see near Tournai is the neo-Gothic castle of the princes of Ligne at **ANTOING**, 5km south of the town. Originally twelfth century, it was the site of some of the first stirrings of rebellion against the Spanish in the mid-sixteenth century, though most of it – aside from the twelfth-century double walls and a sixteenth-century tower – is a nineteenth-century reconstruction. The slow train to Mons stops here, but the castle is only open on Sundays, when there are tours at 3pm, 3.30pm, 4.30pm, 5pm, and 5.30pm.

Mons and around

About half an hour by train from Tournai, the name of **MONS** may be familiar for its military associations. It was the site of battles that for Britain marked the beginning and end of World War I, and in 1944 it was the location of the first big American victory on Belgian soil in the liberation campaign. It has also been a key military base since the last war: SHAPE (Supreme Headquarters Allied Powers in Europe) has its headquarters at Maisières, just outside, providing employment for thousands of Americans and other NATO nationals – something which gives the town a lively, cosmopolitan feel for somewhere so small. It's a pleasant town, too, with a smattering of attractions in itself, and is a useful base for exploring the surrounding countryside.

Arrival, information and accommodation

The **train station** is on the western edge of the town centre, on place Leopold, a ten-minute walk up the hill from the central Grande Place, where at no. 22 you'll find the **tourist office** (daily 9am–6pm; ☎065/33 55 80), with information on the town and around, as well as leaflets detailing the major battlefield sites. There's also a Hainaut regional office at rue des Clercs 31 (Mon–Fri 8am–noon & 1–5pm; ☎065/36 04 64).

There are not many decent reasonably priced **hotels** in the town centre. The *Residence*, a five-minute walk east of the station at rue A. Masquelier 4 (☎065/31 14 03; ③), is the cheapest option. More expensively, there's the *St Georges*, very central at rue des Clercs 15 (☎065/31 16 29; ③–④), and its more luxurious partner hotel, the oddly-named but very friendly *Infohotel*, rue d'Havre 32 (☎065/35 62 21; ⑤), which has pleasant if rather functional doubles with TV and telephone. The tourist office also has details of a handful of **private rooms** and studios for rent, though often only in July and August (②). **Campers** should head for *Camping Communal*, a fifteen-minute walk east of the Grande Place at avenue St-Pierre 17 (☎065/33 79 23). Take rue d'Havre and then avenue Reine Astrid in the direction of Binche/Charleroi; then do a right.

The Town

The **Grande Place** is the centre of most Mons life and activity, its terrace cafés a nice place for an early evening drink. Dominating the square, the fifteenth-century **Hôtel de Ville** is a considerably altered building, its tower dating from the early eighteenth century. Some of the rooms inside are open for guided tours in July and August (1daily; F50), and hold the odd fancy chimneypiece, tapestries and paintings. Outside, on the front wall, there's a fifteenth-century brass monkey that brings good luck to all who stroke him, and has a bald, polished crown as a result.

Walk through to the back of the Hôtel de Ville, via the courtyard and tunnel to the Jardin du Mayeur beyond, and you'll come to the **Musées du Centenaire** (daily 10am–12.30pm & 2–6pm; summer until 5pm on Fri; winter until 5pm on Sun; closed Mon; F60 for all four, F30 for one). This is a complex of four museums under one roof, with displays ranging from ceramics to coins and medals, although the emphasis is on the town's involvement in the two world wars. On the ground floor there's one of the most complete displays in Europe on World War I and the various nationalities involved, and another detailing the American liberation of Belgium in 1944 and 1945. Items include battlefield relics, regimental drums, weapons and uniforms. Other exhibits record life in Mons during the German occupations of both wars, during the second of which (after the French withdrawal in 1940) Mons was virtually deserted by its inhabitants, 2000 remaining out of twenty-eight thousand. On the first floor, the Ceramics Museum features a fine collection of Delftware, over four hundred pieces in all, while the second floor holds a Numismatic Museum, with some eighteen thousand coins and medals, and a Prehistoric Museum of limited appeal.

Around the corner from the Hôtel de Ville, on rue Neuve, the **Musée des Beaux Arts** (same times; F30) has a collection of paintings that ranges from the sixteenth century to the present day. It's not as heavyweight a museum as the one in Tournai, and its permanent collection is in any case only shown in rotation,

---

MONS IN THE WARS

Mons has figured highly in both world wars. During **World War I**, in the latter part of August 1914, the British forces here found themselves outnumbered by the Germans by something like twenty to one. The subsequent Battle of Mons began on August 26, and the British – in spite of great heroics (the first two Victoria Crosses were awarded at Mons) – were inevitably defeated and forced into retreat. The casualties might have been greater. But according to a newspaper article written soon after the battle by the horror-story writer, Arthur Machen, the troops were spared by a host of bow-bearing angels – the so-called **Angels of Mons** – hovering overhead, just at the point when the Germans were about to launch their final attack, causing them to fall back in fear and amazement. Machen later admitted that he had made the whole thing up, but at the time the story took on the status of legend, giving rise to any number of spinoffs, and soldiers (those that were lucky enough) returned home with similar stories of supernatural happenings on the battlefield. The tale also undoubtedly had a morale-boosting effect (and perhaps purpose), giving brief respite at home from the horrible casualty figures that were more normally reported from the front. There's a painting of the event, by one Marcel Gillis, in the Mons Hôtel de Ville.

The town remained in German hands until it was liberated by the Canadians in November 1918. Mons was, however, at the centre of the fighting again during **World War II**. It was occupied by the French on May 10, 1940, but, after a long and vicious German bombardment that went on for nine days, they were forced to withdraw. By the time the Nazis entered the town it had almost entirely been abandoned. Four years later, on September 2, 1944, the Allies took Mons again after more fierce fighting, this time from the air.

much of the museum's space being given over to (often excellent) temporary exhibitions. However, among the things you might be able to view are paintings by Jan Gossaert and Cornelis de Vos, a good selection of works by later Dutch seventeeth-century artists, and more modern canvases by Paul Delvaux and others. There's also a rotating collection of modern sculpture. Next door, down an alleyway, is another museum, though again of rather limited interest, the **Musée de la Vie Montoise** (same times; F30), housed in the Maison Jean Lescarts, which has tidy displays on the development of Mons as a fortress town, local folklore, carnivals and customs.

To the southwest of the Grande Place, along and around rue des Clercs, are the town's best-preserved medieval streets, a string of twisting lanes and alleys that lead up to the Baroque **Belfry** and its gardens, from where there are fine views (daily 10am–5pm). Below, the **Collégiale Ste-Waudru** (daily except Mon 9am–5pm; free) is a good example of the late Gothic style, a massive and majestic church which displays an unusual uniformity in its architecture. There is much to see inside, most importantly the Renaissance works of the local sculptor Jacques du Broeucq, whose alabaster rood loft (1535–39) was broken up in the Revolution, and is now spread around different parts of the church. There are hyper-realistic reliefs in the transepts, choir, and on the high altar, though the most distinguished piece is arguably the swirling *Last Supper* in one of the ambulatory chapels. The **Treasury**, too, is of interest (July & Aug daily 2–6pm; F25), with local goldsmiths' work from the thirteenth to nineteenth centuries.

Behind the church at the foot of rue Notre Dame Debonnaire, the **Musée Chanoine Puissant** occupies a sixteenth-century house known as the Vieux Logis and the adjacent St Marguerite's chapel on rue des Sars (same times; F30). It's made up of the private collection of an eponymous canon, who died in 1934 bequeathing an eclectic mix of chimneypieces, furniture, wrought-iron wares, and drawings from different periods, though mostly sixteenth and seventeenth century. The most impressive item is in the first room of the Vieux Logis – a 1531 wooden ceiling (upright against the back wall) beautifully carved in Renaissance style, taken from a pavilion in town.

Eating and drinking

There aren't a huge number of **restaurants** for a town of Mons' size, and many of the most obvious ones, on and around Grande Place, aren't up to much. Despite its name, the *Copenhagen Tavern*, Grande Place 11, is a good old standard serving a decent array of mid-priced Belgian dishes as well as Danish smörgasbord and the like. The *No Maison* opposite, is much the same sort of place, with reasonably priced daily specials, while *La Trattoria*, Grande Place 31, is the best of a large number of Italian restaurants around here, with fairly good wood-fired oven-cooked pizzas. *La Marchal*, Rampe Ste-Waudru 4, right by the church, is the place to make for if you're willing to spend a little more – wonderful food and, considering the quality of the cooking, moderate prices.

For **drinking**, head for *Atelier*, on the corner of rue de la Grande Triperie and rue des Fripiers, a cosy bar with a good choice of beer; nearby, *La Podo*, rue de la Coupe 43, is a livelier, more youthful hangout with, again, an excellent choice of beers. On Grande Place, *L'Excelsior* is another pleasant place to drink, with a large beer menu and filling snacks.

Around Mons

Mons is usually visited for its surrounding attractions. The nearest and most obvious of these is the **Vincent van Gogh house**, southwest of the city in the suburb of Cuesmes. But there are others besides, notably the castles of **Beloeil** and **Attre** about 15km to the northwest.

Vincent van Gogh and the Borinage

The region immediately west of Mons is known as the **Borinage**, a poor, thickly populated industrial area that in the latter half of the nineteenth century was one of Belgium's three main coal fields, an ugly jigsaw of slag heaps and mining villages that spread toward the French frontier until decline set in early this century. In 1878, after a period in a Protestant school in Brussels, Vincent van Gogh was sent here as a missionary, living in acute poverty and helping the villagers in their fight for social justice – behaviour which so appalled the church authorities that he was forced to leave. He returned the following year and lived in **CUESMES**, on the southern outskirts of Mons – a fact that is, inevitably, opportunistically promoted, but although the connection is important in terms of van Gogh's career – it was here that he first started drawing seriously – there's very little to see. Inspiration to draw came from the hard life of the miners: "J'aime tellement ce triste pays du Borinage qui toujours me sera inoubliable . . . C'est en somme dans le Borinage que j'ai, pour la première fois, commencé à travailler sur nature." The **house** van Gogh occupied (Tues–Sun 10am–6pm; F50) has been restored, but it really is disappointing, with just two standard rooms containing prints of his study-drawings of the period and later famous paintings. Not even "the room as he left it" or a reconstruction of how it was, and no original work. If you're determined to make a thankless pilgrimage, take bus #1 or #2 from outside Mons station (every 30min); it's a ten-minute walk to the van Gogh house from the bus stop.

Beloeil and Attre

Further out of Mons, the château of **Beloeil** (April–Sept daily 10am–6pm; F390 combined ticket for park and château, F100 château only; park daily 9am–8pm) is known as the Versailles of Belgium, an inflated tag that – whatever your views on Louis XIV's palace – is bound to cause disappointment. Built for the aristocratic Ligne family in the late seventeenth century, it's a stately building without question, but the main body was rebuilt after a fire in 1900, and the interior, though lavish enough, with tapestries, paintings and furniture, is run-of-the-mill extravagance, the collected indulgences of various generations of Lignes, who have lived at Beloeil since the fourteenth century. Best parts are the library, which contains twenty thousand volumes, many ancient and beautifully bound, and the eighteenth-century formal gardens outside, the largest in the country, designed by Parisian architect and decorator Jean-Michel Chevotet – though even these are unkempt around the edges and dotted with stagnant ponds. Their grandeur is further diminished by the recreation area and model village in the far corner.

The nearest train station to Beloeil is at **ATH**, connected by hourly train to Mons, a thirty-minute journey; buses leave from outside the station to Beloeil (another half-hour). Allow plenty of time because the buses are fairly irregular. From the stop in the village it's a hundred metre walk to the chateau.

If you want to have a day out, you can visit the château at **ATTRE**, too. Attre is on the Mons–Ath train line, the château about 2km north of the station, or you can take a bus from Ath and save yourself a walk at the other end. The **Château d'Attre** (April–June & Sept–Oct Sat & Sun 10am–noon & 2–6pm; July & Aug daily 10am–noon & 2–6pm, closed Wed; F100, park only F50) is much smaller than Beloeil, more like a country house than a castle. But it has a charm that Beloeil lacks, with a more lived-in, human feel, in part induced by the arrangements of freshly picked flowers chosen to enhance the character of each room. The different styles of the rooms mark not only the passing of time but also the decreasing fortunes of the family that lived here – something that's also explained well on the (obligatory) guided tours.

A neo-Classical structure completed in 1752 on the site of a distinctly less comfortable medieval fortress, the house was a frequent residence of the Archduchess Marie-Christine of Austria and her husband, the governor general of the Southern Netherlands during the reign of Joseph II, and it is filled with their carefully selected furniture. Some of the walls are still covered with the original hand-painted wallpaper (the designs often Chinese in inspiration), some of which is two hundred years old but no less brightly coloured for that. The rooms themselves hold collections of porcelain and silver, as well as paintings by Watteau and other artists of the time. Outside, the grounds hold some deliberately wild "English Gardens", a Romantic "ruin" built at the bottom of the park as a folly, an artificial hill topped with a mock-Swiss chalet and the remains of a tenth-century tower that is said to have been the refuge of a local villain.

Soignies and Ronquières

About 20km north of Mons, **SOIGNIES** is easy to reach from Mons by train, although there's nothing much to bring you here apart from the town's Romanesque church, the **Collégiale St-Vincent** – in the centre of the town, a ten-minute walk from the station along rue de la Station. Dedicated to one St Vincent Madelgar, the husband of St Waudru of Mons, who died here in 677 after founding a monastery, the church was begun in 965 and built over the ensuing three centuries. A squat and severe edifice with two heavy towers, it is sombrely decorated inside, its nave similar to that of Tournai, with Lombardian arches. The transept is eleventh century but now has seventeenth-century vaulting. The oldest section is the huge cavernous choir, dating from 960 and containing one of the church's most outstanding features, a set of Renaissance choir stalls from 1576. Look out also for the fifteenth-century terracotta entombment on the south side of the choir, and the fourteenth-century polychrome Virgin beside the rood screen.

Opposite the church entrance, down a little side street (rue Henri Leroy), is an ancient cemetery with a chapel even older than the church. It contains a tiny archeological museum open only on Sunday afternoon (May–Oct 3–6pm). If you're feeling hungry, grab a cheap meal at the *Croissant d'Or* next to the church.

North of Soignies, **RONQUIERES** is perhaps more interesting, if only because of its one attraction, a curious "lift" or sloping lock for boats travelling on the Charleroi–Brussels canal. When the device was built in 1963 it cut the journey time between Charleroi and Brussels by around seven hours. It consists of two huge water tanks, each 91m long, which shift barges up or down 70m (depending on the change of water level) over a distance of 1500m. A neighbouring tower gives a birds-eye view of the proceedings, and also provides an audiovisual display on the area (May–Aug 10am–6pm; F70). Sadly, though, Ronqières isn't easy to reach from Soignies: you need to take a five-minute train ride to **BRAINE-LE-COMTE** 8km away, and a bus from there (direction Nivelles).

About 12km east of Soignies, parts of the fortified castle of **Ecaussinnes Lalaing** (July & Aug daily except Tues & Wed 10am–noon & 2–6pm; April–June & Sept–Oct Sat & Sun 10am–noon & 2–6pm; F120) date from the twelfth century but the rest has been altered over the centuries up to the eighteenth century. In the hall and armoury there are early sixteenth-century chimneypieces; other rooms contain furniture, glass and Tournai porcelain, and a fifteenth-century kitchen stands as it would have looked then. Ecaussinnes Lalaing isn't easy to get to: again, trains run from Braine-le-Comte but only to Ecaussines-Carrières station, in the industrial township of Ecaussines d'Enghen, about 3km west.

Binche

Halfway between Mons and Charleroi, **BINCHE** is a sleepy little town at the southern end of Hainaut's most decayed industrial region that in February erupts for several days with one of the best, and most renowned, of the country's **carnivals**.

The Town

Most things of interest are at the far end of the **Grande Place** – a spacious square edged by the **Hôtel de Ville**, built in 1555 by Jacques Du Broeucq to replace an earlier building destroyed during an invasion the previous year by Henry II of France. Beyond the Grande Place stands a statue of a "Gille", one of the figures that dance through the city streets during carnival, sandwiched between the dilapidated **Collégiale St-Ursmer** and the **Musée International du Carnaval et du Masque** (Nov–March Mon–Fri 9am–noon & 1–5pm, Sat & Sun 2–6pm; April–Oct Mon–Fri 9am–noon & 2–6pm, Sat 2–6pm, Sun 10am–noon & 2–6pm; F150), which claims to be the only worldwide museum of carnivals in the world. True or not, its collection of masks and fancy dress from carnivals throughout Europe, Africa, Asia and seven Latin American countries is impressive and is complemented by an audiovisual presentation on the Binche carnival and temporary associated exhibitions. Behind the church, a small **park** marks the site of the town's medieval citadel and contains what little remains of the former palace of Mary of Hungary. The park is buttressed by the original **ramparts**, which date from the twelfth to the fourteenth centuries and curve around much of the town, complete with 27 towers.

Practicalities . . . and the carnival

To get to Binche from Mons by train, change at **LA LOUVIERE**; otherwise, bus #22 makes the forty-minute journey every half-hour from outside Mons train station. From Charleroi buses run every hour. The Binche **tourist office** – such as there is one – is located in the Hôtel de Ville on the Grande Place (Mon–Fri 9.30am–12.30pm & 2–5pm; ☎064/33 37 21), a ten-minute walk from the train station. **Accommodation** is a problem: Binche has no hotels, and the nearest

campsite, *Aux Gloriettes*, rue de la Résistance (☎064/33 26 11), is far outside the centre, to the west. For **food**, try the reasonable *Restaurant Industrie*, tucked away in a corner at Grande Place 4, where a hearty meal will cost you F400 or so.

Carnival has been celebrated in Binche since the fourteenth century. The festivities last for several days, getting started in earnest on the Sunday before Shrove Tuesday, when thousands turn out in costume, and leading up to the main events on Shrove Tuesday itself, when the traditional *Gilles* in clogs and embroidered costumes are out from dawn onward. In the morning they wear "green-eyed" masks, dancing in the Grande Place carrying bunches of sticks to ward off bad spirits. In the afternoon they don their plumes – a mammoth piece of headgear made of ostrich feathers – and throw oranges to the crowd (it used to be bread) as they pass through the town in procession.

Charleroi

CHARLEROI stinks. You can smell it as you approach. Belching chimneys dot its horizon, beyond which rise grass-covered slag heaps. Glass works, coal mines and iron foundries have made the town the centre of one of Belgium's main industrial areas, and, although you can reach it easily from just about anywhere in Belgium, there's little reason to do so. It has a couple of decent museums, but these can just as easily be seen using Mons, or even Brussels, as a base. You might, however, find yourself here in the course of travelling down to the Botte de Hainaut to the south, where the countryside is among the province's finest.

The Town

Charleroi divides into two distinct parts: the lower town, where you will probably arrive, and the upper town whose circular **place Charles II** is the city centre. The **Hôtel de Ville**, on the western side, is home to Charleroi's best museum, the **Musée des Beaux Arts** (Tues–Sat 9am–5pm; F50), whose excellent works by Hainaut artists and others who lived or worked in the province can be found at the top of a magnificent Art Deco staircase. There are the naturalistic works of Constantin Meunier depicting life in the mines and factories, romantic paintings by the Charleroi artist François Navez and a number of canvases by Pierre Paulus, whose work combines an earnest attempt to depict the grimy Charleroi industrial landscape with a rather paternalistic view of factory workers in general. There are also paintings by Magritte, notably the whimsical *La Liberté de l'Esprit*, and an indifferent *Annonciation* by Delvaux, as well as an upstairs display devoted to the life and times of one Jules Destrée, a local poet and socialist politician (and good friend of Pierre Paulus), who campaigned hard for improvements in working conditions hereabouts.

Charleroi's other main museum, the **Musée du Verre**, is housed in the *Institut National du Verre* on boulevard Defontaine, on the far side of place Charles II (same times; F50). A fascinating survey of all things glassy, the museum displays many beautiful glass items from different periods: Egyptian jewellery and vases, Roman and Venetian glass, and contemporary glass works, alongside displays dedicated to the material itself – what it is, how it is made, its history, and suchlike. There's also a small archeology museum in the basement.

To Brussels

0   200 m

CHARLEROI

CHAUSÉE DE BRUXELLES

PTE DE WATERLOO

BLVD. G. ROUILLER

BLVD. F. DEWANDRE

RUE DU FORT

RUE DU MAMBOURG

BLVD. SOLVAY

RUE ZENOBE GRAMME

AVE DE WATERLOO

AVE JOS HENIN

RUE ISAAC

RUE DE FORT

Palais des Expositions

UPPER TOWN

RUE LEON BERNUS

BLVD. J. BERTRAND

RUE CHAVANNES

RUE NEUVE

BLVD. P. JANSON

BLVD. JOSEPH II

Palais des Beaux Arts

AVE DE L'EUROPE

RUE DE LA RÉGENCE

RUE LABORATOIRE

RUE DE LA SCIENCE

BLVD. P. JANSON

PL DU MANÈGE

Musée du Verre

RUE TURENNE

BLVD BERTRAND

RUE DUMONCIN

PLACE CHARLES II

Basilique St Christopher

BLVD. DEFONTAINE

AVE G. MICHEL

To Mons

AVE DES ALLIES

Hôtel de Ville

RUE DU GOUVERNMENT

Gare de Ouest

BLVD DE L'YSER

RUE D'ORLEANS

RUE DE LA MONTAGNE

BLVD. AUDENT

RUE BRIGADE PIRON

RUE WILLY ERNST

PLACE DE LA DIGUE

RUE DE DAMPREMY

RUE DE MONTIGNIES

RUE DAGNELIES

To Musée de Photographie

Post Office

BLVD. JOSEPH TIROU

PL ALBERT

RUE DU PONT NEUF

RUE DE MONTIGNY

LOWER TOWN

PLACE BUISSET

RUE LEOPOLD

Tourist Office

QUAI DE BRABANT

River Sambre

BLVD. JOSEPH TIROU

River Sambre

Gare du Sud

The **Musée National de Photographie** (Tues–Sun 10am–6pm; F50) is just outside Charleroi, with 2000 square metres of space devoted to photos and the history of the camera and photography. Take bus #70, #71 or #170 from the Gare du Sud to avenue Paul Pastur 11, Mont-sur-Marchienne.

Practicalities

Charleroi has two **train stations**, the Gare du Sud, where you're likely to arrive, and the Gare de Ouest, in the city centre. The **tourist office** occupies a kiosk in front of Gare du Sud (Mon–Fri 8.30am–noon & 1–5pm; ☎071/31 82 18) and hands out free city maps and the like. Buses run up to place du Manège in the upper town every few minutes throughout the day, and metro trains run to the same square every ten minutes from the adjacent metro station. Failing that, it's only a ten-minute walk. If you want to **stay overnight**, the *Grand Hôtel Buisset*, near the Gare du Sud at place Buisset 2 (☎071/31 45 88; ③), is perhaps the cheapest and most convenient option; another option is the *Pim's Hotel*, across the square at place Buisset 13 (☎071/33 44 40; ⑤).

There are plenty of **restaurants and bars** around place du Manège and in the adjacent streets. Ethnic restaurants predominate: try *Athenes*, place du Manège 19, for excellent, well-priced Greek food, or the *Imperial* next door, which does a good line in home-made Italian dishes – a neat option for a light lunch or big dinner. At the other end of the square, *La Bonne Fourchette*, boulevard Bertrand 55, serves couscous and kebabs, or, if all you want is straight Belgian grub, there's the moderately priced *Le Napoléon*, on place Charles II. Of the **bars**, *Les Templiers*, also on the square, is a convivial place whose *plats du jour* are a good lunch alternative, as is the lunch counter of *Gourmets d'Asie* on place Charles II. Finally, for entertainment, it's well worth checking out what's happening at the **Palais des Beaux Arts**, behind the Hôtel de Ville, on place du Manège. It's Charleroi's – and the region's – cultural and entertainment centre, attracting some of the bigger names in rock music.

Into Brabant: Nivelles and Villers-la-Ville

Travel far north of Charleroi and you cross the border into **Brabant**, whose southern French-speaking districts form a final band of countryside before you enter the sprawl of Brussels, beginning with the characterless splurge of Waterloo (see *"Brussels and Around"*). **Nivelles** is the area's main town, worth a stop on the way north and a short bike ride from the Cistercian abbey ruins at **Villers-la-Ville**.

Nivelles

NIVELLES grew up around its monastery, which was founded here in the seventh century and became one of the most powerful religious foundations hereabouts. Nowadays, most people visit the town for the remains of the former monastery, notably the enormous **Collégiale Ste-Gertrude**, a restored version of a tenth- to twelfth-century original badly damaged in World War II and sadly with little atmosphere or sense of age. It is, however, an interesting building architecturally, a good example of a Romanesque abbey church. Restoration began in 1948 and wasn't finished until 1984. The church is named after the first abbess of the monastery, the daughter of the woman who founded it. It was built in several stages from the tenth century onward and some of its later additions show the influence of the Ottoman architecture of the period. It has two transepts and two choirs at opposite ends and is extremely simple inside, its original flat wooden roof now recreated in concrete. The pulpit in the east choir (the opposite end from which you enter) is by the eighteenth-century Belgian artist Laurent Delvaux. Near the main entrance is a fifteenth-century wooden wagon which carried the shrine of St Gertrude in a procession through the fields once a year. Restored in 1987, it has 24 oak panels along the bottom and 16 along the top, illustrating the life of Gertrude and the miracles she performed. Unfortunately, the original thirteenth-century shrine was destroyed in 1940 and only fragments remain, but a modern replacement has been made and the autumn procession recently revived.

It's worth visiting the church on a guided tour even if you don't understand French, as these take you around parts of the church otherwise out of bounds (for an English tour you have to ring the tourist office ahead – see below). Tours leave roughly every hour (Mon–Fri 10am–4pm, Sat & Sun 2–4pm; F50) and take you first upstairs to the large *Salle Impériale* over the west choir. There are vague plans to house a museum here to contain the thirteenth-century shrine and the wagon panels, among other related miscellany. En route you get a lovely view down over the church from the end gallery. You then pass through the huge Romanesque crypt to visit the interesting **sous-sol archéologique** (excavations), where the foundations of a Merovingian chapel and church (seventh-century) and three Carolingian churches (ninth and tenth century) have been discovered, as well as the tombs of St Gertrude and her relations.

After visiting the church don't miss the **Musée Communal d'Archéologie, d'Art et d'Histoire**, in an ivy-clad house at the end of rue de Bruxelles (daily except Tues 9.30am–12.30pm & 2.30–5pm; F50), which shows items from the end of the Middle Ages to the eighteenth century charting the history of Nivelles – collegiate church, town and region. Much of the material on display has actually come from the church, like the four fifteenth-century Brabantine Gothic statues of the Apostles from the former rood loft, and the Baroque terracotta sculptures by Delvaux. There are also rooms on prehistory and the Gallo-Roman period.

Practicalities

Nivelles' **train station** is ten minutes' walk from the centre of town at the Grande Place, down rue de Namur. The **tourist office** is on the opposite side of the Grande Place to the church, in the corner (Mon–Fri 9am–noon & 1–5pm, Sat 9am–noon; ☎067/21 54 13). There's one reasonably priced **hotel**, the *Commerce*, Grande Place 7 (☎067/21 12 41; ②), although with Brussels so near it's not really worth staying. For **food**, a few doors up from the museum, in the middle of rue Bruxelles, *Le Prevert* bistro is a good place for lunch, with an interesting and varied menu of pasta dishes, *tartines* and salads, and is reasonably priced and popular. Try the *salade wallonie*.

Villers-la-Ville

Some 12km east of Nivelles, accessible by train from Charleroi, the ruined Cistercian abbey of **VILLERS-LA-VILLE** (mid-March to April daily 10am–6pm; May–Aug daily 10am–8pm; Sept daily 10am–6pm; winter Sat & Sun 11am–5pm;

F100) is one of the most haunting and evocative sights in the area. The first monastic community settled here in 1146, consisting of just one abbot and twelve monks. Later the abbey became a powerful local landowner, managing a domain of about 10,000 hectares, with numbers that had risen to about a hundred monks and three hundred lay brothers, bringing in a healthy annual income which funded the construction, from 1200, of most of what you see now. The range of monastic buildings was erected wholly in the thirteenth century; less austere buildings, like the Abbot's Palace, went up in the seventeenth and eighteenth century. In 1796 the monastery was ransacked by French revolutionaries, and later on a railway was ploughed through the grounds.

It's an enormous complex comprising a church, sleeping quarters, refectory, parlour, warming room and workshops. Romanesque, Gothic and Renaissance features remain, with some inevitable nineteenth-century modifications. The buildings are pretty much a ruin, and the site is wild and overgrown, but some kind of mental reconstruction is possible using the numbers on the site and the guidebook available at the entrance.

From the entrance a path crosses the courtyard of honour of the Abbot's Palace to the warming room (27). This was the only place in the monastery where a fire was kept going all winter and it still has its original chimney. It's next to the monks' workroom, so they could keep warm while reading and studying. On the other side is the huge Romanesque–Gothic refectory (26), lit by ribbed twin windows topped with a rose window. It was formerly divided into two naves by vaults, of which you can see the remains of the pillars. Nearby is the kitchen (24) with the main drainage system to the river and a chimney for airing the room. The pantry (22) still has a complete vault intact on a single column. Crossing the court you come to the brewery (14) on the edge of the complex, one of the biggest and oldest buildings in the abbey, in transitional style, with groined vaults, despite its completion at the end of the thirteenth century.

The most spectacular building here, however, is the church, with the dimensions of a cathedral, with pure lines and elegant proportions, and displaying the change from Romanesque to Gothic; indeed, the transept and choir are the first known examples of Gothic in the Brabantine area. It's 90m long, 40m wide and 23m tall at the highest point, with a majestic nave that was supported on strong cylindrical columns. An original feature is the series of bull's-eye windows which light the transepts. Of the original twelfth-century cloister only a pair of twin windows remain (rebuilt in Gothic style from the fourteenth to the sixteenth centuries). Around its edges are tombstones and the tomb of the Crusader Gibert d'Aspremont.

Practicalities

There is no public transport between Nivelles and Villers, though it's an easy and pleasant enough journey by bike. Trains run direct from Charleroi once hourly; from Brussels you have to change at **OTTIGNIES**. From Villers station follow the road which crosses the track in the Monticelli direction and turn right onto the main road. It's a good 20- to 25-minute walk to the abbey.

The **tourist office** is situated in the "Gate of Brussels", a little building to the side which was originally the main entrance. For a good view over the whole area of the abbey complex, take a look from the "bridge" outside the tourist office. If you want to make a day of it, there are fifteen marked **walks** in the vicinity of the abbey. The tourist office or abbey itself has a booklet describing them. There's also a pamphlet (F30, French only) detailing three of the walks. Both publications include map sections. In summer the cloister is used for amateur theatre productions.

South of Charleroi: the Botte de Hainaut

A tongue of land reaching south into France, the **Botte de Hainaut** (Boot of Hainaut) is shared between the provinces of Hainaut and Namur. A natural extension of the Ardennes range further east, though a little flatter and less wooded, it's above all visited for its scenery, although there are a few tangible attractions such as the basilica at Walcourt and the studied prettiness of Chimay. The eastern side of the Botte is crossed by rail tracks that twist their way from Charleroi, passing through the gentle hills around Walcourt, and on to the flatter landscape around Philippeville before reaching the forested area around Couvin. As far as getting to the main centres goes, there is reasonable public transport, with the regular train service between Charleroi and Couvin supplemented by fast and frequent buses connecting Chimay with Couvin and Charleroi – although to tour beyond these a car is desirable. Apart from the region's campsites, decently priced acommodation is rather thin on the ground, and Couvin, with a couple of cheap hotels, is perhaps the best base for seeing the region in depth if you're on any kind of budget.

Walcourt to Mariembourg

The straggling hillside settlement of **WALCOURT**, just across the border in Namur province, is the first town you reach on the train line, a pleasant old place most interesting for its thirteenth- and fourteenth-century **Basilique St-Materne** (daily 10.30am–5pm), which dominates the town from its hilltop location on the Grande Place. Inside, the rood loft is a marvellous piece of work in *Joyeuse Gothique* style, presented to Charles V on the occasion of a 1530s pilgrimage here to the tenth-century Virgin of Walcourt, a wooden statue coated in silver that stands in the transept. An object of considerable veneration even today, the statue is believed to have been crafted in the eleventh century, making it one of the oldest of such figures in Belgium. The treasury, among other items, has a thirteenth-century Cross-reliquary in the style of Hugo d'Oignies (see "Namur" on p.449), a native of Walcourt.

Beneath the church, at the bottom of the wedge-shaped Grande Place, there is a **tourist office** (daily except Wed 10am–noon & 1–5pm; ☎071/61 25 26). The **train station** is 1km north of the centre – turn right out of the car park when you arrive and follow the road up as it curves. If you need to stay, there are two hotels: the *Hostellerie de l'Abbaye*, near the station at rue du Jardinet 5 (☎071/61 14 23; ④), and the *Aigle Noir* by the church (☎071/61 11 39; ④).

Around 5km south of Walcourt – though inaccessible by public transport – the **Barrages de l'Eau d'Heure** is a series of five reservoir lakes (Easter–Sept daily 9am–6pm) that has been turned into a recreation area with boating, windsurfing, etc, and campsites. If you're after water sports it's fine, and you can visit the dam itself (F70) and an audiovisual display on the lakes, which includes a scale model of the site (F120), but they are not especially attractive in themselves.

Fifteen minutes by train from Walcourt, the desultory town of **PHILLIPEVILLE** was built as a fortress by Charles V, and named after his son, Philip II. The only remains of the fortifications are some underground tunnels that once connected a chain of outlying redoubts with the central precinct. There are hour-long guided tours of these in July and August between 1pm and 6pm. Ask at the tourist office, rue de l'Eglise 8 (June–Aug Mon–Fri 9am–noon & 2–5pm; ☎071/66 62 13) for details.

Some 12km south of Phillipeville, **MARIEMBOURG** is an unremarkable little place whose train station adjoins the terminus of the **Chemin de Fer des Trois Vallées**, a refurbished steam engine that chugs its way around the surrounding countryside. One route joins Mariembourg to Treignes in the far east of the region (April–June Sat & Sun 1 daily; July–Aug 1 daily except Fri & Mon); another runs to Chimay (April–Sept Sat & Sun 1 daily). You can buy a return ticket (F240) for either of the two sections and get off en route wherever you want. At Mariembourg some of the trains also connect with trains to and from Charleroi Sud. The steam train runs from April to September, and times are detailed in a very complicated leaflet available from train stations. Outside of these months Mariembourg and Couvin are connected by a regular train.

Couvin and around

Just 12km from France, **COUVIN** is an attractive old place, although beyond its good-looking ancient quarter, set on top of a rocky hill above the main square, place General Piron, there's not much to see. The main feature is the **Cavernes de l'Abîme**, on rue de la Falaise, right in the middle of town by the river, a series of caves that are now home to an exhibition and audiovisual display on prehistoric times (mid-June to mid-Sept daily 10am–noon & 1.30–6pm; Easter to mid-June Sat & Sun only; F120, or F280 combined ticket with *Grottes de Neptune*, see below).

Couvin's **bus and train station** are a five-minute walk from the centre of town, at the end of rue de la Gare. There's a **tourist office** at avenue de la Libération 2 (May–Sept Mon–Fri 9am–noon & 2–5pm; ☎060/34 54 54), very handy for the station, and another, five minutes' walk away in the centre of town at rue de la Falaise 3. Close by, there's the *Hôtel de la Gare* (☎060/34 41 03: ③); otherwise you could try *La Sapinière*, Vieille Route de Rocroy 7 (☎060/34 43 81; ③). Campers should head for *Camping Communal* on rue de la Foulerie. For food, there are a number of lively restaurants on and around place General Piron – try the busy *La Terrasse*, with simple, reasonably priced pasta dishes as well as more substantial items.

Just 3km from Couvin, **PETIGNY** is basically visited for the **Grottes de Neptune** caves (April–Sept daily 9.30am–noon & 1.30–6pm; Oct Sat & Sun only, same times; F200), a well-developed stop on tourist itineraries that includes a twenty-minute boat ride on a subterranean river, and a sound and light show – impressive, if rather slick stuff.

A couple of kilometres further east, just off the main road, **NISMES** is neatly tucked in between the river and a cluster of wooded hills, the most picturesque of the villages around here, complete with the ruins of a seventeenth-century church and a tiny local arts and crafts museum in the stately **Maison des Baillis** (July & Aug daily 10am–noon & 1–5pm; F50). It's possible to rent canoes in the village, and there's a rather cutesy tourist train (April–Sept 9am–6pm; F100) that gives a fifty-minute ride through the surrounding area, passing through the **Viroin-Fagnes nature reserve**. There are several **campsites** – try *Camping Le Sabot* on rue de la Station – and a number of **hotels**, including *du Parc*, by the river (☎060/31 10 22; ③). The most inexpensive **restaurant** is the Slav *Les Grillades des Balkans*, on the main street, with main courses for around F400. For more information there's a **tourist office** on the riverfront (Mon–Fri 9am–noon & 2–5pm; ☎060/31 11 28).

Five kilometres from Nismes, **OLLOY** is a peaceful and prosperous village surrounded by rich farmland. You can rent canoes for use on the swift river here too, and there are three **campsites** – try *des Baudets*, on rue de la Champagne, *Le Rolinvaux*, rue de la Bossette 11, and the smaller *Le Camping Fina* on rue de la Gare. As for **hotels**, you could try the *Rolinvaux*, rue de la Bossette 9 (☎060/39 91 96; ③).

Beaumont to Chimay

Accessible direct by bus from Charleroi, **BEAUMONT** is an old and somewhat dilapidated town sitting on a hill, an important regional stronghold from as early as the eleventh century. Parts of its fortifications are still intact, most notably the **Tour Salamandre** (May–Sept 9am–noon & 2–7pm; F50), a thick-walled rectangular structure that overlooks the river valley from its vantage point a couple of minutes' walk away, signposted from the main square. Inside there's a small museum of regional history, but you really climb the 136 steps for the view.

Fifteen kilometres south of Beaumont, **RANCE** straggles along the main street, an untidy town famous for its red marble quarries, which have supplied buildings worldwide, from Versailles to St Peter's in Rome. It's a subject you can find more out about in the town's **National Marble Museum** (April–Oct Tues–Sat 9.30am–6pm, Sun 2pm–6pm; winter Mon–Sat 8.30am–5pm, closed Sun; F100), housed in the old town hall on the main street.

Chimay and around

Best known for the beer brewed in its local Trappist monastery, the small and ancient town of **CHIMAY** is a pleasant old place, ruled for several centuries by the de Croy family, ever since Charles de Croy was made the first Prince of Chimay by the Emperor Maximilian in 1486. Its finely preserved Grande Place marks the centre of town, an aristocratic square fringed by a harmonious mixture of buildings. In the middle is the **Monument des Princes** of 1852, an allegory representing the town with four members of the princely family. Opposite, the onion-domed **Collégiale Sts Pierre et Paul** is a largely sixteenth-century church, with three bays of the choir remaining from an earlier thirteenth-century structure, that contains the mausoleum of Charles de Croy, a recumbent figure in alabaster dating from 1525.

On the other side of the Grande Place, an elegant sandstone arch leads to the **Château de Chimay** (April–Oct 10am–noon & 2–6pm; obligatory guided visits 10am, 11am, 2pm, 3pm & 5pm; F150), the home of the de Croy family. A considerably altered structure, it was originally built in the fifteenth century, but was reconstructed in the seventeenth century, and badly damaged by fire and rebuilt to earlier plans in the 1930s. Today the main body of the building is fronted by a long series of rectangular windows, edged by the oldest part of what remains, a heavy turreted tower. Inside are mainly old family portraits, although the carefully restored Rococo theatre is worth a look, and there are good views over the river valley and encompassing woods from the gardens at the back.

There are free guided tours and beer tastings at the Chimay monastery's **beer-producing facilities** (Mon–Fri 9am–2pm), 5km east of town, near the village of Baileux. The monastery itself is actually situated 9km away near the village of Forges. Alternatively, 4km away from Chimay, the **Etang de Virelles** is the largest lake in Belgium, a nature reserve important for waterfowl, which have had special protection here since 1985. On the south side of the lake, near the village of **VIRELLES**, there are observation posts (May–Sept daily 10am–6pm; Oct–April Sun only; F80) and a recreation area with canoe and pedal-boat rent (F200 per hour). Guided visits of the reserve are run in June, July and August (F100) – ring Bernard Dubois on ✆071/38 17 61 for details – and you can also see something of the place by means of a special tourist train, which runs from Chimay tourist office throughout the summer (April, May, June, Sept & Oct Sun 3pm; July & Aug Mon–Sat 3pm, Sun 3pm, 4pm, 5pm; F120).

Chimay's **train station** is on the southern edge of town, a five-minute walk from the Grande Place. The **tourist office** is just around the corner from here, at rue des Noailles 4 (Mon–Fri 9am–noon & 1–5pm, plus April–Oct Sat & Sun 10am–noon & 1.30–5pm; ✆060/21 18 46) and has free maps and details of guided tours of the town. There's only one **hotel**, the *Motel de Fagnes* (✆060/21 27 89; ③), a good 25-minute walk southeast of the Grande Place on the road to Couvin, although there are a couple of reasonably priced hotels in Virelles – try the *Hostellerie Le Virelles*, rue du Lac 28 (✆060/21 28 03; ③). **Campers** should use the *Camping Communal*, just outside Chimay on the allée des Princes (April–Oct; ✆060/21 18 43), near a sports complex with swimming pool, shops and its own cafeteria. For **food**, *Au Vieux Chimay*, on the Grande Place, serves excellent homemade meals and snacks, including plenty of things made with the local beer and cheese, and *Aux Armes de Chimay*, also on the Grande Place, has a smaller menu that includes a good variety of regional specialities.

travel details

Trains

Charleroi to: Brussels (hourly; 50min); Couvin (1–2 hourly; 65min); Ligny (hourly; 20min); Lobbes (2 an hour; 20min); Mariembourg (1–2 hourly; 60min); Namur (2 an hour; 30min); Nivelles (hourly; 20min); Ottignies (hourly; 45min); Thuin (2 an hour; 15min); Villers-la-Ville (hourly; 30min); Walcourt (1–2 hourly; 30min).

La Louvière: to Binche (hourly; 10min); Charleroi (2 an hour; 45min).

Mons: to Ath (hourly; 30min); Charleroi (hourly; 1hr 10min); La Louvière (hourly; 20min).

Tournai to: Ath (3 hourly; 20min); Brussels (3 hourly; 1hr).

Buses

Ath to: Beloeil (4 daily; 30min).

Charleroi to: Beaumont (hourly; 30min); Binche (hourly; 40min); Chimay (hourly; 80min); Rance (hourly; 60min).

Couvin to: Chimay (every 2hr; 35min).

Mons to: Binche (2 an hour; 40min).

Soignies to: Le Roeulx (hourly; 15min).

CHAPTER ELEVEN

THE ARDENNES

Some people in the north say that Belgium ends at the Ardennes. And it's true that the region can seem a place apart from the industrial cities of the north and west of the country. It is sometimes painfully difficult to get around – a route that looks direct on the map may involve several changes by bus or train (sometimes both) – and even the major centres of Namur and Liège connect directly with only a few points of interest. Then again, poor communications are a fair guarantee of wild countryside, which is probably why you're here.

Geologically the Ardennes begins in France, enters Luxembourg and extends into Germany, and within Belgian territory is covered by the three provinces of **Namur** in the west, **Luxembourg** in the south and **Liège** in the east. The highest part of the Ardennes is the **Hohes Venns** (High Fens), in the German-speaking far east of the region, beyond which the range links up with the hills of Germany's – and Luxembourg's – Eifel area. But this is not the Ardennes' most attractive or popular corner, which lies farther west, given character and variety by the **rivers** which run through the area. Indeed it's the river valleys which form the real attraction, deep, wooded, winding canyons reaching up to high green peaks – at times sublimely and inspiringly beautiful. The Ardennes' **cave systems**, too, form a major focus, especially those in the Meuse, Ourthe and Lesse valleys, carved out by underground rivers that over the centuries have cut through and dissolved the chalk of the hills, leaving stalagmites and stalactites in their wake.

The obvious gateway to the region is **Namur**, strategically sited at the junction of the Sambre and Meuse rivers – worth a visit in its own right, with some decent museums, a huge citadel and (for the Ardennes) a lively night scene. From Namur you can follow the Meuse by train down to **Dinant**, a scenic – and very popular – journey, going on to explore the **Meuse Valley** south of Dinant by boat or taking a canoe up the narrower (and wilder) River **Lesse**. From here, routes lead east into the heart of the Ardennes, to **Han-sur-Lesse**, surrounded by undulating hills riddled with caves, **Rochefort** – also with caves – and **St-Hubert**, to the southeast, with its splendid Italianate basilica. South, **Bouillon** is similarly picturesque, sited alongside the River Semois, like so many Ardennes towns topped by an ancient citadel city. Farther north, **La Roche-en-Ardennes** is a rustic, hardy kind of town, renowned for its smoked ham and game and seen as something of an Ardennes capital city. North of here, big, grimy **Liège** is also a gateway city, a good stop if you've come down to the region from Maastricht in Holland, to which it's connected by hourly train, and providing easy access to the area around the long-established resort of **Spa**, a little way south. The country-side around here is among the Ardennes' highest, though it's relatively flat and is crossed by major roads. Spa itself still pulls in the crowds, but it's out of curiosity mostly, and there's little, if anything, to see aside from the pretty nearby town of **Stavelot**, with its marvellous carnival.

For **getting around**, buses are for once a better alternative than trains, although services can be sporadic and information difficult to come by – tourist offices usually have a good set of timetables. Most of the major centres have been well developed, and in summer at least resorts like La Roche and Bouillon can be full to bursting. But the crowds are never too oppressive, and in any case the appeal is less one of specific towns, more of outdoor pursuits. Wherever you are, **walking** is the obvious pastime; the really serious can follow the GR Namurois, which runs from Brussels through the three valleys of the Meuse, Lesse and Semois. **Canoes** can be rented at most river settlements, and **mountain bikes** are often available. Cross-country and – in some places – on-piste **skiing** are also popular in winter.

Namur and around

Known as the "Gateway to the Ardennes," **NAMUR** is a logical first stop if you're heading into the region from the north or west, though without a car the dark forests and hills are still a long way off. Even so, the town has a feel of some-where refreshingly free of the industrial belt of Hainaut. There's also plenty to see in what is one of southern Belgium's most pleasant and elegant towns – and in an area of sparse public transport links, Namur is well connected to some far-flung parts of the Ardennes. The town's principal sight is its citadel, one of the most impressive in Europe, wedged inside a fork formed by the Sambre and Meuse rivers. There's also a handful of decent museums, and a nightlife – lent vigour by the presence of the city's university – that is a good antidote to the inevitably rather limited offerings of the region beyond.

> The Namur area telephone code is ☎081

Arrival, information and accommodation

Namur's **train station** is on the northern fringe of the city centre, on avenue de la Gare, two minutes' walk from which is the **tourist office**, at the top of rue Rogier, in a chalet in square de l'Europe Unie (summer daily 9am–6pm; winter daily 9am–5pm; ☎22 28 59). There are more information offices on the other side of the river, just below the citadel. Over the Pont de France on the tip of the "V" made by the confluence of the two rivers (the *grognon* or "pig's snout"), there is

an **information chalet** (June–Aug 9am–5pm) selling combined tickets for town sights, including the citadel and major museums. Across the car park from here, towards the citadel at rue Notre Dame 3, there is a **provincial tourist office**, with information on the whole Namur region (Mon–Fri 8am–noon & 1–5pm; ☎22 29 98).

Namur has relatively few hotels, and **accommodation** can be a problem if you haven't booked, especially in high season. The cheapest hotels, as ever, are close by the train station: of them, the *Queen Victoria*, handily placed opposite the station at avenue de la Gare 11–12, above *McDonalds* (☎22 29 71; ③), is the cheapest, although the *Excelsior*, a few doors along at avenue de la Gare 4 (☎23 18 13; ③), isn't greatly more expensive. More centrally, and somewhat nicer, there's *L'Opéra*, rue Pepin 1 (☎23 17 18; ④), which also has a pleasant bar and good-value restaurant. Finally, if you're after a bit more luxury, and are happy to spend a little more, the *Beauregard*, ten minutes' walk from the centre of town, right on the banks of the Meuse below the citadel, at avenue Baron de Moreau 1 (☎23 00 28; ⑥), has pleasant, large rooms, some with a river-view – and is the home of Namur's casino.

The tourist office has a stock of private **rooms**, which might work out slightly cheaper than the hotels (②), although their location may not be quite as convenient. Failing that, there's a **youth hostel** on the far edge of town at avenue F. Rops 8 (☎22 44 12; ①), on the banks of the Meuse past the casino. Take bus #1, #3 or #4 from the stop opposite the station. There's no lock-out and the hostel, housed in a nice old mansion, has a kitchen, bar and a self-service restaurant. The nearest **campsite**, *Camping des 4 Fils Aymon*, is 10km away at chaussée de Liège 989, in the suburb of Lives-sur-Meuse (April–Sept). Take bus #12 from the bus station, to the right as you walk out of the train station; they run every hour and take about fifteen minutes.

The Town

Central Namur spreads out from around the confluence of the Sambre and Meuse rivers, with the citadel hill on one side of the Sambre, flanking the River Meuse, and the main part of the town centre on the other, the two sides connected by the principal **Pont de France** and the smaller **Pont du Musée**. In the town centre proper, **rue de l'Ange** leads north into **rue de Fer**, Namur's main shopping streets, extending all the way to the train station.

Halfway up rue de Fer, on the right at no. 24, one of the finest of Namur's mansions, the Hôtel de Gaiffier d'Hestroy, houses the **Musée des Arts du Namurois** (Easter–Oct daily 10am–12.30pm & 1.30–6pm; Nov–Easter daily except Tues 10am–12.30pm & 1.30–5pm; F100), has displays of the work of Mosan goldsmiths and silversmiths of the eleventh to thirteenth centuries, though frankly the collections of the Oignie gallery (see over the page) are better. There are also wood and stone sculptures from the fourteenth to sixteenth centuries, paintings and reliquaries from the Collégiale de Walcourt, and a beautiful fourteenth-century ivory portable altarpiece.

West of the Gaiffier d'Hestroy house, on place St-Aubain, Namur's neo-Classical **Cathédrale St-Aubain** is brilliant white inside, with a triumphant, airy feel that forms a suitable backdrop to its paintings from the school of Rubens, including one from the hand of van Dyck. The attached **Musée Diocésain**

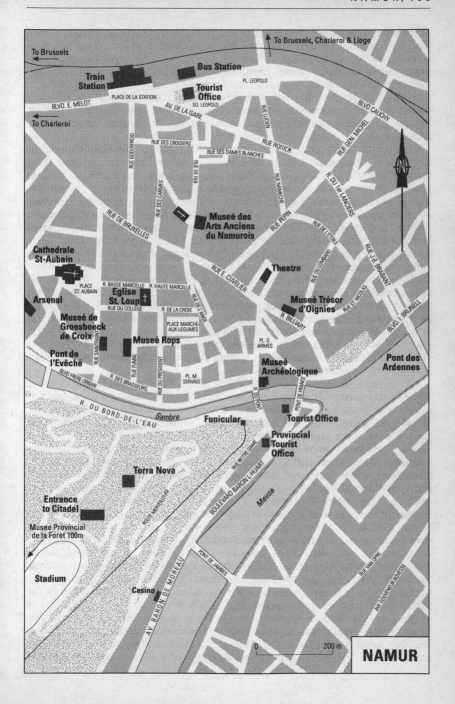

To Brussels, Charleroi & Liege

To Brussels

To Charleroi

Train Station

Bus Station

Tourist Office

PL. LEOPOLD

PLACE DE LA STATION

BLVD. E. MELOT

AV. DE LA GARE

SQ. LEOPOLD

RUE LUCIEN

BLVD CAUCHY

RUE GODEFROID

RUE DES CROISIERS

RUE DES DAMES BLANCHES

RUE ROGIER

RUE GEN. MICHEL

RUE DE FER

RUE DES CARMES

RUE DE BRUXELLES

Museé des Arts Anciens du Namurois

RUE NAMECHE

RUE PEPIN

R. DU 1er LANCIERS

RUE DE L'ETOILE

Cathedrale St-Aubain

PLACE ST. AUBAIN

R. BASSE MARCELLE

R. HAUTE MARCELLE

RUE E. CUVELIER

Theatre

RUE DU LOMBARD

RUE ST. NICOLAS

RUE J-B BRABANT

Arsenal

Eglise St. Loup

RUE DU COLLEGE

R. DE LA CROIX

RUE DE L'ANGE

Museé Trésor d'Oignies

R. BILLIART

BLVD. I. BRUNELL

Museé de Groesbeeck de Croix

RUE SANTRAINT

RUE FUMAL

Museé Rops

PLACE MARCHE AUX-LEGUMES

PL. D. ARMES

Pont de l'Evêché

R. DES BRASSEURS

RUE DU PRESIDENT

PL. M. SERVAIS

Museé Archéologique

RUE DU PONT

Pont des Ardennes

BLVD FRERE-ORBAN

R. DU BORD-DE-L'EAU

Sambre

Funicular

PONT DE FRANCE

Tourist Office

Provincial Tourist Office

Terra Nova

RUE NOTRE DAME

BOULEVARD BARON L-HUART

Meuse

Entrance to Citadel

ROUTE MERVEILLEUSE

Musee Provincial de la Forêt 100m

Stadium

Casino

AV. BARON DE MOREAU

Pont de-Jambes

RUE VAN OPRE

AVE GOUVERNEUR BOVESSE

0   200 m

NAMUR

(Easter–Oct daily 10am–noon & 2.30–6pm; Nov–Easter daily 2.30–4.30pm; closed Mon & Sun am; F50), the cathedral treasury, displays objects from diocesan churches of Namur and Luxembourg provinces, including a golden crown reliquary with thorns from Christ's crown of thorns, a twelfth-century portable altar with eleventh-century ivory carvings, and a silver reliquary of St Blaise. Behind the cathedral on the other side, towards the river, on boulevard Frère Orban beside the river, the **Arsenal** was built at the end of the seventeenth century by Vauban. It was recently restored and is now a university building, but you can go upstairs to see the beamed roof from inside.

Walking down toward the river from here, the **Musée de Groesbeeck de Croix**, at rue Saintraint 3 (daily 10am–noon & 2–5pm, visits on the hour only, closed Tues; F50), is another of Namur's luxury house museums, an opulent Louis XV-style mansion containing seventeenth- and eighteenth-century art objects from the Namur region – clocks, marble fireplaces, furniture, ceramics and floor mosaics. A block from the river, **rue des Brasseurs** is lined with more restored seventeenth- and eighteenth-century houses, and a left turn at rue Fumal leads to the **Musée Felicien Rops** at no. 12 (daily 10am–5pm; closed Tues except during July & Aug; F100), home of an important collection of works by the nineteenth-century Namur illustrator of the same name – paintings, drawings and engravings recording the development of his work. Rops settled in Paris in the 1870s, acquiring a reputation for his dabblings in the occult and his debauched lifestyle, and illustrating works by poets Mallarmé and Baudelaire. He was, apparently, greatly admired by the latter, but he is perhaps better known for his erotic drawings, which show an obsession with the macabre, skeletons and nuns and priests in oddly compromising poses characterizing his later work. He also drew many satirical cartoons, savagely criticizing the art establishment with which he never had much of a rapport.

As you leave place St-Aubain via rue du Collège, the Baroque **Eglise St-Loup** has a theatrical curved roof seen to best effect from the citadel; unfortunately you can no longer go inside. Farther on lies Namur's most stunning museum, the **Trésor d'Oignies** (Mon–Sat 10am–noon & 2–5pm, Sun 2–5pm, closed Tues; F60), housed in the Maison des Soeurs de Notre-Dame at rue Julie Billiart 19 and administered by the nuns of the convent, most of whom speak some English. It's a unique collection consisting of examples of the exquisitely beautiful gold and silver work of the local craftsman Hugo d'Oignies, which were removed here from the abbey of Oignies in Hainaut when threatened by French revolutionary soldiers at the end of the eighteenth century. Hugo d'Oignies was the younger brother of the prior, and he produced these objects between 1230 and 1238. The Mosan gold and silver workers of the twelfth century were renowned, and form something of a transition between Romanesque and Gothic art. Hugo, for example, was open to French influences, and although he perfected Mosan decoration and techniques, he had his own unique style. He was an innovator in the art of filigree, raising the decoration from the background so that the tiny human figures and animals seem to be suspended in space, giving depth to the narrative. He also used the technique of *niello* a lot – a black composition of sulphur or lead filling in engraved lines in the gold. Whatever his style, they're beautiful devotional pieces, most holding holy relics that were brought back from the Holy Land by one Jacques de Vitry, a Parisian ecclesiastic who joined the abbey in 1208. They are rich and elaborate pieces of work, studded with precious and semiprecious stones and display an extraordinary level of craftsmanship, with an exquisite balance between ornament and form. The compositions themselves are lively and realistic, sometimes depicting minute hunting scenes, with animals leaping convincingly through delicate foliage, sometimes engraved with a Christian dedication, or a tiny picture of the artist offering up his art to God in worship. Other treasures on display include a Byzantine Cross, a mitre on illuminated parchment, and another in gold thread.

Around the corner from the museum, the **Eglise Notre Dame** is a late eighteenth-century church with work by Laurent Delvaux. Nearby also, by the Pont du Musée, the former meat hall holds an **Archeological Museum** (Mon–Fri 10am–5pm, Sat & Sun 10.30am–5pm; F40), with a small, rather uninteresting display of prehistoric, Roman and later finds from the locality.

Across the bridge, Namur's **Citadel** (April, May, June & Oct Sat & Sun only 11am–6pm; July–Sept daily 11am–6pm; F195) is inevitably the city's major attraction, and deservedly so, though it has only been open to the public since 1978. Namur's strategic position at the confluence of the Sambre and Meuse rivers, plus the natural defence the sharp junction of the rivers afforded, led to its construction in medieval times, from which parts have been incorporated into the fortifications nearest the "V." The main problem facing successive generations of military engineers including Vauban and the Dutchman Coheoorn, was how to defend the western approach, and the present structure reflects this preoccupation, with the lines of defence becoming more complex and extensive the farther up the "V" you go. There are three main sections to the fortress – the Donjon, whose forbidding walls and gun emplacements date from the eighteenth and nineteenth centuries; the fifteenth- and sixteenth-century Mediane constructions; and the Terra Nova bastion, Spanish works of 1640. By the end of the seventeenth century the Namur citadel was considered one of the most important strongholds in Europe, attracting the attentions of Louis XIV, who besieged the town in 1692 with an army of some twenty thousand men, and of William of Orange just three years later.

The citadel is most easily accessible either by the *téléphérique* cable car (April–Sept daily 11am–7pm; F190 round-trip, F160 one-way), which runs from near the car park just over the Pont du Musée – a long and exhilarating ride; by car, take route Merveilleuse from near the *Beauregard* hotel on the Meuse bank. The entrance fee includes an audiovisual display on the citadel's history, a miniature train ride around the grounds to see the various structures, a guided visit of the deepest underground passages, and access to the fortress's museums. It's an immense complex, and you need two or three hours to cover it thoroughly. A booklet can be bought at the entrance office with the different parts of the site marked, but there are plenty of landmarks dotted around.

A five-minute walk from the cable car terminal is the main entrance, which leaves you in the part of the fortress known as the **Ouvrages à Cornes** – earthworks the shape of horns; turn left and walk around these to where an underground tunnel descends into the Terra Nova barracks – site of the audiovisual show and terminal of the mini-train. From here you can also visit – with a guide – the fortress's underground passages, including the **Galeries Boufflers**, which extend for 300m and include a "War Office" used by Richelieu and Louis XIV. You can see the differences in the tunnels of different periods: ironically the oldest, built in typical Spanish style, are the dryest and best preserved because they were built with two layers of bricks. Also inside the citadel, the **Musée d'Armes et d'Histoire** (Easter–Sept daily 10am–6pm) holds a large collection of artefacts relating to the military history of the area, while just outside, the **Musée de la Forêt**, across the far side of the stadium (April–Oct daily 9am–noon & 2–5pm; F50) has displays pertaining to the wildlife of the Ardennes, in the shape of dioramas and the like.

Eating and drinking

Central Namur is full of decent **restaurants and bars**, and there's no excuse for not eating and drinking well. There are a number of places on and around place Marché-aux-Legumes, in the heart of the old part of town. On the square itself, the *Tavern Alsacienne* serves good basic food at moderate prices, as does the *Restaurant le Rimbaud*, a couple of minutes' walk away at rue de la Croix 58. Also on the square, *La Fondue*, rue St Jean 19, serves excellent fondues. *Rapido Pat*, on rue du Pont, opposite the Archeology Museum, serves pasta, salads, soups, etc, at double-quick speed – a good, fast lunch stop; also good for lunch is L'Ecailler des Halles, rue de la Halle 5, an upmarket deli that has a small, slightly rarefied restaurant with a tasty daily special menu. For vegetarians, the *Maison de l'Ecologie* at rue Basse Marcelle 26, near the cathedral, has a wholefood shop downstairs, and a decent vegetarian restaurant upstairs, *L'Autre Table*, which is open every lunchtime except Sunday and on Wednesday, Thursday, Friday and Saturday evenings. On the other side of the town centre, some of the town's best food is served at *Le P'tit Gris*, rue Rogier 46, a small, unpretentious and very reasonably priced restaurant that's well known locally. Though more of a newcomer, *Brasserie Henry*, right by the cathedral at place St-Aubain 3, is a big loud brasserie in the best tradition, with a French menu that's moderately priced; it also is a good place to people-watch with a **drink**. The *Piano Bar* on place Marché aux Legumes is one of the town centre's liveliest bars, with live jazz Friday and Saturday evenings from about 10pm. On the opposite corner of the square, the *Ratin Tot* is the self-proclaimed oldest bar in town, while *La Rhumière*, just off the square on rue St Jean, has an offbeat decor and clientele.If you're fed up with beer, go to *Les Brasseurs de la Dyle* on rue de la Croix; the owner of the bar has a vineyard in France.

Around Namur: Floreffe, Château de Franc-Waret and south to Dinant

A few kilometres west of Namur, towards Charleroi, the attractively sited abbey of **FLOREFFE** is a possible stop on the way to or from Hainaut. Founded in 1121, little remains of the original complex – the domestic buildings are mainly eighteenth-century – but the **abbey church** is certainly worth the detour, principally for its carved oak choir stalls. The work of one man – Pierre Enderlin – who took sixteen years (1632–48) over them, they're a quite remarkable achievement, in a superb state of preservation and displaying a marvellous inventiveness and intricacy, carved with an array of figures – Biblical characters, eminent and holy persons, some 220 angels – of which each one is different. Many of the faces are obviously portraits, humorous, sometimes satirical in tone, and include a self-portrait of the artist hidden among the rest. Also in the church is a wooden Virgin of Del Cour, carved in 1692, that has been the source, apparently, of many copies. It's an unusual vision of Mary, certainly, a very graceful figure, and the sculpting of her robes is extremely adept. In the restored Romanesque part of the church there is also a small museum, displaying various art objects, though since some were stolen viewing is only permitted on guided tours (on the hour April–June & Sept–Oct daily 1.30–6pm; July & Aug 10.30am–6pm; F60). These are in French, but the guide speaks a little English. An audiovisual presentation picks out the details of the stalls for you to study afterward.

The abbey is also home to the Romanesque **Moulin Brasserie** (daily 11am–6pm; F80), restored in 1972 and famous for three beers. The most distinctive, a dark, sweet ale, is sold here, though it's no longer brewed on the premises. If you're coming from or going to Charleroi by train, you can stop at Floreffe (from the station it's a 15-min walk).

The Château de Franc-Waret

In the opposite direction, just a short distance northeast of Namur (bus #17; 5 daily), the **Château de Franc-Waret** (June–Sept Sat & Sun 2–5.30pm; F100) is another possible day excursion, a classical Louis XV building that was rebuilt in 1750 but which sports two seventeenth-century towers. It houses period French and Dutch furniture, seventeenth-century Brussels tapestries and Flemish paintings.

South to Dinant

The river from Namur to Dinant is arguably the Meuse's best stretch, but even so it's too wide to be all that stunning. You can travel this stretch by boat on Sundays in July and August (F400 one-way, F550 round-trip; ☎082/22 32 15) but it will take a good three hours, and you may be better off simply catching the train if you're only going for the day. On the way (and reachable by bus from Namur or Dinant – 4 daily), **Les Jardins d'Annevoie** are a favourite tourist destination hereabouts, created in 1775 by Charles Alexis de Montpellier and occupying the grounds of an eighteenth-century château (gardens April–Oct daily 9am–7pm; château April–June Sat & Sun only 9.30am–1pm & 1–6pm; July & Aug daily 9.30am–1pm & 1–6pm; gardens F170, gardens & château F200). They're a five-minute signposted walk up the hill from the river, a fifteen-minute walk from **GODINNE** train station, which lies on the other side of the bridge.

A few kilometres further south, a narrow road twists up the valley of the River Molignée, one of the region's prettiest spots, passing beneath the ruins of the **Château du Montaigle**, high above on a rocky outcrop (April–June & Sept–Oct Sat 2–6pm, Sun 11–6pm; July & Aug daily 11am–7pm; F100) – a short walk off the main road. Built originally in the thirteenth century, it was blown up by the French in the sixteenth century and has been like this pretty much ever since. Farther down the valley there's a **campsite**, *Camping de la Forge* (☎082/69 91 36), close to the attractive village of **SOSOYE** and the rather dreary Benedictine neo-Gothic abbey of **MAREDSOUS**, founded in 1872 and enjoying an impressive location towering above the wooded valley. This, despite the location, is an exploitative complex of the worst kind, dominated by a vast acreage of car parks, canteen and gift shop, and not really worth the detour. Even the touted *Maredsous* beer is in fact made off-site at the *Düvel* brewery – although the countryside, it must be said, is sumptuous in the extreme.

Dinant and the Meuse and Lesse valleys

The centre of the Meuse Valley tourist industry, **DINANT** has pretensions to being a very picturesque town, slung along the river beneath craggy green cliffs. But once here the cliffs hem in the town against the river, making it feel gloomy and oppressive, and, in summer at least, there are far too many visitors for a place of its size. There's also surprisingly little to see or do here, and although there are plenty of boat trips down river and on the nearby Lesse (see over the page), transport connections to more interesting places are very limited. Basically, there are more beautiful destinations deeper in the Ardennes, and unless you're passing there's very little reason to stop.

The Town

The **Citadel**, on the central place Reine-Astrid but visible from just about anywhere in town (April–Oct daily 9.30am–6.30pm; Nov–March daily except Fri 10am–noon & 1–4pm; F160 including *téléphérique*; F110 via the steps), is the most obvious – indeed only – attraction in town, and even this is something of a letdown if you've already visited the fortress at Namur. It's reached either by way of the cable car or a flight of four hundred or so steps, cut way back in 1577. The site was previously occupied by a fortified castle, but this was destroyed by the French in 1703 and the present structure was built by the Dutch from 1818 to 1821. The Germans occupied the place briefly in 1914, leading to a fierce battle during which they torched the town and executed hundreds of civilians. The Germans took the citadel again in 1940, and it was the scene of more bitter fighting in 1944 when the Allies took three days to dislodge them. The view from the top is good, while the inside has been turned into what is essentially a historical museum, with models recreating particular battles and the Dutch occupation, and a military section with weapons from the Napoleonic era to the last war. You can also see the wooden beams which supported the first bridge in Dinant, built nine hundred years ago by monks and found again by accident in 1952, as well as prison cells and the kitchen and bakery of the Dutch stronghold.

Immediately below the citadel, Dinant's most distinctive landmark is the originally Gothic church of **Notre-Dame**, topped with the bulbous spire which features on all the brochures. There's not much to see inside – the church has been rebuilt several times – aside from a couple of paintings by Antoine Wiertz, who was born in the town. If you want to see the birthplace of another native of Dinant, **Aldolphe Sax**, the inventor of the saxophone, walk around the corner to rue A. Sax 31 – his house is marked by a neat stained-glass mural of the great man blowing his horn.

There is another **cable car**, or *télésiège*, in Dinant, made up of more rickety two-person contraptions that head up from rue en Rhée (a block back from rue Grande) to the **Tour Mont Fat**, with its fine views, restaurants and kids' attractions (April–Sept daily 10.30am–7pm). However, beyond this you've pretty much seen Dinant, although most people also take in the **Grotte La Merveilleuse** (April–Oct guided visits, in French and Flemish only, on the hour 10am–5pm; F160), across the bridge from the church down route de Philippeville 142. If you're into caves or haven't seen one before, it's worth going, although again there are better ones in the Ardennes proper (principally at Han-sur-Lesse). The caves' most unique feature is the whiteness of their rock formations.

Practicalities

Dinant's **train station** is on the opposite side of the river to the town centre, five minutes' walk across the central bridge. The **tourist office** is a five-minute walk from the main place Reine-Astrid at rue Grande 37 (June–Aug daily 9am–8pm; rest of the year daily 8.30am–noon & 2–5pm; ☎082/22 28 70), one block up from the river. Budget **accommodation** is rather sparse. There are a couple of affordable **hotels** right opposite the station – the *Hôtel de la Gare* (☎082/22 20 56; ④), and the cheaper *Derby* a few doors along (☎082/22 41 96; ③). In town, the *Hôtel de la Couronne* is about as central as it's possible to get – right by the church at rue A. Sax 1 (☎082/222441; ④), and isn't a lot more expensive, and has a nice bar and restaurant to boot. The tourist office also has details of private **rooms**, although there are very few possibilities (③). There is no hostel, although there are two **campsites** – the bucolic but very well-equipped *Camping Villatoile*, south of town beyond Anseremme by the Barrage de Pont-à-Lesse (☎082/22 22 85), and *Camping de Bouvignes,* 2km from the centre on the north side of town (☎082/22 40 02).

As for **eating and drinking**, to cater to Dinant's substantial day-tripper trade, there are plenty of cheap snack bars and the like, although quality restaurants are more thin on the ground. The *Tour Eifel*, to the right out of the station, is a glorified friterie with tables, good for a cheap sit-down lunch. Across the river, *Pizzeria Tivoli*, rue Grande 42, does OK and affordable pizzas, *La Chine*, rue Grande 45, reasonable Chinese food. Good bars are few: *La Clé de Sol*, rue Grande 63, is a pleasant place with a well-priced menu (it also rents out a few rooms); the *Taverne du Palais*, on rue de Palais de Justice, is nice too.

The Meuse Valley

The stretches of the **Meuse** south of Dinant are not the river's most impressive, but the town's wharves are lined with leisure boats pushing **cruises**. There are several different companies, each with boats leaving at different times, though the prices are roughly the same whoever you go with. While the river is not especially picturesque, taking a boat is one way of moving south if that's where you're headed. Destinations include the three places worth visiting on this part of the river: Freyr (F250 round trip), Waulsort (F270) and Hastière (F330); excursions also head out to Heer-Agimont on the French border, although even this far down the scenery is fairly tame, the river wide and gently curving.

If you actually want to have time to visit the above destinations on a day trip, you're better off getting the **GIVET** bus from outside Dinant station, which stops off at each of them (Mon–Fri 12 daily, Sat 7 daily, Sun 4 daily). **FREYR** itself is home to an eighteenth-century château (July & Aug Sat & Sun 2–6pm; F160), pushed up against the riverbank and edged by a small but well-kept formal French garden. On the opposite side of the river, the sheer cliff face is used for training by climbers of the *Club Alpin* school. **WAULSORT**, farther along, is a resort with faded elegance and a yacht club, its riverfront fringed by gracefully aging mansions. Three kilometres away, **HASTIERE** is the most interesting place to stop, due mainly to its Romanesque–Gothic church over the river at **HASTIERE-PAR-DELA**. The **church** (April–June & Sept–Oct daily 2–5pm; July & Aug daily 9am–noon & 2–7pm; free) was built around 1035 and a Gothic choir added in the thirteenth century, though as a whole it's now much restored after destruction by Huguenots in 1568, and again by French revolutionaries two centuries later. It's a typical church of the Mosan Romanesque style, with a flat wooden roof, plain square pillars and Lombard arches, similar to the church at Celles. A faded painting on the triumphal arch dates from the original construction, but the crypt is the oldest surviving part, containing Merovingian sarcophagi. The wooden thirteenth-century stalls are about the oldest in Belgium, with original and unique carvings – some allegorical, some satirical and mocking – a number of which were, in 1443, replaced with a plain triangle since they were considered too disrespectful. An unusual German fifteenth-century calvary hangs above the altar, Christ, Mary and St John standing on a dragon. Near the baptismal font is a beautiful sixteenth-century statue of the Virgin, whose graceful posture has earned it a place in several national exhibitions.

The Lesse Valley

Exploring the valley of the **River Lesse**, which spears off the Meuse a little way south of Dinant, is perhaps the most exciting thing you can do in the area around the town – something most people do in reverse order travelling back down river from Houyet by canoe. There are three companies which run trips, and again prices and options are fairly uniform, the standard trip beginning at Anseremme, where you buy a ticket and take a special morning bus to Houyet, where trips start; trains also leave Dinant for Anseremme and Houyet once hourly. Some companies have lockers and changing rooms at Anseremme, others at Houyet. From Houyet to Anseremme by canoe is 21km and takes about five hours. There are boats for one or two and also large steered "barges" for those who don't feel up to canoeing. There are places to stop for lunch along the way. Groups, by reservation, may leave from Gendron, from where the trip takes about two and a half hours.

The course is wild and winding, with great scenery, though be warned that sometimes it gets so packed there's a veritable traffic jam of canoes. Get to Anseremme/Houyet as early as possible if you want to enjoy the river in peace. For prior reservations and further details call ☎082/22 61 86 or 22 23 25; reckon on paying F500–600 for a single canoe for a day, doubles F700.

Halfway along to Anseremme you pass beneath the **Parc National de Furfooz**, (mid-March to mid-Nov daily 10am–2hr before sunset; F70), scenically the best part of the trip. Occupying a promontory overlooking the Lesse, it's not a large park, and you should allow around ninety minutes to tour its marked circuit of 3.5km. There's not actually a great deal to see, but a scattering of archeological remains and geological formations give purpose to what is a pleasant walk – no more. There are reconstructed Roman baths, from where you can walk up to a high ridge overlooking the river. There are also foundations of a Roman fortress, converted in the Middle Ages and used many times since.

You can also visit the park by train from Dinant. Get off at Gendron-Celles (10min), turn left out of the station, make a sharp left before the bridge into the campsite and then a sharp right under the bridge. A path goes alongside the river for about twenty minutes to the park entrance (car drivers should use another marked entrance on the other side of the park, appoached via the village of Furfooz).

From Gendron-Celles station it's a four-kilometre walk in the opposite direction to the **Château de Veves** (Easter–Oct daily 10.30am–noon & 1–6pm; F120), a renovated fifteenth-century structure set on a ridge overlooking the surrounding countryside. Inside there's an armoury and eighteenth-century period rooms. Two kilometres farther on, **CELLES** is the prettiest village around here, gently filing up the slope of a wooded hill, underneath the huge tower and Lombard arches of the Romanesque **Eglise St-Hadelin**. The church's thirteenth-century stalls are the oldest in the country along with those of Hastière-Par-Delà (see previous page). Celles has one **hotel**, the *Hostellerie Val Joli*, rue St-Hadelin 2 (☎082/66 63 63; ④). There's a **campsite**, near Gendron-Celles station, the *Paradiso* (☎082/66 60 28).

You can also make a canoe trip on another part of the river, up from Wanlin to Houyet, a distance of 12km. If you want to go to a more southern part of the Ardennes, the train from Dinant through Gendron-Celles and Houyet goes on to Bertrix for connections to Libramont, a main train junction, with regular services to Luxembourg, Namur and Virton.

Rochefort and Han

A little distance beyond the source of the River Lesse, to the south, lies one of the Ardennes' most beautiful regions, centring on the tourist resorts of **Han-sur-Lesse** and **Rochefort**. It's a lovely area, but access is difficult from Dinant, and it's in fact easier to go back to Namur and take the train to **Jemelle** (direction Luxembourg), the nearest large train junction; trains also go to Jemelle from Libramont, Liège and Arlon. There are real crowd-pullers like the Han-sur-Lesse caves, the most spectacular in the country, as well as the odd castle, and the surrounding countryside, thickly wooded and with good roads and gentle hills, is perfect for cycling.

As for **transport** in the area, apart from bikes, there are reasonably frequent **buses** between Jemelle station, Rochefort, Lessive, and Han. Also in July and August a special **tourist train** operates twice a day from Rochefort to Lavaux-Ste-Anne – a one-hour journey. It stops at Han, and the RTT at Lessive, but you must begin the journey from Rochefort; details from Rochefort tourist office.

Rochefort

Situated in the midst of some lovely countryside, the small town of **ROCHEFORT** is as good a centre for exploring the Ardennes as you'll find. It's not an especially attractive place in itself, but it does have a good range of cheap accommodation, as well as other facilities like bike rental, and it has none of the crass commercialism of somewhere like Han.

The Town

Rochefort follows the contours of an irregularly shaped hill, its long and pleasant main street, rue de Behogne, slicing through the centre from north to south, although the only things of tangible interest are actually outside the town centre. The main thing to see in the town itself is the **Grotte** (April–Oct daily 9.45am–5.15pm – guided tours run every 45min; F150), a ten-minute walk from the central crossroads, place Albert 1er – walk down rue Jacquet and do the first left up the hill, rue de Lorette, bearing right at the top. First discovered in 1865, the caves are a cold and wild affair, their most impressive feature the huge *Salle du Sabbat* – no less than 85m high. Back at the bottom of the hill, continuing on up rue Jacquet, Rochefort's other main attraction is the ruins of the medieval **Château Comtal** (mid-June to mid-Sept 1–6pm; F60), which offers fine views from its rocky outcrop.

Practicalities

Rochefort's well-organized **tourist office**, rue de Behogne 2 (Mon–Fri 9am–12.30pm & 1–5pm, Sat 10am–12.30pm & 1–5pm, Sun 10am–12.30pm & 1–4pm; ☎084/21 25 37), has information on the town and can make accommodation reservations for no charge, including rooms at a number of bed and breakfast addresses. Of a number of reasonably cheap **hotels** in the centre of Rochefort, *Le Limbourg* (☎084/21 25 37; ③) and the *Central* (☎084/21 10 24; ③), both on place Albert 1er, are both decent alternatives, or there is a couple of cheaper places up rue Jacquet, notably *La Fayette*, rue Jacquet 87 (☎084/21 42 73; ②). In the opposite direction, *La Malle Poste*, rue de Behogne 46 (☎084/21 09 86; ④), is the slightly pricier option, but it is very pleasant, and has an excellent restaurant and a convivial bar attached, with a wide choice of beer. If you're **camping**, there's a convenient site, *Camping Communal*, a five-minute walk from the centre of Rochefort – simply follow route de Marche out of town from place Albert 1er and do the first left after the river, rue du Hableau. There's also an 86-bed **gîte d'étape** nearby, at rue de Hableau 25 (☎084/21 46 04; ①).

For **food**, *Le Luxembourg*, just off place Albert 1er heading towards the tourist office, has a wide-ranging menu, including omelettes and snacks as well as more substantial items. Further down the hill, the restaurant of the *Central* hotel is a decent standby, with tasty and reliable Belgian and French standards, while, in the opposite direction, near the church, the restaurant of the slightly more upscale *Hôtel La Malle Post* serves fine Belgian food – menus from F1000 (see above) – and has a good bar, *La Coterie*, which features over a hundred beers and has occasional jazz evenings.

Han-sur-Lesse

Just 6km southwest of Rochefort, tiny **HAN-SUR-LESSE** is well known for its caves, the most impressive in the Ardennes, with the result that in summer at least the village is packed full with tourists. There are masses of hotels and eating places to absorb the invasion, most in the immediate vicinity of the centre, but the atmosphere, inevitably, may make you want to move on quickly.

Indeed there's not much to actually see in Han apart from the **Grottes de Han**, located outside the village a little way down river (May–Aug trips every half-hour daily 9.30–11.30am & 1–5pm, 6pm in July & Aug; April, Sept & Oct trips every hour daily 10am–noon & 1.30–4.30pm; mid-Feb to March & Nov–Dec trips every 2 hr daily 10am–noon & 1.30–4.30pm; closed Jan to mid-Feb; F275), but in fact accessible from the central ticket office, which dominates the village centre on the corner of rue J. Lamotte – you're taken by special train to the caves' entrance and after the tour are left a little way up the river, five minutes' walk from the village centre.

The caves were discovered at the beginning of the nineteenth century and measure about 8km in length, a series of limestone galleries carved out of the hills by the River Lesse millions of years ago. Tours only visit a small part of the total extent, taking in the so-called Salle du Trophée, the site of the largest stalagmite, the Salle d'Armes, where the Lesse reappears after travelling underground for 1000m (it enters at the Belveux Gap), and the massive Salle du Dome – 145m long and 20m high – part of which holds a small lake.

Han's other attraction is a **wild animal reserve** (same hours as the caves; F185, combined ticket F425) just outside the town, an area of 2.5 square kilometres containing animals which inhabited the Ardennes in prehistoric times – bison, bears and auroch (an ancestor of present-day cattle), along with deer and wild boar. A special bus takes you around the area to seek them out, the whole thing lasting about an hour and a half, and is certainly worth doing if you're travelling with kids – otherwise you might as well concentrate on the caves.

To understand how the caves have formed, go to the **Musée du Monde Souterrain** (July & Aug daily 10am–8pm, April–June & Sept–Nov 10am–6pm; F70), opposite the caves' ticket office at place Theo Lannoy 3, behind the tourist office, a section of which explains the process. Also in the museum are the findings of archeological digs in the region – most were found where the Lesse surfaces again after travelling through the grottoes – among them flints, tools and bone ornaments from the Neolithic period, as well as weapons and jewellery from the Bronze Age.

Practicalities

The cheapest place to stay in Han is the **gîte d'étape**, handily located in the centre of the village, just behind the car park at rue Gîte d'Etape 10 (☎084/37 74 41; ①). There are two **campsites**, both by the river's edge: *Camping le Pirot* and *Camping de la Lesse* (turn right out of the tourist office and walk 100m). **Hotels** have the advantage of being fairly numerous and relatively cheap in Han. The *Hôtel du Luxembourg*, rue d'Hamptay 61 (☎084/37 73 01; ①), is ultra-affordable, with some rooms going for under F1000. With a little more money to spend, the *Hôtel des Ardennes*, right in the centre of town at rue des Grottes 2 (☎084/37 72 20; ②), has a wide variety of rooms and a fairly decent restaurant; the *Henry IV*, five minutes' walk away on rue des Chasseurs Ardennais (☎084/37 72 21; ③), the road towards Rochefort, is also a pleasant spot, and has the advantage of being a little way removed from Han's summer hubbub. There are lots of places to **eat** reasonably, although standards aren't particularly high and prices tend to be inflated almost everywhere. Try *Taverne le Plan d'Eau*, a pleasant spot next to *Le Pirot* campsite.

The **tourist office**, in a chalet opposite the caves' office (May–Sept daily 11am–4pm; ☎084/37 75 96), has cycle tour leaflets and a guide detailing walks in the area. You can also rent **canoes** from an office next to *Le Pirot* campsite (mid-June to mid-Sept daily 10am–6pm; last start at 4pm), making it possible to travel to Lessive by river and return by bike, a journey of two hours in all. It costs from F600 for a two-seater, F400 for a one-seater (bike or tandem available). If you want to rent a **bike** independently, you can do so from the same place, by the hour, half-day or whole day. Costs are F100 an hour, F400 for a day.

Lessive and Lavaux-Ste-Anne

Five kilometres northwest of Han, **LESSIVE** is home to the Belgian space and satellite station or **RTT** (mid-April to end-Oct daily 9.30am–5pm; F150). Topped with three huge antennae, it's something of a local tourist attraction, built here in a sheltered valley, far from wind and phone interference, and because the schist soil is very stable. Here they both broadcast TV programmes and receive and transmit information by satellite. There's an exhibition dedicated to its advanced technology and a museum demonstrating the first telephone and telegraph services. You can also try out a video telephone.

About 5km west of Han, **LAVAUX-STE-ANNE** is home to an originally four-teenth-century **château** (April–Oct daily 9am–noon & 1–6pm; Nov–March 9am–noon & 12.30–5.30pm; F100), surrrounded by a moat, with three fifteenth-century towers and one from the fourteenth century. The exterior has a medieval appearance, and Renaissance buildings surround the sturdy interior courtyard. Inside, there's a **Museum of Nature and Hunting** and a **Museum of the Countryside and Folklore** – neither exactly vital stops, but a reasonable detour if you're in the area.

St-Hubert and around

About 20km south of Rochefort, **ST-HUBERT** is another popular Ardennes resort, named after the patron saint of hunters who is said to have undergone his conversion in the woods nearby, afterwards becoming a monk at Stavelot Abbey. Later, in the seventh century, an abbey was founded here, giving its name to the town that grew up around it – these days one of the more peaceful of the Ardennes settlements, deep in the heart of one of the most thickly forested sections of the region. It's still a popular hunting centre and a great base for some gentle hiking, but its best-known attraction is the **Basilique St-Hubert**, whose grand facade of 1731 is visible from just about anywhere in town. Most of the rest of the church is sixteenth century, Gothic in style, although the crypt's Romanesque arches date back another five hundred years. The slender columns of the ambulatory are one of the church's finest features, a curving corridor of grey and yellow stone with a damaged retable of 24 – albeit spoiled – Limoges enamels in one of the chapels. The recently restored eighteenth-century choir stalls are delightful, too, two meticulously carved cartoon strips tracing the stories of St Hubert and St Benedict.

Practicalities

Next door to the church, the abbey's oldest domestic buildings house the **tourist office** (June–Sept daily 10am–noon & 1.30–5.30pm; rest of the year Sat & Sun only 10am–noon & 1.30–5.30pm; ☎061/61 30 10), which sells maps of the area's marked walks as well as stocking plenty of other Ardennes bumph. The nearest **train station** to St-Hubert is 6km away at Poix-St-Hubert, from where you can either take a bus (Mon–Fri 12 daily, Sat & Sun 4 daily; 15min) or rent a bike to the town, 9km away. There are two central **hotels**, both on place du Marché by the church: the *Hôtel du Luxembourg* (☎061/61 31 77), with a good, family-run restaurant with menus from F485, and the *Hôtel de l'Abbaye*, a little way up the main street (☎061/61 10 23), a nice old-fashioned hotel, also with a restaurant, this time with menus starting at around F390. The nearest **campsite** is on rue de Martelange (☎061/61 12 69), 2km southwest of the town. Around the corner from the *Luxembourg* hotel, about halfway down rue St-Gillies on the right, the

Taverne St-Gillies is another possible place to eat, with a good basic menu that also features couscous and paella should you be fed up with the usual Belgian fare.

Around St-Hubert

St-Hubert is quite a good base for the surrounding area, the highlights of which include excursions to a wild animal park, **Parc à Gibier**, 2km to the north, and, a few kilometres farther north (though within easy cycling distance of the town), to **Fourneau St-Michel** – a centre for ironworking, with an old forge and a museum showing old tools and the like (July & Aug daily 9am–6pm; rest of the year Mon–Fri 9am–5pm, Sat & Sun 9am–6pm; closed Jan & Feb; F100). Part of the same complex, the **Musée de la Vie Rurale en Wallonie** (July & Aug daily 9am–6pm; F100) spreads out over a large area, an open-air museum made up of reconstructions of typical Walloon rural buildings set out by type. There are farmouses and stables, a sawmill and a chapel, along with the usual cafés and restaurants. If you're interested in visiting both Fourneau St-Michel and the Musée de la Vie Rurale en Wallonie, bear in mind that you can buy a combined ticket that entitles you to see all the complex's attractions for F150.

Immediately west of St-Hubert, right by the A11 autoroute, a few kilometres north of the village of **LIBIN**, the **Euro Space Centre** (daily 10am–5pm; F395), is a hugely popular attraction locally. Easily identified by the space rocket parked outside, its hangar-like premises house a hi-tech museum that tells you everything you wanted to know about space travel and the applications of space and satellite technology. There are lots of buttons for the kids to press in the many interactive displays, as well as models of space vehicles and the like, although its lack of English information does make its appeal somewhat limited.

A short drive further on, across the other side of the autoroute, **REDU** is a small village that, like its British counterpart, Hay-on-Wye (with which it has been twinned), is full of bookstores selling new and used books, prints and pictures – a pleasant place, bustling with buyers and browsers in season, although most of the books are inevitably in French or Flemish. Worth the brief detour if you're travelling up the autoroute.

Bouillon and around

Forty-odd kilometres southwest of St-Hubert, close to the French border, **BOUILLON** is a well-known resort centre on the edge of the Ardennes, enclosed in a loop of the River Semois and crowned by an outstanding castle. It's a relaxed and peaceful place, with an easy-going atmosphere about it, and it gives easy access to some lovely walking in the countryside around, which is wilder than that farther north.

The Town

The most distinctive feature of Bouillon is its **Castle** (Dec Wed–Sun 10am–5pm; Jan Sat & Sun 10am–5pm; Feb Mon–Fri 1–5pm, Sat & Sun 10am–5pm; March, Oct & Nov daily 10am–5pm; April–June & Sept daily 10am–6pm; July & Aug daily

9.30am–7pm; F140 or combined ticket with musems F220), set up on a ridge which runs the length of the town. Access is from a road behind (rue du Château), or by a set of steep steps which climb up from Grande Rue, beside the Pont de Liège – the town's main street. The castle was originally held by a succession of independent counts who controlled most of the land around Bouillon. There were five of these, all called Godfrey, the fifth and last of whom left on the First Crusade in 1096, selling his dominions (partly to raise the cash for his trip) to the prince-bishop of Liège. Later on, the castle was confiscated by Louis XIV, and Vauban, his military architect, was charged with modifying it – the results of which are by and large what you see now. It's an intriguing old place, and visits wind through most of its courtyards, along the battlements and towers, and through dungeons filled with weaponry and instruments of torture. A leaflet in English describes the various parts of the structure. The Salle Godefroy, hewn out of the rock and named after the Crusader, contains a statue of the last ruler of Bouillon and an ancient wooden cross in the floor that was only discovered in 1962. The so-called Chair of Godfrey is a lookout, also cut out of solid rock, and one of the oldest parts of the castle.

Down the ridge from the castle, the **Musée Ducal** (April–June & Sept–Nov daily 10am–6pm; July & Aug daily 9.30am–7pm; F120) displays material pertaining to Godfrey's crusades, most notably Eastern art (Byzantine ivory carvings, gold lacquer plates) and medieval items from various local churches, among them Limoges enamels from the thirteenth century. There's also a section of the museum concentrating on the folklore and history of the town and region, a tape recording guiding you from room to room and talking you through the exhibits, which range from a model of the town in 1690 to various period rooms – a weaving room, another devoted to hunting, etc.

Practicalities

A regular bus service connects Bouillon with the train station at Libramont, 30km northeast (Mon–Fri 9 daily, Sat & Sun 3 daily; 50min). There's also an infrequent service from Bertix station, 23km away. The town's **tourist office** is based in the ticket office of the castle (see above for opening times; ☎061/46 62 57), and in July and August there's also an **information chalet** beside the Pont de France (daily 10am–1pm & 2–7pm; ☎061/46 62 89). For **accommodation**, there are a few rooms to let in **private homes**, details of which you can get from the tourist office, and there's a brand new **youth hostel** at chemin du Christ 16, on the opposite hill from the castle (☎061/46 81 37; ①); for a short cut, take the steps up from place St-Arnould, just across the Pont de Liège, which lead there direct. There are also a fair number of **hotels**, of which the *Central Duc de Bouillon*, rue des Hautes Voies 2–4, up the hill from the Pont de Liège (☎061/46 63 20; ③), is one of the most convenient – as is *La Tannerie*, on the waterfront near the Pont de Liège at Quai de la Tannerie 1 (☎061/46 62 27; ③), a hotel-restaurant with a cheap menu too. There is also a good grouping of hotels along Faubourg de France, just beyond Porte de France and the information chalet – try the *Hôtel de France*, Faubourg de France 1 (☎061/46 60 68; ③), or, just along the street at no. 3, the slightly pricier *Auberge d'Alsace* (☎061/46 65 88; ④). The nearest **campsite** is the *Halliru*, next to the river, just south of the town on the route de Corbion (April–Sept) – an easily walkable distance, just along from the far side of the tunnel next to the information chalet. There's a second campsite 1km south of town, *Moulin de la Falize*, at vieille route de France 33, which is well-equipped with a restaurant, swimming pool, tennis courts, etc, and cross-country skiing in winter.

As for **eating**, there are two medium-priced restaurants on the riverside Quai des Remparts – the *L'Acacia* at no. 29, which serves four-course menues for F650 upwards, and *Des Remparts*, at no. 23, with appetizing fish dishes from F400. Just along from *L'Acacia*, the *Roy de la Bière*, Quai des Reparts 34, is a wooden bench bar with a wide choice of beers and an attached mussels-and-chips restaurant – great for lunch. Back down the street, *Le Mont Blanc*, Quai des Remparts 1, has delightful food for F450 or so per dish – a bargain – while around the corner, *La Vieille Ardenne*, Grande Rue 9, has lots of regional specialities and menus from F650, and is also a good place for a drink, with a good list of different beers. For **picnic food**, go to the *Unic* supermarket just next to the Porte de France on the riverfront.

Canoes can be rented from *Les Tritons* (☎061/46 63 91) on the Quai des Saulx near the Pont de Liège and the *Moulin de la Falize* campsite; reckon on F900 for a two-seater per day. The riverscape is gentle and sleepy, the Semois slow moving and meandering; what's more you don't get the kind of canoe traffic jams that occur around, say, Dinant. The most popular excursion is to **POUPEHAN**, 15km down river (see below). **Bikes** can be rented from a Fiat garage a kilometre outside of town, just off the main road to Sedan, although to enjoy the best of the scenery you should really be on foot.

Around Bouillon

The tourist office sells decent walking maps – *Cartes des Promenades du Grand Bouillon* (F60) – with many marked routes, though you shouldn't follow these too slavishly. As long as you have a map and can see where paths exist, you can improvise as you go along. One of the better marked routes is **Route 13**, which runs along the river edge from the Pont de la Poulie behind the castle, ascending for a great view over the valley from the **Rocher du Pendu** (Hanged Man's Rock). You can also simply carry on along the riverbank, though be warned that points that are sometimes marked as river crossings on the map can be no more than boulders or stepping stones, and may be difficult or even non-existent if the river is high (Moulin de l'Epine and one near the Tombeau du Géant are two like this). Whichever way you decide to go, a good place to aim for is the village of **POUPEHAN**, 6km west cross country, an attractive little resort sloping up from the banks of the River Semois. There are five **campsites** in and around the village, including *Le Prahay* on rue Cherizelle (☎061/46 80 31), and several **hotels**, cheapest of which is *La Vallée*, rue du Mont 18 (☎061/46 61 81; ②). You can also rent **canoes** down by the river. Some 4km north, **ROCHEHAUT** is another popular destination, its ancient stone houses surrounded by heavily forested hills. There are a number of campsites here, too, and a couple of cheap hotels – the *Auberge de la Ferme*, rue de la Cense 21 (☎061/46 69 71; ②), and *Pension l'An*, rue du Palis 40 (☎061/46 65 33; ②). Back toward Bouillon, a nice walk is to the **Moulin de l'Epine** (where there's a café-restaurant). From here the high N93 offers a great view of the **Tombeau du Géant**, a conical land mass in a river loop. You could carry on from here to the village of **BOTASSART**.

In the other direction from Bouillon, the Semois twists its way through the village of **DOHAN**, home to a couple of hotels, best of which is the *Auberge Ardennais*, right in the centre of the village (☎061/46 64 28; ④). Before long you reach **HERBEUMONT**, 22km away by road, with its ruined, originally thirteenth-century **Castle**, five minutes' walk from the centre of the village, high on a bluff over the river. It's little more than a shell now, but it's worth the scramble up the hill to get to it, as the views are quite spectacular. There's also a splendid turn-of-the-century **Viaduct**, just outside the village off the main road towards Florenville. There are three **campsites** in the village, best of which is the Champ de Monde, right by the viaduct, as well as a couple of **hotels**, the cheapest of which is *La Chatelaine*, Grand Place 8 (☎061/41 14 22; ③), which also has a **restaurant**. There's also a small creperie, *L'Abri*, just off the main square.

Florenville, Orval, Virton and Arlon

Shortly after rejoining the main N83, **FLORENVILLE**, right on the French border, is a good base for the surrounding countryside, an attractive little town set around a large square and a bustling main street. There's a **tourist office** right on the square (daily 9am–noon & 2–6pm; ☎061/31 12 29), and the venerable *Hôtel de France* on the main street (☎061/31 10 32; ③) makes a nice place to stay, and the *Brasserie du Marché*, on the main square, an amiable place to eat, with plats du jour for just F200 and menus starting at F480.

East of Florenville, beside the main road, the **Abbaye d'Orval** (Easter–Sept daily except Mon 9.30am–noon & 1.30–6.30pm; rest of year daily except Mon 9.30am–noon & 1.30–5.30pm; F80) is a place of legendary beginnings. It was founded, the story goes, when Countess Mathilda of Tuscany lost a gold ring in a lake and a fish recovered it for her, prompting the countess to donate the surrounding land to God for the construction of a monastery. A fish with a golden ring is still the emblem of the monastery, and can be seen gracing the bottles of beer for which the abbey is these days best known.

It's worth a visit if you've got transport, but is otherwise a tedious pilgrimage. Buses run from nearby Florenville, the nearest town on the train network, but they're not at all frequent. Bear in mind also that the abbey is by no means as complete or untouched as it might be. Originally a Benedictine foundation, then Cistercian, it has always been first and foremost a working community, making beer cheese, and bread (samples of which are on sale in the abbey shop), but of the original twelfth- to thirteenth-century buildings, only the ruins of the Romanesque–Gothic church of Notre Dame are left, with the frame of the original rose window and Romanesque capitals in the nave and transept. The rest was rebuilt in the eighteenth century to a design by Dewez, but most of this, too, was destroyed in the French Revolution, and the abbey was left abandoned until 1926, when the Trappist order acquired the property and built on the site to the seventeenth-century plans, creating an imposing new complex, complete with a monumental statue of the Virgin. You can wander around the ruins, and they are picturesque enough, but many of the new buildings are closed to the public. The only parts you can visit are the eighteenth-century cellars – all that is left of the buildings by Dewez – complete with a model of how the abbey looked in 1760, a reading room and an old apothecary.

Virton

The area around Orval is known as the **Gaume**, effectively an extension of the Ardennes, hilly and thickly wooded. **VIRTON**, the main town, is a lively settlement whose compact centre retains the circular shape of its medieval walls, although there's not much, quite frankly, to hold you here for more than an hour or two beyond its one real attraction, the **Musée Gaumais**, situated on the way out of the centre at rue d'Arlon 38 (April–Nov daily except Tues 9.30am–noon & 2–6pm; June–Aug also open Tues; F100). Housed in a spanking new building, its collection of period rooms and prehistoric finds is saved from mediocrity by an outstanding array of iron fireplaces, a local speciality dating from as early as the fifteenth century, some of which are superbly decorated, illustrating biblical themes and the like.

A minor stop on the train line from Libramont and Bertrix, Virton's **train station** is 1km from the centre, straight down avenue Bouvier. The **tourist office** is immediately west of the main square at rue Croix-la-Maire 2 (Mon–Fri 9am–noon & 1.30–5pm, Sat 9am–noon; ☎063/57 89 04). There's one cheap **hotel**, *Le Cheval Blanc*, at rue du Moulin 1 (☎063/57 89 35; ②). For **food**, try the pizzeria *Le Commerce*, close by the main square at rue Charles Magnette 5, or *Au Coin Fleuri*, on the opposite side of the same street, by the church right by the square.

Arlon

The chief town of Luxembourg province, **ARLON** is one of the oldest towns in Belgium, a trading centre for the Romans as far back as the second century AD. These days it's a comfortable, prosperous place, with a relaxed and genial atmosphere that makes for a pleasant, if brief stop – although again there's not a lot to see. The modern centre of the town is **place Leopold**, with the Palais de Justice at one end and a World War II tank in the middle, commemorating the American liberation of Arlon in September 1944. Behind the Palais de Justice, to the left, the **Musée Luxembourgeois**, rue des Martyrs 13 (Mon–Sat 9am–noon & 2–5pm; mid-June to mid-Sept also Sun 10am–noon & 2–4pm; F100), has a good collection of Roman finds from the surrounding area, many of which are wonderfully evocative of daily life in Roman times. There are pieces from the Merovingian era, too, as well as a marvellously realistic sixteenth-century retable.

A couple of minutes' walk from place Leopold, up a flight of steps, is Arlon's diminutive **Grand Place**, where there are more fragments from Roman times, the **Tour Romaine**, in the corner, formerly part of the third-century ramparts. From here, rue des Carmes leads down to the seventeenth-century church of **St-Donat**, which gives good views over the surrounding countryside, and, a little way beyond down rue des Thermes, a few scattered ruins of a first-century **Roman Baths**.

The **train station** is five minutes' walk away from the centre of town, and Arlon's **tourist office**, just off the main square on rue des Faubourgs, next door to the *Café de Nord* (Mon–Fri 8.30am–noon & 1.30–5pm; ☎063/21 63 60). For **accommodation**, the *Hôtel Courtoise*, opposite the station (☎063/22 02 03; ②), is the cheapest and perhaps the most convenient option; the *A L'Ecu de Bourgogne*, on place Leopold (☎063/22 02 22; ④), is rather nicer but somewhat more expensive. For **food**, the *Maison Knopes* on the Grand Place serves excellent crepes, waffles as well as fuller meals, and does a great line in coffee.

Bastogne

Forty kilometres north of Arlon is the important road and rail junction of **BASTOGNE**, best known for its heroic defence by the Americans in December 1944, who held out here against heavy bombardment from the surrounding Germans. A key engagement of the Battle of the Bulge (see below), the American commander in chief's response to the German demand for surrender – "Nuts!" – is one of the more quotable, if apocryphal, of World War II rallying cries. Not surprisingly the town and its environs are full of reminders of the battle. The main square is known as **place McAuliffe** after the American commander, and is the site of an American tank, just around the corner from which the **Musée des Pays d'Ardennes**, on the left a little way down rue de Neufchâteau (daily 9am–4pm; F100), includes a hotchpotch of odds and ends from the war years, includign some touching letters from ex-GIs alongside a disarming array of stuffed Ardennes wildlife.

THE BATTLE OF THE BULGE

Though there's not a lot to see now beyond parked tanks and the odd war memorial, the Ardennes-was the site of some of World War II's fiercest fighting during the **Battle of the Bulge**. The Allied campaign of autumn 1944 had concentrated on striking into Germany from Maastricht in the north and Alsace in the south, leaving a central section of lightly defended front line extending across the Ardennes from Malmédy to Luxembourg. In December 1944, Hitler embarked on a desperate plan to change the course of the war by breaking through this part of the front, seizing Antwerp and forcing the Allies to retreat. In command of the operation was one of his best generals, Von Rundstedt, who hoped to benefit from the wintery weather conditions which would limit Allied aircraft activity. Carefully prepared, Von Rundstedt's offensive began on December 16, 1944, and one week later had created a "bulge" in the Allied line that reached the outskirts of Dinant – though the American 101st Airborne Division held firm around Bastogne. The success of the operation depended on rapid results, however, and Von Rundstedt's inability to reach Antwerp meant failure. Montgomery's forces from the north and Patton's from the south launched a counterattack, and by the end of January the Germans had been forced back to their original position.

The story of the battle is more fully told at the **American Memorial**, situated about 2km outside Bastogne to the northeast, a good fifteen-minute walk from Bastogne-Nord train station. The star-shaped structure, inscribed with the names of all the American states, probably looks a great deal better from the air than it does from the ground, but the panels around the side do an excellent job of recounting different episodes from the battle, and it's possible to climb up onto the roof for a windswept look back at Bastogne and the slag heaps and quarries of the countryside that surrounds it. Next door to the memorial, the **Bastogne Historical Centre** collects together all manner of war-related artefacts – uniforms, vehicles, etc – in an impressive and imaginative display (mid-March to April & mid-Sept to mid-Nov daily 10am–4pm; May & June daily 9.30am–5pm; July & Aug daily 9am–6pm; F245), along with showing a film of the proceedings.

Practicalities

There's not much to Bastogne, and certainly no reason to stay over. The **tourist office** in the middle of place McAuliffe (Mon–Fri 8.15am–noon & 1.15–4.30pm; ☎061/21 27 11) has information on the town. If you get stuck, *Le Bourges*, place McAuliffe 10 (☎061/21 11 00), is the town's cheapest **hotel**, with doubles for F1000 or so; there's a **campsite** about fifteen minutes' walk west of the centre along rue de Marché. For **food**, there are lots of places on and around place McAuliffe. The *Café 1900* does decent light lunches and snacks, as does *Bistro Leo*, just off the square at the top of rue du Sablon. For a full meal, *Restaurant Leo*, housed in an old railway carriage, is excellent and moderately priced, but inevitably very popular.

La Roche-en-Ardenne and around

The unofficial capital of the Ardennes, around 25km northeast of St-Hubert, **LA ROCHE-EN-ARDENNE** is amazingly picturesque, hidden by pressing hills until you're right on top of it and topped by romantic castle ruins. It's a strange mixture: a hidden place, geographically cut off from the rest of the world, yet it teems with people during the summer, fulfilling its role as one of the region's major resorts. It is, however, surrounded by some of the wildest scenery in the Ardennes, and also has – by Ardennes standards – a relatively animated night scene, with plenty of bars and late-night restaurants.

The Town

The centre of La Roche squeezes into one bend in the river, its high street winding between the two bridges, an unashamedly exploitative stretch of shops pushing Ardennes ham and camping gear. That, however, is about it as far as development goes, and the streets around are unspoiled and quiet. The only tangible thing to see is the grass-carpeted **Castle** (July & Aug daily 10am–7pm; April–June & Sept–Oct daily 10am–noon & 2–5pm; rest of the year Mon–Fri 10am–noon & 2–4pm; F70), construction of which began in the ninth century and continued over four hundred years. Destroyed in the late eighteenth century, it remains in ruins. To get there take the steps that lead up from the high street. On the high street itself, the Musée Bataille des Ardennes (daily 9am–6pm; F140), a small collection of military artefacts dedicated to the war years in the Ardennes, is pretty missable, especially if you've been to Bastogne, where they do the same thing much better.

Practicalities

The **tourist office** on the main street at place du Marché 15 (July & Aug daily 10am–6pm, other times daily 10am–noon & 2–5pm; ☎084/41 13 42), has maps and booklets on the town and details of accommodation possibilities. There are loads of **places to stay**, but booking is advisable in season. Across the river, the very pleasant *Luxembourg*, avenue du Hadja 1a (☎084/41 14 15; ②), is one of the town's better-value options, as is the slightly cheaper *Hôtel de Liège*, opposite at rue de la Gare 16 (☎084/41 11 64; ②), while with a little more money, the *Hotel de la Place*, rue de Beausaint 1 (☎084/41 12 52; ④), is a nice old-fashioned hotel, very handily placed, and with an excellent restaurant. The tourist office also has details of plenty of private **rooms** (②). There are no fewer than ten **campsites** in the vicinity, most packed with trailers. Among the closest is a group along rue de Harzé by the Ourthe, north of the town – the *Benelux*, about an 800-metre walk down along rue de la Gare, and *Camping de l'Ourthe*, and *Le Grillon*, just beyond. There are also some in the opposite direction, towards Houffalize – try *Les Templiers*, the first, about 1200m away from the town centre, also by the river, or *Fleur Club* and *Lohan* a little further on.

There are lots of **restaurants** to choose from, mostly along the main street and around the car park-cum-main square, place du Bronze, at the southern entrance of the town centre. *La Sapinière*, just off here at rue Nulay 4, serves great-value classic Belgian country food, as does *Restaurant L'Apero*, rue Clerue 5, a small, family-run restaurant with fine local cooking. Alternatives include the cheap pizzas of the brash *Mezzogiorno*, place du Bronze 1, and the fancier food of the exclusive *Hôtel des Genets* restaurant, overlooking the town from Corniche de Deister 2. If you just want to **drink**, the *Vénetien*, halfway down the main street on the right, is a popular local bar.

Most people come to La Roche to get out to the countryside and walk or canoe. It's possible to rent **canoes** from *Zimmer Sports* opposite the church on the main street. You can also rent **bikes** from M. Hennebert, place du Bronze, or from the *l'Escale* hotel on Quai Gravier, but the area's very hilly – you're better off with a **mountain bike** (also from *Zimmer Sports*). In winter there's cross-country skiing at nearby Samrée. You can buy a combined walking and cycling map (*Carte des Promenades Pedestres et Circuits Cyclotouristes*) from the tourist office in the high street, which can also tell you about the guided walks that are arranged every Tuesday and Thursday in July and August.

Around La Roche

Scenically, the most dramatic thickly forested countryside is southeast of La Roche, in the steep valley of the winding Ourthe, with both road and footpath following the course of the river as far as **MABOGE**, 6km away. From here, two walking routes double back toward the town, while the road veers left to cross the flat uplands surrounding the village of **BERISMENIL**. Halfway to Houffalzie, the village of **NADRIN**, reachable by way of the twice-daily bus to Houffalize, is home to a **belvedere** – actually a high tower with a restaurant attached – from which you can see the Ourthe at six different points due to its meandering course in and out of the tightly packed hills. The belvedere is about 2km from the main road. A couple of kilometres out of Nadrin, a right-turn leads down to the **Barrage de Nisramont**, a dam across the River Ourthe, where there are parking facilities, cafés, etc, and a series of well signposted paths (13km in total) encircling the resultant lake and the various spears of the Ourthe, taking in a number of belvederes and refuges. Walking the entire route takes a good half a day, but be warned that in summer it can get very crowded on the paths. From the dam, the road crosses the river and winds up to Nisramont, shortly before another **belvedere** gives a good view of the barrage and winding valley.

Carrying on to **HOUFFALIZE**, a shabby little resort on both sides of the river valley, you can pick up GR path #57, which follows the Ourthe up toward Liège –

although the stretches north of La Roche are less spectacular. Houffalize itself enjoys a great position, nestling in the valley, but was almost entirely destroyed during World War II when it was the site of a key battle to stop a German advance: a German tank bears testimony. If you want to stay, there are a couple of **hotels**, and a **campsite**, *Camping du Viaduc*, by the river on the Nadrin road.

If you want a shorter walk, the route to **BEAUSAINT**, in open country and along hilltops, is easy. For a full day's walk the most varied is the one toward **HIVES**, part through woods, part high up and in the open.

Moving on from La Roche, eight buses a day (weekends 4) travel the 20km to **MELREUX** train station, where you can pick up trains north to Liège and south of Jemelle. Alternatively six buses a day (weekends 3) head west to **MARLOIE** station, a couple of stops down the line, from where it's possible to hire a bike to visit the caves which lie on the southern outskirts of **HOTTON**, 12km away back toward Melreux (April–Oct daily 9am–6pm; F150); they're noted for their unusual chalk formations – allow around an hour for a visit.

Some 10km north of Melreux, tiny **DURBUY** is a very pleasant large village, surrounded by low-lying wooded hills and set around a large main square, with a tranquil old quarter of narrow cobbled streets and seventeenth-century houses. Without your own transportation it's very difficult to reach – the nearest station is at **BARVAUX**, 4km away, and there are no connecting buses – but it's a pretty place, good for canoeing on the river and gentle walking, and it has stacks of hotels and restaurants so makes a good, if sometimes busy, base for the area. Of the **hotels**, the *L'Esplanade*, on the main street, is good (☎086/21 16 81; ③), or there's the quieter *La Falize* (☎086/21 26 66; ③).

Huy

Midway between Namur and Liège, and easily accessible by train, **HUY** spreads across both sides of the Meuse – aside from Liège, the major centre of the northern Ardennes and worth a stop even if you're only passing through on the way to Liège.

The Town

Most sights are on the opposite side of the river from the train station, principally the **Collégiale Notre-Dame** (Mon–Sat 9am–noon & 2–5pm, Sun 9am–12.30pm & 2–6pm), an imposing Gothic church which occupies a prime site right by the water. Built between 1311 and 1536, it's a superb example of the style, its rose window – restored in 1973 – a dazzling conglomeration of reds and blues, the choir a huge structure, occupying a third of the total nave and cut with slender twenty-metre-high stained-glass windows. On the right side of the nave as you enter, stairs lead down to a Romanesque crypt of 1066, where the relics of Huy's patron saint, St Domitian, were once venerated. His original twelfth-century shrine stands upstairs in the treasury under the rose window (F50), along with three other large shrines from the twelfth and thirteenth centuries, crafted by the Mosan gold- and silversmiths for which Huy was once famous – they're somewhat faded, but the beauty and skill of their execution still shines through.

On leaving the church, walk down the alleyway to the side which leads to the **Porte de Bethléem**, above which is a mid-fourteenth-century central ogival arch decorated with scenes of the nativity. It's a short walk from here across the busy avenue des Ardennes to the nominal centre of town at the **Grand Place**, with its bronze fountain of 1406 showing a representation of the town walls interspersed with tiny statues of the same saints commemorated in the church. The wrought-iron and stone vats were added in the eighteenth century. The square is flanked on the far side by the solid-looking eighteenth-century **Hôtel de Ville**, behind which place Verte gives way to rue St Mengold which in turn leads to rue des Frères Mineurs, on the corner of which is the oldest house in Huy, the **Maison de la Tour** – an example of Gothic civil architecture of the late twelfth century, currently being restored.

At the top of rue des Frères Mineurs, the cloistered former friary of the same name – late seventeenth century – houses the varied exhibits of the **Musée Communal** (April to mid-Oct daily 2–6pm; F60). There is old wine-making equipment, including a winepress of 1719 – wine was a major product of the area from the seventh to the sixteenth centuries – alongside items of daily life, reconstructions of period rooms and displays of ceramics, coins, and religious paintings. The prize exhibit is an oak carving of Christ on the Cross, called the *Beau Dieu de Huy*, a typical Mosan thirteenth-century sculpture.

The last one of Huy's sights worth taking in is its **Citadel** (Easter–Sept daily 10am–6pm, until 7pm in July & Aug; F120), accessible on foot from the Quai de Namur by taking the path up to the left before the bridge, or by cable car from avenue Batta on the other side of the river – cross over the Pont Roi Baudouin and turn left down the riverside Quai du Halage (F80 one-way). Huy's citadel is not actually all that old. Built in the early nineteenth century by the Dutch, the Nazis used it as a prison during World War II, and it's now a kind of museum of that war, with prisoners' cells and the Gestapo questioning room. It's a massive complex, and the marked tour of the seemingly endless galleries is eerie and disorienting.

Practicalities

Huy's **train station** is a short walk from the town centre on place Z. Gramme; walk up rue des Jardins or the parallel avenue Albert 1 until you hit rue St-Pierre and chaussée de Liège, the first major intersection, where you should turn right on to place St-Germain and then turn left. The **tourist office** is across the bridge on Quai de Namur, by the church (July & Aug Mon–Fri 8am–1pm & 2–6pm, Sat & Sun 10am–1pm & 2–6pm; rest of the year Mon–Fri 8am–noon & 1.30–5pm; ☎085/21 29 15). If you want to stay, the cheapest **hotels** are the *Renaissance*, rue des Soeurs Grises 16–18 (☎085/21 28 45; ③), and the *Hôtel de la Collégiale*, right by the church at rue de la Collègiale 5 (☎085/23 06 11; ③), although quite frankly you might just as well stay in Liège, or in a more bucolic location further south. There is an official **youth hostel** 3km outside town – next to a **campsite** (April to end Sept) – at rue de la Paix 3 in nearby **TIHANGE** (☎085/23 10 51; ①), although it's only open during the Easter vacation and in July and August and almost adjacent to a nuclear power station. There's not much in the way of **restaurants**. *Le Jupy*, Quai de Namur 10, is an affable bar that does a large selection of mussels; *Le Febvre*, a few doors down, at no. 15, does delicious two-course menus for a flat F950, while, just off Grand Place at rue Griange 14, *Les Fleurs des Iles* offers a rare chance to try Antilles cuisine. For dessert, or just a snack, *Pastel et Chocolat*, nearby at rue Vierset Godin 2, features brilliant ice cream.

Liège and around

Though the effective capital of the Ardennes, and of its own province, **LIÈGE** isn't the most obvious stop on most travellers' itineraries. It's a large, grimy, industrial city, with few notable sights and little immediate appeal. However, if you're heading down this way from Holland it is hard to avoid – trains on both routes to Luxembourg, for example, pass through the city – and once you've got to grips with its size, Liège even has a few surprises up its sleeve. Certainly, if you're overnighting, you'd be well advised to give it at least half a day before moving on.

Liège was actually independent for much of its history, from the tenth century onward the seat of a line of prince-bishops, who ruled over bodies as well as souls for around eight hundred years. The last prince-bishop was expelled in 1794 by soldiers of revolutionary France, who also torched the cathedral, and Liège was later incorporated into the Belgian state, rising to prominence as an industrial city. The coal and steel industries here actually date back to the twelfth century, but it was only with the nineteenth century that real development of the city's position and natural resources took place – not least under one Charles Cockerill, a British entrepreneur whose name you still see around town. However, the heavy industry Cockerill bequeathed has been in decline, and the city is ringed by the decaying remnants of industrial glories long past.

> The Liège area telephone code is ☎041

Arrival and information

You'll probably arrive in Liège at **Gare de Guillemins**, about 2km south of the city centre. At the station there's a small information office (Mon–Sat 10am–noon & 12.30–4pm), where you can pick up city maps, hotel lists, etc, although for more complete **information** you'll need to go to the main **tourist office** at Feronstrée 92 (Mon–Fri 9am–6pm; April–Oct also Sat 10am–4pm, Sun 10am–2pm; ☎22 24 56), where they also have maps and can advise on accommodation. There's also a **provincial tourist office** in the centre of town at boulevard de la Sauvenière 77 (Mon–Fri 8.30am–5pm, Sat 9am–1pm; ☎22 42 10), although they're normally extremely unhelpful. All trains stop at the Guillemins station, but Liège also has two other stations – **Palais**, on rue de Bruxelles near place St-Lambert, and **Jonfosse**, on rue Stephany, not far from boulevard de la Sauvenière – which handle local trains and connections to Verviers and Eupen to the east, Tournai, Mons and Charleroi in the west.

To get to the centre of town from the station, take bus #1 or #4 to place St-Lambert; the journey by taxi will cost you around F200. In general, **getting around** is easiest on foot in the city centre, which is reasonably compact. However, Liège is a big, sprawling place, and to get from one side of town to the other, or to make a quick short hop, you'll need to take a **bus**. Tickets cost F36 for a journey of any length, either from the driver or one of the ticket booths located at major bus terminals like place St-Lambert, place de la Cathédrale or the train station.

CENTRAL LIÉGE

RUE L'ACADÉMIE

RUE L'ACADÉMIE

St-Servais

Palais des
Princes Évêques

RUE DU PALA

Gare du Palais

RUE DE BRUXELLES

Ste-Croix

RUE HAUTE-SAUVENIÈRE

PLACE
ST-LAMBERT

St-Martin

MONT ST-MARTIN

RUE BASSE SAUVENIÈRE

BOULEVARD DE LA SAUVENIÈRE

Bus
Station

PL. DE LA
RÉPUBLIQUE
FRANCAISE

RUE ST-GANGULPHE

Provincial
Tourist
Office

PLACE XAVIER
NEUJEAN

Theâtre
Royal

St-Jean

PLACE XAVIER NEUJEAN

RUE PONT D'ILE

RUE DE LA CASQUETTE

PASSAGE LEMMONNIER

RUE DE LA

BOULEVARD DE LA SAUVENIÈRE

RUE DES CÉLESTINES

RUE DU MOUTON BLANC

RUE D'AMAY

RUE DE LA CATHÉDRALE

RUE DU POT D'OR

RUE TÊTE DE BŒUF

RUE DU POT-D'AVROY

PLACE
CATHÉDRALE

RUE CH. MAGNETTE

Cathédrale
St. Paul

RUE ST-PAUL

RUE ST. GILLES

BOULEVARD D'AVROY

To the Train Station (1½ km)

To St. Jac

To the Citadel

MONTAGNE DE BUEREN

PLACE DU MARCHÉ

St-Barthélemy

RUE ST-BARTHÉLEMY

Musée d'Architecture

HORS-CHÂTEAU

RUE DES BRASSEURS

Musée Curtis

Musée de la Vie Wallonne

FERONSTRÉE

Musée Ansembourg

RUE HONGRÉE

RUE VELBRUCK

Musée d'Art Religieux et d'Art Mosan

RUE DE LA ROSE

Musée de l'Art Wallonne

Musée d'Armes

RUE ST GEORGE

Tourist Office

RUE DES MINEURS

FERONSTRÉE

RUE DE LA BOUCHERIE

QUAI DE LA GOFFE

Hôtel de Ville

QUAI DES TANNEURS

RUE DE LA CITÉ

RUE LEOPOLD

RUE DE LA MADELEINE

Meuse

PONT DES ARCHES

RUE SOUVERAIN-PONT

RUE ST. PHOLIEN

enis

RUE DE LA CATHÉDRALE

BLVD. DE LA CONSTITUTION

DE LA REGENCE

QUAI SUR-MEUSE

OUTREMEUSE

Post Office

PLACE COCKERILL

PASSERELLE FOOTBRIDGE

QUAI DE GAULLE

BOULEVARD SAUCY

Tchantchès

PLACE DU XX AOÛT

Université

QUAI ROOSEVELT

RUE SURLET

RUE PUITS-EN-SOCK

0   200 m

S CARMES

RUE DE PITTEURS

Musée Tchantchès

(400 m)

To Musée d'Art Moderne (1 km)

Accommodation

Liège's low ranking as a tourist destination means it has relatively few **hotels**, but this also means they're rarely full, especially at weekends; the bulk of the city's visitors are businesspeople and some hotels even close up completely at weekends, although it does mean they're also expensive. The most economical choices are around the train station, either on the station square itself or up rue des Guillemins. The *Couronne*, dead opposite the station (☎52 21 68; ④), is perhaps the most obvious choice, though not the cheapest. The *Univers*, on the corner of rue des Guillemins 116 (☎52 26 50; ④), is much more affordable, and you might prefer to try the *Métropole*, a very short walk away at rue des Guillemins 141 (☎52 42 93; ③), which is slightly cheaper, charging much the same sort of rates as the *Cygne d'Argent*, closer to the centre at rue Beekman 49 (☎23 70 01; ③). Perhaps the most convenient hotel is the *Ramada*, boulevard de la Sauvenière 100 (☎22 49 10; ⑦), although this charges the sort of prices you might expect of a plush establishment geared mainly for businesspeople. The nearest **youth hostel** is 6km south of the city in Tilff (☎88 21 00; ①), easily reachable by train – the site is five minutes' walk from Tilff train station. There are no **campsites** particularly convenient to Liège; the closest is *Camping de l'Allée Verte*, in Visé, fifteen minutes to the north by hourly train (direction Maastricht).

The City

Liège is a large city, and you'd be wise to concentrate your attention on its reasonably compact centre. Situated on the west bank of the Meuse, this divides into two parts – the so-called **new town**, girdled by the traffic artery of boulevard de la Sauvenière, which curls around to the nominal centre of town at **place St-Lambert**; and the **older section**, north of here, with Feronstrée as its spine, right below the steep heights which rise up to the former citadel. Most other places are without interest, though across the river the separate district of **Outremeuse**, on what is in effect an island in the Meuse, might be worth a visit for its tight group of bars and restaurants.

The main squares

The centre of the city is a bit of a mess really, the new and old sections meeting at **place de la République Française**, more of a traffic circle than a square, flanked on one side by the shed-like neo-Classical *Théâtre Royale*, in front of which stands a statue of the Liège-born composer André Grétry (his heart is contained in the urn just below). The square fades seamlessly into **place St-Lambert**, where the city is supposed to have begun – ironic considering its present-day role as a mixture of car parks and bus stops. The **Palais des Princes Evêques** (Palace of the Prince-Bishops), behind, does its best to provide a stately backdrop to the mayhem of the square, but even its vast frontage, built in the early sixteenth century and rebuilt a century later, can't help looking tawdry by association. You can wander into its main courtyard during office hours, though there's not much to see beyond the carved grotesques on its pillars. Cut through the building and you may be able to get into its second court, a smaller, prettier square, planted with greenery.

Old Liège: north of Place St-Lambert

East of the palace, the open space of place St-Lambert narrows to **place du Marché**, another car park in reality, its right side taken up by the eighteenth-century **Hôtel de Ville**. From here, **Feronstrée** leads east, the central spine of the so-called old town, which climbs up the sharp bank from the river to the citadel above. In fact this is a rather grimy affair, and the packed streets of the newer town on the other, southern side of place St-Lambert are more alluring. But the area has the city's densest concentration of museums, and there's a vigorous Sunday morning market, **La Batte**, which stretches along the riverfront all the way from the Quai de la Goffe to the corner of rue Hongrée.

The first turn off Feronstrée to the left, rue des Mineurs, leads up to the **Musée de la Vie Wallonne** (Tues–Sat 10am–5pm, Sun 10am–4pm; F80), one of several museums in the area devoted to aspects of Walloon culture. Housed in the restoration of a former Franciscan friary, there are lots of photographs of nineteenth-century Walloon village life, a reconstruction of a typical Ardennes kitchen from days gone by and displays of tools of various trades, including those used in traditional Ardennes industries like glassblowing and "Dinanderie" or copper-working – once practised in Huy and still a craft of Dinant. There's also a guillotine that used to be set up in place de la République Française. On the whole, though, it's a nostalgic collection, and adds little to understanding current tensions within Belgium.

Almost next door, along rue Hors Château, the **Musée d'Art Religieux et d'Art Mosan** (Tues–Sat 1–6pm, Sun 11am–4.30pm; F50) is another museum focusing on local themes, with a sensitively displayed, roughly chronological assortment of Christian carvings and paintings from the Middle Ages on from Liège and the surrounding area. In Liège, at least, many of the best pieces remain in the churches themselves, but there are one or two nice exhibits from outside the city, including some sixteenth-century polychrome wood carvings of Saint Lambert and Saint Hubert, the latter, the patron saint of hunting in the Ardennes, pictured with his attribute, a stag. There is also a seated Christ from 1240, and the carved *Virgin of Berselius*, an exquisite sculpture in wood from 1530, cherubs stealing from under the Madonna's robes atop a serpent. Among the paintings is a *Virgin with St Donatrice and Mary Magdalen* by the master of St Gudule, as well as landscapes by the early sixteenth-century Antwerp painter Joachim Patenier – lush canvases showing unfolding landscapes of hills and villages that are not unlike the scenes of Bruegel.

Farther along the same street, the four hundred or so steps of the very steep **Montagne de Bueren** lead up to the **Citadel** – not much more than its ramparts these days, which enclose a modern hospital. The views, however, are superlative, worth what is a genuinely lung-wrenching trek, looking right out over the city and the rolling countryside beyond. Afterward you can follow an interesting route back into the centre of the city by way of rue du Pery and rue Volière, which brings you out behind Gare de Palais.

On the opposite side of Feronstrée, farther down, is the third of the area's Walloon museums, the **Musée de l'Art Wallon**, Feronstreé 86 (Tues–Sat 1–6pm, Sun 11am–4.30pm; F80), housed in a modern building by the river. This is a small collection of some quality, comprising nineteenth- and twentieth-century works by French-speaking Belgian artists, and is the best laid-out of all the museums here, arranged chronologically, starting at the top with seventeenth-century paintings and leading down in a descending spiral. The nineteenth- and early twentieth-century sections are strongest, including a number of works by Constanin Meunier – the large *La Coulée à Ourgrée* is one – Antoine Wiertz's fleshy (and enormous) *Greeks and Romans in Dispute over the Body of Patrocles*, and the delicate paintings of women by Armand Rassenfosse. Look out, also, for the small group of works by Delvaux and Magritte, notably the former's wacky *L'Homme de la Rue*, as well as more conventional earlier paintings by the same artist.

Farther along Feronstrée, a little way past the tourist office, the **Musée d'Ansembourg** (Tues–Sun 1–6pm; F50) has been recently renovated and hosts a sumptuous collection of eighteenth-century furniture and decorations in an authentic period setting. Almost opposite, sitting far from the street, the church of **St-Barthélemy** (Tues–Sat 10am–noon & 2–5pm, Sun 1–5pm; F80) is a Romanesque edifice, with a late twelfth-century exterior, that has been pretty much spoiled inside by an insensitive eighteenth-century restoration. Its main feature of interest, however, remains pristinely intact – a bronze baptismal font of 1118. The work of Renier de Huy, it rests on ten oxen and is decorated with a circular relief depicting various baptisms in progress. The figures are graceful and naturalistic, and the oxen bend their heads and necks as if under the weight of the great bowl.

On the riverfront, two further museums may command your interest before you turn around and head back toward the city centre proper – there's nothing else to see in this part of town. The **Musée d'Armes** (Mon, Thurs & Sat 10am–1pm, Wed & Fri 2–5pm, first or third Sun each month 10am–1pm, closed Tues; F50) has, alongside an Ingres portrait of a young and dashing Napoleon, lots of beautifully engraved ornate pistols and rifles from the eighteenth to twentieth centuries – impressive if you're keen on such things – along with examples of military modelling, suits of armour and ancient swords, some dating back to the sixth century. Farther along, the **Musée Curtius** is better (Mon, Thurs & Sat 2–5pm, Wed & Fri 10am–1pm, second & fourth Sun each month 10am–1pm, closed Tues; F50). Housed in a turreted red-brick mansion from the early seventeenth century, it forms the sister collection to the Ansembourg, displaying decorative arts from the environs of Liège up to the nineteenth century, notably the late tenth-century Gospel Book of Bishop Notger, with a contemporary ivory frontispiece, and – in a separate section – a display of glasswork that is one of the world's finest, containing over nine thousand exhibits ranging from European crystal to gorgeous medieval Islamic artefacts.

New Liège: south and west of place de la République Française

Walking in the opposite direction from place St-Lambert takes you into the heart of the **newer part of the city**, bordered roughly by the boulevard de la Sauvenière in the west, and the river and avenue Maurice Destenay to the south. It's in many ways a preferable area to the quarter around Feronstrée, partly pedestrianized, livelier and more engaging, with the bulk of the city's shops, bars, restaurants and nightlife. A short walk from rue Léopold, the church of **St-Denis** (daily 9am–12.15pm & 1.30–6pm), on the square of the same name, is a curious mix of styles, the original, austere pillars of the nave and the brown brick of the base of the tower contrasting markedly with the later ornate stucco topping. At the end of the south aisle, the church's retable is by far its most remarkable feature – an early sixteenth-century work, carved in wood, that stands a good 5m high. The top – and principal – section has six panels showing the Passion of Christ, very Gothic in tone, full of drama, with assertively carved depictions of grieving, leering and abusing humanity. The bottom set of panels is later and gentler in style, with smaller figures, less sensationally observed, telling the story of Saint Denis from baptism to decapitation.

From St-Denis, rue de la Cathédrale leads down to the **Cathédrale St-Paul** (daily 8am–noon & 2–5.15pm), the square in front of which is a busy spot to sit and watch the world go by. The church itself was actually only elevated to cathedral status in 1801, the replacement of an earlier, by all accounts more impressive building that was destroyed in 1794 by revolutionary French guards during the final days of the last prince-bishop. A fairly spartan structure, begun in the fourteenth century and not entirely completed until the nineteenth, it has a couple of notable features, not least the swirling roof paintings of 1570 and a late thirteenth-century polychrome *Madonna and Child* at the base of the choir. But the **treasury** (F50) in the cloisters is of most interest, its small collection including a massive 90-kilogram bust reliquary of St Lambert, the work of a goldsmith from Aachen, dating from 1508 to 1512. It contains the skull of the saint and depicts scenes from his life – the miracles he performed as a boy, his burial in Maastricht and the translation of his body from Maastricht to Liège by St Hubert, who succeeded him as bishop of the area. There are also some lovely examples of ivory work from the eleventh century, and a similarly dated missal, stained by the waters of a 1920s flood in the church.

South of the cathedral, just off avenue Maurice Destenay, the church of **St-Jacques** (Mon–Sat 8am–noon, May–Sept also 5–7pm) is comparable to the cathedral in size and exhibits a transition in styles that varies from the Romanesque west front and pillar bases to the frilly, *joyeuse gothique* of the rest of the church – note the lighter-coloured stone used in the upper levels of the building. The ornate stonework is impressive on its own, as is the painted vaulting of the nave.

There's one other church you should see in the new town, that of **St-Jean** (daily 10am–noon & 2–5.15pm), on place X. Neujean, just off boulevard de la Sauvenière. This was originally a tenth-century church, modelled on Charlemagne's chapel in Aachen – hence the unusual shape – though only the tower remains from the first structure. Inside, behind glass, there's a beautifully carved statue of a Madonna and Child, thirteenth century but still with its original gilt surface, next door to which are two polychrome figures of the Virgin and St John (press the button for lighting), again exquisitely carved and wonderfully preserved.

Over the river: Outremeuse and more museums

The district across the river from the centre of Liège, **Outremeuse**, is supposedly the city's most characteristic neighbourhood, a working-class quarter that's said to be the home of the true Liègeois – it's sometimes known as the "free republic of Outremeuse," in part due to the traditional radicalism of the city's workers. This is a slightly phoney idea these days, not unlike the concept of the Cockney in London, but it is epitomized by the figure known as **Tchantchès** (Liège slang for Francis), the so-called "Prince of Outremeuse." Tchantchès is a character from Liège folklore, an earthy, independent-minded, brave but drunken figure who is said to have been born between two Outremeuse paving stones on August 25, 760; later, legend claims, he was, with the help of his enormous nose, instrumental in the campaigns of Charlemagne. Nowadays Tchantchès can be seen in action in traditional Liège puppet shows; he's also represented in a **statue** on place l'Yser, the traditional place of his death, carried as a symbol of freedom by a woman dressed as a coal miner.

There's a **museum** devoted to Tchantchès nearby at rue Surlet 56 (Tues & Thurs 2–4pm; F20), which displays various artefacts, costumes and other paraphernalia relating to the figure and his life as a puppet character. It's also worth considering a visit to the **Maison de la Métallurgie**, a fifteen-minute walk south at boulevard R. Poincaré 17 (Mon–Fri 9am–5pm; F50), where you can see displays of metalwork and a reconstituted forge from the eighteenth century. Farther south, out of Outremeuse proper, there's another museum, the **Musée d'Art Moderne** in leafy Parc de Boverie, not far from the Palais de Congrès (Tues–Sat 1–6pm, Sun 11am–4.30pm; F50), which displays a permanent collection of fairly minor works by a wide array of recognized modern artists – Picasso, Chagal and Ensor among others – as well as mounting regular temporary exhibitions.

Eating, drinking and nightlife

As with anywhere in Belgium, Liège can be an excellent place to **eat**, and you don't always need to pay through the nose to do so. For lunch, at least, there are lots of places in the centre of town, especially around place de la République Française, offering plats du jour and cheap menus. *Le Tivoli*, across the road from the *Théâtre Royale* on rue G. Clemenceau, has many dishes for under F200, and two-course daily specials for around F250. In the old town, *Le Cheval d'Or* at rue des Mineurs 6 has menus at F395 and F625, as well as dishes (omelettes, etc) that for around F150 make for a good inexpensive lunch-stop between museums. The same can be said for the popular *Taverne des Musées*, around the corner from the tourist office on rue St Georges, where daily specials usually go for under F300.

Au Point de Vue, on place de la République Française, claims to be the oldest tavern in Liège, and its blend of homey bar atmosphere, a local crowd, and cheap lunchtime and evening meals (around F200) is worth experiencing. Not far away, behind the *Théâtre Royale*, the popular *L'Ecailler* , rue des Dominicains 26, is also a good place for fish and seafood, though pricier, with main meals at F600, while, if you're feeling really flush, the *Robert Lesenne* restaurant, in the old part of town at rue de la Boucherie 9, is a well-known and popular local spot for good food. For the last word in traditional Liègeoise cooking, try the buried-away *Mame Vi Cou*, rue de la Wache 9, just off the main squares, where you can try all manner of local specialities at moderate prices.

Bars and nightlife

If none of the above restaurants suit, you'll find plenty more restaurants in the grid of streets that runs north from rue Pont d'Avroy up to rue de la Casquette, which is the city's most popular area for **nightlife**, home to many good bars and clubs as well. Rue Pont d'Avroy itself has lots of **bars**, but they're mostly tacky places, and the best establishments are on the narrower streets behind – though avoid the sleazy rue des Célestines. *L'Aquarelle*, on the corner of rue de Pot d'Or and rue Tête du Boeuf, is a youthful hangout which plays good music – as is *L'Escalier*, rue St Jean-en-Ile. *Le Seigneur d'Amay*, at rue d'Amay 10, is a more sedate, tiny bar, easy to miss, that has an odd baronial feel inside, with imposing wall paintings and impromptu performances at the piano. Five minutes' walk away, *Taverne St Paul*, behind the cathedral a little way down rue St-Paul, is a similarly well-established bar, cosy and friendly, with outside seating and bar snacks at lunchtime. Not far away, *Café des Arts*, on place XX Août, is a popular hangout with students. You might also consider a trip across the river to **Outremeuse**, where rue Roture, a narrow street which spears right off the main shopping thoroughfare of rue Puits-en-Sock, is entirely made up of restaurants and bars. *Pizzeria Comedia*, at no. 38, has reasonably priced pizzas; the *Acropolis* Greek restaurant, at no. 72, offers main courses for F400 or so; *Les Notes en Bulles*, at no. 41, has regional and French dishes from F400.

Listings

Books *Pax*, place Cockerill 4, has a small stock of English paperbacks.

Bureaux de change There's a 24-hr office at Gare des Guillemins.

Buses Timetable information on ☎22 05 51.

Car rental *Avis*, boulevard d'Avroy 238b (☎52 55 00); *Europcar*, boulevard de la Sauvenière 37 (☎22 40 07); *Hertz*, boulevard d'Avroy 60 (☎22 42 73).

Emergencies Police ☎901; ambulance ☎900.

Laundromat *Ipsomat*, Feronstrée 146 (daily 7am–10pm).

Newspapers English-language newspapers are available from the train station bookstand, or in the centre of town from *Bellens*, rue de la Régence 6, or *Libro Plus*, on Feronstrée just before *C&A*.

Post office The main central post office is at rue de la Régence 61 (Mon–Fri 8.30am–6pm, Sat 8.30am–noon).

Telephones There's an office with booths at rue Université 32 (Mon–Fri 8am–8pm, Sat & Sun 10.15am–6pm).

Train enquiries ☎52 98 50.

Travel agents *Nouvelles Frontières*, boulevard de la Sauvenière 32 (☎23 67 67); *Wasteels*, place X. Neujean 25 (☎23 70 26).

East of Liège: Verviers and Eupen

East of Liège, the River Vesdre winds through some lovely wooded countryside, sharp hills plunging down into deep wooded valleys as soon as you get free of the sprawl of Liège. **VERVIERS** is the main town of the Vesdre, a small place of around fifty thousand people that is a good base for the area, though in itself it isn't the sort of place you make a beeline for; indeed you're far better off heading south into the Ardennes proper. However, if you're travelling east into Germany and find yourself here at midday, you may want to stop for lunch, in which case there are a couple of reasonable museums, together worth an hour or so of your time.

The centre of town, five to ten minutes' walk from the train station down past the war memorial, is **place Verte** and – a block away – **place des Martyrs**. Five minutes' walk from the latter, down rue de Collège and left onto rue Renier, is the **Musée des Beaux Arts** (Mon, Wed & Sat 2–5pm, Sun 3–6pm; free), worth visiting for its small, quality collection of paintings, which includes a number of canvases by Dutch artists. Notable among these are a small landscape by Jan van Goyen, a fine crowded *Adoration of the Magi* by Gerrit Dou, a portrait of a child by Cornelis de Vos, as well as later nineteenth-century works by Johan Barthold

Jongkind, such as *The Skaters*. You should also look out for Jan Weenix's portrait of Admiral van Heemskerk, and a room entirely decorated with murals depicting views of the valley of the Vesdre (which runs alongside the museum) and parts of Malmédy by an unknown eighteenth-century artist.

Verviers' other museum, the **Musée d'Archéologie** (Tues & Thurs 2–5pm, Sat 9am–noon, Sun 10am–1pm; free), is of less interest, but it is nearby at rue des Raines 42, so you may as well have a look. Expect a handful of rooms furnished in period style, some weaponry, artefacts pertaining to a local nineteenth- century violinist, Henri Vieuxtemps, and a small collection of Roman coins and other local historical finds.

For maps of the town and other information, the **tourist office** is halfway between place Verte and the station at rue Vieille-Xhavée 11 (Mon–Thurs 9am–12.30pm & 1.30–4.45pm, Fri 9am–12.30pm & 1.30–5pm, Sat 9am–12.30pm & 1.30–4pm; ☎087/33 02 13). The cheapest **hotel** is the *Park*, opposite the tourist office at rue Xhavée 90 (☎087/33 09 72; ②). If you're **eating**, the *Brasserie de l'Europe* on the corner of place Verte is a busy, friendly place with good food and service, and *menus du jour* for around F300; the *Grand Café* around the corner on place des Martyrs, is a good place for a drink and a snack.

Eupen

Trains continue on to **EUPEN**, the landscape unfolding into a gentler affair of undulating pastureland. This again is pleasant enough, but has nothing especially to attract you other than its role as capital of the German-speaking part of Belgium. This area has been largely German since the early nineteenth century, when it was part of Prussia and a policy of enforced Germanization was undertaken. The area was ceded to Belgium under the Treaty of Versailles in 1919, but German is the main language here, both spoken on the streets and used on signs, street-names and menus. Eupen certainly has a definite Teutonic feel, not least in the curvy twin towers of the eighteenth-century church of **St Nicholas** on the main Marktplatz, ten minutes' walk from the train station (5mins from the bus station), which sports some ornate Baroque altarpieces and an extravagant pulpit that could be straight out of provincial Bavaria. Just outside the town, Eupen's main attraction is its **barrage**, a few kilometres to the east (reachable by bus from the bus station), the largest dam in Belgium, with a tower that gives marvellous views over the reservoir below and the area beyond.

South of Liège: Remouchamps, Stavelot, Malmédy and the Hautes Fagnes

Just 20km south of Liège, **REMOUCHAMPS**, connected by reasonably frequent buses or trains to the nearby station of Aywaille, is a small resort on the River Amblève, visited mainly for the **Grottes de Remouchamps** in the centre of town (April–Oct daily 9am–6pm; last departure 1hr before closing; F300). You can see the caves by way of what is claimed to be the longest subterranean boat trip in the world, through beautiful coloured galleries of stalagmites and suchlike.

A few kilometres southeast, **COO** has its own train station and is the site of a rather feeble waterfall surrounded by lovely scenery that gives the excuse for a riot of amusements just off the main street – restaurants, cafés, go-karts, a deer park and a two-person cable car that straddles the road up the mountain (F150 round-trip).

Stavelot

The next stop down the train tracks, **TROIS PONTS**, is the starting point for hourly buses to the busy resort of **STAVELOT**, a ten-minute trip. A small town set on a hill, Stavelot was the scene of fierce fighting during the Ardennes campaign of the last war, and some of the Nazis' worst (in Belgium) atrocities were committed here, mostly by troops scared to death by the American counter-attack. These days Stavelot is a pleasant old place with a former abbey that – with that of nearby Malmédy – was home to a line of powerful abbot-bishops who ran the area as an independent fiefdom from the seventh right up to the end of the eighteenth centuries. Most of the buildings that remain are eighteenth century, but there's a sixteenth-century archway from the original abbey church and some parts have been excavated and there's major work going on to excavate more. Otherwise Stavelot is a nice place just to wander, several of its pretty streets lined by eighteenth-century houses with exposed wooden beams.

The abbey, which dominates the centre of Stavelot, houses a number of different museums, most notably the **Musée Regional d'Art Religieux et de l'Ancienne Abbaye** (April–Oct daily 10am–12.30pm & 2.30–5.30pm; F125), which displays religious art of the Ardennes from the fourteenth to the nineteenth centuries – sculpture, silver and gold carvings, liturgical dress and local history. Other adjoining sections are devoted to the history of the town, its folklore and fine arts. Just over the courtyard, on the second floor of the Hôtel de Ville, the **Musée Guillaume Apollinaire** (July & Aug daily 10.30am–noon & 2.30–5.30pm; F125) was set up to remember the French writer, who spent the sumer of 1899 in the town and wrote many of his poems about Stavelot and the Ardennes. It contains newspaper articles, letters, poems, sketches and photos relating to the man who – despite his premature death – some claim was one of the most influential of early twentieth-century writers. In another wing of the abbey, the **Musée du Circuit de Spa-Francorchamps** contains racing cars and motorcycles from the nearby race track(April–Oct daily 10am–12.30pm & 2.30–5.30pm; Nov–March daily 10am–12.30pm & 2–4.30pm; F125).

A couple of minutes' walk up the hill from here, **place St-Remacle** is the attractive main square. Around the corner, the church of **St-Sebastien** (Mon–Sat 10am–12.30pm & 2–5.30pm; F40) contains a rich treasury, with an enormous thirteenth-century shrine of Saint Remacle, founder of Stavelot abbey in the seventh century; Mosan in style, it's of gilt and enamelled copper with filigree and silver statuettes. To see it you have to knock on a door opposite.

If you can manage it, the best time to be in Stavelot is for its **carnival**, first celebrated here in 1502 and since the early 1900s a renowned annual event, held on the third weekend before Easter, Saturday to Monday evening. The main protagonists are the *Blancs Moussis*, figures with white hoods and long red noses. For more information, consult the **tourist office** in the abbey ticket office (April–Oct daily 10am–12.30pm & 2.30–5.30pm; ☎080/86 23 39). Accommodation is difficult during carnival time, but generally the cheapest **hotel** is the centrally placed *Mal Aime*, rue Neuve 12 (☎080/86 20 01; ②), which also has an affordable restaurant. Alternatives include *Hôtel d'Orange*, a couple of minutes' east of the main square at rue Devant les Capucins 8 (☎080/86 20 05; ④), or the delightful *Maison du Crouly*, on place St-Remacle (☎086/86 41 65; ④). The nearest **campsite** is *Camping des Challes*, near the River Amblève, a fifteen-minute walk east of the centre at route de Challes 5 (April– Nov; ☎086/86 23 31).

For **food**, the *Maison du Crouly* restaurant serves heavyweight regional cuisine for F500 up; *Aux Vieilles Caves d'Artois*, overlooking the abbey buildings at avenue Ferd. Nicolay 7, is a cosy bar with lots of specialist beers and great home-cooked food – menus from F320. *Le Brin de Bruyère*, in an old timbered building along rue Haute, has main dishes from F400 and menus from F550; *La Dolce Vita*, on the corner of place St-Remacle, does reasonable pizzas, if you can't stomach another Belgian feast.

Malmédy

Eight kilometres away, accessible by bus from Stavelot or direct from Spa, **MALMÉDY** is a less immediately attractive town than Stavelot, but it also has a carnival, the *Cwarmê* (though it's less famous than Stavelot's), together with a museum on the subject, the **Musée du Cwarmê** (Mon–Fri 3–6pm, Sat & Sun 2.30–5.30pm; F100), on the third floor of the big white mansion on the central place de Rome. In the same building is the **Musée National du Papier** (July & Aug daily 3–6pm).

Other than the nearby **Cathèdrale**, knocked up in the eighteenth century, there's not much else to Malmédy, and no reason to stay; all in all it's a rather characterless place and useful only as a possible and relatively inexpensive base for the Hautes Fagnes. Should you end up here, there's a **tourist office** right by the church off place de Rome (Mon–Fri 8.30am–noon & 1.30–5pm, Sat 10am–noon & 2–4pm, Sun 10am–noon), and reasonable **accommodation** available at *Hôtel du Centre*, place Albert 1er (☎080/33 73 60; ②), or more expensive *Albert 1er* opposite (☎080/33 04 52; ③). There are a few reasonable **restaurants**: the *Scotch Inn*, on place Albert 1er, has a good choice of beers and light meals and sandwiches; the moderately priced *Au Petit Louvain*, on the main Chemin Rue, is a good choice for evening eating.

Robertville, Reinhardstein Castle and the Hautes Fagnes

The high plateau that stretches north of Malmédy up as far as Eupen is known as the **Hautes Fagnes** or "High Fens", nowadays protected as a national park. This area marks the end of the Ardennes proper, sandwiched between the Eifel hills which stretch into Germany, but is in fact home to Belgium's highest peak, the Signal de Botrange. The rest of the area is boggy heath and woods, windswept and rather wild – excellent hiking country.

ROBERTVILLE, a few kilometres north of Malmédy, is a bland resort that has grown up around the lake created by the **barrage** of the same name. The lake is also the start for a lovely kilometre or so's walk to **Reinhardstein Castle** (also reachable by road from the village of Orvifat, although you have to leave your vehicle half a kilometre from the castle and walk the rest of the way). A squat stone structure nestled in the valley, and still privately owned (mid-June to mid-Sept Sun tours on the hour 2.15–5.15pm; July & Aug also Tues, Thurs & Sat at 3.30pm; F150), the castle was originally built in the fourteenth century and was restored earlier this century, and it now houses the usual array of weaponry and old paintings – an intriguing insight into the life of your average Belgian aristocrat, although not an especially essential detour.

North of Robertville, the **Centre Nature Botrange** (mid-Dec to mid-Nov daily 10am–6pm; F70), provides a focus for explorations of the Hautes Fagnes park, with a small permanent display on the flora and fauna of the area, a coffee shop and bookstore, and, most importantly, a roaring log fire when the weather turns cold. If you're planning a day's walking in the area, you could do worse than leave your car here and take off across the heathy landscape with map for a circular tour. They also rent out bikes and run organized hikes.

A kilometre or so further up the main road, the **Signal de Botrange** is, at 694m, Belgium's highest peak, although the largely flat nature of the Hautes Fagnes means it actually doesn't feel very high at all. A tower marks the spot, plus a restaurant that's ultra-popular with coach parties and walkers.

Spa

SPA was the world's first health resort, established as far back as the sixteenth century: Pliny the Elder knew of the healing properties of the waters here, and Henry VIII, of all people, was an early visitor. Since then it's given its name to thermal resorts worldwide, reaching a height of popularity in the eighteenth and nineteenth centuries, when it was visited by monarchs, statesmen, intellectuals and aristocrats from all over Europe. Later the town went into slow decline – when Matthew Arnold visited in 1860 he claimed it "astonished us by its insignificance" – and the years since have been no kinder, moneyed flashiness replacing glamour, with fast cars and big, pedigree dogs the order of the day. A waft of sophistication comes from the casino in the centre of town, but that's about it, and you'd do better to visit Spa for its access to the countryside around and its small towns, notably Stavelot.

The Town

There's nothing to do or see in Spa. The main thermal baths, **Les Thermes de Spa**, are right in the centre of town on the main place Royale, next door to the casino (Mon–Fri 7.30am–noon & 1.30–4.30pm, Sat & Sun 7.30am–noon), and provide a very grand setting for its arthritis- and hypertension-curing mud and water treatments. A little farther along down rue Royale, to the left, is the **Pouhan-Pierre-le-Grand** – the town's main mineral spring, named after Peter the Great who appreciated the therapeutic effects of its waters and visited often (April–Oct daily 10am–noon & 2–5.30pm; rest of the year daily 2–5.30pm). For just F7 you can get yourself a glass of the water, though it tastes disgusting even if it is very good for you. Spa's waters contain iron and bicarbonate of soda, useful for curing lung and heart ailments as well as rheumatism. There are **four other springs** around Spa: Tonnelet, Barisart, Géronstère and Sauvenière. A little trambus (called a *baladeuse*) plies between them, but they don't normally let you get off to drink and there's otherwise nothing to see. The buses are stationed around the main square, and trips cost about F120 – though there is a variety of itineraries. In the town you can also visit the **Musée de la Ville d'Eau**, back toward the station, opposite rue de la Gare (mid-Sept to mid-Jun Sat & Sun only 2.30–5.30pm; mid-June to mid-Sept daily 2.30–5.30pm; F60). This has posters and objects relating to the resort and its waters, in particular little painted wooden souvenir boxes and other such objects. The museum is situated in the former mansion of Queen Marie-Henriette, and the stables next door have been turned into a **Musée du Cheval** (same times; F40, combined ticket F80).

Practicalities

The **train station** is five minutes west of the town centre, to the left of avenue Reine Astrid. The **tourist office**, in a pavilion opposite the baths at place Royale 41 (July & Aug daily 10am–6pm; other times Mon–Fri 9am–12.30pm & 2–6pm, Sat & Sun 10am–12.30pm & 2–6pm; ☎087/77 25 10) is extremely well stocked with books, walking routes, cycle circuits and maps. Guided walks in the area are organized three or four times a week in July and August with a few during Easter holidays, all free. Spa's cheapest **hotel** is directly opposite the station – the *Chemin de Fer* (☎087/77 14 15; ②). Other options include the slightly pricier *Goliath*, rue G. Bertrand 3 (☎087/77 12 00; ②), and *Le Relais*, place du Monument 22 (☎087/77 11 08; ③), which is very handily placed and very reasonably priced. There are two **campsites** outside Spa, both in the same direction to the southeast of the centre, the nearer of which is *Camping Havette*, rue Chelui 21; follow rue Royale down to where it runs into rue de la Sauvenière, and rue Chelui is a right turn a few hundred metres along. The other site, *Camping du Parc des Sources*, is farther along on rue de la Sauvenière itself, at no. 141.

Among Spa's many **restaurants**, the hotel restaurant, *Le Relais*, place du Monument 22, is perhaps the nicest, with good, reasonably priced food served in convivial surroundings. *La Cortina* in place Royale opposite the casino, serves well-priced spaghetti, pizza and steak on its largely Italian menu – though, oddly enough, it does a wide selection of mussels too. Just along from here, the *Bidule* is a popular bar for evening **drinking**, especially at weekends. A few doors farther along, the *Old Inn* does mussels and other Belgian standards, while around the corner, the *Le Sanglier*, opposite the Pouhan-Pierre-le-Grand spring, is a good local **bar**.

travel details

Trains

Arlon to: Jemelle (6 daily; 50min); Libramont (6 daily; 30min); Luxembourg (hourly; 20min); Namur (6 daily; 1hr 30min).

Dinant to: Anseremme (every 2hr; 10min); Bertix (every 2hr; 1hr 20min); Gendron-Celles (every 2hr; 20min); Houyet (every 2hr; 25min); Libramont (every 2hr; 1hr 40min).

Jemelle to: Antwerp (hourly; 2hr).

Libramont to: Bastogne (every 2hr; 45min); Bertix (every 2hr; 10min); Florenville (every 2hr; 30min); Libramont (every 2hr; 25min); Poix-St-Hubert (every 2hr; 18min); Virton (every 2 hours; 50min).

Liège to: Aywaille (every 2hr; 30min); Barvaux (every 2hr; 1hr); Brussels (hourly; 1hr 10min); Cologne (hourly; 1hr 50min); Huy (every 30min; 20min); Jemelle (every 2hr; 1hr 25min); Leuven (hourly; 50min); Marloie (every 2hr; 1hr 20min); Melreux (every 2 hours; 1hr 10min); Namur (every 30min; 45min); Tienen (hourly; 40min); Trois Ponts (every 2hr; 60min); Verviers (hourly; 18min), change at Verviers-Central for Eupen (hourly; 22min) and Spa (hourly; 30min).

Namur to: Arlon (hourly; 1hr 20min); Charleroi (1–2 an hour; 50min); Dinant (every 30min; 30min); Floreffe (1–2 an hour; 10min); Godinne (every 30min; 20min); Huy (every 30min; 25min); Jemelle (hourly; 40min); Liège (every 30min; 45min); Libramont (hourly; 1hr); Luxembourg (hourly; 1hr 40min).

Rochefort to: Lavaux-Ste-Anne (July & Aug 2 daily; 1hr).

Buses

Bertrix to: Herbeumont (Mon–Fri 6 daily, no weekend service; 40min).

Dinant to: Givet (France) (6 daily; 45min).

Jemelle to: Rochefort (Sept–May Mon–Fri 6 daily, Sat 3 daily, no Sun service; 6min/16min); Han-sur-Lesse (as for Rochefort, 16min). *See also GLT.*

Libramont to: Bouillon (Mon–Fri 9 daily, Sat & Sun 3 daily; 50min).

Liège (Guillemins) to: Remouchamps (6 daily; 35min).

Melreux to: Hotton (Mon–Fri 10 daily; Sat & Sun 5 daily; 5min); La Roche-en-Ardenne (Mon–Fri 8 daily, Sat & Sun 4 daily; 30min).

Namur to: Annevoie (every 2hr; 30min); Floreffe (8 daily; 30min).

Poix St-Hubert to: St-Hubert (Mon–Fri 12 daily, Sat & Sun 4 daily; 15min).

Trois Ponts to: Malmédy (hourly; 10min); Stavelot (hourly; 20min).

Boats

Dinant to: Anseremme (every 20min; 45min round-trip); Freyr (1 daily; 1hr 30min round-trip); Heer Agimont (1 daily in July & Aug; 5hr round-trip); Namur (Sun only; 3hr 30min one way).

CHAPTER TWELVE

LUXEMBOURG

A cross the border from the Belgian province of Luxembourg (with which it has a closely entwined history), the **Grand Duchy of Luxembourg** is one of Europe's smallest sovereign states, a tiny independent principality with a total population of about four hundred thousand, living in an area of just over 2500 square kilometres. As a country it's relatively neglected by travellers, most people tending to dismiss it as a rather dull and expensive financial centre, which is a pity. Compared to much of Europe, its attractions are fairly low-key, and it is pricy, but it has marvellous scenery in abundance: the green hills of the Ardennes spreading over the border to form a glorious heartland of deep wooded valleys spiked with sharp, craggy hills crowned with castles.

The capital, Luxembourg city, home to over one-fifth of the population, lies in the gentler landscape of the south, and as the hub of all public transport routes is almost impossible to avoid if you're not travelling by car. It is based around a dramatically situated fortress city, and still feels more like the grouping of disparate villages it was created from, rather than a major European metropolis (which it isn't) or a leading administrative and financial centre for the EC (which it is). Its handful of sights and rather secretive nightlife can be exhausted in two or three days, but Luxembourg city is more than a bureaucratic centre and as capital of such a small country is a feasible (if expensive) base for visiting the rest of the Grand Duchy.

The **Minett region**, southwest of Luxembourg city, is carved with autoroutes heading south into France, and is home to most of the country's heavy industry, largely concentrated around the Grand Duchy's second city, **Esch-sur-Alzette**. The southeast is far more attractive, with tourism focusing on the vineyards of the River Moselle, whose left bank forms the border with Germany. These slopes hold some pretty towns and the EC's smallest wine industry, which produces some very drinkable (and surprisingly affordable) white and sparkling wines.

The central part of Luxembourg – traditionally known as the **Gutland** – can be reached by way of the spinal road and rail route through Ettelbrück up to Clervaux. This passes through some of Luxembourg's most spectacular scenery, as it heads north into the Eisleck, a region of rich green hills and valleys

---

ACCOMMODATION PRICE CODES

All the **hotels and hostels** detailed in this chapter have been graded according to the following price categories. Note that the prices have been calculated as those for the cheapest double room during high season. For more on accommodation, see p.280.

① Up to F1000 per person.	③ F1500–2000.	⑥ F3000–4000.
② F1000–1500.	④ F2000–2500.	⑦ F4000–5000.
	⑤ F2500–3000.	⑧ F5000 and over.

climaxing in the wooded terrain of the **Luxembourg Ardennes.** For the traveller without wheels, visiting many of the region's attractions can be problematic,
but it is worth the effort. Possible bases include the tiny and ancient abbey town
of **Echternach**, nearby **Diekirch** or **Vianden** to the north, surrounded by high
green hills and crowned by a magnificent castle.

Wherever you decide to go, **getting around** on public transport isn't always easy. Despite (or perhaps because of) the country's size, everything tends to revolve around the capital, and while connections from there to most places (by train or, more usually, bus) are quite good, if not always especially frequent, travelling between the provincial towns and villages can be difficult and involve several transfers. Be patient, and if you can afford to stay there, try and see as much of the country as possible on day trips from the capital. This is quite feasible for many places – nowhere is more than a couple of hours' journey away – although for anywhere north of Echternach you're probably best off staying overnight.

Some history ... and modern Luxembourg

Perhaps the most surprising thing about Luxembourg is that the **modern state** exists at all. Sandwiched between European superpowers France and Germany, Luxembourg is by far the EC's smallest member state and is rare among European principalities in enjoying credibility on the international stage. Most Luxembourgers speak several languages (4 or 5 is usual), and the Luxembourg government is known for its regularly independent line in the EC's Council of Ministers.

While the fortunes of modern Luxembourg have been closely linked to Belgium (through economic union forged in 1921), and, to a lesser extent The Netherlands (partners since 1944 in the Benelux grouping), the region's historical purpose has often been to serve as a gateway for Germany into France and vice-versa. Metz in France is only 60km from Luxembourg city, Trier in Germany about 40km, indeed the road signs here often point to three different countries at once, and it was along these roads that the invading and/or liberating armies came to fashion the face of the modern nation.

Luxembourg city itself came into being as a crossroads. In **Roman times** a settlement was founded at the crucial strategic junction of the trading routes between Trier and Paris and Metz and Liège, and Roman camps were established in the countryside around. Its position at the top of the sheer gorges of the Pétrusse and Alzette rivers meant it could be easily defended – an advantage that was developed when one **Count Siegfried of Lorraine** fortified the place in 963, building the city's first citadel on the Bock cliff. Count Siegfried and his successors ruled the surrounding area from the town as a nominally independent fiefdom of the Holy Roman Empire. Later, in 1354, it became a **Duchy**, the first dukes – John the Blind and his son Wenceslas – extending its lands up to Limburg in the north and down to Metz in the south. In the **fifteenth century** Luxembourg became absorbed, like most of what is now Belgium, into the lands of the House of Burgundy, and its subsequent history mirrors that of its neighbour, becoming part of the Spanish, and later Austrian Netherlands and eventually falling for a short time under the suzerainty of Napoleon. The Congress of Vienna decided to create the **Grand Duchy of Luxembourg**, and though the country remained nominally independent, the throne was assumed by William I of the House of Orange-Nassau, the monarch of the new united kingdom of The Netherlands. At this time Luxembourg's borders included parts of what is now the Belgian Ardennes, now the *province* of Luxembourg – a situation which changed with the establishment of the Belgian state in **1830**, when this western area was handed over to Belgium and the smaller eastern section became what is the present-day country.

Cross-border links remain very strong, however, with Arlon on Belgium acting as a dormitory town for workers in Luxembourg and students in both countries daily crossing the border to study. In 1992, the state railway company, *CFL*, purchased an abandoned station at Audun-le-Tiche in France to reopen a line serving French commuters, the first European company to operate a rail line in another EC state.

Close ties with its neighbours have not spared Luxembourg from the upheavals of the **twentieth century**. In 1940, it was invaded by Germany and incorporated into Hitler's Third Reich and the royal family and government fled to Lisbon. The Luxembourgish language was banned and young Luxembourgish conscripts were sent to fight at the Russian front. Liberation by US forces came in September 1944, when Luxembourg witnessed some of the bitterest fighting of **World War II** – during the freezing winter of 1944 to 1945 the key engagements of the **Battle of the Bulge** were decided here. This is not an episode the country wishes to forget, and there are a number of museums honouring the (mostly American) dead.

Modern Luxembourg is a constitutional monarchy, ruled at present by Grand Duke Jean (born 1921), who came to the throne in 1964 and is married to

---

LUXEMBOURG'S LINGUISTIC MIX

Luxembourg city is one of the centres of the EC (partly because founder-member of the EC, Robert Schumann, was a Luxembourger), as well as being among Europe's leading financial cities. This gives the place a curiously international flavour, enhanced by the fact that although everyone speaks the indigenous language Lëtzebuergesch (a Germanic language, inherited from the Frankish dialects of the Moselle region), most speak at least two or three other languages as well.

Most education is in **French** and **German**. French is the official language of the government and judiciary, but German is spoken with equal ease by all Luxembourgers. **English** is very widely understood and spoken well, especially by the younger generation, many of whom also speak **Italian** and **Portuguese**, a reflection of several decades of southern European immigration into the Grand Duchy. Indeed Portuguese is a dominant language in a few areas, such as the château town of Larochette.

Under this linguistic pressure, the indigenous language, **Lëtzebuergesch**, might have been expected to die out. However, this has not been the case, and Lëtzebuergesch is spoken not only by well-established Lëtzebuergers but also by immigrants who want to get on in local society. In fact, the language has been a uniting factor, as the national motto, seen carved on buildings around the country, has it: *Mir wölle bleiwe wat mer sin* – "We want to stay what we are".

A smattering of **Lëtzebuergesch** does no harm:

Moien	*Good morning/ hello*	Entschëllest	*Excuse me*
		Wanneschglift	*Please*
Äddi	*Goodbye*	A patt	*A drink*
Merci (villmols)	*Thank you (very much)*	Ech verstin näischt	*I don't under-stand anything*
Pardon	*Sorry*	Ech verstin iech nët	*I don't under-stand you*

Josephine-Charlotte, the daughter of the late Belgian king, Leopold II. The grand duke has a twelve-member cabinet of ministers, selected from a directly elected chamber of deputies, based in the capital's rue du Marché-aux-Herbes. Luxembourg politics has a relaxed feel, with a number of green and special interest parties vying with the more established centre-left and conservative parties, and the telephone directory lists direct lines for all ministers – although whether any ever actually answer is another matter.

LUXEMBOURG CITY

The city of **LUXEMBOURG** is one of the most spectacularly sited capitals in Europe. The valleys of the Alzette and Pétrusse rivers, which meet here, cut a green swathe through the city, their deep canyons providing it with an almost perfect strategic location. It's a tiny place by capital city standards, and broadly divides into three distinct sections: the old centre on the northern side of the Pétrusse valley, the modern quarter on the opposite bank, and the valleys far below, a curious mixture of huddles of houses, vegetable beds and parkland, banking steeply up from the tame trickle of the city's two rivers to the massive bastions that secure the old centre.

The **old centre**, high up on a tiny plateau no more than a few hundred metres across, is not actually very noticeably old, but its tight grid of streets are home to most of the city's sights (such as they are), and it's a pleasant, lively area by day. Everything you might want to see is within easy walking distance, although to be honest, there's nothing remarkably rivetting.On the opposite side of the Pétrusse, connected by two main bridges, the Pont Adolphe and Pasarelle, lies the **more modern part of the city** – home to the city's train station, the majority of its cheap hotels and most of its crime, although any crime statistics probably have more to do with the Luxembourgers' tendency to report every petty misdemeanour than with a genuinely high incidence of violent crimes. **Down in the valley**, between the two bridges is a natural, very welcome, city centre park. A little way east of the Pasarelle bridge, edging around to the jutting outcrop of the Bock bastion, the cluster of houses known as **Grund** is an almost villagey enclave, once the home of Luxembourg's working classes, nowadays rather gentrified. To the east of Bock is the neighbourhood of **Clausen**, to the north **Pfaffenthal**, while on the far side of the Alzette valley is the **Kirchberg plateau**, home of the **Centre Européen** and joined to the old centre by way of the imposing modern span of the Pont Grand-Duchesse Charlotte.

Arrival and information

Luxembourg's **airport**, Findel, is 6km east of the city on the road to Trier. There are a number of ways of getting into town from here. **Bus #9** runs every twenty minutes between the airport and the stands to the right of the train station; it takes thirty to forty minutes and costs a flat F35 (the price of an ordinary city bus ticket) plus an extra F35 for any large items of luggage. There are also *Luxair* buses to the same place, which are faster (15min) but more irregular, about a dozen services a day connecting with major flight arrivals and departures; it costs

LUXEMBOURG

To the Campsite

ROUTE D'ECHTERNACH

RUE DE ROLLINGEGRUND

RUE DE MUHLENBACH

Alzette

COTE D'EICH

AUTOROUTE

AVENUE PASTEUR

RUE DE ROLLINGERGRUND

ROUTE D'ARLON

PONT G.-D CHARLOTTE

AVENUE KENNEDY

RUE DU FORT NIEDERGRUNEWALD

Centre Européen

RUE DU FORT THUNGEN

MILLIONENWEG

RUE JULES WILHELM

RUE MALAKOFF

RUE DE CLAUSEN

RUE DE LA COTE D'EICH

KIRSCHBERG PLATEAU

BOULEVARD PRINCE HENRI

BOULEVARD ROYAL

RUE DES BAINS

RUE BEAUMONT

R. DU DAPLING

PL.DU THEATRE

Musée Pescatore

GRAND RUE

RUE DE LA POSTE

PL. D'ARMES

Tourist Office

Youth Hostel

R.DE LA BOUCHERIE

RUE MARCHE AUX HERBES

MONTEE DE CLAUSEN

Alzette

RUE DE TREVES

PLACE E. HAMELIUS

Post Office

RUE DU CURE

RUE DU CURE

AV. EMILE REUTER

AV. MARIA THERESE

BOULEVARD ROYAL

BLVD. JOSEPH II

RUE ALDRINGEN

RUE LOUVIGNY

RUE CHIMAY

PLACE GUILLAUME

RUE DU FOSSE

RUE NOTRE DAME

BOULEVARD ROOSEVELT

Cathedral

PL.DE LA CONSTITUTION

GRUND

Fortress Walls

Pétrusse

LA PASSERELLE

RD. GEN. PATTON

Alzette

AVENUE DU X SEPTEMBRE

ROUTE D'ESCH

RUE STE ZITHE

AV. DE LA PETRUSSE

BD DE LA PETRUSSE

PL.DES MARTYRS

PL.DE PARIS

RUE D'ANVERS

RUE GLESENER

RUE DE STRASBOURG

RUE JOSEPH JUNCK

BD. D'AVRANCHES

AVENUE DE LA GARE

RUE DU FORT

Pétrusse

AUTOROUTE

ROUTE D'ESCH

RUE D'EPERNAY

RUE DU COMMERCE

RUE DE HOLLERICH

PLACE DE LA GARE

AVENUE DE LA LIBERTE

Train Station

To the Campsite

F120 a head. Before collapsing into a taxi bear in mind that Luxembourg's are extremely expensive, and even the locals – some of the richest citizens in Europe – think twice before calling a cab. From the airport, expect to pay F500–600 to the station, F600–700 into the city centre.

The **train station**, situated in the city's modern quarter, a ten- to fifteen-minute walk from the city centre proper, is a convenient place to find yourself: all of the city bus lines operate from here, and most of the more inexpensive hotels are located in the streets around; the station has a bureau de change and left luggage office (see "Listings").

There are branches of the **national tourist office** at the airport (daily 10am–6.30pm; ☎40 08 08) and just outside the station on the right (daily 9am–noon & 2–6.30pm; ☎48 11 99). These have city maps, and can change money and advise on and book accommodation. There's also the busier **city tourist office**, in the old centre on place d'Armes (Oct–May Mon–Sat 9am–1pm & 2–6pm; June–Sept Mon–Fri 9am–7pm, Sat 9am–1pm & 2–7pm, Sun 10am–noon & 2–6pm; ☎22 809 or 27 565), which offers basically the same facilities.

City transport and tours

Luxembourg has a reasonable **public bus system**, but it is such a small city, with such a compact centre, that the only time you'll need to take a bus is either between the centre and the station (though even this is easily walkable), or out to the airport, campsites or wooded periphery. The main route hubs are the stops to the right of the train station as you come out (the other side is for buses travelling outside the city limits), and place E. Hamilius in the city centre, by the main post office. Basically all buses from the train station go to the city centre. Tickets on the buses cost a flat F35, however far you travel; day tickets are available for F140, and are bought from bus drivers, as are the good-value ten-ride tickets, one of which could suffice for a couple of people staying in the city for two or three days. Flights of steps lead down into the valleys, and the city council has also built a free elevator connecting place St-Esprit with Grund (daily 6.30am–3.30am).

To orient yourself you may want to take a **guided tour**. There are the usual bus tours, run by, among others, *Voyages H. Sales* at rue du Curé 26 (☎46 18 18), which will whisk you around the main city and suburban sites in a few hours, every morning between April and October – reckon on paying around F300 a head. There's also a **miniature train** – "Luxembourg Live" – which travels along the floor of the Pétrusse valley from the Pont Adolphe to Grund and up to the plateau du Rham, giving you a good view of the city fortifications. The train leaves at regular intervals throughout the day during the summer from place de la Constitution, where you buy tickets; it costs around F250 per person for the ninety-minute tour.

Accommodation

As the extremely expensive capital of an expensive country, you are not going to find any **accommodation** bargains in Luxembourg city, and are more than likely to end up paying over the odds for an indifferent room in the seedy station neighbourhood, where most of the cheaper hotels congregate. There are a number of reasonable options down rue Joseph Junck, immediately opposite the station. The *Century*, at no. 6 (☎48 94 37; ③), and the slightly nicer *Chemin de Fer*, next door at no. 4 (☎49 35 28; ③), are fair; further down the street at no. 36, there's the *Zurich* (☎49 13 50; ③), and, at no.34, the *Axe* (☎49 09 53; ③), which also has some triples. Other alternatives around the station include the *Alfa*, place de la Gare 16, (☎49 00 01; ③); the slightly cheaper *Red Lion*, five minutes away at rue Zithe 50 (☎48 17 89; ③); and the *Bristol* at rue de Strasbourg 11 (☎48 58 29; ③) – though avoid the other hotels on this street as they (like the street) are decidedly seedy.

With a little more money to spend, you could try the *Italia*, opposite the *Red Lion* at rue d'Anvers 15–17 (☎48 66 27; ⑤), where the rooms have private bath, TV and phone. It also has an excellent (if slightly arrogant) Italian restaurant downstairs (see "Eating, drinking and nightlife"). There's also the *Marco Polo*, rue du Fort Neipperg 27 (☎406 41 41; ⑥), or, if you don't mind staying a little out of the city centre, the pleasant *Siewebeuren*, rue des Septfontaines 36, Rollingergrund (☎44 23 56; ④), which has a popular local restaurant (take bus #2). Failing that, it doesn't cost as much as you might think to stay right in the centre of things, at the *San Remo*, place Guillaume 8–10 (☎47 25 68; ④), or at the also relatively reasonably priced (considering the location) *Français*, which is about as central as you can get at place d'Armes 14 (☎47 45 34; ⑥).

Hostels and camping

The official Luxembourg **youth hostel** is beyond the Bock fortress on the Montée de Clausen at rue du Fort Olisy 2 (☎22 68 89; ①), close to the Mousel brewery. Open all year, it's reachable from the train station by taking bus #9 or #16; on foot it takes about twenty to twenty-five minutes from the station.

There are a couple of seasonal **campsites** within reach of the city centre. The closest and most pleasant, *Grungewald*, is north of the centre on the edge of the Grungewald forest area, just past Dommeldange off route d'Echternach; a short ride on bus #20 or about a thirty-minute walk from the city centre. Dommeldange is also connected to the train station by train (direction Ettelbruck). Another, less sheltered site, *Bon Accueil* (☎36 70 69), is south of the city in the suburb of Alzingen, to which there are three or four buses an hour from the stop to the left of the station as you walk outside. There's also a third site, *Kockelscheuer* (☎47 18 15), further out of the city to the southwest – bus #2 from the train station.

The City

The centre of Luxembourg isn't as ancient as you might expect – most of the medieval city was destroyed by a gunpowder explosion in 1554, and what you see now dates from a seventeenth-century remodelling. Most of the ramparts and bastions, too, were knocked down in 1867, the city centre's encircling boulevards were built on their foundations, though enough survives to give a clue to the city's awesome defensive capabilities.

The centre of Luxembourg is made up of two squares, the most important of which is **place d'Armes**, a shady oblong fringed with cafés and fast-food restaurants and home of the city tourist office at its eastern end. Around the corner, the **Ratskeller** on rue de Curé (summer Mon–Sat 10am–12.20pm & 2–6pm; F40) holds a model of the Luxembourg fortress and shows some slides, while to the north, concentrated mainly on **Grande Rue**, are the city's principal shops. On the southern side of rue du Curé a small alley cuts through to the much larger **place Guillaume**, the site of Luxembourg's main general market on weekday mornings and flanked by the bland buildings of the city authorities. In the centre is a statue of William II and a memorial to the nineteenth-century Luxembourg poet Michel Rodange.

A block away from place Guillaume, the **Palais Grand-Ducal** (which should be open again now after a recent restoration) was built originally as the town hall, a replacement for a previous Gothic structure that perished in the 1554 explosion, but was adopted by the Luxembourg royal family as their residence in the nineteenth century. A Renaissance edifice, the left-hand side of which dates from the sixteenth century, its facade is oddly Moorish in style, turreted and lined with pilasters and arabesques. There used to be tours throughout the summer, but at the time of writing it wasn't known whether or not these would be re-established when the restorations are finished.

To the right of the palace, an extension of 1743 houses the Luxembourg chamber of deputies. Walk up in the opposite direction and turn right, and you're in the oldest part of the city, the **Rocher du Bock**, where in 963 Count Siegfried decided to build the fort that was to develop into the modern town – of which there are scanty remains. An ideal defensive position, it was subsequently expanded upon by just about every major European power, not least by Vauban for the French in 1648, who made Luxembourg into one of the most strongly defended cities in Europe. The streets here cling to the edge of the plateau, overlooking the sharp drop below, at the bottom of which nestle the slate-roofed houses of Grund.

Of the fortifications which remain in Luxembourg, the largest and most accessible are the **Bock casemates** (March–Oct daily 10am–5pm; F50) – defensive positions carved out of the rock that were impossible to demolish without removing the foundations on which this part of town rests. Used as bomb shelters during World War II, their galleries honeycomb the long protrusion of the Bock, which slopes out into the valley. Actually they're a rather damp and drafty way to spend half an hour, and there's nothing much to see beyond a few rusty old cannons, but the views both ways, looking out over the spires and aqueducts of the city's green heart, are fine – across to the Kirchberg plateau to the northeast, south to the plateau du Rham and its Vauban-built barracks.

From the Bock casemates you can follow the pedestrian **chemin de la Corniche** to place St-Esprit and more fortifications, where the bastions of the **Citadelle du St-Esprit**, built in 1685 by Vauban, now form a grassy park with once again great views over the valley and the Passarelle bridge, which leads south toward the station from here. There are more casemates on the southern side of the city centre, the **Casemates de la Pétrusse** (Easter, Pentecost & July–Sept only; F50), hollowed out by the Spanish in 1674 and accessible by way of some steps off place de la Constitution. If you've already visited the Bock, however, you should give these a miss and stick your head around the door of the city's **Cathédrale Notre-Dame**, whose slender black spire dominates the city's puckered skyline. Actually it isn't a very interesting church, a rather perplexing building that went up in 1613 to 1618 in a mixture of styles varying from the Gothic vaulting of its interior, supported by massive pillars, to its eastern end Renaissance porchway. In the crypt you'll notice the tomb of John the Blind, who died at Crécy in 1346.

Back in the old part of town, the **Musée National** (Tues–Fri 10am–4.45pm, Sat 2–4.45pm, Sun 10am–11.45pm & 2–5.45pm; free) occupies a number of converted patrician mansions on the left side of **Marché aux Poissons**, the main square of the old town. A large and rather rambling museum, it gives something of a lowdown on the city's – and country's – history. On the first floor there are fragments of medieval sculpture, and, among many Roman archeological exhibits, finds from – and models of – the palace at Echternach, including funerary monuments, bronze figurines, a weathered marble bust of Septimus Severus and much else besides. Upstairs, on the third floor, you'll find rooms containing prehistoric and geological collections, arrays of fossils – dull stuff mainly, laid out in a deadening, classroom environment – and a popular and decorative arts section, with recreations of eighteenth- and nineteenth-century domestic rooms, including the inevitable apothecary's shop. The arms section has models of the city's fortifications, parts of which are much the same as they look now, many rifles, pistols and armour, and a room detailing the Luxembourg royal lineage. The fourth floor holds fine art, with an average set of mainly Netherlandish paintings ranging from the thirteenth to the nineteenth centuries. There are canvases by Cranach and Cornelisz van Haarlem, and Flemish paintings by Joos van Cleve and Quentin Matsys, notably a very expressive *Presentation in the Temple*. Later Dutch works include a soft *Young Girl on the Balcony* by Ferdinand Bol, a portrait by Hals, genre scenes by Jan Steen and Adrien van Ostade, and Brouwer's *Mussel Eater*. Finally, on the top floor of the museum there's a zoology collection, which – like the prehistoric material – has the distinct whiff of the science lab about it, with an unpleasant, rather archaic assortment of stuffed ostriches, owls, apes, wolves, deer, bison and just about anything that has ever swum, strolled, run or flown in the Luxembourg forests.

Cut behind the museum through the old seventeenth-century **Porte du Pfaffenthal** and follow the road around past the originally eleventh-century **Trois Tours** (on the right) up to Côte d'Eich, a little way down which is the **place du Théâtre**, a small square named after the old Capuchin convent here that has been converted to a theatre. It's home to a small flea market on the second and fourth Saturday of each month.

Over on the other side of the city centre from here, across boulevard Royale, home to most of the city's offshore banking businesses, is Luxembourg city's other main museum, the **Musée Pescatore,** currently occupied by the royal family while they wait for the renovations of the Palais Grand Ducal. Once they move out, temporary exhibitions and summer displays of its modest permanent collection of fine art, including canvases by Dou, David Teniers and Courbet, should recommence

Outside of the city centre there's not much to see. Deep down in the valleys, the so-called "suburbs", old working-class communities gradually turning into yuppie enclaves, merit a stroll – they're very peaceful and hold some of the city's prettiest corners. Take the elevator from place St-Esprit down to **GRUND** and turn right to the park area, where you'll find the old fourteenth-century chapel of **St-Quirin**, and, following the river along the rue Munster, the **Tuteshall**, an art exhibition space housed in a former prison.

Alternatively head in the other direction to **CLAUSEN**, where rue de la Tour Jacob, across the river from the **Mousel Brewery** holds some of the city's best **bars.** Fans of EC institutions, if such people exist, can continue back up out of the valley onto the plateau of **Kirchberg**, to the east, to feast their eyes on Eurocrats at work in the 22-storey **Centre Européen**, made up of the EC Atomic Energy Centre, the European Investment Bank and the European Court of Justice. Potentially more interesting is the nearby **Trois Glands** area, where there are plans to turn the strange seventeenth- to nineteenth-century fortress of **Thungen** into a cultural centre to designs by I. M. Pei – the renowned designer of the Louvre's glass pyramid.

Eating, drinking and nightlife

Luxembourg city isn't a cheap place to **eat**, and even the ethnic restaurants and station-area dives can seem pricy. If you can only afford to **snack**, butchers and bakeries will often make up sandwiches. For burgers, look no further than the *McDonalds* and *Quick* on place des Armes. Keep an eye out too for *Gromperenkichelse* – potato cakes usually served with apple sauce. In winter, stalls sell *Glühwein*, hot wine mulled with cloves.

If you have more money, its worth splurging here, as the city has a much greater variety of restaurants than you'll find in the rest of the country. Many are located in the tawdry station area, but they're not particularly cheaper than places across the river, where the quality is likely to be better.

For lunch, the *Brasserie Chimay*, rue de Chimay 15, just off place d'Armes, is central and unpretentious, serving good-quality filling plats du jour; and, on the other side of the centre, near place d'Armes, there's a a cluster of lively bars and restaurants around rue des Capuchins and rue des Bains. At rue des Bains 23, the *Brasserie des Bains* sells good pasta and wood-fired oven baked pizzas; *La Grotta*, also on rue des Bains, has affordable pasta dishes; and the *Maison des Brasseurs*, Grande Rue 48, specializes in sauerkraut. *Um Dierfgen*, côte d'Eich 6, is also good, a bar and restaurant open both lunchtime and evening, and serving light meals and omelettes. A little more expensively, the bar of *Club 5*, rue de Chimay 5, is one of the city centre's trendier hangouts, with an excellent and not overpriced restaurant upstairs; the house speciality is *carpaccio* – thin slices of raw beef served with fries and salad. *Times*, rue Lovigny 8, is more upmarket, but also does good *carpaccio*; *Yucatan*, rue Notre Dame 13, is a trendy Mexican eatery, with good-value daily menus.

On the other side of the river, near the station, the restaurant of the *Hotel Italia*, at rue d'Anvers 15–17, is a favourite with the city's professional classes, a pricy option but the best one if you're after a good-value splurge; you won't get away for much less than F1000 a head for two courses with drinks, but the service is impeccable and the surroundings reasonably unpretentious. Also not far from the station, *Le Journal* is a relaxed bar – which, as its name suggests, also stocks a wide range of the day's international press for client's reading – offers drinks, and high quality, good-value food such as *carpaccio* and steaks.

Further out, *Siewerburen*, at rue des Septfontaines 36 in **Rollingergrund** is a good place to treat yourself to local cuisine but is also pretty expensive. If you have your own transport, you could head for the **Bambusch** woods where *Juegdschlass*, at rue des Sept-Arpents 44, offers country cooking down a forest road less than half an hour from the city centre on bus #2 – though you'll need to book (☎33 31 37).

Bars and nightlife

Luxembourg is a city which keeps much of its entertainment behind closed doors, and, as such, it's not the most exciting night-time city in Europe. The station area is home to sleazy nightclubs, best avoided unless you're actively seeking the low-life. Thankfully there are some convivial **bars**, all within easy walking distance of each other. In the city centre, *Interview*, just up from the post office at rue Aldringen 21, and *Um Piquet*, around the corner at rue de la Poste 30, are two lively watering-holes, popular with Luxembourg's young and alternative crowd. At the junction of rue des Capuchins and rue Beaumont, the *Vis à Vis* bar is another good place for a drink, as is *Le Villon*, up the street. Down in the valley, the **Grund** neighbourhood harbours a few spots worth checking out: *Bei der Infirmière*, on rue de Trèves, is an amiable little bar; *Scotts*, by the bridge, is a pubby English bar where ex-pats congregate for draught Guinness and bitter and Sunday brunch (popular this last, so book the night before). On a slightly different note, the *Café des Artistes*, at Montée du Grund 2, is the place to go if you like piano and traditional songs. If you don't, try the *French Café* in rue Munster instead.

There are more decent bars further east in **Clausen**, notably *Malou*, rue de la Tour Jacob 57, long a meeting place of Luxembourg's small intellectual community; *Pygmalion*, rue de la Tour Jacob 19, is an Irish bar open till 1am weekdays and 3am weekends; and *Melusina*, on the same street at no. 145, has live jazz and folk music most nights. *Casablanca*, on the station side of the valley at boulevard d'Avranches 36, has a basement bar with live music, usually jazz, an upstairs restaurant and discos at weekends.

Listings

Airport enquiries ☎48 11 99 or 48 79 93.

Airlines *British Airways*, rue Notre Dame 15 (☎22 088); *Icelandair* rue Glesener (☎40 27 272); *Luxair*, Findel airport (☎47 98 23 12); *Sabena*, Grande Rue 70 (☎21 212).

American Express, Close to the train station at rue Origer 6–8 (Mon–Fri 9am–1pm & 2–5pm, Sat 9am–noon; ☎49 60 41).

Bike rental 8 rue Bisserwe in Grund (☎ 47 96 2382), at F100 an hour, F250 for a half day and F400 a day (discounts available for groups and under 26s).

Bureaux de change Although Luxembourg is an international banking centre changing money is not always easy. A Eurocheque card is useful and can be used in some (but certainly not all) machines, including at the *Caisse d'Epargne de l'Etat* branch in place Guillaume II. You can change money outside banking hours at the tourist information office on place de la Gare (for times see "Arrival and information"), or at the office inside the station itself, though for poor rates (Mon–Sat 8.30am–9pm, Sun 9am–9pm).

Car rental *Avis*, place de la Gare 2 (☎48 95 95), and at the airport (☎43 51 71); *Budget*, at the airport (☎43 34 12); *Europcar*, route de Thionville 88 (☎48 76 84), and at the airport (☎43 45 88); *Hertz*, avenue de la Liberté 25 (48 54 85), and at the airport (☎43 46 45).

Car parks There are three central underground car parks, one off to the right of boulevard Royale near the post office, another on place du Théâtre, and a third off rue Notre Dame. Cost per hr F25, for 8hr about F185.

Chemist Dial ☎012 for details of late-opening chemists.

Cinemas These often show films in English. There are seven screens in the place d'Armes cinema; around the corner in the place du Theatre, the *Cinémathèque* has a varied programme of international classics. The monthly *City* booklet has listings.

Doctor Dial ☎012 for details of English-speaking doctors.

Embassies *Belgium*, rue des Girondins (☎44 27 46); *Ireland*, route d'Arlon 28 (☎45 06 10); *Netherlands*, rue C.M. Spoo 5 (☎27 570); *UK*, boulevard Roosevelt 14 (☎ 29 864); *USA*, boulevard E. Servais 22 (☎46 01 23).

Emergencies ☎012.

Hospital The Clinique Ste-Elisabeth at avenue Emile Reuter 19 (☎45 05 81) is about the most central city hospital.

Launderette *Quick Wash*, rue de Strasbourg 31.

Left luggage There's a luggage office at the train station, open daily 6am–10pm and charging F60 per item. There are also lockers (F40–60).

Newspapers English-language newspapers are available from the train station newsstand the day after publication.

Police rue Glesener 58–60 (☎40 91 91).

Post office The main post office is on place Emile Hamilius (Mon–Fri 7am–8pm, Sat 7am–7pm). There's also an office opposite the train station (daily 6am–8pm).

Swimming pools There are excellent facilities at the rue des Bains pool (Tues–Fri 9am–9.30pm, Sat 8am–8pm, Sun 8am–noon), where a swim costs F100, baths F50, shower F25, steam bath F250 and massage F300. There is also a solarium. There's also an Olympic-sized pool out at Kirchberg, close to the Centre Européen (Mon noon–10pm, Tues–Fri 8am–6.30pm, Sun 9am–1.30pm).

Telephones Both post offices have booths for making international calls.

Train enquiries The office in the station is open daily 7am–8pm (☎49 24 24 or 499 05 72).

Travel agents *Nouvelles Frontières*, boulevard Royale 25 (☎46 41 40); *Sotour*, place du Théâtre 15 (☎46 15 14); *Wasteels*, place de la Gare 4 (☎48 63 63).

THE GRAND DUCHY

Luxembourg is a city soon exhausted, and it's a good idea to spend some time while you're here seeing something of the **rest of the country**. The minor attractions of the south and centre are best seen on day-trips, although the lovely scenery of the Ardennes region, up north, merits at least an overnight stay. If you don't have your own transport, you won't have much option, as public transport connections are poor.

The Luxembourg **rail network** reaches up through the centre of the Grand Duchy, connecting the capital with Ettelbruck, Clervaux and Kautenbach in the north (branch lines run from Ettelbruck to Diekirch and from Kautenbach to Wiltz), and extending arms down to Esch-sur-Alzette in the south, and Wasserbillig on the Moselle – from which trains run on to Trier and Koblenz. You're bound at some point to have to take a **bus**, many of which are also run by *CFL* and supplement the sparse rail system.

Without a car, though, you're not going to be able to do much touring in a day. It's better to select a centre and see as much on foot as is practical – no great hardship in the more scenic parts of the country.

In the south of the country, it's the **Moselle** which is of most interest, mainly for the vineyards of the Luxembourg wine industry. To the north, the first major rail junction is **Ettelbruck**, which, although not of interest in itself, provides access by bus to the first taste of the country's finest scenery, for which **Diekirch**, 5km east, is a possible base, home to the country's largest brewery and a decent museum remembering the Battle of the Bulge, much of which was fought in the surrounding area. Further east, **Echternach** is a pretty place built around an ancient abbey and is close to the rolling hiking country of the area known, with some exaggeration, as **Petite Suisse**. To the north, **Vianden,** one of Luxembourg's most popular resorts, lies in the heart of the Ardennes, surrounded by craggy green hills and topped by a glowering, newly restored castle. It's a possible centre for seeing the best of the countryside around – the castle of **Bourscheid** a little way southwest, the tiny settlement of **Esch-sur-Sûre**, clasped in the horseshoe bend of its river and the village of **Clervaux**, also with its castle – though this last is on the main rail line from Luxembourg and easily seen on a day-trip.

Southern Luxembourg: the Moselle and industrial Southwest

The **south** of Luxembourg is the country's least appealing region, with relatively dull scenery and – southwest of Luxembourg city – much of its industry around the grim town of **Esch-sur-Alzette**. The western bank of the **River Moselle,** which for 25km or so forms the border between Luxembourg and Germany up as far as Wasserbillig (where it spears off toward Trier), is the sole highlight, its gentle slopes covered with vineyards which produce the grapes for Luxembourg's tiny **wine industry**. All of the wine produced is white, and most is good quality, varying from fruity Rieslings to delicate Pinot Blancs and flowery Gewurztraminers, as well as some excellent, underrated *méthode champenoise* sparkling wines. There are a number of producers, and their *caves* are open in season for tours and tasting – and buying if you're keen.

The **southwestern corner** is reasonably easily seen by train – there are regular connections to Esch – but for the Moselle you ideally need a car. Although buses and (in summer) boats run up and down the river, public transport links are infrequent and don't always tie in very conveniently with the sometimes awkward opening hours of the various *caves*.

The Luxembourg Moselle

If you are constrained by timetables, **REMICH** is probably the easiest place to reach from Luxembourg, and is as good a place as any to see something of the wine industry. It's also a major stop for the ferry boats that ply up and down the river during the summer, connecting Remich with Schengen to the south and Grevenmacher, Wormeldange and, eventually, Trier (Trèves) to the north (see "Travel Details" for the full picture on schedules).

There's not much to Remich in itself, which is a fairly typical border settlement, full of duty-free shops hawking cigarettes and booze to bargain-hunting Germans. But the town is headquarters of the Moselle wine industry, and the **Caves St Martin** (April–Oct daily 9–11.30am & 1.30–5.30pm; F80), a mainly sparkling wine producer, fifteen minutes' walk north from the centre of town on the left of the main road, offers one of the region's most interesting *caves* tours, taking in the minutiae of the *méthode champenoise* process, which at St Martin is still carried out in a fairly traditional way – the bottles, for example, are still turned by hand. The polyglot guides are informative and entertaining, and, like most of the wineries, there's a free tasting afterwards of the excellent St Martin product.

If you want to **stay** in Remich, there's the very cheap *Hôtel de la Poste* at place du Marché 16 (☎69 81 33; ①); or, with more money, the *Hôtel Beau-Sejour*, at Quai de la Moselle 30 (☎69 81 26; ④), the *Hôtel des Vignes* at route de Mondorf 29 (☎69 90 28; ④), or the more expensive still *St-Nicolas* at Esplanade 31 (☎69 83 33; ⑤).

Walk for twenty minutes in the other direction from the centre of Remich, and you can indulge in more wine-tasting. The village of **BECH-KLEINMACHER** is home to the **Musée A Possen** (mid-March to end Oct daily 2–7pm; F100), a small museum of wine and folklore, housed in the former home of a local vinegrower. Prefaced by a short slide show (in English) giving background on the industry, a number of authentically shabby rooms attempt to recreate life for wine growers in centuries past, with pin-neat bedrooms, a loom and spinning wheel, a kitchen with its walls blackened by cooking, and a facsimile bar and displays of winemaking equipment. Exit is through a real wine bar where you can sample (at a price) some of the local wines or *eaux de vie*.

Further up river from Remich, the pretty village of **EHNEN** has yet another museum devoted to the wine industry, the **Musée du Vin** (April 1–Oct 31 daily except Mon 9.30–11.30am & 2–5pm; F60), on the main street. Housed in the rather less decrepit mansion of another local wine baron, this is a rather more organized, less nostalgic affair than the Musée A Possen, with informative exhibits in the old fermenting cellar detailing various aspects of the wine-making process, past and present. If you feel like hanging around, the *Bamburg*, route du Vin 131 (☎76 022; ④) is a pleasant hotel with a good restaurant. WORMELDANGE, the next village along, strung out beside the river for a good kilometre, gives the opportunity to visit another working wine producer, the Caves Cooperatives (May–Aug daily 9am–5pm; F80), housed in the big pink building on the far side of the village. If by this time you're too befuddled to make it back, head for the *Koeppchen Hotel*, Berreggaass 9 (☎76 046; ③).

GREVENMACHER, about 10km on from Wormeldange, is the capital of the Luxembourg Moselle and its most pleasant town, with a small but lively pedestrianized centre set up above the river. There are more wineries here, the most prominent of which is the Caves Bernard Massard (April–Oct daily 9–11.30am & 1.30–5.30pm; F80), on the southern side of the town centre, right next to the main street and river – follow rue de Trèves from the bus stop and turn left as if to go over the bridge. Like the St Martin *caves*, Bernard Massard is known for its sparkling, *méthode champenoise* wine, though it is a much bigger concern, producing around four million bottles a year to St Martin's eight hundred thousand or so. It shows in the production methods, which are far more automated, which makes it a less interesting – and shorter – tour (though it is preceded by a short slide show) and a less palatable product, sampling of which goes on in the slick hospitality suite afterward.

The Bernard Massard organization is also responsible for Grevenmacher's other attraction, the Jardin des Papillons, on the other side of the town at the far end of route de Trèves (April to mid-Oct daily 9.30am–5.30pm; F160), where around forty species of butterfly are viewable in a specially created (28°C constant) hothouse. There's a lush array of flowers and plants, and at certain times of year you can watch the butterflies hatching, but it's rather overpriced – although you do get yet another free glass of wine as well.

Grevenmacher is an appealing place to stay, although it's not very easy to get to from Luxembourg city – basically you have to take a train to the next town north, WASSERBILLIG, and a bus from there (12 buses daily; 10min). There's a campsite, the *Route du Vin*, in Grevenmacher on the northern edge of town, next to the butterfly park, and a youth hostel (☎75 222) a short walk up rue de Centenaire from the bus stop on route de Trèves. As for hotels, there's the *Mosellan*, at rue de Trèves 35 (☎75 157; ③), and *Le Pigalle* at rue de Thionville 30 (☎ 75 106; ③), which also offers food.

MONDORF-LES-BAINS, "inland" to the west from Remich, is the country's major spa town, attracting the rich of several countries who come to take the cure and play the Casino-2000, and less wealthy Luxembourgers who can receive a prescription from their doctor to spend time there for free. At the spa, found in an attractive 36-hectare park, mineral water emerges at a steady 24°C. Visitors are attracted by Mondorf's reputation as a sports centre, especially for equestrian events, and horses can be rented at the nearby Elvange.

Perhaps not surprisingly, Mondorf has hotels at all prices. The cheapest is the *International*, avenue Fr. Clement 58 (☎67 421; ②). Other possibilities are the smart *Dolce Vita*, avenue Dr. Klein 4 (☎68 073; ④), and, next door, the *Beau-Séjour* (☎68 077; ④).

The southwest

The area immediately southwest of Luxembourg city is pretty dire, an iron ore mining region whose heavy industry and urban sprawls are best glimpsed from a train window on the way to somewhere else. ESCH-SUR-ALZETTE is Luxembourg's second biggest city, with a population of around twenty-five thousand including a large number of Italians, drawn to the *Arbed* steelworks before banking in Luxembourg replaced steel in Esch as the country's main source of income. Esch in recent years has become an exercise in urban regeneration, whose pedestrianized zone around the main street, rue de l'Alzette, contains some of the best and most reasonable shopping, some good cafés and the feel of well-being that other cities in Europe's rust belts might envy. But there's no reason to get off the train unless you want to visit the **Musée National des Mines**, devoted to the mining history of the area, in the nearby town of **RUMELANGE** (Easter–Oct daily 2–6pm, Nov–Easter second Sat & Sun of each month 2–6pm; F100). Situated in a disused mine shaft, close to 1000m deep, guided tours of the museum last an hour and a half, and include displays of ancient and modern tools, photos and charts, and assorted machinery from the nineteenth and twentieth centuries.

There are also one or two places you might want to visit if you're travelling with kids. Northeast of Esch, the **Parc Merveilleux** at nearby **BETTEMBOURG** (April–Oct daily 9.30am–6pm; F120) is a very popular summer target of Luxembourg families, its large site containing a children's zoo, miniature train rides and lots of Disneylandish attractions. In the other direction, **RODANGE** is home to a contraption known as **Train 1900** (May–Sept Sun only at 3pm & 4.20pm; F150), a steam train that runs around the nearby Titelberg hill – the site of some scant traces of Roman occupation. Rodange is, like Esch, connected with Luxembourg by rail, and the steam train departs from a (marked) point fifteen minutes' walk away from the train station.

Central Luxembourg: Ettelbruck, Diekirch and Echternach

Heading north from the capital, Luxembourg's landscapes grow more spectacular, although you have to get some distance from the city before the scenery is anything but tame. The main road and rail lines run parallel, shadowing the course of the Alzette river. **MERSCH** is the first town that feels totally free of the sway of the capital, and the first real stop on the train line, though it's a rather unenticing place, with little to attract you beyond some rather thin remains of a **Roman villa**, southwest of the centre on rue des Romains. If you have your own transport, you might want to make a detour from here down to one of the country's most beautifully sited **youth hostels**, housed in the old castle of **Hollenfels**, 10km southwest of Mersch (☎30 70 37; ①).

Also worth a stop, just off the main road between the capital and Echternach, is the **Château de Bourglinster**. Set in a wooded valley, the chateau is kept in excellent condition by the state, and used as a space for art exhibitions and chamber music concerts. The château also has an expensive restaurant, but you could save on sleeping money by staying in the village's **youth hostel** at 2 rue de Gonderange (☎78 146; ①).

Ettelbruck

Situated at the meeting point of the Alzette and Sûre river valleys, **ETTELBRUCK** is an important provincial centre, a town of around 6500 people that occupies a central position in the country and is an important road and rail junction. Once again, there's not really much to see in the town: Ettelbruck suffered heavy damage during the fighting of late 1944 and is pretty much without historic interest beyond a few mementoes of the war – a **memorial** in the shape of a parked US tank out on the Diekirch road, and a **Musée Patton** at the junction of Grande Rue and rue du Canal (mid-July to Sept daily 1–6pm; F50). But you may find yourself here at least briefly. There's a **tourist office** in Ettelbruck's train station (Mon–Fri 8.30am–noon & 1.30–5pm), though for **accommodation** you're better off staying in Diekirch (see below) unless you're hostelling. Ettelbruck's **youth hostel** is on rue Grande-Duchesse Josephine-Charlotte (☎82 269; ①).

Diekirch

Five kilometres east, and easily accessible by bus or train from Ettelbruck station, **DIEKIRCH** is a more appealing place, although it too suffered during the 1944 fighting. However, it is a good base for seeing some of the surrounding area (with a couple of good campsites), and it does have one or two things to see of vague interest.

One of these, the **Musée de la Bataille des Ardennes**, 200m from the main square of place Guillaume, on the right up Montée de la Seitert (Easter–Oct 31 daily 10am–noon & 2–6pm; F120), provides an excellent historical survey of the Battle of the Bulge in Luxembourg, with a special, if rather adulatory, emphasis on the liberating US troops. The photographs on display steal the show, showing both sets of troops in action and at leisure, some recording the appalling freezing conditions of December 1944, others the horrific state of affairs inside the medics' tent. There's a variety of dioramas, many modelled diligently on actual photographs (which are often displayed alongside), along with a hoard of military paraphernalia – explosives, shells, weapons and personal effects doled out to both American and German soldiers (prayer books, rations, novellas, etc). There's also a display entitled "Veiner Miliz", which details the activities of the tiny Luxembourg resistance movement based in Vianden.

Diekirch's second museum, the **Musée Mosaiques Romaines**, is on the other side of the square (Easter–Oct daily 10am–noon & 2–6pm; F20) – two rooms basically, each featuring a reasonably well-preserved Roman floor mosaic, one from 150 AD, the other from around the third century, found on a site in the centre of Diekirch, just off rue Esplanade, together with a handful of other arte-facts. The best mosaic is the one in the right-hand room, its design centring on a two-faced depiction of Medusa. Alongside it are a couple of skeletons, one still in its original wooden coffin, that were also found nearby.

There are more skeletons on the other side of the pedestrianized town centre, in the church of **St-Laurent** (daily 10am–noon & 2–6pm; free), 100m east of the other main square, place de la Libération, at the top of the main shopping street of Grande Rue. A turreted church, some parts of which date back to the ninth century, you can climb down via a side door to an eerily lit set of medieval tombs that have been discovered under the floor.

Practicalities

Diekirch's **bus and train station** is five- to ten-minutes' walk south of the centre of town on avenue de la Gare, next door to the Diekirch brewery – the country's largest beer producer – although buses also stop outside the *Kremer* hotel in the centre. The **tourist office** is on the corner of place Guillaume (Mon–Fri 9am–noon & 2–7pm; ☎80 30 23), and can help with maps and accommodation. Of the town's **hotels**, the *Hôtel de la Paix*, around the corner from the tourist office on place Guillaume, is the cheapest (no phone; ②), but it's pretty seedy. Rather nicer are two hotels opposite the bus station – the *Au Bon Accueil*, avenue de la Gare 77 (☎80 34 76; ③), and the *Hôtel de la Gare*, avenue de la Gare 73 (☎80 33 05; ③). The town's two **campsites** – *de la Sûre* and *Op de Sauer* – are handily placed a few minutes' walk from the centre by the river; follow the road 100m east from the *Hôtel Europe*, cross over the bridge and take the riverside path. There's also another site, the *Gritt*, a few minutes by bus toward Ettelbruck in **INGLEDORF**, which has a lovely location, also by the river. There aren't huge **eating** alternatives in Diekirch: you could try the reasonably priced pizzas and pasta in the *Rialto*, at Grande Rue 15, or the more traditional and the slightly more expensive Luxembourg fare at the excellent *Brasserie du Commerce*, at the top end of Grand Rue on place de la Libération.

Diekirch makes a good base for touring the surrounding area, either by car or by bike: you can rent **bikes** from the *de la Sûre* campsite. Between May and November the same office also rents **canoes** for travelling down river to Dillingen or Echternach – an easy and safe but exciting trip; reckon on about six hours to reach Echternach.

Echternach and around

Ten kilometres or so east of Diekirch, the Sûre becomes the border between Luxembourg and Germany, edging an area known – rather optimistically – as **Petite Suisse**, or "Little Switzerland", for its thickly wooded hills and rocky valleys. **ECHTERNACH** is the main centre of this region, a town of around four thousand people that is one of Luxembourg's prime resorts. Echternach grew up around an abbey that was founded here in 698 by one Saint Willibrord, a Yorkshire missionary monk who went on to become famous for curing epilepsy and cattle – skills which are commemorated by the renowned hour-long dancing procession around the saint's tomb and town centre, annually on Tuesday after Pentecost.

The centre of town is the wedge-shaped **place du Marché**, an elegant conglomeration of ancient buildings, most notable among which is the fifteenth-century turreted old **town hall**, with its Gothic loggia of 1520. A short walk east of here there's a **Musée de Préhistorie** on the right-hand side of rue du Pont (April–Oct daily except Mon 10am–noon & 2–5pm; F40). But the town's real attraction is the **Abbey** itself, just off place du Marché to the north, signalled by the spires of its enormous **church**. This has had a long and rather varied history. The original church of St Willibrord was a much smaller affair, but it was destroyed by fire in 1016, and a new structure was erected later that century. Restored in 1862, it was later rebuilt to the former eleventh-century plan after sustaining heavy bomb damage during the Battle of the Bulge in 1944, and reconsecrated in 1952. It's a simple basilical structure with a Romanesque arched nave, and it can't help but feel like a reconstruction. Downstairs the crypt is the only major part of St Willibrord's church to have survived. Dating from around 900, its whitewashed walls are home to some unfinished frescoes and the primitive coffin of the saint himself, covered by an ornate canopy made in 1906.

The huge abbey complex spreads out beyond the church to a set of formal gardens by the river, its mainly eighteenth-century buildings used for a variety of secular activities these days. One houses the **Musée de l'Abbaye** (daily 10am–noon & 2–5pm; F40), which contains more fragments of St Willibrord's first monastery and church – foundations mainly, along with some rather macabre eighth-century tombs complete with skeletons. The rest of the museum is well laid out and has some high quality exhibits. Highlights include a piece of mosaic flooring from Echternach's Roman villa (see below) and various examples of medieval calligraphy and illumination, including the eleventh-century *Codex Aureus* of Echternach, whose superb jewelled cover, from 990, was the work of a Trier craftsman.

Practicalities

There's not much else to see in Echternach beyond the abbey, but like Diekirch it is one of Luxembourg's best – and prettiest – countryside bases. The **bus station** is five minutes from the centre of town, down the long rue de la Gare, a lively street lined with tourist boutiques and hotels. The **tourist office** is opposite the abbey church (Mon–Fri 9am–noon & 1–5pm, Sat until 6pm, when closed go to *Hôtel Regine*; ☎72 230), and has maps of the town and information on **accommodation**. Echternach has loads of **hotels**, many along rue de la Gare, among which there are a number of reasonable options: try the *Regine* at no. 53 (☎72 077; ③) and the *Pavillon* at no. 2 (☎72 98 09; ③), or the very cheap *Aigle Noir* at no. 54 (☎72 383; ①-②). The *Petite Poète* on place du Marché (☎72 072; ②) is very central and serves hearty meals. There's a **campsite** (☎72 272) 300m beyond the bus station following the river out of town, and a **youth hostel** at rue André Deutscher 9 (☎72 158; ①) – follow the street that runs south from the corner of place du Marché and rue de la Gare.

For **food**, the *Benelux* restaurant on the same corner is very reasonably priced, as is the *Hôtel de l'Abbaye* restaurant on rue la Gare, with plats du jour and fixed-price menus, and the *Hôtel du Commerce* on place du Marché, which serves a three-course special. For snacks, or just a drink, use the *Bit Beim Dokter* bar, up by the tourist office, which serves sandwiches and light meals for under F200.

Around Echternach

About a kilometre south of Echternach, following the road to **LAUTERBORN**, a large artificial **lake** provides good, if crowded, distraction on hot summer afternoons. Nearby lie the remains of a mainly second-century **Roman villa**, though these are very scant – more or less the foundations only.

Further afield, west into the heart of Petite Suisse, back toward Diekirch, the village of **BERDORF** is a popular climbing centre and a good starting point for gentle hikes into the craggier reaches of the region – paths are marked clearly and take you through some delightful spots. One destination might be the castle at **Beaufort**, about 6km west (April 1–Oct 25 daily 9am–6pm; F60), which enjoys a marvellous location overlooking the surrounding wooded hills. The site was originally a Roman encampment, and the oldest part of the castle dates from the mid-twelfth century; later parts were added in 1380 and 1500. It's no more than a ruin now, but you can wander through the site freely, enjoying the views and poking around the crumbling nooks and corners, which in fact simply fell into ruin through disuse and neglect – the building saw nothing of any kind of fighting, apparently, until hit by shells during the Battle of the Bulge.

There's a **youth hostel** in Beaufort village, a pleasant modern affair at rue de l'Auberge 6 (☎86 075; ③). If you want a destination for moving on to, there's another castle at **LAROCHETTE**, a few kilometres south of Beaufort, poking out of the trees high above what is a very pretty little town. This one is a ruin, too, but the later section has been restored and now has regained its roof and turrets. If you like the place, you could stay at the **youth hostel** at Osterbour 45 (☎87 081; ③), or, more upmarket, the *Hôtel du Château* (☎87 009; ④) or *Hôtel de la Poste* (☎87 006; ④). There are also two **campsites** – *Auf Birkelt* (☎87 90 40) and *Bourpësch* (☎ 87 137).

Northern Luxembourg: Vianden, Esch, Wiltz and Clervaux

The **northern** part of Luxembourg, within the narrowing neck of the country's triangle, is its most spectacular region, repeating the scenic highlights of the Belgian Ardennes. Again, transport connections are difficult without a car, and it's far enough from the capital to make day-trips not nearly so feasible or enjoyable. You should pick one centre as a base and see what you can do from there.

Vianden

Though it's not centrally placed, the best base for seeing the Luxembourg Ardennes is **VIANDEN**, close to the German border. A tiny place, not much more than a village really, Vianden is probably the most strikingly sited of all Luxembourg's provincial towns, and it consequently gets very crowded with tourists in summer. Confined by a bowl of green wooded hills, it spreads up the slope from the River Our, in part still surrounded by ramparts and totally dominated by the newly restored castle, which towers on the hill immediately above.

The main street curves down to the river, almost entirely lined by hotels and restaurants and finishing up at the bridge, on which a Rodin bust of **Victor Hugo** signals a **house** (in part now the tourist office) that was the part-time home of the French writer between 1862 and 1871. Hugo has since become Vianden's most famous adopted son, and his house has been turned over to a museum (April–Oct daily 9.30am–noon & 2–6pm, closed Wed outside July & Aug; F25) commemorating his stay here, with many letters and copies of original poems and manuscripts, including his "Discourse on Vianden", written in 1871. There are also photographs of the town during the nineteenth century, and sketches by the great man of local places of interest – the castles at Beaufort and Larochette, for example. Sadly, though, there's no furniture left from Hugo's time, apart from his bedroom, complete with original bed.

There are **two other museums** in Vianden, one of Dinky toys at rue du Sanatorium 29 (April–Oct daily 2–6pm; F30), and another of "Rustic Arts" at Grande Rue 98 (Easter–Oct daily 10am–noon & 2–6pm; F80). But Vianden's major sight is inevitably the **castle** itself (March & Oct daily 10am–5pm; April–Sept daily 10am–6pm; Nov–Feb daily 10am–4pm; F110), recently open in its entirety following a very thorough restoration, before which much was in ruins. Originally a fifth-century structure, the present building dates mostly from the eleventh century and shows features from the Romanesque style to the Renaissance. It was the home of the counts of Vianden, who ruled the town and much of the area around during the twelfth and thirteenth centuries until falling under the sway of the House of Luxembourg in 1264. Later, in 1417, the Nassau family took over the building, and it remains the property of the grand-ducal family. It forms a very large complex, the renovation sensitively done, though the crowds trooping through the pristine halls and galleries can't help but dispel any atmosphere that might have been left. On display are the inevitable suits of armour and suchlike, but much has just been left empty, notably the long Byzantine Room, with its high trefoil windows open to the air, and the next-door octagonal upper chapel, surrounded by a narrow defensive walkway. There are, too, exhibits on the development of the building, detailing its restoration, and on the history of the town, and some rooms that have been in part furnished in period style – the Banqueting Hall and the huge Counts' Hall, decorated with seventeenth-century tapestries – though the piped music is an odd (and unwelcome) accompaniment. For a more authentic mustiness, peek down the well just off the old kitchen, its murky darkness lit to reveal profound depths, and leave through the unrestored Gothic dungeon – perhaps the most evocative part of the entire building.

Beyond the castle it's the countryside around Vianden which beckons most positively – something you can survey from the hill above by taking the **Télésiège** or cable car to its 450-metre-high summit (Easter–Oct daily 9.30am–7pm; F140 return). This runs from a station on rue du Sanatorium, just off rue Victor Hugo on the western edge of the town centre. At the top there's a restaurant with a terrace; you can also walk down to the castle by way of a footpath.

Practicalities

Buses to Vianden stop on the far eastern edge of town on the route de la Frontière, about five minutes' walk from the **tourist office** in the centre by the bridge (daily except Wed 9.30am–noon & 2–6pm; ☎84 257), which has copious information, maps, etc. **Accommodation** isn't too much of a problem – virtually every other building in Vianden is a **hotel** – although during the high season you'd be wise to reserve in advance. Among the cheaper alternatives on the castle side of the river are *Hôtel Collette*, Grande Ruc 68–70 (☎84 004; ③), *Hôtel Réunion*, Grande Rue 66 (☎84 155; ③), and the *Café de la Poste*, Grande Rue 10 (☎84 209; ③). On the other side of the river, is the *Auberge de l'Our*, just over the bridge on the right at rué de la Gare 35 (☎84 675; ③), also home to a well-priced and popular restaurant. There are any number of other possibilities on both sides of the road as far as the bus station. for example the *Petry*, rue de la Gare 15 (☎84 122; ②). There's also a **youth hostel** nicely placed at the top of Grande Rue, right below the ramparts of the castle at Montée du Château 3 (☎84 177; ①). The nearest **campsite** is *Op dem Deich*, by the river near the bus station; there are also two other campsites further on down the road to Echternach – *De l'Our* and *Du Moulin* – though all are closed from January to April.

Most of the hotels have **restaurants**, and these form the bulk of the town's eating options. The *De l'Our* hotel by the bridge serves a good array of Luxembourgeois specialities, though its terrace by the river means it gets very crowded; its **bar** is also about the most convivial and cheapest place to drink in Vianden. On the other side of the river, the *Café de la Poste* on Grande Rue offers reasonably priced set menus, the *Hôtel Bingen*, further up, charges a little more.

If you're loaded, you might try the rather swankier surroundings of the *Auberge de la Château* restaurant further up Grande Rue – though avoid the hotel itself, which is unfriendly and overpriced.

West from Vianden: Bourscheid, Esch and Wiltz

The only way to go from Vianden and remain in Luxembourg is **west**, a route which takes you through the best of the Ardennes scenery, though you'll need a car to do it comfortably – if at all. The castle at **Bourscheid** (March 1–Sept 30 daily 10am–7pm; F80) provides one of the most spectacular stops if you do have wheels: perching high above the surrounding wooded hills, it's without question the most superbly sited of all Luxembourg's castles. The first proper fortifications were erected here around the year 1000, when a stone wall was substituted for a previous wooden structure, though nothing much is left of this period and most of the later buildings you see now went up during the fourteenth century. It's entirely ruined these days, and there's not much to see beyond the shape of the walls and the odd tower, and some dusty artefacts in the gabled late fourteenth-century Stolzembourg house. But the views, as you'd expect, are stunning.

Below the castle, the River Sûre winds a picturesque route through its valley – a beauty spot you can take most advantage of from a couple of **campsites** situated right by the river in **BOURSCHEID MOULIN** – the *Moulin* and *Um Gritt*. In the opposite direction, the road continues up toward the village of **BOURSCHEID** proper, on the way to which there's another **campsite**. From here, you can follow the Sûre to **ESCH-SUR-SURE**, a small village of just three hundred people with a fame out of all proportion to its size, mainly due to its gorgeous site within an ox-bow loop in the river. Once here, there's nothing to see in particular, and Esch itself, once you get into its few streets, is not even especially attractive. But the location is a fine one, surrounded by a high wall of green in its sheltered position at the bottom of the valley. The castle above, perched on two entirely separate crags, each part of which you can wander around, dates from the tenth century and has been lying in ruins for a couple of hundred years now – and it shows. The centrally-placed *Hôtel des Ardennes* at rue du Moulin 1 is about the cheapest place to stay (☎89 108; ②): its prices include breakfast, and it also has a cheap self-service restaurant and snack bar. Other options include the *Hôtel de la Sûre* at rue du Pont 1 (☎89 110; ③) or the pricier *Hôtel du Moulin* (☎89 107; ⑤). Even if you can't afford to stay here, you might like to try its **restaurant**, which serves some intriguing local specialities. There are two campsites, *Im Ahl* and *Saendgen*.

For those with a car or bike, the hilly country **west of Esch** is worth visiting. Take the road to the **Pont Misère barrage** across the river, a dam that has created a popular stretch of water meandering through several valleys that's popular with watersports enthusiasts, who congregate on the village of **INSENBORN**, only 6km from Esch, and **LULTZHAUSEN**. Just outside Insenborn, the *Hôtel du Lac*, Bonnal 1 (☎89 064; ③), has a **campsite** in its grounds and serves reasonably priced **meals**. For those returning to the main Luxembourg road, the back routes via Arsdorf offer fine rural views.

About 10km north of Esch, **WILTZ** is one of the larger, but not one of the Grand Duchy's most appealing centres, by and large a sprawl of unchecked development. But its upper town, high on the hill above, holds one or two items of mild interest around its **château**, a largely seventeenth-century building now, though built on twelfth-century foundations. High above the wooded valley, the somewhat overzealously restored château, looking like a transplant from the Loire valley, is home to the Wiltz **tourist office** (summer daily 2–6pm; ☎95 74 44) and **two museums**, one yet another tired display devoted to the **Battle of the Bulge** (June to mid-Sept daily 10am–noon & 1–5pm; F50), the other – much better – a **Musée Arts et Métiers** (Easter–June daily 2–5pm; July & Aug 10am–noon & 1.30–5.30pm; Sept 2.30pm; F40), with ceramics, agricultural tools, basketwork and a huge still. Part of the château gardens are laid out for performances of the town's **music festival** during July and August – a nice setting – while **paths** lead down into the wooded grounds below.

It's not really worth stopping in Wiltz unless the festival is on, as for most of the year it's a fairly dead place. If you do come while the festival's in progress there's a **campsite** open for the duration 200m up Grande Rue on the left. For **food**, the *Zumm Treffpunkt*, on Grande Rue close to the château, is good and cheap, especially if you opt for a pizza.

Clervaux

About 15km from Wiltz, in the far north of Luxembourg, **CLERVAUX** is another small town topped with a castle and built around a loop in the river. Clervaux's **castle** dates from the twelfth century but was rebuilt in the seventeenth century and after considerable damage in the last war, as is recounted in the obligatory and rather unimaginative **Battle of the Bulge Museum** across the atmospheric, cobblestone, ivy-clad castle courtyard (June daily 1–5pm; July to mid-Sept daily 10am–5pm; mid-Sept to May Sun 1–5pm; F40). Another part of the castle holds a **museum of models** (same times and price), with dusty maquettes of all the castles of Luxembourg in a series of large echoing rooms.

The castle is also home to the **tourist office** (daily except Sun 2–5pm; ☎92 072), which has details on accommodation in Clervaux – there are plenty of **hotels** for a place of this size, of which the *Des Ardennes*, Grande Rue 22 (☎92 254; ③), is the most central. There's also a **campsite**, *Reillerweiller*, about 2km out of town on the Vianden road, beside the river. The best place **to eat** in a town of pricy restaurants is the *Splendid*, Grande Rue 32. Clervaux is on the main rail line, but bear in mind that it's a good ten-minute walk into town from the **station**.

travel details

Trains

Luxembourg to: Arlon (11 daily; 20min); Brussels (for Amsterdam) (11 daily; 2hr 30min); Clervaux (hourly; 1hr 5min); Diekirch (change at Ettelbruck) (8 daily; 40min); Ettelbruck (hourly; 35min); Kautenbach (hourly; 1hr); Koblenz (8 daily; 2hr); Liège (for Maastricht) (7 daily; 2hr 30min); Namur (11 daily; 1hr 45min); Trier (8 daily; 45min); Wasserbillig (8 daily; 30min); Wiltz (change at Kautenbach) (8 daily; 1hr 10min).

Buses

Diekirch to: Echternach (10 daily; 35min); Vianden (hourly; 20min).

Ettelbruck to: Clervaux (2 daily; 1hr); Diekirch (6 an hour; 10min); Echternach (10 daily; 45min); Esch-sur-Sûre (4 daily; 40min); Vianden (12 daily; 30min).

Grevenmacher to: Echternach (12 daily; 40min).

Luxembourg to: Diekirch (8 daily; 1hr 20min); Echternach (12 daily; 1hr 10min); Mondorf(hourly; 30min); Remich (hourly; 45min); Vianden (2 daily; 55min).

Remich to: Grevenmacher (5 daily; 30min); Wasserbillig (5 daily; 40min); Wormeldange (5 daily; 15min).

Wasserbillig to: Echternach (12 daily; 30min).

Wiltz to: Esch-sur-Sûre (4 daily; 25min).

Ferries

Schengen–Remich–Wormeldange–Greven-macher–Wasserbillig–Trier (mid- April to end Sept roughly 6 weekly). For full timetable details of the Moselle ferry boats, contact *Navigation Touristique de l'Entente de la Moselle Luxembourgeoise*, route de Thionville 32, Grevenmacher (☎75 82 75).

PART FOUR

THE
CONTEXTS

THE HISTORICAL FRAMEWORK

What are now known as the countries of Belgium, Luxembourg and the Netherlands didn't reach their present delimitations until 1830. Until then their borders were continually being redrawn following battles, treaties and alliances, and, inevitably, what follows is an outline of the history of the whole region, rather than an individual country-by-country guide. The term "Holland" refers to the province – not the country – throughout.

BEGINNINGS

Little is known of the prehistoric settlers of the Low Countries, their visible remains largely confined to the far north of the Netherlands. Here, mounds known as *terpen* were built to keep the sea at bay in Friesland and Groningen, and in Drenthe megalithic tombs, *hunebeds*, stretch scattered across a low ridge of hills, the *hondsrug*, north of Emmen.

Clearer details of the Low Countries emerge at the time of Julius Caesar's conquest of Gaul in 57 to 50 BC. He found three tribal groupings living in the region: the mainly Celtic **Belgae** (hence the nineteenth-century term "Belgium") settled by the Rhine, Maas and Waal to the south; the Germanic **Frisians** living on the marshy coastal strip north of the Scheldt; and the **Batavi**, another Germanic people, inhabiting the swampy river banks of what is now the southern Netherlands. The Belgae were conquered and their lands incorporated into the imperial province of **Gallia Belgica**, but the territory of the Batavi and Frisians was not considered worthy of colonisation, and these tribes were granted the status of allies, a source of recruitment for the Roman legions and curiosity for imperial travellers. In 50 AD Pliny observed "Here a wretched race is found, inhabiting either the more elevated spots or artificial mounds . . . When the waves cover the surrounding area they are like so many mariners on board a ship, and when again the tide recedes their condition is that of so many shipwrecked men".

The **Roman occupation** continued for 500 years until the legions were pulled back to protect the heartlands of a crumbling empire. But despite the length of their stay, there's precious little left to indicate their presence, with the notable exception of the odd stretch of city wall around Tongeren and the beautiful baths at Heerlen in Limburg, one of the main Roman settlements. As the empire collapsed in chaos and confusion, the Germanic **Franks**, who had been settling within Gallia Belgica from the third century, filled the power vacuum to the south, along with their allies the Belgae, and established a **Merovingian** kingdom based around their capital in Tournai. A great swathe of forest extending from the Scheldt to the Ardennes separated the Frankish kingdom from the more confused situation to the north and east, where other tribes of Franks settled along the Scheldt and Leie, Saxons occupied parts of Overijssel and Gelderland, and the Frisans clung to the shore.

Towards the end of the fifth century, the Merovingians extended their control over much of the rest of what is now north and central France, and in 496 their king, Clovis, was converted to Christianity, a faith which slowly filtered north, spread by energetic missionaries like Saint Willibrord, first bishop of Utrecht from about 710, and Saint Boniface, who was killed by the Frisians in 754 in a final act of pagan resistance before they too were converted. United by faith, the whole region was soon to be united in a single kingdom under **Charlemagne**, son of Pepin III and king of the west Franks from 768.

In a dazzling series of campaigns, Charlemagne extended his empire south into Italy, west to the Pyrenees, north to Denmark and east to the Oder, his secular authority bolstered by his coronation as the first Holy Roman Emperor in 800, a title bestowed on him by the Pope in order to legitimise his claim as the successor to the emperors of Imperial Rome.

The strength and stability of Charlemagne's court at Aachen spread to the Low Countries, bringing a flurry of building of superb Romanesque churches like Maastricht's St Servaas, and a trading boom, utilizing the region's principal rivers. However, unlike his Roman predecessors, Charlemagne was subject to the divisive inheritance laws of the Salian tribe of Franks, and after his death in 814, his kingdom was divided between his grandsons into three roughly parallel strips of territory, the precursors of France, the Low Countries and Germany.

THE GROWTH OF THE TOWNS

The tripartite division of Charlemagne's empire placed the Low Countries between the emergent French- and German-speaking nations, a dangerous location which was subsequently to decide much of its history, though this was not apparent in the cobweb of local alliances that made up early feudal western Europe in the ninth and tenth centuries. During this period, French kings and German emperors exercised a general authority over the region, but power was effectively in the hands of local lords who, remote from central control, brought a degree of local stability. From the twelfth century, feudalism slipped into a gradual decline, the intricate pattern of localized allegiances undermined by the increasing strength of certain lords, whose power and wealth often exceeded that of their nominal sovereign. Preoccupied by territorial squabbles, this streamlined nobility was usually willing to assist the growth of towns by granting charters which permitted a certain amount of autonomy in exchange for tax revenues, and military and labour services. The first major cities were the **cloth towns** of Flanders, particularly Ghent, Bruges and Ieper, which grew rich from the manufacture of cloth, their garments exported far and wide and their economies dependent on a continuous supply of good-

quality wool from England. Meanwhile, their smaller northern neighbours concentrated on trade, exploiting their strategic position at the junction of several of the major waterways and trade routes of the day.

Predictably, the economic interests of the merchants and guildsmen of the cities often clashed with those of the local lord. This was especially true in Flanders, where the towns were anxious to preserve a good relationship with the king of England, who controlled the wool supply, whereas their count, a vassal of the king of France, was often embroiled in the dynastic conflicts between the two monarchs. As a result, the history of thirteenth- and fourteenth-century Flanders is punctuated by sporadic fighting, the fortunes of war oscillating between the cities and the nobility.

BURGUNDIAN RULE

By the late fourteenth century the political situation in the Low Countries was fairly clear: five lords controlled most of the region, paying only nominal homage to their French or German overlords. In 1419 **Philip the Good** of Burgundy succeeded to the countship of Flanders and by a series of adroit political moves gained control over Holland, Zeeland, Brabant and Limburg to the north, and Antwerp, Namur and Luxembourg to the south. He consolidated his power by establishing a strong central administration in Bruges and restricting the privileges granted in the towns' charters. During his reign **Bruges** became an emporium for the Hanseatic League, a mainly German association of towns who acted as a trading group and protected their interests by an exclusive system of trading tariffs. The wealth of Bruges was legendary, and the Burgundian court patronized the early and seminal Nederlandish painters like Jan van Eyck and Hans Memling, whose works are displayed in Ghent and Bruges today.

Philip died in 1467 to be succeeded by his son, Charles the Bold, who was killed in battle ten years later, plunging his carefully crafted domain into turmoil. The French seized the opportunity to take back Arras and Burgundy and before the people of Flanders would agree to fight the French they kidnapped Charles's daughter, Mary, and forced her to sign a charter that restored the civic privileges removed by her grandfather Philip.

THE HABSBURGS

After her release, Mary married the **Habsburg** Maximilian of Austria, who was forced to assume sole authority when Mary was killed in a riding accident in 1482. Today, her tomb stands beside that of her father in the Onze Lieve Vrouwekerk in Bruges. Maximilian continued to rule until 1494, when he became Holy Roman Emperor and transferred control of the Low Countries to his son, Philip the Handsome, and subsequently to his grandson **Charles V**, who in turn became King of Spain and Holy Roman Emperor in 1516 and 1519 respectively. Charles was suspicious of the turbulent burghers of Flanders and, following in Maximilian's footsteps, favoured Antwerp at their expense. Indeed, the great Flemish towns of Ghent and Bruges were in decline, their economies undermined by England's cloth-manufacturing success and Bruges suffering from the devastating effects of the silting of the river Zwin, whose estuary connected the town to the sea. **Antwerp** became the greatest port in the empire, part of a general movement of trade and prosperity away from Flanders to the cities to the north.

Charles was keen to assert Habsburg authority over the merchant cities of the Low Countries, but regardless of his display of force, a spiritual trend was emerging that would question not only the rights of the Emperor but the power of the Church itself.

STIRRINGS OF THE REFORMATION

An alliance of church and state had dominated the medieval world: pope and bishops, kings and counts were supposedly the representatives of God on earth, and crushed religious dissent wherever it appeared. Much of their authority depended on the ignorance of the population, who were entirely dependent on their priests for the interpretation of the scriptures, their view of the world carefully controlled.

There were many complex reasons for the **Reformation**, the stirring of religious revolt that stood sixteenth-century Europe on its head, but certainly the **development of typography** was a key. For the first time, printers were able to produce relatively cheap Bibles in quantity, and the religious texts were no longer the exclusive property of the church. A welter of debate spread across much of western Europe, led initially by theologians who wished to cleanse the Catholic church of its corruptions, superstitions and extravagant ceremony; only later did many of these same thinkers decide to support a breakaway church. Humanists like **Erasmus of Rotterdam** (1465–1536) saw man as the crowning of creation rather than the sinful creature of the Fall; and, most importantly, in 1517 **Martin Luther** produced his 95 theses against indulgences, rejecting among other things Christ's presence in the sacrament of the Eucharist, and denying the Church's monopoly on the interpretation of the Bible. His works and Bible translations were printed in the Netherlands and his ideas gained a following in a group known as the Sacramentarians. They, and other reforming groups branded as **Lutheran** by the Church, were persecuted and escaped the towns to form fugitive communes where the doctrines of another reformer, **John Calvin** (1509–64), became popular. Luther stated that the Church's political power was subservient to that of the state; Calvin emphasised the importance of individual conscience and the need for redemption through the grace of Christ rather than the confessional. The seeds of Protestantism fell on fertile ground among the merchants of the cities of the Low Countries, whose wealth and independence could not easily be accommodated within a rigid caste society. Similarly, their employees, the guildsmen and their apprentices, had a long history of opposing royal authority, and many were soon convinced of the need to reform an autocratic, venal church. In 1555, Charles V abdicated, transferring his German lands to his brother Ferdinand, and his Italian, Spanish and Low Countries territories to his son, the fanatically Catholic **Philip II**. The scene was set for a massive confrontation.

THE REVOLT OF THE NETHERLANDS

On his father's abdication, Philip decided to teach his heretical subjects a lesson. He garrisoned the towns of the Low Countries with Spanish mercenaries, imported the Inquisition and passed a series of anti-Protestant edicts. The opposition to these measures was, however, so widespread that he was pushed into a tactical withdrawal, recalling his soldiers and transferring control to his sister Margaret in 1559. Based in Brussels, the equally resolute Margaret implemented the policies of her brother with gusto. In 1561 she reorganized the church and created fourteen new bishoprics, a move that was construed as a wresting of power from civil authority, and an attempt to destroy the local aristocracy's powers of religious patronage. Protestantism and Protestant sympathies spread to the nobility, who petitioned Philip for moderation but were dismissed out of hand. In 1565 a harvest failure caused a winter famine among the workers, and in many towns, particularly Antwerp, they ran riot in the churches, sacking them of their wealth and destroying their rich decoration in the **Iconoclastic Fury**.

The ferocity of this outbreak shocked the higher classes into renewed support for Spain, and Margaret regained the allegiance of most nobles – with the principal exception of the country's greatest landowner, Prince William of Orange-Nassau, known as **William the Silent** (though William the Taciturn is a better translation). Of Germanic descent, he was raised a Catholic but the excesses and rigidity of Philip had caused him to side with the Protestant movement. A firm believer in individual freedom and religious tolerance, William became – and for the Dutch remains – a symbol of liberty; but after the Fury had revitalized the pro-Spanish party, he prudently slipped away to his estates in Germany.

Philip II saw himself as responsible to God for the salvation of his subjects and therefore obliged to protect them from heresy. In 1567, keen to take advantage of the opportunity provided by the increased support for Margaret, he appointed the **Duke of Alva**, with an army of 10,000 men, to enter the Netherlands and suppress his religious opponents absolutely. Alva's first act was to set up the **Council of Blood**, which tried and condemned 12,000 of those who had taken part in the rioting of the year before. The policy briefly worked: when William attempted an invasion from Germany in 1568 the towns, garrisoned by the Spanish, offered no support. William waited and conceived other means of defeating Alva. In April 1572 a band of privateers entered Brielle on the Maas and captured it from the Spanish. Known as *Waterguezen* or sea-beggars, these

commando-style units initially operated from England, but it was soon possible for them to secure bases in the Netherlands, whose citizens had grown to loathe Alva and his Spaniards.

The revolt spread rapidly: by June the rebels controlled the province of Holland and William was able to take command of his troops from Delft. Alva and his son Frederick fought back, taking Gelder, Overijssel and the towns of Zutphen and Naarden, and in June 1573 Haarlem, massacring the Calvinist ministers and most of the garrison. But the Netherlanders retaliated: utilizing their superior naval power the dykes were cut and the Spanish forces, unpaid and threatened with destruction, were forced to withdraw. Frustrated, Philip replaced Alva with Luis de Resquesens, who initially had some success in the south, where the Catholic majority were more willing to compromise with Spanish rule than their northern neighbours.

William's triumphant relief of Leiden in 1574 increased the pride of the rebel forces, and when de Resquesens died in 1576, his unpaid garrison in Antwerp mutinied and attacked the town, slaughtering some 8000 of its people in what was known as the **Spanish Fury**. Though Spain still held several towns, the massacre alienated the south and pushed its peoples into the arms of William, whose troops now controlled most of the Low Countries. Momentarily, it seemed possible for the whole region to unite behind William, and the various provinces signed the **Pacification of Ghent** in 1576, an agreement that guaranteed freedom of religious belief. However, differences between Protestant north and Catholic south proved irreconcilable, with many Walloons and Flemings suspicious both of William's ambitions and his Calvinist cronies. Consequently, when another army arrived from Spain, under the command of Alexander Farnese, Duke of Parma, the south was reoccupied without much difficulty, beginning a separation that would lead, after many changes, to the creation of two modern countries.

In 1579 seven provinces (Holland, Zeeland, Utrecht, Groningen, Friesland, Overijssel and Gelderland) signed the **Union of Utrecht**, an alliance against Spain that was to be the first unification of the Netherlands as an identifiable country – the **United Provinces**. The agreement stipulated freedom of belief in the provinces, an important step since the struggle against Spain wasn't simply a religious one: many Catholics disliked the Spanish occupation and William did not wish to alienate this possible source of support. This liberalism did not, however, extend to freedom of worship, although a blind eye was turned to the celebration of Mass if it was done privately and inconspicuously, giving rise to the "hidden churches" found throughout the country.

THE SPANISH NETHERLANDS (1579–1713)

In 1579, representatives of the southern provinces of Hainaut, Artois and Douai signed the **Union of Arras**, a Catholic-led agreement that declared loyalty to Philip II and counterbalanced the Union of Utrecht in the north. Subsequently, Alexander Farnese used this area as a base to reconquer the cities of Flanders, recapturing Antwerp after a long siege in 1585. He could go no further north – his enemies were too strong, and the shape of the **Spanish Netherlands**, roughly today's Belgium and Luxembourg, was decided, ruled by a Habsburg governor in Brussels. Although the Spanish were prepared to permit some degree of economic and political autonomy, they were determined to eradicate Protestantism, and in the last years of the sixteenth century thousands of weavers, apprentices and skilled workers – the bedrock of Calvinism – were obliged to leave, moving north to fuel the economic boom in the province of Holland. It took a while for this migration to take effect, and for several years the Spanish Netherlands had all the trappings – if not, increasingly, the substance – of success, the successors of Philip II, the Archdukes Isabella and Albert, presiding over a brief artistic flourish centred on **Rubens** and his elite circle of friends in Antwerp.

The Spaniards resumed their campaign against the Protestant north in 1621, part of a general conflict, the **Thirty Years' War**, that devastated much of Europe. It was a military disaster and the victorious Dutch were strong enough to insist on the closure of the Scheldt to sea traffic from Antwerp in the **Peace of Westphalia** of 1648. The city was ruined and simply withered away, while the southern provinces as a whole had suffered terribly for their loyalty to the Habsburgs: highwaymen infested the roads, trade had almost disappeared, the population had been halved in Brabant, and

acres of fertile farmland lay uncultivated. But the ruling families seemed proud to appear to the world as the defenders and martyrs of the Catholic faith – and those who disagreed left.

Politically dependent on a decaying Spain, economically ruined and deprived of most of its more independent-minded citizens, the country turned in on itself, sustained by the fanatical Catholicism of the Counter-Reformation. Religious worship became strict and magnificent, medieval carnivals were transformed into exercises in piety, and penitential flagellation became popular, all of which was encouraged by the Jesuits.

The number of **Jesuits** was extraordinary. France as a whole only had 2000, the Spanish Netherlands 1600, and it was here they wrote their most important works, exercised their greatest influence and owned vast tracts of land. Supported by draconian laws that barred known Protestants from public appointments, declared their marriages illegal and forbade them municipal assistance, the Catholic priests overwhelmed the religious opposition and in half a century transformed this part of the Low Countries into an introverted world shaped by a mystical faith, where Christians were redeemed by the ectasy of suffering.

The visible signs of the change were all around, from extravagant Baroque churches to crosses, calvaries and shrines scattered across the countryside. Literature disappeared, the sciences vegetated and religious orders multiplied, all at the time the Dutch were building the greatest fleet in the world. In painting, artists – such as Rubens – were used to confirm the ecclesiastical orthodoxies, their canvases full of muscular saints and angels, reflecting a religious faith of mystery and hierarchy; others, such as David Teniers and the later Bruegels, retreated into minutely observed realism.

The Peace of Westphalia freed the king of France from fear of Germany, and the political and military history of the Spanish Netherlands after 1648 was dominated by the efforts of Louis XIV to add the region to his territories. Fearful of an over-powerful France, the United Provinces, England and Sweden, amongst others, determinedly resisted French designs, fighting a long series of campaigns which began with the **War of Devolution** in 1667 and ended with the **War of the Spanish Succession** from 1702 to 1713. At one time or another, all of the region's major cities were besieged and badly damaged, and only with the **Treaty of Utrecht** in 1713 did the French abandon their attempt to conquer the Spanish Netherlands, which now passed under the control of Emperor Charles VI of Austria.

THE UNITED PROVINCES (1579–1713)

In order to follow the developments of the sixteenth and seventeenth centuries in what is today the Netherlands, it's necessary to have an idea of the organization of the **United Provinces**. Holland, comprising North and South Holland, was by far the dominant province economically and politically. The provinces maintained a decentralized independence, but as far as the United Provinces as a whole were concerned, what Holland said, went.

The assembly of the provinces was known as the **States General**, and met at The Hague; it had no domestic legislative authority, and could only carry out foreign policy by unanimous decision. The role of **Stadholder** was the most important in each province, roughly equivalent to that of governor, though the same person could occupy this position in any number of provinces. The Council Pensionary was another major post and in both cases the man who held the title in Holland was a powerful statesman.

In 1584 a French Catholic tricked his way into William's court in Delft and shot him, his family receiving the reward Philip II had promised for such an assassination. As William's son **Maurice** was only 17, control of the United Provinces was handed to **Johan van Oldenbarneveldt**, later Council Pensionary of Holland. Things were going badly in the fight against the Spanish: Nijmegen had fallen and Henry III of France refused help even with the offer of sovereignty. In desperation the United Provinces turned to Elizabeth I of England, who offered the Earl of Leicester as governor general. He was accepted but completely mishandled the situation militarily, alienating the Dutch into the bargain. Oldenbarneveldt and Maurice took over and had great success in routing the Spanish from much of the country. By 1609 the English had defeated the Spanish Armada and Philip II was dead; the **Twelve Year Truce** was signed and the United Provinces were consolidated.

THE EARLY SEVENTEENTH CENTURY: INTERNAL DISCORD AND FURTHER FIGHTING

In the breathing space created by the truce, the long-standing differences between Maurice and Oldenbarneveldt polarized. An obscure argument within the Calvinist church on predestination proved the catalyst of Oldenbarneveldt's downfall.

The quarrel, between two Leiden theologians, began in 1612: Armenius argued that God gave man the choice of accepting or rejecting faith; Gomarus, his opponent, that predestination was absolute – to the degree that God chooses who will be saved and who damned with man powerless in the decision. This row between the two groups (known respectively as Remonstrants and counter-Remonstrants) became closely linked to the political divisions of the early seventeenth century. When a synod was arranged at Dordrecht to resolve the matter, the State of Holland, led by Oldenbarneveldt, refused to attend, insisting on Holland's right to decide its own religious orthodoxies. He and his fellow deputies supported the provincial independence favoured by Remonstrant sympathisers, whereas Maurice sided with the counter-Remonstrants who favoured a strong central authority. The counter-Remonstrants won at Dordrecht: Maurice, with his troops behind him, quickly overcame his opponents and had Oldenbarneveldt arrested. In May 1619 he was executed in The Hague "for having conspired to dismember the states of the Netherlands and greatly troubled God's church".

With the end of the Twelve Year Truce in 1621, fighting with Spain once more broke out, this time part of the more general **Thirty Years' War** (1618–48), a largely religious-based conflict between Catholic and Protestant countries that involved most of western Europe. In the Low Countries, the Spanish were initially successful, but they were weakened by war with France and by the fresh attacks of Maurice's successor, his brother Frederick Henry. From 1625, the Spaniards suffered a series of defeats on land and sea that forced them out of what is today the southern part of the Netherlands, and in 1648 they were compelled to accept the humiliating terms of the **Peace of Westphalia**. This was a general treaty that ended the Thirty Years' War, whose terms recognised the independence of the United Provinces and closed the Scheldt estuary, an action designed to destroy the trade and prosperity of Antwerp. The commercial expansion and pre-eminence of Amsterdam was assured, and the Golden Age began.

THE GOLDEN AGE

The brilliance of **Amsterdam**'s explosion on the European scene is as difficult to underestimate as it is to detail. The size of its merchant fleet had long been considerable, bringing masses of Baltic grain into Europe. Even the determined Spaniards had been unable to undermine Dutch naval power, and following the effective removal of Antwerp as a competitor, Amsterdam became the emporium for the products of north and south Europe and the new colonies in the East and West Indies. Amsterdam didn't only prosper from its markets – her own ships carried the produce, a cargo trade that greatly increased the city's wealth. Dutch banking and investment brought further prosperity, and by the mid-seventeenth century Amsterdam's wealth was spectacular. The Calvinist bourgeoisie indulged themselves gently in fine canal houses and commissioned their reflections in group portraits. Civic pride burgeoned, and if some were hungry, few starved, with the poor cared for in municipal almshouses. The arts flourished and religious tolerance stretched even to the traditional scapegoats, the Jews, many of whom quickly became enterprising merchants. Huguenot refugees from France were drawn to the city, along with Protestants escaping persecution in the Catholic south.

One organization that kept the country's coffers brimming throughout the Golden Age was the **East India Company**. Formed by the newly powerful Dutch Republic in 1602, the Amsterdam-controlled enterprise sent ships to Asia, Indonesia, and as far as China to bring back spices, woods and other assorted plunder. Given a trading monopoly in all lands east of the Cape of Good Hope, it had unlimited military powers over the lands it controlled, and was effectively the occupying government in Malaya, Ceylon and Malacca. Twenty years later the **West Indies Company** was inaugurated to protect new Dutch interests in the Americas and Africa. Expending most of its energies in waging war on Spanish and

Portuguese colonies from a base in Surinam, it never achieved the success of the East India Company, and was dismantled in 1674, ten years after its small colony of New Amsterdam had been captured by the British – and renamed New York. Elsewhere, the Netherlands held on to its colonies for as long as possible – **Java** and **Sumatra** were still under Dutch control after World War II.

A constant problem in the seventeenth century was the conflict between central authority and provincial autonomy. Although the **House of Orange** had established its royal credentials, many of Holland's leading citizens were reluctant to accept its right to power. On William II's death in 1650 the state of Holland used the fact that his heir was still an infant to force through measures abolishing the position of Stadholder, thereby reducing the powers of the Orangists and increasing those of the provinces, chiefly Holland itself.

Holland's foremost figure in these years was **Johan de Witt**, Council Pensionary to the States General. He guided the country through wars with England and Sweden, concluding a triple alliance between the two countries and the United Provinces in 1678. This didn't succeed, however, and when France and England marched on the Provinces two years later, the republic was in trouble. The previous victories had been at sea, and the army, weak and disorganized, could not withstand an attack. The country turned to **William III of Orange** for leadership and Johan de Witt was brutally murdered by a mob of Orangist sympathisers in The Hague. By 1678 William had defeated the French and made peace with the English – and was rewarded (along with his wife Mary) with the English crown ten years later.

THE AUSTRIAN NETHERLANDS (1713–1794)

The transfer of the country from Spanish to Austrian control made little appreciable difference: there were more wars and more invasions – principally the **War of the Austrian Succession** in the 1740s – and a remote central authority continued to operate through Brussels. The strength of the region lay in its agriculture, which easily survived the various armed incursions, though the country remained vitrified and stagnant – only three percent of the population were literate, workers were forbidden to change towns or jobs without obtaining permission from the municipal authorities, and skills and crafts were tied to particular families.

This sorry state of affairs began to change in 1753 with the arrival of a new governor, the Count of Cobenzl, who was determined to shake the country from its torpor. He initiated an ambitious programme of public works, including extensive road and canal construction, organized financial incentives to industry, and took a firm line with his clerical opponents, who tried to encourage the population to thwart him in his aims.

In 1780, Emperor **Joseph II** came to the throne, determined to organize further reforms himself. Authoritarian and impulsive, his efforts to "root out silly old prejudices", as he put it, resulted in a deluge of edicts and decrees that managed to offend most of the country's major groups – from peasants to nobility, bureaucrats to traders. Pandemonium ensued, and opposition crystallized around the Flemish lawyer Francois Vonck, whose liberal-minded **Vonckists** were countered by the conservative **Statists**. The latter, with the assistance of the priests, raised the peasantry to arms and encouraged them to attack the Vonckists, who were killed in their hundreds. The country was in turmoil and when Emperor Joseph died in 1790, his successor, Leopold, was quick to withdraw many of the reforming acts and send in his troops to restore order.

THE UNITED PROVINCES IN THE EIGHTEENTH CENTURY

Though King William had defeated the French, Louis XIV retained designs on the United Provinces. When William's grandson inherited the Spanish throne and control of the Spanish Netherlands in 1700, Louis forced him to hand the latter over to French control. This threatened the balance of power in Europe, and the Provinces, England and Austria formed an alliance against the French and so began the **War of the Spanish Succession**, a haphazard series of campaigns distinguished by the spectacular victories of the Duke of Marlborough – Blenheim, Ramillies, Malplaquet – that dragged on till 1713 and the **Treaty of Utrecht**.

The fighting drained the United Provinces' riches and a slow economic and political decline began, accelerated by a mood of unadventurous conservatism that reflected the development of an increasingly socially static society, with power and wealth concentrated within a small elite.

Effectively freed from the threat of foreign conquest by the treaty of 1713, the next decades were marred by internal fighting between the Orangists and the pro-French ruling families (who called themselves "patriots"). The situation deteriorated even further in the latter half of the century and the last few years of the United Provinces were dogged by interminable rivalry and conflict.

In 1795 the French, aided by the Patriots, invaded, setting up the **Batavian Republic** and dissolving the United Provinces and much of the control of the rich Dutch merchants. Effectively part of the Napoleonic empire, the Netherlands were obliged to wage unenthusiastic war with England, and in 1806 Napoleon appointed his brother Louis as their king in an attempt to create a commercial gulf between the country and England. Louis, however, wasn't willing to allow the Netherlands to become a simple satellite of France; he ignored Napoleon's directives and after just four years of rule was forced to abdicate. The country was then formally incorporated into the French Empire, and for three gloomy years suffered occupation and heavy taxation to finance French military adventures.

Following Napoleon's disastrous retreat from Moscow, the Orangist faction once more surfaced to exploit weakening French control. In 1813, Frederick William, son of the exiled William V, returned to the country and eight months later, under the terms of the **Congress of Vienna**, was crowned King William I of the United Kingdom of the Netherlands, incorporating both the old United Provinces and the Spanish (Austrian) Netherlands. A strong-willed man, he spent much of the later part of his life trying to control his disparate kingdom, but he failed primarily because of the north's attempt to dominate the south. The southern provinces revolted against his rule and in 1830 the **Kingdom of Belgium** was proclaimed.

THE AUSTRIAN NETHERLANDS (1794–1909)

Occupied by French Republican armies in 1794, the Austrian Netherlands were annexed the following year, an annexation that was to last until 1814. The **French** imposed radical reforms: the Catholic church was stripped of much of its worldly wealth, feudal privileges were abolished, a consistent legal system was formulated and, most unpopular of all, conscription was introduced, provoking a brutally repressed Peasants' Revolt in 1798. Napoleon, in control from 1799, also rebuilt the docks of Antwerp and forced the Dutch to accept the reopening of the Scheldt, but, with the exception of a radical minority, the French occupation remained unpopular.

Following the battle of Waterloo, the great powers decided to give William I's German lands to Prussia and in return presented him with the newly independent **Grand-Duchy of Luxembourg**. This was a somewhat confused arrangement, as the Duchy was detached from the rest of the Low Countries constitutionally and pushed into the German Confederation at the same time as it shared the same king with the old United Provinces and Austrian Netherlands.

Indeed, the main concern of the great powers was to create a buffer state against any possible future plans the French might have to expand to the north. With scant regard to the feelings of those affected, they therefore decided to establish the **United Kingdom of the Netherlands** under the control of William I. But the king failed to calm the anxieties of his southern subjects and in 1830 **revolution** broke out in Brussels. Aided by the French, the revolutionaries managed to resist Dutch invasion and in January 1831 the **Conference of London** reluctantly agreed to recognize Belgium's independence, insisting it be classified a "neutral" state, ceding to it the western segments of Luxembourg, and digging out the uncle of Queen Victoria, Leopold of Saxe-Coburg, to present with the crown.

Shrewd and capable, **Leopold I** (1830–65) was careful to maintain his country's neutrality and encouraged an industrial boom that saw coal mines developed, iron-making factories established and the rapid expansion of the railway system. Politically, a strictly limited fran-chise ensured the domination of the middle classes, who divided into two loose groups, the one attempting to undermine Catholic influence and control over such areas as education, the other profoundly conservative in its desire to maintain the status quo.

Leopold II's (1865–1909) long reign was dominated by similar themes, and saw the emergence of Belgium as a major industrial power. However, the 1860s and 1870s also witnessed the first stirrings of a type of **Flemish nationalism**, which felt little enthusiasm for the unitary status of Belgium, divided as it was between a French-speaking majority in the south of the country – the **Walloons** – and the Dutch-speakers of Flanders, Antwerp and Limburg in the north. Then in the early 1900s the king's personal ownership of the Belgian Congo led to a scandal when the level of exploitation, slavery and atrocity became too great to ignore. The Belgian state took over the administration of Leopold's fiefdom in 1908.

THE NETHERLANDS: 1830 TO THE PRESENT DAY

A final invasion of Belgium in 1839 gave William most of Limburg, and all but ended centuries of changes to borders and territory. The Netherlands benefited from this new stability, the trade surplus picked up and canal building opened Rotterdam and Amsterdam to the North Sea. The outstanding political figure of the times, **J. R. Thorbecke**, formed three ruling cabinets (1849–53, 1862–66 and 1872, in the year of his death) and steered the Netherlands through a profound change. The political parties of the late eighteenth century had wished to resurrect the power and prestige of the seventeenth-century Netherlands; Thorbecke and his allies resigned themselves to the country's reduced status of a small power and eulogized its advantages. For the first time, from about 1850, liberty was seen as a luxury made possible by the country's very lack of power, and the malaise which had long disturbed public life gave way to a positive appreciation of the narrowness of its national existence. One of the results of Thorbecke's liberalism was a gradual extension of the fran-chise, culminating in the Act of Universal Suffrage in 1917.

At the outbreak of **World War I** the Netherlands remained neutral, but suffered privations as a result of the Allied blockade of ports through which Germany might be supplied. Similar attempts to remain neutral in **World War II** soon failed: the Germans invaded on May 10, 1940, destroying Rotterdam four days later. The Dutch were quickly overwhelmed, Queen Wilhelmina fled to London, and opposition to Nazi occupation was continued by the Resistance. Instrumental in destroying German supplies and munitions, they also helped many downed airmen escape back to England. A heavy price was paid for their contribution to the war effort: 23,000 resistance fighters were killed in the war years. In Amsterdam, the old Jewish community, swollen by those who had fled Germany to escape the persecution of the 1930s, was obliterated, leaving only the deserted Jodenhoek and the diary of **Anne Frank** as testament to the horrors.

Liberation began in autumn 1944 with **Operation Market Garden**. This was a British plan to finish the war quickly by creating a corridor stretching from Eindhoven to Arnhem, gaining control of the three main rivers en route, isolating the occupying forces to the west in the Netherlands and pushing straight into Germany. It was a gamble, but if successful would hasten the end of hostilities. On September 17 the 1st Airborne Division parachuted into the countryside around Oosterbeek, a small village near the most northerly target of the operation, the bridge at **Arnhem**. German opposition was much stronger than expected, and after heavy fighting the Allied forces could only take the northern end of the bridge. The advancing British army was unable to break through fast enough, and after four days the decimated battalion defending the bridge was forced to withdraw.

With the failure of Operation Market Garden, the Allies were obliged to resort to more orthodox military tactics to clear the south and east Netherlands of the Germans, a slow process that took all the winter and spring of 1945. As the assault was concentrated on Germany itself, the coastal provinces of the country were left alone, but they suffered terribly from lack of food and fuel. Finally, on April 5, 1945, the German army surrendered to the Canadians at Wageningen.

The postwar years were spent patching up the damage of occupation. Rotterdam was rapidly rebuilt, and the dykes blown in the war to slow the German advance repaired. Two events were to mar the late 1940s and early 1950s: the former Dutch colonies of Java and Sumatra, taken by the Japanese at the outbreak of the war, were now run by a nationalist Republican government in Java that refused to recognize Dutch sovereignty. Following the failure of talks on Dutch control the troops were sent in; world opposition to this was strong, and after much condemnation and pressure the Dutch reluctantly handed over their colonies.

Back at home, tragedy struck on February 1, 1953 when an unusually high tide was pushed over Zeeland's sea defences by a westerly wind, flooding 40,000 acres of land and drowning over 1800 people. The response was to secure the area with the **Delta Project**, closing off the western part of the Scheldt and Maas estuaries with massive sea dykes. A brilliant and graceful piece of engineering, the main storm surge barrier on the Oosterschelde was finally completed in 1986.

Elsewhere rebuilding continued; in Amsterdam all the land projected in 1947 for use by the year 2000 was in fact used up by the "garden cities" of the dormitory suburbs by 1970, and the polder towns on the reclaimed stretches of Flevoland also expanded. But growth wasn't only physical: the social consciousness and radicalism of the 1960s reached the country early, and the word of the psychedelic revolution was quick to catch on. It was quick to fade, too, replaced by the cynicism of the 1970s, but one manifestation of the spread of radical thinking that had some tangible positive results was the **squatting movement**, which precipitated major riots in Amsterdam and other cities throughout the late 1960s and early 1970s. The squatters and other activists won considerable success in attempting to prevent the wholesale destruction of low cost urban housing, a move that would have turned the country's city centres into places where only the rich could afford to live.

Today, the country's finely balanced system of proportional representation forces almost continuous political compromise and debate, but brings little rapid change, politics and politicking seeming a bland business conducted between the three main parties, the

Protestant-Catholic CDA coalition, the **Liberal VVD** and the **Socialist PvdA**.

A governmental system that has so effectively incorporated the disparate elements of a modern and diverse state — Catholic and Protestant, management and union, city and country, socialist and conservative — has earned the Netherlands a well-deserved reputation for comfortable complacency, and outbreaks of opposition, when they do appear, on such items as eco-issues, housing and racism, provoke a mad rush to the bargaining table.

BELGIUM AND LUXEMBOURG IN THE TWENTIETH CENTURY

King Leopold died in 1909, to be succeeded by his nephew **Albert**, whose reign was dominated by **World War I**. Indifferent to Belgium's proclaimed neutrality, the German invasion of 1914 extended over almost all of the country, the exception a narrow strip of territory around De Panne, where Albert was forced to move to continue his administration. For four years, the northern stretches of the lines of trenches which separated the opposing armies from the North Sea to Switzerland crossed Belgium, following roughly the path of the river Yser and the Yserkanaal, through Nieuwpoort, Diksmuide and Ieper. The violation of Belgian neutrality and Albert's spirited resistance attracted worldwide sympathy and admiration. The principal engagements on Belgian soil took place in the bulge in the line around Ieper, where a series of futile, bloody battles came to epitomise the pointlessness of the war and the tactical stupidity of its generals.

After the war, Belgium received extensive reparations from Germany including the slice of land around Eupen. In November 1919, King Albert addressed parliament to announce a package of radical reforms that included universal suffrage and equal rights for the two national languages. Perhaps surprisingly, this proclamation sharpened the embryonic tensions between the Walloon and Flemish sections of the population — for although the Flemings had accepted the domination of the French-speakers without much protest for several centuries, as their province became more prosperous, so they grew in self-confidence, becoming increasingly unhappy with their social and political subordination.

In the 1930s, **Fascism** drew some ten percent of the vote in both the Walloon and Flemish communities, though for very different reasons: the former for its appeal to a nationalist bourgeoisie, the latter for its assertion of "racial" pride amongst an oppressed group.

In May 1940, the **Germans** launched their sudden, surprise attack on the Netherlands and Belgium. This time there was no heroic resistance by the Belgian king, who to many seemed only too prepared to surrender — and subsequently collaborate — and the entire country was occupied within three weeks. As in the Netherlands, it took time for the Belgians to adjust to the new situation, but by 1941 a Resistance movement was organising acts of sabotage against the occupying forces. The **liberation** came some four years later, in the autumn of 1944, and, with the exception of the Battle of the Ardennes (the Bulge) and damage to the port of Antwerp, went relatively smoothly.

After the liberation, the Belgians set about the task of economic reconstruction, helped by aid from the United States, but hindered by a divisive controversy over the **wartime activities of King Leopold**. Many felt his prompt surrender to the Germans was cowardly and his subsequent willingness to work with them treacherous; others pointed out his efforts to increase the country's food rations and his negotiations to secure the release of Belgian prisoners. Inevitably, the complex shadings of collaboration and forced co-operation were hard to disentangle, and the debate continued until 1950 when a referendum narrowly recommended his return from exile as king. Leopold considered this insufficient recommendation and abdicated in favour of his son, the present king, **Baudouin**.

The development of the postwar Belgian economy follows the pattern of most of western Europe — reconstruction in the 1950s; boom in the 1960s; recession in the 1970s; and retrenchment in the 1980s. Significant events have included an ugly, disorganized and hasty evacuation of the Belgian Congo in 1960, the transformation of Brussels from one of the more insignificant European capitals into the home of the EC and NATO, and acute labour unrest in the Limburg coalfield in the early 1980s, following plans to close most of the remaining pits. But, above all, the postwar period has been dominated by the increasing **tension between the Walloon and Flemish communities**. Every facet of Belgian life is now dogged by the prerequisites of bilingualism – speeches in parliament have to be delivered in both languages, and every instance of the written word, from road signs to the yellow pages, has to be bilingual as well. Politically, the parties reflect three broad ranges of opinion – conservative, liberal and socialist – but they are also divided into Flemish- and French-speaking sections, further complicating the structure of national administrations from an already complex system of proportional representation. In 1962 the Linguistic Divide (or Language Frontier) was formally delineated and in 1980 central government was partially regionalized, with major areas of administration transferred to regional councils. In many ways, therefore, Belgium is a divided society, the two linguistic groups viewing each other with suspicion punctuated by hostility – a situation which began to take on the dimensions of a crisis in the early 1990s as it became increasingly impossible to govern and at the same time appease the country's various factions. In 1991 the fall of Wilfred Martens' government led to elections that saw increased representation for the right-wing separatist Flanders parties, among other fringe groups, although a coalition of mainstream right- and left-wing forces was eventually formed and continues somehow to hold the country together. It seems in fact that the majority of Belgians want to remain as one nation, and there were large demonstrations in Brussels in 1992 in support of just that. However, as the country slides ever further into recession (Belgium is the EU's most in-debt member), its future as one nation is looking increasingly uncertain.

LUXEMBOURG

The second half of the nineteenth century had seen Luxembourg's poor, agricultural economy transformed by the discovery and mining of **iron ore deposits**, and by 1939 the Grand Duchy was the world's seventh largest producer of steel. Occupied in both world wars, the Luxembourgers put up a stubborn resistance, leading to many brave acts of defiance and considerable loss of life. The Battle of the Ardennes (the Bulge) was a major disaster and, as the war ended in 1945, one third of the country's farmland lay uncultivated, the public transportation system in ruins, and some 60,000 people homeless.

In the **postwar years**, reconstruction was rapid and the government wisely pursued a policy of industrial diversification that has made the country one of the most prosperous parts of Europe. Disappointed by the results of neutrality, Luxembourg also joined the EC and NATO and is now home to many major Community departments. The present Grand-Duke and Grand-Duchess are Jean and Josephine Charlotte of Nassau.

AN INTRODUCTION TO DUTCH AND BELGIAN ART

The following piece is the very briefest of introductions to the subject, designed to serve only as a quick reference on your way round the major galleries. For more in-depth and academic studies, see the recommendations in the "Books" listings, p.541. For where to find the paintings themselves, turn to the hit list at the end.

THE EARLY FLEMISH MASTERS

Until the sixteenth century the area now known as the Low Countries was in effect one country, the most artistically productive part of which was Flanders in modern Belgium, and it was there that the solid realist base of later Dutch painting developed. Today the works of these early Flemish painters, known as the **Flemish Primitives**, are relatively sparse in the Low Countries, and even in Belgium few collections are as complete as they might be – indeed, many ended up as the property of the ruling Habsburgs and were removed to Spain. Most major galleries do, however, have a few examples.

Jan van Eyck (1385–1441) is generally regarded as the originator of Low Countries painting, and has even been credited with the invention of oil painting itself – though it seems more likely that he simply perfected a new technique by thinning his paint with the recently discovered turpentine, thus making it more flexible. His fame partially stems from the fact that he was one of the first artists to sign his work – an action that indicates how highly his talent was regarded in his own time. Van Eyck's most famous work is still in the Low Countries, the altarpiece of St Baaf's Cathedral in Ghent, known as the *Adoration of the Mystic Lamb*. It was debatably painted with the help of his lesser-known brother, Hubert, and was revolutionary in its realism, for the first time using elements of native landscape in depicting Biblical themes. His work was also rich in a complex symbolism, whereby everyday objects take on a disguised, usually religious meaning, the nature of which has generated analysis and discussion ever since. Van Eyck's style and technique were to influence several generations of Low Countries artists.

Firmly in this Eyckian tradition were the **Master of Flemalle** (1387–1444) and **Rogier van der Weyden** (1400–64). The Flemalle master is a shadowy figure: some believe he was the teacher of van der Weyden, others that the two artists were in fact the same person. There are differences between the two, however. The Flemalle master's paintings are close to van Eyck's, whereas van der Weyden shows a more emotional and religious intensity; few of his more important paintings remain in Belgium. Van der Weyden influenced such painters as **Dieric Bouts** (1415–75), who was born in Haarlem but was active in Leuven (where his *Altarpiece of the Sacrament* remains in the St Pieterskerk) and is recognizable by his stiff, rather elongated figures and horrific subject matter against carefully drawn landscapes. **Petrus Christus** (d.1472), a contemporary of Bouts, was also influenced by van der Weyden and van Eyck: he was the next painter of importance to work in Bruges after van Eyck, and may have been his pupil. His portraits have a directness and simple clarity, but with the exception of a *Lamentation* in the Musée d'Art Ancien, Brussels, most of his masterpieces are now outside the Low Countries. **Hugo van der Goes** (d.1482) was the next Ghent master after van Eyck, most famous for the *Portinari Altarpiece* in Florence's Uffizi. After a short painting career, he died insane, and his late works have strong hints of his impending madness in their subversive use of space and implict acceptance of the viewer's presence. Few doubt that **Hans Memling** (1440–94) was a pupil of van der Weyden. Active in Bruges throughout his life, he is best remembered for the pastoral charm of his landscapes and the quality of his portraiture, much of which survives on the rescued side panels of triptychs. The museum named after him in Bruges has an excellent survey of his work. **Gerhard David** (d.1523) moved to Bruges in 1484, and was the last of the great painters to work in that city, before it was overtaken in prosperity by Antwerp – which itself became the focus of a more Italianate school of art in the sixteenth century.

Hieronymus Bosch (1450–1516) lived for most of his life in Holland, though his style is linked to that of the Flanders painters (see below). His frequently reprinted religious allegories are filled with macabre visions of tortured people and grotesque beasts, and appear at first faintly unhinged, though it's now thought that these are visual representations of contemporary sayings, idioms and parables. While their interpretation is far from resolved, Bosch's paintings draw strongly on subconscious fears and archetypes, giving them a lasting, haunting fascination.

THE SIXTEENTH CENTURY

Meanwhile, there were movements to the north of Flanders. **Geertgen tot Sint Jans** "Little Gerard of the Brotherhood of St John" (d.1490), a student of **Albert van Ouwater**, had been working in **Haarlem**, initiating – in a strangely naive style – an artistic tradition in the city that would prevail throughout the seventeenth century. **Jan Mostaert** (1475–1555) took over after Geertgen's death, and continued to develop a style that diverged more and more from that of the southern provinces. **Lucas van Leyden** (1489–1533) was the first painter to effect real changes in northern painting. Born in Leiden, his bright colours and narrative technique were refreshingly new at the time, and he introduced a novel dynamism into what had become a rigidly formal treatment of devotional subjects. There was rivalry, of course. Eager to publicize Haarlem as the artistic capital of the northern Netherlands, Carel van Mander (see below) claimed Haarlem native **Jan van Scorel** (1495–1562) as the better painter, complaining, too, of Lucas's dandyish ways.

Certainly van Scorel's influence should not be underestimated. At this time every painter was expected to travel to Italy to view the works of Renaissance artists. When the Bishop of Utrecht became Pope Hadrian VI, he took van Scorel with him as court painter, giving him the opportunity to introduce Italian styles into what had been a completely independent tradition. Hadrian died soon after, and van Scorel returned north, combining the ideas he had picked up in Italy with Haarlem realism and passing them on to **Maerten van Heemskerck** (1498–1574), who later went off to Italy himself in 1532, staying there five years before returning to Haarlem.

Bruges' pre-eminence in the medieval Low Countries gradually began to give way to Antwerp, and the artists who worked there at the beginning of the sixteenth century combined the influence of the Italian painters with the domestic Flemish tradition. **Quinten Metsys** (1464–1530) introduced florid classical architectural detail and intricate landscape backgrounds to his works, influenced perhaps by the work of Leonardo da Vinci. As well as religious works, he painted portraits and genre scenes, all of which have recognizably Italian facets, and paved the way for the Dutch genre painters of later years. His follower, **Joos van Cleve** (c.1485–1540/1), painted in a similarly refined and realistic manner. **Jan Gossaert** (d. c.1523) made the pilgrimage to Italy, and his dynamic works are packed with detail, especially finely drawn classical architectural backdrops. He was the first Low Countries artist to introduce the subjects of classical mythology into his works, part of a steady trend through the period towards secular subject matter, which can also be seen in the work of **Joachim Patinir** (d.c.1524), who painted small landscapes of fantastic scenery.

The latter part of the sixteenth century was dominated by the work of **Pieter Bruegel the Elder** (c.1525–69), whose gruesome allegories and innovative interpretations of religious subjects are firmly placed in Low Countries settings. Most famous are his paintings of peasant lowlife, though he himself was well connected in court circles in Antwerp and, later, Brussels. **Pieter Aertsen** (c.1508–75) also worked in the peasant genre, adding aspects of the still life: his paintings often show a detailed kitchen scene in the foreground, with a religious episode going on behind. Towards the latter half of the century the stylized Italianate portrait was much in vogue, its chief exponents being **Adrien Key**, **Anthonis Mor** and **Frans Pourbus**.

RUBENS AND HIS FOLLOWERS

Pieter Paul Rubens (1577–1640) was the most influential Low Countries artist of the early seventeenth century and the most important exponent of Baroque painting in northern Europe. Born in Siegen, Westphalia, his parents returned to their native Antwerp when Rubens was a child. He entered the Antwerp Guild in 1598, became court painter to the Duke of Mantua in 1600, and until 1608 travelled extensively in Italy, absorbing the art of the High Renaissance and classical architecture. By the time of his return to Antwerp in 1608 he had acquired an enormous artistic vocabulary: the paintings of Caravaggio in particular were to influence his work strongly. His first major success was *The Raising of the Cross*, painted in 1610 and kept today in Antwerp cathedral. A large, dynamic work, it caused a sensation at the time, establishing Rubens' reputation and leading to a string of commissions that enabled him to set up his own studio. The *Descent from the Cross*, his next major work (also in the cathedral), consolidated this success: equally Baroque, it is nevertheless quieter and more restrained.

The division of labour in Rubens' studio, and the talent of the artists working there (who included Antony van Dyck and Jacob Jordaens) ensured a high output of excellent work. The degree to which Rubens personally worked on a canvas would vary – and would determine its price. From the early 1620s onwards he turned his hand to a plethora of themes and subjects – religious works, portraits, tapestry designs, landscapes, mythological scenes, ceiling paintings (including that of the Banqueting Hall in Whitehall, London – a commission for Charles I, by whom he was knighted) – each of which was handled with supreme vitality and virtuosity. From his Flemish antecedents he inherited an acute sense of light, and used it not to dramatize his subjects (a technique favoured by

Caravaggio and other Italian artists), but in organic association with colour and form. The drama in his works comes from the tremendous animation of his characters. His large-scale allegorical works, especially, are packed with heaving, writhing figures that appear to tumble out from the canvas.

The energy of Rubens' paintings was reflected in his private life. In addition to his career as an artist, he also undertook diplomatic missions to Spain and England on behalf of the governors of Holland, and used the opportunities to study the works of other artists and – as in the case of Velázquez – to meet them personally. In the 1630s, gout began to hamper his activities, and from this time his painting became more domestic and meditative. Hélène Fourment, his second wife, was the subject of many portraits and served as a model for characters in his allegorical paintings, her figure epitomizing the buxom, well-rounded women found throughout his work.

Rubens' influence on the artists of the period was enormous. The huge output of his studio meant that his works were universally seen, and widely disseminated by the engravers he employed to copy his work. Chief among his followers was the portraitist **Antony van Dyck** (1599–1641), who worked in Rubens' studio from 1618, often taking on the depiction of religious figures in his master's works that required particular sensitivity and pathos. Like Rubens, he was born in Antwerp and travelled widely in Italy, though his initial work was influenced less by the Italian artists than by Rubens himself. Eventually van Dyck developed his own distinct style and technique, establishing himself as court painter to Charles I in England, and creating portraits of a nervous elegance that would influence the genre there for the next hundred and fifty years. Most of his great portraiture remains in England, though his best religious works – such as the *Crucifixion* in Mechelen cathedral and a *Lamentation* in Antwerp's Museum voor Schone Kunsten – can be found in Belgium.

Jacob Jordaens (1593–1678) was also an Antwerp native who studied under Rubens. Although he was commissioned to complete several works left unfinished by Rubens at the time of his death, his robustly naturalistic works have an earthy – and sensuous – realism that's quite distinct in style and technique.

Other artists working this part of the Low Countries during the early seventeenth century were also, understandably, greatly influenced by the output of Rubens' studio. **Gerhard Seghers** (1591–1651) specialised in painting flowers, usually around portraits or devotional figures painted by other artists, including Rubens himself.

Theodor Rombouts (1579–1637) was strongly influenced by Caravaggio following a trip to Italy, but changed his style to fall in line with that of Rubens when he returned to Antwerp from Holland. **Jacob van Oost the Elder** chose to live and work in Bruges: his delicate work embraces Dutch and Italian elements. **Frans Snyders** (1579–1657) took up the genre of the still life where Aertsen left off, amplifying his subject – food and drink – to even larger, more sumptuous canvases. He too was part of the Rubens art machine, painting animals and still life sections for the master's works.

THE DUTCH GOLDEN AGE

Carel van Mander (1548–1606) had a tremendous impact in Holland at the beginning of the sixteenth century. A Haarlem painter, art impresario, and one of the few chroniclers of the art of the Low Countries, his *Schilderboek* of 1604 put Flemish and Dutch traditions into context for the first time and specified the rules of fine painting. Examples of his own work are rare, but his followers were many, among them **Cornelius Cornelisz van Haarlem** (1562–1638), who produced elegant renditions of Biblical and mythical themes; and **Hendrik Goltzius** (1558–1616), who was a skilled engraver and an integral member of van Mander's Haarlem academy. These painters' enthusiasm for Italian art, combined with the influence of a late revival of Gothicism, resulted in works that combined Mannerist and classical elements. An interest in realism was also felt, and, for them, the subject became less important than the way in which it was depicted. Biblical stories became merely a vehicle whereby artists could apply their skills in painting the human body, landscapes, or copious displays of food – all of which served to break religion's stranglehold on art, and make legitimate a whole range of everyday subjects for the painter.

In Holland (and this was where the north and the south finally diverged) this break with tradition was compounded by the **Reformation**: the austere Calvinism that had supplanted the Catholic faith in the northern provinces had no use for images or symbols of devotion in its churches. Instead, painters catered to the public, and no longer visited Italy to learn their craft; the real giants of the seventeenth century – Hals, Rembrandt, Vermeer – stayed in the Low Countries all their lives. Another departure was that painting split into more distinct categories – genre, portrait, landscape, etc – and artists tended (with notable exceptions) to confine themselves to one field throughout their careers. So began the greatest age of Dutch art.

HISTORICAL AND RELIGIOUS PAINTING

If Italy continued to hold sway in the Low Countries it was not through the Renaissance painters but rather via the fashionable new realism of Caravaggio. Many artists – Rembrandt for one – continued to portray classic subjects, but in a way that was totally at odds with the Mannerists' stylish flights of imagination. Though a solid Mannerist throughout his career, the Utrecht artist **Abraham Bloemaert** (1564–1651) encouraged these new ideas, and his students – **Gerard van Honthorst** (1590–1656), **Hendrik Terbrugghen** (1588–1629), and **Dirck van Baburen** (1590–1624) – formed the nucleus of the influential **Utrecht School**, which followed Caravaggio almost to the point of slavishness. Honthorst was perhaps the leading figure, learning his craft from Bloemaert and travelling to Rome, where he was nicknamed "Gerardo delle Notti" for his ingenious handling of light and shade. This was, however, to become in his later paintings more routine technique than inspired invention, and though a supremely competent artist, Honthorst remains somewhat discredited among critics today. Terbrugghen's reputation seems to have aged rather better: he soon forgot Caravaggio and developed a more personal style, his lighter, later work having a great impact on the young Vermeer. After the obligatory jaunt to Rome, Baburen shared a studio with Terbrugghen and produced some fairly original work – work which also had some influence on Vermeer – but few of his paintings survive today, and he is the least studied member of the group.

But it's **Rembrandt** who was considered the most original historical artist of the seventeenth century, painting religious scenes throughout his life. In the 1630s, the poet and statesman Constantijn Huygens procured for him his greatest commission – a series of five paintings of the Passion, beautifully composed and uncompromisingly realistic. Later, however, Rembrandt received fewer and fewer commissions, since his treatment of Biblical and historical subjects was far less dramatic than that of his contemporaries. It's significant that while the more conventional Jordaens, Honthorst and van Everdingen were busy decorating the Huis ten Bosch near The Hague for patron Stadholder Frederick Henry, Rembrandt was having his monumental *Conspiracy of Claudius Civilis* (completed for the new Amsterdam town hall) rejected – probably because it was thought too pagan an interpretation of what was an important symbolic event in Dutch history. **Aert van Gelder** (1645–1727), Rembrandt's last pupil and probably the only one to concentrate on historical painting, followed the style of his master closely, producing shimmering Biblical scenes well into the eighteenth century.

GENRE PAINTING

The term **genre** refers to scenes from everyday life, a subject that, with the decline of the church as patron, became popular in Holland by the mid-seventeenth century. Many painters devoted themselves solely to such work. Some genre paintings were simply non-idealized portrayals of common scenes, while others, by means of symbols or carefully disguised details, made moral entreaties to the viewer.

Among early seventeenth-century painters, **Hendrik Terbrugghen** and **Gerard Honthorst** spent much of their time on religious subjects, but also adapted the realism and strong chiaroscuro learned from Caravaggio to a number of tableaux of everyday life. **Frans Hals**, too, is better known as a portraitist, but his early genre paintings no doubt influenced his pupil, **Adriaen Brouwer** (1605–38), whose riotous tavern scenes were well received in their day and collected by, among others, Rubens and Rembrandt. Brouwer spent only a couple of years in Haarlem under Hals before returning to his native Flanders to influence the younger **David Teniers** (1610–90), who worked in Antwerp, later in Brussels. His earlier paintings are Brouwer-like peasant scenes, his later work more delicate and diverse, including *Kortegaardje* – guardroom scenes that show soldiers carousing. Like Brouwer, **Adriaen van Ostade** (1610–85) studied under Hals but chose to remain in Haarlem, skilfully painting groups of peasants and tavern brawls – though his later acceptance by the establishment led him to water down the realism he had learnt from Brouwer. He was teacher to his brother **Isaak** (1621–49), who produced a large number of open-air peasant scenes, subtle combinations of genre and landscape work.

The English critic E. V. Lucas dubbed Teniers, Brouwer and Ostade "coarse and boorish" compared with **Jan Steen** (1625–79), who, along with Vermeer, is probably the most admired Dutch genre painter. You can see what he had in mind: Steen's paintings offer the same Rabelaisian peasantry in full fling, but they go their debauched ways in broad daylight, and nowhere do you see the filthy rogues in shadowy hovels favoured by Brouwer and Ostade. Steen offers more humour, too, as well as more moralizing, identifying with the hedonistic mob and reproaching them at the same time. Indeed, many of his pictures are illustrations of well-known proverbs of the time – popular epithets on the evils of drink or the transience of human existence that were supposed to teach as well as entertain.

Gerrit Dou (1613–75) was Rembrandt's Leiden contemporary and one of his first pupils. It's difficult to detect any trace of the master's influence in his work, however, Dou instead initiating a style of his own – tiny, minutely realized, and beautifully finished views of a kind of ordinary life that was decidedly more genteel than Brouwer's, or even Steen's for that matter. He was esteemed, above all, for his painstaking attention to detail: he would, it was said, sit in his studio for hours waiting for the dust to settle before starting work. Among his students, **Frans van Mieris** (1635–81) continued to produce highly finished portrayals of the Dutch bourgeoisie, as did **Gabriel Metsu** (1629–67) – perhaps Dou's greatest pupil – whose pictures often convey an overtly moral message. Another pupil of Rembrandt's, though a much later one, was **Nicholaes Maes** (1629–93), whose early paintings were almost entirely genre paintings, sensitively executed and again with a moralizing message. His later work shows the influence of a more refined style of portrait, which he had picked up in France.

As a native of Zwolle, **Gerard ter Borch** (1619–81) found himself far from all these Leiden/Rembrandt connections, and despite trips abroad to most of the artistic capitals of Europe, he remained very much a provincial painter all his life, depicting Holland's merchant class at play and becoming renowned for his curious doll-like figures and his enormous ability to capture the textures of different cloths. His domestic scenes were not unlike those of **Pieter de Hooch** (1629–after 1684), whose simple depictions of everyday life are deliberately unsentimental, and, for the first time, have little or no moral commentary. De Hooch's favourite trick was to paint darkened rooms with an open door leading through to a sunlit courtyard, a practice that, along with his trademark rusty red colour, makes his work easy to identify – and, at its best, exquisite. That said, his later pictures reflect the encroaching decadence of the Dutch republic: the rooms are more richly decorated, the arrangements more contrived and the subjects far less homely.

It was, however, **Jan Vermeer** (1632–75) who brought the most sophisticated methods to painting interiors, depicting the play of natural light on indoor surfaces with superlative skill; it's for this and the curious peace and intimacy of his pictures that he is best known. Another recorder of the better-heeled Dutch households, and, like de Hooch, without any overt moral tone, he is regarded (with Hals and Rembrandt) as one of the big three Dutch painters – though, he was, it seems, a slow worker, and only about forty small paintings can be attributed to him with any certainty. Living all his life in Delft, Vermeer is perhaps the epitome of the seventeenth-century Dutch painter – rejecting the pomp and ostentation of the High Renaissance to quietly record his contemporaries at home, painting for a public that demanded no more than that.

PORTRAITURE

Naturally, the ruling bourgeoisie of Holland's flourishing mercantile society wanted to put their success on record, and it's little wonder that portraiture was the best way for a young painter to make a living. **Michiel Jansz**

Miereveld (1567–1641), court painter to Frederick Henry in The Hague, was the first real portraitist of the Dutch Republic, but it wasn't long before his stiff and rather conservative figures were superseded by the more spontaneous renderings of **Frans Hals** (1585–1666). Hals is perhaps best known for his "corporation-pictures" – portraits of the members of the Dutch civil guard regiments that had been formed in most larger towns while the threat of invasion by the Spanish was still imminent. These large group pieces demanded superlative technique, since the painter had to create a collection of individual portraits while retaining a sense of the group, and accord prominence based on the importance of the sitter and the size of the payment each had made. Hals was particularly good at this, using innovative lighting effects, arranging his sitters subtly, and putting all the elements together in a fluid and dynamic composition. He also painted many individual portraits, making the ability to capture fleeting and telling expressions his trademark; his pictures of children are particularly sensitive. Later in life, his work became darker and more akin to that of Rembrandt.

Jan Cornelisz Verspronck (1597–1662) and **Bartholomeus van der Helst** (1613–70) were the other great Haarlem portraitists after Frans Hals – Verspronck recognizable by the smooth, shiny glow he always gave to his sitters' faces, van der Helst by a competent but unadventurous style. Of the two, van der Helst was the more popular, influencing a number of later painters and leaving Haarlem while still young to begin a solidly successful career as portrait painter to Amsterdam's burghers.

The reputation of **Rembrandt van Rijn** (1606–69) is still relatively recent – nineteenth-century connoisseurs preferred Gerrit Dou – but he is now justly regarded as one of the greatest and most versatile painters of all time. Born in Leiden, the son of a miller, he was apprenticed at an early age to **Jacob van Swanenburgh** – a then quite important, though uninventive, local artist. He shared a studio with **Jan Lievens**, a promising painter and something of a rival for a while (now all but forgotten), before going up to Amsterdam to study under the fashionable **Pieter Lastman**. Soon he was painting commissions for the city elite and an accepted member of their circle. The poet and statesman Constantijn Huygens acted as his agent, pulling strings to obtain all of Rembrandt's more lucrative jobs, and in 1634 he married Saskia van Ulenborch, daughter of the burgomeister of Leeuwarden and quite a catch for the still relatively humble artist. His self-portraits at the time show the confident face of security – on top of things and quite sure of where he's going.

Rembrandt would not always be the darling of the Amsterdam smart set, but his fall from grace was still some way off when he painted the *Night Watch* – a group portrait often associated with the artist's decline in popularity. Although Rembrandt's fluent arrangement of his subjects was totally original, there's no evidence that the military company who commissioned the painting were anything but pleased with the result. More likely culprits are the artist's later pieces, whose obscure lighting and psychological insight took the conservative Amsterdam burghers by surprise. His patrons were certainly not sufficiently enthusiastic about his work to support his taste for art collecting and his expensive house on Jodenbreestraat, and in 1656 possibly the most brilliant artist the city would ever know was declared bankrupt, dying thirteen years later, as his last self-portraits show, a broken and embittered old man. Throughout his career Rembrandt maintained a large studio, and his influence pervaded the next generation of Dutch painters. Some – Dou, Maes – more famous for their genre work, have already been mentioned. Others turned to portraiture.

Govert Flinck (1615–60) was perhaps Rembrandt's most faithful follower, and he was, ironically, given the job of decorating Amsterdam's new town hall after his teacher had been passed over. He died before he could execute his designs, and Rembrandt was one of several artists commissioned to paint them – though his contribution was removed shortly afterwards. The work of **Ferdinand Bol** (1616–80) was so heavily influenced by Rembrandt that for a long time art historians couldn't tell the two apart. Most of the pitifully slim extant work of **Carel Fabritius** (1622–54) was portraiture, but he too died young, before he could properly realise his promise as perhaps the most gifted of all Rembrandt's students. Generally regarded as the teacher of Vermeer, he forms a link between the two

masters, combining Rembrandt's technique with his own practice of painting figures against a dark background, prefiguring the lighting and colouring of the Delft painter.

LANDSCAPES

Aside from Bruegel, whose depictions of his native surroundings make him the first true Low Countries landscape painter, **Gillis van Coninxloo** (1544–1607) stands out as the earliest Dutch landscapist. He imbued the native scenery with elements of fantasy, painting the richly wooded views he had seen on his travels around Europe as backdrops to Biblical scenes. In the early seventeenth century, **Hercules Seghers** (1590–1638), apprenticed to Coninxloo, carried on his mentor's style of depicting forested and mountainous landscapes, some real, others not: his work is scarce but is believed to have had considerable impact on the landscape work of Rembrandt. **Esaias van der Velde**'s (1591–1632) quaint and unpretentious scenes show the first real affinity with the Dutch countryside, but – though his influence, too, was great – he was soon overtaken in stature by his pupil **Jan van Goyen** (1596–1656), a remarkable painter who belongs to the so-called "tonal phase" of Dutch landscape painting. Van Goyen's early pictures were highly coloured and close to those of his teacher, but it didn't take him long to develop a markedly personal touch, using tones of greens, browns and greys to lend everything a characteristic translucent haze. His paintings are, above all, of nature, and if he included figures it was merely for the sake of scale. Neglected until a little over a century ago, his fluid and rapid brushwork became more acceptable as the Impressionists rose in stature.

Another "tonal" painter and a native of Haarlem, **Salomon van Ruisdael** (1600–70) was also directly affected by van der Velde, and his simple, atmospheric, though not terribly adventurous, landscapes were for a long time consistently confused with those of van Goyen. More esteemed is his nephew, **Jacob van Ruisdael** (1628–82), generally considered the greatest of all Dutch landscapists, whose fastidiously observed views of quiet flatlands dominated by stormy skies were to influence European painters' impressions of nature right up to the nineteenth century. (Constable, certainly, acknowledged a debt to him.)

Ruisdael's foremost pupil was **Meindert Hobbema** (1638–1709), who followed the master faithfully, sometimes even painting the same views (his *Avenue at Middelharnis* may be familiar).

Nicholas Berchem (1620–83) and **Jan Both** (1618–52) were the "Italianizers" of Dutch landscapes. They studied in Rome and were influenced by Claude, taking back to Holland rich, golden views of the world, full of steep gorges and hills, picturesque ruins and wandering shepherds. **Allart van Everdingen** (1621–75) had a similar approach, but his subject matter stemmed from travels in Scandinavia, which, after his return to Holland, he reproduced in all its mountainous glory.

Aelbert Cuyp (1620–91), on the other hand, stayed in Dordrecht all his life, painting what was probably the favourite city skyline of Dutch landscapists. He inherited the warm tones of the Italianizers, and his pictures are always suffused with a deep, golden glow.

Of a number of **specialist seventeenth-century painters** who can be included here, **Paulus Potter** (1625–54) is rated as the best painter of **domestic animals**. He produced a fair amount of work in a short lifetime, most reputed being his lovingly executed pictures of cows and horses. The accurate rendering of **architectural features** also became a specialized field, of which **Pieter Saenredam** (1597–1665), with his finely realized paintings of Dutch church interiors, is the most widely known exponent. **Emanuel de Witte** (1616–92) continued in the same vein, though his churches lack the spartan crispness of those of Saenredam. **Gerrit Berckheyde** (1638–98) worked in Haarlem soon after, but limited his views to the outside of buildings, producing variations on the same scenes around town.

In the seventeenth century another thriving category of painting was the **still life**, in which objects were gathered together to remind the viewer of the transience of human life and the meaninglessness of all worldly pursuits: often a skull would be joined by a book, a pipe or a goblet, and some half-eaten food. Again, two Haarlem painters dominated this field: **Pieter Claesz** (1598–1660) and **Willem Heda** (1594–1680), who confined themselves almost entirely to these carefully arranged groups of objects.

THE EIGHTEENTH CENTURY

With the demise of Holland's economic boom, the quality – and originality – of Dutch painting began to decline. The delicacy of some of the classical seventeenth-century painters was replaced by finicky still lifes and minute studies of flowers, or finely finished portraiture and religious scenes, as in the work of **Adrian van der Werff** (1659–1722). Of the era's big names, **Gerard de Lairesse** (1640–1711) spent most of his time decorating the splendid civic halls and palaces that were going up all over the place, and, like the buildings he worked on, his style and influences were French. **Jacob de Wit** (1695–1754) continued where Lairesse left off, receiving more church commissions as Catholicism was allowed out of the closet. The period's only painter of any true renown was **Cornelis Troost** (1697–1750), who, although he didn't produce anything really new, painted competent portraits and some neat, faintly satirical pieces that have since earned him the title of "The Dutch Hogarth". Cosy interiors also continued to prove popular, and the Haarlem painter **Wybrand Hendriks** (1744–1831) satisfied demand with proficient examples.

French influence was dominant in the area that was to become Belgium. Artists such as **Jan Joseph Horemans I** and **Balthasar van den Bossche** took the Flemish genre painting of the previous century and made it palatable for Parisian tastes. Towards the end of the century neo-Classicism became the vogue, and the entire period was marked by the weakening of domestic tradition in favour of external influences. **Laurent Delvaux** (1696–1778) was also an important figure during this period, a Flemish sculptor who produced a large number of works for Belgian churches, including the pulpit of Ghent's cathedral and other pieces in Brussels.

THE NINETEENTH CENTURY

HOLLAND

Johann Barthold Jongkind (1819–91) was the first great artist to emerge from nineteenth-century Holland, painting landscapes and seascapes that were to influence Monet and the early Impressionists. He spent most of his life in France and his work was exhibited in Paris with the Barbizon painters, though he owed less to them than to the landscapes of van Goyen and the seventeenth-century "tonal" artists.

Jongkind's work was a logical precursor to the art of the **Hague School**, a group of painters based in and around that city between 1870 and 1900 who tried to re-establish a characteristically Dutch national school of painting. They produced atmospheric studies of the dunes and polderlands around The Hague, pictures that are characterised by grey, rain-filled skies, windswept seas, and silvery, flat beaches – and that, for some, verge on the sentimental. **J. H. Weissenbruch** (1824–1903) was a founding member, a specialist in low, flat beach scenes dotted with stranded boats. The banker-turned-artist **H. W. Mesdag** (1831–1915) did the same but with more skill than imagination, while **Jacob Maris** (1837–99), one of three artist brothers, was perhaps the most typical Hague School painter, with his rural and sea scenes dominated by gloomy chasing skies. His brother, **Matthijs** (1839–1917), was less predictable, ultimately tiring of his colleagues' interest in straight observation and going to London to design windows, while **Willem** (1844–1910), the youngest, is best known for his small, unpretentious studies of nature.

Anton Mauve (1838–88) is a better known artist, an exponent of soft, pastel landscapes and an early teacher of van Gogh. Profoundly influenced by the French Barbizon painters – Corot, Millet *et al* – he went to Hilversum in 1885 to set up his own group, which became known as the "Dutch Barbizon". **Jozef Israëls** (1826–1911) has often been likened to Millet, though it's generally agreed that he had more in common with the Impressionists, and his best pictures are his melancholy portraits and interiors. Lastly, **Johan Bosboom**'s (1817–91) church interiors may be said to sum up the nostalgia of the Hague School – shadowy works, populated by figures in seventeenth-century dress, that seem to yearn for Holland's Golden Age.

Vincent van Gogh (1853–90) was one of the least "Dutch" of Dutch artists, and he lived out most of his relatively short painting career in Belgium and France. After countless studies of peasant life in his native North Brabant – studies which culminated in the sombre *Potato Eaters* – and a spell in the industrial Borinage area of southern Belgium, he went to live in Paris with his art-dealer brother, Theo. There, under the influence of the Impressionists, he lightened his palette, following the pointillist work of Seurat and "trying to render intense colour and not a grey harmony". Two years later he went south to Arles, the "land of blue tones and gay colours", and, struck by the harsh Mediterranean light, his characteristic style began to develop. A disastrous attempt to live with Gauguin, and the much-publicized episode when he cut off part of his ear and presented it to a woman in a nearby brothel, led eventually to committal to an asylum at St-Remy, where he produced some of his most famous, and most Expressionistic, canvases – strongly coloured and with the paint thickly, almost frantically, applied.

Like van Gogh, **Jan Toorop** (1858–1928) went through multiple artistic changes, though he didn't need to travel the world to do so; he radically adapted his technique from a fairly conventional pointillism through a tired Expressionism to Symbolism with an Art Nouveau feel. Roughly contemporary, **G. H. Breitner** (1857–1923) was a better painter, and one who refined his style rather than changed it. His snapshot-like impressions of his beloved Amsterdam figure among his best work and offered a promising start to the new century.

BELGIUM

Until the coming of the Kingdom of Belgium in 1830, French styles of painting remained the most significant – neo-Classicist painting, chiefly that derived from Jacques Louis David, was particularly popular in first part of the century. David's pupil, **François Joseph Navez** (1787–1869), was the most important of his followers working in Belgium, furthering the influence of neo-Classicism via his position as director of the Brussels academy. With independence from Holland, came, as might be expected, a rise in nationalism – artists such as **Gustave Wappers** (1807–74) leading a movement that favoured a romantic interpretation of historical events, idealizing both recent and medieval history. **Antoine Wiertz** (1806–65) was celebrated for his grandiose romantic canvases, and **Henri de Braekeleer** (1840–88) for his Dutch-inspired interiors and landscapes. Indeed landscape painting underwent a resurgence of popularity throughout Europe in the mid-nineteenth century, and Belgian artists once again reflected the tastes and movements of France, with artists like **Théodor Fourmois** and **Eugène Huberti** involved with the Barbizon group, and **Emile Claus** (1849–1924) adapting French Impressionist ideas into an individual style known as Luminism. **Paul-Jean Clays** (1819–1900), **Louis Artan** (1837–90) and **Theodoor Baron** (1840–99) also took their lead from the Impressionists, but retained a distinctive local approach.

One artist who stands out during this period is **Constantin Meunier** (1831–1905), a painter and sculptor whose naturalistic paintings and sculptures of brawny workers and mining scenes were the perfect mirror of a fast-industrializing Europe – and Belgium. Much of Meunier's work depicts life in the industrial parts of Hainaut, notably the Borinage, and there are good collections of it all over Belgium, not least in Brussels.

Perhaps the best known Belgian artist of the late nineteenth century is **James Ensor** (1860–1949). Ensor, who lived in Ostend for most of his life, painted macabre, disturbing works, whose haunted style can be traced back to Bosch and Bruegel and which was itself a precursor of Expressionism. He was active in a group known as **Les XX** (*Les Vingt*), which organized exhibitions of new styles of art from abroad, and greatly influenced his contemporary Belgian painters.

THE TWENTIETH CENTURY

HOLLAND

Most of the trends in the visual arts of the early twentieth century found their way to Holland at one time or another: of many minor names, **Jan Sluyters** (1881–1957) was the Dutch pioneer of Cubism. But only one movement was specifically Dutch – **de Stijl** (literally "the Style").

Piet Mondrian (1872–1944) was de Stijl's leading figure, developing the realism he had learned from the Hague School painters – via Cubism, which he criticized for being too cowardly to depart totally from representation – into a complete abstraction of form which he called **neo-plasticism**. He was something of a mystic, and this was to some extent responsible for the direction that de Stijl – and his paintings – took: canvases painted with grids of lines and blocks made up of the three primary colours and white, black and grey. Mondrian believed this freed the work of art from the vagaries of personal perception, and made it possible to obtain what he called "a true vision of reality".

De Stijl took other forms, too: there was a magazine of the same name, and the movement introduced new concepts into every aspect of design, from painting to interior design to architecture. But in all these media lines were kept simple, colours bold and clear. **Theo van Doesburg** (1883–1931) was a de Stijl co-founder and major theorist: his work is similar to that of Mondrian except for the noticeable absence of thick, black borders and the diagonals that he introduced into his work, calling his paintings "contra-compositions" – which, he said, were both more dynamic and more in touch with twentieth-century life. **Bart van der Leck** (1876–1958) was the third member of the circle, identifiable by white canvases covered by seemingly randomly placed interlocking coloured triangles.

Mondrian split with de Stijl in 1925, going on to attain new artistic extremes of clarity and soberness before moving to New York in the 1940s and producing atypically exuberant works such as *Victory Boogie Woogie* – so named because of the artist's love of jazz.

During and after de Stijl, a number of other movements flourished, though their impact was not so great and their influence largely confined to the Low Countries. The Expressionist **Bergen School** was probably the most localized, its best-known exponent **Charley Toorop** (1891–1955), daughter of Jan, who developed a distinctively glaring but strangely sensitive realism. **De Ploeg** (The Plough), centred in Groningen, was headed by **Jan Wiegers** (1893–1959) and influenced by Kirchner and the German Expressionists; the group's artists set out to capture the uninviting landscapes around their native town, and produced violently coloured canvases that hark back to van Gogh. Another group, known as the **Magic Realists**, surfaced in the 1930s, painting quasi-surrealistic scenes that, according to their leading light, **Carel Willinck** (b.1900), reveal "a world stranger and more dreadful in its haughty impenetrability than the most terrifying nightmare".

Postwar Dutch art began with **CoBrA**: a loose grouping of like-minded painters from Denmark, Belgium and Holland, whose name derives from the initial letters of their respective capital cities. Their first exhibition, at Amsterdam's Stedelijk Museum in 1949, provoked a huge uproar, at the centre of which was **Karel Appel** (b.1921), whose brutal Abstract Expressionist pieces, plastered with paint inches thick, were, he maintained, necessary for the era – indeed, inevitable reflections of it. "I paint like a barbarian in a barbarous age," he claimed. In the graphic arts the most

famous twentieth-century figure is **M. C. Escher** (1898–1970).

As for **today**, there's as vibrant an art scene as there ever was, best exemplified in Amsterdam by the rotating exhibitions of the Stedelijk or the nearby Overholland Museum, and some of the numerous private Amsterdam galleries. Of contemporary Dutch artists, look out for the abstract work of **Edgar Fernhout** and **Ad Dekkers**; the reliefs of **Jan Schoonhoven**; the multi-media productions of **Jan Dibbets**; the glowering realism of **Marlene Dumas**; the imprecisely coloured

LOW COUNTRIES GALLERIES: A HIT LIST

HOLLAND

In **Amsterdam**, the *Rijksmuseum* gives a complete overview of Dutch art up to the end of the nineteenth century, in particular the work of Rembrandt, Hals, and the major artists of the Golden Age; the *Van Gogh Museum* is best for the Impressionists and, of course, van Gogh; and, for twentieth-century and contemporary Dutch art, there's the *Stedelijk*. Within easy reach of the city, the *Frans Hals Museum* in **Haarlem** holds some of the best work of Hals and the Haarlem School; also in Haarlem, the *Teyler's Museum* is strong on eighteenth- and nineteenth-century Dutch works. In **Leiden**, the *Lakenhal* has works by, among others, local artists Dou and Rembrandt, and the *Centraal* in **Utrecht** has paintings by van Scorel and the Utrecht School. Also in Utrecht, the *Catherine Convent Museum* boasts an excellent collection of works by Flemish artists and by Hals and Rembrandt.

Further afield, **The Hague**'s *Gemeente Museum* owns the country's largest set of Mondrians, and its *Mauritshuis* collection contains works by Rembrandt, Vermeer and others of the era. The *Boymans van Beuningen Museum* in **Rotterdam** has a weighty stock of Flemish primitives and surrealists, as well as works by Rembrandt and other seventeenth-century artists; and nearby **Dordrecht**'s *Municipal Museum* offers an assortment of seventeenth-century paintings that includes work by Aelbert Cuyp, and later canvases by the Hague School and Breitner.

The *Kroller-Muller Museum*, just outside **Arnhem**, is probably the country's finest modern art collection, and has a superb collection of van Goghs; a little further east, **Enschede**'s *Rijksmuseum Twenthe* has quality works from the Golden Age to the twentieth century.

BELGIUM & LUXEMBOURG

Brussels' *Musées Royaux des Beaux Arts* together comprise an excellent survey of Low Countries painting: the Flemish Primitives, Bruegel and Rubens in the *Musée d'Art Ancien*, Ensor, Magritte and Delvaux in the *Musée d'Art Moderne*. **Antwerp's** *Museum voor Schone Kunsten* has everything from Flemish Primitives to nineteenth-century masters, with all the great names – van Eyck, van der Weyden, Rubens, van Dyck, Jordaens, Brouwer, Teniers, Ensor and Delvaux – getting a look in. The *Mayer van den Burgh* museum has work by Quentin Matsys and Bruegel, and the *Onze Lieve* cathedral two of Rubens' seminal works. The *Memling Museum* in

Bruges has some of the artist's best works, housed in a magnificent medieval hospice; the *Groeninge Museum* also has work by the Flemish Primitives: van der Weyden, van der Goes, Gerhard David and an important van Eyck. Van Eyck's greatest work, *The Adoration of the Mystic Lamb* is housed in St Baaf's Cathedral in **Ghent**.

Luxembourg isn't well served in terms of great collections, although the *Musée National* in Luxembourg city has recently taken custody (for seven years) of the Bentick-Thyssen collection of mainly Dutch and Flemish art – a marvellous coup for a museum whose own array of art is fairly mediocre.

geometric designs of **Rob van Koningsbruggen**; the smeary Expressionism of **Toon Verhoef**; and the exuberant figures of **Rene Daniels** – to name only the most important figures.

BELGIUM

As in Holland, each of the major modern movements had its followers in Belgium, and each was diluted or altered according to local taste. **Expressionism** was manifest in a local group of artists established in Laethem St Marten in Flanders, most eye-catching of which was the work of **Constant Permeke** (1886–1952), whose bold, deeply coloured canvases can be found in many Belgian galleries. **Surrealism** also caught on in a big way, perhaps because of the Flemish penchant for the bizarre and grotesque. **René Magritte** (1898–1967), one of the leading lights of the movement, was born and trained in Belgium and returned there after being involved in the movement's birth in 1927. His Surrealism is gentle compared to the work of Dalí or de Chirico: ordinary images are used in a dreamlike way, often playing on the distinction between a word and its meaning. His most famous motif was the man in the bowler hat, whose face was always hidden from view. **Paul Delvaux** (1897–1989) adopted his own rather salacious interpretation of the movement – a sort of "What-the-butler-saw" Surrealism.

Most of the interwar artists were influenced by van Doesburg and de Stijl in Holland, though none figured highly in the movement. The abstract geometrical works of **Victor Severanckx** (1897–1965) owed much to de Stijl, and he in turn inspired the postwar group known as **La Jeune Peinture**, who along with CoBrA (see above) were the most notable artists working in the country, the antecedents of the Abstract Expressionists of the 1950s. While none of the CoBrA artists achieved the fame of Karel Appel, **Pierre Aleckinsky** is perhaps the best known among the Belgians.

Contemporary Belgian painting seems to have turned away from "movements" in favour of individualism and community art, a trend underlined by the fact that there are separate Flemish amd Walloon ministries of culture. Even so, the country has produced few artists of recent note, and it seems left to Holland to remain at the vanguard of the contemporary Low Countries art scene.

BOOKS

HISTORY

Pieter Geyl *The Revolt of The Netherlands 1555–1609; The Netherlands in the Seventeenth Century 1609–1648* (Cassell/ Barnes & Noble). Geyl's two volumes of history present a concise account of the Netherlands during its formative years, chronicling the uprising against the Spanish and the formation of the United Provinces. Without doubt the definitive books on the period.

Geoffrey Parker *The Dutch Revolt* (Penguin). Compelling account of the struggle between the Netherlands and Spain. Perhaps the best work of its kind.

J. H. Huizinga *Dutch Civilisation in the Seventeenth Century* (Collins/Ungar o/p). Analysis of life and culture in the Dutch Republic by the late, widely respected historian.

J. L. Price *Culture and Society in the Dutch Republic in the Seventeenth Century* (Batsford/ Scribner o/p). An accurate, intelligent account of the Golden Age.

Simon Schama *The Embarrassment of Riches: An Interpretation of Dutch Culture in the Golden Age* (Collins/Univ. of California Press). The most recent – and one of the most accessible – works on the Golden Age, drawing on a huge variety of archive sources. Justifiably the biggest selling book on Dutch history ever written.

Sir William Temple *Observations upon the United Provinces of The Netherlands* (OUP/ Gregg International). Written by a seventeenth-century English diplomat, and a good, evocative account of the country at the time.

Dedalo Carasso *A Short History of Amsterdam* (Amsterdam Historical Museum). Brief account written from a left-wing perspective, well illustrated with photos of artefacts from the Amsterdam Historical Museum.

Geoffrey Cotterell *Amsterdam* (Saxon House/ Little, Brown o/p). Popularised, offbeat history giving a highly readable account of the city up to the late 1960s.

E. H. Kossmann *The Low Countries 1780–1940* (OUP, UK). Gritty, technically detailed but ultimately rather turgid narrative of the Low Countries from the Austrian era to World War II. Concentrates on the narrow arena of party politics.

A de Meeüs *History of the Belgians* (Praeger o/p). Entertaining if rather confused attempt at an exhaustive history of the Belgians, from "prehistoric dawns" to modern times. Good on incidental detail.

Michael Glover *A New Guide to the Battlefields of Northern France and the Low Countries* (Michael Joseph, UK). Battlefields guide that is not entirely devoted to the Low Countries but has substantial sections on the conflicts at Bastogne, Arnhem, Ypres and Waterloo. Deliberately readable, well illustrated, and an essential handbook if you're exploring the region.

ART AND ARCHITECTURE

Max J. Friedlander *From Van Eyck to Bruegel* (Phaidon/Cornell Univ. Press). Definitive and learned account of the early Flemish masters, though stylistically and factually (in the light of modern research) beginning to show its age.

Walter S. Gibson *Bosch* (Thames & Hudson). Standard introductory work on the late fifteenth-century painter.

Gregory Martin *Bruegel* (Thames & Hudson). Good introduction to the religious paintings and genre scenes of Pieter, the most well-known and influential of the Bruegels.

Eugene Fromentin *The Masters of Past Time: Dutch and Flemish Painting from Van Eyck to Rembrandt* (Phaidon/Cornell Univ. Pres.). Entertaining essays on the major Dutch and Flemish painters.

R. H. Fuchs *Dutch Painting* (Thames & Hudson). As complete an introduction to the subject – from Flemish origins to the present day – as you could wish for in a couple of hundred pages.

Jacob Rosenberg et al. *Dutch Art and Architecture 1600–1800* (Penguin). Full and erudite anthology of essays on the art and buildings of the Golden Age and after. Strictly for dedicated Dutch art fans.

Christopher White *Rembrandt* (Thames & Hudson). The most widely available – and wide-ranging – study of the painter and his work.

Svetlana Alpers *Rembrandt's Enterprise* (Thames & Hudson/Univ. of Chicago Press). Intriguing study of Rembrandt, positing the theory – in line with the recent findings of the Leiden-based Rembrandt Research Project – that many previously accepted works are not by Rembrandt at all but merely the products of his studio.

Pierre Cabanne *Van Gogh* (Thames & Hudson). Standard mix of art criticism and biography, drawing heavily on the artist's own letters, which are published in the UK by Flamingo at £3.50.

Irving Stone *Lust for Life* (Methuen/NAL Dutton). Everything you ever wanted to know about Vincent van Gogh in a pop genius-is-pain biography.

Wolfgang Stechow *Dutch Landscape Painting of the Seventeenth Century* (Phaidon £7.50). All-encompassing rundown on the many and varied landscapists of the Dutch Golden Age.

Alastair Smart *The Renaissance and Mannerism outside Italy* (Thames & Hudson/Harcourt Brace). A very readable survey that includes lengthy chapters on van Eyck and his contemporaries, their successors, Bosch and Bruegel, and the later, more Mannerist-inclined painters of the Low Countries. A fine introduction to a lengthy period.

H. L. C. Jaffe *De Stijl: Visions of Utopia* (Phaidon/Abbeville Press). A good, informed introduction to the movement and its philosophical and social influences.

Christopher White *Peter Paul Rubens: Man and Artist* (Yale Univ. Press). A beautifully illustrated introduction to both Rubens' work and social milieu.

Kenneth Clark *Civilization* (Penguin). This includes a warm and scholarly rundown on the Golden Age, with illuminating insights on the way in which the art reflected the period.

SPECIFIC GUIDES

Guus Kemme (ed.) *Amsterdam Architecture: A Guide* (Thoth). Illustrated guide to the architecture of Amsterdam, with potted accounts of the major buildings.

Christian Rheinwald *Amsterdam Art Guide* (Art Guide Pubs). Comprehensive guide to the city's galleries, shops and contact points for both artists and those wanting to tour the art scene.

Jan Stoutenbeek et al. *A Guide to Jewish Amsterdam* (De Haan). Fascinating, though perhaps over-detailed, guide to just about every Jewish monument in the city. Purchase a copy before you leave from the *Netherlands Board of Tourism*, or in better Amsterdam bookshops.

LITERATURE

Jerome Brouwers *Sunken Red* (Peter Owen). A best-selling novel in Holland that tells a bleak tale of a child's imprisonment in Japan during World War II.

Simon Carmiggelt *Kronkels* (De Arbeiderspers o/p). Simon Carmiggelt wrote these short pieces, usually concise, wry anecdotes concerning everyday Dutch life, for *Het Parool*, an Amsterdam daily newspaper he helped to found. This is the second collection of what he termed his "slight adventures".

Hugo Claus *The Sorrow of Belgium* (Penguin/Pantheon). One of the Dutch language's foremost novelists, and another concerned with the subject of the effects of World War II in the region, this very successful novel charts the growing maturity of a young boy living in Flanders under the Nazi occupation. A huge book, it gets to grips well with the guilt, bigotry and mistrust of the period, causing an uproar when first published seven years ago, although Claus's style is somewhat dense to say the least.

Anne Frank *The Diary of a Young Girl* (Pan/Pocket Books). Lucid and moving, the most revealing thing you can read on the plight of Amsterdam's Jews during the war years.

Nicolas Freeling *A City Solitary; Love in Amsterdam; Cold Iron; Strike Out Where Not Applicable* (Penguin/Carroll & Graf). Freeling writes detective novels, and his most famous creation is the rebel cop, van der Valk, around whom a successful British TV series was made. These are light, carefully crafted tales, with just the right amount of twists to make them classic cops 'n' robbers reading – and they sport some good Dutch and Belgian locations.

Etty Hillesum *Etty: An Interrupted Life* (Granada/Pocket Books). Diary of a young Jewish woman uprooted from her life in Amsterdam and taken to Auschwitz, where she died. As with Anne Frank's more famous journal, penetratingly written – though on the whole much less readable.

Richard Huijing (ed and trans.) *The Dedalus Book of Dutch Fantasy* (Dedalus). A fun and artfully selected collection of stories that contains contributions from some of the greats of Dutch literature, including a number whose work does not as yet appear in translation anywhere else.

Margo Minco *Bitter Herbs* (Penguin). A diary that traces Minco's experiences as a young Jewish girl in wartime Breda and Amsterdam. *The Glass Bridge* and *An Empty House* (Peter Own/Dufour), two novels, also concentrate on the plight of Dutch Jews during the last war. *The Glass Bridge* sold half a million copies in Holland, and *An Empty House*, its sequel follows the main character back to Amsterdam, where she tries to pick up the pieces of her life.

Harry Mulisch *The Assault* (Penguin/ Pantheon). Set part in Haarlem, part in Amsterdam, *The Assault* traces the story of a young boy who loses his family in a Nazi reprisal-raid. A powerful tale, made into an excellent and effective film. Mulisch's later novel, *Last Call*, is a more introspective, less specifically Dutch work, more concerned with metaphysical questions concerning the nature of reality and fiction.

Multatuli *Max Havelaar: or the Coffee Auctions of the Dutch Trading Company* (Penguin/Univ. of Massachusetts Press). Classic nineteenth-century Dutch satire of colonial life in the East Indies. Eloquent and, at times, amusing.

Cees Noteboom *Rituals* (Penguin/Louisiana Univ. Press). An absorbing, sparsely written novel, by perhaps the most well-known name in current Dutch literature, that maps the empty existence of a rich Amsterdammer who dabbles in antiques. The later *In the Dutch Mountains* (Penguin) is similarly aloof in style, and not directly about Holland, but it is nonetheless compelling at times, casting up offbeat philosophical musings like pearls. Noteboom's latest novel, *The Following Story* (Harvill), continues with the author's favourite themes of memory, and the nature of reality.

Jona Oberski *Childhood* (Hodder & Stoughton/NAL Dutton). First published in 1978, this is a Jewish child's eye-witness account of the war years, the camps and executions. Written with feeling and precision.

Janwillem van de Wetering *Hard Rain* (Gollancz/Ballantine). An offbeat detective tale set in Amsterdam and provincial Holland. Like van de Wetering's other stories (sadly only available in the US), it's a humane, quirky and humorous story, worth reading for characters and locations as much as for inventive narrative.

Jan Wolkers *Turkish Delight* (Marion Boyars). Wolkers is one of the Netherlands' best-known artists and writers, and this is one of his early novels, examining closely a relationship between a bitter, working-class sculptor and his young, middle-class wife. It's not one of his best books by any means, but at times shows flashes of Wolkers' typically sardonic wit.

LANGUAGE

Throughout **Holland**, and in the **northern part of Belgium** (chiefly the provinces of Flanders, Antwerp and Limburg), the principal language is **Dutch**. Most Dutch-speakers, particularly in the main towns of Holland and in the tourist industry, speak English to varying degrees of excellence. The Dutch have a seemingly natural talent for languages, and your attempts at speaking theirs may be met with bewilderment.

Though around sixty percent of Belgians speak Dutch, the other forty percent speak a **dialect of French** known as **Walloon**, and live in Brussels and the country's southern provinces, known logically enough as Wallonia. Walloon is almost identical to French, and if you've any previous knowlege of the language, you'll be readily understood.

French is also the most widely spoken language of **Luxembourg**, along with German – although most Luxembourgers also speak their indigenous language of **Letzeburgesch**, a dialect of German.

DUTCH

Dutch is a Germanic language – the word "Dutch" itself is a corruption of *Deutsche*, a label inaccurately given by English sailors in the seventeenth century. Though the Dutch are at pains to stress the differences between the two languages, if you know any German you'll spot many similarities. As noted above, English is very widely spoken, but in smaller towns and in the countryside, where things aren't quite as cosmopolitan, the notes that follow will prove handy; they can be supplemented with the detailed "Food Glossary" on p.36-37.

Of the **phrase books and dictionaries** available, *Dutch at your Fingertips* (Routledge) is the most up-to-date and useful companion. To continue your studies, take a look at *Colloquial Dutch* (Routledge).

PRONUNCIATION

Dutch is pronounced much the same as English. However, there are a few Dutch sounds that don't exist in English, which can be difficult to pronounce without practice.

Consonants

v is like the English f in **f**ar

w like the v in **v**at

j like the initial sound of **y**ellow

ch and *g* are considerably harder than in English, enunciated much further back in the throat; in Amsterdam at least, where the pronunciation is particularly coarse, there's no real English equivalent. They become softer the further south you go, where they're more like the Scottish lo**ch.**

ng is as in bri**ng**

nj as in o**ni**on

Otherwise double consonants keep their separate sounds – *kn*, for example, is never like the English "knight".

Vowels and Dipthongs

Doubling the letter lengthens the vowel sound:

a is like the English **a**pple

aa like c**a**rt

e like l**e**t

ee like l**a**te

o as in p**o**p

oo like p**o**pe

u is like the French t**u** if preceded but not followed by a consonant (eg *nu*); it's like w**oo**d if followed by a consonant (eg *bus*).

uu the French t**u**

au and *ou* like h**ow**

ei and *ij* as in f**i**ne, though this varies strongly from region to region; sometimes it can sound more like l**a**ne.

oe as in s**oo**n

eu is like the dipthong in the French l**eu**r

ui is the hardest Dutch dipthong of all, pronounced like h**ow** but much further forward in the mouth, with lips pursed (as if to say "oo").

DUTCH WORDS AND PHRASES

Basics and greetings

yes	*ja*	do you speak English?	*spreekt u Engels?*
no	*nee*	I don't understand	*Ik begrijp het niet*
please	*alstublieft*	women/men	*vrouwen/mannen*
(no) thank you	*[nee] dank u* or *bedankt*	children	*kinderen*
hello	*hallo* or *dag*	when?	*wanneer?*
good morning	*goede morgen*	I want	*ik wil*
good afternoon	*goedemiddag*	I don't want	*Ik wil niet. . .(+verb)*
good evening	*goedenavond*		*ik wil geen. . .(+noun)*
goodbye	*tot ziens*	how much is. . .?	*wat kost. . .?*
see you later	*tot straks*		

Finding the way

how do I get to. . .?	*hoe kom ik in. . .?*	left/right	*links/rechts*
where is. . .?	*waar is. . .?*	straight ahead	*recht uit gaan*
how far is it to. . .?	*hoe ver is het rnaar. . .?*	platform	*spoor* or *perron*
far/near	*ver/dichtbij*		

Money

post office	*postkantoor*	cashier	*kassa*
stamp(s)	*postzegel(s)*	ticket office	*loket*
money exchange	*wisselkantoor*		

Useful words

good/bad	*goed/slecht*	cheap/expensive	*goedkoop/duur*
big/small	*groot/klein*	hot/cold	*heet/koud*
open/shut	*open/gesloten*	with/without	*met/zonder*
push/pull	*duwen/trekken*	here/there	*hier/daar*
new/old	*nieuw/oud*	men's/women's toilets	*heren/damen(s)*

Days and times

Sunday	*Zondag*	Saturday	*Zaterdag*	minute	*minuut*
Monday	*Maandag*	yesterday	*gisteren*	hour	*uur*
Tuesday	*Dinsdag*	today	*vandaag*	day	*dag*
Wednesday	*Woensdag*	tomorrow	*morgen*	week	*week*
Thursday	*Donderdag*	tomorrow	*morgenochtend*	month	*maand*
Friday	*Vrijdag*	morning		year	*jaar*

Numbers

When saying a number, the Dutch generally transpose the last two digits: eg, *drie gulden vijf en twintig* is *f*3.25.

0	*nul*	9	*negen*	18	*achttien*	80	*tachtig*
1	*een*	10	*tien*	19	*negentien*	90	*negentig*
2	*twee*	11	*elf*	20	*twintig*	100	*honderd*
3	*drie*	12	*twaalf*	21	*een en twintig*	101	*honderd een*
4	*vier*	13	*dertien*	30	*dertig*	200	*twee honderd*
5	*vijf*	14	*veertien*	40	*veertig*	201	*twee honderd een*
6	*zes*	15	*vijftien*	50	*vijftig*	500	*vijf honderd*
7	*zeven*	16	*zestien*	60	*zestig*	1000	*duizend*
8	*acht*	17	*zeventien*	70	*zeventig*		

FRENCH

French – or, more properly, the Walloon dialect of French spoken in Belgium's south – isn't language, despite the number of words shared with English, but learning the bare essentials is not difficult and makes all the difference. Even just saying "*Bonjour Madame/Monsieur*" when you go into a shop and then pointing will usually get you a smile and helpful service. People working in hotels, restaurants, etc, almost always speak some English and tend to use it if you're struggling – be grateful, not amused.

Differentiating words is the initial problem in understanding spoken French – it's very hard to get people to slow down. If, as a last resort, you get them to write it down, you'll probably find you know half the words anyway. See also French "Food Glossary", p286-287.

Of the available **phrase books and dictionaries**, *The Penguin French Phrase Book* does the job well enough. To actually learn the language, try *French in three months* (Hugo) which is a useful primer.

PRONUNCIATION

One easy rule to remember is that **consonants** at the ends of words are usually silent. *Pas plus tard* (not later) is thus pronounced pa-plu-tarr. But when the following word begins with a vowel, you run the two together: *pas après* (not after) thus becomes "pazapre'.

Consonants

Much as in English, except that: *ch* is always sh, *c* is s, *h* is silent, *th* is the same as t, *ll* is like the y in yes, *w* is v, and r is growled (or rolled).

Vowels

These are the hardest sounds to get right. Roughly:

a as in h**a**t

e as in g**e**t

é between g**e**t and g**a**te

è between g**e**t and g**u**t

eu like the **u** in h**u**rt

i as in mach**i**ne

o as in h**o**t

o, au as in **o**ver

ou as in f**oo**d

u as in a pursed-lip version of **u**se

More awkward are the **combinations** in/im, en/em, an/am, on/om, un/um at the ends of words, or followed by consonants other than n or m. Again, roughly:

in/im like the **an** in **an**xious

an/am, en/em like the d**on** in D**on**caster when said with a nasal accent

on/om like the d**on** in D**on**caster said by someone with a heavy cold

un/um like the **u** in **u**nderstand.

FRENCH WORDS AND PHRASES

Useful Words and Phrases

Excuse me	*pardon*	good morning/ afternoon	*bonjour*
Do you speak English?	*Vous parlez anglais?*	good evening	*bonsoir*
yes	*oui*	good night	*bonne nuit*
no	*non*	How are you?	*Comment allez-vous?/ Ça va?*
I understand	*Je comprends*		
I don't understand	*Je ne comprends pas*	Sorry	*Pardon, Madame/ je m'excuse*
OK/agreed	*d'accord*		
please	*s'il vous plaît*	Leave me alone (aggressive)	*Fichez-moi la paix!*
thank you	*merci*		
hello	*bonjour*	Please help me	*Aidez-moi, s'il vous plaît*
goodbye	*au revoir*		

Finding the way

How do I get to...?	*Comment est-ce que je peux arriver à .. ?*	far	*loin*
		left	*à gauche*
Where is . . .?	*Où est . . .?*	right	*à droite*
How far is it to .. .?	*Combien y a-t-il jusqu' à près/pas loin*	straight on	*tout droit*
		behind	*derrière*

Basics and Greetings

now	*maintenant*	big	*grand*
later	*plus tard*	small	*petit*
man	*un homme*	a lot	*beaucoup*
woman	*une femme*	good	*bon*
here	*ici*	bad	*mauvais*
there	*là*	hot	*chaud*
open	*ouvert*	cold	*froid*
closed	*fermé*		

Days and Dates

Sunday	*dimanche*	Friday	*vendredi*	tomorrow morning	*aujourd'hui matin*
Monday	*lundi*	Saturday	*samedi*	hour	*heure*
Tuesday	*mardi*	today	*aujourd'hui*	day	*jour*
Wednesday	*mercredi*	yesterday	*hier*	week	*semaine*
Thursday	*jeudi*	tomorrow	*demain*	month	*mois*

Numbers

1	*un*	11	*onze*	21	*vingt-et-un*
2	*deux*	12	*douze*	22	*vingt-deux*
3	*trois*	13	*treize*	30	*trente*
4	*quatre*	14	*quatorze*	40	*quarante*
5	*cinq*	15	*quinze*	50	*cinquante*
6	*six*	16	*seize*	60	*soixante*
7	*sept*	17	*dix-sept*	70	*soixante-dix*
8	*huit*	18	*dix-huit*	75	*soixante-quinze*
9	*neuf*	19	*dix-neuf*	80	*quatre-vingts*
10	*dix*	20	*vingt*	90	*quatre-vingt-dix*

95	*quatre-vingt-quinze*
100	*cent*
101	*cent-et-un*
200	*deux cents*
300	*trois cents*
500	*cinq cents*
1000	*mille*
1,000,000	*un million*

GLOSSARIES

ABDIJ Abbey or group of monastic buildings.

AMSTERDAMMERTJE Phallic-shaped objects placed alongside Amsterdam streets to keep drivers off pavements and out of canals.

BEIAARD Carillon chimes.

BEGIJNHOF Similar to a *hofje* but occupied by Catholic women (*Begijns*) who led semi-religious lives without taking full vows.

BELFORT Belfry.

BURGHER Member of the upper or mercantile classes of a town in the fifteenth to eighteenth centuries, usually with certain civic powers.

FIETSPAD Bicycle path.

GASTHUIS Hospice for the sick or infirm.

GEMEENTE Municipal: eg *Gemeentehuis* – town hall.

GEVEL Gable. The only decoration practical on the narrow-fronted canal house was on its gables. Initially fairly simple, they developed into an ostentatious riot of individualism in the late seventeenth century before turning to a more restrained classicism in the eighteenth and nineteenth centuries.

GILD Guild.

GERECHTSHOF Law Courts.

GRACHT Canal.

HALLE Hall.

HIJSBALK Pulley beam, often decorated, fixed to the top of a gable to lift goods, furniture etc. Essential in canal houses whose staircases were narrow and steep, *hijsbalken* are still very much in use today.

HOF Courtyard.

HOFJE Almshouse, usually for elderly women who could look after themselves but needed small charities such as food and fuel; usually a number of buildings centred around a small, peaceful courtyard.

HUIS House.

JEUGDHERBERG Youth hostel.

KERK Church; eg *Grote Kerk* – the principal church of the town; *Onze Lieve Vrouwe kerk* – church dedicated to the Virgin Mary.

KONINKLIJK Royal.

LAKENHAL Cloth hall. The building in medieval weaving towns where cloth would be weighed, graded and sold.

LUCHTHAVEN Airport.

MARKT Central town square and the heart of most Dutch communities, normally still the site of weekly markets.

OMMEGANG Procession.

POLDER An area of land reclaimed from the sea.

POSTBUS Post office box.

PLEIN A square or open space.

RAADHUIS Town hall.

RANDSTAD Literally "rim-town", this refers to the urban conurbation that makes up much of North and South Holland, stretching from Amsterdam in the north down to Rotterdam and Dordrecht in the south.

RIJKS State.

SCHEPENZAAL Alderman's Hall.

SCHOUWBURG Theatre.

SIERKUNST Decorative arts.

SCHONE KUNSTEN Fine arts.

SPIONNETJE Small mirror on canal house enabling occupant to see who is at the door without descending stairs.

SPOOR Platform (on a train station).

STADHUIS The most common word for a town hall.

STICHTING Institute or foundation.

STEDELIJK Civic, municipal.

STEEN Fortress.

VOLKSKUNDE Folklore.

VVV Dutch tourist information office

WAAG Old public weighing-house, a common feature of most towns – usually found on the Markt.

ABBAYE Abbey.

AUBERGE DE LA JEUNESSE Youth hostel.

BEAUX ARTS Fine arts.

CHÂTEÂU Mansion, country house, or castle.

COUVENT Convent, monastery.

DEGUSTATION Tasting (wine or food).

DONJON Castle keep.

ÉGLISE Church.

ENTRÉE Entrance.

FERMETURE Closing period.

FOUILLES Archeological excavations.

GALLO-ROMAIN Period of Roman occupation of Gaul, from the first to fourth century AD.

GARE Station.

GÎTE D'ÉTAPE Basic hostel accommodation, primarily for walkers.

GOBELINS Most famous tapestry manufacturer, based in Paris, whose most renowned period was in the reign of Louis XIV.

HALLES Covered market.

HÔTEL DE VILLE Town hall.

JOURS FERIÉS Public holidays.

MARCHÉ Market.

PLACE Square.

PORTE Gateway.

PTT Post office.

QUARTIER District of a town.

SORTIE Exit.

SYNDICAT D'INITIATIVE Tourist office.

TOUR Tower.

ARCHITECTURAL TERMS

AMBULATORY Covered passage around the outer edge of the choir of a church.

APSE Semicircular protrusion at (usually) the east end of a church.

ART DECO Geometrical style of art and architecture popular in the 1930s.

ART NOUVEAU Style of art, architecture and design based on highly stylized vegetal forms. Popular in the early part of the twentieth century.

BAROQUE High Renaissance period of art and architecture, distinguished by extreme ornateness, exuberance and complex spatial arrangement of interiors.

CABINET-PIECE Small, finely detailed painting of a domestic scene.

CARILLON A set of tuned church bells, either operated by an automatic mechanism or played by a keyboard.

CARYATID A sculptured female figure used as a column.

CAROLINGIAN Dynasty founded by Charlemagne; late eighth to early tenth century. Also refers to art, etc, of the time.

CLASSICAL Architectural style incorporating Greek and Roman elements – pillars, domes, colonnades etc – at its height in the seventeenth century and revived, as **Neoclassical**, in the nineteenth century.

CLERESTORY Upper story of a church, incorporating the windows.

FLAMBOYANT Florid form of Gothic (see below).

FRESCO Wall painting – durable through application to wet plaster.

GABLE The triangular upper portion of a wall – decorative or supporting a roof. See *Gevel*, above.

GOTHIC Architectural style of the thirteenth to sixteenth centuries, characterized by pointed arches, rib vaulting, flying buttresses and a general emphasis on verticality.

MEROVINGIAN Dynasty ruling France and parts of Germany from sixth to mid-eighth centuries. Refers also to art, etc, of the period.

MISERICORD Ledge on choir stall on which occupant can be supported while standing; often carved with secular subjects (bottoms were not thought worthy of religious ones).

NAVE Main body of a church.

NEOCLASSICAL Architectural style derived from Greek and Roman elements – pillars, domes, colonnades, etc – popular in the Low Countries during French rule in the early nineteenth century.

ROCOCO Highly florid, light and graceful eighteenth-century style of architecture, painting and interior design, forming the last phase of Baroque.

RENAISSANCE Movement in art and architecture developed in fifteenth-century Italy.

RETABLE Altarpiece.

ROMANESQUE Early medieval architecture distinguished by squat forms, rounded arches and naive sculpture.

STUCCO Marble-based plaster used to embellish ceilings, etc.

TRANSEPT Arms of a cross-shaped church, placed at ninety degrees to nave and chancel.

TRIPTYCH Carved or painted work on three panels. Often used as an altarpiece.

TYMPANUM Sculpted panel above a church door.

VAUBAN Seventeenth-century military architect – his fortresses still stand all over Europe and the Low Countries.

VAULT An arched ceiling or roof.

INDEX

HELP US UPDATE

We've gone to a lot of effort to ensure that this second edition of *The Rough Guide to Holland, Belgium and Luxembourg* is completely up-to-date and accurate. However, things do change — places get "discovered", bars and restaurants close, transport connections change — and any suggestions, comments or corrections would be much appreciated.

We'll credit all contributions, and send a copy of the next edition (or any other Rough Guide if you prefer) for the best letters. Please mark all letters *Rough Guide Holland Belgium & Luxemboug Update* and send to:

Rough Guides, 1 Mercer Street, London WC2H 9QJ
or, Rough Guides, 375 Hudson Street, 4th Floor, New York NY10014

DIRECT ORDERS IN THE UK

Title	ISBN	Price
Amsterdam	1858280869	£7.99
Australia	1858280354	£12.99
Barcelona & Catalunya	1858280486	£7.99
Berlin	1858280338	£8.99
Brazil	0747101272	£7.95
Brittany & Normandy	1858280192	£7.99
Bulgaria	1858280478	£8.99
California	1858280907	£9.99
Canada	185828001X	£10.99
Corsica	1858280893	£8.99
Crete	1858280494	£6.99
Cyprus	185828032X	£8.99
Czech & Slovak Republics	185828029X	£8.99
Egypt	1858280753	£10.99
England	1858280788	£9.99
Europe	185828077X	£14.99
Florida	1858280109	£8.99
France	1858280508	£9.99
Germany	1858280257	£11.99
Greece	1858280206	£9.99
Guatemala & Belize	1858280451	£9.99
Holland, Belgium & Luxembourg	1858280877	£9.99
Hong Kong & Macau	1858280664	£8.99
Hungary	1858280214	£7.99
Ireland	1858280958	£9.99
Italy	1858280311	£12.99
Kenya	1858280435	£9.99
Mediterranean Wildlife	0747100993	£7.95
Morocco	1858280400	£9.99
Nepal	185828046X	£8.99
New York	1858280583	£8.99
Nothing Ventured	0747102082	£7.99
Paris	1858280389	£7.99
Peru	0747102546	£7.95
Poland	1858280346	£9.99
Portugal	1858280842	£9.99
Prague	185828015X	£7.99
Provence & the Côte d'Azur	1858280230	£8.99
Pyrenees	1858280524	£7.99
St Petersburg	1858280303	£8.99
San Francisco	1858280826	£8.99
Scandinavia	1858280397	£10.99
Scotland	1858280834	£8.99
Sicily	1858280370	£8.99
Spain	1858280818	£9.99
Thailand	1858280168	£8.99
Tunisia	1858280656	£8.99
Turkey	1858280885	£9.99
Tuscany & Umbria	1858280915	£8.99
USA	185828080X	£12.99
Venice	1858280362	£8.99
West Africa	1858280141	£12.99
Women Travel	1858280710	£7.99
Zimbabwe & Botswana	1858280419	£10.99

Rough Guides are available from all good bookstores, but can be obtained directly in the UK* from Penguin by contacting:

Penguin Direct, Penguin Books Ltd, Bath Road, Harmondsworth, West Drayton, Middlesex UB7 0DA; or telephone our credit line on 081-899 4036 (9am–5pm) and ask for Penguin Direct. Visa, Access and Amex accepted. Delivery will normally be within 14 working days. Penguin Direct ordering facilities are only available in the UK.

The availability and published prices quoted are correct at the time of going to press but are subject to alteration without prior notice.

For USA and international orders, see separate price list

DIRECT ORDERS IN THE USA

Title	ISBN	Price
Able to Travel	1858281105	$19.95
Amsterdam	1858280869	$13.95
Australia	1858280354	$18.95
Berlin	1858280338	$13.99
Brittany & Normandy	1858280192	$14.95
Bulgaria	1858280478	$14.99
California	1858280907	$14.95
Canada	185828001X	$14.95
Corsica	1858280893	$14.95
Crete	1858280494	$14.95
Cyprus	185828032X	$13.99
Czech & Slovak Republics	185828029X	$14.95
Egypt	1858280753	$17.95
England	1858280788	$16.95
Europe	185828077X	$18.95
Florida	1858280109	$14.95
France	1858280508	$16.95
Germany	1858280257	$17.95
Greece	1858280206	$16.95
Guatemala & Belize	1858280451	$14.95
Holland, Belgium & Luxembourg	1858280877	$15.95
Hong Kong & Macau	1858280664	$13.95
Hungary	1858280214	$13.95
Ireland	1858280958	$16.95
Italy	1858280311	$17.95
Kenya	1858280435	$15.95
Mediterranean Wildlife	1858280699	$15.95
Morocco	1858280400	$16.95
Nepal	185828046X	$13.95
New York	1858280583	$13.95
Paris	1858280389	$13.95
Poland	1858280346	$16.95
Portugal	1858280842	$15.95
Prague	185828015X	$14.95
Provence & the Côte d'Azur	1858280230	$14.95
St Petersburg	1858280303	$14.95
San Francisco	1858280826	$13.95
Scandinavia	1858280397	$16.99
Scotland	1858280834	$14.95
Sicily	1858280370	$14.99
Spain	1858280818	$16.95
Thailand	1858280168	$15.95
Tunisia	1858280656	$15.95
Turkey	1858280885	$16.95
Tuscany & Umbria	1858280915	$15.95
USA	185828080X	$18.95
Venice	1858280362	$13.99
Women Travel	1858280710	$12.95
Zimbabwe & Botswana	1858280419	$16.95

Rough Guides are available from all good bookstores, but can be obtained directly in the USA and Worldwide (except the UK*) from Penguin:

Charge your order by Master Card or Visa (US$15.00 minimum order): call 1-800-255-6476; or send orders, with complete name, address and zip code, and list price, plus $2.00 shipping and handling per order to:
Consumer Sales, Penguin USA, PO Box 999 – Dept #17109, Bergenfield, NJ 07621. No COD. Prepay foreign orders by international money order, a cheque drawn on a US bank, or US currency. No postage stamps are accepted. All orders are subject to stock availability at the time they are processed. Refunds will be made for books not available at that time. Please allow a minimum of four weeks for delivery.

The availability and published prices quoted are correct at the time of going to press but are subject to alteration without prior notice. Titles currently not available outside the UK will be available by January 1995. Call to check.

* For UK orders, see separate price list

You are
A STUDENT

You travel
THE WORLD

You want
TO SAVE MONEY

Here's
how

The International
Student Identity Card

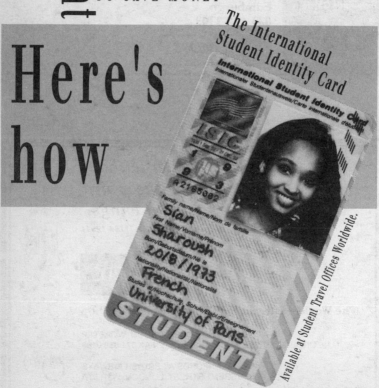

Available at Student Travel Offices Worldwide.

Entitles you to discounts and special services worldwide.